Special Operations in World War II

C&C

CAMPAIGNS & COMMANDERS

GREGORY J. W. URWIN, SERIES EDITOR

CAMPAIGNS AND COMMANDERS

GENERAL EDITOR

Gregory J. W. Urwin, *Temple University, Philadelphia, Pennsylvania*

ADVISORY BOARD

Lawrence E. Babits, *East Carolina University, Greenville*
James C. Bradford, *Texas A&M University, College Station*
Robert M. Epstein, *U.S. Army School of Advanced Military Studies, Fort Leavenworth, Kansas*
David M. Glantz, *Carlisle, Pennsylvania*
Jerome A. Greene, *Denver, Colorado*
Victor Davis Hanson, *California State University, Fresno*
Herman Hattaway, *University of Missouri, Kansas City*
J. A. Houlding, *Rückersdorf, Germany*
Eugenia C. Kiesling, *U.S. Military Academy, West Point, New York*
Timothy K. Nenninger, *National Archives, Washington, D.C.*
Bruce Vandervort, *Virginia Military Institute, Lexington*

SPECIAL OPERATIONS IN WORLD WAR II

British and American Irregular Warfare

Andrew L. Hargreaves

UNIVERSITY OF OKLAHOMA PRESS | NORMAN

Library of Congress Cataloging-in-Publication Data

Hargreaves, Andrew L., 1981–
  Special operations in World War II : British and American irregular warfare / Andrew L. Hargreaves. — First edition.
     pages cm. — (Campaigns and commanders ; volume 39)
  Includes bibliographical references and index.
  ISBN 978-0-8061-4396-5 (hardcover : ISBN 978-0-8061-9406-6 (paper) 1. World War, 1939-1945—Commando operations—Great Britain. 2. World War, 1939-1945—Commando operations—United States. 3. Great Britain. Army—Commando troops—History—20th century. 4. United States. Army—Commando troops—History—20th century. 5. Special forces (Military science)—Great Britain—History—20th century. 6. Special forces (Military science)—United States—History—20th century. I. Title.
  D794.5.H36 2013
  940.54′1241—dc23
                                    2013016698

Special Operations in World War II: British and American Irregular Warfare is Volume 39 in the Campaigns and Commanders series.

The paper in this book meets the guidelines for permanence and durability of the Committee on Production Guidelines for Book Longevity of the Council on Library Resources, Inc. ∞

Copyright © 2013 by the University of Oklahoma Press, Norman, Publishing Division of the University. Paperback published 2024. Manufactured in the U.S.A.

All rights reserved. No part of this publication may be reproduced, stored in a retrieval system, or transmitted, in any form or by any means, electronic, mechanical, photocopying, recording, or otherwise—except as permitted under Section 107 or 108 of the United States Copyright Act—without the prior written permission of the University of Oklahoma Press. To request permission to reproduce selections from this book, write to Permissions, University of Oklahoma Press, 2800 Venture Drive, Norman OK 73069, or email rights.oupress@ou.edu.

Contents

List of Figures	vii
Preface	ix
Acknowledgments	xv
List of Acronyms	xvii
Introduction	3
1. The Inception and Employment of Commando and Ranger Formations	17
2. The Inception and Employment of Special Forces	54
3. Anglo-American Cooperation and Interdependency	110
4. Command and Control	142
5. Misapplication, Misuse, and Disuse	180
6. The Impact of Specialist Forces	203
7. Cost-Effectiveness	241
Conclusion	270
Appendix A. Organizational Charts	283
Appendix B. Estimates of Manpower within Anglo-American Specialist Formations	289
Notes	301
Bibliography	347
Index	395

Figures

A.1. Special Service Brigade Organization, November 1940   284
A.2. Special Service (Commando) Organization,
      February 1944   285
A.3. Command Arrangements for Specialist Formations,
      Mediterranean Theater, April 1944   286
A.4. Anglo-American Special Forces Command Organization
      for the Invasion of France, June 1944   287
B.1. Comparison of Manpower in Commando (or Ranger)
      Formations and Special Forces   297
B.2. Comparison of Manpower in British and
      American Specialist Forces   299

Preface

Over the course of the past eighty years, special forces—highly trained, specially selected military units tasked with performing unconventional and often high-risk missions—have gradually emerged as a recognizable and valued genus of military formation. Although their historical lineage is complex, at heart their origins lie in the Second World War. Between 1939 and 1945 such units, for the first time, were comprehensibly developed and extensively used in order to undertake a wide range of activities in support of conventional military operations.

If one were to consider modern military operations by relying solely upon the media and popular literature, special forces and elite light infantry rapid-reaction forces would feature so prominently as to give an impression not only of indispensability but also of ubiquity. Such is the attention lavished upon them that the general public might be forgiven for erroneously thinking that the exclusivity suggested by such terms as "unconventional," "irregular," "special," or "elite," which in many regards define these units, are misnomers. In spite of the seemingly never-failing popularity of this subject in nonscholarly works of popular history, the *academic* study of specialist formations and irregular warfare has remained as broadly elusive and as specialist as the practitioners of special operations themselves. This volume serves to help redress this balance by offering a comprehensive study of the development, application, and value of Anglo-American commando and special forces formations from 1943 to 1945.

The origins of this work lie in a PhD thesis completed at the Department of War Studies, King's College London, and in light of the perennial restrictions of all academics—time, money, space, and access to materials—the work is not without its limitations. It is important to recognize these from the outset.

The task confronting any historian investigating this subject is by no means an easy one. Even by employing relatively strict definitions and restricting the examination to British and American forces alone, the researcher faces some daunting hurdles. The problem posed by the significant number of different independent formations, each needing to be identified and analyzed, is only magnified by the sheer range of missions that each conducted across a range of different theaters and operational environments. Source materials also present many a headache, and any researcher of this subject must thus be prepared to cast his or her net far and wide. In one sense, sources are in abundance, necessitating a protracted trawl through unsubstantiated narratives and popular works abounding with exaggeration, sentimentality, and romanticism in order to find the occasional gem. In another sense, they remain frustratingly sparse. Given the sensitivity and secrecy of their work, specialist formations rarely made the best record keepers, and their small scale and heterodox establishments seldom produced the voluminous amounts of material one might find emanating from other regular military outfits. Both facts are further compounded by the ephemeral existence that many of these units had during the Second World War.

In terms of primary research, the bedrock for this study consists of those official documents and private papers found at the British National Archives at Kew; the Imperial War Museum, London; the Liddell Hart Center for Military Archives at King's College London; the British Library; and the U.S. National Archives and Record Administration in College Park, Maryland. The significant amount of material concerning British specialist formations found in the American archives, and vice versa, alone provides sufficient justification for the Anglo-American approach that has been adopted within this study.

The only significant archival source neglected during researching this work was the U.S. Army Military History Institute in Carlisle, Pennsylvania, in particular the papers of William J. Donovan held there. This exclusion was an unfortunate result of the aforementioned limitations of time and funding, but given the wide range of materials found from other sources, it is the hopeful expectation that this has not adversely affected the overall conclusions of the current work.

Although efforts were made to be as broad and inclusive as possible here, it would have been wildly impractical to cover all the many, varied groups and organizations charged with undertaking irregular, covert, clandestine, or subversive actions during the Second World War within one volume. It was thus desirable to separate the commandos and special forces from other espionage, "cloak and dagger," and subversive agencies. This work focuses on those specially organized and clearly identifiable units comprising uniformed servicemen trained to undertake irregular or high-risk military tasks. It does not, therefore, attempt to analyze in detail the broader activities undertaken by the likes of the British Special Operations Executive (SOE) and Secret Intelligence Service (SIS), or the U.S. Office of Strategic Services (OSS). The body of academic literature dealing with these organizations collectively dwarfs those few works focused on specialist formations. Similarly, while modern interpretations of what constitutes "special operations" have a tendency to include a range of activities broadly grouped as "nonmilitary special operations" or "operations other than war"—undertakings such as propaganda and psychological operations—including these activities, or the organizations created for their conduct, was also impracticable here. Such activities and the considerations influencing their conduct were far removed from those performed by commandos and special forces. These restrictions notwithstanding, as a number of specialist formations arose under the wider aegis of such organizations, OSS in particular being central to the American experience, the study of groups like these remains essential to this work.

With similar limitations in mind, the present volume is not the place to delve into a discussion of the many complex debates related to the activities and effectiveness of the various partisan and resistance movements that sprang up in the occupied territories. This point notwithstanding, as many wartime special forces worked closely with indigenous movements (performing "unconventional warfare," as this role is doctrinally referred to as today), with such a mission being the raison d'être of certain units, it is absolutely necessary to examine those special forces that provided military organization, training, and leadership to indigenous partisan movements.

When special operations were conducted at depth, they were almost totally reliant on a vast amount of support furnished by the Allied Air Forces—often coming from the RAF's Special Duty or the USAAF's "Carpetbagger" squadrons. Given the importance of these actions, it is regrettable that it has not been possible to examine these within this volume—nor, for that matter, the actions of other air force "specialist" units such as the 1st Air Commando Group in Burma or those airmen taking part in the Dambuster or

Doolittle Raids. Equally, it has been necessary to omit discussion of certain naval formations that possessed something of a nonregular organization or mandate, such as the fast PT boat or midget submarine flotillas. The missions and composition of these formations, though certainly of a nonregular nature, turned on a range of variables different from those affecting other specialist formations. There are, for instance, quite pronounced differences in the nature of missions performed, the manner in which personnel were recruited and trained, and the nature and composition of the enemy faced, each of which make their inclusion problematic in a volume such as this.

The focus here thus remains on Anglo-American approaches to commando and special forces, two subtly different genres of formation representing two sides of the same coin. The closely symbiotic nature of their wartime relationship makes it imperative to give equal attention to both of the genres when considering specialist forces as a whole. However, in so doing, some clarification is necessary, particularly regarding distinctions with other wartime light infantry formations. Although the commandos and rangers both shared a degree of common ground with the airborne forces, mountain units, and Chindit formations, it was necessary to exclude each of these formations from this study. While this decision has implications for the work's conclusions, particularly in terms of making cost-effectiveness calculations, their inclusion was undesirable, given the inherent distinctions that existed between their core missions and sizes of their establishments and those of the British commando and American ranger variety of unit. This point is explained in greater depth in the introduction that follows.

Because of limitations imposed by the size of this work, the demands of research, and the desirability of cohesion, the current volume is restricted to a treatment of Anglo-American endeavors alone. It was unfeasible to extend the scope to include other Commonwealth, Dominion, and Allied specialist forces—let alone those of the Axis powers, which were by no means inactive in these areas. In contextual terms the omission of Australian and New Zealand specialist units (notably "Z" Special Unit, the Australian Independent Companies, and the "Coast watchers"), which carried out various raids and reconnaissances against the Japanese, are perhaps most acutely felt. However, not only would their inclusion distract from the assessment of specialist formations through the lens of Anglo-American cooperation, but, more significantly, it would have presented significant research hurdles, as doing justice to the subject would have required accessing primary materials held in Australasia. It is with regret that this volume also perpetuates an endemic issue with Anglo-American historiography by ignoring the Soviet Union's experiences with specialist units and partisans. The fact remains, however, that the inclusion in any such work of the Soviet Union—a power that, for example, by Operation Bagration of 1944 was employing upward of 300,000 partisans behind the enemy lines—would distort, if not entirely eclipse, any of the more nuanced conclusions made about the Anglo-American application of specialist formations.

One thing that might strike a reader of this text is that it is a work of "traditional" military history, insofar as it does not employ the theoretical structure or emphasis on issues such as race, class, or gender so prevalent in much of the current historiography. This was a conscious decision. Although adopting such an approach, specifically one that placed a greater focus on the cultural aspects of the Anglo-American relationship, would certainly have had its merits, doing so would have distracted from the main research objectives of this work and would have demanded a vastly expanded manuscript. Thus the primary focus here is on the military aspects of the subject (such as operations, command and control, alliances, and military effectiveness). Given the fragmented and inadequate state of existing academic literature, taking such an approach was entirely necessary. Only once the foundations of the subject have been firmly laid (and, at root, military operations *are* the foundations of this particular subject) can one turn to other avenues of research.

One final concession should perhaps be that in any single volume of this nature it is impossible to provide detailed information about every unit, operation, or personality involved. This work is based on a great deal of archival research and on the long-drawn-out navigation of innumerable primary and secondary published materials of varied quality and worth. The material that has made it into this volume is dwarfed by that which has not. For the most part, therefore, what have been used here are specific examples to reinforce general themes and provide an indication of trends rather than exotic character portraits, detailed dissection of tactical minutiae, or overblown narratives of acts of great daring: such approaches are more than catered to by the existing body of literature.

The focus of this work is to explore British and American approaches to special forces and commando formations during the Second World War. It studies the inception, use, and evolution of these units, and in so doing it serves to examine how and why they were created. It examines the distinctions between the commando and special forces genres of unit and how these developed, as well as analyzing how the employment of them evolved during the course of the war (chapters 1 and 2). It examines how the Anglo-American alliance functioned in the application and evolution of these units, and it highlights and assesses the significance of the extensive cooperation and interdependency between Britain and America in these fields (chapter 3). It addresses command perceptions and the manner in which these formations were controlled during the course of the war (chapter 4), going on to address the notion of their "correct" employment and application, accounting for any limitations and failings therein (chapter 5). Having done this, the work draws conclusions about the value and effectiveness of these units and examines their impact upon the course of the Second World War (chapters 6 and 7).

Acknowledgments

Despite the inherently solitary nature of the beast, the completion of this work either could not have occurred, or at least would have been made inherently more difficult, without the help and support offered by a number of individuals.

My sincere thanks go to the longtime support of my PhD supervisor, Professor Brian Holden Reid of King's College London, for his counsel, patronage, and guidance, which stretched over the better part of a decade. His help was quite instrumental in the development of my work. Also from the Department of War Studies, King's College London, I owe a debt of gratitude to Professor (Emeritus) Michael Dockrill, Dr. Steve Weiss, and Professor Bill Philpott for their guidance and support. I would also like to thank Professor Hew Strachan of All Soul's College, Oxford University, whose supervision of my master's dissertation helped germinate a number of ideas influencing my later work. Thanks are also due to Major-General Julian Thompson, visiting professor at the Department of War Studies, and Professor David Reynolds of Christ's College, Cambridge, for conducting my viva examination and giving me food for thought in the process. I would be remiss if I did not mention the support of my long-time friend Dr. Patrick Rose, for providing both a perfect sounding board for my ideas and, more importantly, welcome distraction where needed.

Whilst researching this work I was fortunate enough to have had the pleasure of meeting the late M. R. D. Foot ,who kindly agreed to discuss both his virtually unparalleled knowledge of SOE as well as his own wartime experiences as an intelligence officer in the SAS Brigade. Professor Foot was also instrumental in introducing me to the late Lord George Patrick John Rushworth Jellicoe, KBE, DSO, MC, with whom I feel privileged to have shared some correspondence relating to his wartime role as commander of the Special Boat Squadron.

Thanks are due to the staff and trustees of the Liddell Hart Center for Military Archives, King's College London, for granting me permission to use their collections while researching this work.

I would also like to recognize the helpful and knowledgeable staffs of the Imperial War Museum, the British National Archives at Kew, and the U.S. National Archives and Records Administration (NARA II) in College Park, Maryland.

The final and most heartfelt thanks must go to my long-suffering family, without whose love, patience, and financial help the completion of this work would never have been possible.

Thank you, one and all.

Acroynyms

AAI	Allied Armies Italy
ACO	Adviser on Combined Operations
AFHQ	Allied Force Headquarters [Allied headquarters for the Mediterranean theater]
AGWAR	Adjutant General, War Department [U.S.]
AIB	Allied Intelligence Bureau
APD	Fast destroyer transport ship
ATB	Amphibious Training Base
BAF	Balkan Air Force
BPB	Boom Patrol Boat
CBI	China-Burma-India [Theater]
CCO	Chief of Combined Operations
CCOR	Chief of Combined Operations Representative
CGS	Chief of General Staff
CIA	Central Intelligence Agency
C in C	Commander in Chief
CIGS	Chief of the Imperial General Staff
CNO	Chief of Naval Operations [U.S.]
CO	Commanding Officer
CODC	Combined Operations Development Center
COHQ	Combined Operations Headquarters
COI	(Office of . . .) Coordinator of Information [U.S.]
COPP	Combined Operations Pilotage Parties
COS	Chiefs of Staff [British]
COSSAC	Chief of Staff to Supreme Allied Commander
COSU	Combined Operations Scout Unit
DCGS	Deputy Chief of the General Staff
DCO	Director(ate) of Combined Operations
DDO	Deputy Director of Operations
DMI	Director of Military Intelligence
DMO	Director of Military Operations
DNI	Director(ate) of Naval Intelligence

DDOD(I)	Deputy Director of Operations Division (Irregular) [Admiralty]
EMFFI	Etat-majeur des Forces Françaises de l'Intérieur [Fighting French General Staff]
ETO	European Theater of Operations
ETOUSA	European Theater of Operations United States Army
FFI	Forces Françaises de l'Intérieur
FSSF	First Special Service Force
G-2	Intelligence Staff Branch
G-3	Operations Staff Branch
GHQ	General Headquarters
GOC	General Officer, Commanding
G(RF)	General Staff (Raiding Forces) Branch
GS(R)	General Staff (Research)
ILRS	Indian Long Range Squadron
ISTDC	Inter-Service Training and Development Center
JCS	Joint Chiefs of Staff [U.S.]
LAF	Libyan Arab Force
LCI	Landing Craft Infantry (Gunboats)
LCOCU	Landing Craft Obstacle Clearance Unit
LCN	Landing Craft, Navigation
LFA	Land Forces Adriatic
LRDG	Long Range Desert Group
MEDTO	Mediterranean Theater of Operations
MEF	Middle East Forces
MI(R)	Military Intelligence (Research)
MTB	Motor Torpedo Boats
MU	Maritime Unit [OSS]
NATO	North African Theater of Operations
NCDU	Naval Combat Demolitions Unit [U.S.]
NCO	Noncommissioned Officer
NORSO	Norwegian Special Operations [Group]
OC	Officer Commanding
OG	Operational Group(s) [OSS]
OSS	Office of Strategic Services
PAIC	Persia and Iraq Command
PPA	Popski's Private Army

RAF	Royal Air Force
R&D	Research and Development [OSS Branch]
RCNVR	Royal Canadian Navy Volunteer Reserve
RCT	Regimental Combat Team
RF	Raiding Forces
RM	Royal Marines
RMBPD	Royal Marine Boom Patrol Detachment
RN	Royal Navy
RSR	Raiding Support Regiment
SA	Special Activities [COI Branch]
SAARF	Special Allied Airborne Reconnaissance Force
SACO	Sino-American Cooperative Association
S&R	Scouts and Raiders [U.S.]
SAS	Special Air Service
SACMED	Supreme Allied Commander, Mediterranean
SACSEA	Supreme Allied Commander, South East Asia
SBS	Special Boat Section [also Squadron and later Service]
SBU	Special Boat Unit
SEAC	South East Asia Command
SF	Special Forces
SFHQ	Special Forces Headquarters
SHAEF	Supreme Headquarters Allied Expeditionary Forces
SI	Secret Intelligence [OSS branch]
SIG	Special Interrogation Group
SIS	Secret Intelligence Service
SO	Special Operations [OSS branch]
SOE	Special Operations Executive
SOF	Special Operations Forces
SOG	Small Operations Group
SPOC	Special Projects and Operations Center
SRD	Services Reconnaissance Department [AIB branch responsible for sabotage]
SRS	Special Raiding Squadron [also Sea Reconnaissance Section, forerunner of SRU]
SRU	Sea Reconnaissance Unit
SS	Special Service [not to be confused with German Schutzstaffel in this instance]

SSO	Strategic Services Officer [OSS]
SSRF	Small Scale Raiding Force
TOE	Table of Organization and Equipment
UDT	Underwater Demolition Team
USAAF	United States Army Air Force
USANIF	United States Army—Northern Ireland Forces
USFOR	United States Forces
USMC	United States Marine Corps
USN	United States Navy

Special Operations in World War II

Introduction

Today Special Forces or Special Operations Forces (SOF) are well regarded, well understood, and arguably indispensable components of modern military force structures. Though historically complex, the principal foundations for the modern conception of these units lie, in both theory and practice, within the 1939–45 experience. Proportionately small in establishment, these formations were made up of specially selected volunteers led by men with dynamic and innovative, albeit often unconventional, personalities. Each of these units trained in a curriculum foreign to conventional units; placed a premium on individual initiative and rigorous planning; and sought to conduct a diverse range of operations, in uniform and often at depth, that fell beyond the capabilities of existing conventionally organized, trained, and equipped formations.

Although irregular warfare and special operations during the Second World War are the subjects of a large body of literature, coherent academic analysis of the rise, evolution, deployment, and value of specialist formations has for the most part remained elusive. While certain units (such as the British Special Air Service or the U.S. Army Rangers) and certain operations (such as the Dieppe raid) have attracted a host of works of dramatically varying levels of scholarship and quality, other units and operations have received little or no attention. The historical neglect of certain significant wartime American special forces (such as the Operational Groups or the Alamo Scouts) is glaring.[1] Furthermore, the number of sources that narrowly chart the history of a specific unit or operation is disproportionately larger than that of the works that attempt to engage with the broader phenomenon of specialist formations during the Second World War.

The literature of specialist formations is all too often focused on tactics, tradecraft, and the dissection of operational minutiae; it rarely examines broader issues such as the mechanics of the creation and use of these units, the evolution of their purpose and application, or their utility and value. As Colin Gray claimed in an excellent and all too uncommon study of the strategic dimension of special operations: "For every thousand pages in the literature [of special operations] which recount the deeds of derring-do, there is scarcely one page that troubles to ask whether these deeds made much of a difference to the course and outcome of a conflict."[2] Furthermore, although a modest number of scholarly studies do illuminate the history of the specialist formations of either Britain or the United States during the Second World War,[3] very few analyze the developments of the two allies collectively. Yet such joint analysis is quite essential, particularly for an understanding of the American adoption and use of specialist formations. During the Second World War, the Anglo-American "special relationship" resulted in close and, at times, almost symbiotic links between the specialist formations of the two nations. On a number of occasions this relationship and the direct interplay and cooperation between various British and American units had a great bearing on the manner of their inception, evolution, and application.

When addressing this subject it is also important to consider the two distinct varieties of specialist unit that emerged during the Second World War: special forces (or SOF, in modern American vernacular) and commando-style elite light infantry units.* Broadly considered, the two genres of formation had different-size establishments, comprised different "types" of individual, undertook different missions, utilized different methods, operated at different depths of deployment, and had different command and control arrangements. Despite such points of variance, the two genres, linked by broadly irregular mandates, represented two sides of the same coin. Because of the closely entwined nature of their relationship—certain special forces, for instance, evolving in direct response to changes within commando units—it is imperative to give equal

---

*Henceforth the term "commando'" (without capitalization) will refer to all units, British and American, of the elite light infantry variety. The term "ranger" (without capitalization) will be used to refer exclusively to American units of that same variety. "Commando" and "Ranger" (capitalized) will refer to specific formations adopting those names. The umbrella term "specialist formations" will be used to collectively encompass both special forces and commando units.

attention to both the commando and special forces genres of formation when examining this subject. By adopting a holistic approach that engages with the inception, evolution, use, and value of *both* British and American special forces *and* commando formations, this work serves to address some of the broader deficiencies surrounding the subject's existent literature.

There can be a great deal of ambiguity surrounding such potentially esoteric terms as "irregular warfare," "unconventional warfare," or "special operations." As Thomas Mockaitis emphasized, "The language of irregular warfare has become as elusive as the guerrillas themselves."[4] Colin Gray similarly noted the "peril" of defining "special operations," arguing that "the exclusiveness that must characterize any good definition is contrary to the very spirit of special operations."[5] Official twenty-first-century definitions of "special operations" thus tend to be suitably broad, placing emphasis on the diversity and flexibility of the units charged with their conduct. The 2003 U.S. Joint Chiefs of Staff definition, for example, holds that special operations are "operations conducted in hostile, denied, or politically sensitive environments to achieve military, diplomatic, informational, and/or economic objectives employing military capabilities for which there is no broad conventional force requirement. . . . Special operations differ from conventional operations in degree of physical and political risk, operational techniques, mode of employment, independence from friendly support, and dependence on detailed operational intelligence and indigenous assets."[6] While such definitions certainly serve to highlight the multifaceted nature and roles of modern specialist formations, such breadth does little for the study of those units of the Second World War except muddy an already unclear pool of water.

Within the historiography of this subject, a relatively common trend of analysis has been to examine units of a particular modus operandi selectively. A number of works, for example, are confined to the study of those units that conducted operations "behind enemy lines." Although operations in depth, broadly considered, are often a characteristic of special operations, they are not a universal constant and are thus inadequate as the sole point of definition for all specialist formations and activities. Equally prevalent is a potentially more undesirable tendency to focus exclusively upon the "raid" as a "would-be hegemonic broad class of special operations activities."[7] Yet it remains important to emphasize that the legacy of special operations goes beyond those infamous and well-publicized actions of derring-do that tend to overshadow the more mundane day-to-day or inconspicuous activities of these units. To escape such a "raid" and "behind enemy lines" myopia, it is essential to also examine the much broader remit of specialist activities, including, but not limited to, intelligence activities, work alongside indigenous populations, and the distinct tasks undertaken by maritime-oriented special forces.

Another mechanism often used to examine this subject is through consideration of military "elites." Elite bodies of soldiers are as old as war itself, men more talented, better trained, or better equipped than their counterparts who would be assigned the most important missions of their day.[8] Eliot Cohen identified three main criteria that define an elite unit: the perpetual assignment of hazardous and unusual missions; the conduct of such missions that "require only a few men who must meet high standards of training and physical toughness, particularly the latter;" and a "reputation—justified or not—for bravura and success."[9] If one applies these points to special forces and their commando brethren, then most such units can be considered elites, but not all elites are specialist formations. Special forces are more than units that purely wage war at a high standard; they wage a unique form of warfare that separates them from conventionally oriented bodies. They, as John Gordon clarified, are "'elite' in the qualitative sense of their choice of personnel and excellent preparation, but they were 'special' in the functional military sense of what they did."[10] Although the British Commandos and the American-ranger variety of formations of the Second World War both shared a degree of common ground with other so-called elite light infantry units—most notably with airborne or mountain formations—their core roles were fundamentally different, something that makes the inclusion of these other "elites" impracticable.

In the early stages of the war, the nascent airborne formations had a certain commonality with commando and special forces units. Their selection of high-quality volunteers and the rigorous training of these was certainly analogous, and in the British instance the first parachute unit raised stemmed directly from the conversion of an Army Commando.[11] Furthermore, on three separate occasions early British airborne units undertook raids clearly falling within the definition of special operations,[12] and later in the war they were arguably as susceptible to being "misused" as conventional infantry as were the varied commando and ranger formations. These points notwithstanding, raids and other special operations were never intended to be the principal occupation of airborne formations. The few raids undertaken by a proportion of the early airborne community were primarily mounted by way of experiment—helping to ascertain and define what the precise role of these units should be. They were a means of amassing experience about the conduct of airborne operations and were not reflective of a definitive mission statement for airborne forces.[13] The utilization of the parachute or glider was intended merely as a means of transportation, and once these airborne formations reached the ground, they were primarily intended to serve as normal (albeit light) infantry as part of the larger conventional battle.[14]

Alongside this fundamental discrepancy in core role is the fact that the Anglo-American airborne formations were ultimately firmly structured around divisional- and corps-scale establishments that enabled attacks to be mounted *in force* against an open (vertical) flank.[15] The size of airborne formations, which reached army scale by August 1944, dramatically exceeded the war establishment of even the largest specialist formation. Bracketing airborne units alongside specialist formations would thus impede and inappropriately distort analysis into the impact and cost-effective worth of the latter variety of units. This fact, alongside the fundamental divergence of role, confirms that the inclusion of airborne formations within this study is undesirable.

For much the same reasons the Chindits, which were organized by General Orde Wingate and practiced long-range penetration in Burma in 1943–44, do not feature in this work. In light of both the relatively common "behind enemy lines" and "elites" focus on this subject, occasionally the Chindits are placed within the same bracket as other special forces and commando units. This association is not warranted. Their official designation of "special force" and their role behind the enemy line in Burma notwithstanding, the long-range penetration role of the Chindits is not broadly comparable to the activities of other special forces operating in depth; the Chindits sought to hold ground and fight rather than to raid and harass.[16] As Julian Thompson asserted, the Chindits were a "conventional force" fighting "conventional battles."[17] Another notable point of separation, as emphasized by Scott R. McMichael, is that, unlike many specialist formations, only some 5 percent of the Chindits were volunteers; on the whole they were "perfectly ordinary soldiers from perfectly ordinary battalions assigned to Wingate to be prepared for extraordinary tasks."[18] Alongside both of these factors is the issue of proportionality of scale, which undoubtedly serves as the clearest justification for the exclusion of the Chindits from this volume. The scale of the Chindit expeditions (some 3,000 men involved in the first, and some 20,000 men involved in the second) would eclipse any other specialist operation in depth.[19] Although it is thus unwarranted to include the Chindits within this volume, it is nevertheless important to examine their intended American "equivalent:" the 5307th Composite Unit (Provisional), known either as Galahad in official communiqués or, more commonly, as Merrill's Marauders. Notwithstanding that the Marauders were initially raised with the intention of serving as an "American Chindit" and were partly trained under Orde Wingate in such a capacity, their ultimate employment in a medium-range spearheading role had greater similarities to the roles undertaken by other commando and ranger formations than to the work of the Chindits. Furthermore, it is not without significance both that the Marauders were an all-volunteer force and that they consisted of noticeably smaller numbers than did the Chindits.[20]

Although not strictly a point of definition in the categorization of specialist formations, the scale or size of establishment of a unit is an important consideration. Special forces and commando units, the latter of which generally being larger, are in many ways characterized by exclusivity and restricted numbers. Although the scale of establishments and operational commitment of these units during the course of the war often had notable variation—ranging from mere handfuls of men to concentrations upwards of 2,000—such numbers, kept in perspective, were rarely exceeded, and as individual formations their proliferation was in no way comparable to the aforementioned examples of either the Chindits or airborne formations. Issues of scale have, however, clouded some treatments of this subject. Robin Neillands, for example, claimed that "Special Forces units were not always small. Few of them come out of the Second World War with a higher reputation than the mighty United States Marine Corps [USMC]."[21] Neilland's inclusion of the entire USMC as a special force betrays the sheer broadness, and concomitant inadequacy, of his definition. Certainly the amphibiously trained men of the USMC fulfilled a role above the most basic conventional doctrine, but not in such a manner that they could be considered either a commando or a special force. Within the larger USMC, however, the creation both of Raider battalions and the Amphibious Reconnaissance Company (later Battalion) are certainly illustrative of specialist formations.

With these broad limitations in mind, one of the best, and more succinct, definitions of specialist formations that can be applied to this study is that offered by John Gordon in his excellent study of British special forces in the Desert War. He states that these units were "not civilian saboteurs but uniformed soldiers specifically organized to carry out the high-risk functions of raiding, harassing, and intelligence gathering on the flanks or behind enemy lines. Their creation was predicated upon the assumption that the missions they undertook either fell outside the 'normal operations of war' or else were impossible for standard units to perform efficiently within time and space constraints."[22] It is upon this suitably broad definition, closely relevant to the range of operations as undertaken by both commando and special forces during the Second World War, that this work shall continue.

Although the Second World War represents the beginnings of modern special forces and commando units, it would be erroneous to ignore the fact that both Britain and America had rich historical backgrounds of undertaking irregular and unconventional activities before 1939. Equally it should be axiomatic that certain activities that became the wartime preserve of specialist formations—such as raids, clandestine intelligence gathering, or the provision of military support and leadership to indigenous populations—were not in any way "new" at the outbreak of the Second World War: in one way or another such tactics have always been part of organized armed conflict.

British history from the sixteenth century onward is full of examples of such activities; one only need look at the campaigns of Sir Francis Drake, General James Wolfe, or Lord Thomas Cochrane, or to examine the methods utilized in the Peninsular War or during the "Great Game" on the Indian frontiers,[23] to see such a legacy.[24] Nor is it without significance that the British had a long history of being on the receiving end of irregular warfare, and their perception of the potential efficiency of such activities was certainly affected by their experiences in America, South Africa, Palestine, the Northwest Frontier, and Ireland.[25] Upon the shelves of many an interwar staff college or officers' mess bookshelf one would have likely found well-thumbed copies of the likes of C. E. Callwell's seminal appraisal of colonial low-intensity operations, *Small Wars* (1896), or Deneys Reitz's *Commando* (1929), which recounted his experiences as a guerrilla in the Boer War.[26]

At the outset of the Second World War, perhaps the most prominent British memories of waging irregular warfare came from the exploits of T. E. Lawrence during the Arab Revolt in the First World War. In a conflict infamous for stalemated battles of attrition, the paucity of irregular operations ensured that the exploits of Lawrence stood out like a beacon. While the effectiveness of Lawrence's "sideshow of a sideshow" is debatable, his activities did, nevertheless, prove to some of the military establishment the potential benefits of these operations: that a small, low-cost commitment of men and material organized to conduct a campaign of mobile attacks could produce a disproportionate impact; and that "small teams of advisers and leaders, provided with money and basic weapons, can weld untrained, undisciplined, indigenous volunteers into an effective military force."[27] Lawrence "provided both glamour and intellectual sinew to the theory of guerrilla warfare."[28] His exploits, and more importantly the literature and publicity that followed them, would ensure that the potential for irregular activities had been realized by some, although by no means all, British military theorists and practitioners before 1939.[29]

Britain entered the Second World War with a military that was conducive toward the development and exploitation of irregular means: the country had both a small and decentralized military well experienced in the rigors of colonial warfare and a strategic culture that placed a premium on surprise, maneuver, and peripheral attack.[30] The British strategic perspective, epitomized by the likes of J. S. Corbett and Captain B. H. Liddell Hart, held that "when Britain had employed troops outside Britain they had been most effective when they had been used in amphibious roles to raid the enemy's coastline and compel him to withdraw forces which might otherwise have been used to fight Britain's continental allies, to cripple the enemy's fleet by destroying his naval bases, or to capture his overseas colonies."[31] Nor had Britain forgotten the lessons of its irregular past. When considering the future of infantry in 1933, Liddell Hart advised that the "infantry soldier needs to revive the tradition of the Peninsular skirmisher, but also to carry it to a higher pitch. He should profit by the lessons of irregular warfare so that he may develop the rusefulness and the ground-craft of the guerrilla fighter." Hart believed that an infantryman who was *"tria juncta in uno*—stalker, athlete, and marksman" could "seize or create many opportunities for vital intervention on the modern battlefield." Such a recommendation encapsulated many of the virtues later exhibited among those personnel of the wartime specialist formations.[32] The prominent vein of irregular actions occurring throughout British military history ensured that by the outbreak of the Second World War the British "way in warfare" was inherently amenable to the creation and employment of specialist formations.

Before the Second World War the United States also had a long history of irregular warfare. Colin Gray has gone as far as suggesting that in its colonial phase the United States "all but invented irregular warfare in modern times."[33] Light infantry "ranger" companies first developed in North America in the seventeenth century as a means of emulating Native American tactics and making up for the deficiencies of British regulars when fighting in frontier warfare. Although Colonel Benjamin Church can correctly be identified as the father of American rangers, the more influential irregular formation predating the creation of the United States was the Rangers of Major Robert Rogers, who fought for the British during the Seven Years' War. Rogers's exploits certainly inspired the creation of similar formations in the American War of Independence from the Continental Army (such as the Rangers of Thomas Knowlton), as well as from their Loyalist opponents (such as the Queen's Rangers, which Rogers himself commanded).[34] Though George Washington deliberately structured the Continental Army to fight pitched battles in the established "regular" manner of European armies, the recurrent use of elite light infantry alongside the strategy of "partisan war" pursued by the likes of Nathanael Greene and such subordinate leaders of his as Francis Marion and Thomas Sumter are certainly illustrative of an early American proclivity toward the irregular.[35]

By the start of the nineteenth century, "ranger" units had been revived to help patrol the American frontier on horseback, Congress authorizing six such companies in 1812 and approving the short-lived Mounted Ranger Battalion for the same purpose in 1832 after the Black Hawk War. This pattern continued into the American Civil War, during which time it has been estimated that "more than 400 . . . military organizations called themselves 'ranger' units."[36] In that war, spontaneous local events and the April 1862 Confederate Partisan Ranger Act would ensure that the Confederacy, in particular, would utilize various sorts of irregular forces in their efforts to defeat the Union. Robert R. Mackey has drawn attention to three different varieties of irregular tactics employed during the "uncivil war": guerrilla tactics (of "people's war"), partisan warfare of a more organized variety, and cavalry raids. Though meeting with some success—such as the raids conducted by the partisan rangers of John S. Mosby—this form of warfare was ultimately found to be unsuccessful, being tarnished by an inability to exert control over the depredations of some of the more freebooting "bushwhackers" (as typified by the infamous actions of William C. Quantrill and his men) and, more generally, being defeated by effective counters from the Union.[37] Despite the colorful reputations amassed by the partisans and rangers of the Civil War, the net result was that the U.S. Army emerged from the conflict firmly behind a tradition laid out by Ulysses S. Grant, viewing the use of irregulars "as nothing more than bandits with Southern sympathies."[38]

In spite of such plentiful experience in undertaking irregular warfare, the years after the Civil War saw the U.S. Army much more likely to be on the receiving end of irregular action, as seen in both the Indian and Philippine wars. While these conflicts certainly proved challenging, the regular U.S. Army was nonetheless able to deviate from and adapt its European-style methods in order to overcome the difficulties posed by foes using irregular methods.[39] In spite of this, lessons about the potential efficiency of waging irregular warfare never reverberated in the collective consciousness.

Perhaps more than anything else it was the American experience of the First World War that helped propel the U.S. military toward eschewing unconventional war. After 1918 the U.S. Army was forced to cease thinking of itself as a frontier constabulary and to redefine its mission as that of fielding a mass force capable of battling any other modern army in the world. Combined with the fact that during the First World War the United States suffered no Somme or Passchendaele, this meant that by 1939 America was, militarily speaking, not seeking unorthodox solutions to large-unit warfare in the same manner that the British were prone to doing. By the eve of the Second World War, therefore, the American "way of warfare" was firmly committed to the notion of applying "mass and concentration in the manner of U. S. Grant."[40] The American orientation toward the mass of the citizen army remained pronounced, and the U.S. Army's "long-standing suspicion of elite forces" was arguably greater than ever.[41] Simply put, in spite of such rich historical experience, it is not possible to surmise that Americans were as amenable as the British toward irregular warfare.

Despite such pronounced divisions in their respective attitudes toward irregular warfare in the interwar period, neither Britain nor the United States had, with a couple of exceptions, made any significant doctrinal or organizational strides in the field of irregular warfare before the start of the Second World War. Within Britain, perhaps the most notable exception to this was the 1938 establishment of a new branch of the General Staff concerned with researching irregular methods and guerrilla warfare. This small branch, known initially as GS(R) and later renamed MI(R), was headed by Colonel J. C. F. Holland. An officer of some experience, Holland had served in Arabia and, later, in Ireland, where he had been wounded during the "troubles."[42] At the hands of Holland and the likes of Major Colin Gubbins, who later became head of the Special Operations Executive (SOE), this branch produced documents such as *The Art of Guerilla Warfare* and the *Partisan Leader's Handbook*. These publications, which drew upon recent experiences of irregular warfare, succinctly laid out principles for individuals and small groups "working by stealth on acts of sabotage"; for larger groups "working as a band under a nominated leader, and employing military tactics, weapons etc."; and for the operations of large guerrilla forces whose "strength necessitates a certain degree of military organization in order to secure their cohesion and to make and carry out effectively a plan of campaign."[43]

MI(R) would eventually merge with Section D, a small section of the Secret Intelligence Service (SIS) that had been raised in March 1938 for the conduct of sabotage, and a department of the Foreign Office known as Electra House, which dealt with propaganda, to form the nucleus of the SOE in the summer of 1940.[44] The existence of such departments immediately prior to the outbreak of the Second World War illustrates both that the British were beginning to attach certain priorities to irregular warfare and that they were attempting to translate some of their previous experiences into practical lessons.

Progress was not, however, uniform across the board. Despite such developments, during the interwar period Britain had struggled to prepare and fund a "striking force" of Royal Marines designed for raiding operations, which had been recommended in a 1924 committee chaired by Admiral Charles Madden and, more reprehensibly, in the first months of the war foolishly chose to disband the Inter-Service Training and Development Center (ISTDC) that had been created in 1937 to prepare plans for combined operations.[45]

Although before 1939 America had made no effort to research irregular methods in the same manner as did Section D or MI(R), a number of developments in the prewar USMC are, however, certainly of note. Prior to the outbreak of the Second World War, elements of the USMC had gained firsthand experience of irregular warfare both in China and in various Caribbean "banana republics." Dozens of amphibious landings were made in Haiti and Nicaragua, and Marines were establishing pacification programs and running special anti-bandit groups to help combat guerrilla activities. Furthermore, efforts had been made to translate lessons learned during such activities into (albeit tentative) doctrine, resulting in the publication of the *Small Wars Operations* manual in 1935.[46] Also worthy of mention are the experiments and doctrinal developments by the USMC in the field of amphibious operations during this period, which resulted in strides having been made in such areas as "submarine reconnaissance for improved intelligence . . . and experimenting with the specialist groups needed to control naval gun fire and close air strikes accurately."[47]

While historically noteworthy, such interwar studies and advances from both Britain and the United States would have little direct application to the development and employment of specialist formations during the Second World War. These initiatives were insufficient to suggest that before the war either nation placed any great faith in the potential of special operations. The fact remains that in 1939 neither power had formed any specialist unit nor did they have any coherent plans to do so. This is both significant and—given how unprepared both nations were for the outbreak of war—not unsurprising. The importance of any interwar studies, as well as the significance of any prior historical experience or national predisposition in these fields, thus becomes greatly lessened. It was the unique conditions and circumstances of the Second World War that would encourage both Britain and America to ultimately adopt specialist formations. At the start of the war neither nation had any practical doctrine or any vast reserves of firsthand experience in the conduct of irregular warfare upon which to base their first specialist formations. In the adoption of these units, both Britain and the United States would initially be in the same position of having either to invent or assimilate such capabilities.

This work thus serves to examine how, from such a "cold start" in 1939 and 1941 respectively, Britain and the United States would go on to successfully conceive, develop, and utilize a wide variety of commando and special forces units to take on a multitude of tasks across practically every theater of operation during the Second World War. The existent historical record regarding this subject tends to make assumptions that the prewar patterns and attitudes held by Britain and America toward these formations continued into the Second World War. It suggests that the British, historically familiar as they were with raiding operations and decentralized autonomous groupings, resorted swiftly and adapted well to the development and use of specialist formations during the war. The British found in these operations, in the opinion of Alexander Clifford, a "buccaneering, marauding, piratical sort of game which Englishmen took to like a duck to water. They discovered a talent and a liking for it, a heritage . . . [from] four centuries of pioneers, explorers, travellers, colonists, eccentrics, individuals."[48]

It is often conversely assumed that the American prewar aversion toward irregular warfare continued during the war itself. The assumption thus follows that specialist formations were neither favored nor widely adopted by the United States during the Second World War.[49] Indeed, extant appraisals seem to suggest that the American "way of war" had difficulty embracing or utilizing specialist formations.[50] The strategic perception of the United States was notably sceptical of "Britain's tangential, 'soft-underbelly,' 'closing the ring' approach to waging war," an approach in which the potential for specialist operations was quite prominent.[51] America instead favored a strategy that ignored the periphery and extraneous activities in place of a concentrated annihilative strike, reliant upon an "overwhelming quantity of . . . firepower and logistical capacity," against the enemy heartland—an approach in which the potential value of specialist formations would appear to be much less pronounced.[52]

Such a traditional appreciation, however, neglects some central factors related to the creation and use of specialist formations during the Second World War. It is important to recognize that although broadly committed to a more undeviating "way of war," the United States would swiftly develop an understanding of the potential value of employing specialist formations for the furtherance of the application of mass conventional force. Understanding that beaches had to be reconnoitered, fortifications stormed, flanks protected, and advances screened, they recognized the value of specialist formations in providing for such needs and in serving as an ancillary to their "way of war." Furthermore, while it is true that America, on the whole, was reluctant to become embroiled in peripheral activities, they *did*, however, show a marked willingness (for both political and military reasons) to employ and exploit specialist formations—just as the British did—in peripheral theaters such as Yugoslavia, Greece, Scandinavia, and the Far East. Specialist formations transcended traditional strategic impediments, and the employment of these units could circumvent national strategic perceptions and policies.

The broader realities of U.S. strategy in the Second World War have colored and distorted analysis of the American adoption and utilization of specialist formations. Their military culture and strategic priorities were not impediments toward their development and application of specialist formations. Ultimately, American specialist units would proliferate, in numerical terms, almost as extensively, and in practical terms as effectively, as they did among the more culturally predisposed British. What the divergence of military cultures and strategic approaches between Britain and the United States *did* do, however, was affect how each power would perceive virtually all aspects of the inception, use, and evolution of these units. The result was that between Britain and the United States there would be a range of different attitudes, policies, and motivations behind the inception, expansion, organization, proliferation, command and control, and disbandment of these units—not to mention a range of divergent ideas and priorities concerning the respective roles, methods, and employment of both commandos and special forces.

CHAPTER 1

THE INCEPTION AND EMPLOYMENT OF COMMANDO AND RANGER FORMATIONS

The years 1939–45 bore witness to several significant innovations that revolutionized the art of war. The advent of specialist formations was one such development. The global scope of the Second World War provided an unprecedented set of opportunities for the conduct of irregular operations, encouraging the exploitation of depth and the periphery. Overstretched lines of communication combined with an almost limitless number of potentially vulnerable flanks to present a range of fertile targets for saboteurs, raiders, and other irregular bodies. The increasingly complex nature of warfare and the range of different operational environments confronting the combatants made specialization desirable, if not inevitable. Meanwhile, various technological advances and refinements increased the potential application of small bands of highly trained personnel. Technology such as gliders and transport aircraft, the parachute, motor vehicles, submersible craft, and fast shipping facilitated the insertion, supply, and recovery of irregular groups. Parallel advances in man-portable radio telegraphy enabled such groups to be controlled and directed and facilitated the better undertaking of intelligence-gathering missions, while developments in weaponry, such as light machine guns and plastic explosives, permitted mere handfuls of men to cause levels of destruction and attrition disproportionate to their numbers.

Nothing spurred the creation of specialist formations within the first years of the Second World War, however, so much as exigency. These formations arose from the weakness and limitations (both real and imagined) of conventional forces and a lack of opportunity to use the latter. Defeat in France and the Low Counties and continental exclusion following Dunkirk in the summer of 1940 undoubtedly caused Britain to opt "for the 'British way in warfare' from necessity, not choice," and paved the way for the creation of an extensive range of unconventional forces.[1] As Barry Posen contended in reference to interwar doctrinal developments, "Organizations innovate when they fail."[2] A combination of fear, surprise, impotence, and conventional defeat gave Britain the impetus to develop the Commandos, the Special Operations Executive (SOE), and a range of smaller irregular "private armies," all within a few weeks in June 1940. The reverses of Dunkirk, Greece, and Narvik (and soon afterward Crete, Tobruk, and Singapore) reinforced all too vividly the specter of the Somme and Passchendaele. Small bands of specially selected men willing to take great risks for low outlay were thus naturally attractive. Not only did they offer a means of regaining the strategic initiative, but through action they could personalize conflict, create heroes, and provide a glimmer of hope in an otherwise bleak outlook.

The Advent of British Commando Formations

Though short lived, the Independent Companies were the first genuine British specialist formation created during the Second World War.[3] Their genesis came in April 1940, following suggestions made by Colonel Colin Gubbins of MI(R). Gubbins had long held an interest in irregular warfare, having served both in northern Russia during the civil war in 1919 and in Ireland during the interwar period. He would go on to become a prominent figure in the irregular warfare community during the Second World War, developing not only the Independent Companies but also the Auxiliary Units (a civilian stay-behind force that was to be used in the event of a German invasion of Britain), before being appointed head of SOE in 1943. The Independent Companies developed from Gubbins's complex notion that units of select volunteers could serve as "guerrillas" in occupied territories while supplementing their strength by raising additional "bands" from among indigenous populations.

Within only five weeks ten Independent Companies had been formed from the Territorial Army and other sources, each company comprising volunteers able to "fend for themselves" and (preferably) skilled in "stalking" and "ambushing."[4] By May five of these hastily raised, trained, and equipped companies had arrived in Norway in an attempt to delay the German advance toward Narvik.[5] Though certainly ambitious, Gubbins's ideas would ultimately prove premature. The use of uniformed soldiers to raise and harness indigenous guerrilla forces, a role in modern military parlance known as "unconventional warfare," was something that would not properly develop until the later stages of the Second World War. With hindsight, sending personnel with negligible specialist instruction, equipment, or knowledge of either Norway or the Norwegian language to operate behind enemy lines in groups of nearly three hundred men has all the hallmarks of an ad hoc and amateurish effort. With scant opportunity for anything irregular, the Independent Companies were thus "squandered in main force operations, where they lacked the numbers, fire-power and logistical support necessary for sustained combat operations."[6] This pattern of commando-style formations evolving from their originally intended role and toward conventional occupations within the main battle would, for both British and American units, often recur. Yet in spite of the evident mismatch between concept and reality, the creation of the Independent Companies illustrates just how rapidly elements of the British military establishment were willing to apply MI(R)'s prewar research on irregular means.[7]

The Independent Companies were followed by the Army Commandos, credit for whose formation falls to Lieutenant Colonel Dudley Clarke, a knowledgeable and very influential officer who had experienced counterinsurgency firsthand while serving as a staff officer in Palestine following the Arab rebellion. Just two days after Dunkirk, on June 5, 1940, after discussing the need to maintain offensive action with Field Marshal Sir John Dill, vice chief of the Imperial General Staff (CIGS), to whom he was military assistant, Clarke proposed the formation of "Commando" forces.[8] He sought to re-create the Boer *Kommando*, "to aim," he wrote, "mosquito stings with telling effect on the ponderous bulk of a German Army stretched invitingly along a coastline which might soon reach from Narvik to Biarritz."[9] On June 8 the Commando concept was given official approval, and ten Commandos, each comprising five hundred volunteers, were authorized.

It is significant that Clarke's proposals were submitted in a favorable military and political climate. Even as Clarke was presenting his idea, Prime Minister Winston Churchill was thinking on similar lines. On June 6, 1940, the prime minister wrote to his chief of staff,

Major General Hastings Ismay, suggesting that Australian formations due to arrive in Britain (but that were subsequently diverted to the Middle East) should be organized into lightly armed "striking companies," each of 250 men of the "hunter class," capable of both reacting quickly against enemy landings and developing a "reign of terror" against enemy-occupied coastlines with "butcher and bolt" raids.[10] A foremost champion of specialist formations, Churchill ultimately advocated establishment of both the Commandos and SOE. David Stafford attributed this support to "Churchill's romanticism, which enlarged and fed upon his own memories of quasi-guerrilla fighting on the north-west frontier and in South Africa, and upon the legacy of T.E. Lawrence and the revolt in the desert."[11] Churchill's personal desire to avoid the stalemated campaigns of attrition of the First World War, combined with "a profound conviction that, as an underdog, Britain in 1940 had to mobilize every form of warfare that it could, however unconventional," resulted in a great deal of enthusiasm for embracing irregular solutions to Britain's strategic dilemmas.[12]

Even as the Commandos were being established, Churchill continued to urge the creation of further specialist formations. Unashamedly influenced by his perception of how the German armed forces operated,[13] on June 18, 1940, he would ask General Ismay about his ideas for "storm troops": "We have always set our faces against the idea, but the Germans certainly gained in the last war by adopting it, and this time it has been a leading cause of their victory. There ought to be at least 20,000 Storm Troops or 'Leopards' drawn from existing units, ready to spring at the throat of any small landings or descents."[14] The prime minister expressed similar perceptions to his secretary of state for war, Anthony Eden, to whom he wrote on August 25: "How strongly I feel that the Germans have been right, both in the last war and in this, in the use they have made of storm troops. . . . The defeat of France was accomplished by an incredibly small number of highly-equipped *élite*, while the dull mass of the German Army came on behind, made good the conquest and occupied it."[15]

With the decision to raise Commandos taken, Dudley Clarke was appointed to head a new War Office section, MO9, responsible for both raising these units and preparing cross-channel raids. Given the magnitude and inherently interservice nature of the task facing Clarke only one week later, on June 14 it was thought necessary to place MO9 under the aegis of Lieutenant General Sir Alan Bourne, who, alongside his position of adjutant general of the Royal Marines, was accordingly appointed "commander of raiding operations." This arrangement was also short lived, and it took only one month for it to be superseded by the appointment of Admiral Roger Keyes as director of combined operations (DCO) on July 17. At the age of sixty-eight, Keyes was perhaps not the most obvious choice to head a dynamic new organization responsible for, among other things, Commando raids. His most prominent qualification for the position, his vast naval experience notwithstanding, was the fact that he had planned and commanded the 1918 Zeebrugge Raid—a relatively rare example of a combined operation in the First World War and one not dissimilar to some of the tasks being projected for the Commandos.[16] The establishment of the Combined Operations organization, which would become more vibrant after October 1941 when under the charge of Louis Mountbatten, was a seminal point in the history of British specialist formations; it would coordinate, and provide essential support for, the establishment and application of both the Commandos and a variety of special forces.

Given the dire strategic situation Britain faced in the summer of 1940 and a concomitant scarcity of trained personnel and equipment, the formation of the first Commandos faced a number of hurdles. As no existent formation could be diverted from home defense, it was thought axiomatic that the Commandos be formed as entirely new entities.[17] The resulting call for first-class personnel aggrieved many regular unit commanders, who, preoccupied with mobilizing and equipping their own units, were understandably reluctant to give up their best officers and men. However, spurred on by the strategic realities of the time, that "raids must necessarily be the British Army's main offensive contribution for the present," the formation of the Commandos was granted high priority and much opposition was accordingly brushed aside.[18] By June 1940 the Independent Companies had become somewhat redundant, and thus, despite their general lack of specialist training, they were immediately latched onto as a source of personnel for the Commando initiative. In November 1940, when a sufficient number of Commandos had been raised, Admiral Keyes thus decided to group them, together with the remaining Independent Companies, into Special Service (SS) Battalions. (Hereinafter the initials SS refer to "Special Service" rather than their more common use for the

German Schutzstaffel.) As with so many of the early Commando developments, this arrangement would prove short lived, and in February 1941 the SS Battalions were restructured and reverted to being called "Commandos," with the Independent Companies therein formally merged into their establishment. (See appendix A for an organizational chart of this arrangement.)

When considering the creation of the Commandos, it might appear strange that the Royal Marines were not chosen as the source of recruits. During the interwar period, the Marines were certainly the most advanced service as far as amphibious operations were concerned, and they, as stipulated by the Madden Committee of 1924, filled an explicit wartime role of supplying the Army "with units for special duties for which Naval experience is necessary"—something clearly in line with the tone of the Commando program.[19] The decision not to use the Royal Marines appears even more puzzling given the fact that in the summer of 1940 the provisional Royal Marine Brigade was "technically available," having participated in the occupation of the Faroe Islands and the invasion of Iceland in April and May 1940 respectively. Their availability and doctrinal mandate aside, the decree that the Commandos should be formed as entirely new units was considered absolute, placing the men of the Royal Marines "severely off-limits."[20] It was a judgment that caused a degree of offense to many Marines, who saw the Commando role of amphibious raiding as being a central part of their own raison d'être. Ultimately this decision helped ensure that for the first two years of the war the Royal Marines Division, which was founded in September 1940 (just prior to elements of it participating in a failed operation against Dakar), faced a frustrating and ill-defined existence before Royal Marines were finally permitted to join the Commando organization in 1942.

The roles intended for the first Commandos in the summer of 1940 were as indistinct as those of the original Independent Companies. The Commandos were expected to undertake dual, but seemingly opposed, roles of the "striking companies" of Churchill's "butcher and bolt" policy and serving as "leopards" that could act as a defensive mobile reserve with the capacity to "pounce" on any German landing against Britain.[21] The latter "leopard" role would continue until invasion fears were allayed, but it rapidly became considered secondary to what was regarded as being the main role of the Commandos: small-scale amphibious raids of limited duration—variously termed "tip and run," "butcher and bolt," and "smash and grab" operations.[22] It was made explicit that a Commando was "not expected to resist an attack or to overcome a defense by formed bodies of troops . . . success must depend on speed, individual ingenuity and dispersion."[23] The tenor of this latter point should be borne in mind when considering the subsequent evolution of the Commando role.

Despite the necessity that had spurred their creation—the perceived need to strike back at the enemy in a series of pin-prick raids—the early Commandos performed few of these operations, and lack of experience, equipment, and inadequate training ensured that those operations that did take place in 1940 were invariably unsuccessful. The first cross-Channel raid to be undertaken, Operation Collar on the night of June 23/24, 1940, was conducted by No. 11 Independent Company, a composite force made up of volunteers from Nos. 6, 7, 8, and 9 Independent Companies. The operation consisted of four separate landings against beaches in the Pas-de-Calais area of France and was undertaken with the intention of gathering intelligence and seizing prisoners. Although being of some worth in terms of propaganda and proving that troops could technically be landed in France (perhaps an unsurprising lesson as the raid occurred only weeks after Dunkirk, and one that in any case proved short lived as German coastal defenses improved), the raid was sloppily executed and entirely unspectacular in terms of military results. Dudley Clarke, who had joined the raid to see his new initiative in action, was very almost hoist with his own petard, becoming the only casualty after his ear was grazed by a stray bullet from a chaotic skirmish.[24]

The first true "Commando" raid, however, was Operation Ambassador, undertaken by No. 3 Commando and No. 11 Independent Company on the night of July 14/15 against Guernsey, one of the recently occupied Channel Islands. The results were even more disappointing than Collar, the lowlights including a landing being made on the wrong island (Sark) and three men having to be left stranded because it was belatedly discovered that they could not swim. In the words of Lieutenant Colonel John Durnford-Slater of No. 3 Commando, Ambassador was "a ridiculous, almost a comic, failure. We had captured no prisoners. We had done no serious damage. We had caused no casualties to the enemy. . . . A youth in his teens could have done the same."[25] Such amateurish operations unsettled even the prime minister, who was quick to vow that there should be no more "silly fiascos. . . . The idea of working all these coasts up against us by pin-prick raids . . . is one to be strictly avoided."[26]

These initially disappointing operations severely curtailed the ad hoc opportunistic small-scale raids that some had envisioned as being the prime occupation, and one of the key benefits, of the Commandos. These setbacks further reinforced the necessity for comprehensive planning prior to a raid as well as the importance of both a thorough selection procedure and a rigorous training program for all Commando personnel. These requirements alone were sufficient to stall further Commando raids from Britain until March 1941. Churchillian rhetoric aside, the "reign of terror" was slow in coming, and the prospect of coordinated coastal raiding operations from mainland Britain would remain elusive. Rather than small-scale raiding, the weighty demands of interservice and interagency cooperation thus ensured that Combined Operations Headquarters (COHQ) increasingly favored larger preplanned "set-piece" raids that encompassed, and exceeded, the deployment of entire Commandos. The larger raids conducted from Britain in the period 1941–42, such as the successful raid targeting industry on the Norwegian Lofoten Islands (Operation Claymore) in March 1941, the raid against the harbors and fish-oil factories on Vaagso Island (Archery) in January 1942, or the audacious attack on the docks of St. Nazaire (Chariot) in March 1942 do, nevertheless, illustrate that in this period the Commandos generally conformed to their original role as being "pin-prick" raiders, even if they were not deployed in the frequency or scale originally intended.[27]

Although regular small-scale raids by Commando elements based in Britain were infrequent, in late 1940 it was hoped that the Mediterranean and Middle East might provide a more fertile climate for amphibious raiding. With such motivations in mind, three Middle East Commandos (Nos. 50, 51, and 52) were locally raised from personnel serving in Egypt and Palestine. The first months of 1941 saw No. 50 Commando held in a defensive capacity in Crete and Egypt, while Nos. 51 and 52 Commandos were deployed in protracted operations in East Africa—which, although successful, were along the lines of those that any infantry battalion could undertake.[28] Despite such lackluster employment hardly being suggestive of an apposite strategic climate for raiding forces, in February 1941 it was nevertheless decided to send Nos. 7, 8, and 11 Commandos from Britain to the Middle East. Ready for deployment in March 1941, these Commandos were administratively grouped with the Middle East Commandos to form "Layforce," named after their commander, Colonel Robert Laycock.

For the Layforce Commandos general inexperience, inadequate numbers of naval transports, and a lack of air superiority transpired to abort most of their planned operations. Of those undertaken—such as the actions of No. 50 (ME) Commando against the Greek island of Kastelorizo in February 1941; the No. 7 Commando attempt on Bardia, Libya, in April 1941; or the Litani River (in Lebanon) operation of No.11 Commando in June 1941[29]—none, as General Claude Auchinleck would admit, "was a great success."[30] Perhaps most illustrative of the confused employment of Commandos in this theater, however, was the use of Nos. 7 and 50/52(ME) Commandos as part of the rear guard covering the evacuation of Crete in May 1941. This task was born of necessity, and although well performed, marked a conventional and inappropriate (although not necessarily unwarranted) use of specialist formations that were ill equipped and too lightly armed for the task.[31] Following Crete, the Layforce group was disbanded, with large numbers of its personnel migrating into alternative irregular outfits. Robert Laycock would go on to have a very great bearing on the evolution of the Commandos—peaking with his appointment as Chief of Combined Operations (CCO) in October 1943—but the unhappy fate of his Commando group is reflective of early tribulations in undertaking raids and harnessing specialist units. Thus, while Commando deployments in the Mediterranean and Middle East of 1941 were certainly more varied than those launched from the British Isles, they were, nonetheless, fraught with many of the same difficulties and frustrations.

By 1942 the expediency of hitting back at the enemy in a series of pin-prick raids was gradually being replaced with a desire to gain experience in, and to prosecute, large-scale amphibious actions to facilitate the commencement of conventional operations. In such a climate the amphibious experience and capabilities of the Commandos were at a premium, and their potential value in spearheading or supporting major amphibious assaults was becoming clear. Such was the perceived value of utilizing Commandos in this capacity that in March 1942 Field Marshal Alan Brooke, the CIGS, recommended that eighteen Commandos be raised by April 1944, with the expectation that there be four Commandos per assault division in any future large-scale amphibious landings.[32]

Charles Messenger has claimed that No. 5 Commando's participation in the May 1942 Madagascar landings "marked the first occasion when the Commandos were used in what was to become their fundamental role, the spearheading of major amphibious assaults on opposed shores."[33] In chronological terms this statement is accurate, but in doctrinal terms it is the use of Nos. 3 and 4 Commandos in securing the flanks of the Dieppe raid on August 19, 1942, that most adequately highlights this transition.

The Dieppe raid has been the subject of significant academic debate and controversy over both its objectives and subsequent worth.[34] Although important lessons about amphibious operations were undoubtedly learned from the action, taken in isolation it is impossible to avoid the conclusion that the raid was a costly failure. While earlier raids on Vaagso and the Lofotens had involved a sizable commitment of forces and naval vessels, Dieppe was something much more ambitious. Not simply a Commando raid, it was the boldest combined operation thus far undertaken in the war.[35] Early plans for the operation did not even include Commandos within the order of battle, as it was envisioned that airborne forces would be suitable for protecting the flanks of the raid. Given the nascent state of airborne operations at this time, it was probably fortuitous that unsuitable weather conditions precluded this option. In the event, a total of three Commandos would take part in the raid: Nos. 3 and 4 Commandos and the newly created Royal Marine A Commando (subsequently renamed No. 40 Commando). At Dieppe their employment was to be supportive of, but strictly ancillary to, the main landings made by the 2nd Canadian Infantry Division.

Dieppe was not an auspicious debut for the Royal Marine Commandos. Tasked with undertaking sabotage tasks in the harbor subsequent to the initial landings, the Marines more generally acted as a floating reserve for the central landing. As a result of the difficulties experienced during the initial assault, however, the Commando was only tentatively committed in such a capacity. Coming under heavy fire while attempting to land, the unit was only saved from horrendous casualties by a hastily ordered withdrawal that claimed the life of Lieutenant Colonel Joseph Picton-Phillips, its commanding officer. Nos. 3 and 4 Commandos were each tasked with more autonomous duties during the raid. They were to silence two coastal batteries that might threaten the main landings: No. 3 Commando was tasked with neutralizing the Berneval battery to the east of Dieppe, while No. 4 Commando landed to the west of the town to tackle the battery near Varengeville-sur-Mer. Although No. 3 Commando was unable to destroy the guns at Berneval, in part because of problems experienced coming ashore at the correct position, the handful of personnel able to reach the target were nevertheless able to provide sufficient distraction and prevent its operation against the main landings.[36] Without any doubt the standout success of an otherwise dire operation was No. 4 Commando's successful "textbook" attack on the Varengeville-sur-Mer battery.[37] More than anything else this action highlighted the versatility of employing Commandos in support of larger amphibious operations. The subsequent COHQ report of the raid surmised that it was the success of the Commandos on the flanks of the raid that "allowed the operation of our ships off Dieppe for all the nine hours."[38] The lesson that Commandos could act as "perfect flank guards" for conventional operations was disseminated to, and understood by, British and American planners alike.

The Advent of American Ranger Formations

Despite the many limitations of the early Commandos and the initial raiding program, the inception of these units had a profound significance in paving the way for the creation of several other specialist formations on both sides of the Atlantic. Even if America did not share the same institutional aversion as the British toward attrition and the big battle, after Pearl Harbor it found itself in much the same position as Britain had been in 1940: shocked, outnumbered, and conventionally defeated, it was unable to come to grips with the enemy on a large scale.

Prior to Pearl Harbor, the United States was already well aware of Commando developments. Britain had provided America with information on their establishment, organization, and methods and, more significantly, had permitted both William J. Donovan's Coordinator of Information (COI), the forerunner of OSS, and USMC representatives to observe and receive training from the Commandos.[39] Lessons learned during these early American tours undoubtedly had a direct influence on the advent of the first American specialist formation created during the Second World War: the USMC Raiders. James Ladd has claimed that the Raiders were created "largely on the basis" of reports made by two marine captains, Samuel B. Griffith II and W. M. Greene, Jr., who had received Commando training in Scotland.[40] Although these were noteworthy, of even more significance was the lobbying of Captain James Roosevelt, the eldest son of the president, who had toured the Commandos while working for Donovan's COI. Illustrative of the power of social positioning, in January 1942 Captain Roosevelt submitted a proposal directly to Major General Thomas Holcomb, the commandant of the Marine Corps, that outlined his ideas for a unit "for purposes similar to the British Commandos and the Chinese Guerrillas."[41] Although Holcomb expressed reservations based on a belief that any existent Marine unit could perform the proposed tasks, the scheme received obvious fillip when Captain Roosevelt again bypassed red tape to submit the proposal to his father.[42]

While not comparable to Churchill, President Franklin D. Roosevelt certainly had some natural inclination toward irregular warfare. During the First World War, as assistant secretary of the navy he was responsible for overseeing the Office of Naval Intelligence, and consequently, as David Stafford has claimed, "Roosevelt liked secrets."[43] His willingness to appoint his friend "Wild Bill" Donovan as COI (and later as head of OSS) and his enthusiasm about the Marine Raiders is certainly representative of this. That his son's proposal also referenced the example of the Chinese guerrillas likely struck a further chord with the President in light of his meetings with Lieutenant Colonel Evans F. Carlson, USMC. Carlson was Roosevelt's prewar military observer in China who, having observed the Chinese guerrillas in action against the Japanese, had become "convinced that guerrilla warfare was the wave of the future" and had discussed such matters with the President.[44]

Equally if not more important than both the British example and Chinese lessons in aiding the inception of the USMC Raiders, however, were prewar USMC forays into "rubber boat" companies. As early as 1940 General Holland M. Smith, commanding the 1st Marine Division, had experimented with such companies to conduct raids and diversions from fast destroyer transports, known as APDs, in Fleet Landing Exercises. By 1941 this concept had evolved, and General Smith, now commanding the Amphibious Force Atlantic Fleet, selected the 1st Battalion, 5th Marines, to become an independent "APD battalion" under Lieutenant Colonel Merritt Edson. Following Pearl Harbor and Captain Roosevelt's suggestions, this battalion was renamed the 1st Separate Battalion, and a sister battalion was created using a proportion of its personnel as a nucleus. On February 16, 1942, the 1st Separate Battalion was redesignated a Raider Battalion; three days later the 2nd Battalion followed suit.[45] Edson would command the 1st and Carlson the 2nd Battalion. James Roosevelt and Samuel Griffith II, both of whom had observed Commando training firsthand less than six months before, became their executive officers.

The U.S. Army's first specialist unit of the Second World War was the 1st Ranger Battalion. Its creation owes much more to the British model than did the Marine Raiders. The U.S. Army first came into contact with the Commandos during tours of the British Combined Operations Headquarters (COHQ) in January 1942, but it was not until April 1942, when General George C. Marshall visited London, that the U.S. Army was first spurred to emulate British capabilities. Following his tour of COHQ, General Marshall became convinced that Commando raids served as an important mechanism for making a "preliminary active front" of continental European coastlines. He believed that attaching American service personnel to COHQ would provide a solid means of gaining much needed combat and amphibious experience.[46] It was thus proposed that a small number of American soldiers undertake Commando training (akin to an arrangement made with the USMC six months earlier), a proportion of whom could then be used to form the nucleus of an "American Commando," while the remainder would be returned to the United States to serve as "Commando instructors" who would train Army Ground Forces personnel in combined operations techniques. On the back of such suggestions, eight officers from the U.S. Army, Navy, and Marines under Colonel Lucian K. Truscott, Jr., were attached to COHQ.[47] Subsequently, on May 26, 1942, having witnessed British developments, Truscott recommended to the Joint Chiefs of Staff that there be the immediate formation of an "American Commando." In light of earlier suggestions, this was immediately agreed to.[48]

The 1st Ranger Battalion was thus activated on June 19, 1942; its ranks comprised 488 volunteers taken from U.S. Army personnel then stationed in Northern Ireland. In line with the British approach, it was thought desirable to create an entirely new unit rather than risk destroying the integrity of an existing formation. Although the Rangers were to closely mirror the Commando model and were placed under the British SS Brigade for "training and tactical control," conscious efforts were made to retain the American identity of the force as much as practicable. It was made explicit that the U.S. 34th Infantry Division (then stationed in Ireland) would remain responsible for all administration and supply, and it was hoped that American equipment and tactical doctrines would be retained as much as feasible.[49] This was of course in line with wider American motivations to remain as independent of the British as possible. The title "Ranger" was chosen for the new unit precisely because of its North American associations; a name such as "American Commando" held undesirable connotations of subservience.

Marshall's 1942 visit to Britain also laid the foundations for the advent of another unique specialist formation. During his visit to COHQ, Marshall had been introduced to a British scientist named Geoffrey Pyke, who had devised a plan for a special snow vehicle, code-named Plough. Pike envisioned specially trained personnel using the Plough to raid vulnerable German possessions in Norway or other snow-covered environments. However, given Britain's limited manufacturing capabilities at the time, it was evident that, if constructed, the Plough would need to be developed in America. As such, it was suggested to Marshall that the U.S. Army might also take responsibility for raising the personnel who would undertake the scheme. Marshall was enthused and sent Lieutenant Colonel Robert T. Frederick from the Operations Division of the General Staff to make an assessment of the project's viability. Although this appraisal identified some limitations in the plan, Marshall remained keen, and in June 1942 he placed Frederick in charge of creating what would become known as the First Special Service Force (FSSF).[50]

The FSSF was created as a joint American-Canadian formation. The Canadian contingent became involved partly from a desire to develop their own specialist capabilities, of which they provided no other example during the war, and partly because of the Canadian Army's suitability for training and operating in winter conditions.[51] Initial recruiting for the force was, at least for the American contingent, fraught with problems. While the Canadian "half" was composed of hand-picked and qualified volunteers, much of the initial American contingent was made up of "a collection of marginal types culled from stockades and unit rejects . . . [who] were low on the scale of intelligence in the US Army."[52] Frederick had to fight numerous bureaucratic battles to help rectify the situation, which arose principally because of a common reluctance to release high-quality personnel from regular units for indistinct purposes. Prescribed and heavily favored by the British, yet executed in a joint manner by Canada and America, the inception of the FSSF was, in both conception and composition, uniquely representative of an international effort.

Offspring of divergent military cultures and—potentially more significantly—born at different stages of the war, the motivation behind Britain's creation of the Commandos and America's adoption of the Rangers, and to a lesser extent the FSSF and Raiders, was notably different. The Commandos (the total number of which consistently outnumbered ranger units) were raised at a time of strategic desperation, and as such there was some gravitas behind their creation: they were viewed as an important striking arm that could help wrest back the strategic initiative. The various ranger-style formations, on the other hand, were conceived at a time when the strategic situation was, although still taxing, by no means as desperate as it had appeared in the summer of 1940. From the outset the 1st Ranger Battalion was perceived as a transitory "training and demonstration unit": as a means of providing employment and experience for a proportion of personnel before the brunt of conventional U.S. forces had an opportunity to fight in a style more synonymous with the American "way of war."[53] The Ranger participation in the British raiding program was in line with Marshall's initial intention: they represented "the first step in a program . . . for giving actual battle experience to the maximum number of personnel of the American Army."[54] It is no coincidence that the Ranger's inception coincided with Army Ground Forces establishing its first Amphibious Training Center at Camp Edwards, Massachusetts.[55]

Given British influence on the creation of the U.S. Army Rangers, it is perhaps not surprising that their function and employment would closely follow the evolution of their British counterparts. The first operational deployment involving Ranger personnel, and the only time the 1st Rangers would serve in an amphibious raid, occurred when fifty Rangers took part, via attachment to various elements (predominantly No. 3 Commando), in the Dieppe raid. Even before the completion of their formal training, therefore, the Rangers had begun to emulate the Commandos' transition toward spearheading roles. Had they not done this, they may swiftly have become redundant. Operation Torch would soon enable a much larger proportion of the U.S. Army to gain practicable combat experience without the need for such "training and demonstration" units.

Reorganization and a Transition of Role

For both the Commandos and Rangers, the Dieppe raid created a model for future deployments and altered their inherent function; they began to be perceived, and used, as shock troops to tackle difficult tactical objectives for the furtherance of conventional operations, rather than serving as independent raiding specialists. The landing of Nos. 1 and 6 Commandos "at the head of the hunt" during Operation Torch was the first significant deployment of the Commandos in a landing where the objective was to stay ashore rather than withdraw.[56] Deployed in a spearheading capacity with the leading elements during the assault, the Commandos were not subsequently withdrawn; they were, instead, retained for operations at the front. With a few exceptions, such as Operation Bizerte—No. 1 Commando's December 5, 1942, attempt to turn the enemy's sea flank in support of 36th Infantry Brigade—these Commandos spent six months serving in a light infantry capacity in the front lines.[57] Such deployments were in direct contrast to those early conceptions for the Commandos, which explicitly stated that they were "not expected to resist an attack or to overcome a defense by formed bodies of troops."[58]

The first deployment of the 1st Ranger Battalion as a complete unit also ocurred during the Torch landings, when it was tasked with neutralizing the coastal artillery at Fort de la Pointe, which overlooked the harbor of Arzew.[59] Subsequent to the initial assault, however, the role of the Rangers became ill defined and experienced "the phenomena of 'mission creep.'"[60] After undertaking a number of more mundane activities, the Rangers were ultimately attached to the U.S. 1st Infantry Division, under which, like the Commandos, they would fight "a dozen soldiers' battles." Although their nighttime raid on Station de Sened and their seizure of the Djebel el Ank Pass during this campaign would emphasize the Rangers' talents in night infiltration and assault, the more common deployments of the 1st Rangers in North Africa were of a conventional infantry capability.[61]

Despite operating against a very different enemy in different operational environments, the employment of the USMC Raiders in the Pacific war would largely mirror the same patterns of evolution that the Commandos and Rangers were undergoing in Europe and North Africa. In light of the imprecise blend of Commando and Chinese guerrilla influences that had helped shape their inception, the exact purpose for which the USMC Raiders had been created was somewhat unclear. Given this, the two initial battalions were each strongly influenced by their respective commanding officers' perspective as to what their function should be. Lieutenant Colonel Evans Carlson's progressive ideas about guerrilla warfare and devolved leadership for the 2nd Battalion were at odds with Lieutenant Colonel Merritt Edson's more conventional methods for the 1st Battalion and went some way to ensure that although the "battalions bore the same name . . . they could hardly have been more dissimilar."[62] The 1st and 2nd Raider Battalions were first deployed, independent of one another, in August 1942. On August 7, with clear parallels to the commando role emerging in Europe, the 1st Battalion attacked the small island of Tulagi in the Solomon Islands, spearheading the first U.S. amphibious landings of the war.[63] Ten days later the 2nd Battalion raided Makin Atoll in the Gilbert Islands via submarines, with the aims of destroying the garrison, gaining intelligence, and drawing Japanese attentions away from Guadalcanal.[64] Although the raid would to an extent prove the validity of the raiding and scouting concepts that Carlson had been expounding for his unit, the operation itself was beset with problems brought about by poor intelligence and general inexperience, thus drawing parallels with the limitations of early British raids. Makin would, however, remain the only operation of this kind undertaken in the Pacific war.[65]

Following these operations, one after the other, both Raider battalions were deployed to Guadalcanal. There, both 1st Battalion's "copy-book hit-and-run" amphibious raid against Tasimboko village of September 8, 1942,[66] and 2nd Battalion's landing and protracted long-range patrol near Aola Bay throughout November, illustrated the Raider potential in specialist deployments.[67] Their far more common deployments, however, akin to the use of Rangers and Commandos in North Africa, were conventional infantry tasks. Although in numerous aggressive patrols, and in actions such as the defense of "Edson's Ridge" in September 1942, the Raiders performed admirably, Lieutenant General Thomas Holcomb would echo the sentiments of many Raider critics when he stated that "such tasks could just as well be performed by any marine rifle battalion."[68] Nevertheless, Tulagi, Makin, and Guadalcanal had highlighted the potential versatility and value of the Raiders, and following these campaigns it was subsequently decided to expand their establishment with the creation of the 3rd and 4th Raider Battalions in Samoa and California, respectively.

The European-oriented Commandos and Rangers were also expanding and facing reorganization at this time. The operational employment of these units in the North African campaign had broadly overstretched their capabilities. As light infantry forces they lacked the firepower, transport, medical, and logistical facilities to deal with protracted operations and suffered accordingly. Despite the difficulties experienced, Operation Torch and North Africa had cemented the commando and ranger transition in role as it became clear that both "raiding for the sake of raiding was unlikely to be undertaken" and "Commandos must be prepared to carry out a role as specialized and highly trained infantry, possibly for protracted operations."[69] In preparation for future deployments, steps were thus undertaken to reorganize the Commandos on more regular lines so as to render them "capable of taking part in operations subsequent to the assault."[70] The likes of Robert Laycock, again at the helm of a provisional Commando brigade, and Lord Louis Mountbatten, who had replaced Keyes as CCO in October 1941, therefore made the decision to group the Commandos into four SS brigades, to make them "administratively as well as operationally self-contained"; their war establishments received an increase in support weaponry and transport "to enable commandos to remain in contact with the enemy during daylight and after surprise has been lost"; and what was called a "holding Commando" was established to help alleviate the significant problems with replacing specially trained personnel following casualties.[71]

The North African campaign had similarly demonstrated the potential of the U.S. Army Rangers in initial amphibious assaults and in post-landing operations. The Rangers became viewed as highly trained "all-around infantrymen."[72] Such was their perceived value that at the start of 1943 it was decided to expand the concept, and the 3rd and 4th Ranger Battalions were accordingly raised by taking a nucleus of 1st Ranger personnel and bulking them up with recruits taken from U.S. Army personnel in North Africa. This expansion was not, however, in any way illustrative of a fundamental shift in the U.S. Army's attitude toward these units. Despite the ever-growing opportunities for conventional formations to gain combat experience, these new Ranger battalions were still created with the expectation of their being able to function as a training vehicle. As General George C. Marshall, army chief of staff, signaled General Dwight D. Eisenhower upon their creation: ". . . after [the] need for these battalions is passed personnel therein might be returned to parent organizations so that personnel might attain highest rating commensurate with proven ability."[73]

Following the cessation of operations in North Africa, and thinking in a vein similar to the British regarding their Commando formations, Lieutenant Colonel William O. Darby, commanding the 1st Ranger Battalion, had become convinced that his unit had to develop a greater capacity to operate in a conventional infantry role. With a background as an artillery officer, Darby had a "fetish for firepower," and he gradually undertook measures to transform the Rangers "into a light combined arms team." Prior to participating in the invasion of Sicily, mortars of the 83rd Chemical Warfare Battalion were attached to the Rangers, in what was to become a permanent arrangement, and later, for the invasion of Italy, Darby introduced a "cannon company" to his command that consisted of four 75mm guns mounted on half-tracks.[74] Making such tactical concessions was, however, the limit of Darby's powers to reorganize the Rangers. Despite significant lobbying, he was not authorized to instigate any more substantial changes akin to those being made by Laycock and Mountbatten to the Commandos. The Ranger establishment was to remain firmly provisional.

As the war moved across the Mediterranean, the prospect of an amphibious assault on Sicily ensured the Rangers and Commandos again coming to the fore. Tasked with securing defensive batteries overlooking the main landing beaches, the missions for Nos. 3, 40 (RM), and 41 (RM) Commandos during the invasion of Sicily already had a ring of familiarity about them.[75] During the operation, these tasks were quickly accomplished, and having helped to secure the beachhead, the Commandos were subsequently swiftly withdrawn from the line to prepare for forthcoming operations against Italy—quite unlike what had occurred in North Africa (and would in many future landings). The only exception was No. 3 Commando's participation in a costly amphibious "right hook" to secure a bridge, the Ponte di Malati, in conjunction with airborne forces on July 14.[76] The Rangers were similarly employed during the Sicilian assault: the 1st and 4th Battalions spearheaded the landings at Gela to secure the coastal defenses while the 3rd Rangers attacked beach defenses at San Mollarella.[77] After these actions it was initially hoped that the Rangers would help further the offensive, but neither the 1st nor 4th Rangers could keep pace with Patton's "reconnaissance in force," and thus their time was spent undertaking marginal tasks before they too were withdrawn in readiness for the invasion of the Italian mainland. Among the various Commandos and Rangers employed in Sicily, the actions of the 3rd Rangers were something of an exception: continuing to keep pace with Truscott's 3rd Infantry Division, the unit was widely deployed in frontline duties and would be among the first units to reach Messina.

For Britain and America alike, the invasion of Sicily (code name Operation Husky) served to further reinforce the potential value of commandos and rangers in supporting and hastening amphibious assaults. With the invasion of France on the horizon, these units were thus placed at a premium and it was deemed advisable to expand the number of such formations to cater to the need for future landings.[78] For the British, the most obvious manner of facilitating this expansion was to authorize the direct conversion of existing Royal Marine battalions into seven additional Royal Marine Commandos (to join the two already in existence). This was a move that initially brought much resentment from the all-volunteer Army Commandos, who believed "that units of conscripted marines could not be expected to maintain the high Commando standards."[79] Such animosity was, however, short lived and was gradually suppressed by the sensible grouping of Royal Marine and Army Commandos together in the same SS Brigades, a move that fostered mutual respect and esprit de corps.

Observing the Husky landings, U.S. Army Brigadier General Norman D. Cota echoed the sentiments of the British and singled out the importance of "improved Ranger Activities" in the success of the amphibious assault. He accordingly deemed Rangers "vitally necessary" for future landings. Cota went on to recommend that further Ranger battalions be raised "at least two per 'assault division' . . . without delay" for the invasion of France.[80] Unlike with the British, however, this request met with a "cold reception" from

Army Ground Forces, which still viewed the Rangers as transient expedients contradictory to the favored mobilization of large numbers of homogenous conventional formations. Rangers were recognized as valuable for the assault but not for subsequent roles.[81] It was only following concerted pressure from ETOUSA (European Theater of Operations, United States Army), and particularly the likes of Cota, who had worked with COHQ, that the formation of the 2nd and 5th Ranger Battalions at Camp Forrest, Tennessee, in April and September 1943, respectively, was grudgingly accepted.[82]

The increased premium placed on amphibious landings alongside the commencement of protracted overland operations led to a discernible shift in the core roles of commando and ranger formations. As one Commando officer would comment, after Sicily "the war had . . . reached a stage where raiding was nearly finished with. . . . There might still be small-scale reconnaissance raids, but there would be no more Vaagso's or Dieppe's."[83] Laycock predicted that "such raids as do take place are likely to be on a larger scale, of long duration and of immediate strategic importance."[84] Instead of conducting "hit-and-run" raiding operations or even spearhead operations, where withdrawal was possible, the Commandos would, with the commencement of offensive overland operations, be increasingly called upon to undertake more protracted deployments. Their "hit-and-run" repertoire was gradually being replaced by "hit-and-hold" or "bite-and-hold" operations. For the invasion of Italy the 1st, 3rd, and 4th Ranger battalions (which tellingly had been formally designated Ranger *Infantry* Battalions in August 1943) were deployed at Salerno alongside Nos. 2 and 41 (RM) Commandos to protect the flanks of X Corps. After spearheading the initial landings, the Commando units held the flanks for twenty-one days before being relieved. Salerno thus provides good illustration of a consistent problem with the use of such formations in protracted operations. Despite the changes made to their establishments, these light infantry forces could never hope to emulate the organization and firepower of conventional forces.[85] Darby summed up the situation well when he wrote: "All my soldiers were rugged raiders, but we lacked enough artillery for a full-scale defense. We were equipped to hit and run but not to stick it out in a slogging match against forces armed with medium and heavy artillery outnumbering us at least eight to one."[86]

The transition of role to "bite-and-hold" is perhaps best illustrated by Operation Devon, the October 3, 1943, landing of Nos. 3

and 40 (RM) Commandos and the Special Raiding Squadron (a lineal descendant of the 1st SAS Regiment, which at this time was deployed in a Commando capacity) at Termoli to outflank the German lines on the Adriatic coast of Italy. In this operation the Commandos took the town independently and held it doggedly, with the minimum of support, for three days against repeated counterattacks until eventually being relieved by the British 78th Division's coastal drive.[87] Operation Devon, in the opinion of Julian Thompson, was a "classic example of employing commandos."[88] More generally, however, in Italy, as in North Africa, the Commandos would undertake a number of more protracted, less specialized deployments that saw them operate in a manner more akin to conventional infantry battalions. A fine illustration of one such deployment is the five weeks that No. 40 (RM) Commando spent on the line at the Garigliano River.

Despite the limitations in deploying commando formations in protracted defensive operations without support, by 1944 many such units were, nevertheless, "fully prepared to undertake any normal infantry tasks."[89] Completely comprehending their evolving role, many Commandos actively undertook measures to adapt and prepare themselves for such tasks. In February 1944, for example, Colonel John Frederick "Ronnie" Tod, commanding No. 9 Commando, actually requested that his men each have opportunity to spend time in the line before future deployments in order to give them "time to appreciate the nature of the tasks before them, learn the working and routine organization of life in the line, and become accustomed to working with other units in the Field Army."[90] Despite a gradual acceptance of more conventional activities, it nonetheless remained clear that the best advantage offered by commandos was to capitalize on their highly-trained personnel and to utilize them as elite spearhead and shock troops in amphibious operations, deployments over difficult country, infiltrations, nighttime operations, and operations requiring the elimination or capture of specific objectives such as forts, bridges, roads, and coastal defenses. The expansion of both Commando and Ranger programs in preparation for the invasion of France epitomizes the value attributed to these formations in such roles.

Joining the Commandos and Rangers in Italy at this time was the American-Canadian First Special Service Force. The FSSF's originally intended role of conducting raids and protracted operations against Norway had been put aside within only six months of its formation.

The force had faced intractable problems with both the readiness of the Plough and with political disputes with the Norwegian government-in-exile over the destruction of industry.[91] Lack of a clear role prompted the FSSF to supplement its already accomplished Arctic warfare expertise with a training schedule that included both parachuting and amphibious techniques. The delay in being operationally committed led, in the opinion of Scott McMichael, to a training program that "in terms of intensity, difficulty, variety, and scope, far surpassed that experienced by any other regiment or division in the US Army during the war."[92] With no opportunity to deploy against Norway, the force was first used in August 1943 in a "traditional" commando spearhead capacity during the assault on Kiska in the northern Pacific Aleutian Islands. However, as the Japanese had abandoned Kiska, this entirely unopposed landing can be regarded as being little more than a training exercise. Following this brief deployment, the force was offered to various theater commanders in the hope of attaining more permanent employment.[93] Two potential opportunities for the FSSF emerged: deployment with the Fifth Army in Italy, with an aim to utilizing the force's unique skills in the Apennines; or, as requested by General Henry Maitland Wilson, commander in chief Middle East Forces (C in C MEF), deployment along the Dalmatian coast to serve alongside Yugoslav partisans in a guerrilla capacity.[94] The sheer divergence between these two potential deployments highlights not only the indistinctness of the force's role but also the expected versatility of its capabilities.

Ultimately it was operational necessity, particularly General Mark Clark's shortage of personnel, that forced the decision and saw the FSSF deployed to Italy, where it was hoped that the unit could "provide extremely valuable leavening for normal divisions" and make up for a general deficiency in knowledge about fighting in mountainous and winter conditions.[95] Upon its arrival in Italy the force was swiftly put to use. In December 1943 it was tasked with taking, by nighttime infiltration/assault, the peaks of Monte la Difensa and Monte la Remetanea, key positions in Field Marshal Albert Kesselring's Bernhardt Line, which formed part of the heavily fortified Winter Line running across the width of Italy. The attack on Monte la Difensa required the force to make a seemingly impossible nighttime mountain ascent with ropes to tackle a difficult fortified objective. The assignment was, in the opinion of McMichael, "fully suited to the FSSF," taking advantage of its "special training in night fighting, mountain climbing, cold weather, and lightning assault."[96] Less flair was called for in its subsequent attack on Monte la Remetanea, a successful albeit bloody frontal assault. These actions, alongside those other duties the force performed in the Italian mountains over the next month, were certainly difficult propositions but were, nevertheless, of the shock troop variety. Once the peaks had been taken they had to be held—actions that precipitated a costly period of protracted mainline deployment for the force.[97]

Anzio was the next notable deployment for both the U.S. Army Rangers and the FSSF. The 1st, 3rd, and 4th Rangers and Nos. 9 and 43 (RM) Commandos were all used in the initial assault. The Commandos, which were employed "almost as an afterthought" as a blocking force for the landings, were, as at Sicily, swiftly withdrawn from the beachhead after only three days—although two Commandos would later return to the beachhead to help hold its left flank once it became threatened.[98] The Rangers, on the other hand, were not relieved after the initial landings but instead were used both to expand the beachhead and subsequently to help hold the line against enemy counterattacks. At Anzio the mismatch between Ranger capabilities and their current duties had disastrous consequences. On January 31, 1944, the 1st and 3rd Rangers attempted to infiltrate enemy lines to seize the town of Cisterna, which was held, unbeknownst to them in light of inadequate intelligence, by a superior, strongly fortified, and alert enemy force. With their infiltration detected, at Cisterna the two Ranger battalions were ambushed, encircled, and decimated.[99] The 4th Rangers, although avoiding this battle, was absorbed in protracted deployments alongside the 504th Parachute Infantry Regiment and the FSSF, and having sustained heavy casualties, was disbanded in March 1944 with a proportion of its personnel being retained as reinforcements for the FSSF.[100]

Such was the stock of the FSSF following the feat of Monte la Difensa that at Anzio it was given responsibility for an eight-mile frontage, representing over one quarter of the entire beachhead and double that held by the 3rd Infantry Division (albeit covering an area unsuited to mobile operations and thus unlikely to be directly counterattacked).[101] During this period in the line, the force performed effectively, masking its numerical inferiority by consistently maintaining aggressive nighttime fighting patrols along the Mussolini

Canal.[102] At the same time, in preparation for the Anzio breakout, Colonel Frederick had prepared his unit for mobile combined arms operations.[103] It was a prudent move. In the subsequent drive on Rome the FSSF formed part of the task force leading the advance, and having helped capture key bridges en route, would be among the first units to arrive in the city.[104]

The ultimate evolution of commando roles is best illustrated by the employment of these units during the invasion of France and in the subsequent campaign across northwestern Europe. Operation Overlord, the June 6, 1944, invasion of Normandy, was the culmination of months of planning and undoubtedly represented the most climactic event facing the Western Allies during the war against Germany. The roles Commando and Ranger formations would play in the operation were similar to those that they had performed in other amphibious landings, but with one notable difference: in Normandy they were not called upon to be the "tip of the spear." As a 21 Army Group staff study into the employment of commandos and rangers completed in the last days of 1943 concluded, these units "may well have a vital influence on the success of the assault" if employed to move "rapidly across the difficult country in rear of the beaches" or against "definite objectives."[105] The first waves landing in France were thus drawn from regular divisions that had long prepared for the amphibious assault, with the Commando formations being tasked with more explicit D-day objectives.

During the Normandy invasion, both the 1st and 4th SS Brigades (each composed of four Commandos) deployed in a now classic manner, acting against specific points of resistance to hasten the formation of the beachhead. The SS Brigades landed just behind the leading assault waves, with No. 46 (RM) Commando actually landing the next day. The Commandos of 1st SS Brigade were tasked with helping to secure Oiustreham and linking up with the 6th Airborne Division to anchor the left flank of the invasion.[106] The Commandos of 4th SS Brigade would join them on this flank after having, for the first hours of the invasion, operated independently against individual points of resistance. Perhaps the most difficult task fell to No. 47 (RM) Commando, which was to capture Port-en-Bessin and link up with U.S. formations moving east from Omaha Beach. After the initial assault, and despite some premature predictions that they would be withdrawn to Britain to reorganize and refit, both brigades were deployed in the front line in conventional tasks until the buildup reached a stage where their withdrawal was feasible.[107] This only occurred after the SS Brigades had spent eighty-three days in contact with the enemy, more time than any other British formation.[108]

During the drive on Germany, the Commando virtuosity in spearheading tasks made the obvious transition to overland infiltration and assault. The effectiveness of the Commandos in such tasks is well illustrated by their advances across the flooded terrain of the lowlands; the 4th SS Brigade's November 1944 attack on Walcheren Island, strategically located at the mouth of the River Scheldt; Operation Widgeon, the March 1945 crossing of the Rhine, in which the 1st Commando Brigade (formerly 1st SS Brigade; the SS Brigades were all diplomatically renamed Commando Brigades in December 1944) attacked and held the town of Wesel; or Operation Enterprise, the seizure of bridges over the Elbe in April 1945.[109]

D-day saw the 2nd and 5th Ranger Battalions deploy in an archetypal spearhead and flankguard capacity. During the planning stages of the Neptune (the code name for the assault phase) landings, the German battery and casemates at Pointe du Hoc, situated between and overlooking both Utah and Omaha Beaches, were singled out as the only objective "which is both suitable for a Commando or Ranger task and also vital to the Operation."[110] The assault on these formidable cliff-top defenses by elements of the 2nd Rangers remains illustrative of a model application of ranger formations in support of an amphibious landing.[111] The remainder of the 2nd Rangers landed with the 5th Rangers among the early waves at Omaha beach, and amid the carnage and chaos on the beaches, the small-group cohesion and training of the Rangers helped regain the momentum and open up the beachhead for further reinforcements. The D-day assault was the very raison d'être of the 2nd and 5th Rangers, and its successful completion created a void for further Ranger employment. In the days following the invasion, Colonel Earl Rudder, commanding the 2nd Rangers, petitioned for his command to be returned to Britain, reinforced, and withheld for future specialist deployments.[112] Such lobbying was, however, unsuccessful, and like the Commandos (and many parachute and glider-borne troops that took part in the initial assault), the Rangers were retained at the front for more conventional tasks.

After their D-day tasks had been accomplished, the Rangers had a brief period out of the line for reinforcement and were then deployed in a largely conventional manner in the reduction of Brest and subsequently in the advance toward Germany.[113] Like their Commando counterparts, however, the Ranger battalions were still called upon, albeit more infrequently, to supplement these more conventional deployments with shock troop roles to tackle difficult objectives. The 2nd Ranger Battalion's seizing and holding of Hill 400, also known as Castle Hill, near Bergstein in December 1944 provides good example of such a deployment,[114] as does the 5th Rangers's costly four-kilometer infiltration to capture and hold the Irsch-Zerf road for nine days in February 1945.[115]

Two months after the invasion of Normandy, the FSSF participated in the Anvil/Dragoon landings against the South of France. During the initial assault, the force was used in a spearheading capacity to seize the coastal batteries on Ile du Levant and Ile de Port Cros, situated on the left flank of the invasion beaches.[116] The FSSF was not, however, used in the main landings and was not deployed on mainland France until breakout had occurred. The subsequent deployment of the force during the so-called Champagne campaign was very conventional and became more of "an extended route march than a battle."[117] In December 1944, in a climate where the majority of other commando and ranger formations were being deployed conventionally, the FSSF was disbanded. Lack of a clear role, increasing headaches over the multinational composition of the unit, and a general manpower shortage all contrived to give this step certain inevitability.

Exceptions to the Rule

By late 1942 a common pattern for the employment of commandos and rangers in the European theaters had been established that saw their primary occupation evolving from independent raiding toward spearhead and shock troop roles alongside greater participation in the main battle. This pattern was not, however, entirely uniform, and throughout the war a number of Commandos, both individually and in brigades, continued to undertake independent specialized deployments more analogous to their original conception. The theater of operation in which these units operated, unsurprisingly, had significant ramifications for their employment. Operating in Italy and the Adriatic, 2nd SS Brigade (composed of Nos. 2, 9, 40

(RM) and 43 (RM) Commandos) undertook a diverse range of operations that, alongside more protracted conventional deployments, included numerous raids and independent actions. Its operations from the island of Vis against enemy forces on the Dalmatian coast and later tasks in Albania and Greece in close coordination with special forces and partisans, in particular, were representative of a distinctly different manner of deployment from those the Brigade had performed on the Italian mainland. In the opinion of one Commando officer, the Balkans offered a "setting for true Commando operations [which] couldn't have been bettered"; such periphery theaters permitted Commandos to be deployed, almost as originally intended, to raid coastlines and support indigenous partisan forces with the goal of tying down disproportionate numbers of enemy manpower and material.[118]

The Commandos of the 3rd SS Brigade—Nos. 1, 5, 42 (RM) and 44 (RM) Commandos—which were deployed to the Far East in January 1944 similarly undertook, albeit sporadically, a more diverse set of operations than their comrades employed in Europe. The Arakan coastline and the numerous rivers in Burma offered the potential for coastal raiding, as well as spearheading projected amphibious assaults and river crossings.[119] Even given these more apposite conditions, however, there could be definite commonality between the use of these Commandos and that of formations deployed in Europe. The January 1945 operations against the Myebon Peninsula, conducted in support of the 25th Indian Division, for example, have clear parallels. Of particular note, and illustrative of their shock troop role, was the accomplishment of Nos. 1 and 5 Commandos in January 1945—the critical seizure and holding of Hill 170 near Kangaw—an action bearing considerable similarities to the 2nd Rangers' seizure of Castle Hill in the Hurtgen campaign one month earlier.[120]

In addition to these aforementioned "regular" establishment Commandos serving under the SS Brigade organization, a number of other Commandos existed that possessed unique capabilities or operational responsibilities beyond the normal. One such unit was No. 10 (Inter-Allied) Commando. Raised in June 1942, it was made up of foreign nationals, each organized into troops along national lines. Personnel included French, Belgian, Dutch, Norwegian, Polish, Yugoslav, and "X troop" (later known as No. 3 "Miscellaneous" Troop), which was formed from enemy aliens. Never intended to deploy as a complete unit, the personnel of the Commando would be attached, either as individuals or troops, to other formations, specialist and otherwise, for deployment. Personnel of the Commando were thus employed in a wide variety of tasks, taking part in numerous raids—such as Bruneval, St. Nazaire, and Dieppe—as well as in conventional operations in Italy, France, and Holland.[121]

No. 12 Commando had been raised from Irish and Welsh regiments with the intention of being a "normal" Commando, but experiencing difficulties coming up to establishment, it was retained outside the SS Brigade organization and placed directly under COHQ for special duties. In its deployments No. 12 Commando was unusually malleable, and throughout 1941–44 it would continue to undertake various small-scale raids within the original Commando mandate, at a time when the majority of other Commandos were in the process of making the transition to more conventional deployments.[122]

In late 1943 No. 12 Commando and the French and "Miscellaneous" troops of No. 10 (IA) Commando were grouped together as "Layforce II" under Major P. Laycock (brother of Robert Laycock, then CCO) and assigned responsibility for undertaking the majority of the Operation Hardtack reconnaissances and Manacle (or Candlestick) raids proposed against the Channel coast prior to D-day. Because of security concerns, the main purpose of such operations was deceptive: to indicate other landing sites, test general defensive readiness, and draw attention away from clandestine reconnaissance activities. In December 1943 six Hardtack operations were successfully launched, with Brigadier John Durnford-Slater subsequently remarking that "there is no doubt that the mounting of these raids achieved considerable success, provided first-class experience both for planning and execution, and have raised the morale of the units participating, to an incredibly high degree. This applies especially to the French, who were suffering from a long period of continued disappointments."[123] By the start of 1944, however, the majority of other such proposed operations were being aborted as a result of unsuitable weather conditions.[124] Shortly before D-day No. 12 Commando was disbanded as surplus to requirement; the commencement of continental operations made small-scale coastal raiding unnecessary, and to have altered No. 12 Commando's under-strength establishment to deal with the rigors of more conventional deployments would have been a difficult and unwarranted course of action.

No. 14 Commando was raised in November 1942 with the intention of becoming an "Arctic Commando" for deployment against German forces occupying Norway.[125] With an establishment of only two troops, the Commando had an international makeup, with personnel coming from the Royal Navy, the Canadian Army, and a select number of Norwegians all chosen for their "experience in mountain or snow conditions or for their knowledge of canoeing."[126] The first troop of the Commando was a "boating troop," intended to operate, somewhat redundantly, in a manner analogous to existent maritime special forces. Its structure was, however, fraught with a number of intractable problems. As Captain Noel Andrew Croft, commanding, was to claim: "Never in my life have I met a set-up more conducive to failure.... [We] were not exactly a cohesive, well adjusted marine unit, which our dangerous mission really demanded, and none of the men had any battle experience at all."[127] Problems of "differences in languages, outlook and rates of pay" made certain that it was "impossible to foster a proper esprit de corps," and in February 1943 the troop was disbanded and its personnel amalgamated into No. 12 Commando. No. 14 Commando's second troop was conceived to be a "ski troop," with a mandate not dissimilar to that of the significantly larger FSSF. Like the FSSF, however, this troop would never deploy as initially intended, and in mid-1943 it was disbanded, with the remainder of its personnel joining the Lovat Scouts training in Canada for winter operations.[128]

No. 30 (Assault) Commando (known for a time as the Special Engineering Unit) bore few similarities to the other Army and Royal Marine Commandos, being notably different in size, composition, and role.[129] Formed in August 1942 on the recommendation of the personal assistant of the director of naval intelligence (DNI), Commander Ian Fleming (later to gain fame as an author and the creator of James Bond), the unit was intended to mimic the operations that the German Abwehrkommando had employed in Yugoslavia and Greece.[130] Operating closely with the DNI, the unit was to act as an "intelligence assault unit," to be "employed both before a landing and, in a tactical role in conjunction with the first assault, going for enemy Headquarters and attempting to obtain enemy cyphers, equipment, instruments, papers, or other intelligence data as required."[131] In addition to this "authorized looting," the unit would carry out demolition and counterdemolition operations ahead of the main advance as well as protecting "white list" VIPs.[132]

No. 30 Commando was divided into three troops, one each from the British Army, Royal Marines, and Royal Navy. Personnel from this unit first deployed during Operation Torch and subsequently saw action in Sicily, Italy, the Aegean, and on the Dalmatian coast. Prior to Operation Overlord, the Royal Marine element was reorganized as 30 Assault Unit (AU), which, in close coordination with their DNI counterparts, continued to operate with advancing Allied formations until the end of the war.[133]

Despite the exceptions noted above, the majority of commando formations followed a pronounced trend that saw their role evolve away from the conduct of independent raiding and related enterprises and move closer toward that of more conventional "shock troops." This pattern, seen with both the Commandos and U.S. Army Rangers, was also apparent with the other specialist formations modeled on elite light infantry.

As contrasted with the war in Europe, the war against Japan would ultimately promote somewhat different experiences for the application of ranger formations. The initial employment of the USMC Raiders following Guadalcanal did, however, broadly conform to the pattern witnessed in Europe: the four battalions were widely used in both an amphibious spearhead capacity (as against the Russell Islands in February 1943 or against Bougainville in November 1943) and in more protracted conventional infantry tasks (as on New Georgia).[134] While the Raiders' unconventional attitude and training generally served them well, the Pacific War was gradually outpacing opportunities for their deployment. The emerging series of "island hopping" campaigns would certainly call for great amphibious virtuosity, but the nature of the small islands and atolls, the huge distances between the chains, and the heavily fortified enemy—who expected to fight to the last man—simply did not offer specialist forces the opportunity to independently raid and harass. While in the European and Mediterranean theaters commando and ranger formations fitted well into an Anglo-centric amphibious doctrine that placed a premium on speed and surprise, in the Pacific theater the Raiders were found to be largely incompatible with the USMC and U.S. Navy and their doctrine that focused on firepower.

The strategic realities of the Pacific war transpired to degrade role of the Raiders, whose lack of firepower, mobility, and an inability to sustain losses could not be offset by training and esprit de corps alone.[135] Following deployment on Guadalcanal, Carlson had recommended that "our military units must be mobile, flexible, persistently aggressive, clever and must possess as much fire power as is commensurate with mobility."[136] By emphasizing mobility, flexibility, and a continued light infantry role, Carlson was effectively shunning the conventionalization in establishment that both Darby's Rangers and the Commandos had undertaken. He had also misread the nature of the war evolving in the Pacific. Technological and doctrinal developments such as the use of the "amphibian tractor and improved fire support . . . removed the need for the light assault units envisioned by Holland Smith at the beginning of the war."[137] Requirements for assault troops and spearheaders in landings were being fulfilled by the better equipped conventional Marine units, of which detractors of the Raiders had long stated were already an amphibious elite. Under such circumstances, the decline of the Raiders became inevitable, and they were gradually conventionalized and ultimately disbanded in February 1944, their personnel amalgamated into the newly re-formed 4th Marine Division.

Despite the incompatibility of the ranger concept in the Central Pacific, in September 1944 the 6th Ranger Battalion was created to cater to specialist operations in the southwestern Pacific. Technically not related to the other Ranger battalions except in name, the 6th Rangers were created from a "batch conversion" of the 98th Field Artillery Battalion. General Walter Krueger, a foremost American champion of specialist formations, had conceived of the battalion in an effort to furnish his Sixth Army with a force capable of undertaking independent offensive tasks analogous to those expected of early Commandos. As with the other Ranger battalions, much of the 6th Ranger's deployment would be in a spearheading capacity. Three days before the invasion of Leyte in the Philippines in October 1944, the Rangers landed to secure the outlying islands of Dinagat, Guiuan, and Homonhon, possession of which by the Japanese potentially threatened the main landings.[138] Similarly, before the Luzon landings the Rangers were tasked with the capture of the undefended Santiago Island but were then left with noncombatant roles, such as acting as headquarters guards, during the main amphibious assault.[139]

What made the 6th Rangers unique in comparison with their counterparts, both British and American, was that they were never called upon to conduct protracted conventional infantry duties after the assault. This was not due to any overarching decision, however, but was a manifestation of various factors: the nature of operations in the Philippines favoring decentralized control and small groups; a comparative lack of other specialist formations in the theater removing competition for specialist tasks; and, perhaps most significantly, the military situation on the ground in the Philippines never being desperate enough to warrant the use of the Rangers in such a capacity. In the Philippines the 6th Rangers seldom deployed as a complete unit, and often in company-size or smaller formations, the unit undertook roles "so broad as to defy definition." Its most famous action, and the subject of much literature and film, was their masterful infiltration of Japanese lines to raid the Cabanatuan prison camp to rescue Allied prisoners of war in January 1945.[140]

The last originally conceived American commando-style formation raised during the war was the 5307th Composite Unit (Provisional), a unit also referred to as Galahad but probably better known as Merrill's Marauders (a name coined by a journalist). Its inception stemmed from decisions made at the August 1943 Quebec Conference, code name Quadrant, at which Orde Wingate had so impressed the Americans with his concept of long-range penetration that the U.S. Army agreed to form an American Chindit "counterpart." Instead of taking Wingate's lead and converting conventional infantry units into jungle specialists, however, the army issued a call for volunteers with combat and jungle experience. The result was recruits from three different sources: 960 men from the Caribbean defense command; 970 men from Army Ground Forces; and 674 battle-tested men from the South Pacific.[141] Although by late 1943 the precedent of volunteerism for specialist units had become well established, there remained no guarantee that the most suitable men would be put forward, and the recruiting process for the Marauders, akin to that of the FSSF, met with a number of problems. Of his new command one Marauder officer, Charlton Ogburn, would remark that "an assemblage of less tractable-looking soldiers I had never seen." Ogburn believed that instead of issuing a call for volunteers it would have been more profitable to have used an existent and cohesive unit with jungle training, such as the 33rd Infantry in Trinidad, for the task.[142] That this did not occur had much to do with the U.S. Army's perception of the Marauders as being a fleeting expedient.

From the outset the Marauders' role was focused on protracted infiltration and penetration of enemy lines, their initial training being based on the assumption that they would operate in a manner analogous to Wingate's Long Range Penetration Groups. The unit's function altered, however, once its command ceded from Wingate to General Joseph Stilwell in early 1944. The Marauders would become what Otto Heilbrunn dubbed a "Medium Range Penetration Group" with a task "closer to that of the Rangers than to that of the Chindits."[143] From February 1944 onward Stilwell employed the Marauders, in conjunction with Chinese formations, as a spearheading and encircling force for his Burma Road offensive.[144] The Marauders' campaign, heavily intertwined with both the actions of OSS-led Kachin guerrillas and Chinese regulars, would involve an advance of over 750 miles and culminated in their most notable success, the seizure of the important landing ground of Myitkyina.[145] Throughout their operations the Marauders were subjected to massive levels of attrition from both disease and malnutrition, as well as from casualties sustained performing countless blocking operations. Such was their wastage rate that while engaged at Myitkyina some 2,000 new volunteers were hastily organized and committed, with only a modicum of training, as wholesale reinforcement for the second and third Marauder battalions, while all the remaining Marauder veterans were integrated into the first battalion.[146] These losses ultimately became unsustainable, and in August 1944 the Marauders were disbanded. This move certainly correlated with the spirit in which the unit was raised—as a provisional and expendable expedient.[147] A number of the Marauder survivors would subsequently join the newly formed 475th Infantry Regiment, which formed part of the 5332nd (Provisional) Brigade, better known as the Mars Task Force, which worked alongside Chinese formations to eventually open up the Burma Road.

Despite some points of divergence in the experience of these various Commando and ranger formations, and in spite of the fact that such units were often initially intended to fulfill slightly different roles, their actual deployments and the manner in which their role evolved followed a common pattern. This was a result both of the close relationship between Britain and the United States in the inception of these units, in particular the influence of the Commando model on the Americans, as well as being a natural consequence of their evolving in a similar manner to the same battlefield requirements. The evolution of commando roles closely mirrored transitions in the overall strategic picture. Peripheral and independent raiding operations were at a premium when the Allies were understrength and on the strategic defensive. Up until mid/late 1942, therefore, many of the commando units, both existent British examples and emergent U.S. varieties, were employed (albeit often infrequently) in raiding activities, as evident in the cross-Channel and Norwegian activities of the Commandos; the Raider raid on Makin; or even the Rangers' participation in the Dieppe raid. After this point, however, the raison d'être of the majority (although not all, as with the 6th Rangers or No. 12 Commando, for example) of Anglo-American commando and ranger formations began to shift in conjunction with changes in the strategic situation.

Gradual mobilization and a transition to the offensive ensured that the war could be fought, as in the favored American tradition, with an emphasis on firepower and overwhelming quantitative superiority. In such a climate, expedient irritant raids by relatively large light infantry formations became distinctly secondary to operations in direct support of the main effort. Increasingly wedded to the main battle, these forces were prone to be viewed as elite infantry, as shock and assault troops to be used at the front or on the flanks of conventional deployments. Dieppe, North Africa, and Sicily had proven the potential value of using them to tackle difficult objectives and, most important, to spearhead amphibious assaults. The expansion and modification of both the Commando and Ranger programs subsequent to Operation Husky epitomizes the perceived desirability of maintaining commandos for such tasks. The ever-looming specter of an invasion of France gave obvious fillip, particularly in the United States, to the development and retention of these formations after raiding no longer became a necessary or viable proposition.

The fact cannot be escaped that the United States created the majority of its Ranger formations with a definite understanding that these units were only temporary and expendable expedients that would fill a gap until conventional arms were ready and able to engage the enemy with mass and firepower. While America was certainly willing to embrace these formations, it did so for distinctly limited ends. Ranger formations were perceived as temporary expedients, as mechanisms for gaining experience, a means for aiding the prosecution of amphibious warfare and as facilitators for the "American way of war." Subsequent to these goals being attained, when conventional formations had gained experience and were able to conduct operations at the scale and duration required, there was a definite awkwardness in the ability and willingness of the United States to adapt its ranger formations to alternate applications. This discomfort is illustrated both in the general absence of U.S. ranger-style formations undertaking independent or raiding operations and in the American attitude toward disbanding these units. Once the USMC was in a position to mount its Central Pacific drive, the Raiders were surplus to requirement; once the U.S. Army had its foothold in France, the FSSF was disbanded and the 2nd and 5th Rangers fought desperately for specialized employment; and once the Marauders and 1st, 3rd, and 4th Rangers had sustained heavy casualties, it was deemed wiser to disband rather than reconstruct them.

The proliferation of ranger-type formations in the period 1942–44, while never quite keeping pace with the development of the British Commandos, is certainly illustrative of the U.S. willingness to develop these units. Despite this, by late 1944 the overwhelming majority had been disbanded or deployed to extinction. The number of men in ranger formations peaked in mid-1943, with approximately 6,630 personnel involved, but by the start of 1945 this figure had declined to 1,350. Their pattern of proliferation was quite distinct from that of the British, whose Commandos gradually increased until they peaked in late 1943/early 1944 with approximately 9,100 men involved. This number did not drop substantially until the end of the war.* The British retained their enthusiasm for the Commandos throughout the war, and compared to the United States, were much more inclined to utilize them both in independent tasks, as seen in their operations from Vis and in Greece, and in the main battle, as seen in their lengthy deployments in both Italy and northwestern Europe.

As emphasized at the outset of this chapter, the evolution and development of commando and ranger formations was closely linked to the proliferation and use of special forces. Almost in tandem with the decline of larger, light infantry commando formations conducting independent direct action, reconnaissance, and coup de main raids was the rise of smaller, more specialized, and flexible special forces with a mandate for such activities. The two events were not unrelated. Usurping some of the more traditional commando roles,

---

*See appendix B for further details.

special forces would often prove themselves a more versatile and cost-effective alternative to the committal of commando elements. With their raiding role in decline, the commandos were, nevertheless, able to prove their worth in other tasks. However, the more they performed shock troop or conventional tasks, the more they had to adapt, doctrinally and via reorganization of establishment; and the more they adapted, and the greater their successes in these tasks, the more likely it was that they would be utilized in such a capacity again. Examination of the inception and manner of employment of special forces is thus an important component in understanding the evolution of the Anglo-American commando and ranger formations.

Chapter 2

The Inception and Employment of Special Forces

Alongside witnessing the advent of commando formations, the summer of 1940 also saw the emergence of the special forces genre of unit—broadly separated from their commando cousins by being of a smaller scale, operating with a greater degree of autonomy, and undertaking a more diverse range of specialized tasks. While the majority of wartime commando and ranger formations followed a discernible pattern of inception and employment, the creation and use of special forces, conversely, was notably more complex and idiosyncratic.

Born of the Desert: Britain's First Forays

The Second World War was the nursery of modern special forces, and for Britain the Desert War was the cradle. The campaign waged between 1940 and 1943 in Egypt, Libya, and Tunisia bore witness to the advent and steady proliferation of a variety of unorthodox bodies. The nature of the Desert War provided uniquely apposite circumstances and variables for the creation of special forces: it was a conflict of logistics, vast distances, open flanks, and overstretched lines of communication that provided many accessible targets for raids and reconnaissance. Although in terms of composition, methods, and outlook there was notable diversity among the individual heterodox units "born of the desert," each exhibited certain uniform characteristics that remain cornerstones of the special forces genus of military formation.[1]

One almost constant theme in the inception of the first British special forces was the initiative and driving force provided by individual innovatory actors. Often a relatively junior officer, an "errant captain," these individuals so often not only conceived of the original idea for a unit but also subsequently proved instrumental in both orchestrating its establishment and in directing its operations in the field. As General Sir John "Shan" Hackett, who as a lieutenant colonel in the Desert War commanded Britain's first dedicated special operations command branch, would observe:

> It is often the appearance of the unusual person on the scene which causes the opportunity or the requirement to be first recognized. It is his own proposals which are often seen to be the best (and sometimes the only) way of doing what ought to be done and if he is the best person available to take charge (as he is sometimes the only one) the project is likely to be handled in the way he proposes. This is often how private armies are born.[2]

In reference to military reform in the interwar period, Barry Posen highlighted the significance of both the role of the civilian reformer and the "maverick" military officer as prime motivators for change.[3] The role and prominence of the "errant captain" in the inception of special forces in the early stages of the Second World War arguably conforms to such a pattern. Irrespective of how innovative the scheme of an "errant captain" or how persuasive his character, little would have come from such ideas were it not for support received from the higher echelons of command. Determined and innovatory individuals could not hope to overcome the obstacles of orthodoxy alone. In the creation of these units, backing was often needed from a sympathetic, or equally innovative, "champion," a senior officer who was well positioned both to lift "red tape" to establish units in the first instance and, subsequently, to provide backing and patronage for the unit while in the field. For, as Alan Millett and Williamson Murray emphasized in application to the interwar period, "new ways of fighting" cannot "take root within existing military institutions" without "the emergence of bureaucratic acceptance by *senior* military leaders."[4] Within the creation of British special forces every "errant captain" had his "champion," without whom nothing would have been possible.

In the summer of 1940, in the very same climate of desperation that was sweeping Whitehall following Dunkirk, General Archibald Wavell, commander in chief Middle East, was faced with rapidly changing strategic circumstances. He was thus both willing and able to serve as "champion" for the first of Britain's wartime special forces. The man, the "errant captain," responsible for the creation of this force was Major Ralph Bagnold of the Royal Signals.

Since 1927 Bagnold had been an avid traveler of the Libyan Desert and was a prominent member of the Zerzura Club of prewar explorers. Bagnold's desert expeditions had furnished him with a virtually unrivaled expertise in the travel and negotiation of deserts and had fostered within him an almost pathological interest in the physics of sand.[5] In 1939, while serving with the 7th Armored Division in the Middle East, Bagnold drew upon his prewar expertise to consider the military potential for small forces working in depth across the desert. While many of his contemporaries regarded the southern desert flanks of Cyrenaica to be impassable, Bagnold understood what a potentially fertile environment the Libyan Desert could provide for the operation of small-scale and autonomous long-range desert patrols holding a raiding and intelligence-gathering mandate.

Working up his concepts into a proposal, which he would admit were something of a revival of the ideas behind the Light Car Patrols that had been used against the Senussi Arabs in 1915, Bagnold would twice submit these to the general officer, commanding (GOC), 7th Armored Division. In November 1939 the ideas were presented to Major General Percy Hobart and, subsequently, in January 1940, to his successor, Major General Michael O'Moore Creagh.[6] On both occasions, however, Bagnold's proposals were rejected as being premature at a time when Mussolini, though saber rattling, had yet to reveal his intentions.[7] The scheme not only appeared to be an unwarranted drain on the scarce manpower and material resources in theater, but there was further concern that such undertakings might provoke Italy into decision. Furthermore, there existed a notable margin of scepticism about the potential efficiency of Bagnold's scheme at this time: the type of enterprise being proposed was quite unprecedented, and few minds could grasp the potential for a unit operating across the inhospitable vastness of the inner Libyan Desert.[8]

The Italian declaration of war in June 1940 was the catalyst for the acceptance of Bagnold's proposals. With Italy as a belligerent the strategic landscape had dramatically altered: 30,000 British personnel in Egypt were suddenly facing some 350,000 Italians, while in the Sudan some 2,500 British and 4,800 Sudanese confronted 250,000.[9] Exacerbating this precarious situation was the fact that the British remained broadly in the dark about Italian operational capabilities and intentions. Bagnold's scheme offered General Wavell a potentially valuable solution to the two pressing problems of physical weakness and intelligence shortcomings.

The archetypal soldier-scholar, Wavell was perhaps uniquely amenable and positioned to serve as "champion" for Bagnold's scheme. During the interwar period, not only had Wavell had various correspondence with the likes of T. E. Lawrence, Basil Liddell Hart, and J. F. C. Fuller on subjects such as a "motor guerrilla" that could "gather information and harass the enemy's rear elements," but he had also experienced irregular warfare firsthand during the Arab revolt in Palestine.[10] Furthermore, he had a history of giving license to unorthodox personalities and of granting such characters a degree of latitude for irregular schemes. In 1938, while serving as British commander in Palestine, Wavell had granted Captain Orde Wingate (later of Chindit infamy) permission to form his British-Jewish Special Night Squads—an effective if unconventional solution to the problems of Arab guerrilla raids.[11] Given the difficult situation that Wavell faced in the summer of 1940, Bagnold's idea, which greatly appealed to his "imagination and love of the unorthodox," was naturally attractive.[12] Meeting with Wavell only thirteen days after the Italian declaration of war, Bagnold came away with an enthusiastic carte blanche for his scheme. Even given the exigency of the situation, it remains fair to assert that this would not have occurred without both Bagnold's "driving power and importunity" for his concept and Wavell's patronage and willingness to support Bagnold in the face of his own crippling shortages of personnel and equipment.[13]

Bagnold had only a short space of time with which to recruit and prepare his force, which was initially dubbed the Long Range Patrols before becoming the Long Range Desert Group (LRDG) in October 1940. After some diplomatic deliberation, it was arranged that Bagnold's first cohort of recruits would be drawn from volunteers from the New Zealand Division. These personnel would be formed around, and directed by, an experienced nucleus of personnel assembled by Bagnold from an assorted collection of such prewar friends, colleagues, and fellow explorers as Pat Clayton, Bill Kennedy Shaw, and (later) Guy Prendergast.[14] After its initial series of operations, the LRDG would recruit additional patrols from Guards, Yeomanry, and Southern Rhodesian regiments.

The LRDG was created with the expectation of fulfilling two immediate goals not readily attainable by other means: providing a reliable source of "human intelligence" to monitor Italian intentions in southern Libya and acting as a force multiplier by harassing far-flung Italian outposts in inner Libya to unnerve the enemy, disrupt their plans, and make them alter their dispositions.[15] The LRDG would ultimately straddle these two principal responsibilities, which required both intelligence-gathering and offensive capabilities, with great flexibility. Throughout the course of the Desert War the operations of the LRDG remained uniquely broad; in the words of one LRDG officer, they simply were "of infinite variety."[16] The most widely undertaken occupation of the unit was its provision of long-range reconnaissance, intelligence gathering, and information reporting. Of particular note were the almost continuous clandestine "road watches" that it mounted along the main coastal road between Cyrenaica and Tripolitania from February 1942 onward. Such was the intelligence value attributed to these operations that they would absorb much of the LRDG's time and often took precedence over other activities in 1942.[17]

With expertise furnished by its nucleus of prewar desert travelers and enhanced via the attachment of other specialists, such as officers from the Egyptian Desert Survey, the LRDG was able to supplement its provision of military intelligence with topographical survey, map making, and reports on "going"—valuable activities that helped chart the largely unknown terrain west of the Egyptian frontier. LRDG patrols also performed useful service undertaking pathfinding and scouting tasks for both Eighth Army and Free French units.[18] The group's long-range patrols, capable of covering over 3,500 miles in a round trip, also provided a reliable means of transporting agents of the Special Operations Executive (SOE), Secret Intelligence Service (SIS), and MI9 (the agency responsible for escape and evasion and rescuing prisoners of war), as well as the personnel of the Libyan Arab Force (LAF) Commando and L Detachment Special Air Service (SAS), for much of its formative year in the desert. The unit's expertise further ensured that its personnel were valued as instructional troops, often being called upon to teach conventional and specialist units alike the arts of desert travel, navigation, and signals, as well as producing training pamphlets on such subjects.[19] Such many and varied demands on the small unit were, at times, quite exacting.

Although well within its initial mandate, offensive action by the LRDG generally came secondary to intelligence tasks, being largely limited to opportunistic and extracurricular actions rather than those preplanned strikes as undertaken by other special forces in theater. However, there were occasional exceptions to this general rule, such as in November 1940, when patrols performed a series of raids on Italian strongholds in cooperation with the Free French, most notably attacking the fort of Murzak in the Fezzan and serving as an advance guard for Colonel Jacques-Philippe Leclerc's capture of the Kufra Oasis.[20] Furthermore, so long as it did not compromise their intelligence activities, most patrols were given carte blanche for "piracy" and harassment of the enemy during their deployments.[21] Fluctuations in the strategic situation could, however, shift the priority from intelligence operations toward offensive activities, and vice versa. For example, in both February 1941, following the shock arrival of the Afrika Korps, and again in September 1941, following the commencement of the Crusader offensive, aggressive actions were given priority.[22] While for much of 1942, on the other hand, the significance of the intelligence gained by the "road watch" generally ensured that intelligence gathering took precedence.

After only a very short period of operations, Bagnold's unit met with tangible success and was thus able to carve out a clear niche for itself. In the immediate wake of Bagnold's early successes, GHQ Middle East Forces (MEF) pressed with alacrity for the expansion of the original Long Range Patrols to form the LRDG. This decision was taken at a time when a number of other proposals for expanding upon the long-range patrol concept were being aired. In October 1940 Major Orde Wingate arrived in theater at the behest of Wavell and brought with him a proposal to operate in southern Libya with a "fully mechanized desert force" of divisional strength that would utilize highly mobile columns supported by organic reconnaissance and tactical aircraft.[23] Although many of the themes of these plans were later brought to fruition in Wingate's work in both the Sudan and Burma, for the Desert War they were wildly impracticable. They failed to recognize the precarious manpower and resources situation in theater; the physical and logistical limitations of operating in the desert; and the significance of keeping operations to a small scale—a central tenet of special forces success. Despite such clear limitations, Bagnold was nevertheless taken by some aspects of the scheme and accordingly proposed a "modified Wingate," whereby the LRDG would be expanded into a self-supporting "desert striking force" possessing, in smaller numbers than Wingate had proposed, its own artillery, light armor, infantry, and close air support.[24] Although more realistic and informed than Wingate's original concept, such a proposal was still fanciful, and little came of it aside from some minor experiments whereby the LRDG employed a handful of light tanks and low-caliber guns and, more successfully, obtained two light aircraft for its own "private airforce."[25]

In lieu of such ambitious schemes, Bagnold was promoted out of the LRDG in order to examine the potential of forming upwards of five more LRDG-equivalent units for operations in the African and Syrian deserts.[26] The only formation ultimately to be created from this initiative, however, was the Indian Long Range Squadron (ILRS). Of the ILRS, formed in mid-1941 from volunteers from Indian cavalry regiments, the expectation was that the unit might undertake LRDG-style operations for the Persia and Iraq Command (PAIC). With little of such work available, however, in October 1942 the largely underemployed ILRS was transferred to the Libyan desert, placed under LRDG control, and used to undertake medium-range reconnaissance for the Eighth Army. As the lines moved toward Tunisia, the ILRS would later be tasked with helping to escort elements of General Leclerc's command across the Fezzan. Following this brief period of activity, the duties of the ILRS once again became more mundane, including escorting officers on tour, enforcing traffic controls for contraband goods, and assisting in internal security police work.[27] Eventually, with the close of operations in the desert, the squadron was returned to India and remained unemployed until May 1944, when it was used to "patrol the Persian-Afghan-Russian border zone . . . to discourage Soviet attempts to infiltrate clandestine takeover forces into this oil-rich area."[28]

Although those former efforts to directly expand the LRDG had been thwarted because of the realities of the operational situation in theater and a general deficit in manpower and resources, wider enthusiasm toward special operations and the proliferation of irregular bodies had not been curtailed. Indeed, the continued successes of the LRDG had fostered a definite climate of acceptability toward irregular ideas and independent formations; the group's work would thus provide obvious stimulus for the establishment of other irregular units in theater. It was in such an atmosphere that in the summer of 1941 GHQ MEF agreed to give another "errant captain" license for one more "private army": the Special Air Service (SAS).

Although the SAS would develop in the wake of successes attained by the LRDG and in an environment broadly supportive of irregular enterprises, the more precise root causes for its creation stemmed from perceived inadequacies in the establishment and use of the Layforce Commandos. Lieutenant Archibald David Stirling (who never used his first name, which he shared with his father) of No. 8 Commando was, like many men of Layforce, frustrated by the infrequency and inadequacy of Commando operations in theater. He became convinced that the use of Commandos was fundamentally flawed, most crucially over the issue of scale. While recuperating in the hospital following a mishap experimenting with parachutes, Stirling devised a proposal for the formation of a small unit that, he believed, would be capable of undertaking a broader and more flexible range of offensive actions than had heretofore been possible with a Commando. In July 1941 he presented this proposal, as SAS mythology has it, in a characteristically unorthodox manner direct to the highest local authorities: General Claude Auchinleck, C in C MEF, and his chief of staff, General Neil Ritchie.[29] Coming at a time when the Crusader offensive was being planned and in an atmosphere in which plans for an increase in special operations were regularly being discussed, Stirling's move was both well timed and sensibly directed. As Tim Jones states, it was "fortuitous that he [Stirling] was in the right place at the right time for such heterodox thinking to be accepted by top-level decision makers."[30] In a manner directly analogous to Bagnold's experience with Wavell one year previously, Auchinleck was willing to act as "champion" for Stirling's scheme, accordingly promoting him to captain and granting him a small establishment for his unit. The force would be named L Detachment, SAS Brigade, a title coined by Dudley Clarke to lend a margin of truth toward a deception scheme he had devised to convince the Axis of the existence of an entire airborne brigade in theater.[31]

Helped greatly by popular literature, Stirling and his proposals have attained almost mythological status. Illustrative of the aggrandizement of the man is Mike Morgan's contention that Stirling "ranks alongside Hannibal and Wellington as one of the most extraordinary gifted and original military thinkers of all time."[32] Such opinions notwithstanding, the central themes of Stirling's proposal cannot be considered to be entirely original: the LRDG had been operating in small groups in this theater for over a year, while the February 1941 raid (code name Colossus) on the Tragino aqueduct in Italy, undertaken by lineal forebears of the Parachute Regiment, had already proven the potential of utilizing the parachute for sabotage in depth.[33] In an overall assessment Stirling's idea has a wealth of different origins,[34] but perhaps most important was the influence of his colleague, and fellow Commando officer, Lieutenant John Steel "Jock" Lewes. Following the disbandment of Layforce, Lewes had established himself as an exponent of the nighttime raid in a number of forays near Tobruk, and it was he who had been directed to undertake the trials with parachutes that had preceded Stirling's proposal.[35] Furthermore, once the SAS was raised, it was Lewes who devised practically all formative training schemes and tactics.[36] This was certainly not lost on Stirling, and after Lewes's untimely death in an early raid, Stirling himself wrote that "Jock could far more genuinely claim to be the founder of the SAS than I."[37]

Rather than dwell unnecessarily on proportioning credit for the creation of the SAS, it is most profitable to view its inception as a partnership. Michael Asher painted an eloquent picture of the SAS emerging from the creative tensions existing between two different personalities: "the analytic perfectionist" Lewes and the "romantic visionary" Stirling.[38] Stirling's own personal contribution was perhaps most acute, as was the case with most "errant captains," in having "the tenacity to drive it [the idea] through an unwilling and therefore unresponsive higher headquarters."[39] Stirling had not only this determination but also the guile to sidestep opposition—as well as the fertile social connections to gain favor among the higher echelons. Had Stirling not had these, it seems unlikely that it would have been possible for him to bring his concept to the field.

Central to Stirling's proposal for the SAS was his idea that the scale of Commando operations was incompatible with the realities of the strategic situation in the Middle East. He was emphatic that a smaller unit could undertake raiding operations more efficiently than a Commando. Like many of the men in Layforce, Stirling had been frustrated by the constant cancellation of operations, and he believed that the smaller a unit's deployments, the less likely it would be that the headaches of logistics, transportation, and administration would impede employment. By dividing his men into a number of small patrols, each of approximately five men, Stirling believed it would be feasible to engage a much wider range of targets than had been possible with the Commandos; moreover, he foresaw that the use of such autonomous groups simultaneously against different targets would magnify the disruptive and destructive effects of each raid and further increase the moral attrition of the enemy. Furthermore, by confining individual attacks to a small scale, it was more likely that each would attain tactical surprise, thereby increasing their margin of success, while at the same time reducing the potential cost of men and material lost should an operation fail.[40] The ultimate success of the SAS in the Desert War would, on the whole, validate this cost-effective logic.

L Detachment's first operational deployment was a set-piece attack on airfields near Gazala/Tmimi in conjunction with Auchinleck's Crusader offensive of November 1941. Lack of experience in desert travel and an early fascination, in all quarters, with the potential of the parachute (influenced not least of all by Germany's use of Fallschirmjäger against Crete) ensured that this operation would be the first British operational parachute jump undertaken in the Middle East theater (and only the second-ever operational jump, following Colossus). As it turned out, however, atrocious weather conditions, relatively concentrated enemy ground-to-air defenses, and broad inexperience in all aspects of airborne operations all transpired to turn this operation into a disaster.[41] Thirty-four of the fifty-five men dropped were killed or captured, while the objectives remained unscathed.

The history of the SAS may well have ended here were it not for the resilience and inventiveness of the survivors. When those L Detachment personnel who had survived the drops were picked up for exfiltration out of the desert (as had been prearranged) by the LRDG, the foundations for a new tactical approach were laid that almost certainly saved Stirling's force from disbandment. During the return to Cairo, Stirling and the LRDG patrol commanders came to the conclusion that much could be gained from the LRDG transporting the SAS to, as well as from, their objectives, which the SAS would infiltrate to attack on foot.[42] Following a very brief period of recuperation, Stirling's remaining men would swiftly embark upon such a series of joint operations. Not only did this move demonstrate Stirling's "most extraordinary" characteristic of being able to "bounce back after the most dismal failures," it also highlighted his merits as a tactician. Between December 13 and 15, 1941, LRDG patrols transported L Detachment men to raid enemy airfields at Sirte, Tamet, and Agheila. These operations were extremely successful; some sixty-one enemy aircraft were destroyed on the ground and various points of the enemy's rear areas shot up. In one stroke Stirling's original concept had been broadly validated, and the short-term continuation of his force, at least, was assured.[43] The advent of this tactical approach also dramatically altered both the pace and volume of special operations undertaken in theater.

As a result of the startling successes of L Detachment's December operations, the decision was taken to formalize the partnership between the LRDG and SAS into what Eric Morris has called "a marriage not of mutual convenience but of complementary skills and expertise."[44] The SAS would take advantage of a safer and more efficient manner of transportation, navigation, and administration, while the LRDG would receive help in facilitating its offensive duties, which would allow it to focus increased attention upon its intelligence-orientated mandate.[45] Such benefits notwithstanding, for the LRDG the arrival of the SAS must be viewed as something of a mixed blessing, in light of the increased burden it placed on the Group. For at least five months the expanding SAS force would be almost wholly dependent on LRDG patronage for navigation, signals, and transportation. Even in the summer of 1942, when L Detachment had secured its own transportation and had amassed much experience in desert travel, the reliance upon the LRDG in matters of logistics (and to a lesser extent navigation and signals) would continue.[46]

As compared to the myriad of tasks undertaken by the LRDG, the role of the SAS in the desert was comparatively simple; its members were fundamentally aggressive albeit versatile raiders, unflatteringly described by General Auchinleck as being of "the thug variety."[47] The principal target of the SAS, and one it excelled at tackling, were enemy aerodromes and associated aircraft. Against these targets, small parties operating on foot employed hand-placed demolition charges (the "Lewes" bomb of their own design) and met with broad success.[48] Despite the obvious value of such work, Stirling remained wary of his unit becoming docketed at GHQ as being solely capable of attacking airfields. Constantly conscious of the importance of remaining flexible in order to ensure the greatest potential employment of his force, Stirling actively sought to expand the repertoire of targets his unit could attack. In January 1942, to help facilitate attacks on the harbors of, and shipping at, Benghazi and Buerat, Stirling secured the attachment of elements of the 1st Special Boat Section (discussed later) to L Detachment.[49] Undeniably expansionist in his desires, at this time Stirling was able to further increase the size of his command via the attachment of Free French parachutes from 1 Infantérie de l'Air.

It was with a similar motivation to develop new means and methods that Stirling sought to utilize the advantage offered by personnel of the Special Interrogation Group (SIG). Raised in April 1942, the SIG was an independent unit of platoon strength made up of fluent German linguists, mainly Palestinian Jews of German descent and formerly of No. 51 (ME) Commando. Led by Captain Herbert Buck, the British officer who had conceived of the force, the unit would don enemy uniforms and masquerade as Afrika Korps personnel to infiltrate enemy lines and undertake intelligence and sabotage tasks.[50] Securing the temporary attachment of the SIG to the SAS in June 1942, Stirling hoped that the unit could "escort" a group of the Free French paratroopers through enemy lines to facilitate a raid against Derna. The result of this audacious scheme was, however, unfortunate. The commonly accepted view of events is that treachery within SIG ranks, resulting from a German NCO acting as something of a double agent, compromised the operation and led to the majority of the force being captured or killed.[51] Equally ill fated was the SIG's participation in leading the deception to facilitate a large-scale raid on Tobruk in September 1942, Operation Agreement. During this failed attack, the SIG, whose personnel likely harbored no doubts about their likely fate in the event of capture, was decimated by heavy casualties. Although at times certain special forces would don civilian clothes or reap the benefits of ambiguous uniforms, actually employing enemy uniform to masquerade as enemy soldiery was, in Anglo-American special forces, limited to the SIG—perhaps not surprisingly, as fighting in enemy uniform violates the laws of armed conflict.[52]

Like the LRDG, the SAS also had an instructional role and trained various personnel in demolitions and parachuting.[53] As the SAS grew in size and ambition, GHQ MEF began to pay increased attention to Stirling's force. In particular, and reflective of an endemic fascination with the potential for airborne operations, eyes turned toward the SAS's nascent airborne talents.[54] Despite their first operation having been a disaster, Stirling had nonetheless been insistent that all SAS recruits train in the use of the parachute, as it would help maintain the flexibility of his unit for future operations and was a solid means of gauging the mettle of any recruit. The SAS had thus developed a parachute training facility at Kabrit, the only such example in the Middle East at this time. In light of this, in mid-1942 it was even suggested that L Detachment be made responsible for training, and providing the nucleus of, an entire airborne brigade.⁵⁵ Adamant that this would be to the detriment of his unit, and claiming that the use of his men in such a manner would be analogous to "using medical specialists as stretcher bearers," Stirling was able to consistently lobby against such dramatically expanded duties.⁵⁶ Ultimately, however, it was the range of SAS operational obligations and the regular margin of success they attained that was sufficient to prevent the SAS from being saddled with large-scale instructional commitments. This fact notwithstanding, the unit's facilities, which had gradually been stiffened by specialist Army and RAF instructors to become No. 4 Parachute Training School RAF in May 1942, continued to be utilized for all parachute instruction undertaken in theater until the end of that year.⁵⁷

"Errant captains" were rarely as instrumental in the creation and operation of their units as was Vladimir "Popski" Peniakoff, commander in the Desert War of both the LAF Commando and, subsequently, what came to be known as "Popski's Private Army." In both instances he "created, controlled, directed and inspired" his formations.⁵⁸ Working in Egypt before the war, in 1940 Popski had gained a commission in the LAF but soon became frustrated by the lack of action. He thus proposed using his prewar knowledge of desert travel and of the Cyrenaican Arabs and their language to establish an intelligence network "covering the Jebel Akhdar from Derna to Benghazi" and sought "to take control of the friendly Arab tribes in that area." In April 1942, in a climate of desperation following Field Marshal Rommel's recent advances, Popski was granted permission to form the LAF Commando for these purposes. It was a grand-sounding name for a unit composed of Popski, one Arab officer, a British sergeant, and twenty-two Arab soldiers that served, in Popski's words, as little more than a "personal bodyguard."⁵⁹ The main occupation of the LAF Commando was to be embedded in, as opposed to patrolling, the Jebel Akhdar to fulfill an intelligence collecting, analyzing, and disseminating function. Beginning in May 1942, the unit began to undertake more aggressive roles when Popski was ordered to spread "alarm and despondency" and target enemy fuel supplies—something it did very successfully on May 19, 1942, when it sabotaged an Italian petrol dump at El Qubba, destroying an estimated 100,000 gallons of petrol.⁶⁰ The LAF Commando, alongside the LRDG, also had a role in assisting Advance A Force (a branch of MI9 in theater) in aiding evaders and escaped POWs to get back to Allied lines.⁶¹

Almost six months after the LAF Commando's inception, it was disbanded. When Popski returned from deployment, Colonel John Hackett, heading the newly established Raiding Forces branch of GHQ MEF, suggested "that a unit operating on the lines of Popski's parties but with bigger means and transport of its own" might be able to do useful service harassing the enemy's withdrawal following El Alamein.[62] Popski sought to fulfill this proposition commanding a LRDG squadron, believing that so doing he "would achieve results far greater than if . . . saddled with the responsibilities of a unit" of his own.[63] This did not, however, transpire, and consequently, on November 3, 1942, No. 1 Demolition Squadron, or "Popski's Private Army" (PPA), was established as the smallest independent unit in the British Army, and Popski was given fourteen days to recruit, equip, and organize his twenty-man "army."[64] The rapid creation of PPA as an autonomous motorized special force at this late stage in the campaign highlights the ascendancy and continued desirability of such methods in the Desert War, even after the strategic initiative had been regained following the victory of the Second Battle of El Alamein.

However, in the short space of time that it took PPA to be raised, equipped, and deployed, the Eighth Army had liberated Cyrenaica, and the purpose for which PPA had been formed had ceased to exist. The move toward Tunisia meant PPA would be operating over unfamiliar terrain without the benefit of Popski's unique contacts; furthermore, the shortening of Axis lines of communication made certain that gasoline supplies (which, in light of El Qubba, Popski was viewed as somewhat of a specialist at attacking) were becoming both less of a problem for Rommel and less accessible to raiders.[65] Rather than being disbanded, PPA found alternative employment operating in close conjunction with the LRDG (to which it was briefly attached), performing reconnaissance and topographical survey. Later, operating independently, and more by accident than design, PPA was the first complete Eighth Army unit to link up with the First Army, from whose lines it would subsequently focus on "harassing enemy convoys and on raiding headquarters and landing-grounds."[66]

The Desert War was a theater uniquely appropriate for the proliferation and use of special forces. Here such units were able to gain a gradual but definite ascendancy over their Commando counterparts. Just as L Detachment rose from remnants of the original Layforce

Commandos, it was equally fitting that the newly expanded 1st SAS Regiment, created in September 1942, came up to establishment from the disbandment of an underutilized Middle East Commando (or, as it had become known, the 1st SS Regiment).[67] The importance of the SAS gaining regimental establishment almost exactly one year after its first operation should not be underestimated—validating special forces tactics, ending much of the talk of private armies, and showing that, in the desert at least, these bodies were preferable to other irregular means.

Donovan, OSS, and America's First Forays

While the American adoption of ranger formations was inherently linked to the example of the British Army Commandos, the American conception of special forces units arose, for the most part, independently of the British. Unlike the eclectic, ad hoc, and grassroots process that led to the creation of many British formations, the majority of U.S. special forces capabilities arose under the aegis of one organization: William J. Donovan's COI/OSS. As coordinator of information (COI), and later head of the Office of Strategic Services (OSS), Donovan fulfilled an important role in developing American specialist warfare capabilities.

By the summer of 1940 the colorful William "Wild Bill" Donovan had already had an illustrious career. An influential Wall Street lawyer and then a U.S. Attorney, Donovan was also a man of action, having won the Medal of Honor in 1918 while leading an assault against a fortified position in France. As a member of the Ivy League social elite, Donovan possessed the social connections, intellect, and political savvy necessary to effectively fight the many jurisdictional battles he would face at the helm of COI and OSS. Despite their being from differing political parties, he and President Roosevelt, who greatly valued Donovan's advice on foreign affairs, had forged a good personal relationship. In July and December 1940, at the suggestion of Frank Knox,[68] secretary of the U.S. Navy and friend of Donovan, President Roosevelt authorized Donovan to embark upon a worldwide fact-finding tour of British military and subversive commands, during which he fostered a clear idea of America's need to develop both intelligence and covert operations capabilities.[69] Having subsequently convinced the president of such a point, in July 1941 he was appointed coordinator of information (COI) by Roosevelt, with the mandate to "direct the New Deal's excursion into espionage, sabotage, 'black' propaganda, guerrilla warfare, and other 'un-American' subversive practices."[70] Despite having inherited many such ideas from the British, as Alfred Paddock emphasized, only someone of Donovan's "stature, perseverance, and personal dynamism could have successfully applied those unorthodox concepts in the face of the intense opposition and competing bureaucratic interests."[71]

Three months after becoming COI Donovan began moves to define his "special operations" responsibilities, and in October 1941 he established the SA/G (Special Activities/Goodfellow) Section—so named after the section head, Millard Preston Goodfellow, with the responsibility of making arrangements for guerrilla and special operations. Discussions within this branch, which were led by Lieutenant Colonel Robert Solborg and Captain James Roosevelt (the latter being influenced by his recent observations of British developments), aired the possibility of raising 2,500 "elite troops" that could serve as guerrilla battalions behind enemy lines.[72] However, it was not until December 22, after Pearl Harbor had thrust America into the war, that Donovan was formally able to outline the SA/G Section's responsibilities, which as well as subversive and fifth column activities included proposals for guerrilla warfare, specifically the "establishment and support of small bands of local origin under definite leaders" and "the formation in the United States of guerrilla forces military in nature."[73]

By May 1942 Donovan had modified such ideas and proposed the formation of numerous region-specific "guerrilla battalions," each made up of highly trained and linguistically talented personnel.[74] At this time, however, these schemes were rejected by the War Department, not only because (akin to the early British Independent Companies) they were somewhat impracticable, but also because there was significant opposition toward a quasi-civilian agency undertaking military operations over which the War Department would have no direct jurisdiction. In spite of this, any concerns toward such activities as being "un-American" had been largely suppressed.[75] Even Henry L. Stimson, secretary of war, who had famously taken the moral high ground in 1929 when claiming that "gentlemen do not read each other's mail" upon abolishing the peacetime Black Chamber code-breaking agency, concurred with the basic ideas presented by Donovan, writing to him that "the conduct of organized sabotage in areas occupied by the enemy has become an essential mode of warfare."[76]

It was only with the creation of OSS in June 1942, however, that Donovan was officially able to assume responsibility for "special operations," forming the Special Operations (SO) branch (from the nucleus of the SA/G Section) with a mandate for its conduct. Progress was, however, slow. It was not until December 23, 1942, almost exactly a year after the SA/G Section's responsibilities had first been outlined, that the JCS permitted OSS to undertake approved "special operations," including clandestine sabotage, psychological operations, the orchestration and conduct of coup de main attacks, and guerrilla warfare. There remained, however, a continued aversion to involving significant numbers of U.S. service personnel in such activities, and it was made explicit that "personnel to be provided for guerrilla warfare will be limited to organizers, fomenters, and operational nuclei."[77] Despite this limiting proviso, special forces units were a natural concomitant of this directive; the idea for "operational nuclei" ultimately taking flight with the creation of various OSS Operational Groups (OGs). The OGs were the most significant American special forces units created during the war, each comprising small numbers (four officers and thirty men per group) of highly trained bilingual (often first-generation) uniformed soldiers; with their role of acting as "nuclei" for indigenous guerrilla movements, they typified the dominant American notion of special operations.[78] The idea behind the OGs correlated well with broader American policies: for a small manpower commitment, trained American representatives backed by the "arsenal of democracy" could harness indigenous support, and with almost Wilsonian aspirations for self-determination, help these occupied peoples liberate themselves from occupation.

There remained, however, significant opposition to Donovan forming a "private army," and considerable red tape had to be surmounted before OSS had access to anything approaching its own military units. Despite having received authorization for the OG concept, OSS was not yet permitted to begin recruiting.[79] The catalyst for the concerted creation of the OGs came only in April 1943, when General Eisenhower at Allied Force Headquarters (AFHQ), having been given an outline of OSS capabilities, requested the dispatch of "four to eight operational groups or nuclei, to be used as organizers, fomenters and operational nuclei in areas adjacent to this theater."[80] On May 13, in the expectation of similar requests from other theater commands, the OGs were granted branch status within OSS—initially being subordinate to the larger Special Operations (SO) branch—and were thus enabled to recruit personnel and deploy them in the field.[81] Recruiting for the OGs from the U.S. Army thus began, first with native Italian speakers and subsequently extending to French-, German-, Norwegian-, Yugoslav-, and Greek-speaking personnel.[82] Although many of OSS's moves in the Second World War were strongly influenced by the British, the composition and mandate for the OGs was unique. The OGs were a solely American endeavor. Britain formed no comparable formation, in either organization or raison d'être, during the war.

Transition and Change: Special Forces in the Mediterranean and Italy

The Desert War had highlighted the potential of special forces in both independent action and in support of the main campaign. It had created, as Gordon contended, a "cult of special forces," and "by spring 1943 their prestige virtually ensured that new roles would be found for them as the war shifted to the other side of the Mediterranean.'[83] However, it was abundantly clear that the uniquely apposite circumstances and conditions of the Desert War would not be replicated in other theaters and that special forces would thus have to adapt both their establishments and methods to new roles and operating conditions. As eyes turned toward the conduct of operations in Continental Europe, the British conception of autonomous special forces had to adapt to operations occurring at an increased depth and involving an increased level of cooperation with indigenous guerrilla movements.

In March 1943 after some debate, in which both disbandment and a transition to noncombatant were swiftly ruled out, it was agreed that the LRDG's experience in conducting independent operations in depth, and its excellent navigation and signaling skills, would make the unit ideal liaison troops for operations alongside partisans in Greece and the Balkans.[84] To help facilitate such roles, and thus increase the versatility of the unit, the LRDG underwent a period of supplementary training that included basic language skills, parachuting, mountaineering, skiing, and small-boat work, this last under the instruction of the Special Boat Squadron, or SBS

(Squadron), to be discussed below.⁸⁵ After such preparations, the LRDG, alongside the SBS (Squadron), formed part of Raiding Forces Aegean, with an initial task of landing on a number of small Greek islands to act as an "advance guard" for the arrival of larger British forces en route.⁸⁶

The primary role of the LRDG in Greece and the Aegean remained that of intelligence gathering and reconnaissance. Offensive operations and liaison with partisans were considered secondary tasks.⁸⁷ On various Aegean and Yugoslavian islands LRDG patrols would undertake valuable "shipping watches," reporting the movement of enemy shipping and personnel and directing RAF or Royal Navy strikes against these.⁸⁸ Deployment to the Aegean did, however, embroil the LRDG in the desperate efforts to cling to the "island prizes" that had been cheaply gained with the Italian capitulation. In such a climate the LRDG was drawn into a number of inappropriate deployments, such as its casualty-rife attack on the island of Levitha in October or its use in the defense of Leros in November 1943. Subsequent LRDG operations would highlight the continued versatility of the unit, as its patrols were gainfully employed throughout Greece, Albania, and Yugoslavia in both intelligence, pathfinding, and advance guard tasks (occasionally in depth via parachute), as well as the undertaking of more aggressive activities both independently and alongside various conventional, indigenous, and other Allied specialist formations.

Before the close of operations in North Africa, the newly expanded SAS Regiment would undergo many organizational changes in an effort to adapt to post-desert operations. The predominant catalyst for change was the capture of David Stirling, the architect and leader of the SAS, while on an operation in early 1943. The removal of such a significant and influential figure from the scene created genuine complications in long-range planning for the unit.⁸⁹ The lack of a similar unifying figure following Stirling's capture was a real limitation: Stirling's spiritual (but not technical) successor, Major Robert Blair "Paddy" Mayne, lacked Stirling's social connections and skills of high-level diplomacy and was unable, or unwilling, to argue for the retention of the force in its existent form.⁹⁰ Although there was faith placed in SAS methods, as seen with both the 1st SAS's regimental expansion and the creation of the 2nd SAS Regiment under Lieutenant-Colonel William Stirling (brother of David) at AFHQ in early 1943, it was widely understood that aggressive autonomous raids on assets in the enemy's rear, the primary occupation of the SAS in the desert, would become much more difficult in other, less apposite theaters. High-level discussions at Casablanca in February 1943 favored splitting the SAS "into a normal SS unit [i.e., a Commando] for raiding overseas and a small SS squadron for small-scale sabotage-and-scuttle raids."[91] The decision was consequently made to divide the 1st SAS Regiment into two independent formations: the Special Raiding Squadron (SRS) under the command of Mayne and the Special Boat Squadron (SBS) under Major George Jellicoe. Between these two formations and the newly created 2nd SAS Regiment, there would be significant diversity in both missions and employment.

When the SRS was created in February 1943, it was decided that it should "form a unit of similar characteristics [to a Commando] in the near future," and with this in mind planners assigned the unit a commando-style spearheading role in the invasion of Sicily.[92] In preparation for such a role, the SRS underwent amphibious training and made alterations to its organization and tactical approach. Its small jeep-borne patrols were largely dissolved and replaced with a troop-centric establishment in which each troop was equipped with a mortar, engineer, and signals section.[93] During Operation Husky, the SRS took to the commando role with élan and skilfully neutralized the Cape Murro di Porco coastal batteries during the initial assault. Links with the Commandos were further strengthened when the squadron was deployed in a nominal brigade with Nos. 3 and 40 (RM) Commandos under Brigadier John Durnford-Slater for the commencement of the Italian offensive, taking part in operations in the "toe" of Italy and later participating in the Termoli landings.[94] The SRS severed its links with the commando model in December 1943 when it was decided to revive the 1st SAS Regiment for operations in support of the invasion of France, a decision that resulted in the SRS being transferred to Britain, where it was expanded and renamed.

The function of the Special Boat Squadron, defined at the same time as the SRS, was much more closely related to those Casablanca plans for a "small SS squadron for small-scale sabotage-and-scuttle raids." Its general mandate was to undertake independent small-scale raids on land-based targets that could be approached amphibiously as well as undertaking "attacks on shipping and harbor installations."[95] The offensive employment of the SBS was broad: the unit would undertake various small-scale sabotage raids against Sicily, Sardinia, Crete, and in the Aegean and Adriatic; participate in larger combined operations, as it did in its attack on Simi in July 1944; and perform more protracted duties, both independently and in support of conventional forces, as during the liberation of Greece or in the Eighth Army's actions near Lake Comacchio.[96] The SBS was not, however, of the "thug variety," and its more cerebral capabilities were well illustrated by its use in political liaison groups with surrendering Italian garrisons in the Aegean, and with partisan formations in Greece and Yugoslavia, and its participation in widespread ferrying, reconnaissance, and shipping watch operations. In many deployments the SBS worked very closely with the LRDG, and in both the Aegean and, later, the Northern Adriatic, the two units worked "together in harmony," sharing and complementing each other's responsibilities perfectly.[97]

The 2nd SAS Regiment was raised in early 1943 with the core of its personnel coming from the British-based Small Scale Raiding Force (SSRF). The SSRF, in turn, had its origins in an SOE-maintained mission that was formed in the spring of 1941 from a small nucleus of men from No. 7 Commando. The mission covertly operated a small vessel, the *Maid Honor*, off the coast of West Africa to perform a variety of roles, including agent transport and reconnaissance.[98] Returning to Britain at a time when Mountbatten as CCO sought to raise a small "amphibious sabotage force" capable of undertaking pin-prick coastal raids without many of the bureaucratic complications confounding larger Commando deployments,[99] the "*Maid Honor* Force" thus provided the perfect nucleus for what in March 1942 became the SSRF.[100]

The raison d'être of the SSRF was small-scale "smash-and-grab" operations, principally directed at prisoner capture for intelligence purposes, and throughout 1942 the unit was relatively widely employed in such a capacity.[101] Although generally successful, by the end of the year a number of factors transpired to threaten the force's existence. An unsuccessful raid near the Cherbourg Peninsula on September 12 resulted in the loss of eleven men from the small unit, including both Major Gustavus March-Philipps and Captain Graham Hayes, the unit's commander and second-in-command respectively.[102] The loss of such experienced personnel, architects of the unit's existence, hit the small force hard, and analogous to the situation with L Detachment SAS after its first raid, it is testament to the character of the remainder of the personnel that the unit was not dissolved there and then. Instead, in November 1942 the unit was actually expanded beyond its initial establishment via the attachment of personnel from No. 12 Commando and was subsequently placed under the command of Lieutenant Colonel William "Bill" Stirling, brother of David Stirling.[103] Although organizational politics were undoubtedly involved, Bill Stirling's appointment was not solely an act of nepotism: he came to the post with a sound grounding in irregular operations, having been chief instructor at the first Special Training School established at Lochailort in Scotland in 1940.[104] In spite of the expansion of the SSRF, its operations were increasingly being curtailed by the strategic situation and the fear that its very modest results did not justify its stirring up of the enemy's coastline. Thus, when Generals Eisenhower and Harold Alexander at AFHQ began to call for the formation of an SAS-style organization under their command in Algiers, the personnel of the underemployed SSRF, conveniently commanded by David Stirling's brother, became the obvious candidates to be sent to North Africa to form the nucleus of the 2nd SAS Regiment.[105]

The 2nd SAS's first operations from North Africa and Malta were small reconnaissance raids undertaken against the small Mediterranean islands of Pantellaria (code name Snapdragon) and Lampedusa (Buttercup), actions which no doubt benefited significantly from the presence of experienced SSRF hands.[106] Plans to employ the 2nd SAS overland in Tunisia in a manner analogous to the 1st SAS in the desert were, however, generally thwarted by unsuitable terrain, few accessible targets, and a more concentrated enemy. Prior to the invasion of Sicily, Bill Stirling pressed, in a similar manner as his brother would have, for a wide-ranging deployment of his regiment and recommended the dispatch of large numbers of small autonomous groups via parachute in a concentrated effort to overwhelm enemy lines of communication on the island.[107] He believed, somewhat naively, that in Sicily and Italy "jeep patrols brought in by WACO gliders could fight their way to vital objectives with explosives by the ton. In concert with a major operation, mountainous areas could be infested with small parties, which if sufficiently numerous, will saturate completely local defenses, and paralyse communications unhampered."[108]

The scale, depth, and ambition of these proposals were a marked departure from previous SAS operations, and they were ultimately rejected both because of a lack of transport aircraft and because of an unwillingness to employ the SAS in penny packets. In any case, Stirling's Sicilian ambitions occurred only in token form, with two small operations mounted in direct support of the invasion: Narcissus, a naval assault on a lighthouse in the south, and Chestnut, a largely ineffective parachute deployment targeting lines of communications in northern Sicily. The regiment also conducted two more indirect operations in support of the invasion: Waterlily, targeting railroads in Genoa, and Hawthorn, against Sardinian airfields.[109]

Following the disappointment of Sicily, Bill Stirling was quick to critique what he regarded as the lackluster use of his command. He was adamant that a more concerted employment of the SAS would have led to strategically valuable results. For the invasion of Italy Stirling thus repeated his suggestions for a wide and coordinated deployment of his regiment. In a series of hastily prepared plans, he proposed supporting conventional landings in the south of Italy via the dispatch of numerous small SAS teams to target enemy rail networks and lines of communication, principally in an area enclosed by La Spezia, Bologna, and Florence.[110] Nonetheless, similar limitations as those before Sicily saw to it that only five small parties were dropped in support of the landings at Salerno. A frustrated Stirling argued that what was required was "not five parties ill-equipped, but 50 or 100 parties with adequate equipment" to effectively disrupt enemy communications and isolate and delay reinforcement to a beachhead. He argued that had this been laid on, German supply and reinforcement to Salerno "by rail . . . would have been negligible. Telephone communication, power supplies and road transport would have been reduced to a state of chaos."[111] That the unit was not deployed as such at this time was, however, a result of more than a lack of enthusiasm on the part of AFHQ: material constraints on aircraft were severe; intelligence about rear areas was scant; and the Italian partisans were only in their formative periods.

With hindsight and an understanding of the problems in deploying, supplying, and coordinating even a handful of small groups working in depth, it seems likely (assuming all parties could be equipped and deployed as intended) that following an initial impact, which may well have caused surprise and briefly impeded enemy communications, the effect of these groups would have been short lived; would have been underexploited by other arms; and would have been swiftly suppressed with significant loss to the SAS.

At this stage of the war SAS operations were still a very new concept, and parachute operations in Italy were far removed from the vehicular patrols that had operated so successfully in the desert. The potential gains expounded by Stirling were largely theoretical, and there was certainly no tangible evidence that such activities would be able to cripple enemy communications to any great extent. The high command cannot be blamed for not being willing to risk squandering this unit, and the resources to support it, on such ambitious schemes.

After the initial landings in Italy, therefore, the 2nd SAS Regiment spent much of its time operating in the manner of a reconnaissance squadron, undertaking foot and jeep patrols at the immediate front of conventional Allied units.[112] Proportions of the unit were also deployed in the Termoli landing alongside the SRS, and a number of smaller raids were launched from the sea against targets on Italy's eastern coastline. Those few specialist deployments that were undertaken, such as those in support of Salerno or, later, the handful of operations conducted for the benefit of the Anzio landings did, however, show that there was some potential in using small groups, in concert with larger conventional landings, for disruption and harassment behind the enemy lines.[113]

Beginning in September 1943, personnel of the OSS Operational Groups also began to deploy against Italy and the Western Mediterranean islands (the OSS Special Operations branch—under whose mandate the OGs then came—had been "caught short" by the invasion of Sicily, and despite requests from the U.S. Seventh Army, was unable to launch any concerted operations during that campaign).[114] Personnel were deployed to Sardinia and, in October, to Corsica to help ensure the complicity of the Italian garrison and harass the German withdrawal following the armistice.[115] An OG detachment was also landed at Salerno, with the optimistic intention of liaising with any partisans encountered, but in the face of German counterattacks it spent its time gathering tactical intelligence and marshaling local logistical support.[116] From October 1943 both the "French" and "Italian" OGs, often working in close cooperation with the Free French Bataillon de Choc,[117] began to mount, from Corsica (which had become their branch headquarters), a number of small-scale reconnaissance, shipping watch, and offensive sabotage raids against the coasts of southern France, northwestern Italy, and various small western Mediterranean islands.[118]

Having missed out on taking part in the invasion of Sicily, Popski's Private Army also deployed against the Italian mainland. Landing with the 1st Airborne Division at Taranto in September 1943, the small unit's *modus operandi* remained largely unchanged from what it had been in North Africa. As Popski stated, "A fluid military situation and dry weather had presented us with golden opportunities for worrying the Germans inside their own territory," and in such activities, widely undertaken in the "heel" of Italy, PPA met with a fair margin of success.[119] Remaining under the aegis of the British Eighth Army throughout its drive up the east coast of Italy and into Austria, the unit would utilize its mobile autonomous patrols of proportionately heavily armed jeeps to conduct both "alarm and despondency" harassment and intelligence-gathering activities behind the enemy line, as well as occasionally serving in a short-range reconnaissance capacity for conventional formations.

Special Forces in France

The activities of the SAS in the Desert War, Sicily, and Italy were sufficient to attract the attention of the planners for Operation Overlord, who were desperate to leverage every possible advantage to help ensure success in Normandy. Accordingly, in early 1944 the 2nd SAS and SRS were dispatched to Britain to form the SAS Brigade, which would include the two British regiments (the SRS being renamed 1st SAS Regiment) alongside two Free French parachute regiments (known as the 3rd and 4th SAS) and a Belgian parachute company (known as 5th SAS, despite its smaller establishment). General Bernard Montgomery believed that the SAS Brigade could "assist in forming a wide and sustained belt of small independent parties round the 'Overlord' bridgehead area" that would obstruct German lines of communication and delay the movement of German mobile reserves to the beaches during the early stages of the operation.[120] Although this certainly bore some similarities to Bill Stirling's suggestions made in Italy, it lacked the crucial element of depth. Montgomery's scheme represented a fundamentally tactical deployment of the SAS that was widely thought to be unsuitable for a myriad of reasons, including "security, unsuitability of terrain, the difficulty of the force being landed and resupplied in this area, shortage of aircraft around D-Day and the unlikelihood of the force achieving results commensurate with casualties."[121] Although such a use of the brigade may have caused localized confusion and discomfort for German formations in the beachhead areas, it would have been very difficult to mount, and with virtually nonexistent Resistance infrastructure at the edge of the battle area, impossible to sustain. It could have potentially resulted in the destruction of the entire SAS brigade.

Although by this stage of events the SAS was increasingly regarded as a useful and effective formation, this same respect did not extend in all quarters to a widespread knowledge and understanding of its roles and potential employment. Montgomery's suggestions were made in the face of a growing body of understanding, emanating from AFHQ in Algiers, about the best use of the SAS. In January 1944 AFHQ, under the advisement of Stirling and Co., had recommended that "the most suitable employment for the Regiment is in small [3–5 man] long range raiding parties in a strategic rather than tactical role."[122] A slightly later appraisal, again contradicting Montgomery's projected use of the brigade, stated that "the SAS task is to break the weakest link in the chain of enemy communication and to keep that link broken. The weakest link and the most effective point of attack coincide—usually between 75 and 150 or more miles behind the line."[123] It was not until May 1944 and after much heated debate, during which Bill Stirling resigned, that plans for SAS employment in France were altered to a "strategical role in back areas. . . . To harass enemy lines of communication" and "in conjunction with SOE to link up with and assist the . . . French resistance."[124]

Elements of the SAS Brigade were dispatched into France in depth from the eve of D-day onward. Although very varied, the brigade's role in that campaign can be broadly divided into three categories, which were not mutually exclusive: sabotage and small-scale offensive operations from relatively static bases or "strongholds" in enemy territory; roving flying column operations or "peripatetic affairs"; and operations in direct support of organized guerrilla movements.[125] The use of bases by the brigade, established at various locations in depth from June 7 onward, represented one of the more controversial changes in the SAS's modus operandi. The "strongholds" were intended to serve as mounting bases for operations and as havens at which supplies could be stored and Resistance forces given instruction.[126] Despite being an important requirement for undertaking protracted operations in depth, the development of such strongholds—which were moved in accordance with the tactical situation—arguably sinned against the well-established maxims of small scale, surprise, and mobility that had dominated earlier successful SAS operations. That some of the strongholds, most infamously that of Operation Bulbasket, which was established near Poitiers, were compromised and attacked by superior forces before they could be relocated, resulting in heavy SAS losses, certainly opens up debate, not so much as to whether strongholds should have been used, but whether so many men should have been employed from static locations while undertaking conspicuous offensive actions and at the same time employing so few defensive measures.[127]

A further limitation was that many of the early SAS operations in France were hamstrung by a lack of mobility in the field; the general absence of jeeps, in the opinion of Roger Ford, "certainly detracted from their effectiveness."[128] Once the strategic situation had become more fluid, however, it was possible for the SAS to deploy some mobile patrols in harassment operations. One such operation was Wallace-Hardy of August 1944, commanded by Major Roy Farran. This action, as a December 1944 report from SHAEF (Supreme Headquarters Allied Expeditionary Forces) reflected, "proves that with correct timing and in suitable country (with or without the active help of the local population) a small specially trained force can achieve results out of all proportion to its numbers." The report continued, saying that it "must surely rank as one of the most successful actions ever carried out by a small harassing force behind the enemy lines; the losses sustained were extremely low."[129] The difficulty of timing such operations to capitalize on a fluid operational situation would, nonetheless, inhibit the widespread exploitation of such methods in France.

Alongside undertaking harassment and working with the French Resistance from strongholds, the SAS Brigade was also tasked with a number of unique deployments: Haft and Defoe were reconnaissance operations specifically intended to relay targeting information to the Allied air forces; Titanic-4 was a deception operation in which six SAS men were dropped on the eve of D-day alongside large numbers of dummy paratroopers to suggest a large-scale airborne assault; while Operation Gaff saw a patrol tasked with the assassination of Field Marshal Rommel.[130] The latter operation is an example of an infrequent task for wartime special forces: the deliberate targeting of enemy leaders for assassination or kidnap.

Other examples of such activities are Operation Flipper—a disastrous November 1941 attempt, targeting Rommel, undertaken by former personnel of No. 11 Commando who had formed something of a "private army" under Lieutenant Colonel Geoffrey Keyes;[131] the kidnapping of the Persian pro-Axis General Fazlollah Zahidi in late 1942 by SAS captain Fitzroy Maclean; SOE's kidnap of General Heinrich Kreipe on Crete in April 1944; and, most famously, SOE's 1942 targeted killing of Reinhard Heydrich in Prague.

It is interesting to note the general absence of similar operations undertaken by American wartime special forces. The closest they came to such tasks involved the Alamo Scouts (to be discussed later) in May 1944, an aborted operation to kidnap Lieutenant General Hatazo Adachi in New Guinea.[132] Conversely, it was much more likely for U.S. specialist formations to face deployment helping to counter such activities, with both the U.S. Army Rangers and USMC Raiders occasionally being used as headquarter guards, and the Alamo Scouts forming part of General Walter Krueger's personal bodyguard and escort in New Guinea.[133] The deliberately planned interception of Admiral Isoroku Yamamoto's aircraft in April 1943 by USAAF aircraft based on Guadalcanal, which is occasionally cited as an example of a special operation, does however largely dispel the notion that there was any cultural perception of such operations as being somehow "un-American."

In addition to its more familiar harassment and aggressive coup de main operations, the SAS Brigade in France had a common mandate to organize, train, and provide junior leadership to indigenous guerrilla movements. While the French SAS regiments, obviously benefiting from their knowledge of the French language and people, were widely employed in such activities in Brittany (as at the Operations Samwest and Dingson bases), there was a definite reluctance to burden the British SAS regiments with such tasks lest they unduly detract from their independent offensive activities.[134] Soon after D-day, Brigadier Roderick W. McLeod, commanding the SAS Brigade, warned that the SAS "are military forces carrying out military as opposed to political tasks" and advised that they should not be employed "more than necessary" in organizing partisan formations.[135] Other SOE and OSS groups had a much clearer mandate to work directly alongside the Resistance in France.

One such group, whose raison d'être was undertaking activities alongside indigenous partisan movements, was the inter-Allied

SOE/OSS Jedburgh Teams. Though bearing certain conceptual similarities to both the early ideas for the Independent Companies and the work of SOE Mission 101 and Gideon Force in Ethiopia in 1940–41,[136] the idea for the creation of the teams that made up the group can be traced back to May 1942 discussions between two SOE regional directors, Majors Peter Wilkinson and Robin Brook. If indigenous partisan movements were to be of benefit to conventional Allied operations, Wilkinson and Brook understood that there was a cardinal requirement for guerrilla bands to be adequately equipped and properly directed. They thus proposed the formation of dedicated specialist groups that could be dispatched, in uniform, into occupied territories to arm, exploit, and coordinate indigenous forces in concert with the conventional campaign.[137] This concept was tested and validated in front of an international audience in the Spartan exercises of March 3–11, 1943.[138] The OSS, Free French, and Belgian representatives observing the exercises were all suitably impressed with the concept and accordingly agreed to participate directly in the SOE initiative.[139] The project, soon named Jedburgh, thus became a multinational endeavor, and recruiting proceeded from SOE, OSS, Free French, Dutch, and Belgian sources with the expectation that three-man teams would be created, each consisting of one SOE or OSS officer, one bilingual officer (preferably a native of the occupied nation), and one trained radio operator.[140]

Dispatched into France both independently and alongside SAS and OG missions from the eve of D-day on, the principal function of the Jedburghs remained that as first expounded in May 1942: they were to "make contact with local authorities or existing SOE organizations, to distribute the arms, to start off the action of the patriots, and, most particularly, to arrange by W/T [wireless telegraphy] communication the dropping points and reception committees for further arms and equipment."[141] Once contact had been made with partisan formations, the Jedburghs had three key areas of responsibility: "liaison," "organization," and "leadership."[142] They were to instruct, organize, and equip the partisans while at the same time advising SHAEF on their capabilities. The Jedburghs would also act as reception bodies for both SAS and OG elements, and they were subsequently capable of acting in a liaison capacity between these groups and the Resistance.[143] The Jedburghs themselves, however, were considered too small and "too precious" to participate directly in offensive operations,[144] which would be handled by the SAS and OGs.[145]

The other Anglo-American special forces widely employed in support of the invasion of France were the "French" and (in light of a lack of opportunity for their original mission) "Norwegian" OSS OGs. As has been previously noted, the OSS OGs were created to serve as "operational nuclei" for guerrilla formations: providing a bilingual nucleus of military professionals to raise, train, support, and operate indigenous forces. The OGs nonetheless retained a versatile mandate and were also tasked with undertaking independent direct action and coup de main missions in a manner similar to those missions of the SAS. There remained, however, some clear points of difference between the SAS and OGs. Most obvious were the linguistic talents of the OSS men and their more explicit focus on operating alongside partisan formations.[146] Yet despite this, the OGs did not generally employ vehicles in the same manner as did the SAS, for mobile harassment, and an OSS assessment of operations in France would later indicate that in the breakout and pursuit stages of operations, this absence of vehicles certainly "limited their usefulness."[147]

It is interesting to note that although America was willing to emulate and develop most special forces roles as exhibited by the British, it never sought to mirror the British proclivity for mobile harassment actions. This absence is perhaps most attributable to a divergence of perception about the roles of these units. The British conception of special forces was forged from the successful and highly mobile operations undertaken in the desert. The United States never had such a learning experience, and by the time of its entry into the war the potential for such activities had declined (although, as proven by the likes of the SAS or PPA, had not entirely disappeared). American perceptions of special forces were instead forged at a time when partisan-sponsored actions were coming to the fore: special forces were thus viewed primarily as a reserve that could be used to harness indigenous forces in support of the main effort rather than as actors capable of independent effect. As such, there would be no requirement for U.S. special forces to be independently mobile after initial insertion: they would operate until they were overrun by conventional arms, at which point their mission would be accomplished. This American perception of the principal role of special forces remained throughout the war and beyond.[148]

The initial concept for the use of the OGs in France proposed that they should infiltrate the coastal areas to "conduct hit and run warfare on advance enemy munitions and oil dumps, supply columns, armored columns, and communications."[149] It was a mission that simply did not correlate with the original designs for "operational nuclei." As with some of the earlier schemes proposed for the SAS Brigade, such shallow deployment in a heavily defended area where the majority of the civilian population had been removed would doubtless have resulted in only fleeting gains and would likely have led to heavy casualties among the groups. As had occurred with the SAS, such ideas were discarded before the invasion, and ultimately the OGs were tasked with operating as a "strategic reserve" that could be dispatched after the initial landings into areas where a clear need for their capabilities had been identified.[150] By deploying proportionately heavy weaponry, including machine guns, mortars, and modest antitank weaponry, the OGs were particularly well suited for reinforcing and providing "stiffening" for both Jedburgh Teams and the French Resistance (as seen with Operations Percy Red or Louise, for instance). Although it had been projected that the OGs could undertake those offensive and coup de main operations that the Jedburghs were unsuited for, few such deployments occurred in France. Most commonly, working closely with the Resistance, OGs would undertake harassment operations (such as Operations Christopher or Adrian) and perform "counter-scorch" missions in an effort to protect infrastructure from potential German "scorched earth" operations (as with Operations Patrick, Lindsay, or Donald.)[151] In France there was no "typical" deployment for the OGs per se. The objectives and results of each operation were greatly affected by the time at which they were deployed, the area to which they were dispatched, and the state of readiness and composition of the partisan formations therein.

It will be noted that there existed a certain inexplicit overlap between the varied roles and responsibilities of the OGs, Jedburghs, and SAS Brigade in France. This duplication of effort, exacerbated by command and control problems (discussed in a later chapter), particularly over responsibilities in dealing with the Resistance, was at times a source of confusion and animosity in the field. Jedburgh Team Hugh, which parachuted into central France near Châteauroux in June, for instance, was particularly critical of the Bulbasket mission of the 1st SAS, with whom it worked. The team's after-action report stated that "we never considered that uniformed troops, foreign to the country and its language, could carry out sabotage in better conditions than the resistance. On the contrary, they attract far more remark, and consequently draw danger not only on themselves, but also on all the Maquis in the region. . . . The employment of 'Jeeps' by the SAS at that early stage, showed how little they appreciated the true position."[152]

The manner in which the SAS dealt with the Resistance was a particular matter of contention for the Jedburghs. With scant regard for politics, the SAS was generally willing to "assist any group, no matter what its political persuasion, to obtain arms if it showed any sign of wanting to use them to kill Germans."[153] Jedburgh Team Frederick found it "very difficult" to work with the SAS Operation Samwest operation in northern Brittany because "they had ideas about arming the partisans and rather intruded on our job. We do not mind the maximum number of men being armed naturally, but when hasty preparations are made and the parachutings fail the effect is bad on the Maquis."[154] In the field the SAS was also prone to take command of the Resistance, something that ran contrary to the Jedburghs' mandate to only provide direct leadership when essential. Furthermore, it was a role that, as William Mackenzie emphasized, the "admirable thugs of the SAS were not selected or trained for . . . some of their rank and file seem to have been a little heavy-handed in their dealings with the natives."[155] Such problems were not, however, universal. For example, in stark contrast to Jedburgh Team Frederick's findings, Team George found the SAS Dingson base in Southern Brittany very capable of operating with the Resistance, claiming they "worked wonderfully . . . [the SAS] was never a nuisance or a burden to us."[156]

Following the breakout of Normandy and the development of a fluid Allied offensive, the opportunity to use special forces in depth declined with the advancing front. In this situation the function of the SAS, after some speculation, became the provision of jeep-based reconnaissance at the point of advancing Allied armies.[157] In a manner akin to the use of 2nd SAS Regiment in Italy during 1943, the role of the SAS became "similar to that of a reconnaissance regiment, as there was not . . . any requirement for jeep parties to break through and operate behind the lines."[158] The exception to these later deployments in Belgium, Holland, and Germany were the actions of Major Farran's newly created 3rd Squadron of the 2nd SAS. In December 1944 this squadron began conducting operations in depth in northern Italy, often working alongside Italian partisans.[159]

After operating in France, a number of Jedburghs were deployed to Holland, seven teams were dropped in support of Operation Market Garden, and others were sent to Italy, Yugoslavia, and Burma.[160] Plans for Jedburgh deployments in Denmark, China, and Malaya, although advanced, were never put into effect.

Special Forces in the Balkans, Far East, and the Pacific

Although the use of OSS OGs in France well highlights their function alongside partisan elements, it is their extensive, but all too commonly ignored, employment in other theaters that best highlights their overall versatility. The earliest OG deployments were in the Italian theater but initially bore little relation to their principal mandate to set up and lead indigenous guerrilla forces. The January 1943 conception of the OGs nonetheless advised that until work could be conducted with indigenous guerrillas, the groups should aim to "supplement the work of invasion forces and sabotage units and, in the interim, . . . be used in commando and combined operations work on 'one shot targets' or 'coup-de-main' projects."[161] Having participated in the October 1943 liberation of Corsica, helping both to gain the complicity of the Italian garrison and subsequently in harrying the German withdrawal, the OGs subsequently made the island their headquarters for "French" and "Italian" OG operations. From Corsica the groups, often in cooperation with Free French forces, mounted what were judged to be a number of "highly successful and effective" small-scale reconnaissance, shipping watch, and offensive sabotage raids against the coasts of southern France, northern Italy, and various western Mediterranean islands.[162] It was not until July 1944 that AFHQ became willing to exploit the value of Italian partisans, and coinciding with the upsurge in partisan activities elsewhere in Europe, these OGs began to undertake the tasks that they had originally been created for. From August 1944 onward small teams of OGs were thus widely deployed throughout northern Italy and Slovenia in an effort to coordinate and support partisan formations and disrupt enemy communications.[163]

The most varied OG operations were undertaken by the "Greek" and "Yugoslav" groups. In early 1944 just over a hundred OG personnel were sent to the island of Vis in the Adriatic to serve alongside No. 2 Commando. In this deployment their role became similar to that as performed by the LRDG and SBS in the Aegean, including offensive raids against neighboring islands and shipping, often mounted alongside both the Commandos and Yugoslav partisans, as well as the establishment of radio stations and shipping watches.[164] From April 1944 the "Greek" OGs were deployed as part of the larger Noah's Ark operation to harass the German withdrawal from Greece. Inserted into Greece, the OGs conducted a protracted series of operations to interdict key highways and railroads and provide "supporting fire" and assistance to the *andartes* partisans.[165] In these actions the OGs often worked in cooperation with elements of the British Raiding Support Regiment (RSR).

Raised in October 1943, the RSR was created to provide additional fire support to the partisans and specialist units forming part of both Raiding Forces Middle East and Force 133 (SOE) in the Adriatic.[166] The RSR was organized into five individual "batteries": A battery was made up of heavy machine guns, B battery of three-inch mortars, C battery of light antiaircraft guns, D battery of antitank guns, and E battery of mountain artillery. So equipped with a range of proportionately heavy direct- and indirect-fire weaponry, the RSR was also capable of undertaking independent offensive action missions, as seen with its late 1944 operations along the Dalmatian coast and its participation in the Noah's Ark operations in Greece.[167]

Arriving in Britain in December 1943, the "Norwegian" OGs, like both the First Special Service Force and No. 14 Commando before them, had little opportunity to deploy against Norway. Instead, a deficit of trained personnel available for deployment to France would ensure that they deployed alongside the "French" OGs. This was a course of action which showed that although the linguistic talents of the OGs were not always of tangible value, the personnel involved were sufficiently versatile. It would not be until early 1945 that the men of the "Norwegian" OGs, reorganized into the NORSO (Norwegian Special Operations) Group, were able to deploy, albeit on a limited scale, against the German forces in Norway for the conduct of coup de main operations against rail networks and bridges.[168]

The Far Eastern theater would become as prolific a playground for Allied special forces as was France and the Mediterranean. The initial shock of Japanese gains in theater had resulted in the ad hoc proliferation of "mobs for jobs," which was a spirit certainly analogous to that occurring in the Desert War 1940–41.[169] A fine example of such a pattern can be seen with the creation of Force Viper during the Japanese invasion of Burma in January 1942. Created in Ceylon under Major Duncan Johnston, Force Viper consisted of a composite group of Royal Marines, formerly of Mobile Naval Base Defence Organisation 1,[170] who volunteered to patrol the Gulf of Martaban to help prevent the advancing Japanese from encircling the retreating British forces. Utilizing an improvised flotilla (consisting of motor launches and a paddle steamer), Force Viper would harass the Japanese advance, guard the flanks of the retreating 17th Indian Infantry Division across the Irrawaddy River, and conduct raids and demolitions with Major Mike Calvert's 2nd Burma "Commando" (another scratch force).[171] Of the 107 men of "Viper" who embarked on these operations, 58 eventually made it back to India, where the ad hoc force was disbanded.[172] Equally illustrative of the impromptu and somewhat amateurish proliferation of irregular formations in the early stages of the war against Japan were the hastily arranged stay-behind parties orchestrated by No. 101 Special Training School of SOE, which sought to conduct harassment and sabotage operations among indigenous guerrillas following the Japanese advances in Malaya.[173]

In September 1942, before the concept behind the formation of the OGs had properly been solidified, OSS activated its first operational detachment of the war, appropriately known as Detachment 101. This group, which would ultimately represent the most extensive American special forces "unit" of the Second World War, began as a group of fewer than thirty men seeking to conduct intelligence and sabotage operations in General Stilwell's China-Burma-India (CBI) theater. Ultimately deployed against northern Burma beginning in late 1942, the detachment forged links with anti-Japanese Kachin tribesmen, whom it armed and formed into units of "Kachin Rangers." The detachment was initially focused on establishing intricate intelligence networks, but gradually, and especially with the commencement of Stilwell's Burma Road offensive in September 1944, broadened its role, placing the emphasis on ambushing and harassing Japanese forces and on providing guides and screens for both British and Chinese regular forces as well as for the Chindits and Merrill's Marauders.[174] Over the course of the war Detachment 101 underwent significant expansion, with its ranks approaching some 1,000 men by the end of the war. Simultaneous to this growth, the detachment became the nominal OSS mounting authority in theater, and with the subsequent attachment of both the OSS Maritime Unit (discussed below) and OG veterans from Europe, its potential repertoire of roles further increased.[175]

Over the course of its operations Detachment 101 also established an extensive network for the recovery of Allied pilots downed over Burma, and this network succeeded in returning an impressive 425 downed airmen to Allied lines.[176] Furthermore, on the eve of the Japanese surrender a number of personnel formerly of Detachment 101 (which had been deactivated in July 1945 following the close of the Burma campaign) were chosen to parachute into Japanese POW camps to help ensure the correct treatment of the Allied prisoners being held there.[177] Aiding the escape and evasion of personnel stranded behind enemy lines or facilitating the repatriation of the captured was an infrequently assigned mission for special forces; for instance, the likes of the LRDG, SAS, and PPA were occasionally called upon to assist MI9 with such duties in North Africa and Italy. Such missions were, however, the sole focus of the Special Allied Airborne Reconnaissance Force (SAARF). Established by SHAEF on March 29, 1945, and beginning its short period of operations on April 25, SAARF deployed three-man multinational "contact and reconnaissance teams" (arranged in a structure broadly comparable to the Jedburgh Teams and comprising British, U.S., French, Belgian, and Polish personnel) by both parachute and overland infiltration into German POW camps.[178]

In southern Burma SOE (which after the creation of South East Asia Command [SEAC] became known, in theater, as Force 136) was paralleling Detachment 101's operations in the north and were broadly successful in harnessing the local Karen populations to create guerrilla forces. Of particular note is Operation Character of February 1945, which saw Force 136, supported by Jedburghs, sponsor and lead a large-scale Karen uprising across southern Burma to harass the withdrawal of the Japanese 15th Division.[179] Also of significance in this theater was V Force, operating specifically along the Indo-Burmese border. Originally created in April 1942 as the vaguely titled Assam Organization from a collection of British Army personnel and elements of the Assam Rifles (armed police), the unit's purpose was to recruit local tribesmen and operate as a postoccupational stay-behind force. Deployment saw "this polyglot band of endearing thugs," at times working alongside both OSS

Detachments 101 and 404 (the latter the OSS mounting authority in southern Burma and Southeast Asia),[180] do "magnificent work" for the British Fourteenth Army by providing accurate, if occasionally sporadic, intelligence on enemy movements; acting as guides and pathfinders; and more generally in harassing the enemy.[181]

Throughout the war various efforts were made to train and assist the Chinese in waging guerrilla warfare. As early as the start of 1941 it had been decided that SOE should "offer more active military help to China by providing modern explosives, leadership and coordinated planning for Chinese sabotage and irregular Guerrilla forces." Coming before Pearl Harbor, such initiatives were conducted covertly, under the guise of Danish industrial interests.[182] Once the war with Japan broke out, SOE Mission 204 was established. Including a number of former Layforce Commando personnel and the likes of Michael Calvert, who had been training irregular forces in Australia, Mission 204 sought to establish a demolitions and irregular warfare training school on the Indo-China border and raise a Chinese commando group.[183] The overall effectiveness of such early British initiatives was, however, slight, being marred by Chinese suspicions of British motives. Ultimately it was America that worked most closely with the Chinese in the field of unconventional warfare.

In China the U.S. Navy operated a somewhat similar organization to OSS Detachment 101 under Commander Milton E. Miles (who served under Tai Li, Chiang Kai-shek's head of military intelligence). First known as U.S. Naval Group China, before being renamed Sino-American Cooperative Organization (SACO), this organization served primarily as a joint intelligence-gathering initiative but also had some responsibility for training Chinese guerrillas. SACO was also assigned the unique duty of establishing meteorological stations in China and providing trained weathermen to monitor developing weather patterns for the benefit of Allied air and naval operations in the Pacific.[184]

As the war against Germany was nearing its conclusion, other American personnel, from both the OSS OGs and the Scouts and Raiders (discussed below), were sent to the Far East to train Chinese Commandos. In April 1945 it was expected that twenty Chinese Commandos could be trained and equipped by August. Although progress was hindered by the obtrusive animosity and suspicions endemic to the China-Burma-India theater, from July 1945 a few missions involving Chinese Commandos, working under American supervision, were launched in an effort to interdict the retreating Japanese.[185]

Perhaps the best example of a versatile independent American special forces unit raised during the war was the Sixth Army Special Reconnaissance Unit or, as it was better known, the Alamo Scouts. The Alamo Scouts arose to fill a gap caused by inadequacies of available conventional forces in the Southwest Pacific, and the motivation, if not the mechanism, behind the unit's creation was certainly analogous to that behind the establishment of the LRDG in 1940.[186] Its "champion" and, in the American model, architect of its design was Lieutenant General Walter Krueger, GOC Sixth Army, who in late 1943 was "concerned about the lack of reliable ground intelligence available to his command.... Such intelligence was hard to obtain in the dense jungles of the Southwest Pacific."[187] Although Krueger benefited from intelligence from both the Australian Coastwatchers and U.S. maritime-oriented special reconnaissance units, problems with the dissemination of such intelligence led Krueger to identify a need for a special intelligence unit that would be at his personal disposal.[188] In November 1943, having canvassed ideas from other specialist formations, Krueger tasked Lieutenant Colonel Frederick Bradshaw with creating the Alamo Scouts Training Center (Alamo being the code name of the Sixth Army) in New Guinea.[189]

The purpose of the training center was to qualify Sixth Army volunteers "for the efficient performance of scouting and patrolling duties under all conditions of terrain, weather, and vegetation found in the Southwest Pacific; and to train teams capable of landing near, and reconnoitring, areas of future operations."[190] Only a proportion of the personnel graduating from the center would be formed into Alamo Scout units, while the remainder were returned to their units to disseminate the techniques learned. This approach was unique to American formations, and as has been noted, it was also the motivation behind the creation of the U.S. Army Rangers: to improve the whole by training the few.

The primary purpose of the Alamo Scouts was, like the LRDG, the provision of human intelligence via small four- to eight-man patrols and the undertaking of road and coastal watches.[191] Deployment in the Southwest Pacific ensured that the unit had a strong amphibious focus; it was called upon to supply military intelligence, furnish information on beaches and topography (as at

Leyte), and prepare maps. Deployment in the Philippines saw the unit's role expand, liaising with guerrillas and organizing intelligence networks. Although the scouts were "specifically indoctrinated with the idea of avoiding combat except when essential to the accomplishment of their mission," their inherent flexibility ensured that small-scale raids, roving ambushes, and demolitions were all part of their intended repertoire. The October 1944 raid on a prison camp on Moari in New Guinea to rescue thirty-two natives is a good example of their more aggressive capabilities. They were also excellent guides for conventional and specialized forces alike—something well illustrated by the pre-mission reconnaissance and guidance they provided the 6th Rangers in its raid on the Cabanatuan prisoner of war camp.[192]

Offensive Maritime Special Forces

In addition to the various special forces mentioned above, both Britain and America would develop an extensive range of maritime-oriented special forces. As compared to the broad, and at times indistinct, roles of land-oriented special forces, maritime special forces tended to have better defined and more individualistic roles that were subject to much less transition over the course of operations. Despite this, with little or no precedent to follow, the earliest maritime-focused special forces were, like the first land-oriented examples, by no means inflexible in the roles that they were intended to undertake.

The first British maritime special force conceived during the war was the Special Boat Section. Its July 1940 inception occurred, in a manner analogous to many other early British formations, at the hands of an "errant captain": Lieutenant Roger Courtney, a prewar game hunter and experienced canoeist.[193] While a member of No. 8 Commando training in Scotland, Courtney drew upon his passion for small boats and developed ideas about the military potential of canoe-mounted raids and reconnaissance. Exhibiting the necessary streak of unorthodoxy, he promptly illustrated these ideas to sceptical superiors with a successful, albeit unusual, demonstration. Without seeking permission, Courtney paddled out to a Royal Naval ship moored off the coast, boarded the ship undetected, and stole a gun cover as evidence of his feat. Upon revealing his achievements to the higher powers, he was granted the opportunity to affect another demonstration, during which he paddled up to another ship and placed chalk marks at the points where he would have placed limpet mines.[194] This succeeded in impressing Admiral Keyes who, as DCO, promoted Courtney to captain and authorized him to raise a twelve-man "folbot section" for his Commando.[195] In February 1941 Courtney's group was sent to the Middle East with the Layforce Commandos. By April the unit had become administratively divorced from Layforce and was attached, as an independent entity, to the 1st and 10th Submarine Flotillas in Alexandria and Malta, respectively, and was renamed the 1st Special Boat Section (SBS).[196]

Throughout 1941 the 1st SBS was widely deployed from submarines, with the unit receiving carte blanche to undertake operations during submarine sorties as and when opportunities arose. In early 1942 the unit was increasingly deployed from fast Motor Torpedo Boats (MTBs). For over a year the small unit undertook an extensive range of successful operations that broadened its initially envisioned role to include beach reconnaissance, pilotage, sabotage operations, raids, and personnel transport.[197] At the start of 1942 Courtney and a number of other key officers were recalled to Britain in order to help facilitate the creation of a second SBS unit. For those SBS personnel remaining in the Mediterranean, this move heralded a period of closer association with the SAS, with whom they shared a base in Kabrit.[198] While those overland SAS operations which sought to directly utilize SBS canoe "pairs," such as the attacks on Bourat and Benghazi, would be largely ill fated, principally as a result of the undesirability of carrying canvas boats in the back of trucks, the SBS continued to operate independently, albeit with a fair few tribulations, throughout the Mediterranean until late 1942.

As if to highlight the inevitability of the SBS idea, almost concurrent to the creation of Courtney's unit from No. 8 Commando, No. 6 Commando had also independently conceived of and created its own folbot troop, known as 101 Troop, for much the same purpose. Operating from mainland Britain, however, the troop was not afforded the same ad hoc flexibility that the 1st SBS received during its attachment to submarines in the Mediterranean. 101 Troop's operations were confined to sporadic attacks on enemy shipping using limpet mines and limited reconnaissances of the French coastline. Both such tasks were commonly hampered by unsuitable weather and water conditions.[199] In May 1942 calls for the expansion of the SBS led to a degree of rationalization, and 101 Troop was redesignated 2nd SBS. Subsequently sent to the Mediterranean, 2nd SBS was able to mirror the versatility of its forebear by carrying out a number of diverse intelligence- and offensive-oriented missions.

Soon after the 2nd SBS's creation, and somewhat muddying the previous attempt at rationalization, Major Guy Courtney, brother of Roger, formed Z SBS. Retaining close links with submarine flotillas, Z SBS undertook many clandestine reconnaissance and transportation roles across the Mediterranean. Most notably, the unit helped facilitate two diplomatically important missions in October 1942: the clandestine landing of General Mark Clark to meet with French representatives in North Africa followed by the recovery of General Henri Giraud from France.[200] Later, in 1944, when deployed to the Far East, A, B, and C SBS groups, each formed around a nucleus of experienced SBS personnel who had served in Europe, managed to maintain a flexible and innovative approach to both offensive action, reconnaissance, and transportation tasks when working along the Arakan coastline and the Chindwin and Irrawaddy Rivers.[201] Z SBS, also sent to the Far Eastern theater in the middle of 1944, remained somewhat independent and primarily focused on conducting clandestine ferrying and other operations for SOE's Force 136.[202]

Soon after the inception of the SBS and 101 Troop, yet more maritime special forces with an offensive mandate developed, each justifying their independent existence by the provision of either a niche role or technique. In November 1940 another "errant captain," Royal Marines Major H. G. "Blondie" Hasler, "a natural small boat man" who sought to emulate Italian "human torpedo" techniques, wrote a paper to the Admiralty "proposing a method of attack on ships in harbor employing a type of single-seater submersible canoe manned by a shallow water diver." Analogous to the fate of Bagnold's first suggestions for the LRDG, both this paper and a subsequent one, submitted in May 1941, that emphasized reconnaissance, were rejected as being impracticable and unwarranted.[203] It was not until the effectiveness of Italian developments were vividly illustrated by the successful use of hand-placed limpet mines against the battleships *Queen Elizabeth* and *Valiant* in Alexandria Harbor on December 14, 1941, that the Admiralty was suitably shocked into action.[204]

Hasler was subsequently attached to the Combined Operations Development Center (CODC) with the assignment "to study, coordinate and develop all methods of stealthy seaborne attack by very small parties." Having spent much time developing and submitting to trial an explosive motorboat of the kind that had been developed by the Italians (and was given the cover name Boom Patrol Boat [BPB]), Hasler believed the best way to employ these craft would be to use "cockle" canvas canoes alongside them to help them negotiate boom defenses around enemy harbors. Believing that it was necessary to develop the use of cockles and BPBs within a single unit so as to ensure the best possible cohesion, on July 6, 1942, Mountbatten would accordingly authorize Hasler to recruit forty-six men and form the Royal Marine Boom Patrol Detachment (RMBPD).[205] The niche specialization and sole operational occupation of the detachment, and that in which Major Hasler hoped to gain a level of proficiency unsurpassed by any other existing formation, was the attack of dock installations and ships in harbor utilizing new CODC technologies.[206]

The first deployment of the RMBPD, Operation Frankton, was easily the most noteworthy action of the unit. Mounted in December 1942, it was a bold but costly attempt to attack blockade-running shipping in the docks of Bordeaux. Although neither the target nor method of attack was truly unique (in April 1942 men of 101 Troop had sunk a 7,000-ton tanker in Boulogne harbor using such means[207]), in both depth of deployment and in proposed method of exfiltration, however, the operation is almost without parallel.[208] Transported via submarine to the mouth of the Gironde River, the unit deployed two-man canoes in an effort to paddle the entire length of the watercourse to reach their targets before having to escape and evade overland through occupied France to Spain. Out of the ten "cockleshell heroes" who launched their canoes, it was a feat ultimately managed by only Hasler and his partner Bill Sparks, the other members either being caught and then executed or dying of hypothermia.[209] In late 1943 the RMBPD was sent for service with Raiding Forces Middle East where they would undertake a number of sporadic deployments, the most notable of which being their successful attack on two German destroyers near the island of Leros in the Aegean in June 1944, which facilitated the SBS (Squadron) and Greek Sacred Squadron's[210] raid on the island of Simi in July.[211] The area in which the RMBPD was most active, however, was the nonoperational provision of personnel for the development and trial of new equipment and technologies, such as the BPBs and the "sleeping beauty" submersible attack craft.[212]

Another offensively minded British maritime special forces formation with a niche role was the Sea Reconnaissance Unit (SRU).[213] Predictably, the idea for this unit's inception came from one junior officer: Lieutenant Bruce S. Wright of the Royal Canadian Naval Volunteer Reserve (RCNVR). An experienced prewar swimmer, in January 1941 Wright found himself patrolling a Newfoundland harbor boom when he was struck with the idea that teams of "abalone divers" could be used to infiltrate harbors and attack shipping therein with mines placed by hand. After submitting his ideas to COHQ, Wright was eventually called to Britain to demonstrate his proposed methods. Upon his arrival, Mountbatten sent him to the RMBPD to see if they could adapt themselves to his techniques. It was, however, soon to become apparent that the requirements asked of canoe specialists were not the same as those of combat swimmers. Mountbatten accordingly permitted Wright to form a forty-man unit from scratch, and Hasler dutifully helped him recruit his force.[214]

Like the RMBPD, the SRU had gained establishment by forging a unique tactical approach to existent tasks. Its niche was the use of both surface and underwater combat swimmers to undertake offensive and intelligence tasks against "objectives not otherwise attainable by canoes or other craft."[215] With water conditions in Britain being far from ideal for the training of such a unit, the SRU was dispatched to the warmer waters first of California and later Nassau to perfect this new technique. Although such training accustomed the unit to tropical conditions, it would ultimately preclude its employment in cold-water operations undertaken from Britain before D-day.[216] The unit was not operationally deployed until February 1945, when it was placed under SEAC. In Burma the SRU retained its unique tactical approach when undertaking small-scale reconnaissance and offensive raids against river and shoreline targets.[217]

Joining these other maritime special forces in the Far East in early 1945 was Royal Marine Detachment 385. Raised in March 1944, the detachment was to specialize in the full gamut of small-boat work, including offensive, intelligence, and transportation tasks.[218] Made up of eight troops, each of thirty men, the unit conducted operations that required greater strength than was possible with the other, smaller maritime special forces.[219] The size of Detachment 385's troops and the nature of their deployments had definite similarities to the actions of a "special" OSS OG that had been raised in early 1944 for reconnaissance and ferrying operations in southern Burma.[220]

In contrast to the British, the United States developed *offensive* special maritime capabilities comparatively late in the day, and when it did so, it was heavily influenced by the British. This delay ensured, however, that when America began to develop such capabilities they occurred in a centralized manner, as had also happened with the OSS OGs. The OSS Maritime Unit (MU) was a rational alternative to the cumbersome variety of disparate formations that had proliferated in Britain. Despite the confusing nomenclature, the MU was not a coherent formation per se but was instead, as with the OGs, an operating branch of OSS comprising a collection of different elements each responsible for either a different operational niche or area of operation.

The creation of the MU owes much to the British example. In February 1942 Commander H. G. A. Woolley, an experienced British naval officer and adviser on combined operations to the British Joint Staff Mission in Washington, was loaned to Donovan's COI to advise "on British methods of training operatives and raiding forces." In late April 1942 Woolley suggested that COI establish a maritime training school for clandestine agents, and thus, with his guidance, "Area D" was created on the Potomac near Quantico.[221] By January 1943 this fledgling organization had become the OSS MU, and placed under the aegis of the larger SO branch, it began to take responsibility for the development of specialized equipment and the organization of operational units. In June 1943 the MU was granted independent branch status within OSS that enabled it to put personnel into the field.[222]

The MU held three broad responsibilities: "clandestine ferrying," "maritime sabotage," and, from October 1943 (following a split with the main OSS Research and Development [R&D] branch), the trial and development of new technologies in a manner similar to the relationship between the RMBPD and the CODC.[223] The "clandestine ferrying" branch of the MU was broadly responsible for providing for all OSS small-boat needs, including the infiltration of clandestine personnel and the supply of guerrillas. The first deployment of the MU in this role came with the establishment, in Cairo, of a clandestine ferry service for Greece and the Aegean. This role was, however, limited by an absence of suitable craft and competition with various other agencies charged with the same role, including Z SBS and the Admiralty's Levant Schooner Flotilla, which operated a small number of commandeered caïques in the Aegean Sea.[224]

In October 1943 the MU created a "special maritime group" closely mirroring the role and composition of the British SRU. This group underwent offensive swimming and "frogman" training in close conjunction with the SRU in both California and Nassau before a proportion of it was dispatched to Britain for deployment. Use from Britain was, however, greatly hamstrung by a number of problems with weather and water conditions (as also experienced by the SRU), which were exacerbated by the general absence of U.S. shipping from which to mount independent operations. The latter fact was a common impediment for the use of U.S. maritime special forces in all theaters except the Pacific.[225] Mirroring the fate of the SRU, this group was subsequently sent to Burma in an effort to extend Detachment 101's operational repertoire, and, later still, elements would join an expanded MU organization serving in Ceylon as a part of OSS Detachment 404 to conduct clandestine transportation tasks analogous to those performed by Z SBS for SOE's Force 136.[226]

The individual MU group that had the most frequent, and in many ways most versatile, deployments was that commanded by U.S. Navy Lieutenant Richard Kelly in the Italian theater. Working from June 1944 on, this group benefited considerably from the attachment of experienced Italian personnel formerly of the San Marco Battalion to its ranks.[227] The first missions for this group were the Ossining series of operations conducted against the coastline of northern Italy and Istria, which, somewhat analogous to early SBS deployments, involved seaborne infiltration for the destruction of coastal roads and railways.[228] This group was subsequently widely employed in a range of offensive, intelligence-oriented, and ferrying tasks that were conducted alongside, or for the benefit of, partisans, Allied subversive agencies, and other special forces.[229]

Beach Reconnaissance, Assault Pilotage, Demolitions, and Deception

Not all specialist seaborne units were created with offensive activities in mind; in general terms the requirement for beach reconnaissance and assault pilotage provided greater impetus for the creation of specialist maritime forces. In this field Britain and America simultaneously developed parallel capabilities, albeit independently of one another. The British pioneer in this area was (Herbert) Nigel

Clogstoun-Willmott of the Royal Navy. Having taken part in the Norwegian campaign of 1940, Willmott well understood both the complexities of amphibious warfare and the value of beach reconnaissance in its conduct.[230] In March 1941 Willmott was appointed navigational officer for proposed amphibious landings against Rhodes. In this position he persuaded GHQ MEF to allow him to personally conduct a clandestine survey of the island's beaches via canoe—arguably a questionable decision as far as operational security was concerned. Willmott successfully undertook this task with Major Roger Courtney of the SBS serving as his paddler and bodyguard.[231] Had landings against Rhodes actually been undertaken this effort would doubtless have been of value: as it turned out, however, the venture was little more than a unique experiment. Although Willmott and Courtney subsequently maintained some unofficial liaison, and the SBS's occasional conduct of some limited military reconnaissances notwithstanding, there were no concerted moves to develop a dedicated beach reconnaissance and survey capability at this time.[232]

The requirement for such units received increased attention following the inadequacies of hydrographical and beach intelligence before the Dieppe raid, where the gradients of the beaches had infamously been calculated from prewar postcards.[233] With Operation Torch in the pipeline, the need to rectify such deficiencies was pronounced. In mid-September 1942 Willmott, who had briefly been working alongside the LRDG, was thus instructed to raise an outfit to fulfill these tasks. The resulting formation, which was made up of naval volunteers who had been trained by the SBS in small-boat techniques,[234] would initially comprise two curiously code-named groups: Koodoo, which was to perform pre-invasion reconnaissance; and Inhuman, which was to undertake approach marking and pilotage.[235] The employment of these two groups prior to the invasion of North Africa is best viewed as an experiment. In light of security concerns, Koodoo's reconnaissances were limited to those that could be undertaken by submarine periscope alone, while the small Inhuman party was insufficient in size to perform pilotage for all units, some of which would subsequently be landed on the wrong beaches, up to twelve miles away from their objectives. These points notwithstanding, both groups performed as well as could have been expected given their ad hoc nature, and from their perspective "the Assault operation was a great success."[236] Following Torch, Koodoo/

Inhuman was disbanded, but the value of such units had been firmly established. Subsequently, on November 27, 1942, Willmott was given responsibility for overseeing the creation of nine units dubbed Combined Operations Pilotage Parties (COPPs).[237] Their role, as broadly defined, was to "provide all the non-air-photo reconnaissance required" on both main and subsidiary beaches before an assault, and during the assault to provide "pilotage, assault marking, demolition guides, mine guide, and Royal Engineer assault guide duties."[238]

From the invasion of North Africa onward (inclusive of Koodoo/Inhuman's forays), such roles were considered to be essential prerequisites for all major amphibious undertakings. COPPs were thus utilized in all major European amphibious landings (excluding Anvil/Dragoon) and would participate widely in numerous smaller operations occurring in the Adriatic, Aegean, and Mediterranean. Prior to the Normandy landings COPP teams undertook both offshore soundings from specially modified LCNs (Landing Craft, Navigation), as well as shoreside canoe and swimmer reconnaissances that were launched from newly developed "X-Craft" four-man submersibles. Later, during the subsequent drive on Germany, the European COPPs were called upon to undertake reconnaissances of the Rhine and Elbe Rivers. In the Far East, meanwhile, further COPP teams had been deployed since autumn 1944 in preparation both for projected amphibious landings and numerous river crossings.[239] This theater would also see COPPs occasionally perform a number of more diverse activities that were removed from their initial mandate. Examples of such missions include COPP 3's demolition of mines and stakes obstructing a landing on the Myebon Peninsula in January 1945 and COPP 9's overland reconnaissances undertaken in conjunction with OSS agents and indigenous forces in April 1945.[240]

American developments in beach reconnaissance and pilotage occurred at almost the same time as the first British developments. Army and Marine Corps landing exercises conducted on New River, North Carolina, in July-August 1941 had highlighted the initial requirement for these units.[241] Consequently, Colonel Lewis B. Ely of the army was assigned the task of developing reconnaissance and beach marking capabilities, and he began trials on a variety of techniques, including the deployment of small reconnaissance groups from submarines. Rudimentary assault pilotage techniques began to be developed from March 1942 from the "boat pool" of the Amphibious Training Base (ATB) on Solomons Island, Maryland,

and subsequently, at Ely's recommendation, another ATB was set up in Little Creek, Virginia, where assorted volunteers created the Amphibious Scout and Raider School (Joint) on August 15, 1942.[242] The Scouts and Raiders (S&R) trained at this school represented the first American maritime special force of the war. The unit's operational forte was shoreline reconnaissance, beach survey, and assault pilotage. The "Raider" element of their training (and nomenclature) was largely only for self-preservation.[243]

The first operational deployment of S&R personnel was, like Koodoo/Inhuman, in Operation Torch, where teams had the objective of cutting harbor booms and antisubmarine nets before providing pilotage.[244] Later S&R personnel, often in close cooperation with the COPPs, undertook similar activities throughout the Mediterranean and Adriatic, as well as performing soundings prior to Overlord.[245] As was common to many special forces, the S&Rs also had a significant training and instructional mandate; their school at Fort Pierce, Florida, provided instruction to the 2nd and 5th Rangers, the FSSF, and the USMC Reconnaissance Companies.[246] In July 1943 S&R instructors, alongside Australian personnel, were also responsible for the creation of the relatively short-lived Special Service Unit 1 in the Southwest Pacific to perform amphibious scouting. This unit later provided the nucleus of instructors for the Alamo Scouts.[247] The range of tasks that S&R-trained personnel ultimately undertook was exhaustive and included employment as "UDTs, Scout Intelligence Officers, Beachmasters and Control Officers." Toward the end of the war twenty S&R men, under the name Amphibious Roger, were sent to join SACO in China to help train Chinese guerrillas.[248]

To cater to operations in the Pacific, the USMC also sought to develop its own independent special amphibious reconnaissance capabilities. By October 1942 a comprehensive document on reconnaissance patrols landing on hostile shores had been drafted that highlighted the need to develop mechanisms for tactical and hydrographic beach reconnaissance, assault pilotage, deception operations, and small-scale direct action missions.[249] This document served as a call to arms. In January 1943 the USMC created the Amphibious Reconnaissance Company under Captain James Logan Jones. Working in the Central Pacific, the Reconnaissance Company shared a number of the roles with the Underwater Demolition Teams (UDT), albeit often maintaining a more clandestine focus. In addition, the company was capable of undertaking both overland reconnaissance and modest offensive tasks (as they were called upon to undertake against Apamama Atoll, comparatively close to Tarawa, in November 1943).[250] With the development of the Central Pacific drive, this unit was gradually expanded, first with the creation of a second company and later gaining battalion strength. The unit's growth and employment in numerous amphibious landings in the Central Pacific was in direct contrast to the comparative decline of the USMC Raiders, but it remains illustrative of the fact that, despite an apparent suspicion toward elite units, the USMC was still willing to utilize such formations should necessity determine it.[251]

Another pressing problem confronting the Allies that specialist seaborne units arose to help alleviate was overcoming underwater, beach and shoreside obstacles and defenses (both natural and manmade) that might impede amphibious landings. On May 6, 1943, Admiral Ernest J. King, commander in chief U.S. Navy, issued a directive proposing the training of men for permanent naval demolition units.[252] King was sparked into this by an "urgent requirement" for approach channels to be opened up for the landings on Sicily.[253] To this end, a scratch unit, three officers and fifteen men, of U.S. Navy SeaBees (Construction Battalion personnel) was formed as Demolitions Unit No.1 at the Solomons Island ATB, given basic instruction, and deployed to the Mediterranean. Although the unit was not needed for the Sicily landings, belying prior expectations, the potential for such units had nonetheless been identified, so that when the men returned to the United States they became the nucleus for the newly authorized Naval Combat Demolition Units (NCDUs), each of one officer and five men.[254] In establishing the NCDUs the Navy turned toward their bomb disposal expert, Lieutenant Draper L. Kauffman, who had honed his skills in London during the blitz as an officer in the Royal Navy Volunteer Reserve before being commissioned into the U.S. Navy and selected to head the bomb disposal school at the Washington Naval Yard. In July 1943 Kauffman was appointed commander of the NCDUs and was given responsibility for establishing a training school at the Fort Pierce ATB.[255]

The direct British "equivalent" of the NCDUs were the Landing Craft Obstacle Clearance Units (LCOCUs), initially referred to as both RN Boom Commando and Boom Clearance Parties. Like their NCDU counterparts, these units developed just before the invasion of Sicily.[256] The Boom Commandos were originally designed to "open" enemy harbor booms and use them to the advantage of assaulting forces, but this "floating obstacle" role was soon considered to be of secondary importance to the "removal of underwater obstacles" that was thought "much more likely to be required for any major amphibious operation in Northern Europe." Destroying a "runnel" in a sandbank impeding landing craft during Operation Husky proved the worth of this small unit, so in late June 1943 the force was expanded into six sections, each composed of one officer and ten men.[257] Subsequent to the Sicily landings both British and American units were utilized, with varying levels of responsibility, in every major amphibious landing occurring within the European and Mediterranean theaters. Their work was gradually supplemented, occasionally by direct attachment, by personnel of the U.S. Army Corps of Engineers, the Royal Engineers, and the Royal Marine Engineer Commandos, who took responsibility for demolitions above the high watermark in the assault.[258] It was not until shortly before the invasion of Normandy, however, that interservice cooperation on these tasks was firmly established and "gap assault" teams were created from a combination of both naval and army personnel.[259]

Although the S&R concept had expanded to the Southwest Pacific with the creation of the 7th Amphibious Force Special Service Unit 1 in March 1943 under Commander William B. Coultas, and the USMC had created their Reconnaissance Company, on the whole the development of specialist reconnaissance and demolitions units in the Pacific Theater was, given the potential requirement, surprisingly slow in coming.[260] The real catalyst for change, the identification of need, stemmed from assaults on the atolls of Tarawa and Makin in November 1943. The difficulties experienced in crossing the coral reef at Tarawa, in particular, illuminated "the crying need for scout-swimmers."[261] Although immediately prior to the assault Admiral Chester W. Nimitz "had directed his own gunnery officer Captain Tom B. Hill to assemble a beach reconnaissance and demolition unit," time was too short for it to be properly used in the operation.[262] Following Tarawa and Makin, Rear Admiral Richmond Kelly Turner, commander Fifth Amphibious Force, conducted an analysis of lessons learned and identified the cardinal requirement for a naval demolition and reconnaissance unit. Subsequently, on December 26, 1943, Turner called for the formation of nine UDTs and the creation of an experimental and tactical underwater demolition station on Hawaii.[263] Following some initial guidance from the NCDU teams at Fort Pierce and the USMC Reconnaissance Company in Hawaii, the first UDTs were established. Each made up of one hundred men of all ranks, their creation absorbed a large quantity of NCDUs. By May 1944 the NCDU program at Fort Pierce was absorbed by the larger UDT organization.[264]

Formed from a combination of personnel that included men of the NCDU, the S&Rs, and the OSS MU, the UDTs had a broad range of capabilities. Nomenclature aside, their role was not limited to demolitions but also included reconnaissance and pilotage activities. The first UDT deployments came with Operation Flintlock against Roi Namur and Kwajalein in the Marshall Islands. Despite these operations being somewhat ad hoc because the "teams lacked permanence, cohesion, discipline and military experience," they did, however, prove the "value of night reconnaissance in rubber boats" and of obstacle demolitions and thus promoted the development of more UDTs.[265] Unlike the prevailing clandestine, nighttime approach to reconnaissance and pilotage tasks that dominated all amphibious operations before Overlord in the European and Mediterranean theaters, the methods of the UDTs in the Central Pacific, in correlation with the prevailing amphibious doctrine that sacrificed surprise for firepower, were more overt in focus, often conducted in daylight under the cover of supporting fire. The exception to this general rule was UDT 10, which, formed from a nucleus of OSS swimmers who had trained with the SRU, also undertook a number of clandestine reconnaissance tasks from submarines, as seen before the landings on Palau, Yap, and Truk.[266] After their inception, UDTs were employed in every major amphibious operation occurring in the Pacific theater. Their value is reflected by the rapid expansion of their establishment. By the time of the invasion of Okinawa in April 1945, a total of eight different teams were supporting the amphibious landings, the largest ever UDT deployment. By the end of the war, thirty-two different UDTs had been raised. Although not all teams would see action, the organization ultimately involved over 3,000 American personnel and is thus illustrative of the single largest specialist formation raised by the United States during the course of the Second World War.

The increasing importance of amphibious operations during the war not only called for beach reconnaissance, combat demolitions, and pilotage roles, but also for deception and diversion operations. In April 1942 COHQ created Camouflage Training and Development Center B (also known under the code name Light Scout Car Training Center) to train units to conduct sonic, aural, visual, and wireless *tactical* deceptions before amphibious landings.[267] These British developments, which resulted in a unit subsequently dubbed Combined Operations Scout Unit (COSU),[268] were sufficient to attract the attention of U.S. Naval Lieutenant Douglas Fairbanks, Jr., who had been serving as a liaison officer at COHQ.[269] After observing British developments, Fairbanks returned to the United States, and no doubt drawing upon his celebrity as a prewar Hollywood star, was able to convince Rear Admiral Hewitt, at that time preparing for the North African landings, to form an American counterpart unit. Hewitt subsequently took the proposal to Admiral King, who, in March 1943, authorized the formation of the U.S. Navy Beach Jumpers, with a similar mandate to the existent British outfit.[270] Subsequently the COSU and Beach Jumpers were both employed as part of the A Force deception plans for the amphibious landings against Sicily and Italy. They also operated in the Adriatic, and cooperating with the likes of S&R teams, extended their range of tasks to include "beach reconnaissance, landing and recovering agents behind enemy lines, recovering downed pilots, and supporting prisoner escape networks."[271]

Although this chapter has only covered the inception and employment of Anglo-American special forces in broad brushstrokes, it is evident that, in comparison to the commando and ranger variety of unit, the processes behind the inception and use of the various special forces were considerably more complex. The speed and extent to which British specialist formations proliferated during the first years of the war is illustrative both of desperation and of a cultural proclivity for such means. Special forces developed from both high-level policy decisions and the grass-roots ideas of junior officers. The latter ad hoc, informal process of innovation and acceptance, based on the relationship between "errant captains" and "champions," was uniquely British. There were no American counterparts to the likes of Bagnold, Stirling, Courtney, Hasler, or Wright, who acted as both innovators and practitioners. For the United States it was so often the higher commander who played the essential "founding father" role for the creation of these units, as evidenced by Donovan's role with COI/OSS groups; General Marshall laying the foundations for both the Rangers and the FSSF; or General Walter Krueger's raising the Alamo Scouts and the 6th Rangers.

As nascent creations, the roles of the earliest special forces, such as the LRDG or 1st SBS, were uniquely broad. These units initially offered unknown potentials, and their ad hoc and highly idiosyncratic patterns of inception would ensure that their exact function and projected manner of employment was left largely undefined. In their formative periods, therefore, there was a certain proclivity to view these units, often derisively, as "private armies": as temporary, small-scale expedients that did not require an explicit expression of purpose. Perhaps more than anything else, it was the rise and use of such formations in the Desert War that was of the greatest significance in defining the genre of special forces. Successes in both offensive and intelligence-gathering tasks led to both the expansion and legitimization of these units. By the end of 1942 the majority of them had escaped the "private army" stigma and were increasingly viewed as useful, if not essential, adjuncts to conventional operations.

That the growth and legitimization of offensively oriented special forces shadowed the transition of the commando role was no coincidence. Special forces such as the SAS and SSRF were created because of growing frustrations with the ability of commando formations to undertake raiding operations at the required frequency, scale, and depth. That special forces were proving themselves to be more cost effective, versatile, and simpler alternatives to the committal of commando formations certainly hastened the general evolution of the commando role. For many special forces, however, small-scale autonomous raiding, the brief raison d'être of commando formations, would represent only one occupation within a much broader range of other responsibilities.

In many regards the proliferation and use of special forces was in direct contrast to that of commando and ranger formations. While from the summer of 1944 onward commando, and particularly ranger, formations faced a gradual decline in deployment and even disbandment, the various special forces, conversely, continued to grow in both establishment (with units such as Royal Marine Detachment 385 or the SAARF being created at a relatively late stage in the conflict) and use, as the concerted employment of various special forces in virtually all theaters throughout 1944–45 attests. This divergence in employment is most pronounced in the American example. While in 1945 the personnel employed in U.S. ranger-style formations had declined to approximately 1,350 men, the number of men in U.S. special forces was at an all-time high of approximately 6,770 men, a figure—greatly engorged by the size of the UDT organization—that even exceeded the comparative number of 3,870 men within the British special forces at this time. It is therefore clear that, contrary to much historical opinion and unlike with the rangers and commandos, Britain and the United States equally embraced both the development and use of special forces.

The roles and employment of special forces evolved alongside transitions in the overall strategic picture. Besides heralding the formal transition of commandos and rangers toward spearheading and flank guard duties, the amphibious invasions of North Africa and Sicily also witnessed the creation and employment of dedicated special forces to cater to the need for hydrographical and topographical reconnaissance, underwater and shoreside demolitions, assault pilotage, and deception operations. Similarly, while the stresses and strains of protracted overland campaigns propelled commando formations into more conventional deployments, they offered special forces the potential to conduct operations in depth to support main-force activities in a more indirect manner. Most significantly, perhaps, was the gradual inclusion and coordination of special forces activities with emergent partisan movements. The "great partisan summer" of 1944 saw a distinct acceleration in the employment of special forces in such a capacity, as Allied subversive agencies aimed to coincide the upsurge of partisan activities across Europe with the invasion of France in order to recoup the greatest disruptive benefit to the German war effort. Before this date, and despite some concerted lobbying from the likes of the SAS and OGs in Italy, special forces were rarely able or permitted to deploy in depth at the scale that they desired.

In the later stages of the war, operations alongside partisan formations became both more common and an increasingly important function for many special forces, even for those units without an original mandate for such roles. Operating in depth, special forces were increasingly called upon to act as political liaison groups. As Mackenzie stated, "The guerrilla leader, and the officer attached to him, had to be as much politician as soldier, and it was rarely possible to undertake serious operations without considering political consequences."[272] The dispatch of Major Jellicoe of the SBS into Rhodes to negotiate with the Italian garrison soon after Italy's surrender is a prime example of such a role, as is the dispatch, with similar motivations, of Lieutenant Colonel Serge Obolensky of the OSS OGs to both Sardinia and Corsica. Special forces such as the LRDG, SBS, and OGs also undertook civil affairs and "hearts and minds" operations, helping to gain the complicity and support of local populations by the provision of supplies and medical care. One good, albeit by no means exclusive, example of such a role was the OSS OG Operation Antagonist, in which an OSS medical officer was dispatched into France to support the Percy Red OG mission and organize medical services to the Maquis and the local population.[273]

Links with partisans was a natural concomitant to operating in depth; a nucleus of preexisting indigenous support being an important prerequisite for the committal of uniformed special forces. The use of special forces in enemy-controlled territory with no such nucleus of support imposed severe limitations on the activities that they could expect to undertake. Conversely, with indigenous guerrilla formations in existence (or in sparsely populated areas such as the Libyan Desert), the potential for special forces became widely extended. Deployment of special forces alongside partisans was often a mutually beneficial arrangement. Indigenous forces provided special forces with guides, intelligence, and, if properly equipped and trained, additional manpower for security cordons and reception committees. In so doing, they thus freed up special forces personnel for other activities. Special forces, for their part, could provide partisans with guidance, training, direction, leadership, equipment, and "stiffening."[274] Such roles became common for both the SAS and LRDG, and they were the raison d'être for the likes of the Jedburgh Teams, the OSS OGs, and the British RSR.

In a number of areas Britain and America raised special forces for similar purposes, particularly those units dealing with beach reconnaissance, pilotage, underwater demolitions, and deception tasks. Furthermore, as the examples of the Jedburghs and SAARF highlight, they even formed units of a multinational composition. Despite this, and unlike the clear inter-Allied commonality within commando and ranger formations, there were certain notable differences between both the variety of special forces that Britain and America raised and in the manner in which they operated. There was, for example, no American effort to deal with autonomous mobile harassment operations widely undertaken by the likes of the SAS or PPA; no comparable effort to emulate to quite the same extent the broad gamut of tasks performed by British maritime special forces; no units utilizing enemy uniforms, such as the SIG; and little effort to decapitate enemy leadership via assassination or kidnap. That the United States did not undertake such roles, or form specialized units for their conduct, was partly due to its cultural perception as to what acceptable roles for these formations were, but was also greatly affected by the nature of the strategic situation when the units were being conceived.

Conversely, among the British there was no concerted effort to emulate either the strategic reserve role of the OGs or their bilingual talents for dealing with indigenous forces; nor was there the same proclivity to create special forces from institutions such as the S&R School or the Alamo Scouts Training Center, which could both train units and help disseminate their specialist techniques; nor did the British, largely because of the drastically different amphibious warfare doctrine that developed in Europe, make any effort to emulate the size, scale, or methods of UDT operations. Despite these doctrinal and organizational differences, one cannot escape the prevailing impression of just how close the Anglo-American alliance was in the field of specialist forces and irregular warfare.

CHAPTER 3

Anglo-American Cooperation and Interdependency

It is a widely established truism that by 1944 the U.S. military had matched, and was beginning to exceed, the British contribution to fighting the Second World War. Britain was gradually becoming the lesser partner of the global alliance. Study of the fields of irregular warfare and specialist formations, however, presents a quite different picture. During the course of the Second World War, Britain not only helped America identify a need for specialist formations but also willingly supplied them with the model on which to base their first nascent creations. Britain provided America with establishments, equipment, instructors, and the means through which experience could be gained in this field. Moreover, British hegemony in irregular operations survived the more general decline of Britain's strategic contribution. This chapter utilizes specific examples to assess the value and importance of the British model and experience, and willingness to share, on the American creation and use of ranger and special forces. It examines the notion of the "special relationship" in irregular warfare and the manner in which the two allies cooperated with one another in the field. By addressing the issues of allied interdependence and the effects of cross-fertilization of ideas, personnel, doctrine, and equipment, a close, almost symbiotic relationship between the two nations becomes clear.

The scale and importance of the Anglo-American military alliance during the Second World War is an exhaustively covered subject, and discussion of the broader issues of alliance strategy and diplomacy has little place here. It suffices to acknowledge that this alliance was, diplomatically and militarily speaking, one of the closest and "most successful in modern history."[1] In such a climate, at least a degree of cooperation and mutual dependency between the specialist formations of Britain and America was inevitable. It is equally unsurprising that Britain would dominate this alliance when it was first cemented. Britain's two years of practical experience in raising, training, organizing, equipping, and, most important, deploying specialist formations contrasted favorably against the practically nonexistent American record on the issue before their entry into the war. The significance of this early British lead is obvious but should not be underestimated. Militarily speaking, the armed forces of the United States entered the war deficient in most areas, and in December 1941, compared to a mobilized and combat-experienced Britain, America was the junior partner in the relationship.

Teaching America to Fight Dirty

Cooperation between Britain and the United States in the field of irregular warfare and specialist formations preceded American entry in the war. During the period 1940-41, as David Reynolds has emphasized, "the co-operative element [between the two nations] was paramount. Both countries faced common military and ideological threats at a time when their strengths and weaknesses were unusually complementary."[2] Among other things, these threats caused the United States to seek British advice on irregular and subversive warfare, clandestine intelligence, and raiding operations prior to Pearl Harbor. Knowledge of such areas would allow the country to prepare for, and theoretically embark on, actions against Germany while retaining an isolationist stance.

The earliest moves made by the United States to learn about British approaches to, and experiences of, irregular warfare came from William Donovan. In both July and December 1940 Donovan toured British military commands with the intention of learning "as much as he could about British secret intelligence, special operations, psychological warfare and guerrilla units."[3] The lessons he learned during these visits were soon put to practical effect when the President appointed him coordinator of information and head of an office by that name (COI) in July 1941. From the outset Donovan saw close liaison with his British counterpart organizations to be an essential requirement to the success of his command, and he accordingly sought to develop a symbiotic bond with them.[4] The British organizations, including the Special Operations Executive (SOE), Combined Operations Headquarters (COHQ) and, to a lesser extent, the Secret Intelligence Service (SIS), were accommodating, and each was willing to forge a relationship with Donovan and tell him all that he wanted. From the outset COI gained "complete entrée into the operations and techniques [that the British] . . . had developed during the preceding years." However, British willingness to share this knowledge was no act of charity, and the cost of COI's education would be the United States yielding a degree of control over its activities to the British. Despite this, it was evident that the United States had "little to lose and years to gain" by such propositions and was thus initially willing to "surrender independence for rapid learning."[5]

From September 1941 SOE began offering concerted specialist training to COI personnel. As sending large numbers of personnel to Britain would have been impracticable at this time, a decision was made that such training would be best achieved by establishing a dedicated special school in Canada (known as School 103, or Camp X), at which a nucleus of British experts could provide training to American recruits and lay the "foundations for an American capability in secret warfare." Although not opened until December 9, 1941, at which stage it would have been politically acceptable for such camps to have been formed within mainland USA, Camp X was, in the opinion of David Stafford, a "godsend" to Donovan's fledgling organization.[6] With the impediments of neutrality removed, in early 1942 COI established, in Virginia and Maryland, its first U.S. camps, to which SOE would continue to furnish the "key instructors." Even when OSS was created and established its first independent training schools in July 1942, there was a continued reliance upon a British curriculum and on the rotation of these British instructors.[7] The impact of the British on the fledgling COI, and later OSS, should not be undervalued. As Richard Harris-Smith contended: "The British felt that OSS, in its formative stages, 'could not have survived' without their aid. Donovan knew this as well."[8] Were it not for the British example and willingness to share with their new wartime ally, it is certainly conceivable that OSS, or at least its special operations capabilities, would not have existed at all.

In addition to clandestine intelligence, subversion, and sabotage, the United States also took a prewar interest in British raiding operations and the Commandos. As has already been noted, British influence on the establishment of all U.S. ranger-style formations during the war was quite evident, and, like COI, the seeds of this process were sown early. In the summer of 1941 a contingent of U.S. Marines headed by General Julian Smith had toured Britain and, in so doing, had observed the Commandos and been provided with detailed information on their organization and establishments.[9] It was subsequently arranged that forty USMC officers and NCOs be attached to No. 3 Commando (recently returned from the Lofotens raid) for two months' training. For their part, the Commandos were said to have "greatly welcomed" such an opportunity to share their experiences with the U.S. marines and glean what they could of American equipment and doctrines.[10] Although at least a proportion of the motivation and ideas for the USMC Raiders stemmed directly from this successful arrangement, subsequent British contact with and influence on the Raiders was negligible. The USMC only ever sent two groups of marines to Britain for Commando training (the aforementioned 1941 group and another in April 1942), and thus even before the Raiders had been operationally deployed in August 1942, all direct contact with the British Commandos had effectively ceased.[11]

The U.S. Army first came into contact with the Commandos during tours of COHQ in January 1942, but it would not be until Lucian Truscott's COHQ staff was formed that the army began to show any real interest in the Commandos. The creation of the 1st Ranger Battalion, in both theoretical and practical terms, closely mirrored the Commandos: the Ranger Table of Organization and Equipment (TOE) closely followed the Commando War Establishment; the battalion's training occurred at British hands at the Commando school at Achnacarry and in exercises with formed Commandos in Scotland; and, for the purposes of tactical control, it was placed under the British SS Brigade Headquarters.[12] Despite such influence, the U.S. Army remained keen for the Rangers to keep as much of their American identity as possible. They hoped "that all applicable American doctrines and methods will be retained, but the special doctrines and methods developed by the British will be adopted whenever necessary."[13] There was an implicit expectation, which was to be often repeated, that the British model could be improved upon.[14]

When first considering the formation of American special units to operate in small groups behind enemy lines, Donovan also gained initial inspiration from the Commandos. Having come into contact with the early Commandos during his 1940 visits to Britain, Donovan had come away enthused, viewing the Commandos as a unique model of aggressiveness and irregularity. As soon as he was appointed COI in July 1941, Donovan thus made a special request that Dudley Clarke (at that time serving in Cairo) prepare some "notes on Commandos" for him.[15] In dealing with this request the British seem to have held an incorrect impression that the United States had already made some progress in this field, believing it "unwise" to provide them with a "paper entitled 'A Suggested Procedure for starting Commandos in the USA Army,' as they may feel that we are trying to teach our grandmother to suck eggs."[16] Nonetheless, a more modestly entitled paper was dutifully prepared by Clarke and COHQ personnel and submitted to Donovan.

Donovan remained impressed with the Commando concept, and in July 1942, following the establishment of OSS, he dispatched a group under Colonel John "Iron Mike" O'Daniel to observe and report upon the Commandos. This mission's findings were, however, less than complimentary:

> The [Commando] personnel are not up to the qualifications as laid out in the directive setting up the service. As planned the men should be able to handle every type of vehicle, every type of weapon. They should be able to handle boats, to swim, to know thoroughly demolition and communication. Actually the men are small, scrawny individuals but extremely powerful and in better shape than anything we have attained with our own troops. They are stupid, act like sheep, and have the mentality of a Carolina nigger.[17]

It was an analysis obviously marred by a false and unrealistic perception of what the Commandos were and what they could achieve (which itself resulted from the original, optimistic training mandate setting up the Commandos[18]), and colored by a number of less than glowing appraisals of the early Commando raids. The report cited, for example, the damning fact that some Commandos could not swim and were left behind in the "Guernsey fiasco"; it mentions inexperience at Vaagso, and is critical of the heavy losses at St. Nazaire, but shows little sense of what was achieved by any of the raids. This OSS report concluded that "if Americans are to develop these units, these should be trained as the British say their Commandos are trained, but actually are not."[19]

OSS was imposing unfair criteria upon which to gauge the capabilities of the Commandos;[20] they were not looking for an example of an elite light infantry raiding formation, which is what the Commandos were, but were instead seeking an example of a more autonomous and flexible type of unit capable of undertaking complex, protracted operations behind the lines. Donovan was looking for examples of units that he could relate to his concepts, expounded as early as October 1941, for "guerrilla battalions." The reports made on the Commandos were, nevertheless, certainly of importance in ultimately shaping the approach that OSS eventually adopted toward direct action units. Despite Donovan's earlier interest, therefore, when the Operational Groups (OGs) were ultimately formed, they were fundamentally different from the Commandos in both composition and role. This point notwithstanding, a number of OGs would still ultimately benefit from attending the Commando training establishments in Scotland, as well as British parachute facilities at Ringway, near Manchester, and various other SOE training schools for more specialized instruction.

Although the British may not have influenced the creation of OSS overland special forces to any great extent, their influence on OSS maritime-oriented specialist capabilities was very great indeed. In both practical and theoretical terms the OSS Maritime Unit (MU) owed more to the British example than any other element of COI/OSS. In February 1942 Royal Navy commander H. G. A. Woolley was attached to COI to provide advice on methods of maritime transport and agent infiltration. By April Woolley had established the Area D training facility on the Potomac near Quantico. This decision permitted extensive instruction in British special maritime methods to be provided and, consequently, really illuminated COI as to the "wide possibilities which lay ahead" in offensive maritime activities.[21] Such was his influence in this capacity that in January 1943, when the MU was formally established as an operational branch of OSS, Woolley was appointed branch commander.[22] That Woolley was granted the unique privilege of heading a foreign unit (a post that he held until October 1943, when he would become liaison officer between Donovan and Brigadier Laycock, CCO) is illustrative of just how symbiotic the relationship between Britain and America in the development of these units could be.

The OSS MU London branch was established in June 1943 and, unsurprisingly, developed strong links with its British counterpart organizations. In the belief that they had "everything to gain" from forging close relations with the British, the MU personnel immediately toured various British specialist units, including the Special Boat Sections (SBS), the Combined Operations Pilotage Parties (COPPs) and the Royal Marine Boom Patrol Detachment (RMBPD), and finding some "damned good allies" therein, received "general instruction" on British techniques and methods.[23] In a familiar pattern, the Americans hoped that attachment to these elements would enable them to "learn, perfect, and if possible better the [British] ... technique in Small Boat Operations."[24] Despite the disparity in relative size and levels of experience, the various British special maritime formations, and COHQ in general, also had much to gain from cooperating with the MU, principally benefiting from an exchange of information and equipment, not to mention welcome reinforcement to overstretched operational requirements.[25]

With such motivations in mind, COHQ and OSS were able to establish an "efficient exchange arrangement" whereby the "COSD [Combined Operations Supply Depot] would supply MU and other U.S. groups wherever possible and in turn ... OSS and other U.S. groups such as the USMC, NCDU [Naval Combat Demolitions Unit], etc. would meet the requirements of CCO in various theaters."[26] Arrangements such as this would help lead to a greater degree of standardization of specialist equipment, and ergo methods, between Anglo-American specialist maritime formations.[27] Ultimately, however, the London MU had little opportunity to conduct operations from Britain, being hindered both by increasingly unsuitable strategic circumstances and by a general absence of U.S. naval support. In what would become a common theme for maritime special forces, British patronage thus became a cornerstone for the MU's deployment. As the MU freely recognized, without the "generous and understanding help" of their British counterparts it would have been "able to do very little, if anything."[28]

Once America entered the war, exchanges of personnel and equipment between British and American subversive agencies and specialist formations became much more common. These arrangements were an obvious ancillary to the wider trends of Allied cooperation, epitomized by the establishment of the Combined Chiefs of Staff, and would grow stronger and more efficient as the war progressed. One of the more significant arrangements in this field was the March 1942 creation of the Chief of Combined Operations Representative (CCOR) staff in Washington, D.C., which would be loosely paralleled by Colonel Lucian Truscott's American staff in London, established the following month. This arrangement served to keep both nations abreast of developments in amphibious techniques and equipment and permitted the exchange of advice on "all matters of combined operations," including the development of commandos and special forces. Despite the absence of a direct American equivalent to COHQ, forcing CCOR to cover much ground "by personnel contacts," the arrangement worked well, and a standing practice of monthly exchange visits and tours of experimental and training areas was established. The CCOR staff found the "Americans . . . only too keen to help . . . by keeping us informed of their developments."[29]

The British naval-oriented special force with the most intensive relationship with the U.S. military was the Sea Reconnaissance Unit (SRU). Because of the unsuitability of British coastal waters for the training of combat swimmers, CCOR in Washington arranged for the SRU to conduct its training on the Californian coast. Based at the USMC's Camp Pendleton, the SRU developed its own training regime independent of the Americans but was aided by the attachment of a liaison officer, Captain E. H. "Dutch" Smith, USMC, who helped Lieutenant Bruce Wright develop his exercises.[30] At Pendleton the SRU came into contact with both the 4th Raider Battalion and the emergent USMC Reconnaissance Company, which provided the British outfit with much "valuable and willing assistance" and would cooperate in various exercises, experiments, and training procedures.[31]

In October 1943, following discussions between Donovan and Mountbatten, the OSS MU raised a forty-man combat swimmer unit along SRU lines.[32] This MU group set up its training establishment only 150 yards away from the SRU base at Pendleton and would copy that unit's training program "in every respect," with Captain "Dutch" Smith becoming the MU training officer.[33] Wright provided comprehensive "information regarding the objectives and schedules of their training," and for a two-month period the two units operated closely with one another, mutually investigating the still unexplored area of underwater and surface swimming for sabotage and reconnaissance.[34] The SRU benefited as much from the relationship as did the MU, and Laycock (who had replaced Mountbatten as CCO) was quick to express to Admiral King the "great value . . . of] the liaison afforded with U.S. Units working on similar lines."[35] Upon completion of its training in California, the OSS group followed the SRU to Nassau, and later a group of nine men were sent to Britain. Ultimately this relationship, which was so solid in training, never extended to operational deployment.[36]

Although the influence of British models and assistance on the American adoption and development of irregular capabilities during the period 1940–43 was pronounced, the pattern of the British "teacher" and American "student" was not uniformly correct. In the areas of beach reconnaissance, assault pilotage, and combat demolitions American capabilities and methods were developed either independently or through direct, mutually supportive collaboration with the British. The manner in which the U.S. Naval Combat Demolitions Units (NCDUs) and British Landing Craft Obstacle Clearance Units (LCOCUs) developed is illustrative of this. In January 1943, following a tour of British establishments, U.S. Navy captain Alfred G. Hoel submitted a report that served to enlighten the U.S. Navy Engineer Board on early British experiments into underwater demolitions and provided notes on their training of what were first called Boom Commandos and later renamed LCOCUs.[37] Hoel's recommendations were followed by a combined mission consisting of Major C. E. Kennedy, U.S. Army, and Major R. R. Fairbairn of the Royal Engineers that was sent to the Maryland and Fort Pierce Amphibious Training Bases (ATBs) in early 1943 to advise on "special demolition problems." It was this mission that subsequently helped forge the NCDU syllabus and help train the first ad hoc group for Operation Husky.[38] Despite providing such assistance, the British were by no means further advanced nor more experienced in these fields than were the Americans. Their first Boom Commandos were neither trained nor ready for deployment until February 1943 and would amass no operational experience until the invasion of Sicily, at which stage the first NCDU had been created. From mid-1943 onward, therefore, there was much liaison between British and American groups and regular exchange visits at which information and methods were shared.[39] Furthermore, once the Underwater Demolition Team (UDT) organization emerged to cope with the exigencies of the Pacific War, the British capacity to be "student" was well highlighted, as the British undertook initiatives to learn and assimilate the emerging American techniques, lessons, and equipment.[40]

Cooperation and Conflict

As soon as OSS began considering the conduct of clandestine subversion, sabotage, intelligence, and special operations in earnest, it was clearly essential that the closest possible relationship with

Britain be maintained to avoid the risk of compromise, competition, and redundancy. SOE or OSS independence would be impracticable and could lead to confusion and chaos.[41] Thus, as soon as OSS was created in June 1942 its alliance with SOE was swiftly cemented, and plans for worldwide collaboration were established. Donovan and his then British counterpart at SOE, Sir Charles Hambro, immediately proposed dividing up the world to establish global spheres of cooperation and responsibility for the conduct of special operations by the two organizations. Ratified in September 1942, the SO/SOE Agreement "set forth the basic elements of co-operation in every theater of war, [it] was based upon the general principle that Americans would control areas specifically designated as spheres of American influence, while SOE would control special operations in areas dominated by the British."[42] India, East and West Africa, the Balkans, the Middle East, and Western Europe were to be the province of SOE, while OSS was to have authority over special operations in China, Manchuria, Korea, Australia, the Atlantic Islands, Finland, and North Africa. Other areas were placed under joint control.[43] This agreement was not, however, definitive, and in areas where one nation held "responsibility" the other could still provide liaison and assistance. The "U.S. could assign its own Mission, with headquarters, stations and agents to British territory, to operate under direction and control of the British 'controller'; and vice versa. Differences of opinion would be referred to Washington and London, respectively."[44]

With this agreement in place, the Special Operations (SO) branch of OSS began to make preparations for commencing operations in various theaters. In December 1942 Donovan sent his SO branch chief, Ellery C. Huntington, Jr., on a three-month tour of Europe, Africa, and the Middle East to prepare infrastructure for the conduct of SO activities (under whose broader control both the OGs and MU were originally placed). Huntington initially believed that SO should not be "'an adjunct' of SOE and must remain independent of the British."[45] At this early stage, however, the junior status of OSS rendered such desires almost totally impracticable, and thus when the SO London branch was established, although technically being separate from the British, not only was it organized in a manner "exactly similar" to the operational division of SOE but it was also placed under their British counterpart's charge. Needing to redress his early expectations, Huntington subsequently hoped that by June

1944 OSS would be "reasonably experienced" to become fully independent.[46] By the later stages of 1943, however, it was becoming gradually apparent that in such an important theater independence for either SOE or OSS would be quite inappropriate and, in time, almost perfect synergy between the two organizations would be achieved. In January 1944 the relevant sections of SOE and OSS in Britain became integrated into the SOE/SO organization (rechristened Special Forces Headquarters [SFHQ] in April 1944) and were placed under the control of Supreme Headquarters Allied Expeditionary Forces (SHAEF). SOE was willing to grant OSS a greater share of responsibilities at this stage the American agency was increasingly proving its value to the British, specifically in its provision of funds, manpower, staff assistance, supplies for resistance groups, communication infrastructure, and, most significantly, by providing aircraft for the insertion and supply of agents and groups.[47]

Attempts at a similar merger between SOE and OSS in Algiers were initially problematic. The SOE section in this theater (known under the designation AMF) was wary of the "American temperament [that] demands quick and spectacular results," which it believed contrasted negatively with its own "long-term and plodding" approach. It believed there were a number of "dangers" to OSS independence:

1. "The irresponsibility of OSS.
2. "Their permanent hankering after playing cowboys and red Indians.
3. "Their unlimited dollars.
4. "The political necessity of paying spectacular dividends.
5. "Their capacity for blundering into delicate European situations about which they understand nothing."[48]

Though such ill feeling did not last long, these negative perceptions highlight the fact that even as late as September 1943 SOE still considered itself as providing the brains and experience to any enterprise, viewing OSS as immature, inexperienced, and merely a source of money and resources. OSS, on the other hand, still very much the junior partner, was critical of being hamstrung by SOE: the first American officer dropped into France in June 1943, for example, operated firmly under SOE auspices, and future American deployments were delayed by SOE insistence that OSS agents be screened and trained at British installations before deployment.[49]

Such a policy was not, however, a result of British arrogance. As late as 1944 even those formations that had been trained by American instructors in American training camps would still find that they benefited greatly from supplementary training received either from direct contact with British specialist formations or through attending British advanced training establishments. OSS captain John Tyson reported to the chief of the SO branch in July 1943 that "the training any prospective SO agent has received in our Washington schools prior to his arrival in this [ETO] theater is entirely inadequate and no trainees should be considered for field operations until they have had further training in this theater, which in many cases will involve a period of three months."[50] To have deployed personnel with OSS training alone was thought to be suicidal. Major Herbert Brucker, an OSS SO agent dispatched to France in early 1944, would admit that "SOE training was far superior. It made most of my OSS/SO stateside training seem amateurish."[51] Aaron Bank, wartime Jedburgh and the postwar "father of U.S. Special Forces," believed that despite his formative OG training in America (Bank was originally a member of the "French" OGs before transferring to the Jedburghs) he had only received the "real McCoy" upon arrival in Britain.[52] This view is reinforced by William Colby, wartime Jedburgh, leader of the NORSO mission and later head of the CIA, who freely cited American inexperience and claimed that it was from the British that "we learned all the dark arts."[53]

As a whole, however, it was increasingly understood that between SOE and OSS cooperation was more beneficial than conflict and that independence for either agency was impracticable. The first quarter of 1944 thus saw SOE, OSS, and other Allied subversive and specialist commands become increasingly well integrated. The multinational Jedburgh program serves as a fine illustration of the positive application of the close SOE/SO alliance that had developed in both Britain and North Africa. In the training of these groups, first in Scotland and later in Milton Hall near London (and, for some teams, Algiers), the British were dominant and were fully prepared to share their experience and methods with the men of the other nations involved. The American contingent, meanwhile, more than pulled their weight in regard to the supply of weaponry and equipment, thereby ensuring that "no Jed was without his American parachute boots, satchel and carbine." Throughout the program, "all forms of segregation by nationality were very deliberately avoided if not actually banned. . . . the

Jeds were quartered together, trained and messed together and, in all matters of food, equipment and privileges, were treated identically."[54] This served to create a climate of "remarkable corporate spirit," in which it was possible to form the individual teams by self-selection on the basis of personal relationships.[55] For the most part cooperation between the various nationalities taking part in the Jedburgh program was remarkably harmonious, with any animosity taking the form of healthy rivalry analogous to that "between different regiments in the same brigade, or different ships in the same squadron."[56]

On the whole, SOE and OSS cooperation in Europe was particularly smooth, well organized, and controlled. This is not to suggest that the Anglo-American SOE/OSS relationship was entirely devoid of tensions in Europe. It was not. As U.S. involvement, particularly in areas of logistics and material support, dramatically increased, British unwillingness to fully relinquish the reins would lead, in certain areas, to a degree of competition, conflict, and confusion. The regions where these problems were most acute, leading to the conduct of some independent unilateral operations, were Yugoslavia, Romania, and toward the end of the war Southeast Asia. These tensions were, however, directed primarily at strategic and political issues relating to postwar policy, and although certainly affecting wider SOE and OSS policies, they were not of any immediate concern to the elements of those organizations that dealt with the functioning of specialist formations.

In the Far East, on the other hand, and reflective of the generally strained relations between the Allies in theater, the relationship between Allied irregular elements was "never free of antagonism."[57] Although the June 1942 SO/SOE Agreement established Burma as a theater of joint SOE/OSS responsibility, there were significant tensions in the application of this policy. Clinging to the possessions of Empire, the protective British sought to retain a significant measure of control over independent American intelligence and subversive operations in the Far East. However, unlike in Europe, where the British had over a year and a half of experience in irregular and special operations before American entry, in the war against Japan the British "lead" was considerably narrower, and the general absence of subversive and special operations infrastructure at the time of Pearl Harbor ensured that in the Far East the British had little justification to claim that they were more experienced than their emergent American counterparts.

This much more balanced situation ensured that when OSS Detachment 101 began to commence operations in northern Burma in September 1942, it did so as an explicitly separate entity from SOE; coming under General Stilwell's Northern Combat Area Command rather than the British GHQ-India. At this early stage of OSS operations, such independence from the British was unique and was thus likely a source of much of the subsequent friction. When it was first created, OSS Detachment 101 had nonetheless had a close relationship with the British. Its initial cadre had been trained at Camp X in Canada, and in recruiting personnel for its first operations it relied heavily on British and Anglo-Burmese officers and men.[58] In a parallel arrangement, the British-controlled V Force included a handful of American personnel, which would cede to Detachment 101's control in early 1944.[59] Despite being independent of SOE, Detachment 101 would retain close liaison with them, sharing training establishments and jointly recruiting personnel. Even though there could be a degree of duplication of effort as well as disharmony in the first Detachment 101 deployments, resulting principally from personality conflicts, these early arrangements were generally acceptable to those in the field.[60] The historian Christopher Thorne, in fact, took time to acknowledge that Detachment 101 (alongside the USAAF and RAF relationship in theater) provides rare evidence of good relations in a theater in which Anglo-American relations were continually afflicted by tension and animosity.[61]

The principal problems between irregular groups in the Far East arose at the higher echelons of command. In early 1943 SOE withdrew some of its teams from northern Burma, leaving Detachment 101 as the dominant subversive and irregular organization in the area. When Detachment 101 sought to solidify this position and expand the scope and scale of its operations, inter-Allied tensions increased. The British, GHQ-India in particular, resented the prospect of relinquishing all control of irregular activities in northern Burma to an independent American group, while the infamously Anglophobic General Stilwell "felt that the risk of OSS coming under British political domination outweighed the advantages that would accrue from expanded operations." By the summer of 1943 the relationship between OSS and the British in theater was "so bad that the status of Detachment 101 itself was being seriously impaired and its very existence was in danger."[62] It would not be until the end of that year that these tensions began to dissipate.

At the August 1943 Quebec conference Donovan had taken the opportunity to broach OSS's difficulties with Mountbatten and would subsequently, in a visit to India in November, get Mountbatten to tentatively assent to an expansion of OSS operations. Consequently, when in December 1943 P Division was created, which served to coordinate all Allied subversive, irregular, and special operations units under Mountbatten's South East Asia Command (SEAC), Detachment 101 was recognized as the sole Allied agency responsible for conducting irregular operations in northern Burma in support of CBI forces and was permitted to expand accordingly, something aided by Stilwell having "used all his influence to have . . . [SOE] removed from the Kachin Hills."[63] To deal with OSS operations in other areas of Southeast Asia, which were firmly dominated by the British, it was deemed inappropriate to expand Detachment 101, and it was instead decided to create another, more diplomatically acceptable OSS group, Detachment 404, which operated in "sufferance" directly under SEAC rather than Stillwell's CBI. The *War Report of the OSS* goes as far as suggesting that "had inter-Allied relationships been harmonious in the China-Burma-India Theater, it is probable that Detachment 404 would never have been created. Instead, OSS operations in the territory of the South East Asia Command would almost certainly have been conducted from an expanded Detachment 101."[64]

As a general rule, however, the most strained relations that OSS would have with the British were not concerned with special operations but rather with espionage and secret intelligence.[65] There was a relatively pronounced body of opinion within OSS that suggested that "in intelligence, the British are just as much the enemy as the Germans."[66] As a statement made by an unnamed member of OSS in North Africa points out: "This British intelligence service [SIS] holds itself aloof from the SOE as from us, and it is a question whether the worst enemy of the SOE is the Germans or the SIS. . . . SIS is an imperialistic organization closely tied to the Foreign Office, and together they form the only British outfit which, in my opinion, we have any reason to mistrust."[67] The same individual, however, paints a very different picture as regards SOE: "Probably one of the happiest unions in the history of international relations was that which existed, and still exists, between OSS and our British counterpart, the SOE. In my experience we worked in complete harmony and unison. Any difficulties which arose, and there were very few, were between individuals regardless of nationality and not between nationalities."[68]

As close as the Anglo-American alliance was, it was by no means innate, and "the indoctrination in 'allied' thinking would take time to develop and vigilance to maintain."[69] In the earliest stages of the alliance the British had a tendency to look down upon American soldiery as lacking in the training, discipline, and diplomatic savvy that would enable the soldiers to undertake raiding and special operations independently and unsupervised.[70] In late 1942, for example, when General Eisenhower at AFHQ in North Africa had expressed a desire for a raiding unit to be formed under his command, he had hoped that it would include American personnel, but the British immediately considered such a move to "be ill-advised" for a number of reasons: the naval forces used for transport would be entirely British; the British had more experience and more trained personnel available; and inter-unit transfers of personnel with other British formations (the 1st SAS Regiment was cited) would be easier with a British unit. Furthermore, in light of the "backward state of training of the American troops," it was recommended both that the unit should be, if not entirely British, at least have a British nucleus, and that independent American deployments should not occur until they had more trained and experienced personnel.[71] Illustrative of the sway of such British arguments was the fact that the unit that ultimately arose to fulfill Eisenhower's wishes was the 2nd SAS Regiment, comprised entirely of British personnel. This decision likely helped prompt Eisenhower to subsequently request the dispatch of the first OSS OGs to his theater.

The most acute military animosities to trouble the wartime Anglo-American alliance would occur at the highest levels of command over matters of strategic direction; perhaps the most notable conflicts resulted from the incompatibility between American desires to prosecute an invasion of France at the earliest possible moment and the British proclivity toward an opportunist strategy involving the Mediterranean and other periphery theaters. As small-scale, generally low cost, and potentially autonomous bodies, specialist formations often transcended strategic debates about the committal of forces and offered a means of applying force on almost a global scale without traditional impediments. The employment of specialist formations would thus commonly circumvent national strategic policy, offering Britain a medium through which its more ambitious tangential "Churchillian" strategies could be embraced without significant diplomatic backlash and affording the United States opportunity to undertake operations in theaters in which the committal of conventional formations was shunned.

Fine illustration of this fact can be seen with the U.S. policy toward Greece and the Balkans. Following his 1941 tour of the Middle East, Donovan had returned to America with "a strong endorsement of the Churchillian view of the Balkans as the 'soft underbelly' of the Axis."[72] Retaining such convictions, in August 1943, at a time when the likes of Eisenhower, Marshall, and Roosevelt were grudgingly assenting to the diversion of only a small number of USAAF aircraft to these theaters, Donovan would submit a proposal to the Joint Chiefs of Staff (JCS) asking for permission for OSS to begin operating against Greece and the Balkans. The JCS approved Donovan's plans but issued a strict proviso that such "activities should be of such a character as will involve no commitment on the part of the United States. They should be directed solely to assisting in the defeat of the Axis Powers" and be in support of all indigenous elements "without regard to their ideological differences, or political programs."[73] The latter part of this order, regarding the provision of apolitical support to guerrilla movements, is illustrative of an area of notable difference between British and U.S. irregular policies. Despite early sentiments from Churchill that Britain would "support the devil" to fight Hitler, British policy generally preferred to divert supplies away from any elements that might act against their postwar interests. OSS, on the other hand, generally favored following the broader U.S. policy of postponing political considerations until after the war.[74] The British were selective in their dealings with partisan elements, whereas the United States at least attempted to remain apolitical and was generally willing to deal with any group showing a willingness to fight the enemy. The variation between these approaches was, on occasion, a source of tension between the Allies, but in light of the invariably close relations and integrated command arrangements between OSS and the British, such divergences seldom led to any great complications and did not subvert the overall effectiveness of Allied support to indigenous movements.

Issues of grand strategy and politics aside, between the men at the "sharp end" of Anglo-American special operations there was little reciprocal animosity. As General Omar Bradley, no stranger to high-level Allied antagonisms, stated: "The suspicions and jealousies that split us centered largely in the headquarters commands. The nearer one went to the front the more comradely were our relations."[75] This sentiment was echoed in a letter Peter Wilkinson of SOE wrote to his wartime OSS colleague Franklin Lindsay regarding the

> splendid . . . mutual trust and cooperation which existed between all of us "in the field." . . . There is abundant reference to the sickening intrigues, etc., Anglo/American, OSS/SOE rivalries and the rest of it in London and Washington and at Headquarters, that I think it is important for someone to say loud and clear that in the field it was completely otherwise and we were not only indifferent to who got the credit, but resolved above all never to let each other down.[76]

Animosities that did occur among British and American personnel were most prevalent during times of inactivity or training rather than during operational deployment, and these stemmed primarily from respective differences in military uniform, equipment, discipline, and pay between the troops.[77] Between personnel in the Anglo-American specialist formations, however, such divergences were generally overshadowed by a camaraderie stemming from a shared culture of volunteerism, a sense of belonging to an elite, and an esprit de corps forged both from strenuous and selective training and from undertaking unique and dangerous tasks in the field. As Serge Obolensky, training "Norwegian" and "French" OGs in England before D-day, remarked in an unintended rebuttal to the contemporary British gripe that American GIs were "oversexed, overpaid and over here": the OGs were "popular with the girls. Their pay was much higher than in the British army. . . . And yet there was a certain mutual respect . . . between them and the British."[78]

Collaboration in the Field

The act of British and American specialist formations training together led to some strong ties developing between the personnel of the two nations. It would, however, be the stresses and strains of participating in combined special operations that most readily led to Anglo-American personnel developing bonds that could transcend national identities. The first operational deployment involving both British and American specialist personnel were the fifty men from the 1st Ranger Battalion who "forged a bond in blood with the Commandos" during the Dieppe raid.[79] In line with the policy that the Rangers should closely mirror the Commandos, the majority of the Rangers deployed at Dieppe, four officers and thirty-six men, would be attached to Lieutenant Colonel Durnford-Slater's No. 3 Commando; four Rangers were attached to No. 4 Commando and six to various elements of the 2nd Canadian Division. Before the operation those Rangers attached to the Commandos had a brief opportunity to train with them, so that during the operation they could be fully integrated in with the Commando troops. They were "treated as equals, ... given meaningful assignments, and in some cases were incorporated into the British Commando system of 'Jack and John' [a buddy system] with one Ranger working with one Commando."[80] In the opinion of Captain Roy Murray, the senior Ranger officer on the raid, the Rangers "actually became part of 3 Commando," and Murray made a point of reporting to Lieutenant Colonel Darby, commander of the 1st Ranger Batallion, the "most friendly spirit [that] prevails between the 3 Commando and the Rangers."[81]

The Dieppe raid transpired to be the only operation in which, as was originally envisioned, "the Rangers fought as students of the British."[82] The invasion of North Africa provided the Rangers with ample opportunity to gain combat experience without being attached to the British raiding program. Despite undertaking similar roles during Operation Torch, there was scant cooperation or even liaison between the Rangers and Commandos in North Africa. The invasion did, however, bear witness to a unique Anglo-American integration within the ranks of Nos. 1 and 6 Commandos. Prior to the invasion, in August 1942, the 168th Regimental Combat Team (RCT) of the U.S. 34th Infantry Division was sent to Scotland to undertake amphibious and mountain warfare training and to participate in exercises and rehearsals in conjunction with the Commandos.[83] Following the conclusion of these exercises, it was decided that elements of the 168th RCT should be incorporated into both Commandos to form composite units for the Torch landings. This decision was taken for two main reasons: first, to improve inter-Allied cooperation in the Eastern Task Force landings and, second, to help maintain the illusion, taken for political reasons, that the invasion was a wholly American affair.[84]

The Torch landings saw ten troops of No. 1 Commando and four of No. 6 Commando variously integrated with British and U.S.

RCT personnel.⁸⁵ This Anglo-American composition was retained after the initial landings, and British and American sections again fought together under the same banner in both No. 1 Commando's "amphibious left hook," Operation Bizerte, in December 1942 and in No. 6 Commando's actions against the aerodrome at Bône.⁸⁶ Although reports from this period generally speak of a high esprit de corps and a degree of mutual respect between the men in these formations, the British did note certain problems in regard to the comparable quality of the American personnel over the hand-picked and highly trained Commandos. Captain Philip Dunne, for example, spoke negatively of the RCT personnel "whose training and discipline is greatly inferior to the English Commando troops."⁸⁷ The U.S. personnel working with No. 6 Commando were returned to their units in December 1942, although sixty-nine American volunteers remained with No. 1 Commando until the end of January 1943 as they conducted front-line duties.⁸⁸ Thus ended a unique, and for the main part either ignored or misunderstood,⁸⁹ historical example of the successful integration of British and American personnel within a specialist formation and serves to highlight the willingness and ability of both nations to cooperate closely with each other in the field in commando tasks. Such instances of short-term integration were, nevertheless, the exception and not the rule.

Despite the notable commonality between the evolutionary paths of the various Anglo-American commando and ranger formations, direct cooperation between these units in the field was a rare occurrence. The closest instance was Operation Avalanche, the September 1943 amphibious landings against Salerno, during which the Commandos and Rangers were jointly tasked with spearheading the assault and securing the left flank of the beachhead. Prior to the landings, and in preparation for their tasks, "Ranger Force" (as the grouping of the 1st, 3rd, and 4th Ranger Battalions had begun to be called, unofficially) and Nos. 2 and 41 (RM) Commandos swapped personnel and liaison officers; "Ranger Force" HQ employed "several British officers," including Royal Artillery and Royal Navy fire observation officers, while the Commandos received similar personnel as well as the attachment of six 4.2-inch mortars from "Ranger Force"'s U.S. 83rd Chemical Mortar Battalion.⁹⁰

Possibly the closest coordination occurring between Commandos and Rangers, however, came from the short-lived, and desperately ad hoc, 29th Rangers. In late 1942, with the 1st Rangers operating in North Africa, it was proposed that another Ranger battalion be formed in Britain for training and instructional purposes under the tactical control of the British SS Brigade.[91] Consequently, on February 1, 1943, the U.S. 29th Infantry Division, the only American combat division in Britain at the time, consented to sending 10 officers and 166 men to Achnacarry for Commando training.[92] Upon completion of its training, the understrength 29th Rangers (made up of only a headquarters and two rifle companies) were attached for further instruction to No. 4 Commando, with whom it quickly established good relations.[93] Subsequently, in October 1943, various elements of the 29th Rangers were attached to Nos. 10 (IA), 12, and 14 Commandos and would participate in a number of small-scale raids against the enemy in Norway and France.[94] During such operations, which aside from Dieppe represented the only time that Rangers participated in the raiding program, the 29th Rangers built up a good reputation with the Commandos, "who praised them highly."[95] After these attachments, however, and with the 2nd and 5th Ranger Battalions having been raised in America, the 29th Rangers was disbanded, with the men returning to their original units.

To have taken this course of action with a trained and partially experienced unit at a time when two new Ranger units were being formed in the United States from raw material was a somewhat surprising and not altogether cost-effective move. The 29th Ranger's disbandment was based on three principal factors: first, an adherence to the original Ranger concept, which explicitly viewed these units as a training vehicle whereby the men therein would be returned to their units once they had received training and gained experience on raids; second, a bureaucratic reason, that the Ranger war establishment would only allow for a total of two Ranger battalions to be based in Britain; finally—a plausible judgment, as identified by Robert Black—that the 29th Rangers was disbanded because it was expected that those battalions training in the United States at the time were "better trained than those who had been trained by the Commandos."[96] The latter judgment, for which there was no solid basis and, as will be noted, was considered largely fallacious by the Rangers themselves, was clearly motivated by the U.S. Army's desire to maintain their own identity for the Rangers and their belief that they could take what they required from the British model and improve upon it.

The 2nd and 5th Rangers were thus raised and conducted the majority of their core and formative training in the United States. When the 2nd Rangers arrived in Britain in late 1943, followed shortly after by the 5th Rangers, it was intended that the units should participate in the COSSAC (Chief of Staff to Supreme Allied Commander) Raids and Reconnaissance Program preceding the invasion of France. To this end, the Rangers were attached to COHQ for planning, and elements were tentatively assigned to the various raids—Forfar, Manacle, Candlestick, and Hardtack—planned for the early 1944 lunar dark periods.[97] However, in light of their lack of combat experience and general unfamiliarity with the equipment and landing craft involved in raiding operations, it was not thought possible for the Rangers to undertake these activities independently.[98] To better prepare themselves for such tasks, they thus underwent a brief period of instruction on raiding techniques from the experienced personnel of No. 4 Commando at Dartmouth, and Eisenhower granted "blanket authorization for necessary supplies" to enable the conduct of their raids.[99] Only following these measures was it deemed possible to assign Rangers a clear role in the raiding program. It was subsequently proposed that in certain operations, such as Hardtack 22 and Candlestick 4, a relatively substantial number of Rangers (between seventy and a hundred men) would have the dominant responsibility for undertaking the raid, with the British contribution being solely limited to providing transport and Commando guides. In any event, however, bad weather combined with a growing disinclination toward raids made certain that each of the pre-D-day operations that the Rangers were due to participate in were either canceled or aborted.[100]

With any pre-invasion role negated, from February 1944 the Rangers underwent formal training at the Commando Training Center in Scotland, where they were able to forge closer links with the British. This training, in the opinion of the 5th Rangers, was considered invaluable: "The hills of Scotland proved to be more than anything that had been encountered in former Ranger training [in the United States], and here Rangers were made or lost. . . . Too much can not be said for the Scotland training. To it, many of the Rangers owe their lives and their success."[101] In April 1944 Ranger links with COHQ were formalized, and after a number of requests, Lieutenant Colonel Earl Rudder, commanding the 2nd Ranger Battalion, was authorized to communicate with, and draw supplies from, COHQ directly. This arrangement facilitated a greater degree of contact between the Commandos and Rangers and enabled the sharing of experience and information in advance of their D-day tasks.[102] In spite of such a healthy vein of cooperation having developed between the two nations in the areas of training, exchanges of equipment, and operational planning, once the invasion of France commenced there was an almost total absence of further contact between the Ranger formations and British units, specialist or otherwise.

The various OSS OGs were probably the closest approximation to an all-embracing American special forces unit during the Second World War, and despite having broken free of any British model and developed a uniquely American raison d'être, they would remain closely associated with their British counterparts in a wide variety of operational deployments. In mid-1943 the 2nd SAS Regiment and the "Italian" OGs were both aiming to conduct similar operations against Northern Italy, and in the spirit of cooperation both Bill Stirling and Serge Obolensky, commanding the respective groups, decided to meet with one another for a mutual exchange of ideas and to establish mechanisms for combined planning.[103] In October 1943 such arrangements bore fruit when personnel of the two units cooperated in a joint series of operations directed at contacting, and aiding the rescue of, escaped prisoners of war on the behalf of A Force (MI9).[104] These operations, code-named Simcol by OSS and Jonquil by the SAS, saw three small groups, comprising a combination of both SAS and OG personnel, being inserted amphibiously along the Adriatic coastline of Italy to coincide with the dispatch, via parachute, of eleven OG men near Chieti. Despite ultimately being only partially successful, these actions nonetheless emphasized the viability of SAS and OG cooperation.[105]

Following Simcol/Jonquil, greater efforts were made for collaboration between the two units, and officers from the respective "planning and operations sections" were exchanged.[106] By the start of 1944 this arrangement had resulted in the two units jointly conceiving a series of "coordinated tactical operations in Northern Italy" aiming to target enemy communications in support of Anzio.[107] As it turned out, however, as was noted in the previous chapter, the majority of such proposals were rejected. Shortly before the 2nd SAS's transfer to Britain ended this brief but fertile period of cooperation, it was even suggested that Stirling might command a grouping of the 2nd

SAS, OGs, and the French Bataillon de Choc for operations in support of the Anvil/Dragoon landings in the South of France.[108]

Given the fledgling degree of cooperation between the OGs and SAS in Italy, it is curious to note the general absence of a similar relationship in their deployments in France. Despite OG operations being closely wedded to the actions of both the partisans, Jedburghs, and, via a convoluted command structure, the SAS Brigade, the OGs had negligible direct cooperation with their British SAS "counterparts" in France and only a modicum with the French SAS Regiments in Brittany. Before the invasion, however, elements of the OGs had certainly sought a closer relationship with the SAS, with the likes of Major Edwin Black, responsible for OG planning at SHAEF's Special Forces Headquarters (SFHQ), suggesting the establishment of a joint SFHQ-SAS committee and the attachment of SAS officers to SFHQ for training.[109] In light of the complex command arrangements and the degree of mutual interorganizational suspicion that was endemic to the pre-invasion planning for these groups (issues to be addressed in the next chapter), such suggestions were, however, largely ignored. Once in the field, different areas of operation, different timetables of insertion, and a slight diversity in roles generally transpired to preclude significant contact between the SAS and OGs. On the few occasions when OGs did come into contact with the SAS, such as with the OG Operations Adrian, in the Haute-Vienne department, or Percy Red, near Dijon, any collaboration was opportunistic and strictly tactical.[110]

Although the "French" and "Italian" OGs forged a modest bond with their SAS colleagues, and in the Far East Detachment 404's OGs had infrequent collaboration with varied British specialist elements based in Ceylon,[111] it was the "Yugoslav" and "Greek" OGs that ultimately had the closest and most frequent cooperation with their British counterparts. In January 1944 12 officers and 120 men of these OGs were sent to Vis alongside No. 2 Commando and placed under the tactical control of Brigadier Thomas Churchill's 2nd SS Brigade. Living and working closely together on Vis ensured the development of close bonds between the British and American personnel. Michael McConville, a Royal Marine Commando officer on Vis, found the OGs "refreshingly frank." When first deployed to the island "they admitted cheerfully to complete inexperience, they would put themselves in the hands of Jack Churchill [commanding No. 2 Commando]. If he thought their concepts sound, well and good. If not, they would do whatever he advised." The Commandos on Vis accordingly would provide an improvised training program for the OGs, during which "American open-mindedness and enthusiasm continued to impress."[112] In return for such instruction, the OGs would, with their linguistic talents, help foster smooth relations with their Yugoslav hosts and provide interpreters for operations in conjunction with partisans.[113]

From Vis the OGs mounted a number of operations alongside the Commandos, notable examples being the January 26, 1944, raid on the island of Hvar, where thirty OGs joined No. 2 Commando in the attack,[114] or the March 1944 raid on Solta in which almost the entire OG complement on Vis cooperated with the Commandos on what was later dubbed a "model combined operation."[115] The OGs also acted in a supportive capacity, and on raids against Mljet and Brač in May and June 1944, respectively, provided "headquarters security" for the Commandos' attacks.[116] In April 1944, when offensive raids from Vis were being curtailed by inadequate and out-of-date intelligence, Major Philip G. Lovell of the OGs suggested to Brigadier Thomas Churchill that his men could help alleviate this deficiency by establishing wireless coast-watch stations on outlying islands. In so doing, the OGs created and ran a complete operations room on Vis that became the "intelligence and planning center" for both OSS and the Commandos.[117] On the whole, as was acknowledged by both parties, the relations between the OGs and Commandos on Vis were excellent and the planning and execution of their operations against the Dalmatian coast well integrated.[118]

The OGs on Vis also developed close relations with the British Raiding Support Regiment (RSR) for whose heavier weapons troops they would often provide escort and security.[119] In May 1944 this relationship was further strengthened when the "Greek" OGs joined elements of the RSR undertaking Noah's Ark operations in Greece. When the two units were deployed together their actions in the field were tactically mutually supportive. During Operation Kirkstone of June 1944, which targeted rail networks north of Kaitsa, for example, the OG men undertook reconnaissance tasks and provided close protection for RSR mortar teams and demolition parties.[120] Living and working together behind enemy lines led to the OGs and RSR personnel developing some very close bonds. In the opinion of OG Captain Cronje, the men "get along very well. No distinction is made between the two groups."[121] The OGs praised the RSR as being "highly skilled and tremendously effective in support of the Operational Groups and *Andartes* [partisans], and were likewise a fine example of aggressive and competent soldiering."[122] The only American gripe about operating with these British elements seems to have been directed, as was quite common, toward the quality of the food and cigarettes available.[123] Personnel of these "Greek" OGs would subsequently operate with the LRDG, who provided both guides and reception committees to OGs operations in exchange for the attachment of OG men to serve as interpreters.[124] These varied deployments provide clear illustration of harmonious, multifaceted cooperation between British and American specialist formations in both training for, planning, and executing operations.[125]

As contrasted with other OSS elements, the MU's direct relations with the British in the field were limited by the branch's own lack of activity. The closest operational link occurred in Italy, with the MU headed by U.S. Navy lieutenant Richard Kelly. As was the case with the MU groups based in Britain, this unit remained heavily reliant on the use of Royal Navy fast surface craft for its operations, but unlike Britain there remained ample opportunities for deployment in the Mediterranean.[126] By August 1944 a successful series of operations in which Kelly's MU provided clandestine transportation for various British agencies had proven "the feasibility of cooperating with the British and obtaining their wholehearted aid in MU operations."[127] The MU was subsequently placed under the general control of the Eighth Army, and its operations became closely integrated with the work of SOE, MI9, and Popski's Private Army (PPA). By 1945 this group had become so well regarded by the British that it was appointed the "responsible boating organization" for British-dominated operations around Lake Comacchio in northeastern Italy, a commitment that would see it work in close cooperation with the Commandos, Combined Operations Pilotage Parties (COPPs), and the SBS (formerly Squadron, now Service).[128] In addition to such activities, this Italian MU also lent personnel to the LRDG to serve as liaison officers and translators for their September 1944 operations in Istria;[129] later still it worked alongside PPA in its operations around the mouth of the Po River and during its advance toward Venice.[130]

Cooperation with the MU was also seen in the Far East. While in discussion with General Donovan in late 1943, Mountbatten made a request for personnel to help share the burden of undertaking beach reconnaissance tasks in SEAC, as he believed that it was "impossible, and improbable," that the COPP Depot in Britain would be able to provide sufficient personnel to accommodate the demand.[131] Donovan assented, and by the start of 1944 MU personnel destined for the Far East were introduced to COHQ specialist personnel in London and given "complete explanations of CCO techniques and equipment."[132] Upon their arrival in Asia the MUs, who would remain heavily reliant on British shipping (particularly submarines), forged close relations with their British counterparts, and both parties benefited from "a mutual exchange of facilities and an opportunity to compare respective methods of operation."[133] Although tactical-level cooperation between the MUs and their British counterparts within SEAC was rare, there remained a notable amount of combined planning and operational-level integration between these units.[134]

As the previous chapter noted, Britain and the United States had simultaneously yet independently developed the COPP and Scouts and Raider (S&R) maritime special forces to deal with the pressing problems posed by amphibious reconnaissance and assault pilotage. Despite the notable absence of an Allied interchange of ideas in the inception process of these units, ultimately a pronounced spirit of Anglo-American cooperation developed within these fields. The first use of these units during the Torch landings against North Africa included a pronounced degree of Allied integration in pilotage tasks. The American S&Rs were responsible for the pilotage and guidance of No. 1 Commando's landing,[135] while the British forebears of the COPPs, the Koodoo/Inhuman parties, conversely guided the landing of the 1st Rangers at Arzew.[136] Following Torch, with further major combined amphibious landings looming, the development of a standardized Allied approach to beach reconnaissance and pilotage became essential. As soon as the COPPs were formally created, it was recommended that U.S. Navy lieutenant George Hoague "be represented on the [COPP] Training Sub-Committee."[137] Meanwhile, the likes of U.S. Army captain George Bright were schooled in British techniques before being sent to the S&R School.[138]

In April 1943 S&R personnel were dispatched to Malta to help alleviate the shortage of COPPs available for reconnaissance and pilotage tasks against Sicily. To the overstretched British, whose lack of properly trained personnel had been exacerbated by the loss of a number of COPP personnel in pre-Husky reconnaissances, the prospect of reinforcement was greeted with enthusiasm. Upon the arrival of the Americans in Malta, however, the British impression of the state of the S&Rs' training and equipment (much of which had been left in the United States because of an oversight) was generally unfavorable.[139] Lieutenant Neville Townley McHarg, commanding COPP 4, believed the S&Rs' methods of operating "a portable echo sounding set from a rubber dingy" to be unsuitable for pre-invasion tasks, as they were "much too clumsy for use from submarines and their silhouette too big to escape detection on well guarded beaches."[140] Thus, it would not be until the S&Rs had received instruction from the British on their favored reconnaissance tactic of utilizing canoes launched from submarines that the American personnel were ultimately able to participate alongside the COPPs in the Sicily reconnaissances.[141] Subsequently, both prior to and during the landings against Salerno and Anzio, there was much closer cooperation, in both reconnaissance and pilotage tasks, between the COPPs and S&Rs. In addition, before the Anzio landings a general shortage in COPP teams ensured that the S&Rs also worked closely with Z SBS.[142]

Preparations for the invasion of France provided further incentive for the development of a harmonious allied approach to COPP and S&R tasks. Following their participation in the Anzio landings, two S&R teams (each of one officer and four men) were sent to Britain to be stationed with the COPPs preparing for pre-invasion tasks. It was initially hoped that these S&R personnel would work alongside COPP 2—later expanded into the 712th LCP (Landing Craft, Personnel) Survey Flotilla—in undertaking hydrographical soundings, but a range of factors ultimately transpired to deny the concerted use of S&Rs in such a capacity.[143] Because of yet another "apparent error in their orders," the S&Rs had arrived in Britain without any of their special stores or equipment and would thus remain heavily reliant on British generosity and patronage. Although the Admiralty was willing to provide a Landing Craft, Navigation (LCN), for the S&Rs (when combined together the two S&R teams were only of sufficient size to man a single boat), it was thought unwise to have a single American craft operating in an otherwise exclusively British flotilla. Furthermore, unlike COPP 2, the S&Rs were not thought properly trained in the specialist techniques of taking soundings and sonic bearings from LCNs, nor were they trained in the use of the "X-Craft" submersible that other COPP teams were utilizing for the pre-invasion reconnaissances.[144]

These limitations, combined with the fact that many of the projected tasks were adequately provided for by existent British formations, made certain that the ultimate employment of the S&Rs from Britain was limited to sporadic sounding tasks undertaken by individuals paired with COPP personnel.[145] Although Britain thus dominated pre-invasion special reconnaissance operations for both the British and American beaches in Normandy, on D-day itself the pilotage tasks performed by these units were generally conducted along national lines, with only a handful of British personnel working alongside U.S. naval forces.[146] The obstacle clearance missions carried out by the American NCDUs and the British LCOCUs, meanwhile, were carried out exclusively along national lines.

Between the Anglo-American specialist formations of the Second World War there was certainly a strong vein of cooperation and, on occasion, dependency between the two allies. The significance of the Anglo-American alliance in the evolution of wartime specialist formations was acute. For the United States it was crucial. Had it not been for the British example and willingness to share both knowledge and experience and thereby encourage the United States to embark on irregular ventures, it seems unlikely that America would have participated in this field to the extent which it ultimately did so. This is particularly apparent in the motivations behind the U.S. adoption of ranger-style forces; but it also applies, at least in part, to their establishment of OSS and its ancillary special forces such as the MU or OGs. Although the United States proved more than capable of raising specialist formations in response to specific exigencies (as with the Alamo Scouts) or to make provision for certain tasks (such as amphibious reconnaissance and demolitions), had an accessible British model not been in existence it would appear that American forays into irregular warfare would have been significantly subdued.

In application to the alliance as a whole, David Reynolds emphasized that "ultimately, the British needed the Americans more than the Americans needed the British."[147] In application to the albeit niche area of specialist formations, however, this seems to be reversed, with Britain remaining the dominant partner throughout the war. During the formative periods of practically all American specialist formations, the British were further advanced. The years

1942–43 have been called "the period of British strategic hegemony," and the development of specialist formations certainly appears to mirror this.[148] The paths that America would have to follow in order to catch up with the British lead required them to bow to experience, accept an initial position as student, and to an extent sacrifice control for knowledge. William Casey, wartime branch chief of the OSS Secret Intelligence (SI) European Theater of Operations (ETO) and later director of the CIA, summed up the situation well: "The British had everything which we still lacked: experience, seasoning, tradition, trained talent, contacts in Europe they had spent three years rebuilding. To some extent the haughtiness they displayed to OSS was justified. . . . British objections to our intrusions made sense. . . . Nevertheless, British aloofness and often downright hostility brought its own host of problems."[149]

In the British-dominated European and Mediterranean theaters, therefore, U.S. formations were heavily reliant on British patronage and would often have to conform to British standards and doctrines in order to gain employment. There are numerous examples of this occurring: OSS agents being subject to SOE vetting and training before their dispatch to the Continent; the U.S.-trained 2nd and 5th Rangers being trained by Commandos before they could be committed to the pre-D-day raiding program; or the S&Rs having to perfect British submarine-launched reconnaissance techniques before they could be employed before Husky. The British model prevailed to dominate the American practice of special operations.

With a few exceptions, such as Detachment 101 in Burma, it would not be until 1944 that the United States had become sufficiently experienced and mobilized to be in a position to properly contest the British lead in irregular operations. By this stage, however, independence was largely impracticable, and parity was becoming a practical reality. Once America had two years' of experience under *its* belt, it began conducting almost the full gamut of specialist activities in practically every theater of operation. David Reynolds has claimed that in Europe D-day "proved the fulcrum" for a transition toward American dominance, and it is by no means a coincidence that concerted American use of special forces, often matching British contributions, occurred primarily *after* D-day.[150] By 1945 it was clear that in the broader alliance Britain had become the junior partner, and although Britain never quite relinquished its wartime dominance in irregular fields, it is certainly worth acknowledging that by 1945 U.S. special forces units, but not the ranger formations, were as widely employed as their British counterparts.

The British had a substantial role in influencing, both actively and passively, the Americans in their adoption of specialist formations and development of irregular capabilities. Despite the best efforts of the U.S. military to take only what they needed from the British model and to retain their national identity (which certain formations like the OGs managed to do), the British laid the foundations for many American units. While the British commonly provided the model, the knowledge, the experience, and occasionally the means for the American creation and deployment of specialist formations, American value to the British, with few exceptions (such as the sharing of NCDU and UDT techniques, or the accommodation of the SRU in California), may appear more intangible. The greatest contribution of the United States to British irregular efforts was in alleviating the burden of mounting operations and the provision of additional personnel for their conduct, something particularly valued following the dramatic expansion of effort that both the harnessing of indigenous partisans and the conduct of large-scale combined amphibious assaults required. Also of great significance was the United States providing Britain with welcome reinforcement in aircraft, supplies, and resources through which the prosecution of plans with partisans could be expressed; furthermore, when the Americans were sufficiently experienced, their contribution to developing and providing new tactics and equipment such as firearms, explosives, radios, swim fins, breathing apparatus, and small surface and submersible craft was also highly valued.

One perception that prevailed in certain quarters throughout the war was that the British supplied the brains and the experience and the Americans the resources.[151] In the field of specialist formations this perception was partially borne out. British "brains" and "experience" are well illustrated, and in the areas of supplying aircraft and equipment for protracted operations in depth, from mid-1944 onward, the United States certainly took on much of the burden. There were, however, exceptions to both these trends, where American "brains"—as evidenced by the examples of the S&Rs, NCDUs, and UDTs—were certainly welcome, and where the British certainly pulled their weight in the provision of training establishments and operational craft for deployments. Mackenzie emphasized well this complex interdependency when he noted, in regard to the close relationship between SOE and OSS: "OSS could hardly move without British organization and British knowledge, cramping though it sometimes found them: SOE drew largely on American stores, above all on American aircraft, and American brains and energy contributed much to the liveliness of an organization which might have easily become narrow and over-tired as the war went on."[152]

Viewing the Anglo-American relationship through the lens of special operations illuminates a number of clear examples of integration and very close cooperation between British and American personnel at the grassroots level in both training, planning, and (albeit less frequently) operational deployment. The strains of shared suffering in both training and the rigors of battle led to relationships developing between the men of the two nations that often transcended national identity. It is not without significance that, as Kenneth Macksey emphasized, much "extensive cementing" of the Anglo-American "alliance at ground level was performed by the arbiters of raiding."[153] Nor is it without significance that the overwhelmingly good relations between British and American specialist formations rose above many of the more general animosities that troubled the broader alliance. The small-scale and cost-effective nature of special forces provided a politically acceptable mechanism through which both Britain and the United States could conduct military operations and covert diplomacy on a global level without many of the traditional limitations or dilemmas that troubled alliance strategy. Although representing only a tiny area of a global alliance, the field of specialist formations provides a window into what at times was model cooperation between Britain and the United States. Had the alliance not functioned as smoothly and as successfully as it ultimately did, it is clear that the U.S. adoption and development of specialist formations would have been severely curtailed; and had this occurred, with the full burden of mounting irregular operations falling on the British, it is equally likely that their enthusiasm for such ventures would have been significantly reduced. Simply put, the Anglo-American alliance was an essential factor in forging the manner and extent to which both nations adopted, developed, and utilized specialist formations and waged irregular warfare. The successes attained in developing and practicing a fundamentally new way of waging war ultimately demonstrate the overall flexibility, innovatory prowess, quality, and adaptability of *both* allies during the Second World War.

CHAPTER 4

COMMAND AND CONTROL

The command and control of specialist formations presents what is perhaps a uniquely difficult prospect. For, to be effective, such command and control require, almost at the same time, two seemingly contradictory and often intractable mechanisms. On the one hand is the requirement for a malleable, innovative, and loose approach to command that gives a degree of independence and autonomy to discrete units so as not to stifle individual initiative and flexibility. On the other hand is the even greater requirement for a suitably restrictive, centralized control mechanism capable of harnessing these units and directing their actions to the best benefit of greater operational and strategic plans, lest they become wasteful or redundant or come into conflict with other activities. Centralization is also important so as not to unnecessarily burden small operational units with dilemmas such as administration and logistics, while at the same time not allowing these units to place undue strain upon the conventional channels having to provide for them. These requirements and the best method of employing these formations were, however, far from understood at the outset of the Second World War. There was little or no precedent in place to guide commanders on how irregular forces should be organized, directed, and controlled. Mechanisms, methods, and practices for the effective command, administration, and application of these formations all had to be virtually invented over the course of the war. (See appendix A for various organizational charts of the command hierarchies highlighted in this chapter.)

Perceptions and Attitudes toward Specialist Formations

Although at times enthusiastic, command preconceptions of specialist formations were, more often than not, marked with scepticism and animosity. Military resentment of the unconventional is understandable. The unique composition, recruitment practices, missions, equipment, discipline, and methods of administration that separated specialist formations from conventional forces led to suspicion, while their exclusivity and the aura of either mystery or, conversely, pronounced publicity surrounding them undoubtedly fostered an impression of favoritism and led to resentment. Mass armies do not like elites; the very existence of elites is an implied slur on the martial and "nonspecial" attributes of everybody else. The result, as Peter Fleming had contended, was that the "unorthodox warrior always fights on two fronts."[1] For every Churchill, Wavell, or Gubbins, those "champions" of specialist formations, "a thousand regular officers existed," in both Britain and the United States, "who, wedded to conventional military tradition disdained irregular warfare."[2]

Friction with the irregular characters attracted toward these units and so often prominent among their ranks went no way to improving matters, and much animosity, as a 1944 Admiralty paper noted, was directed at such a "gallant madman . . . for he is himself unorthodox, impatient of discipline and invariably ignorant or casual regarding service custom and procedure, so that unless properly led and instructed he gives offence through this same casualness or ignorance."[3] The expansionist and "prima donna" behavior so often associated with these individuals was particularly resented and, if unchecked, could rapidly escalate "to an active and mutual antagonism with negative consequences for operations."[4] To an extent, therefore, irregular units brought on many problems for themselves. Bill Stirling of the 2nd SAS Regiment, for example, was commonly regarded as a difficult character who was not well liked by regular staff branches. A GHQ Middle East Forces (MEF) assessment of June 1943 cited the "earned unpopularity" of Stirling's unit, while even fellow irregular warriors such as David Lloyd Owen of the Long Range Desert Group (LRDG) privately remarked that Stirling was a "tiresome bragging type" whose unit was "universally disliked."[5]

Although a number of specialist formations received highlevel support from "champions" in their inception, it should not be assumed that these units faced fewer obstacles. The opposite may well be the case. Staffs and subordinates charged with dealing directly with the demands of irregular units were seldom enthusiastic about catering to the needs of the "playthings" or "pets" of politicians and high commanders.[6] Unorthodox and relatively junior officers bypassing bureaucratic normalcy, and getting a "direct line" to the top could be the cause of significant resentment and jealousies among command hierarchies. As Prime Minister Churchill observed in reference to the Commandos, "resistances . . . increased as the professional ladder was descended."[7] Such opposition had the potential to cause genuine problems for the use of specialist formations, for as Bill Stirling expressed while vying for the employment of the 2nd SAS in support of the invasion of Sicily, "when the staff . . . gets between the [higher] commander and SAS Regiment, the latter has little prospect of useful employment."[8]

Overcoming the obstacles of orthodoxy was not easy, yet with time and, most important, tangible successes in the field, progress was made. The LRDG's early successes opened up many orthodox minds within GHQ MEF to the potential of special forces and helped ensure that by Operation Crusader they were willing to sponsor other specialist ventures to aid their offensive. The Commando successes at Vaagso, the Lofotens, and St. Nazaire similarly gave a boost of confidence in the Commando idea, which had been flagging as a result of the negligible value of their first operations. The American experience holds similar comparisons: the actions of the USMC Raiders on Tulagi and Guadalcanal were sufficient, not only to temporarily silence some of those critics who had steadfastly resisted the idea of an elite within an elite, but also to lead to an expansion of the concept; the Rangers' performance in North Africa "won over their superiors,"[9] while the First Special Service Force's (FSSF) assault on Monte la Difensa and Monte la Remetanea made certain that General Mark Clark saw the group as "idealized."[10] Successes aside, certain units were held in higher esteem within the establishment purely because of the roles that they undertook. Opposition to units focused on intelligence gathering or reconnaissance was significantly less acute than that toward those "pirates" or "thugs" engaged in the "ungentlemanly" pursuits of raiding and harassment.[11] Similarly, conventional mindsets were more prone to accept the military value of commando formations or "shock troops" for hazardous tasks than they were of special forces performing nonregular missions.[12]

Alongside a lack of sympathy and support for specialist formations lay another, more serious, but not always unrelated, problem: a lack of knowledge and understanding about their function and potential utility. Colin Gray has emphasized a "trained incapacity, a *déformation professionelle*, on the part of conventional military minds to grasp the principles of special warfare.... If superior commanders do not appreciate or do not like what special operations forces might do, the strategic utility of those forces will be strictly moot."[13] The proliferation of special forces and commandos in the Second World War represented a fundamentally new approach to warfare, utilizing new methods and equipment and occurring at an unprecedented depth. The mechanisms by which to control and wield this new weapon were by no means innate, and there was little precedent in place to guide commanders and staffs on the best approach. Broader understanding of the potential offered by irregular units would only develop when experience was amassed and as dedicated command branches and staffs were created to direct these formations.

Combined Operations Headquarters, the Special Service Brigades, and the Command and Control of British Commandos

The most significant wartime command arrangement for British specialist formations was Combined Operations Headquarters. Developing immediately after the inception of the Commandos, as part of its broader mandate, COHQ had the responsibility for both the administration, training, and tasking of the Commandos under its SS Brigade Headquarters, and for the planning and mounting of amphibious raids from Britain. However, in actually fulfilling this directive, COHQ faced many bureaucratic difficulties. Its creation as a brand new agency answerable only to the Chiefs of Staffs (COS) had antagonized a number of powerful figures in a sceptical Whitehall, and with the earliest Commando raids having proved to be of dubious worth, the confidence in Admiral Keyes's ability to conduct these operations notably declined. By September 1941 it was decreed that no amphibious operation, however small, could be mounted by COHQ against the Channel coasts without the express authority of both GHQ Home Forces and the COS. The COHQ role thus became limited to planning, training for, and providing advice on raiding operations—powers that were technically shared by Home Forces, with regional Home Commands having the mounting authority for operations launched from their areas of responsibility.[14] Only against the enemy in Norway, an "administratively easy target" because it came under the jurisdiction of the Commander in Chief (C in C) Home Fleet, was COHQ able to undertake raiding without the "web of conflicting red tape."[15] At this time operations against the Channel coastline, the originally envisioned target for Commando raids, were heavily hamstrung by the lack of "any precise system for planning, mounting and executing" such operations[16]—a fact that Keyes vehemently emphasized in the parting shot he delivered to the House of Commons upon his dismissal as DCO: "Inter-services committees and sub-committees had become the dictators of policy instead of the servants of those who bore full responsibility; by concentrating on the difficulties and dangers of every amphibious project ... the planners have succeeded in thwarting execution until it is too late."[17]

The subsequent and somewhat controversial appointment of Lord Louis Mountbatten as adviser on combined operations (ACO, later CCO) in October 1941 injected the organization with a new aura of vitality. In March 1942 Mountbatten was promoted to vice admiral, granted a chair on the COS Committee, and appointed "the sole co-ordinating authority for all raids on the western seaboard of Europe." Despite COHQ's increasing powers, Mountbatten's ability to conduct regular raids remained hindered by significant bureaucratic hurdles. Any COHQ plan still had to be submitted for approval by the COS Committee (but no longer GHQ Home Forces) and, if authorized, would then be placed under the command of a Naval Home Port commander in chief for execution. Furthermore, this naval commander, three Army Home Force commanders (Southern, South-Eastern and Eastern), and RAF authorities could all veto the execution of an operation.[18] In July 1942 a frustrated Mountbatten complained that he "found it difficult to translate this responsibility [for raiding operations] into practice because of the system of divided control which at present guides operations of this nature." He recommended that a new streamlined system be instigated that would, if not grant him executive powers, at least make the process of planning and mounting operations reliant upon the "smallest number of authorities that is permissible."[19]

Mountbatten was a keen advocate of the idea of conducting fortnightly raids against the Continent but found such ambitions greatly hamstrung by the convoluted command procedures through which even minor raids were authorized. As part of his suggestions for administrative reforms, Mountbatten thus proposed a "more flexible procedure for planning and approving" minor raids and suggested retaining one Commando in readiness at Portsmouth with the necessary naval links already in place so that operations could be planned and mounted quickly after receiving only oral approval from the COS.[20] Such suggestions led to the establishment of the Small Scale Raiding Force (SSRF) in March 1942 as a means of swiftly undertaking minor raids with a minimum of red tape. The SSRF initially worked directly under the CCO, but its ability to conduct frequent operations was further enhanced when it was placed under the operational control of Commodore John Hughes-Hallett's Force J, a move that gave the SSRF access to a dedicated naval planning staff with a greater capacity to mount operations.[21] Hughes-Hallett described this arrangement, stating that "we hardly ever interfered with the military part of the plan. We did find it necessary however to go into considerable detail in connection with navigational problems, and escort and cover, and it was not in the least surprising that the Small-Scale Raiding Forces should have failed to achieve anything so long as they were entirely independent."[22]

Gradually the divergent requirements of SIS and SOE activities transpired to make the conduct of even minor raids from Britain problematic once again. There was mounting concern from these agencies that COHQ raids were making the insertion of agents and the gathering of clandestine intelligence, particularly on the lightly defended Brittany coastlines, more difficult. Because the SSRF held a virtual monopoly over small-scale COHQ raiding in these areas, it was its activities that became a catalyst for debate over the relative priorities of raiding operations on the one hand versus clandestine intelligence and sabotage activities on the other.[23] The subsequent debate was extensive, but it ultimately concluded in favor of SIS, whose intelligence was deemed more valuable than that obtainable by the "smash-and-grab" methods of the SSRF. The COS therefore decreed that in the event of conflicts between SOE, SIS, and COHQ, SIS would "ordinarily be given priority" and appointed the C in C Home Fleet to mediate over any further conflicts of interest between these different agencies.[24] The activities of the SSRF were thus heavily curtailed, and with its principle advantages subverted—notably the ease and frequency in which operations could be executed—the unit's raison d'être ceased to exist, and it was ultimately disbanded.[25]

As preparations for the invasion of France increased, even more stringent controls upon amphibious raiding operations from Britain were necessary lest they jeopardize or preclude essential reconnaissance, compromise invasion plans, or unfavorably alter the disposition of enemy forces and defenses. Furthermore, as clandestine reconnaissance operations by units such as the British Combined Operations Pilotage Parties (COPPs) and the U.S. Scouts and Raiders (S&Rs) were increasingly coming to the fore, it became necessary to establish mechanisms by which their operations could be properly directed toward answering specific questions posed by the supreme commander and his intelligence and planning staffs.[26] In October 1943, therefore, the COSSAC (Chief of Staff to Supreme Allied Commander) Raids and Reconnaissance Committee was established as the chief arbitrator of all raiding operations within COSSAC's sphere. Although the planning and mounting of raids would technically remain a COHQ responsibility, the committee's role would be "to allot priorities for and co-ordinate all such raids and to ensure that the best use was made of all means and resources available."[27] This arrangement was both sensible and constructive, and at the suggestion of Admiral Bertram Ramsay, additional "reconnaissance committees" were established on the staffs of other theater commanders.[28]

The transition of the Commando role away from independent raiding activities and toward spearheading and protracted light infantry tasks necessitated changes in the manner in which the Commandos were organized, administered, and controlled. Participation in the North African campaign had highlighted many limitations with the Commando organization, not least of all the restrictions of being reliant upon the Britain-based SS Brigade Headquarters for the administration of individual Commandos in the field. Before the invasion of Sicily, therefore, Brigadier Laycock established a subordinate SS Brigade HQ under AFHQ to act as a theater-wide body to coordinate the assignment of the Commandos and deal with their administrative concerns. He also strove to alter the Commando war establishment to ensure that each individual Commando possessed adequate "transport and administration personnel for maintaining themselves in the field," lest they incur the charge of being "parasites" constantly reliant on the patronage of neighboring field formations.[29]

The creation of six more Royal Marine Commandos in August 1943 (joining the two already in existence by this point) provided even greater impetus for an effective command structure capable of orchestrating the deployments of various Commandos, potentially separated by large geographical distances, and catering to their specific needs. As the use of the SS Brigade HQ subdivision was deemed to have worked well in Sicily, in October 1943 it was decided to group all full-establishment "regular" Commandos into four individual SS Brigades (each consisting of four Commandos) and place all of these under a newly established SS group based in Britain and headed by Royal Marines general Robert Sturges. This move would decentralize administration and help alleviate the problems of reinforcement, logistics, and command and control, which were becoming exacerbated by the increasingly large distances separating the individual Commandos when on operational deployment.[30]

Attached to various divisional, corps, and army commands, in the field the SS Brigade organization remained flexible. In France and northwestern Europe the deployment of SS Brigades was relatively conventional. From June 8, 1944, onward the Commandos of the 1st and 4th SS Brigades deployed under 21 Army Group as complete units, maintaining a similar relationship with their brigade as that which a conventional infantry battalion would have with an infantry brigade.[31] For the 2nd SS Brigade in Italy and the Mediterranean and to a lesser extent the 4th SS Brigade in SEAC, however, cohesive deployments of Commandos directly under a brigade was a rarer occurrence. The 2nd SS Brigade's individual Commandos, in particular, were often separated from their brigade HQ for protracted periods, working in subdivisions widely dispersed throughout Italy, the Balkans, and Greece.[32] In such instances brigade HQs merely served as a theater-level administrative and advisory post on the best methods of deploying Commandos in an independent manner; individual Commandos were granted much more latitude, retaining only loose links with the brigade through the exchange of liaison officers.[33] Although the comparatively small SS Brigade staffs were placed under such great strain in such circumstances, they nevertheless played an essential role in orchestrating the deployment of Commando formations, particularly when making provision for the reinforcement of individual Commandos or supervising their attachment to other field formations.[34]

Overall, the SS Brigade structure can be viewed as highly successful. It was a flexible arrangement capable of adapting to both independent activities and more conventional mainline deployments.

It helped mold the Commandos into the British order of battle for conventional operations; eased the attachment of Commandos to field formations and, equally important, the attachment of supporting arms to the Commandos themselves;[35] and helped alleviate interservice tensions when integrating Army and Royal Marine Commandos. As the war progressed, the powers of SS Brigades to train, plan for, and administer individual Commandos would steadily increase. For example, by the closing stages of the war the 3rd Commando Brigade HQ (as the SS Brigades were renamed in December 1944) in India, had developed auxiliary sections encompassing, among other things, a "holding Commando" for reinforcement, a Royal Marines Engineer Commando, various brigade defense sections, and a medical Commando, as well as quartermasters, provost marshals, and workshops.[36] The SS Brigade performed an important role in coordinating the actions of the Commandos, aiding their employment, and providing for their logistical and administrative needs; but most significantly it performed an essential role in advising higher commanders on the Commandos' "employment and technique."[37] Furthermore, adopting a more conventional organization alongside Commando successes in spearheading and assault roles helped submerge much of the opposition and suspicion previously directed at Commando formations.[38]

The Command and Control of American Ranger Formations

Although in many areas there was a close commonality between the Commandos and the U.S. Army Rangers, one of the most notable points of divergence was in the manner in which the formations were administered and controlled; and it is fair to say that the Rangers suffered from the absence of a similar arrangement to that of COHQ and the SS Brigades. Throughout the war the Rangers lacked a formally constituted command structure that could give them legitimacy, provide high-level representation, advise higher commanders on their capabilities and tactics, set organizational and doctrinal precedents, and provide for their logistics and administration. All Ranger formations were directly attached to field formations, commonly at divisional level or lower, and with the possible exception of the 6th Rangers, there was no real effort to instruct higher bodies on Ranger capabilities or employment, nor was there any adequate apparatus for their administration. Consequently, the tasking and use of Ranger formations became solely dependent on the willingness of the higher headquarters, to which they were attached, to employ them.

In April 1943, prior to the invasion of Sicily and following the creation of the 3rd and 4th Rangers, Colonel William Darby had requested (almost simultaneously with the creation of the first nominal SS Brigade under Robert Laycock) that a "Ranger Force" headquarters be authorized to provide for the "direction of training and operations and for the purpose of facilitating administration of the three battalions." However, unlike Laycock's suggestions, Darby's requests were rejected, with the explanation that the Rangers were "considered to be of a transient nature and to have no permanent place in army organization." The "Ranger Force" that did deploy in Sicily was thus merely a cosmetic grouping with no separate headquarters, no special powers, and no formally appointed commander (although Darby, as CO 1st Rangers, was de facto commander of all three battalions).[39] Following Sicily, there were further calls for the creation of a formal "Ranger Force" headquarters and the acknowledgment of the battalions as a permanent organization. Major Roy Murray, CO 4th Rangers, rose above his station to argue audaciously with General Lesley J. McNair, commanding Army Ground Forces, that such a headquarters was essential and that it should be "patterned after the British Combined Operations staff, to handle the administrative problems, intelligence, long range planning, the allocation of assignments to the various battalions, and, most important, to decide if the assignment is a proper one for Rangers."[40] Darby, echoing such sentiments, went as far as suggesting to General Eisenhower that "if . . . it is the opinion of the War Department that battalions of this nature are not permanent, it is requested that these battalions be disbanded and reformed as a regularly approved organization with a table of organization already fully recognized by the War Department."[41]

Lieutenant General George S. Patton, Jr., was firmly behind the proposals of the Rangers, and "in view of the excellent work performed by these units while under . . . [his] command," he recommended that the battalions "be consolidated into a Ranger Regiment, given suitable headquarters" under the command of Darby and be permanently assigned to his Seventh Army for operations.[42] Despite such high-level support, General McNair remained adamant that these units were only provisional expedients and accordingly rejected all such proposals. The only concession ultimately made was allowing the Rangers to establish a small provisional tactical headquarters before the invasion of Italy. Later, before the Anzio operation, General Mark Clark promoted Darby to colonel and allowed him to establish a temporary headquarters, called 6615th Ranger Force, Provisional.[43] In its brief existence, however, this grouping had no real authority aside from administration and tactical considerations, and in no way did it compare to an SS Brigade.[44] In May 1944, prior to the deployment of the 2nd and 5th Rangers in the invasion of Normandy, another ad hoc provisional Ranger group was established under Lieutenant Colonel James E. Rudder (who outranked Major Max Schneider, his counterpart in the 5th Rangers), yet this too remained solely concerned with logistics and administration and ceased to operate shortly after D-day.[45]

The refusal to grant the Rangers a permanent headquarters to formalize their command and control provides a clear illustration of the dominant U.S. perception of ranger formations as ephemeral bodies for which there was little requirement once conventional arms had come into contact with the enemy. Although this overarching policy precedent would have notable implications for the "correct" employment of the Rangers (as the next chapter will highlight), it did not, however, universally impede the development of effective command structures. The 6th Ranger Battalion's command arrangements are of particular note and surpassed those that had developed for the other Ranger battalions in Europe. The first important difference between the 6th Rangers and the other battalions was a result of theater-specific conditions of the Southwest Pacific and the Philippines, which promoted an inherent focus on the use of small groups and encouraged decentralized control.[46] The second and more significant factor was that the 6th Rangers, like the Alamo Scouts, maintained a close and constructive relationship with the man ultimately responsible for its tasking: General Krueger, GOC Sixth Army. Having personally orchestrated the establishment of the 6th Rangers in the first instance, Krueger was unwavering in his support for the unit—something that helped guarantee the development of uncomplicated and effective command paths between his G-2 (Intelligence branch) and G-3 (Operations branch) infrastructure and Colonel Henry Mucci's Rangers. Such a relationship was undoubtedly central to the success of the 6th Rangers during the Cabanatuan prison raid.[47]

In contrast to the Army Rangers, the command and control of both the First Special Service Force (FSSF) and Merrill's Marauders was comparatively conventional. The FSSF was organized into three nominal "regiments" and a "group HQ" under Colonel Frederick and was perpetually deployed as a complete unit via direct attachments at the divisional and corps level.[48] The Marauders was comparably structured, consisting of three "battalions" and a headquarters. Furthermore, in light of being the only U.S. ground forces in the China-Burma-India (CBI) theater, they operated under an uncomplicated chain of command, serving directly under General Stilwell's Northern Combat Area Command. Although both the Marauders and FSSF each had a composition and role largely foreign to conventional arms, the scale of their establishments and organization was certainly more familiar. Both units were loosely based around the "triangular" system adopted by conventional U.S. Army units, and because each unit possessed its own headquarters element, the command and control of the Marauders and FSSF and their integration into operations involving field formations was an inherently easier proposition than it was for many other specialist formations. That is not to discount, however, a proportion of problems endemic to the use of these formations in an irregular manner. The rigors of the long-range penetration activities participated in by the Marauders in particular required the development of more unconventional procedures to provide for the use of columns widely reliant on air supply and often separated from one another, and the unit's headquarters, by both distance and the limitations of communications in Burma.

Somewhat ironically considering its disbandment, it was the USMC Raiders that had the clearest command and control mechanisms of all of the U.S. ranger formations. The initial command arrangements for the first two Raider battalions reflected the idiosyncrasies of their commanding officers. In their deployments against both Tulagi and Guadalcanal, Colonel Merritt Edson's 1st Raider Battalion fitted smoothly into the existing infrastructure of the 1st Marine Division. The 2nd Raiders under the more unconventional Evans Carlson, by comparison, conducted the Makin raid under the direction of Admiral Nimitz's Pacific Fleet and would go on to maintain looser and more irregular command structures during their time on Guadalcanal. Of particular note are the command arrangements, which were made for Carlson's "long patrol" from Aola Bay in November and December 1943.[49] While the operation was authorized and overseen by General Alexander Vandergrift, commanding the 1st Marine Division, Carlson was granted a rare level of autonomy for its conduct. Although maintaining regular contact with the Divisional Operations branch, forwarding situation and intelligence reports and organizing resupply missions, Vandergrift explicitly ordered that his staff make no effort "to give him [Carlson] anything whatever in the way of orders or instructions."[50] As the success of this operation was in large part due to Carlson's irregular talents, credit must also fall upon the flexible and open-minded command and control system of the 1st Marine Division and its willingness to give Carlson the latitude through which his methods could be exploited.[51]

In March 1943, following Guadalcanal and the creation of two more Raider battalions, the decision was taken, almost at the same time as Darby's proposals for the reorganization of the Rangers were first rejected, to organize the heretofore independent Raider battalions into the First Marine Raider Regiment. In September 1943 the 2nd and 3rd Raiders were removed from this command and placed under the newly created Second Regiment. Both organizations served to coordinate the administration, but not operational control, of the individual battalions. Ironically, this positive development actually marked the beginning of the end for the original raider concept, as more orthodox officers came into the organization and proceeded to place the battalions on a more conventional footing.[52] This step toward conventionalization was a leap toward the ultimate disbandment of the Raiders; the removal of the likes of Carlson from the organization (via promotion) providing, in the opinion of one Marine officer, "a momentary glimpse of the dark side of the upper levels of the Marine Corps showing inflexibility of thought and a compulsive suspicion of all things new and untried."[53]

The Command and Control of British Special Forces, 1940–1944

As a whole, the deployment of commando and ranger formations in close conjunction with the main battle was effectively achieved, and aside from administrative and bureaucratic dilemmas, would cause relatively few problems during the war. The same, however, cannot be said for the command and control of special forces (or for those comparatively few instances in which commando formations deployed in an irregular manner). Operating in depth, highly individualistic, and employing even more unfamiliar methods and equipment, the use and control of special forces was uniquely complicated. As nascent creations special forces offered largely unknown potentials, and initially the best manner by which to utilize them was to provide them with significant latitude to plan and conduct their own operations. Although leadership should not be confused with command and direction, during the formative period of a number of special forces the two things were often symbiotic.[54] The relationship between the "errant captain" and the "champion," so apparent in the creation of British special forces, was significant in defining early mechanisms for the command and control of these formations. The system was inherently directed toward informal procedures: individual units would be provided with a loose mandate, time frame, or area of operations and then given autonomy, within these restrictions, to plan and conduct operations as they saw best. Such arrangements were often resented and helped germinate the corrosive—if not always inaccurate—notion of the "private army."

When Ralph Bagnold established the LRDG, he immediately sought "GHQ control" directly under Wavell.[55] He assumed that only by being responsible to the highest practicable authority in theater would it be possible for his unit to be correctly deployed, with its activities wedded into the broader operational and strategic picture.[56] In forging this arrangement, Bagnold had set a precedent, and thus when Stirling established L Detachment, wary of "how fatal it would be . . . to be put under any existing branch or formation," he attained a similar arrangement with Auchinleck.[57] For much of their time in the Desert War both the LRDG and L Detachment SAS would work independently under GHQ MEF (with liaison officers attached to the Western Desert Force/Eighth Army) with little formal organization of command and control. Each unit was responsible for its own administration and training. The LRDG conducted planning alongside the director of military operations (DMO),[58] albeit often with a great deal of liaison with and direction from the Intelligence branch, while the SAS was generally responsible for its own planning within the remits of broad directives as laid out by the DMO.[59] Because of the unique conditions of the Desert War— the barren terrain, vast distances, open lines of communication, expansive flanks, and a strategy uncomplicated by inhabited areas—autonomous raiding was eminently possible and profitable. The command arrangements for these special forces, as was admitted by Lieutenant General R. L. McCreery, CGS MEF, "may be untidy in principle but in practice it works."[60]

Beginning in mid-1942, however, the proliferation of these units made necessary a tighter manner of command and control, not only to protect them from competition and overlap but also, and more important, so as to not jeopardize, detract from, or impede conventional operations, lest "plans of enormous moment [be] spoiled by the wild depredations of a handful of adventurers."[61] As the "raiding circus" began to get out of hand, the former informal autonomous mechanisms of control began to falter. Moves were thus undertaken to formalize the command and administration of special forces in the Middle East, and it was thought desirable to provide one body the authority to coordinate the activities of all the disparate groups in the theater. The first efforts to do this occurred in April 1942, when the LRDG was made responsible for the coordination of all activities "behind the enemy's lines" in Libya, including, while in the field, all desert special forces, as well as the Middle East Commando and agents from SOE, SIS, and MI9. Given the experience of the LRDG and the infrastructure that had developed to provide for its operations, this was ostensibly a sensible arrangement. In practice, however, the move was soon found to be impracticable, as it placed too much of a burden on the LRDG and threatened to diminish its operational efficiency.[62]

By August 1942, following extensive discussion with the relevant parties, it was decided to appoint an officer at GHQ MEF with the specific duty to coordinate the various desert special forces.[63] In addition, to further streamline this process, it was thought essential to amalgamate the 1st SBS, L Detachment SAS, and 1st SS Regiment (Middle East Commando), in order to increase cooperation and eliminate competition over resources and targets.[64] Although both David Stirling of the SAS and Lieutenant Colonel John A. Graham, commanding the 1st SS Regiment, sought control of this grouping, Graham had neither Stirling's flair for backdoor lobbying nor his social contacts and record of success with which to back up his plea. One day after Graham submitted his proposal, Stirling, in characteristic style, offered his riposte in a letter to Winston Churchill, to whom he had been introduced in August 1942.

In making his grab for expansion Stirling undoubtedly greatly benefited from having allowed Winston Churchill's son Randolph to "join" his unit in a May 1942 raid against Benghazi. Following this undertaking, Randolph dutifully recounted all to his father in a suitably embellished letter that reads like a *Boy's Own* novel.[65] Thus, when the Prime Minister visited the Middle East in August 1942, he accordingly invited both Stirling and SAS captain Fitzroy Maclean (also on the Benghazi raid and with whom, as a member of Parliament, Churchill was already acquainted) to dine with him. In the opinion of David Hoe, Stirling's biographer, this meeting "alone could be important to the long-term survival of the unit."[66] In his subsequent letter to the Prime Minister, Stirling argued that not only should L Detachment be enlarged but also suggested "control to rest with the Officer Commanding 'L' Detachment and not with any outside body superimposed for purposes of co-ordination. . . . The planning of operations to be carried out by 'L' Detachment to remain as hitherto the prerogative of 'L' Detachment."[67] Stirling would win his point about expansion when in late September the 1st SS Regiment and the SBS were formally incorporated into the 1st SAS Regiment, but even he could not avert the need for a coordinating branch for all special forces in the theater.[68]

In September 1942 a general staff branch under the DMO, GHQ MEF, was established to coordinate the various desert special forces. This branch, known as G(Raiding Forces) or G(RF), became the responsibility of Lieutenant Colonel John "Shan" Hackett, whose duties were "to rationalize the kaleidoscope of special forces without diminishing the priceless individuality of the men in each," to improve inter-army cooperation, to make special operations more palatable to high command, and to ensure that individual unit commanders would not be able to harass army or theater commanders without first going through him.[69] Unfortunately, this branch was not operationally ready in sufficient time to prevent the abject failure of a September 1942 coordinated series of raids involving all of the special forces in the Middle East. The miscarriage of these operations would, nonetheless, dramatically highlight the necessity behind the creation of the G(RF).

Soon after the fall of Tobruk in June 1942, Lieutenant Colonel John Edward Haselden, yet another adventurous prewar Arabist, who since 1940 had been widely involved in undertaking intelligence operations in theater, conceived of an idea for a small-scale raid on the port. He envisioned that a small force, heavily reliant on surprise, might be able to infiltrate the town and sabotage fuel dumps and port facilities. However, this potentially attractive idea soon became distorted, as the scheme escalated into a much larger combined operation. Operation Agreement, into which the plan evolved, was a complex scheme that would see the German-speaking Special Interrogation Group (SIG), masquerading as the enemy, "escort" a larger assault force, predominantly composed of 1st SS Regiment personnel and disguised as prisoners of war, directly into Tobruk.[70] Occurring simultaneously would be an amphibious assault launched against the harbor by a force made up of the 11th Royal Marine Battalion and a group of Argyll and Sutherland Highlanders guided by SBS personnel. Instead of seeking to sabotage a few fuel tanks, Haselden and his engorged force were now expected to capture and hold Tobruk for twelve hours while ships and harbor installations were destroyed in detail.[71] In addition, to further increase the disruptive effect of this operation—which was being launched in an effort to blunt any further attacks by Rommel—it was decided to simultaneously mount a number of subsidiary attacks: a raid on Benghazi (Operation Bigamy) by a force comprised predominantly of L Detachment SAS; a raid on Jalo (Operation Nicety), undertaken by the Sudan Defense Force; and a LRDG raid on Barce (Operation Caravan).[72]

Undertaken in September 1942, each of these operations would, with the exception of Caravan, prove to be costly failures. The attack on Tobruk was a disaster. Very little was achieved to compensate for the loss of one cruiser, two destroyers, four motor torpedo boats, and two Fairmiles motor launches sunk, and 280 naval officers and men, 300 Royal Marines and 160 soldiers killed or captured.[73] The SIG leading the deception was decimated, and Haselden was killed. Bigamy and Nicety were equally ill fated. The failings of the September raids were all too clear: the raids had no single commander and were instead all run by an ad hoc committee; they were too ambitious and too complex (resulting in the failure to achieve the all-important synchronicity); and they would ultimately rely upon good fortune for success.[74] Aside from slipshod organization and planning, the most cited reason for failure was the atrocious operational security surrounding the raids.[75] As a result of the cumbersome number of people intimately involved in the planning of these operations, it is a commonly made allegation that Axis intelligence was aware of the operations up to ten days before they commenced.[76] British intelligence, however, must also shoulder some of the blame, as information about enemy strengths, defenses, and dispositions were each woefully inadequate. The raids' failure, of Operation Agreement on Tobruk in particular, proved that complex operations could not be run by an array of disparate groups and highlighted the need for a "properly constituted planning staff" of a limited number of select personnel.[77] Hackett's G(RF) thus began its existence with vivid illustration of its importance.

The historian John Gordon has claimed that the "chief flaw of the desert special-operations venture" was the failure to devise controlling apparatus to "keep pace with ... proliferation." While admitting that the G(RF) was valuable, he speculated on "how much more effective it might have proved had it been expanded into something more substantial—a 'Joint Desert Special Operations Command.'"[78] Such a move, however, was neither practicable nor strictly necessary in the unique conditions of a theater that, for the most part, welcomed autonomy and freedom of action. If there was a flaw in command, it was not the absence of a complex controlling body, for ultimately the G(RF) was more than adequate in dealing with the single-service and predominantly British special operations occurring in theater, but it was in the late development of any controlling apparatus. Had the G(RF) been created earlier it would have helped ensure the best possible application of special forces, may have prevented some of the wilder schemes (not least such debacles as Operation Agreement), and would have led to a better organized and more cost-effective use of personnel and resources.

Despite the increasing requirement for coordination of the planning, administration, and tasking of special forces, it still remained important to provide them with a degree of independence, flexibility, and latitude for both the planning and mounting of operations. Much was gained, particularly in harassment and "alarm and despondency" operations, by assigning units broad areas of operational responsibility in which they could have a virtually free hand. Winston Churchill summed up this truism well when he asserted: "If you want to use the inventiveness and audacity of the people who are best adapted for the job ... you must give a good deal of latitude lower down in how they operate."[79] The G(RF) system was effective not least of all because Hackett, something of a kindred soul to the "errant captains" under his charge, had a sound understanding of their roles and tactics. Under the G(RF) the individual units retained their independence and Hackett was "reluctant to try to impose too much control," understanding that in the field "faced by situations that changed rapidly, the special-force commander on the spot sometimes seemed the individual best qualified to make decisions about what targets to hit."[80] This was a sensible arrangement given the absence of accessible, real-time, and secure means of communication through which timely orders could be delivered to units operating hundreds of miles away behind the enemy's line.

The Desert War proved that so long as their area of operation is clearly defined and broad controls are placed on their deployment, granting special forces freedom of action and autonomy within a given area could certainly be very effective. The opportunities for adopting such an approach were, however, largely particular to the unique conditions of the Desert War—and, later, to a lesser extent those in Burma. As a rule, the more complex or important the issue at hand, the less potential there was for autonomous activities by special forces. When real estate became limited, controls on these units became essential, if for no other reason than to prevent them from being a nuisance and attempting to coerce higher commanders into accepting missions of dubious worth and limited operational value. Because of the many and complex variables affecting the deployment of special forces in depth in other theaters—such as conventional offensives, politics, partisans, the limited availability of transport or support resources, and the necessity for security and deception—special operations increasingly required more coordination and control in both planning and execution, not just for tidiness and efficiency, but for the most successful prosecution of Allied strategy.

The G(RF) branch set a precedent for the effective control of special forces, but it became redundant soon after its creation, as special operations were curtailed following the advances of the Eighth Army after the Second Battle of El Alamein and the commencement of Operation Torch in November 1942. With an eye toward future deployments, on March 8, 1943, Lieutenant Colonel H. J. Cator was appointed to command a new GHQ ME subdivision named Headquarters Raiding Forces. The G(RF) branch was absorbed by this move to "centralize and improve" the administration, reinforcement, logistics, and discipline of its special forces.[81] This organization was also short lived and was broken up by the separation of the units under its charge for differing deployments in the Eastern and Western Mediterranean. In September 1943 this branch's lineal, but not direct, descendent—Raiding Forces HQ Aegean—was created under Brigadier D. J. T. Turnbull. Responsible to GHQ ME, this branch was to maintain the same relationship with its varied special forces that an infantry brigade HQ maintained with an infantry battalion.[82]

In performing its duties Raiding Forces HQ Aegean suffered some notable teething problems, with the "amount of muddled thinking" dictating its early actions being likened, disparagingly, to the "early days of the war."[83] The experienced hands of the LRDG in particular were not impressed by its activities and resented having to be reliant upon it for logistics and intelligence. David Lloyd Owen, commanding the LRDG from November 1943, believed that "inexperience and a lack of knowledge" led to Raiding Forces not appreciating the "intricate and careful planning that is essential for success of LRDG patrols."[84] This was exacerbated by the fact that Turnbull, by all accounts no John Hackett, was personally inexperienced, knowing "nothing about any form of special work." The situation was only partially resolved by the appointment of Lieutenant Colonel Guy Prendergast, formerly in command of the LRDG, as Turnbull's second in command.[85] Although the wider direction of the Aegean "folly" was not the fault of Raiding Forces HQ, nor of the units therein, in the earlier stages the branch did little either to promote suitable, or prevent inappropriate, deployment of the formations under its charge. Early raids in the Aegean were plagued by the very problems that Raiding Forces HQ had been established to prevent. Operations were "poorly coordinated, without central planning," with the individual special forces generally operating independently of one another with much "'overlapping, wastage, and friction.'"[86] Gradually, however, this branch grew more successful, and as broader ambitions in the Aegean were curtailed, the personnel of Raiding Forces were increasingly used as intended.

The Command and Control of American Special Forces, 1942–1944

Although U.S. ranger-style formations were hindered by the absence of a direct equivalent to either COHQ or the SS Brigade, many U.S. special forces benefited greatly from William Donovan's OSS as an organization dedicated to their interests. OSS provided a centralized unifying body for American special operations that, in terms of administering and directing disparate special forces on a global scale, certainly had the potential to be a more efficient arrangement than the cumbersome multiagency approach of the British. As early as May 1942 Donovan clearly understood the need for a centralized approach to irregular activities. A COI memorandum stated that "decentralization into isolated groups engaged on independent and unrelated missions is improper. A definite command in the military forces should be created to plan and conduct this type of warfare through the war. Without such centralized planning and control, the full possibilities of sabotage and guerrilla warfare cannot be utilized."[87]

In the process of developing American special forces capabilities, OSS bears more similarities to COHQ than it does to their more obvious counterparts of either SIS or SOE. The fierce opposition that Donovan as COI faced in June 1941, particularly over his proposals for special operations or so-called supplementary activities, was certainly analogous to that which Keyes first faced when appointed DCO.[88] Nor was the opposition confined solely to Washington. Suspicion and animosity precluded OSS development in both the Pacific and Far Eastern theaters. The starkest opposition came from General Douglas MacArthur, who saw OSS requests to operate in his theater as "an outrageous infringement upon his own territory."[89] Although certainly not adverse to irregular actions, as exhibited by his sponsorship or endorsement of the Philippine guerrillas, the Allied Intelligence Bureau (AIB) in Australia, the Alamo Scouts, and the 6th Ranger Battalion, MacArthur was reluctant to cede control to what he saw as being a suspicious external agency with dubious political motives, and he accordingly barred all OSS elements from the Southwest Pacific theater.[90] OSS operations in the Central Pacific were also heavily curtailed by Admiral Nimitz, limiting their participation to only the Maritime Unit (MU) and Research and Development (R&D) branches. This move was, however, based more on a lack of requirement and opportunity than from any particular animosity.[91]

Similarly at odds with OSS was General Stilwell. Fundamentally an orthodox soldier, he was "fervently prejudiced against 'irregular' military activity" and disparaged "guerrilla tactics as 'illegal action' and 'shadow boxing.'"[92] Although willing to grant Commander

Milton Miles's Naval Group China (later known as SACO) "free and exclusive control over special operations in CBI," Stilwell was initially unwilling to award the same access to OSS Detachment 101. Naval Group China "enjoyed virtual autonomy as far as any American military authority in Asia was concerned, both because of Tai Li's [head of the Chinese intelligence service as recognized by the Chungking government] directorship and because the Navy Department in Washington fully supported Miles' position." For operations in China OSS had no choice but to accept Miles as a nominal regional head until 1944.[93] Detachment 101 was thus confined to operating in Burma and maintained very little contact with SACO. This separation was not, as is sometimes believed, a result of any interservice divisions or tensions. In reference to Miles, Major Carl F. Eifler (commanding Detachment 101) claimed they "hit it off from the moment we met," but the pair swiftly came to a mutual agreement that "we could work a lot better and accomplish more if we worked together but gave the opinion to the outside world that we disliked each other." At its heart this separation was a fundamentally political move for the benefit of the Chinese, who were suspicious of Eifler's associations with supposedly untrustworthy British.[94]

With any conflict with the Chinese averted, Stilwell ultimately embraced Detachment 101 in Burma and gave them a "free hand" to operate independently, sending Eifler into the jungle with the mandate that all he wanted to hear from them were "booms."[95] Detachment 101 was thus able to establish a main base station at Nazira in the Assam from which to direct its operations in the field. This centralized command system worked well, but with 101's dramatic expansion to meet the needs of Stilwell's Burma Road offensive, it began to become overstretched. It was thus deemed necessary to develop an "area control" system by which northern Burma was divided into four regions, each under an individual commander responsible for all subsidiary 101 activities within his area. This was a logical and very effective method of dealing with the complications of expansion; it removed the burden from Nazira and greatly improved communications and logistical arrangements, and the rewards, as Lieutenant Colonel William R. Peers, who had replaced Eifler at the helm of Detachment 101 in 1943, stated, "were initiative and flexibility such as we had never known."[96]

Within Europe, no doubt affected by the British influence, attitudes toward OSS were significantly mellowed. The first overseas

COI branch in London was small, "characterized by informality," and had no "elaborate chain of command."⁹⁷ By the summer of 1942, however, with the creation of OSS "the presence of such an independent quasi-civilian agency, conducting highly operational activities" was becoming "incompatible with the rigid organizational pattern" rapidly enveloping the theater. In order to alleviate these tensions and promote more efficient operational mechanisms, in February 1943 OSS/London began to request incorporation into the theater framework via "militarization," a process granted on June 4, 1943, when OSS/London was officially recognized as a military detachment and made responsible to the Assistant-COS, G-2 (Intelligence branch) ETOUSA (European Theater of Operations United States Army).⁹⁸ Such a move, mirrored in other theaters, provided OSS with the all-important Table of Organization and Equipment (TOE) and an allotment for the recruitment and promotion of personnel. This reorganization was not, however, a panacea for OSS inexperience, and in many of its first operational deployments the initial position of OSS was "inevitably that of a new agency about whose functions and relative position neither its own members, nor those to whom it was immediately responsible were sure."⁹⁹

In May 1943 the OSS Operational Groups (OGs) were awarded branch status, which authorized them to dispatch personnel into the field. When deployed in a theater, the OGs operated under their own "area staff" responsible for controlling "all Groups operating within and from the Theater." This staff nonetheless remained subservient to the larger SO (Special Operations) branch headquarters for all matters of planning, administration, tasking, and direction.¹⁰⁰ Soon after the OGs first took to the field, this arrangement was deemed undesirable. The "general character and duties" of the OGs were thought to be so divergent from the rest of OSS that many OGs "felt they had little in common" with the larger organization.¹⁰¹ Furthermore, there was a genuine concern that the SO branch did not sufficiently understand the qualifications or mandate of the OGs.¹⁰² Lieutenant Colonel Russell Livermore, commanding the first operationally deployed OGs in Corsica, highlighted the need for "a good tough guy with some rank as head of OG who is not afraid to yell bloody murder and protect our rear in matters of allotment, etc. . . . Having much trouble here with command and administrative channels within OSS, it being a crazy civilian agency. I hope to get OG reorganized in this theater as a regular military regiment with a different name and under OSS command only at the very top."[103]

On the basis of such justifications, on June 21, 1944, the various OGs in the Italian and Mediterranean theater were placed on a more military footing and renamed Companies A (Italian), B (French), and C (Yugoslav and Greek) of the 2671st Special Reconnaissance Battalion Separate (Provisional). This reorganization was undertaken for a variety of reasons: to improve the planning and application of the OGs, to make their use more palatable to the military high command, to remove suspicion over their utility, and to ease the attachment of groups to higher formations for operational control. Rather naïvely, it was also hoped that the reorganization would help protect OG personnel from Hitler's Commando Order (Kommandobefehl) if personnel were captured.[104] The latter point undoubtedly weighed heavy on the minds of OG personnel in the summer of 1944 because in March a group of fifteen OG personnel had been compromised, captured, and subsequently executed while attempting to destroy railway tunnels near La Spezia in Operation Ginny II.[105]

The gradual separation of the OGs from the SO branch was completed in November 1944 with the creation of the OG Command under Livermore. This, as per Livermore's suggestions, represented a separate "military unit" of OSS responsible directly to Donovan.[106] These moves toward independence for the OGs increased the potential for their employment and gave them greater powers and a more efficient structure for the conduct of operations. The extensive and widespread deployment of the OGs from the summer of 1944 onward reflects the effectiveness of these measures.

Joint and Combined Special Operations

By the start of 1944 the gradual rise of partisan activities, alongside a concomitant increase in the deployments of SOE, OSS, and the varied special forces in the Mediterranean theater, increasingly highlighted the importance of coordinating the activities of all Allied irregular elements working "behind enemy lines" under one clear banner to improve their administration and tasking. By February 1944 the volume of work these varied elements were generating "had increased to such an extent and had become interwoven with such high level policy decisions" that it was necessary to establish several regional staff branches to specifically coordinate the conduct of "special operations" (defined by AFHQ as those "military operations within or behind enemy lines").[107] The staff branches were Special Operations G-3 Algiers (AFHQ), for coordinating operations in the Western Mediterranean and the South of France; Special Operations G-3 15 Army Group, for operations in support of the Allied Armies in Italy (AAI); and Force 266, for operations in Yugoslavia and Albania.[108]

In April 1944 Special Operations: Mediterranean was established under British Major General W. A. M. Stawell to coordinate these three separate branches, and the forces within their respective areas of operation, under one head; prepare plans and initiate these for higher command approval; advise AFHQ on the capabilities and availability of these forces; coordinate such activities with commanders of lower echelons; and allot priorities for use of air and naval craft.[109] Stawell would be the "technical adviser" to General Henry Maitland Wilson, supreme Allied commander Mediterranean, on special operations and was to act as "commander of such SOE/OSS units as are not assigned to subordinate commands, and controller of all special operations and SOE/OSS activities in the Mediterranean."[110] Although Special Operations: Mediterranean was a joint Anglo-American branch, OSS remained somewhat aloof, retaining an independent headquarters, headed by Colonel Edward Glavin, directly under AFHQ. While this alternative channel did not cause any significant complications for the deployment of the OGs and MUs, it did, nonetheless, remain an extra bureaucratic hurdle for coordination with wider OSS activities.[111]

Command arrangements had to adapt swiftly to alterations in the strategic situation and did so dramatically in mid-1944. The stepping up of activities in the Balkans necessitated the creation of the Balkan Air Force (BAF) in June 1944, with responsibility over all trans-Adriatic operations. With this move, Force 266 was disbanded, and the forces previously under its charge (including a number of Commandos, the LRDG, OGs, and the RSR) became the responsibility of Land Forces Adriatic (LFA), a subdivision of BAF headed by Brigadier George Mark Oswald Davy, an individual familiar to many of these special forces, having previously served as director of military operations at GHQ MEF during the Desert War.[112]

By far the most important organizational changes occurred as the Allies prepared to invade France in 1944. Here the magnitude of events at hand necessitated concerted efforts to centralize the control of the special forces that would be used in depth to support the invasions. Yet in spite of the strategic importance of the theater, mechanisms for the coordinated control of special forces and the Resistance in France were established relatively late in the day; the initially confused plans for the use of the SAS Brigade and the OSS OGs in France being symptomatic of this delay. It was not until May 1944 that the inter-Allied branches of Special Forces Headquarters (SFHQ) in London and the Special Projects and Operations Center (SPOC) in Algiers (formerly the AFHQ-controlled G-3 Special Operations branch) were established under SHAEF. These two organizations would coordinate the planning, dispatch, administration, and control of SOE/OSS agents and their Jedburgh and OG special forces in the north and south of France, respectively, and, most important, would advise the Supreme Commander about the capabilities both of these units and of the Resistance, and provide him with the means of employing them for best effect.

From July 1944, however, the command and control of the Jedburghs and OGs became more complex as the direction of the Resistance, SFHQ, and SPOC ceased to be the direct responsibility of SHAEF and was placed under the Etat-major des Forces Françaises de l'Intérieur (EMFFI), commanded by Free French general Marie-Pierre Koenig.[113] Although this transition in command was not fully implemented until mid-August, the timing of the reshuffle created disruption and many bureaucratic headaches. Kenneth Macksey has claimed that "the unevenness of clandestine performance [in France] must largely be laid at the door of the Allied Higher Command. . . . Had [EMFFI command] been implemented when FFI [Forces Françaises de l'Intérieur] was formed in March all might have been well, since the new headquarters would have had time in which to shake down after being pitched into action."[114] Instead, experienced staff officers from SOE and OSS faced notable problems working in a foreign bureaucracy with inexperienced French officers.[115] Although a historical study by S. J. Lewis has discounted the damage caused by this transition, claiming that it was "largely a political and cosmetic measure, because Koenig's deputies from SOE and OSS maintained the mechanisms of command, communication, and supply"; its timing was, nevertheless, ill thought out and was, in the opinion of Roger Ford, "counter-productive, causing disruption and confusion at a critical time."[116]

A further source of difficulties affecting the command and control of the Jedburghs and OGs in France stemmed from the patchy relations existing between SPOC and SFHQ. While those OGs that operated from Algiers under SPOC benefited from an existent and "splendid" staff experienced in OG operations who "properly understood the manipulation of the OG as a weapon" (something to be expected of a branch that had formerly been Special Operations G-3, Algiers), those OGs working from Britain under SFHQ, on the other hand, were hindered by the absence of proper infrastructure and were forced to rely on planning and administrative staffs who had little "proper understanding of the function" of the OGs. The situation for the OGs in Britain was subsequently aggravated when their CO, Lieutenant Colonel Serge Obolensky, an officer well experienced in OG work, accompanied his men into the field, leaving the administration of his groups to the SO branch.[117] It is interesting that while the OGs worked better from SPOC than SFHQ, the reverse was true for the Jedburgh Teams, whose entire infrastructure began and largely remained in Britain. Teams were only sent to Algiers in April, and SPOC was unable to develop a proper staff to deal with their coordination and dispatch. As one Jedburgh subsequently reflected, the "greatest mistake" of SPOC was "the lack of one head. Duplicity or even triplicity of command . . . leads only to confusion and lack of clear directives. . . . The lack of an administrative officer to look after the Jeds in the field was a big mistake. The Jed officer cannot be expected to do briefing, resupply, and field telegrams, as well as administration."[118]

Such confused command arrangements risked leading to misunderstanding and confusion between the Jedburghs and OGs in the field and on occasion led to potentially disastrous situations, as occurred on June 8, when Jedburgh Team Quinine arrived at the same drop zone as OG Emily without any prior warning and with neither group having knowledge of the other's mission or intentions.[119] It could also lead to a degree of resentment between groups because of the differing procedures of allotting supplies and aircraft priorities. Jedburgh Team Willys, for example, was aggrieved that OGs Louise and Betsy, with whom it worked closely, "seemed to receive everything they requested from Algiers almost as soon as the ink was dry on the signals pad" while it "had to wait, sometimes for weeks, for scraps."[120]

The problems with the command and control of the SOE/OSS units were exacerbated by the separation of the SAS Brigade from the SFHQ and SPOC infrastructure. Upon its creation in March 1944 the SAS Brigade came under the control of I Airborne Corps. This was not an entirely new precedent. In Italy both the 2nd SAS and the Special Raiding Squadron (formerly 1st SAS) had come under the command of the 1st Airborne Division for a short period of time, an arrangement that Major General Frederick Browning, GOC Airborne Forces, believed would "make best use of the troop carrying aircraft available."[121] The suitability of this arrangement for operations in depth in France is, however, debatable. Philip Warner suggests that the brigade was placed under I Airborne Corps because "neither 21 Army Group nor SHAEF . . . were prepared to take the SAS under direct command, and in fact Airborne was the only Headquarters with the transport, knowledge, and experience for the job."[122] The greatest limitation with this situation, as Terence Otway points out, was that the main focus of I Airborne Corps was directed toward the use of "regular" airborne formations and that the command was never in full "possession of all the facts, political as well as military, that would enable them to suggest the most valuable employment of SAS troops on strategical objectives."[123] Under Airborne HQ, however, the SAS Brigade was able to retain a great deal of independence, receiving direct guidance from SHAEF and undertaking most of its own planning, intelligence analysis, and operational command and control.

The SAS Brigade nonetheless remained "on the horns of a bureaucratic dilemma," and the lack of clear links with SFHQ was certainly an issue (the absence of links with SPOC in Algiers was of less significance, as the SAS did not deploy extensively in the South of France). SAS Brigade independence led SFHQ to perceive the SAS as "a potential usurper and drain on scarce resources" rather than as an organization with complementary aims and methods to its own.[124] Such mutual suspicion and antagonism prevented the establishment of a joint SAS-SFHQ committee, and aside from the permanent attachment of an SAS staff officer, Lieutenant Colonel Ian Collins, to SFHQ to help plan the SAS role in "strategical resistance" operations, there was no direct communication between SFHQ and the SAS Brigade.[125] Being forced to thus rely upon improvised and informal command arrangements, relations between the SAS, the OGs, and the Jedburghs were prone to be marred by confusion in planning, a duplication of effort, and a margin of competition for aircraft sorties and supplies—factors all to the detriment of their effective tasking.¹²⁶ In the field, meanwhile, these command and control problems could lead to practical difficulties resulting from such things as different signal procedures, supply arrangements, and aircraft allotments.¹²⁷

The convoluted manner via which irregular elements and Resistance formations were controlled in France also led to problems in synchronizing their activities with the operations of field formations. Military formations in the field were only able to communicate with, and receive reports from, the Jedburghs and OGs via SFHQ or SPOC and through Special Forces Detachments, which were placed in army and army group headquarters and with field formations. But the Special Forces Detachments themselves, and ergo the field formations, had no direct means of communicating with the Jedburghs or organized partisan groups without first going through the overstretched SFHQ and SPOC networks, which were continually plagued with problems with both the quality of communications and the sheer volume of signals needing to be analyzed.¹²⁸ The result of this inadequate system ensured that in France most Allied officers, "particularly at the senior levels . . . remained unaware of the capabilities of SOF [Special Operations Forces] teams beyond postlinkup tactical assistance."¹²⁹ In light of the nascent nature of special operations in depth, the magnitude of operations occurring, and the complicated problems of joint and combined operations, such problems would have been hard to avoid entirely, but their effects could have been significantly lessened had a unified command system, properly wedded to the strategic decision-making process, existed.

The Command and Control of Maritime Special Forces

The pattern, visible from 1943 onward, that saw heretofore autonomous special forces become increasingly centralized under dedicated command branches is equally apparent among the varied maritime special forces. In the wake of the rampant proliferation of these units, each under COHQ, in June 1943 Mountbatten called for the centralization of each of these groups under a single coordinating authority. He believed such a move to be essential in order to "avoid overlapping and duplication of function" and lead to "a simplification and standardization of training."¹³⁰ This arrangement would also remove the burden of administration from small operational units, a move welcomed by the likes of Lieutenant Commander Willmott, commanding the Combined Operations Pilotage Parties (COPP) Depot, for example, who had already complained that "successive storms from on high . . . [were] increasingly hard and wearing to resist" and had requested that he be permitted to "dissociate myself entirely from questions of equipment and facilities."[131] By July 1943 Mountbatten's proposals had been formalized, and HMS Rodent, better known as the Small Boat Unit (SBU), was created to centralize the administration (if not the training or operational control) of the many disparate maritime special forces.[132]

The SBU also fulfilled an important role as an educator, informing and instructing higher commands, via COHQ, about the functions and availability of its units. The significance of this should not be underestimated. For instance, before the invasion of Sicily it was thought that the COPPs had been underutilized by naval authorities not "properly aware of their function and purpose." Yet by October 1943 their capabilities were "generally understood and appreciated," with the SBU helping to make it "clear that these units are not a clandestine free-lance party sent out by the Admiralty, but a section of the Naval Forces with a definite function and duty to perform in preparation for the Assault."[133] Despite its varied benefits, by mid-1944 the declining requirement for special maritime operations from Britain had made certain that the SBU had become largely redundant, and in August it was subsequently disbanded. Running concomitant with the SBU in Britain was the Admiralty's cumbersomely titled Deputy Director of Operations Division (Irregular), or DDOD(I), branch. Created in May 1943, this branch sought to coordinate and provide for the Royal Navy's irregular shipping needs (primarily agent transport and supply) from Britain and within the Mediterranean. At various stages SBU formations had had contact with DDOD(I), and with the decline of the SBU's responsibilities, DDOD(I) lobbied for the transfer of various SBU naval units to its command. It would ultimately succeed in gaining control of both the Royal Marine Boom Patrol Detachment (RMBPD) and SOE's maritime assets in the summer of 1944.[134]

Before the SBU was disbanded, however, many of its charges had been sent to the Far East as a result of Mountbatten's call for "*his* boys" to join him in his new appointment as supreme Allied commander, Southeast Asia (SACSEA).[135] Following the arrival of these units, Mountbatten established the Small Operations Group (SOG) to coordinate their activities.[136] Mountbatten's motivations behind its creation were much the same as they had been in 1943 when he had created the SBU: he considered such a group essential to help avoid confusion; to reduce the number of independent organizations with which higher commanders had to deal; to "simplify administration and provide a common base"; and to "ensure that as far as possible training and equipment of parties were standardized and that all units benefited from the experience gained in operations and training."[137] Furthermore, like the SBU, the SOG would be extremely important in fostering an "increased appreciation" among higher commands as to the roles of the formations under its charge.[138]

The SOG was an Admiralty-dominated organization: commanded by two Royal Marine officers, Colonel H. T. Tollemache and Lieutenant Colonel Hasler (formerly of the RMBPD), and operating under the overall control of the C in C Eastern Fleet (later East Indies Fleet). As such, the Army personnel of the SBS were concerned about the lack of a "friend at court" and feared being "discarded" under this regime.[139] As experienced units they, and a proportion of the COPPs, were also "inclined to be a little scornful" of the new SOG organization. Particularly distasteful were suggestions that the experienced SBS and COPP training staffs in Britain be disbanded and that the SOG be solely responsible for the training of all new recruits for these formations. Such a move, the SBS argued, would be to the clear detriment of the overall quality of their units.[140] Although such concerns were in part alleviated by the transfer of essential personnel from Britain to join the SOG training sections, they did, however, prompt Major Guy Courtney's Z SBS (undoubtedly the maritime formation most closely resembling a "private army" by this stage of the war) to shun the SOG entirely and instead seek employment directly under SOE's Force 136.[141] In orchestrating operational deployments the SOG was flexible, capable both of attaching its units under corps or divisional jurisdiction (commonly under XV Corps in the Arakan), as well as remaining capable of planning and mounting independent operations of its own creation or those directly devised by Mountbatten or the C in C Far Eastern Fleet.[142]

The activities of the SOG, alongside Force 136, OSS, SIS, and V-Force in SEAC were all coordinated, in a manner analogous to the Special Operations: Mediterranean organization, by the theater-wide

P Division headed by Royal Navy captain G. A. Garnons-Williams. Established in December 1943, P Division would coordinate and approve plans for all "British and American quasi-military organizations and irregular forces" within Mountbatten's command.[143] The command arrangements of the SOG and P Division are together illustrative of how far the methods of administering and controlling disparate special forces had evolved toward the end of the war. They were dedicated yet uncomplicated command branches, directly responsible to the highest practicable authorities. By centralizing and coordinating the planning, administration, and deployments of special forces, they helped ensure their most efficient application and avoided the risks of compromise, duplication of effort, and competition. Furthermore, these organizations played a vital role in making other commands aware of the capabilities and existence of specialist formations and helped reduce much of the animosity directed toward them. At the same time, however, they also remained broadly flexible, providing enough latitude to their subordinate formations so as to neither stifle initiative nor sacrifice the esprit de corps of individual units.

The all-embracing and more rational nature of the OSS MU branch diluted much of the need for the United States to develop command arrangements similar to the British SBU and SOG; it was an inherently sound and efficiently organized structure for the training, supply, and dispatch of special maritime personnel on a global scale. Moreover, possessing OSS branch status, as did the OGs, further streamlined the manner by which MU operational parties could be attached to other commands (such as G-3 Special Operations, 15 Army Group in Italy, or Detachments 101 and 404 in the Far East) for deployment.[144] In the Mediterranean non-OSS American maritime special forces were integrated into a Special Operations subsection of the War Plans Section of the U.S. Eighth Fleet. This section, something of an equivalent to the Admiralty's DDOD(I) branch, was charged with devising and developing plans for naval diversions, amphibious raids, and cover and deception plans. Through this mechanism both the Beach Jumpers and attached Scout and Raider (S&R) personnel operated under the direction of Task Group 80.4, a small flotilla with a mandate for deception operations and air-sea rescue.[145]

Ultimately the most prolific deployment of U.S. special maritime formations occurred under the extensive Underwater Demolitions

Team (UDT) organization that developed in the Central Pacific theater. The first UDT deployments in January 1944 during Operation Flintlock against the Marshall Islands were somewhat uncoordinated affairs, in which the UDTs were not adequately integrated into the main landings. Lessons were, however, learned from this, and following lobbying from the commander of UDT-1, more efficient arrangements were made, particularly in the area of signals and communications, which led to greater coordination of UDT activities with the overall landing plans.[146] In spite of this, up until the capture of Leyte in December 1944, each UDT was managed independently of one another under the "administrative cognizance of Commander Amphibious Forces, U.S. Pacific Fleet," namely Admiral Richmond Kelly Turner, and each was independently assigned to various Task Force commanders for operational deployment. This was not the most efficient arrangement. The lack of centralized procedures made the training and administration of the teams difficult and cooperation and any institutional sharing of information and techniques between units much more problematic.[147]

It was not until shortly before the Lingayen Gulf landings on Luzon in January 1945 that a new UDT command mechanism developed with the appointment of Captain B. Hall Hanlon as commander Underwater Demolition Teams, Amphibious Forces, U.S. Pacific Fleet. This new UDT command put the UDTs, their fast transport craft, and Close Fire Support Groups—most commonly comprising destroyers and Landing Craft Infantry (Gunboats) LCI(G)—all under one head and allowed a flexible and effective tactical framework to develop that "provided almost instantaneous response on order from a central authority and that could take care of predictable exigencies" before and during an assault.[148] Later still, in June 1945, in readiness for the projected invasion of the Japanese Home Islands, the UDT command was enlarged, with the teams divided into two operational squadrons and placed under a UDT flotilla under U.S. Navy captain R. H. Rogers, who would have "direct command" of all UDTs and any ships "in which these teams are embarked."[149] The development of command arrangements was thus able to keep pace with the extensive growth of the UDT organization. What had begun as a collection of autonomous formations individually operating under one body had, in under two years, become a large and efficient joint command organization that encompassed not only the personnel of the special forces but also the resources and personnel involved in their transportation and support.

The importance of clear command structures was essential to the correct application, and therefore the effectiveness and value, of wartime specialist formations. The development of clear methods and structures of command and control for these units during the Second World War followed a prominent learning curve. Early command approaches for specialist formations were often widely inadequate, either being too restrictive and convoluted or, conversely, too informal and decentralized. In time, however, the structures of the control and employment of specialist formations became more professional and efficient: an expected concomitant to the growing martial proficiencies of the Allies. Specialist formations were increasingly integrated into regular military mechanisms, and as this occurred understanding about their existence, methods, and utility naturally increased, while reservations about and antagonism toward them declined. As Field Marshal William Slim well emphasized, "It was not until the activities of all clandestine bodies operating in or near our troops were coordinated, and where necessary controlled, through a senior officer on the staff of the commander of the area, that confusion, ineffectiveness, and lost opportunities were avoided."[150] It was natural that proper command channels and "educated consumers" would develop with time; once knowledge had been amassed, people with direct experience had risen in rank, lessons had been learned, and organizations to advise higher commands about the potential of special operations had developed.

Under certain circumstances it could well be argued that excessive "layers" of command and attendant bureaucracy risked inhibiting the responsiveness of special operations. There was undoubtedly a certain beauty to the simplicity with which many operations were mounted during the Desert War, with largely autonomous special forces capable of a swift response when directed by the highest echelons of theater command. The responsiveness of special operations in such a situation indeed contrasted favorably with the many bureaucratic hurdles that faced special operations from Britain at the same time. A December 1942 letter to Mountbatten (as CCO) draws particular attention to the seeming ease with which elements of the SBS (at the time attached to L Detachment SAS) had raided aerodromes in Crete in June of that year. These raids, the letter remarks with some apparent astonishment, were prepared in only three days, during which time aerial photographs were analyzed, plans formulated, and personnel found and then trained. The letter's author, Major Ian Collins (who later, as a lieutenant colonel, would serve with the SAS Brigade), believed that: "An interesting comparison might be made with the time it takes us to mount an operation [from Britain] . . . , and does, I think, need full consideration, especially when it is borne in mind that nearly all the mounting had to be arranged by one person."[151]

Contrasting the command and control arrangements of the SAS Brigade in 1944 with those of its SOE/OSS counterparts serves as further illustration of the possible ills of excessive "layers" of command and control. The SAS Brigade, working loosely under I Airborne Corps, can be considered to have been somewhat more efficient in mounting operations and securing the delivery of equipment and armaments to its parties in France than were some of the Jedburgh Teams or OSS OGs purely because it had a comparably smaller and simpler staff organization. This point notwithstanding, as M. R. D. Foot, a former intelligence officer of the SAS Brigade, reminds us: "SAS's problems were complicated enough—about a dozen different authorities had to consent to every new SAS venture."[152]

Given the number of competing interests, alongside the greater potential for political and diplomatic ramifications, the time taken to organize operations in certain theaters (such as from Britain before the opening of the second front) were understandably much greater than they were in more remote theaters. Special operations in the Aegean (a campaign that Winston Churchill initiated with the instruction "improvise and dare"[153]) or the Adriatic, for example, were capable of being mounted with comparative ease because of the existence of dedicated command branches that were able to operate in relative autonomy without excessive interference from actors with conflicting interests. As a rule, the complexity of mounting special operations was directly proportionate to the complexity of the strategic or operational situation that they sought to assist. Relative autonomy was really only possible in areas where special operations represented the dominant form of operation.

Thus, although the uniquely apposite circumstances of the Desert War highlighted the fact that special forces could be profitably employed autonomously and with very loose command mechanisms, as a whole, however, this arrangement was not practicable. As the Allies regained the initiative the autonomy of these units had to decline, not only to make best use of them in less suitable theaters, but also to prevent competition, tie these units into the regular battle, and prevent them from jeopardizing other operations. Strict control was difficult but essential. By the start of 1943, therefore, it was becoming widely accepted that the best manner for special forces to be used was to form dedicated command branches, responsible to the highest possible authority in theater, to provide for their administration and coordination. Such moves centralized (and to an extent conventionalized) their establishments, reduced animosity (via a reduction of their freebooting or "bandit" image), and led to the better tasking of these units, thereby increasing their potential value. Despite this, the more successful of these organizations still granted individual formations a notable margin of latitude for planning, training, and tactical control.

Commensurate with the transition and conventionalization of their role, the command and control of commando formations gradually became, at least in the British example, adapted to a more regular brigade organization, a move that increased their opportunity to undertake protracted deployments and operate in support of the conventional battle. Many British specialist formations were fortunate to have arisen under the patronage of COHQ, which, as an organization with a chair on the Chiefs of Staff Committee, could look after their interests directly and lobby for their employment. The lack of anything approaching the British COHQ and SS Brigade organization was clearly to the detriment of the command and control of most U.S. ranger-style formations. The American perception of elite light infantry units as temporary expedients largely precluded the establishment of any centralized or theater-level command infrastructure to provide for the command and administration of these units. The absence of clear arrangements through which higher commands could be advised on the tasks, capabilities, requirements, and availability of these units, as well as the lack of any formal mechanism through which their activities could be planned and vetted, would (as the next chapter will highlight) place unnecessary complications on the proper application of these formations. Such omissions were the most severe for the U.S. Army Rangers, afflicting both the First Special Service Force (FSSF) and Merrill's Marauders to a somewhat lesser extent because of their more "familiar" organizational structures. Of the U.S. ranger-style formations, it was only the 6th Rangers and USMC Raiders that were ultimately able to forge a workable integrated command and control system; the former because the unique conditions of theater and the patronage of General Walter Krueger, the latter, ironically, stemming from USMC motivations not to embrace the irregular but to conventionalize it.

In the field of special forces, however, U.S. command and control mechanisms were, as a whole, very effective and, in places, more efficient than those of the British. Their later entry into the Second World War enabled America to learn from the mistakes its ally had made before them. The U.S. induction to irregular warfare would avoid many of the pitfalls and problems that the British had previously experienced with the command and control of special forces; the United States was able to avoid the depredations of the "private army" and circumvent many of the interagency and interservice command and control complications. The existence of OSS as a body to centralize a large proportion of American special operations (not to mention intelligence activities too) was of the utmost importance for the effective command and control of many U.S. special forces, ensuring that the command infrastructure for operational units such as the OGs and MUs were actually in place *before* the units took to the field; this was something that, because of the exigencies surrounding their inception, was so often not the case with early British formations, which were subjected to much trial and error before a workable framework for their command would develop. The effective control of U.S. special forces would, of course, also follow a learning curve. Even with command infrastructure in place it would take time for the best arrangements to be established—a point well illustrated, for example, both by the frustrations that the OGs had working under the SO branch and by the late development of a unified UDT command. As a whole, however, it seems clear that this curve was significantly shallower for the United States than it had been for the British.

Even with the existence of organizations such as COHQ and OSS, the command and control of specialist formations during the Second World War was certainly hindered by the existence of many cumbersome and confused organizations, each with vested irregular interests, which coexisted uneasily in a climate of mutual suspicion and secrecy. Unity of command among these varied irregular groups, in the midst of the many other complexities facing the Allies in the Second World War, was, with the exception of the Southwest Pacific (due to Krueger's and MacArthur's sponsorship and direct control of units that they had explicitly authorized), an unreasonable and unobtainable goal. It would have required a massive effort, a total upheaval of early mechanisms—not to mention a clear idea of what specialist formations were for and what they could achieve— to have developed a unified (let alone Allied) "joint special operations command" or equivalent organization. Given the complex interservice and interorganizational problems to surmount, as well as the political and military complications of total war, these limitations are understandable. With no preexistent doctrine in place to guide how to control and use specialist elements, these had to be discovered almost by trial and error. The command and control of the Anglo-American specialist formations must be viewed as evolutionary, gradually becoming more efficient and effective as the war progressed. When it is considered that it was not until 1987 that both Britain and the United States established integrated joint-service organizations for the control of SOF (the British Special Forces directorate and the U.S. Special Operations Command), the achievements in developing complex command branches and control mechanisms for the nascent creations of the Second World War, well exemplified by the SOG and P Division or the extensive UDT organization, appear quite considerable.

CHAPTER 5

MISAPPLICATION, MISUSE, AND DISUSE

With one eye firmly on the past, Colin Gray made the observation that specialist formations are "probably uniquely vulnerable to misunderstanding and misapplication."[1] The study of Anglo-American specialist formations of the Second World War certainly seems to bear out this contention. Within the history—be it narrative, war diary, or biography—of almost every wartime commando or special forces formation there is mention, however fleeting, of their having been used inappropriately, tasked with undertaking an unsuitable role, or frustrated by unemployment or neglect. The "correct" use of specialist elements assumes many factors: a well-defined and clear-cut role and doctrine for their employment; a dedicated command and control organization to provide for their implementation; an educated consumer versed in, and amenable to, their employment; an equally informed or innovative practitioner; and apposite circumstances and means available for their use. The interaction between these variables, which gradually evolved over time and were subject to a notable margin of fluctuation, largely determined the manner in which specialist formations were utilized during the course of the war. This chapter examines where and why the misuse and disuse of specialist formations occurred and, in so doing, highlights how such occurrences were part of greater evolutionary processes governing their application.

Command Misapplication

The previous chapter illustrated two distinct limitations: first, that command preconceptions toward specialist elements could be rife with suspicion and animosity; and second, that the manner in which specialist elements were directed and controlled was seldom clear cut, well understood, or at least in their formative stages particularly efficient. These limitations alone could be of clear impediment to the "correct" application of specialist formations. Unless given a distinct carte blanche for autonomy of action (a rare but not unprecedented occurrence), specialist formations remained reliant upon sensible "tasking" for their use. This in turn had, as a cardinal requirement, direction from higher commanders who, if not adverse to their existence, were at least educated in their use. As Gray states: "The strategic utility of special operations forces depends at least as much on the imagination and competence of their political and military masters as it does on their tactical effectiveness."[2] One of the clearest reasons for the misuse or disuse of specialist formations stemmed, dislike and distrust aside, from widespread ignorance and misunderstanding among higher echelons as to the existence, purpose, and manner of employing irregular forces.

As nascent creations, an element of ignorance and confusion in the use of specialist formations was to be expected. There were no manuals at Camberley or Leavenworth (let alone at Sandhurst or West Point) to advise on their employment, and there was no guarantee that even after efforts were taken to instruct conventional elements in special operations—via such means as the establishment of dedicated command branches, the exchange of liaison officers, and the distribution of instructional materials—that these would be understood, let alone embraced. Ignorance, distrust, and misunderstanding led, at various stages, to misuse and misapplication.

The protracted and, at the time, much-derided deployments of Nos. 1 and 6 Commandos in the line during the North African campaign were, for example, in the opinion of the Commandos, caused by the "ignorance of all staffs to understand the roles of Commandos."[3] As Colonel Robert Laycock subsequently stated, force commanders "are only too willing to use Commandos to their best advantage during the initial landings, but . . . subsequently they regard them as unwanted and unnecessary units, with the result that Commandos are invariably allotted tasks for which they are neither organized, trained nor equipped, and which would be better undertaken by regular infantry."[4] These North African deployments were, however, both educational and symptomatic of a wider learning process about the use of these formations. Reflecting upon and understanding the difficulties that they had faced in such deployments, the Commando structure was accordingly altered to better deal with protracted deployments, and by the invasion of Sicily "the conception of Commandos had become definite and well-established. Their organization was well-tried and battle-proved; their capabilities well-known and their limitations appreciated."[5]

Similarly instructive was the misuse of the Long Range Desert Group (LRDG) in the summer of 1941, when, despite earlier successes, the unit was deployed in both tactical reconnaissance and static defensive roles at the Kufra Oasis, actions deemed inappropriate for a mobile long-range reconnaissance force. In the end, however, such deployments led to no great disaster, and according to David Lloyd Owen, "everyone learnt some excellent lessons from all this . . . the LRDG were seldom again used on tasks best carried out by reconnaissance aircraft or by armored cars."[6] Representations were made to GHQ to try and prevent such a misapplication of the LRDG from happening again, and General Auckinleck "went out of his way to assure . . . [Bagnold] that he would personally see that the unit wasn't mishandled and that we could count on him as a friend."[7] Patrol Commander Michael Crichton-Stuart went as far as stating that "much of the ultimate success of the LRDG could be traced, in retrospect, to the lessons of that 'wasted' summer of 1941."[8]

In some of their earlier deployments the Alamo Scouts of the U.S. Sixth Army also faced similar misapplication. For example, during deployment in Hollandia-Aitape in New Guinea in April 1944, I Corps, which had no experience in their methods, inappropriately used Scout teams in risky tactical combat patrols that merely duplicated the functions of existent regular reconnaissance units.[9] However, as had been the case with the LRDG in 1941, this misapplication was educational and led in part both to the development of more efficient practices for the employment of Scout teams and to the creation of a special staff under Sixth Army's G-2 (Intelligence) Section to coordinate their deployments.

The extent to which misuse was part of the learning process was, however, reliant on the willingness, or ability, of the broader military organization to learn and adapt. Despite having faced problems similar to the Commandos' during their evolution of role during the North African campaign, the U.S. Army Rangers were never able to adapt either doctrinally or organizationally as well as did the Commandos. The constant refusal to make anything more than tactical concessions (in such areas as support weaponry), the rejection of a "Ranger Force" headquarters, and the concomitant absence of a Ranger doctrine, a formal statement outlining their capabilities and limitations, undoubtedly paved the way toward the annihilation of the 1st and 3rd Ranger Battalions during the Battle of Cisterna in 1944. The absence of a proper "Ranger Force" headquarters prevented long-range planning and offered no advice on whether an "assignment is a proper one for Rangers."[10] Their perpetual provisional status saw to it that commanders had no guide toward the employment of Rangers and, consequently, "were left with only a vague, intuitive sense of the purpose of such troops."[11] As a result, the Rangers were prone to face "mission creep," as commanders were inclined to deploy them in the conventional manner with which they were versed.

With these limitations in place, misapplication was made all the more likely. However, as Jeff Stewart has accurately stated, "In order to declare misuse of the Rangers [at Cisterna], it must first be established what their proper use would be. This was never done."[12] While a nighttime infiltration mission the likes of that planned at Cisterna should have fallen within Ranger capabilities, as the 1st Rangers had exhibited in North Africa, by the start of 1944 casualties sustained in protracted deployments in the front lines had degraded the mean quality and experience of the Rangers and made failure at Cisterna all the more likely. Cisterna cannot, however, be blamed on command ignorance. At the time of the battle the 6615th Ranger Force, Provisional, was under the control of General Truscott's 3rd Infantry Division, and neither Truscott, who had first conceived of the Rangers and "knew more about their capabilities and limitations than any other general officer," nor Darby, their commander, actually opposed the deployment; both, as Truscott himself would reflect, "considered the mission a proper one, which should have been well within the capabilities of these fine soldiers."[13]

Misuse thus did not only stem from ill-informed or sceptical higher commanders but also, at times, from the personnel and leaders of the units themselves. Special operations being an emergent genus, not even its practitioners were, from the outset, fully versed in their art or optimum manner of employment. Gray has drawn attention to instances where "opportunities for special operations were arguably lost because no one, including the special warriors themselves, were sufficiently unconventional in their thinking. . . . Unconventional war is a state of mind as well as a mission and a distinctive set of tactics."[14] Certainly a number of commanders charged with leading specialist formations did not adequately understand, or even believe in, their unconventional mandate, and accepting employment in a more conventional manner, were disinclined to push for tasking in the same manner that a more unorthodox character, or an individual better versed in irregular warfare, might have done. Despite the proficiency and professional qualities of specialist formations, it is quite fallacious to assume that all involved, higher commanders and practitioners alike, immediately realized, understood, or cared about the best manner for their employment. The latitude given to certain special forces commanders to perform autonomous acts presupposed that they had the "necessary strategic, tactical and man-management skills"; as Roger Ford assessed in reference to the SAS Brigade in France, "Some did; some did not, and the results their operations produced reflected their abilities."[15]

Such problems were evident in the ranger example; an undoubted concomitant both to the widespread American perception of specialist formations as being fleeting and provisional expedients and to the general absence of "errant captains" or "founding fathers" as seen among the British examples. William Orlando Darby, commander of the 1st, 3rd, and 4th Ranger Battalions, although a justifiably lauded fighting leader, was arguably one such character. Darby had a "conventional outlook" and was, in the opinion of David Hogan, "hardly the maverick one so often finds in command of a special unit. Lacking commitment to a concept of special operations, he perceived his unit more as an elite fighting force than as a formation with a unique mission, and he does not seem to have opposed the use of his men as line infantry," and as has been noted, he did not object to the use of his force at Cisterna.[16] Similar cases could be advanced regarding Merritt Edson of the 1st Raider Battalion, who, like Darby, was undoubtedly a solid fighting leader but lacked the unorthodox streak possessed by Carlson, his counterpart in the 2nd Raider Battalion; equally pronounced is the case of Brigadier Merrill of the Marauders, who was neither unorthodox in outlook nor physically up to the challenge of leading the Marauders in the field (having had two heart attacks while doing so). Furthermore, his close association with General Stilwell did not make him the best man to fight in the Marauders' corner when lobbying for correct employment.[17]

These issues were compounded by the fact that, being perceived as temporary units, many American commanders had no path for advancement within irregular communities. Just as the "errant captain" was foreign to the inception of American specialist formations, once they had proven their mettle William Darby, Robert Frederick, Earl Rudder, Evans Carlson et al. were, albeit often reluctantly, each promoted out of specialist formations and returned to the command of conventional units. Within U.S. specialist formations there were few comparable figures to the Stirling, Courtney, or Churchill brothers who each forged careers at the helm of specialist formations, nor the likes of Orde Wingate, Michael Calvert, Brian Franks, or Derek Mills-Roberts, each of whom, in addition to having amassed practical experience in the field, subsequently commanded and directed these formations at a higher level. There was certainly no American wartime equivalent to Robert Laycock, for example, a man who, in addition to commanding some of the first Commandos, participated in such actions as the evacuation of Crete in May 1941 and the ill-fated "Rommel raid" of November 1941 (after which he was one of only two men able to escape back to Allied lines) and also commanded, on two separate occasions, early attempts at nominal Commando brigades, before eventually assuming the post of chief of combined operations (CCO) that placed him at the helm of all Commandos and ancillary units. Because of both the absence of an equivalent to COHQ, or the SS Brigade, as well as the stigma attached to temporary formations, there was little American equivalent to the "special forces community" of the British (aside from that of OSS, which itself was seen as provisional and treated with suspicion), and their ability to learn lessons and develop clear doctrines suffered accordingly.[18]

Social connections, elite patronage, and the "old boy network" were clearly evident among a number of British specialist formations; with the familiar school tie or membership of the right gentleman's club supplementing many more formal recruitment practices for officers in the earlier stages of the war. As Commando lieutenant Ronald Swayne reflected in reference to the early Commandos, "Commandos tended to be clubs. When we had a vacancy, you could put up suggestions to the colonel. Opinions would be sought, like the blackball system, and each Commando had its own character. No. 8 Commando—Laycock's outfit—had apparently been recruited from a bay window in White's Hotel."[19] OSS officer Franklin Lindsay echoed this sentiment when making a reflection about Fitzroy Maclean, his British colleague in Yugoslavia: "All his officers appeared to be old friends and several had been together in North Africa fighting against Rommel's forces. These British officers who were drawn to irregular operations seemed not only to have been together in early wartime operations but also to have had many close school and family ties. In contrast, in three years overseas I had met only one person I had known before the war."[20]

The Maclean example is particularly pronounced, the "casually opportunist" manner in which he first orchestrated the dispatch of specialist formations to the island of Vis providing a fine illustration of the British social system at work within irregular fields. In late 1943 military activities in support of Tito in Yugoslavia were dominated by a special forces "educated" group of people. Maclean, who had served with the SAS in the Desert War, personally assessed the validity of mounting special operations and raids from Vis with his former SAS colleagues Vivian Street and Randolph Churchill, son of the Prime Minister; and in late 1943 it was he who arranged the deployment of Lieutenant Colonel Jack Churchill's No. 2 Commando to the island on the basis of casually meeting Jack's brother and CO, Brigadier Thomas Churchill (commanding 2nd SS Brigade), at a New Year's Eve party in Molfetta, Italy.[21] All arrangements were put in place before Maclean approached General Alexander for authorization; Alexander subsequently lent him his own airplane to fly to Tehran to discuss this scheme with the Prime Minister.[22]

Within higher circles too the value of preexistent professional and social relationships are clearly discernible in the British example. By means of illustration, when commanding the SS Brigade in Sicily, Robert Laycock—himself well known for recruiting officers from within his wide social circle—reflected that the Commandos were "extremely lucky" that he personally knew each of the Corps commanders: Oliver Lesse of XXX Corps had been adjutant of the Eton College Officer Training Corps when Laycock had attended the school; Miles Dempsey of XIII Corps was Laycock's platoon officer when he had attended Sandhurst; and Brian Horrocks of X Corps had been an instructor at the Staff College when both he and Thomas Churchill (subsequently commanding 2nd SS Brigade) had attended.[23] Aside from the initial Ivy League–heavy recruiting practices of OSS and the "Roosevelt connection" of the 2nd Raiders, there were few comparable examples of such informal social networks at play behind American specialist formations.[24]

Misuse as a Result of Exigency

Misuse based on command antipathy or ignorance was, however, less prevalent than misuse as a result of necessity. Hard-pressed and under-reinforced commanders who had a group of well-trained and experienced men under their charge were often only too willing to thrust specialist units into the breach if expedient, almost regardless of the role they were being asked to perform. In the event of an unfavorable or deteriorating situation on the ground, specialist forces could merely represent a source of readily available manpower. The potential for forces to be misused as such was pronounced, and it would take great wisdom, foresight, and confidence for commanders not to employ specialist elements incorrectly in desperate circumstances, to not ruin a thoroughbred by having it plough the field in absence of a mule. As Scott McMichael observed, "Once a unit arrives in theater—its special capabilities notwithstanding—its availability irresistibly tempts commanders to employ it."[25] Gray similarly contended that "because they are unusually well endowed with warrior virtues, commanders tend to use elite units—and special operations forces—much as teenagers drive sports cars and with similar and predictable results."[26] The attachment of a specialist formation to a field command could result in the force swiftly becoming overworked as the command becomes overreliant on the unit, utilizing its willing and capable "warriors" for every difficult assignment, including more routine activities (such as tactical reconnaissance and combat patrols) that conventional forces would have been more than capable of undertaking.[27]

Such instances occurred almost as soon as the first varieties of specialist units reached the field. The desperate situation on the ground in Norway in 1940, and an absence of alternative resources with which to tackle it, had soon dispelled any notion that the Independent Companies would be able to act as guerrillas, and they were almost immediately used in line infantry duties. The fate of Nos. 1 and 6 Commandos in North Africa was, in a similar vein, partially blamed on an "obvious temporary shortage of Infantry troops in the forward areas."[28] As General Kenneth Anderson, commanding the First Army, wrote to Mountbatten as the Commandos were withdrawn from North Africa, "I know I misused them, strained them to the utmost and kept them far too long. But we were hard pressed in those days, and every single man had to do the job of ten without rest or respite. The Commandos naturally never complained and always fought brilliantly. . . . Alas their losses were heavy. . . . I was sorry to lose them, but glad to be able at last to let them go."[29] The similarly inappropriate use of the 1st Rangers for much of this campaign principally occurred because, as far as General Terry Allen of the 1st Infantry Division (to whom the Rangers were attached) was concerned, "the Rangers were proven troops that were available. Faced with an uncertain battlefield situation, he would not hesitate to throw them into the breach."[30]

Stilwell's mishandling of the Marauders was also comparable. Colonel Charles Hunter, second in command of the unit (but often de facto leader in light of Merrill's ill health), reflected at the end of their campaign that "the unit had been badly misused and had suffered unnecessarily" and placed the blame on the "personality and personal ambition" of Stilwell.[31] The ultimate abuse of the Marauders stemmed from overemployment. Stilwell was too reliant on the unit and used it to the point of decimation. As the only U.S. ground force at his disposal, Stilwell saw the Marauders as a source of dependable personnel that could be used to shore up and rectify deficiencies in his Chinese forces. Such was its perceived value to him that by appointing Merrill, one of his most trusted officers, to the unit's command Stilwell had actively sought to maintain a hand in its planning and to actually prevent its misuse.[32] The first operation of the Maurauders, against Walawbum, was thus conducted as intended: it was a successful medium-range penetration that cost the unit few casualties and, most important, saw it be swiftly relieved by Chinese forces.[33] However, in later operations Stilwell's increasing reliance upon the Marauders would mean his employing it in a series of costly blocking operations without having granted the men adequate time to rest or recover their strength.

Yet in spite of Hunter's claims, Stilwell's overreliance upon and subsequent misuse of the Marauders stemmed principally from the political imperative he faced to keep the only U.S. ground forces in theater employed and to demonstrate to coalition members America's commitment to the war in Burma.[34] It would have been quite unthinkable for Stilwell to have withdrawn the Marauders while continuing to remain reliant on British and Chinese formations under his charge. As Gary Bjorge has asserted, "Without Galahad to help hold up the coalition banner of shared suffering, the combined force would have lacked a crucial unifying element and a catalyst for action"; the unit was thus a victim not so much of hubris as it was of "the exigencies and requirements of coalition warfare and combined operations."[35]

The squandering of a highly trained and experienced corps d'elite in a role that they were neither prepared nor equipped for was, of course, ultimately not cost effective; however, should adverse circumstances require their committal in either alternate roles or in less apposite conditions, the use of specialist formations in such a capacity was not necessarily improper. The use of commando and ranger formations in nonspecialized or inappropriate roles because of operational imperatives was both common and, at times, quite understandable. To be cost effective, specialist formations cannot exist in isolation and must remain subservient to the direction and requirements of the greater campaigns they assist. For example, although the use of Nos. 7 and 50/52 (ME) Commandos to help cover the evacuation of Crete in May 1941 was a role for which they were neither trained—nor, most important, equipped for—and was thus one that ultimately caused the two Commandos significant loss, it was, nevertheless, a role that they undertook with determination and was of value in aiding the evacuation of a number of other personnel from the island. Although both unplanned and expensive, this deployment, so often considered inappropriate, was arguably of more value than these Commandos' earlier "correct," but failed, actions at Kastelorizo in February or Bardia in April 1941. While costly, the use of specialist troops in extremis was not a true misuse; and gradually, particularly following the commando transition in role, the use of specialist personnel in a "fire brigade" or strategic reserve role became more common. In Italy, for example, both the Rangers and the First Special Service Force (FSSF) attached to the Fifth Army were particularly prone to be used as such, the Fifth Army's shortage of personnel meaning that General Mark Clark "could not afford to hold special formations in reserve until suitable missions presented themselves."[36]

The 6th Ranger Battalion was, for a variety of reasons, considered unique among its counterparts as having been the only Ranger battalion to have not been "misused" as line infantry at some stage during the war.[37] Despite this, had the Sixth Army been faced with a desperate operational situation, such as had occurred at Kasserine Pass in Tunisia or on Edson's Ridge in Guadalcanal, or a crippling shortage of personnel, as encountered by the Fifth Army in Italy or the 21 Army Group in northwestern Europe, it seems likely that the 6th Rangers would have been used in any manner possible to alleviate the situation, even if that meant so-called misuse in conventional tasks. To have done so would have been quite correct. Higher and unit commanders alike seemed to have had an appreciation of this. Despite having consistently lobbied for the independent and specialist employment of the Commandos, Laycock clearly appreciated that *in extremis* Commandos could, and should, be used in any capacity. In 1943 he wrote: "SS troops should never be given tasks which could equally be well carried out by Infantry unless the Commander can satisfy himself that . . . There are no other troops available . . . [or that] he, or superior or neighboring Commanders, will not require them for more important specialized tasks at a later stage in the campaign."[38] General Bradley displayed similar logic writing, in reference to parachute troops, that they are "too expensively trained to be spent as conventional doughboys unless an emergency warrants their employment in this way."[39]

Much more damning, and potentially far more damaging than the use of a commando-style light infantry force in a conventional infantry manner when necessity demanded, was the deployment of smaller special forces units in similar circumstances. Few examples illustrate this contention better than the employment of an experienced and intelligence-oriented LRDG squadron in an assault to recapture the island of Levitha in the Aegean in October 1943, a task for which they were untrained, unequipped, and unsuited. The LRDG was desperately opposed to mounting the operation, but "no appeal to the GOC [General Henry Maitland Wilson] would rescind his [somewhat nebulous] orders that it was vital to the Navy that the enemy garrison should be liquidated."[40] As LRDG officer David Lloyd Owen reflected, "We knew the raid was pointless, we knew it violated all the principles by which our small hit-and-run attacks were guided and we had no confidence in its direction by commanders who had few ideas how to handle us." He believed it was a "wicked and misplaced" political move to "to regain by a spectacular success the confidence that Cairo had lost in the direction of the Aegean battle."[41] With no prior reconnaissance having been conducted, and in the face of local German command of the air, the raid was a disaster. Of the fifty men in the raid, forty-one experienced and trained specialists were lost, killed, or captured, more casualties sustained in one operation than the unit had lost in the three years prior. Soon after this unnecessary and costly operation, the LRDG was to suffer another great blow when tasked, alongside elements of the Special Boat Squadron (SBS), again inappropriately—but more understandably because of operational, if not strategic, necessity—with forming part of the garrison on Leros. The fall of the garrison, in November 1943, led to the small unit taking further heavy losses: ten men were killed, including the unit's commander, Jake Easonsmith, and a nearly crippling over one hundred men captured (although a proportion of these would subsequently escape captivity and return to the unit). As the War Diary of the LRDG acknowledged, the garrison duties on Leros were "a gross misuse of LRDG Patrols who were trained and equipped for special tasks, and not for mere garrison duties the job of the normal infantryman."[42]

Clearly, therefore, being held in high regard (which by this stage the LRDG certainly, and quite rightly, was) was no protection against misuse. It could even exacerbate the situation. A unit's prior successes, its reputation or aura of elitism, could provoke false estimations of its abilities. The fate of Ranger Force at Cisterna can be blamed, at least in part, on its track record of success and "their leaders' [including Darby's] absolute faith in the Rangers to accomplish any mission."[43] As if to emphasize this point, General Bradley's memoirs recall that the Rangers "formed as professional combat unit as existed in the American army. . . . the Rangers became so competent that by the war's end I honestly believe there was nothing they could not do."[44] Perception of misuse of specialist formations is, however, often tinged with hindsight and generally follows either tactical failure or heavy casualties. Levitha was an inappropriate role for the LRDG, but had it carried the day and had the attack been a success with little or few casualties sustained, it may well have been regarded as another notable achievement for the versatile formation.

There is a thin line between success and failure in special operations, and even heavy casualties are not necessarily indicative of misapplication: some of the more famous and indeed lauded "correct" deployments of specialist formations (such as No. 2 Commando's March 1942 St. Nazaire raid or the 5th Ranger Battalion's capture of the Irsch-Zerf road in February 1945) could result in quite startling casualties. An officially prepared GHQ MEF appraisal of the Aegean campaign reflected the perception that the Commandos were "in fact expendable and the rule guiding their employment is largely 'Is this operation worth the number of casualties it will cost?'"[45] Such a mentality was certainly a concern. In July 1943 Lieutenant Colonel Bruce Lumsden of the newly formed No. 41 (RM) Commando expressed resentment of an attitude he believed to be prevalent in the SS Brigade, "that unless a Commando Unit has heavy casualties the job is not any good," and gave voice to fears that his unit would be "used in a pointless Operation evolved for the benefit of the Special Service Brigade rather than the furtherance of the job in hand."[46]

The loss of personnel, even proportionally horrendous losses, in the right application was rarely, however, considered inappropriate so long as the ends justified the means. This was an understanding equally applicable to special forces, as perfectly highlighted by a 1943 statement regarding the employment of the SBS (Section): "Forlorn hopes should not be undertaken and that the lives of valuable and highly trained men should not be endangered unless there is reasonable chance of direct success and unless the objective is worthwhile."[47] Furthermore, for special operations, as Gray has asserted: "Tactical failure at the right time, in the right way, and for the right reasons can amount to strategic success."[48] For example, while the June 1944 raid on the island of Brač (Operation Flounced) was a costly "tactical failure" for the Yugoslav partisans, Commandos, and OSS OGs taking part, it did, nevertheless, succeed in its objective of diverting almost 2,000 German soldiers to the Dalmatian coast and away from the offensive on the mainland that was threatening Tito at this time. In the opinion of Michael McConville, at the time an RM Commando subaltern, the raid represented a "worthwhile contribution to the achievement of the overall strategic objective."[49]

Disuse

If losses and certain inappropriate additional duties, such as acting in a "fire brigade" exigency capacity, were to be expected, tolerated, and even made legitimate, what was potentially more damning than use in a nonspecialized role was disuse: holding back valuable formations for an indeterminable amount of time until apposite circumstances for employment developed. There is a fine balance between potentially wasting specialist elements in inappropriate use and negating their value entirely by letting them wither on the vine. Constant deployment of specialist formations was an unattainable goal. To remain "special" they often required at least some (occasionally much) time to recruit and train—and, in the event of casualties, time to refit, reinforce, and recuperate. Yet in instances where specialist formations were underemployed for long periods of time, it is possible to argue that any employment, even if inappropriate, would have been of more value than their not having been used at all. After all, the value of a specialist unit remains proportionate to its use.

A fine example of the ills of disuse is seen with the Middle East Commando (later known as the 1st SS Regiment). Principally recruited from the remnants of the "Layforce" Commandos, predominantly No. 51 (ME) Commando, the unit suffered from an identity crisis, lacked any clearly defined role, and "never had the *esprit de corps* and cohesion of its forebears."[50] Initially it was thought the Commando could be incorporated into the regional SOE pool as a "fifth column force," but such plans came to nought.[51] In March 1942, in an effort to gain employment, "C" Squadron of the Regiment was attached to the LRDG but "met with many misfortunes" because, as the unit's commander stated, "the men of this Regiment have never received training in this type of work and are entirely unsuited for it."[52] In a similar proposal of May 1942 it was suggested that "A" Squadron of the Regiment be deployed in "short or medium range reconnaissance and sabotage activities."[53] This again did not transpire. Inactivity and comparative failures gave ammunition to detractors, while many of the "not unnaturally ... depressed and restless" personnel in the unit applied for transfer to the various other special forces in theater.[54] The 1st SS Regiment was continually frustrated and never able to find suitable employment. Its fundamental problem was one of the unnecessary retention of a Commando-modeled formation in a theater unsuited to its use. One year before its eventual disbandment Laycock had warned that in the Middle East there were simply "too many commandos, and not enough work."[55] GHQ MEF had similarly advised that it was "wasteful to keep first-class material in units whose opportunities for employment are exceedingly rare"; General Auchinleck likening this disuse to "keeping a valuable cow and milking it once or twice a year."[56] Despite these concerns, the regiment was left to languish for over a year, undertaking little worthwhile deployment, before its inevitable disbandment in September 1942 paved the way, almost in Darwinesque terms, for the expansion of L Detachment into the 1st SAS Regiment.

Wartime debate over the relative merits of use over the nonuse of specialist formations is nowhere better illustrated than in the high-level discussions that occurred over the employment of the Canadian-American FSSF. In September 1942 plans for the force to be used against Norway, as had originally been intended, were postponed indefinitely. Rather than disband the formation, General Marshall, Field Marshal Dill, and the force itself all pressured for deployment, in almost any capacity, so as to maintain the unit's esprit de corps, which risked becoming eroded with inaction.[57] Mountbatten and Churchill, among others, on the other hand, were keen that the force's skills in Arctic warfare not be squandered in unrelated deployments, believing that "to yield to impatience seems most unsound militarily" and would, in the opinion of Lieutenant General Frank M. Andrews, be a "grave mistake."[58] With no such deployments on the horizon, however, and the force reportedly "growing stale," the only options available became either deployment in an alternative environment or disbandment. Yet to disband would have had been a total waste of an expensively and intensely trained cohesive unit. While the force's eventual deployments against Kiska, Italy, and France were not as initially envisaged, they each show the merits of use, even if somewhat removed from original intention, over nonuse.

Conversely, withholding smaller special forces that had undergone extensive training from deployment could well be considered preferable to risking their misuse in inappropriate roles or circumstances. A solid example of this is provided by the combat swimmers of the Sea Reconnaissance Unit (SRU), who, following tropical water training in Nassau, were withheld from numerous coldwater deployments from Britain and in the Mediterranean. To have deployed COHQ's only tropically oriented combat swimmers in an ad hoc role (such as clearing mines in French ports) in Europe would have been wholly inappropriate, and it was quite correct that the unit's time was spent in supplementary training until it could be sent to the Far East.[59] Similar restraint of employment was shown with the Combined Operations Pilotage Parties (COPPs) sent to SEAC in early 1944. For over six months these units were widely unemployed, both because of the lack of information about their value and there having been little opportunity for large-scale amphibious operations in this theater at that time. There was concern that if this unemployment continued, the units would be used for "very elementary reconnaissance and pilotage work . . . nothing like commensurate with their training and qualifications," a course of action that would have led to unnecessary risks and would have lowered their "standard and morale."[60] The OSS Maritime Unit (MU) groups deployed to this theater were equally reluctant to undertake nonspecialist occupations for the sake of employment.[61] In light of the potential for future large-scale amphibious operations in this theater, however, the disbandment or transfer of such units was not an option, and they, like the SRU in Britain, were thus prescribed more "imaginative training" so as to retain their standards and keep them occupied until more suitable tasks opened up.[62]

There remains a world of difference between small maritime special forces and large commando formations, like the FSSF, being left idle for extended periods. The forty-man SRU, for example, could be withheld from deployment without being a significant drain on resources and manpower and without hard-up commanders looking to use it; yet to have withheld the deployment of the 2,500 first-rate men of the FSSF for any period of time would have been widely impracticable. Despite this, with pressing exigencies and no opportunity for niche deployment on the horizon, the use of special forces with very specific roles in alternate, yet still related, occupations could also be of value. For example MU Group No. 1 (also known as Group "A"), which had trained in Nassau with the SRU in an offensive-oriented combat swimmer role, was sent to Hawaii in June 1944 and asked to perform a rubber-boat beach reconnaissance of Saipan. Although the group's commander, Lieutenant Arthur O. Choate, objected to the task, stating that it was "unfair to use us to carry out this operation," his objections were, quite reasonably, overruled.[63] At this time in the Central Pacific there was a shortage of personnel capable of undertaking such roles, and the group's specialization remained applicable to the task being asked of them. Furthermore, it was very unlikely that the group would have had opportunity to carry out its original offensive swimming mandate in this theater at that time.

The effective deployment of the smaller and more "niche" formations was certainly hindered by the lack of knowledge about their precise specialties. It was a problem exacerbated by the degree of secrecy, both inevitable and enforced, that surrounded a number of these units. For example, in early 1943 Mountbatten released a paper to theater commanders that outlined the organization and function of the COPPs in an effort to help educate them about their employment.[64] It later transpired, however, that this "TOP SECRET and PERSONAL" document was not circulated beyond the commanders in chief to whom it was addressed, "with the result that planning staffs were not given a clear idea of what a COPP could do."[65] Although the development of dedicated command structures certainly helped educate higher commanders in the potentials of specialist formations, their efforts could still be thwarted by the needs of secrecy and security. Colonel H. T. Tollemache, commanding the Small Operations Group (SOG) in the Far East, believed that this led to "quite straightforward work being considered as 'Black Art' not only by the units themselves, but also by the staffs of the regular formations who could best make use of them."[66] Such problems could be further aggravated by the nomenclature of units and their taking, on occasion, deliberately innocuous names for cover. One can hardly blame poorly informed commanders for wishing to use the Special Air Service in an airborne role or the Alamo Scouts for tactical reconnaissance; wondering what possible utility a Long Range Desert Group could have in the mountains and coastlines of Yugoslavia or Greece; or let alone trying to fathom what duties the Royal Marine Boom Patrol Detachment, Beach Jumpers, or Popski's Private Army had been created to fulfill.

Opportunities and Means for Employment

Disuse was not always a conscious decision, however, and the correct employment of specialist elements required both opportunity and means. Material considerations could be a significant impediment. Most evidently, aircraft and shipping had to be available in sufficient quantities to facilitate not only insertion and exfiltration but also supply and reinforcement. Early Commando operations from both Britain and in the Mediterranean and later operations in the Far East were often hamstrung and confined to a small scale because of an absence of landing craft and supporting shipping (or the unwillingness to risk the loss of what was available).[67] Such shortages could hinder even minor raids, as was found by both the Small Scale Raiding Force (SSRF) in Britain in 1942 and the OSS MU more generally throughout 1944.[68] Competition for resources obviously increased with the commencement of larger and more protracted operations. The invasion of France, in particular, saw the Jedburghs, Operational Groups (OGs), and SAS Brigade all struggling for their allotment of dispatch and supply from the limited numbers of available aircraft.[69] Despite having the declared role of being a "strategic reserve" that could be used subsequent to, and in support of, the main invasions, many of these formations thought that they were committed too late, believing that the delay in their dispatch (which in some cases occurred up to two and a half months after the invasion) was a clear impediment to their effectiveness. The clearest reasons for these delays were material shortages in "lift," poor weather conditions, political considerations, unimaginative tasking, and—as was noted previously—the lack of a unified control system for the disparate groups.[70]

Many of those groups dropped into France as late as August 1944 (particularly those in support of Operation Anvil/Dragoon against the South of France) never had time to adequately perform the role for which they had trained before being overrun by advancing Allied forces. Subsequently, many remained adamant that they would have achieved more had they been dispatched earlier. Jedburgh Team Cecil, for example, which deployed on August 25 to the Aube area, concluded that "we feel it was greatly to be regretted that a very good job was prevented from being an even better one by the failure to send us on, or even before D-Day, by which time we were already fully trained and prepared."[71] Major H. N. Marten, commanding Jedburgh Team Veganin, concurred, stating that the timing of deployment "has been probably the most criminal matter in the whole history of the Jeds.... for some reason the majority of the teams were left waiting until the very last moment before they were sent in and it was impossible for them to do any good whatsoever. ... It was a lamentable appreciation by the higher authorities to delay this departure."[72] Similar claims were made by the OSS OGs. Major Alfred T. Cox, commanding the OGs in the South of France, stated that "all are in unanimous agreement that the teams should have been put into FRANCE much earlier than they were. Everyday spent training the Maquis brought increased dividends in their combat effectiveness."[73] General Frederick Browning, GOC Airborne Corps, would support this opinion when he stated that the "last minute distribution of arms only results in badly trained MAQUIS taking part in actions and being more nuisance than they are worth."[74]

Even those groups dropped earlier were prone to suggest that they would have been better employed up to three months before the invasion of France. Lieutenant William H. McKenzie III, commanding OG Louise believed his operation should have been "laid on during March," as they could "have played a greater part in training and organising Maquis."[75] Roger Ford's later historical appraisal of the Jedburghs shares such perceptions, stating that if there was an "operational flaw, it was the decision . . . not to insert at least some of them before the invasion got underway."[76] Such comments, easy with hindsight, are nevertheless still not necessarily correct. It should not be overlooked that, as SOE's history of the Jedburghs reminds us,

> the Jedburgh Teams [and OGs] formed part of an operational *reserve* of trained personnel. Where the work of interfering with rail and telecommunications could be carried out by existing Resistance Groups, there was nothing to be gained in committing this reserve. On the other hand, there was good deal to be lost by encouraging clandestine Resistance to take overt action before the time was ripe, inviting heavy repressive action from the enemy in areas it was vital to him to control, and risking the breakup of the Resistance Groups.[77]

Although sometimes delayed, which certainly had implications in terms of overall effectiveness, the majority of these formations were not misused; the situation on the ground had to be ripe for the committal of such groups. The dispatch of special forces before the commencement of the invasion would have been costly; they would likely have achieved little and, if detected, risked compromising Resistance networks and invasion schemes alike. Despite this, in alternative theaters where the enemy was less dense and terrain more favorable, early dispatch does seem to have been beneficial. Those Jedburghs later deployed to Burma, for instance, considered that they were more effective precisely because they had more time to operate.[78] It should be noted, however, that Burma was an active theater when these teams were dispatched, and thus much of the complications that prevented dispatch before the invasion of France did not apply.

In a similar vein, although the later actions of the SAS Brigade in northwestern Europe (which were more akin to a conventional reconnaissance force) have been criticized for being a misuse of a "strategic" force in a "tactical" role, this employment, in light of the rapidity of the Allied advance, remained the best use of the SAS at that time. Any "traditional" SAS role in depth (presuming it could be planned and mounted in time) would have been impracticable, and it was believed "doubtful" that operations, mounted with no partisan infrastructure in place and in regions with an assumed 100 percent hostile German population, would have achieved results commensurate with casualties. Such operations would likely have been a waste of resources and would merely have served as a diversion from the main effort.[79] The possible exception, however, might well have been to have made use of such units during Operation Market Garden, to have potentially furthered the advance of XXX Corps or have harassed German counterattacks on the beleaguered airborne units.[80] On the whole, however, at this late stage of the war in Europe to have deployed the SAS in the "strategic" role in depth, for which they had lobbied for some time, would have been a grave misuse. Tactical deployment, so often derided, became the only option lest the SAS face disuse or disbandment.

The specter of disbandment or disuse was a threatening proposition for irregular warriors who, in frustration, were prone to consent, albeit often reluctantly, to almost any task so as to retain their esprit de corps and justify their existence to sceptical superiors. Specialist forces were, as Eric Morris states, "vulnerable to a form of moral blackmail which meant they took on tasks and missions which they were singularly ill-equipped to handle."[81] In fighting for a permanent establishment for his Rangers, William Darby, for example, was unwilling to take too firm a stance against the misapplication of his force lest he denigrate his own arguments about its flexibility and value and thus risk hastening the disbandment of his command.[82] Similarly illustrative of these pressures is L Detachment SAS's disastrous debut operation against the Tmimi/Gazala airfields, which was mounted despite indications that atrocious weather would make successful parachute drops impossible. David Stirling was, however, conscious that if the operation was called off it would not only invalidate his sentiments about the flexibility of the SAS idea (which he had sold partly on the very basis of the constant cancellation of Commando operations in theater) but would also give his detractors the opportunity "to pervert the reasoning for calling off the job and use it as a lever either to have the force disbanded or to make life even more difficult subsequently."[83]

Once units had met with success such pressures could actually increase, leading to the expectation of repeated results. Perhaps it was in such a vein that Stirling, conceivably with an eye to gaining a regimental establishment, agreed to take part in the costly September 1942 raid on Benghazi, an operation that he later claimed sinned against every principle of the SAS.[84] A few months later, with the desire to guarantee the SAS a role in future campaigns, Stirling also pushed his unit hard in operations ahead of the Eighth Army into Tunisia which, in light of more difficult terrain, hostile Arabs, and a more concentrated enemy, were more costly and ultimately led to his own capture. Similar pressures "to keep the SAS on active service" propelled them, much later still, to accept the role of performing tactical reconnaissance for 21 Army Group's advance into Germany.[85] Such demands were, in the words of Julian Thompson,

> a hazard which faces all "special" troops, who by their temperament usually hanker after action. As an advance nears its objective, the amount of suitable "real estate" available for behind the lines operations may be reduced. So the special troops in question will be tempted to take whatever roles, or targets, are on offer. To have left such skilled troops sitting on the sidelines in an advance, where reconnaissance is always at a premium, would have been unthinkable; nor would the SAS have wanted this.[86]

Toward the end of the war, in spite of better command mechanisms and staff practices, there remained the definite prospect of misuse occurring because of an often mutual (consumer and practitioner) desire to keep these formations employed, almost regardless of the circumstances, in order to reap the benefit of their training. In March 1945 the Norwegian Special Operations group (NORSO; formerly the "Norwegian" OGs), commanded by Major William Colby (who would go on to serve as director of central intelligence in 1973), finally able to operate in Norway, mounted Operation Rype to target bridges and disrupt German rail communications. The mission, although achieving its goals, was costly: horrendous weather and inexperienced aircrews caused one aircraft transporting elements of the group to crash into a mountain, with the loss of all on board, and another to mistakenly drop its personnel into Sweden. A member of the OSS planning staff, Lieutenant Colonel Leflesen, commented that in this regard the NORSO mission "represents a sad chapter in the history of our activity, one which I am constrained to add might have been avoided."[87] Although a comparison could be drawn to L Detachment's first operation, also costly in men and machines, the SAS operation, albeit unsuccessful, taken as it was in the desperate days of the 1941 Crusader offensive, was perhaps a risk worth taking. Operation Rype, on the other hand, although technically successful, did not warrant the risks of losing such well-trained and experienced men in the destruction of nonvaluable assets in a strategic backwater at this late stage of the war. Though Rype flew the flag of American participation in the liberation of Norway, a feat well reported by the Norwegian press, on a broader level this mission is indicative of waste and of deployment for the sake of employment.

Throughout the course of the Second World War the experiences of the Anglo-American specialist formations were quite mixed. Although often created with a specific role or speciality in mind, many units would, at least at some point, either find themselves employed in circumstances or undertaking roles that they were not prepared for or experience being withheld from deployment for protracted periods of time. The "correct" use of irregular formations had broad requirements that assumed (1) the existence of informed consumers and practitioners capable of making farsighted and logical decisions and (2) the opportunity and means for employment. In an evolving military situation with a general absence of any clear doctrines or precedents to guide the use of specialist formations, the chances of misapplication and misuse was made all the more likely.

Definition of misuse requires a rigid definition of role, something that was far from prevalent among many of the specialist formations of the Second World War. To remain employed and be of use, specialist formations had to continually adapt and evolve their missions to the requirements on the ground. Charges of misuse were often a counterpart to such transitions of role. When a conversion of role first began to occur, it tended to be branded as abhorrent misuse, but in time, when a unit adapted to its new mission, what was once wrong subsequently became perceived as normal. For instance, the first time the Commandos were faced with conventional, protracted deployments in North Africa, they were broadly ill prepared and suffered accordingly, with claims of misuse soon following. Yet a few months later, with an altered role and modifications having been made to their organization and structure, their future deployments in Italy or northwestern Europe in "shock troop" and "seize-and-hold" operations were considered part of the Commando repertoire without anywhere near as much negative comment.

To remain viable and useful, and not subvert their inherent value of being cost effective (of potentially providing greater result than was the sum of their investment), specialist formations had to remain employed. They had to remain subservient to the necessities and course of the war as a whole. Operational necessity could pervert the ability of specialist formations (particularly those of the commando variety) to deploy in the manner for which they had prepared, and there was an oft-repeated propensity to thrust any available units into the breach whenever battlefield reverses threatened. Commanders under pressure, who had been inadequately briefed about the employment of specialist assets and possessed little appreciation of the "cost" of raising and training these elements, were particularly prone to act as such. Although often proving costly and certainly not cost effective (as will be discussed in a later chapter), these actions were, however, understandable and, at times, quite excusable. Without relying on hindsight, there is great difficulty in actually condemning many of the instances in which specialist forces were "misused" during the Second World War.

Arguably more reprehensible than misapplication, however, was disuse: perpetually delaying the committal of specialist formations, continuously waiting for apposite circumstances, or holding out for a "model mission" that, in an evolving situation, might never occur. The cost of training and equipping a force, not to mention the manpower tied up in its establishment, could represent a noticeable investment, and should no opportunity for it to deploy in the capacity as originally intended arise, any use of the force (as with the FSSF) was arguably preferable to holding potentially large formations in reserve in the hope that opportunities would arise for their use. As misuse is potentially far more threatening for smaller special forces, disuse, even for prolonged periods, is more preferable and excusable.

Misapplication, misuse, and disuse of specialist formations must, therefore, be viewed as an essential component of the broader learning curve regarding their employment over the course of the Second World War. Because of the embryonic nature of specialist formations, the lack of understanding about their use, and—perhaps most important—the exigencies and requirements of total war, misuse was to be expected; and, in evolutionary terms, it cannot always be seen as having been counterproductive.

CHAPTER 6

THE IMPACT OF SPECIALIST FORCES

In January 1981 M. R. D. Foot posed a refreshingly simple question: "Was SOE any good?" Concluding his analysis with an "emphatic Yes," Foot's article remains a relatively rare example of an attempt to contextualize the import of special operations on the course of the Second World War.[1] The present chapter serves to modify Professor Foot's question, to ask: Were the Anglo-American commandos and special forces any good? Focusing on their wartime achievements, the chapter examines their impact in both independent actions and in conjunction with other arms; it surveys not only the direct but also the intangible and more abstract consequences of their deployments and relates these to tactical, operational, and strategic utility. What it does not do, however, is provide a breakdown of the impact, either qualitatively or quantitatively, of individual units or operations, since any attempt to do so would prove exhaustive; instead, specific examples are drawn upon for the purpose of illustrating general themes.

There is an inherent margin of ambiguity in attempting to determine the impact and value of any one element or event during the course of the war as a whole. This fundamental problem in accurately determining impact needs to be highlighted before the question of the value of specialist formations can begin to be addressed. Physical problems are the most obvious: problems that relate to an absence of clear information about costs, losses, and results; that relate to divergences in claims or the lack of adequate after-action reports. Because of indeterminable chains of causation, independent effect is seldom ascertainable. For example, an accurate "tally" of the achievements of the SAS Brigade in France is colored not only by the impact of other specialist formations (the OGs and Jedburghs) but also by the impact of the French Resistance, the SOE/OSS clandestine circuits, the Allied air forces, and, more generally, the movements and actions of conventional forces at the immediate front.

Analytical problems are more complicated still. There is definite difficulty in extrapolating the value of an individual tactical outcome to the course of the wider battle, operation, campaign, or conflict as a whole. While tangible results like the destruction of personnel or materials give some impression of value, ascribing to such isolated activities a margin of effect, or causational impact, upon later events is practically impossible. What precise impact, for instance, does the destruction of a number of aircraft, or the delay of enemy reinforcement, have on the course of a campaign? Even greater difficulty is found when attempting to assess the value of the myriad of intangible, but no less significant, effects that special operations had. What, for example, was the value of Combined Operations Pilotage Party (COPP) reconnaissances of beaches? How important were Underwater Demolition Team (UDT) activities before an amphibious landing? How valuable was the intelligence provided by the Alamo Scouts or Long Range Desert Group (LRDG)? How many lives were saved, how much faster was success achieved by special forces aiding or facilitating conventional deployments? Addressing such questions with any degree of precision remains an inherently difficult proposition.

Underlying such arguments is the expectation of the provision of strategic utility—in other words, effects that shape the course and object of the conflict as a whole.[2] Although it is certainly possible for specialist formations to reap, both actively and passively, strategic benefit (although not decisively so in high-intensity conflict), their means, methods, and tradecraft remain in the tactical sphere. The apparent dichotomy between tactical means and strategic impact is a source of confusion, resulting, at times, in either an underestimation or conversely an inflation of the value of specialist forces and their operations. In their own words, most Second World War practitioners of special operations viewed themselves as "strategic" troops. This perception was, however, principally a result of the depths at which they operated, the duration of their deployments, or the fact that they were commanded at the GHQ level, rather than referring to their utility or the effectiveness of their operations. This fact was likely compounded by the failure of the Anglo-American armies of the Second World War to formally recognize any intermediary, or "operational," level of war, viewing activity up to corps level as tactical and that at army level or higher as strategic.[3]

The perception of special forces as being wholly strategic actors tends to lead both to a condemnation of "tactical" employment, and as has been noted in the previous chapter, to the erroneous impression that their use "as close adjuncts to conventional military efforts ... [was] an abuse or waste of their unique capabilities."[4] Independence in operations was seen as the gold standard, yet to decry operations conducted alongside, or in support of, the conventional battle is not only fallacious but also neglects some of their clearest claims of strategic utility. Colin Gray accordingly believes that "the notion that there is an inherent distinction between strategic and tactical missions is both false and counterproductive."[5] Special operations have the potential for a degree of impact at all levels of war; they "may have strategic value whether they are intended to have immediate effects on a battle, on a campaign, or on a war as a whole.... Moreover, special operations have strategic value whether one uses them on independent missions or whether they coordinate their action with regular forces."[6]

The Impact of Raids and Direct Action

Independent offensive action, typified in the raid, tends to dominate discussion of the impact of special operations. Yet taken in isolation, when totally disconnected from the actions of conventional arms, individual raids by both commandos and special forces had little impact on the Second World War. These operations were often self-declared "pin pricks," which served, as in the initial conception of the Commandos, not so much to cause material attrition as to help strengthen national resolve, regain the initiative, gain experience, and frustrate the enemy. Early examples of raids (from both Britain and the Middle East) were amateurish in conception, of a small scale, invariably unsuccessful, and in general of little inherent military value in terms of material impact. Despite a greater level of proficiency seen in later raids, as well as the concomitant increase in the likelihood of cost-effective attrition, this contention remained largely applicable to individual raids taken in isolation.

Not all raids, however, were conducted on a small scale with limited objectives. A number of commando operations had loftier expectations in mind. A fine example of such an undertaking is the bold Commando raid against St. Nazaire in March 1942.

The motivation behind Operation Chariot was ostensibly strategic in character: to destroy the drydocks of St. Nazaire to deny their use to the battleship *Tirpitz* and so alter the course of the Battle of the Atlantic. Churchill called the raid "a deed of glory intimately involved in high strategy."[7] Although the raid was costly, with 169 men killed and 215 taken prisoner of war, it was undeniably a great success, succeeding spectacularly in its primary purpose of rendering the Normandie dock inoperable for the remainder of the war. With hindsight, however, the raid cannot be seen to have had any significant strategic utility. By 1942 Hitler had no intention of risking his remaining large surface vessels in the Atlantic, nor would the denial of the maintenance facilities at St. Nazaire preclude the *Tirpitz* from operating in the North Sea against convoys bound for Russia. As a result, Gray has called the raid "a heroic example of doing the wrong thing well for the right reason. The raid was a critical blow against the German naval strategy of 1940–41, not of 1942–45."[8] William McRaven, meanwhile, categorically stated that the risks taken in the raid were not worth the potential gains, and he contrasts it unfavorably with the September 1943 X-Craft submersible attack on the *Tirpitz* made by the Admiralty's 12th Submarine Flotilla, Operation Source, which ultimately rendered the ship inoperable with far fewer losses.[9]

Potentially the most directly "strategic" independent special operation carried out in the war was Swallow/Gunnerside, an SOE-sponsored operation conducted in February 1943 against the Vemork hydroelectric plant in Norway, a significant target because of its heavy water by-product (an essential moderating component in the establishment of a nuclear reactor). Arrangements for the mission first occurred in September 1942 when four SOE-recruited Norwegians, code-named Grouse, were parachuted into the vicinity of the plant to provide advance reconnaissance and act as guides for Freshman, a demolitions force of thirty airborne-trained Royal Engineers sent by glider to attack the target in November. While Grouse went to plan, the two gliders carrying Freshman (and one of the Halifax bombers towing them) crashed on approach, with the survivors captured and subsequently executed by the Germans.[10]

Grouse, however, remained in position, and in February 1943 Gunnerside, a force of six SOE Norwegians, was parachuted in as a second strike group to meet with Swallow (as the Grouse group had been renamed).[11] These two groups combined and subsequently successfully attacked the Vemork plant to place it out of action for a number of months. The resultant denial of heavy water production thus went at least some way to preventing German experimentation with atomic weaponry. Considering the obvious ramifications had these been developed, David Stafford believed this "may have been the most important act of sabotage by either side during the Second World War."[12] Illustrative of the problem of ascribing credit in a complex chain of causation, however, is the fact that the German failure to develop atomic weapons had more to do with the lack of heavy water alone. Furthermore, it should be noted that Gunnerside did not permanently stop the plant: credit must be shared with both a subsequent SOE mission in February 1944, when two Norwegians sank, via sabotage, a ferry transporting half a year's heavy water production from the newly repaired plant, and with the USAAF, whose air raids ultimately kept the plant inoperable.[13]

Another raid that had strategic ramifications, and which in choice of target bore certain similarities to Freshman, was Operation Musketoon of September 1942. Here ten members of No. 2 Commando and two SOE Norwegians were transported to Norway via submarine to attack the hydroelectric plant at Glomfjord. The objective, in this instance, was not heavy water but the immobilization of a nearby aluminum plant that was reliant on the energy supplied. The raid was a great success, but after the raid eight members of the force were killed (seven of them by execution after capture), and only four men were eventually able to return to Britain via Sweden. Though heavy in proportion to the size of the force, these losses were more than compensated for by the elimination of an important component of the German war effort. As Kenneth Macksey wrote, "MUSKETOON produced solid results by using a simple formula with a low outlay, and it hit the Germans at a critical moment in the war's development."[14]

On the whole, however, independently strategic special operations were the exception and not the rule. Despite often being perceived as the gold standard, few special operations had the potential for independent strategic effect in a conflict of the scale and intensity of the Second World War. The much more pronounced contribution that special operations made to the strategic situation came when their actions, however individually insignificant, were wedded to the activities of conventional formations and the main campaign. The value of specialist formations acting in a contributory role in facilitating, enhancing, or aiding the development and continuation of conventional operations is potentially much more significant than any independent and self-contained operations divorced from the deployment of conventional arms except in an abstract sense. As Julian Thompson has stated, "Offensive action and intelligence gathering, produce the best 'return' when carried out as adjuncts of the campaign, or battle, being fought or about to be fought, by the main body of the army. There are few examples of offensive action far removed from main force activity producing a good 'return.'"[15] It is through examination of these more direct contributions that the most substantial tangible value of special operations can be seen. As Gray contends, the strategic utility of special operations "depends on the context of war as a whole" and "corresponds to the significance of the grander-scale military operations that they assist."[16] The true strategic value of special operations is not in one annihilatory action that achieves strategic paralysis but, as James Kiras reminds us, in collective strategic attrition to weaken "an adversary's combat power and will to fight."[17]

It is only when raids are taken as a whole that their value becomes more apparent: based on quantity rather than quality, the cumulative effects of these operations could be greater than the sum of their parts. Small-scale raids, often repeated, could produce a very favorable return on investment capable of causing cause clear, albeit localized, damage to the enemy war effort. This is a point well illustrated by the prolific, and often tactically successful, small-scale raids of the SAS during the Desert War. The SAS's most feted achievement, and potentially their most significant achievement during the entire war, was their destruction of an estimated 350 enemy aircraft throughout the campaign.[18] This achievement was undoubtedly significant and greatly aided the beleaguered Desert Air Force by materially helping "to tilt the balance of air power in the Mediterranean Theater."[19] GHQ MEF was of the opinion that the SAS achievements throughout the North African campaign "had a great bearing on the final defeat of the enemy in Tunisia."[20] Even Erwin Rommel would acknowledge their contribution (albeit probably unwittingly conflating their achievements with those of the LRDG), writing in his diary that the SAS "caused us more damage than any other British unit of equal strength."[21] While it is certainly evident that special operations by the likes of the SAS and LRDG in the desert were of clear value in aiding the course of the wider campaign, their achievements should be kept in perspective. They were not, as Mike Morgan has contended, "a phenomenal and decisive contribution to the overall victory."[22] These actions were not decisive acts but ancillary and contributory events to the course and conduct of the main campaign.

For conventional arms, the most beneficial results that special forces and partisans undertaking harassment and interdiction activities in the enemy's rear could achieve came not with material destruction but instead with the disruption of enemy lines of communication and logistics, serving as a force multiplier by performing strikes on targets that negatively affected the enemy's speed of response and ability to maneuver. Although there were numerous instances in which special operations were able (with varying levels of success) to attain such a result, one of the more notable, and indeed contested, examples is the value that SAS Operation Bulbasket had in disrupting the arrival of German reinforcements at the Normandy beachhead. Taken as a case study, it not only emphasizes the potential value of special operations in this regard but also highlights the difficulty of assessing the impact of one event in a broader chain of causation.

Operation Bulbasket was undertaken by personnel from "B" Squadron of the 1st SAS Regiment in the Vienne department of France. The first elements of the mission arrived by parachute in the early hours of D-day, with further reinforcements dispatched over the following week. The broad intention of the mission was to operate against rail and road networks to prevent German reinforcements from reaching the Normandy beachhead. After a fertile few weeks of operations, on July 2 the SAS's base camp was compromised and attacked by a superior force. A total of thirty-three SAS men (and one USAAF pilot who had been picked up by the group) were captured and subsequently executed. Despite this calamity, those personnel who managed to escape the attack were nevertheless able to continue with their original mission, spending a further three weeks targeting rail networks in the area before being ordered to cease operations.

Max Hastings has attributed to Bulbasket part of the credit for the delay of the SS Das Reich Division in reaching the Normandy beachhead. Although the division was delayed significantly by crippled rail networks (primarily caused by air power and Resistance sabotage) and the constant specter of Allied aerial supremacy that prevented daytime movement, Hastings claims that SAS ambushes, attacks on rail links, and, crucially, their tasking of an air strike against a petrol train at Châtellerault, where the fuel reserves for Das Reich was stored, delayed the division's arrival at the front for upward of two or three days of their longer holdup.[23] Even if the SAS's part in the delay was a matter of hours, waylaying such an important division from the Normandy battlefield was significant. Thompson has thus contended that the SAS actions "more than compensated for the [subsequent] virtual elimination of the Bulbasket Team."[24] Roger Ford, on the other hand, attributes Das Reich's delay principally to the Resistance, arguing that it is "difficult to rate it [Bulbasket] as more than a partial success, not only because so many lives were lost in its course and it had to be brought to a premature conclusion as a result, but also because it actually achieved very little in purely military terms."[25] Furthermore, Ford discounts the significance of Das Reich's delay, emphasizing that when the division did arrive in Normandy, it was not committed immediately but was instead held in reserve until early July.[26] These criticisms are, however, somewhat misplaced—overlooking both the fact that it was the SAS who directed the strike at Châtellerault, not the Resistance, and the point that the lateness of Das Reich's committal to the line at Normandy was not by choice but was a necessity because of the disorganized state in which the division had finally arrived at the front.

As a general rule, the use of commando and ranger formations in conjunction with, or in support of, conventional arms would ultimately prove to be of more value than their independent raiding activities. This fact of course underscores their evolution in role: their ultimate occupation as spearheaders, flank guards, and shock troops were all intended to facilitate, or accelerate the pace of, conventional military operations. Commandos and rangers, as a post-Sicily appraisal stated, "assist in keeping the battle in a state of fluidity."[27] Their greatest usefulness, and the raison d'être of many such formations after 1942, occurred when "they came to fight within the larger framework of the big invasions . . . when their place was in the vanguard of the vanguards and on the outer wings of the beachheads."[28] The presence of specially trained and motivated troops on the beaches during, or soon after, the initial assault certainly went some way to overcoming the daunting problems of mounting amphibious operations. Commando and ranger formations would demonstrate a particular usefulness when working on the flanks of landing beaches to tackle important but tactically hard to assail positions, such as defensive coastal batteries.

No. 4 Commando's masterful work at Dieppe and the 2nd Rangers' assault on Pointe du Hoc on D-day provide perhaps the best, though not the only, examples of the utility of employing commandos and rangers acting in such a capacity. The perceived value of such roles is evidenced by the steady proliferation and expansion of these formations between 1942 and 1944 to meet the expected requirements of ever-larger amphibious operations.

In addition to their value in an amphibious capacity, commando formations also displayed their utility in a number of valuable overland deployments where, via infiltration and assault, they helped hasten the development of the conventional battle by the seizure of important objectives. Three solid, although by no means exclusive, examples of commando-type formations proving valuable in such capacity are the assaults by the First Special Service Force (FSSF) on Monte la Difensa and Monte la Remetanea, the capture of which helped crack the Bernhardt Line and increased the tempo of the main battle; the Marauders' seizure of Myitkyina airfield in Burma alongside Chinese regulars, an action that helped open the Burma Road and saw to it that flights over the Hump—the area over the Himalayas that had to be flown across to connect India with China—were shorter and safer by removing Japanese fighter cover over northern Burma; or 3rd Commando (formerly SS) Brigade's seizure of Hill 170 in the Arakan, an action that greatly aided the advance of the 25th Indian Division toward Kangaw. Such examples, in addition to those albeit infrequent amphibious strokes, such as that at Termoli, and the more frequent river crossings, such as 1st Commando Brigade's Operation Widgeon across the Rhine, helped greatly in facilitating operational-level maneuvers and speeding up the pace of the conventional battle. Yet even when very successful, such actions cannot, in the context of the magnitude of other events occurring, really be considered to be, as Hogan claims, "critical to the success of conventional forces."[29]

It was not, however, only in their direct actions against the enemy that specialist formations had value. They were also of notable worth in facilitating the development of new techniques, doctrines, and equipment. Commando raids permitted experience to be gained that could then be translated into valuable lessons and doctrinal advances in areas such as amphibious operations, small-unit battle tactics, and equipment. James Dunning, a wartime member of No. 4 Commando and an instructor at the Commando Training

Center, for example, contended that the Commandos' development of "new and innovative standards in military training" proved that "the benefits and value of the Commandos went beyond the limits of their operation."[30] Early Commando raids were certainly of value in ironing out some of the more pressing problems inherent in the planning and conduct of amphibious operations. The lessons COHQ learned regarding staff practices and interservice cooperation during the Lofotens and Vaagso raids, not to mention the more obvious example of Dieppe, helped establish precedents and mechanisms that were invaluable in planning and mounting future amphibious assaults.[31] It should, nonetheless, be noted that the majority of lessons learned during raiding operations were of a very specific nature that would have little general application. Adrian Lewis went as far as suggesting that because "British experiences in amphibious raids were not directly applicable to large-scale joint amphibious operations" they may have actually "hampered their ability to develop an effective tactical and operational amphibious doctrine," giving them false estimations about the value of surprise and mobility over the benefits of mass and firepower.[32]

The Impact on Intelligence

Although offensive activities tend to dominate much special operations literature, it is equally important to examine the results of their intelligence-gathering activities. Yet doing so is not without complications. For, as John Ferris states, "one rarely has the equivalent of a laboratory experiment in which all other variables remain constant and one can gauge with precision the effect of changes in intelligence."[33] The contribution of special forces to the intelligence picture should not be underestimated. In the opinion of LRDG patrol commander Anthony Timpson, the timely provision of intelligence and information was "the most decisive influence which the LRDG could exert."[34] If the SAS contributed to victory in the Desert War by its regular harassment of enemy lines of communication and its destruction of aircraft, the LRDG easily matched that contribution with its invaluable provision of topographical and human intelligence.

The LRDG "road watch," in particular, has often been hailed as an activity of particular value. By physically charting all east- and west-bound traffic along the arterial coastal roads of Libya, the LRDG helped build up an exceptionally detailed and therefore valuable picture of the supply and reinforcement situation of Axis forces. Brigadier T. S. Airey, director of military intelligence (DMI), GHQ MEF, believed the road watch to be of "quite exceptional importance" and that it provided "an indispensable basis for certain facts on which calculation of enemy strength can be based. Without their reports we should frequently have been in doubt as to the enemy's intentions, when knowledge of them was all important; and our estimate of enemy strength would have been far less accurate and accepted with far less confidence."[35] Subsequent appraisals of the intelligence contribution of the "road watch" were prone to herald it as having been decisive. Trevor James Constable, for example, recounts that "when Ritter von Thoma, Rommel's deputy, was captured . . . the German general was shocked to learn that Monty knew more about the supply status of the *Afrika Korps* than he did. Most of this information reached Monty via LRDG road watch patrols."[36] However, to comprehend the true contribution of the LRDG's returns, it is necessary to consider them against the value of intelligence emanating from other sources.

Placed against the significance of the contribution of signals intelligence, most notably "Y" Service intercepts and "Ultra" decrypts, which were undoubtedly the greatest intelligence sources available to the Western Desert Force/Eighth Army, the contribution of the LRDG is put in better perspective. Despite the fact that the LRDG did not produce the same range of information as signals intelligence, it did, nonetheless, hold a number of benefits over other available intelligence sources. Signals intelligence was not without its limitations. "Ultra" was reliant on what was sent via the Enigma cipher machine and, consequently, could suffer from being patchy, delayed, and open to misinterpretation. "Y" Service, meanwhile, was heavily reliant on suitable conditions for the interception of signals and was often of value only at the tactical level.[37] "Road watches" offered a unique means of verifying intelligence gained from signals intelligence, as well as having the additional advantages of being proactive, regular, almost continuous, and, in light of well-trained practitioners, accurate.[38] Furthermore, the "road watch" was considered highly trustworthy. As a consequence of its clandestine nature and the depth at which it was mounted, as a source it was almost invulnerable to subversion or interruption from enemy deception, radio silence, and other wireless security measures, or camouflage that might mar intelligence from other sources. Moreover, for professional officers, such human, "Mark 1 Eyeball" intelligence provided by trained and uniformed personnel was, despite its depth, highly agreeable—at times a great deal more so than that coming from "Ultra," which for security reasons was occasionally dressed up in the cover of emanating from some dubiously ubiquitous super agent. Of course it is also worth noting that the LRDG patrols themselves provided a wonderful cover, a plausible source that "Ultra" intercepts could be attributed to.

Set against other forms of human intelligence available in this theater, the LRDG returns were particularly favorable. David Hunt, a GHQ MEF intelligence staff officer, claimed that "all the agents' reports ever received through all the cumbrous and many-branched organizations set up for the purposes of espionage put together, never amounted to enough to be weighed in the balance against the information which the Long Range Desert Group supplied."[39] Against photo reconnaissance, the LRDG comes off favorably too. Despite a growing proficiency in aerial reconnaissance in the later stages of the campaign, when working at depth the RAF could never hope to match the range, time on target, and completeness of intelligence attainable by LRDG patrols.

In the uniquely apposite conditions of the Desert War, the LRDG was also of notable value to conventional operations through supplying topographical information and serving as guides and pathfinders. In the later stages of the Desert War, working ahead of the main advance following the victory in the Second Battle of El Alamein, LRDG patrols made daily wireless reports on such things as the going, obstacles, cover, water supplies, and potential sites for landing grounds and dumps; and when returning to friendly lines, patrols conferred with divisional headquarters and erected models and maps to demonstrate possible lines of advance. The LRDG also directly guided conventional units on flanking maneuvers across the desert—as with the 22nd Guards Brigade south of the Jebel Akhdar to the Benghazi-Agedabia road; the 400 km outflanking maneuver of the 4th Light Brigade and the New Zealand Division at El Agheila; the guidance (with the Indian Long Range Squadron) of Free French Forces north from the Fezzan; and, most notably, their discovery of "Wilder's Gap" (named after Captain Nick Wilder, the patrol commander who discovered it) in the Matmata Hills, which allowed the

Eighth Army to circumvent the heavily defended Mareth Line during its advance into Tunisia in March 1943. In reference to the latter achievement, General Montgomery would commend: "Without your careful and reliable reports the launching of the 'left hook' by the N[ew]Z[ealand] Div[ision] would have been a leap in the dark; with the information they produced, the operation could be planned with some certainty and as you know, went off without a hitch."[40] Eric Morris considered its discovery "one of the most important contributions by Special Forces to the land battle in North Africa."[41]

When the LRDG shifted its operations to the islands and coastlines of the Aegean and Adriatic, its "shipping watch" operations (which were occasionally mirrored by the Special Boat Squadron (SBS) and the OSS OGs) continued to be a source of valuable intelligence. For instance, in January 1945 the Balkan Air Force, responsible for all trans-Adriatic operations, reported that: "LRDG patrols on [the] JUG [Yugoslav] coast were only reliable source [of] information [on] enemy and shipping movements in that area. They are an essential preliminary to any operations and [an] important source [of] intelligence."[42]

The closest American counterpart to the LRDG, in both broad modus operandi and results, were the Alamo Scouts, whose combat record and tactical virtuosity is arguably without parallel. Throughout the course of their operations they are believed to have accounted for over five hundred Japanese soldiers killed and over sixty captured (a phenomenal feat in light of the rarity of Japanese prisoners for much of the war), all without the loss of a single man.[43] It is not in these claims, however, that their chief value is to be found. The greatest contribution of the Alamo Scouts was their provision of intelligence for the benefit of the U.S. Sixth Army in the Southwest Pacific and the Philippines. Undertaking tactical reconnaissance, beach survey, liaison with partisans, and pathfinding, as well as important road and coastal watches, they provided direct assistance for General Walter Krueger's offensives and were an undeniable asset in his arsenal. With the establishment of the Special Intelligence Subsection under the Sixth Army's G-2 (Intelligence) Section, Krueger's staff benefited enormously from being able to task and dispatch a "Scout team in any given area on Luzon within 48 hours," either to provide specific intelligence or undertake a gamut of other tasks.[44] Krueger himself would later praise the tremendous value of having a reliable and readily available reconnaissance asset at hand capable of producing a "considerable volume of extremely valuable information."[45]

Another fine example of special forces recouping intelligence returns is provided by OSS Detachment 101 in Burma. After an awkward first year, once the detachment had become properly established, it was estimated that its extensive intelligence networks provided Stilwell "with over ninety percent of the entire Japanese intelligence that they got in the [Northern Burma] area" and was used in the designation of 65 percent of all air attacks mounted in theater.[46] As the unit's commander, Colonel William R. Peers, was keen to emphasize that "considering all of the numerous sources available to that [CBI] command, including Chinese, British and American troops, prisoner of war interrogations, aerial photography and a wide variety of other sources, the magnitude of the 101 intelligence collection effort can be readily appreciated."[47] SOE's Force 136, V Force, and the Sino-American Cooperative Organization (SACO, also known as Naval Group, China) in China each recouped similar benefits in their respective areas of operation, but none quite paralleled the expansive successes of Detachment 101.

Not all intelligence advances attained by specialist formations came from the conduct of clandestine activities. At various times, valuable intelligence was gained as a result of conducting offensive operations; indeed No. 30 (Assault) Commando was created with this specific intention in mind. A good example of an offensive raid undertaken for intelligence purposes was the February 1942 Operation Biting against Bruneval in upper Normandy. This raid was mounted by C Company, 2nd Parachute Battalion, to secure German radar technology.[48] The successful completion of this operation provided, as R. V. Jones claimed, "first-hand knowledge of the state of German radar technology, in the form in which it was almost certainly being applied in our principal objective, the German nightfighter control system."[49] The most startling intelligence benefit accrued from an offensive raid, however, occurred during Operation Claymore, the first Lofotens raid, carried out by Nos. 3 and 4 Commandos in March 1941. Tactically and materially the raid was successful (although the Commandos faced little opposition), yet its real strategic significance came in the seizure of ciphers, documents, and Enigma coding equipment, a haul that significantly aided the evolution of "Ultra."[50] This latter achievement was, however, an unexpected windfall; the seizure of intelligence materials appearing low in the list of priorities when planning the raid.[51] Other operations too could reap unforeseen intelligence gains. While working with his unit north of Taranto in late 1943, Vladimir "Popski" Peniakoff was personally able to seize, via deception and guile, the entire ration strength returns of the German 1st Fallschirmjäger Division—an intelligence coup with such obviously beneficial ramifications that it alone justified the existence of his private army.[52]

Arguably the most significant intelligence activities as performed by special forces were those directed at facilitating and advancing amphibious operations. Solid intelligence about matters such as hydrographics, beach gradients, natural and enemy underwater obstacles, and shoreline defenses, cardinal requirements for the successful prosecution of large-scale amphibious landings, were often obtainable only through the use of units such as the COPPs and Scouts and Raider (S&R) teams. Julian Thompson has claimed that the work of these units "was absolutely indispensable to the success of the amphibious operations carried out by the Allies, of which Normandy was the supreme example."[53] Of perhaps equal significance were the actions of maritime special forces undertaking the tasks of beach clearance, demolitions, deception, and assault pilotage. Fine examples of the value of such operations are seen with the UDT activities before the landings on Guam, after which Admiral Nimitz noted: "Assault operations in the Marianas would have been far more difficult, if not almost impossible, on some beaches without the capable and courageous work of the Underwater Demolition Teams."[54] It is difficult to assess the precise value of these activities, but the consequences of inadequate reconnaissance, pilotage, and other preassault tasks had been displayed all too clearly at, for example, Dieppe or Tarawa. Without such benefits as accrued by the use of special maritime groups, many large-scale landings would have been a significant gamble, and a greater number of casualties would likely have been sustained in their execution. The activities of these formations, if not crucial to success, certainly hastened events and saved lives during some of the most difficult of all military maneuvers.

When considering the contribution that specialist formations made to the intelligence picture, it is also important not to neglect how essential intelligence was to the execution of special operations themselves. Despite the erroneous suggestion one might receive from reading some of the more exciting narratives surrounding this subject, successful special operations were very seldom a result of intuition alone. The majority of operations were directed (with mixed levels of success) by intelligence that emanated from other sources. As was the case with most things related to the tasking and use of specialist formations at depth, wedding these units to the intelligence picture took time to develop and effort to maintain. Incorrect, inadequate, or out-of-date intelligence are perennial perils for the effective execution of special operations, and it is certainly not hard to find examples of failures caused by such shortcomings.

The Impact of Working with Partisans

The principal occupation of a number of special forces was to provide training, "stiffening," and leadership to indigenous partisan movements. In order to examine the impact of these activities, it is necessary to briefly consider the efficiency of the wider partisan movements that they assisted. While any cumulative analysis of the value of guerrilla movements is greatly complicated by a myriad of different military, political, geographical, and chronological variables as affecting each individual movement, it is broadly possible to surmise that their value increased almost universally in proportion to their proximity, in both time and space, to conventional Allied operations. Although the subject is a contentious one, Julian Thompson is right to emphasize the "perfectly respectable point of view which argues that few, if any, resistance movements conducted successful overt military operations, unless operating in concert with a main, conventional force; even if that force was some distance away."[55] Such a consideration is important: overt military operations by partisan formations either had to be in sufficient strength (as in Yugoslavia toward the end of the war) or occur in conjunction with main-force operations to have any chance of significant success and therefore impact. Without sufficient strength, organization, and equipment, or a main force to distract the enemy, guerrilla formations were prone to expend their energies without significant return for the risk.

John Keegan in *The Second World War* is particularly scornful of achievements of SOE (and by association OSS), which he says "largely fails in its claim to have contributed significantly to Hitler's defeat."[56] Keegan bases this contention on three very selective "key events" of resistance warfare against Germany: the actions of the French Resistance (supported by Jedburghs and OGs) in Vercors on D-day,[57] the July 1944 Slovakia uprising, and the August 1944 Warsaw uprising. As each of these events ultimately resulted in brutal and effective suppression, Keegan is led to the conclusion that "the programme of subversion, sabotage and resistance . . . must be adjudged a costly and misguided failure."[58] The brevity and selectivity of such a narrow assessment does not, however, suffice, and it ignores the cumulative effects of partisan warfare on the enemy war effort.

It is certainly true that the use of partisans, sabotage, and subversion never lived up to the idealistic Churchillian rhetoric to "set Europe ablaze" as first expounded in 1940. Fighting alone and reluctant to become embroiled in protracted land battles, Britain was grasping at straws, harboring naive and unrealistic views about how the people of Europe could rise up and virtually liberate themselves from the shackles of Nazism with the minimum of support. While such misguided perceptions arguably lasted longer than they should have, by 1942 the British had begun to perceive partisan movements as the Americans had from the outset: as an ancillary bonus to conventional actions, not a war-winning weapon. The merits of partisan and guerrilla movements should thus be judged on this latter expectation and not on the adolescent view that they could be independently decisive.[59]

Irregular activities in support of the invasion of France provide clear illustration of the utility of partisans acting in support of the regular battle. Of particular note are the large-scale Resistance uprisings in Brittany, which William Casey claimed "must rank among the most brilliant and successful of the war."[60] Their effectiveness was, in no small part, magnified by the timely dispatch of various Jedburgh Teams and a large number of (overwhelmingly French) SAS groups to the area. In Brittany the SAS and fourteen Jedburgh Teams managed to arm and organize over 20,000 maquisards, whose actions were so successful in paralyzing German forces that they were able to protect the flanks of Patton's encircling drive, allowing him to focus on the front, spare his own resources, and speed up his rate of advance.[61] SOE's verdict was that the Jedburghs' contribution, in conjunction with the Resistance and the SAS, "saved the use of at least one Division in the Brittany campaign."[62] Even the impact of just one three-man Jedburgh Team able to orchestrate the timely delivery of Allied resources could be significant. For example, Team Frederick in a ten-week deployment in support of the SAS Samwest base claimed to have trained over 4,000 partisans in Brittany.[63] Resistance activities in support of the landings in the South of France, again aided by Jedburghs and OGs, were equally well praised. General Alexander McCarrell "Sandy" Patch, commanding the U.S. Seventh Army, estimated that the contribution of the Resistance in support of Operation Dragoon as being "the equivalent of four to five Divisions."[64] Certainly no mean feat.

The arrival of uniformed specialist troops in advance of the conventional arms into occupied territories was an act that alone could be sufficient to cause spontaneous indigenous uprisings and an instant uplifting of morale. The French Resistance, for example, was "intoxicated" by the sudden appearance of uniformed SAS, OG, and Jedburgh personnel in their territory. Their arrival, as Paul Gaujac claims, "was a harbinger of liberation and a call to action."[65] An OSS appraisal of OG work in the South of France stated that their "least tangible but probably most important" impact was the "tremendous lift given to the Maquis. . . . Many French leaders have said that even if the men had not carried out a single tactical operation their presence alone was of enormous value."[66] Any assessment of the value of special forces working in such a capacity must, of course, also acknowledge the impact and efficiency of the clandestine circuits of SOE and OSS. The work done by these agencies in contacting, organizing, and preparing the partisans prior to the committal of special forces was very important. For instance, in the first six months of 1944, before any Jedburgh, OG, or SAS element was committed to France, SOE and OSS had arranged that by D-day "about twenty thousand resistance fighters were fully armed; another fifty thousand were armed '. . . in some degree.'"[67] Without such foundations, alongside the continued support offered both by these agencies and by the Allied air forces—the record of which unfortunately lies beyond the scope of this volume—the potential application, and ergo impact, of specialist formations would in many instances have been distinctly lessened.

Previous chapters have highlighted distinct limitations with the employment of large numbers of special forces in support of the conventional Allied effort in France, and it is certainly worth asking whether these units could have been utilized for greater benefit.

James Kiras has taken a narrow and critical view of the use of the SAS Brigade in France, believing few of its actions translated to strategic benefits. He believes that instead of it being used in a reactionary fashion (as a strategic reserve), undertaking an esoteric range of operations, the SAS and other irregular elements should have been used in a concerted and proactive manner, deliberately targeting enemy supply arteries as soon as the invasion commenced. Expanding upon the oft-repeated discussion of misuse that maintains that these units were committed too late, he adds that they were also committed against the wrong sort of targets. Kiras maintains that "the inability of the Allies to conduct a campaign of unconventional attrition prior to and during the Normandy campaign was one of the greatest lost opportunities of the war: a severely weakened *Wehrmacht* might have been overwhelmed by the Allied and Soviet armies on both fronts as early as autumn of 1944."[68]

Such a statement presupposes many things, not least of all being the (quite fallacious) assumption that there was a widespread understanding about the possibilities of "unconventional attrition" and of the role that special forces would occupy therein. Irregular warfare on the scale and depth of that to be conducted during the invasion of France was, in 1944, an entirely new proposition; a lack of knowledge about how this should be undertaken, and corresponding doubts in some quarters about its potential, was therefore quite understandable. The limitations in orchestrating concerted SAS and OG deployments in Italy only five months before the commencement of operations in France illustrate that the "learning curve" dictating their employment had not yet been properly mastered. With such limitations in mind, the use of such a large number of Allied special forces groups (each burdened to some extent by problems resulting from a rapid expansion in establishment, a requirement to develop new methods and tactics, or simply inexperience) in support of the invasion of France appears quite the achievement—highlighting just how far the organization and acceptance of these units had come by this stage.

The assumption that any worthwhile "unconventional attrition" could have occurred before the commencement of the invasion is equally erroneous. Until the mainstay of German forces had been distracted by large-scale continental landings, any irregular activities would have been easily suppressed. This was the precise reason that soon after the landings, once the beachhead had become unexpectedly static, SHAEF ordered a brief suspension of many Resistance activities, to ensure that a potentially valuable weapon for the benefit of the breakout was not prematurely spent. While there were certainly problems with the control and tasking of these formations, and definite limitations with the flexibility of response following the rapidity of the Allied breakout, it is quite unwarranted to engage in counterfactual or hindsight estimations that wrongly assume both that there was a rational and comprehensive construct of special operations in 1944 and that the means and resources (aircraft in particular) for application were all available. Kiras contended that "had the SAS been used to sever some of the tendons of the *Westheer* and been part of an integrated team to run it to ground instead of attempting to demonstrate its own 'strategic' value and prepare for subsequent operations that never materialized, the war might very well have ended earlier, with fewer Allied casualties and a potentially different map of post-war Europe."[69] With this statement Kiras falls into a trap of his own creation: by drawing such idealistic conclusions about the potential for far-reaching and decisive effects, he manages to undermine his own more rational and modest concepts about the value of special operations being strictly ancillary to conventional success.

David Hogan has asserted that "partisan efforts in Italy and the Balkans had only a nuisance value and were rarely tied into the operations of conventional Allied combat units."[70] At times the operations of partisans in the Balkans (or Greece for that matter) were certainly hindered by divergent political motivations and a lack of both weapons and formal military training, but to claim that their effectiveness was only of nuisance value is unconvincing. That these operations were not tied in with an Allied land force (other than rather composite forces predominantly made up of special forces and Commandos in the later stages of the war) should not necessarily detract from their value. The sheer size and frequency of their operations in a theater well suited to guerrilla action ultimately proved a significant thorn in Germany's side. It has variously been estimated that in 1943 up to fifty German divisions (albeit rarely first rate) were tied down in Yugoslavia and Albania on occupational and antipartisan duties: more divisions than faced the Allied armies in Italy at that time.[71]

In a number of cases conflicts of interest and political tensions existing between the Anglo-American special forces and partisan elements could nonetheless be a real impediment to the conduct of operations. In both Greece and Yugoslavia tensions with emergent communist movements severely curtailed the deployment of special forces. Toward the end of the war various LRDG and SBS (Squadron, later Service) personnel in Istria and Yugoslavia were physically detained by partisan forces seeking to gain political capital by downplaying the value of Allied assistance in the liberation of their territories.[72] Being widely made up of bilingual first- and second-generation Americans, the OGs were a particular source of suspicion among the Greek and Balkan partisan movements. Despite proving themselves efficient and versatile in operations from Vis, the use of OGs on the Yugoslavian mainland was heavily curtailed by fears that their arrival would send out the wrong message to the partisan elements.[73] Similar fears about the use of OGs in Greece made necessary the submission of all "Greek" OG personnel to a rigorous vetting procedure to root out any unacceptable political beliefs before they were allowed to be committed.[74] Such precautions were not always unwarranted. First- or second-generation immigrants returning to their former homeland were obviously less likely to be able to remain impartial in delicate political affairs than were nonnative operatives. Furthermore, the guerrillas themselves might treat such individuals with suspicion, not as legitimate representatives of the Allied powers.

The pressure of dealing with partisan movements possessing divergent political and military motivations to their own was an understandable source of frustration for the various special forces. Robert Kehoe of Jedburgh Team Frederick highlighted the pressures his three-man team faced with "discussion, frequent argument, and much diplomatic pressure" and of the need to "try to understand the views of the varied participants in the complex political situation that underlay all of our military operations."[75] Major Roy Farran of the 2nd SAS found that although the Resistance he came into contact with in France were "quite energetic," by no means a universal trait, "the difference between our respective methods made close cooperation difficult, and it was better just to maintain a loose liaison."[76] Similar sentiments were expressed by the commander of OG Operation Peg in France, who believed it would have been more efficient to have dispatched a larger number of OG men (thirty was recommended) rather than having to rely on the "help of untrained [Maquis] men who do not understand what is to be done . . . valuable time is lost telling them what to do and how to do it."[77] Jedburgh Aaron Bank went as far as contending that "OSS would have been more effective in their insurgency and sabotage roles without the collaboration of the local militias."[78]

Many of the young men within special forces units working in Yugoslavia possessed "little or no political experience" themselves and so were shocked when they "found that the amount of help which they received from the Partisans was governed not only by the military situation but also by the political outlook of the Partisan bands themselves."[79] In Albania the Raiding Support Regiment (RSR) were often frustrated by the lackluster behavior of the *andartes* partisans, who were unwilling to harass German forces finally leaving their country. When serving in Albania, Thomas Churchill, commanding the 2nd SS Brigade, was wary that the methods and interests of partisans might be divergent to his own and thus developed a policy of only utilizing partisans in noncritical actions. He believed that "they should always be given a task which did not directly affect our own, one which might lie on a flank, for instance, the success of which would further our combined plans, but the failure of which would not jeopardize our immediate operations."[80] It was perhaps the emergent civil war in Greece between rival ELAS (Greek People's Liberation Army) communist and EDES (National Republican Greek League) republican guerrillas, who were far more interested in fighting one another than the Germans, that would cause some of the most significant problems for special forces attempting to harass and delay German movements in these areas.

Hogan's appraisal of partisan efforts in Italy as having been of little more than nuisance effect is equally unfair. For much of the war, until mid-1944 at least, one can see Hogan's point. The partisans, small in number and largely uncoordinated, were of little significance. From the summer of 1944 onward, however, the emergent Italian partisans began to be of more worth to the Allied armies in Italy. As General Mark Clark assessed it: "The role of the Italian partisans in supplementing the operations of the Allied Armies in Italy has been a most important one. Their attacks . . . during the fall of 1944 and winter of 1944–5 were a constant and serious harassing problem for the enemy."[81] The potential for the concerted committal of uniformed special forces in depth in Italy only became a practicable proposition after the summer of 1944. As SOE and OSS began to make serious efforts to support the Italian partisans, as

Allied command and control arrangements for special forces became more centralized and efficient, and as all parties gained experience in irregular warfare, special forces would become of increased worth to the Allied effort in Italy. In the last year of the war, despite both the reduction in force strengths to cater to expanded operations in France and the perennial impediments of the mountainous Italian terrain and a harsh winter, special operations were, nevertheless, mounted with increased frequency to harass the enemy, coordinate partisan groups, target lines of communication, and supply intelligence.

The competence of partisan formations in Italy was thus, to no small degree, down not only to the equipment supplied by the Allies but also to the direction and molding that came from varied special forces and clandestine elements. Just as General Clark praised the efficiency of the partisans, he also contended that "the outstanding success of partisan operations . . . and the excellent intelligence as to enemy dispositions received was in large measure due to the presence of these [OG] men and their leadership of Partisan formations."[82] It was a pattern that the Germans also observed. In early 1945, at a time when the Allies were stepping up their support for the partisans, Field Marshal Albert Kesselring reported that the Italian partisans were beginning to "show clear results. The execution of partisan operations shows considerably more commanding leadership. Up to now it has been possible for us, with a few exceptions, to keep our vital rear lines of communications open by means of our slight protective forces, but this situation threatens to change considerably for the worse in the immediate future."[83] The "commanding leadership" to which Kesselring referred was due, at least in part, to the various methods, including the use of special forces, with which Allied subversive and specialist elements were attempting to harness the partisan weapon in Italy at this time.

The feat of orchestrating, training, equipping, and leading indigenous partisan formations is perhaps nowhere better observed than in the example of Burma. Detachment 101's contacting and marshaling of Kachin tribesmen into "ranger" units dramatically highlighted the effectiveness of partisans in offensive activities and proved that they could "take the place of sizable regular units." The commencement of Stilwell's Burma Road offensive was the catalyst for an expansion of 101's activities, and by February 1945 over 10,000 "Kachin Rangers" had been raised. Their value to Stilwell's offensive was clear: the partisans acted as a screen and a force multiplier, and they were independently held responsible for some 5,447 known Japanese dead.[84] Merrill would claim that the Marauders' advance on Myitkyina "could not have succeeded without [the] help of 101."[85] Their achievements are put into perspective when it is considered that only 22 U.S. personnel and 184 native guerrillas were killed during the detachment's operations.[86] To put it another way, a battalion-size commitment from the United States had raised a division-size unit from indigenous populations, which had then succeeded in the destruction of over a brigade-size number of the enemy for the loss of less than a company's worth of men. The work of V Force and Force 136 (SOE) in this theater were also of great assistance to the activities of the Fourteenth Army in southern Burma. In addition to providing what at times was significant intelligence, their activities alongside the Karen populations, in particular, produced solid results in both offensive action and screening duties. Force 136's Operation Character from February 1945, for example, marshaled considerable numbers of Karen guerrillas and has been estimated to have accounted for some 10,964 Japanese dead.[87]

Alongside those formations working in Burma, SACO was making a similar contribution in China. SACO's reports of its achievements state that SACO-trained guerrillas "killed over 25,000 enemy troops, wounded 11,642, captured 508 prisoners of war, destroyed 209 bridges, 82 locomotives, 193 ships and river craft, and aided in the rescue of over 76 Allied pilots and crewmen," all achieved without the loss of a single American adviser. Certainly this appears a phenomenal achievement, but these estimates are widely considered to be heavily jaundiced by the Chinese propensity to dramatically inflate claims (it should be remembered that Tai Li, head of Chiang Kai-shek's secret police, was the operational chief of the organization, with Milton Miles serving as second in command). Such is the issue of doubt surrounding these claims that Lance Zedric and Michael Dilley have gone as far as suggesting that SACO's most significant contribution was in its provision of weather reports;[88] while Robert Asprey emphasized that for all of SACO's successes, which he believes "should not have been taken at face value," it was not able to prevent the 1944 offensive against Chennault's airfields.[89]

Force Multiplication and the Disruption of Enemy Plans

Any assessment of the numbers of enemy killed, aircraft sabotaged, intelligence gained, or partisans trained only goes so far in showing the ultimate utility of special operations during the war. An overview of the effects of specialist formations, acting both independently and in conjunction with conventional operations, must also examine the less quantifiable and more abstract manner through which they had strategic utility. One of the clearest benefits to the employment of specialist formations is that they have the potential to act as force multipliers. As Colin Gray asserts, "Special operations can work either as an economical equalizer or, better still, as critical leverage for victory."[90] The LRDG, for instance, was raised with the explicit motivation to undertake operations far and wide so that the Italians would be bluffed into "the impression of British ubiquity throughout the interior of Libya."[91] Although conducting operations of a very modest scale at this time, LRDG actions in the deep interior of Libya certainly helped distract Marshal Rodolfo Graziani during Operation Compass, between December 1940 and February 1941, which led to his decisive defeat and the capture of 115,000 Italian prisoners of war. In General Archibald Wavell's words, the unit made "an important contribution toward keeping Italian forces in back areas on the alert and adding to the anxieties and difficulties of our enemy."[92] The Italian reaction to the incursion of only a handful of men in their rear areas is evidence of what is potentially the most significant impact of special operations: to disrupt enemy plans, prey on insecurities, and coerce an opponent to take excessive precautions against further operations.

Special operations have a definite objective, to compel the enemy to alter their force dispositions unfavorably and expend resources unnecessarily, tying up men and material in wasteful tasks. General John Hackett believed this to be their most significant role, stating after the war that "the aim . . . in using these special forces is to hinder the most effective application of the enemy's resources in war and to secure advantages in the employment of our own."[93] The LRDG's first deployments caused the Italians to increase their defense of far-flung outposts throughout Egypt and Libya, tying up a considerable number of personnel and weakening their defense of the crucial coastal areas.[94] These, and later LRDG and SAS operations, provoked similar responses, promoting among the enemy an ever-growing need to defend and patrol rear areas, something that diverted both manpower, materials, and resources from the front lines. This was a consequence almost as significant as the physical destruction of personnel and resources in the raids themselves. The enemy was forced to waste manpower, resources, and time in what a War Office publication wonderfully described as the "feverish and almost ceaseless search for the Will-o'-the-wisp that flitted about the enemy's back garden while the whole panoply of Allied might was swarming across his front lawns."[95]

Similar motivations also underlay the original Commando raids. When General Alan Bourne was first appointed DCO, he considered the aim of raiding to be twofold: first, the destruction of enemy resources, and second, to "make him expend his resources, and to make his life as hard as possible."[96] Admiral Roger Keyes succeeded him with the directive to continually "harass the enemy and cause him to disperse his forces, and to create material damage."[97] This remained the spirit of practically all cross-Channel raiding and was a goal that was as equally appealing to the Americans upon their entry to the war. When visiting Britain in March 1942, General Marshall had faith that while massing forces prepared for a cross-Channel assault, "continuous raiding" of the French coast would create "a preliminary active front" that would provide combat experience to his soldiers while importantly diverting enemy resources and attention away from the critical situation on the Eastern Front.[98] Soon after this, Churchill wrote to President Roosevelt to advise him that the key goal in the employment of the newly established "Californian Commandos" (USMC Raiders) should be "to make the Japanese anxious for their numerous conquests and prevent them scraping together troops for further large excursions."[99]

The motivation to tie up a disproportionate number of enemy resources was used as a central point of justification for Allied (overwhelmingly British) involvement in the Aegean, Adriatic, and Greece. Beginning in late 1943 in the Aegean and early 1944 on the Dalmatian coast, raids were conducted against German-occupied islands and coastlines with the hope that they would provoke the reinforcement and retention of overstrength garrisons. In this goal the Allied special forces, aided by partisans, were generally successful. Barrie Pitt has estimated that by May 1944 raiding in the Aegean by the SBS (Squadron), the LRDG, and the Greek Sacred Squadron had caused the reinforcement of the Aegean garrisons by over 4,000 extra troops within a period of a month.[100] Not a bad tally for units that, in the case of the LRDG and SBS, numbered no more than around 250 men each. Likewise, those special forces and Commandos on the island of Vis in the Adriatic represented a continued "thorn in the side of the Germans in the Balkans" throughout 1944; their efforts are estimated to have been directly responsible for tying down three German divisions along the Yugoslav coast and forcing another one to be held in reserve, as well as playing a "very notable part" in keeping twenty-five enemy divisions occupied in Yugoslavia in the spring and summer of 1944.[101] Although the Allied specialist formations were only responsible for a token of the larger antipartisan and occupational difficulties that the enemy faced in these areas, in terms of numbers and the materials the enemy was forced to expend in response to such actions, they do appear to have been a worthwhile practice.

The same argument could be made in relation to actions against the Germans in Norway. The January 1942 Commando raid on Vaagso, alongside some of the smaller raids, certainly preyed very successfully on German insecurities, resulting in Hitler dispatching significant resources to Norway in an effort to protect against potential future Allied landings.[102] This raid, alongside other factors such as the Operation Fortitude North deception schemes (as it is quite unconvincing to attribute such dramatic reinforcement to the raid alone), helped confine much of the German surface fleet to Norwegian waters and ensured that by D-day some ten German divisions were left idle in Norway.[103] The strategic benefit this German reinforcement had on the overall Allied war effort was not, however, appreciated by exiled Norwegian prime minister Johan Nygaardsvold, who stated: "'Who could be so blind as to delude himself that this effort could have done anything to shorten the ordeal of Norway? ... the Germans would now strengthen their defenses making the ultimate victory even harder to achieve than it would have been if the raid had never taken place.'"[104] However, as far as Britain was concerned this was an acceptable, even favorable, outcome. The tenor of Nygaardsvold's point would, nonetheless, hold greater resonance in application to other theaters of war in which the Allies *did* intend to conduct conventional operations.

As raids had the power to compel the enemy to alter his dispositions, reinforcement schedules, and fortification schemes, it became absolutely essential that these operations be tightly controlled lest they prompt the enemy to strengthen his defenses in areas potentially to the detriment of the committal of conventional Allied arms. The last thing wanted when planning a large-scale amphibious landing, for example, would be to find out that you faced a stronger or more entrenched enemy because of the uncontrolled activities of a handful of raiders. When considering the relative benefits of small-scale raiding against France in late 1942, Admiral Charles Forbes, C in C Plymouth, doubted whether the advantages of raiding, such as intelligence gains, material destruction, or even the dissipation of enemy manpower, outweighed the disadvantages. Such operations, he believed, would draw the enemy's attention to "weak spots in his defenses," which would have adverse ramifications not only for future amphibious landings but also for destroyer and mine-laying operations off the enemy coast and for the insertion of SIS and SOE agents.[105] Such doubts about the viability of small-scale raids on France increased as preparations for Operation Overlord advanced.

At the start of 1944 Lieutenant General Frederick E. Morgan, COSSAC, was arguing the case for more raids and was "firmly convinced of the necessity for blooding our Rangers and Commandos before the day of battle on which they are destined to perform exploits of which the success must be assured." Instead of curtailing or canceling operations, he believed "that we should redouble our efforts. Not to do this is to leave the German in undisputed possession of his ill-gotten gains and to forgo our only opportunity of giving Commandos and Ranger units much required experience."[106] Such a scheme met with little favor, however, as the potential disadvantages of raiding were seen to outweigh the advantages. By this time various policies affecting raiding had been put in place: all raids with the purpose of "beating up" the enemy had already been stopped; it had been decreed that there were to be no needless operations in the Neptune area (where the Normandy landings were to take place), with the additional proviso that there be at least three cover raids undertaken for every one reconnaissance operation mounted; and it was decreed that no raid would "exceed strength of 100 all ranks," a limitation "imposed with the object of not encouraging the GERMANS to strengthen their coastal defenses."[107]

Even with these limitations in place, and despite the fact that poor weather during the January "dark period" had made sure that few raids were mounted, Major General Francis de Guingand, chief of staff 21 Army Group, began to argue against the necessity of all such raids. He came to "the conclusion that a policy of raiding *anywhere* on the BELGIUM/FRENCH coast is wrong. . . . We have told the enemy that we are going to invade the continent this Spring. I feel that the best way to fox him as regards the sector which we have chosen for the invasion, is to stop raiding altogether" [emphasis in the original]. He argued that all raids risked exposing to the enemy his weaknesses and believed that any information gained from commando raids would not be commensurate with the risks that mounting them entailed. Furthermore, he believed that even cover raids could potentially draw attention to the actual beaches chosen to land on or, more likely, provoke a universal improvement of defenses.[108] Such arguments were considered by the Raids and Reconnaissance Committee and generally accepted, with a large proportion of the initially intended raids subsequently being canceled.

The potential ills of a raid leading to undesirable enemy reinforcement are well illustrated by the aftermath of the August 1942 raid by the 2nd Raiders on Makin. Aside from destruction, the raid had, as an explicit goal, the creation of "a diversion confusing Japanese plans and diverting forces from the stronger concentrations being assembled to attack Guadalcanal in late August." At face value the raid can be said to have succeeded in all its purposes, "inflicting loss of planes, ships, supplies, and men, and diverted ships and aircraft, by causing the formation of a Makin relief force."[109] The latter result would, however, have more significant repercussions. It has been argued that the raid sparked the elaborate fortification and reinforcement of the Japanese garrisons in the Gilbert Islands, most notably on the Tarawa Atoll, which neighbored Makin, and the November 1943 invasion of which was infamously bloody for the U.S. 2nd Marine Division. With this consideration in mind, the historian Joseph H. Alexander believed "the raid accrued no strategic benefit. Quite the opposite: Carlson stirred up a hornet's nest in what had been a quiet, lightly held backwater of the Japanese perimeter."[110]

Just as there are limitations in praising raids for independently causing the enemy to divert his resources (as in Vaagso), there are equal difficulties in proportioning blame for events like Makin. Kenneth Macksey has asked that if the Makin raid sparked the strengthening of defenses, then why was there a delay of a year before the Gilberts were reinforced in earnest? Why did this reinforcement occur at the same time as a more general Japanese transition to the defensive?[111] The strengthening of defenses as the Axis powers were placed on the strategic defensive would have occurred irrespective of the conduct of special operations. As COHQ emphasized in late 1942, the enemy will not "increase his RDF [radio direction finding] cover and CD [coastal defense] Batteries to beat off small parties of men in canoes. Any measures he may take to counter our seaborne activities against his coastal convoys, he will take on their own merits."[112] Furthermore, the Makin raid did result in some positive benefits: it highlighted the limitations of rubber boat landings against atolls and the concomitant necessity for amtracks (amphibious landing craft, tracked)—an important lesson for the assault on Tarawa—and it also provided valuable intelligence for the 27th Infantry Division's eventual invasion of Makin.[113]

The Impact on Morale

In addition to attacking the enemy physically, special operations also assailed his morale. By targeting the enemy in areas that he had heretofore considered as being under his control, special operations could foster paranoia, prey on insecurities, and humiliate. It was thus a relatively common occurrence for various special forces operating in enemy rear areas to be given a significant margin of latitude to create "alarm and despondency" when the opportunity arose. It would, however, be incorrect to assume that the earliest infrequent and amateurish Commando raids had any great effect upon the morale of a triumphant enemy. The psychological toll inflicted by special operations was not properly manifested until the enemy's situation had deteriorated significantly as a result of other factors. On 13 October 1942 Churchill asked Mountbatten to further "intensify his small scale raids" because he "was certain that the Germans were being worried by them."[114] Churchill appears to have been correct. One week later Hitler betrayed his frustration by issuing his infamous Commando order (the Kommandobefehl, which pressed for the execution of all individuals caught waging irregular warfare, irrespective of uniform). Concerted activities in the rear by partisans, special forces, and subversive agencies had awakened latent German insecurities about a repetition of the "stab in the back" myth leading to their 1918 collapse. As irregular activities increased in volume and became progressively wedded to successful Allied offensives, their effect on a harried enemy naturally intensified.[115]

In addition to the long-term assault on enemy morale caused by the threat of constant action from an unknown angle, there was also the potential for more immediate tactical psychological effects, whereby the very presence on the battlefield of elite formations (most commonly of the commando type) could be enough to promote fear among the enemy. The sight of a red or green beret, or hearing shouts of "Commando! Commando!" in the attack (used just as much for maintaining cohesion and an identification of friend and foe as it was a psychological device) could be enough to provoke a response of retreat or surrender among poorly led or haggard troops. At Anzio, for example, during its period holding the beachhead, the FSSF intentionally undertook aggressive patrols in order to gain the moral ascendancy over its German counterparts. The force clearly emphasized its presence with terrifying nighttime raids, deliberately provoking fear among the Germans it faced, who consequently dubbed it the "black devils' brigade." Reg Seekings of the SAS believed elite credentials "made a lot of difference. If the British troops knew they were up against German paratroopers, they were half beaten already. It's the psychological effect you have on ordinary troops. They can't stand up to specialist troops."[116] This is a contention that was vividly illustrated in the Aegean, when Raiding Forces intentionally "created a reign of terror" among the German island garrisons, so that when the island of Samos was attacked, the enemy garrison of twelve hundred men in well-fortified positions surrendered unconditionally "to a trifling Allied force because they were literally frightened for their lives of Raiding Forces."[117]

The value of special operations causing fear among occupying garrisons must, however, be weighed against the potential risk of reprisals against innocent civil populations.[118] William Seymour doubts that any benefits of the earliest Commando raids "justified the reprisals sometimes meted out to the local inhabitants."[119] Despite attempts by political warfare agencies to keep local inhabitants and the enemy informed about the intention of raids, in order that they not unfairly proportion blame, there were occasional mishaps. In the immediate aftermath of the St. Nazaire raid, for example, some French civilians were killed and a large number wounded because of panicked Germans attributing subsidiary and delayed-action explosives to them (the precise number is a matter of debate; Lucas Phillips claims sixteen Frenchmen were killed, whereas Hilary St. George Saunders puts the figure as high as three hundred); in addition some fifteen hundred local men were subsequently arrested and sent to internment camps.[120]

Reprisals against civilians and partisans alike obviously intensified with the commencement of open partisan warfare; because of this, the dispatch of special forces to an area was occasionally resented because of the unwelcome attention that their presence could bring.[121] This point is vividly illustrated in a report that Commissar Mamola of the Second Partisan Sector on Dugi Otok (an island on the northern Dalmatian coast) made to OSS lieutenant John Hamilton. Expressing strong disapproval of the Commando and OG raids against various islands under his command, he asked:

> Why do they want to make raids on these Islands? They plan to come here, make a raid, kill a few Germans, capture 30 to 40 and then return to Vis with all kinds of stories; in the meanwhile the Germans will come over here take this island, burn a few villages, kill our civilians and we will have to run away to another Island. ... Our people must realize that this is NOT SPORT, THIS IS NOT RUGBY!.[122]

The moral cost of the Second World War was very great, and when the grim realities of unconventional warfare are merged with the actions of an enemy wedded to a brutal antipartisan doctrine, such reprisals became practically impossible to avoid.

One of the more intangible benefits resulting from the conduct of special operations was the fillip to morale they could provide to a nation's military and home front. In both Britain and America specialist formations were (and remain) a source of great fascination for the general public. Special operations give the impression of speed, dash, finesse, and adventure; traits rarely associated with the protracted slogging matches of open fronts. As John Newsinger wrote in a unique assessment of this phenomenon: "The story of the SAS in the Second World War is an adventure story. Young ex-public-school boys, the cream of the British race, leading their men in daring, sometimes foolhardy exploits against a brutal enemy."[123] Special operations offered welcome escapism from the realities of modern industrial warfare; they personalized conflict, created heroes, and were a tonic for both conventional defeat and inactivity.[124] For Britain they rekindled the romanticism and spirit of T. E. Lawrence and allayed fears of a recurrence of the horrors of stalemated attrition that characterized much of the First World War.

The creation of popular heroes was of course not limited to specialist formations, but for a time their operations offered a welcome glimmer of hope for harassed, strategically defensive, or stalemated nations. Consequently they became an obvious focal point for both press attention and propaganda. As Colin Gray reminds us, "Special operations can make the point that a powerful and feared enemy can be outfought on his own terms and thereby be denied moral ascendancy."[125] When conventional operations were neither possible nor successful, victories, however slight, could become magnified for the benefit of morale—giving hope and renewed confidence in a nation's martial abilities. Even failure, when occurring in a daring and dramatic fashion, could inspire confidence and was seemingly of little consequence when it came to reportage and mythologizing. Early Commando raids were undertaken, as much as for any other reason, simply "To cheer-up everyone at home."[126] An August 1942 OSS appraisal of the Commandos suggested that their "main purpose . . . is that of publicity."[127] Roger Beaumont even goes as far as suggesting that "the dashing image of the Commandos transcended any resources the Nazis were forced to allocate to defense or damage done."[128]

The United States seized upon the publicity value of special operations to an even greater extent than did the British. As the first ever independent raid undertaken by U.S. specialist formations the raid on Makin by the 2nd Raiders was an ideal candidate for a publicity campaign. Coming at a time when U.S. ground forces had not yet become actively involved in the war, this outwardly very successful, daring raid led by the charismatic and easily heroized Evans Carlson and his swashbuckling Raiders, which included the president's son, obviously received press attention. Admiral Nimitz would later claim that the primary purpose of the raid was "to boost morale."[129] In this goal it certainly succeeded and would make a "news splash" that was "almost as stimulating to morale as the Doolittle air strike over Japan."[130] At the same time as the Makin raid, the U.S. press were also reporting with alacrity the participation of the Rangers at Dieppe. Four U.S. correspondents accompanied the raid (as compared to three Canadian and two British), and the results of their reportage left "an American public . . . cheering offensive action and wanting more." Robert Black estimated that the fifty Rangers participating in the raid "were worth an army division to the American war effort."[131] There would, however, be diplomatic ramifications in this instance, with both Britain and Canada understandably taking umbrage to the disproportionate attention lavished upon the mere handful of Rangers involved in the action.[132]

Perhaps the finest example of a special operation receiving press attention is the 6th Ranger Battalion's raid on the Cabanatuan prison camp in the Philippines, an operation motived more by "sentimental allure" than by any intrinsic strategic priority.[133] Colonel Henry Mucci, commanding the Rangers, certainly understood the benefits of courting the press and had taken four official Army photographers along with his unit on the raid.[134] The operation itself was extremely successful. The Rangers, aided by 300 guerrillas and the Alamo Scouts, liberated over 500 prisoners and accounted for 532 Japanese dead for the loss of a single Ranger and 26 guerrillas killed.[135] The results were a publicist's dream: a deft, tactically masterful mission of mercy to liberate some of the famed prisoners of Baatan. It is of little surprise that MacArthur, himself no novice at publicity and self-aggrandizement, latched onto the raid's success, claiming that "no incident of the campaign has given me such personal satisfaction."[136]

There was also a political agenda in publicizing special operations. To both allies and enemies alike, well-publicized special operations could promote the impression of an energetic and martially talented nation. Raiding operations, most notably Dieppe, helped in some way to protect the British against accusations of inaction regarding the opening of a second front. They were, in the opinion of Brian Villa, "a showpiece for the Americans . . . to dispel the impression of passivity and defensiveness that was doing so much to erode the good opinion of British fighting resolve that Americans had formed during the Battle of Britain."[137] As Churchill admitted, "Small scale raids by the Commandos . . . not only gave us confidence and experience, but showed the world that although beset on all sides we were not content with passive defense."[138] The United States would similarly benefit. The employment of specialist units helped contribute to the appearance of ubiquity: the use of OGs in Yugoslavia and Greece or of Detachment 404 in the Arakan, for example, flew the flag of American participation in theaters where their presence was otherwise negligible. For instance, as the first American ground force in Burma, Merrill's Marauders (whose nonofficial name was itself an invention of correspondents attached to Stilwell's command) had an inherent degree of political capital and would attract "a greater share of attention from the press ... than a similar-sized unit merited anywhere else."[139]

If overused and overpublicized, however, raiding operations could ultimately prove to be a source of clear frustration to the war-weary general public and embattled allies alike; these may come to view such pin pricks themselves as a sign of passivity and reluctance to begin large-scale conventional operations. There was also a real danger that undue publicity would increase the negative perception of specialist elements as being "prima donnas" and thus be the cause of increased resentment among regular troops facing the unglamorous realities of front-line combat. An awareness of this fact certainly developed among the British. After the earliest commando forays, as more servicemen had become actively engaged in combat, the majority of smaller raids were conducted with "the minimum of publicity."[140] As Churchill wrote after Dieppe: "It is natural that there should be some resentment in the Army at the undue emphasis laid upon the work of the Commandos by the Press."[141] The same antipathy was seen within the USMC following the press attention bestowed upon the Raiders after Makin, which many believed was "too extensive, too complimentary."[142] Such resentments are understandable, for as Anthony Timpson of the LRDG asserted when assessing the value of his unit in the Desert War: "Set against Montgomery's nine divisions at Alamein, the nine Italian divisions and the German Panzer Army's five divisions, the glamour which is attached to irregular formations is not entirely fair. An infantryman or trooper or gunner or sapper with his unit could do little but try his best to fulfil his duty and slog it out."[143]

Despite the aggrandizement and mythologizing of specialist achievements prevalent in both wartime and postwar literature (and most commonly found in popular histories narrowly focused on one single unit or operation), it should be considered axiomatic that special operations did not win the war. Their achievements, while often notable, were dwarfed by the sheer magnitude of the conflict. As Field Marshal William Slim stated, "Armies do not win wars by means of a few bodies of super-soldiers but by the average quality of their standard units."[144] In any assessment of the wartime value of special operations, this point must be fully recognized. The achievements of specialist formations must be kept in perspective.

Disconnected from the activities and interests of greater campaigns, the value of special operations were, with a few possible exceptions (such as the seizure of intelligence materials during the Lofotens raid or the strike on the hydroelectric plant at Vemork), of less overall value to the course of the war than were those specialist activities that were wedded (however intangibly and at whatever depth) to the actions of conventional formations. The utility of the majority of pin-prick raids that occurred in the early years of the war were strictly moot, and aside from the occasional tactical coup, even their irritant effect was negligible against a triumphant enemy. The intelligence benefits of these operations were similarly slim. Landing on a coast snatching a prisoner or two was not a war-winning weapon, and against the completeness of signals intelligence, their impact pales in comparison. Perhaps the greatest benefit of such undertakings was that they offered a beacon of hope for the victory-starved people in Britain. It would not be until the enemy had witnessed a general downturn in his strategic position, a result of conventional actions, that such pin pricks began to represent a cumulative threat for the enemy.

There is a certain irony surrounding the use of specialist formations. Although commonly created in the first half of the war as a means of regaining the strategic initiative and of acting as a force multiplier for conventional arms, their greatest effect came once Allied arms had begun to engage the enemy or were already beating the enemy in a position of material and physical superiority. Their greatest impact came in a climate where their unique talents were, if valuable, no longer strictly necessary. Victory in these later circumstances was reliant on conventional arms, and any effects that specialist forces could achieve were strictly supportive. Their utility, with a few exceptions, was reliant upon the performance of regular forces to capitalize on their actions. Forcing the enemy to alter his dispositions, for example, is only of value if regular forces are able to seize the opportunity and strike at a weakened point. Their strategic utility, as Colin Gray asserts, "derives largely from the quality and quantity of performance by conventional forces.... War is a team endeavor. A special operation can open a door, but the regular forces may not be able to follow through."[145]

Taken as a subsidiary to conventional deployments, where an enemy is fully engaged at the front, the whole gamut of specialist deployments have more impact, helping, in various ways, to accelerate the pace of conventional success. Commando and ranger formations were ultimately of more value as elite spearhead and shock troops than they ever were as raiders. That, of course, was the reason for their evolution in role: beaches had to be taken, mountaintops assaulted, and flanks secured. Commando and ranger formations provided numerous examples of such tasks being performed quickly and successfully. Raiding activities by special forces in support of an active campaign could disrupt enemy lines of communication and infrastructure and hinder the enemy's ability to control and reinforce his fighting troops. The threat they posed also necessitated the enemy to waste valuable manpower and resources in guarding rear areas and prompted disproportionately heavy attempts to counter the elements doing the harassment. Such a diversion of effort from the front, exacerbated by the growth of indigenous guerrilla movements, could be as significant as any material destruction that the raids themselves caused. The intelligence benefits of special forces were similarly magnified when working for the direct benefit of conventional formations, a fact well illustrated by the value of the intelligence that the LRDG, Alamo Scouts, or Detachment 101 provided. On occasion the intelligence provided by these units was unique and obtainable through no other source; at other times their intelligence was supportive and of value simply because it could verify existing information.

In 1959 Peter Fleming, who during the war worked for SOE in Norway and Greece and later undertook deception work in the Far East, made the correct prediction that "there will always be controversy about any unorthodox achievements, however valuable they appear to be."[146] Although it is true to say that the Allies would have won the war had they not adopted irregular warfare or employed specialist units, this does not mean, however, that there is no latitude to recognize the contribution that specialist units did make in the Allied war effort. However proportionately small, the actions of specialist formations would each have impact, none independently decisive but all contributory to eventual Allied victory: they could accelerate the pace of success and limit casualties; they could provoke a paranoid enemy into making the wrong move; they were able to wreak material and physical destruction upon the enemy that, at a local level, disrupted his maneuvers and war effort; they could serve as a focal point for allied morale while being corrosive to that of the enemy; they provided a test bed for new doctrines and methods and enabled experience to be gained and disseminated. Even if the impact of these many achievements are impossible to precisely quantify, it appears that when assessed fairly, and not in the fantastical expectation of causing decisive impacts independently, the Anglo-American specialist formations certainly made a valuable contribution to the Allied war effort. So, to answer the question posed at the outset of this chapter—Were the Anglo-American commandos and special forces any good?—it is possible to echo M. R. D. Foot's verdict on SOE and argue an "emphatic Yes."

CHAPTER 7

COST-EFFECTIVENESS

Having highlighted the various achievements of Anglo-American specialist formations of the Second World War and their contribution, albeit proportionately modest, to the Allied war effort, it is now pertinent to ask: Were they cost-effective? Was the expenditure and effort exerted in their creation, deployment, and use proportionate with the results that they achieved? To use a framework similar to that which Julian Thompson used to judge effectiveness, was the "return" gained by these units worth the "investment"?[1] Such calculations embrace not only the question of specialist "achievements" but also wider issues related to the policies that Britain and America adopted toward the procurement, proliferation, expansion, and disbandment of these formations. Such calculations are not easy, however, and any assessment of an individual unit's cost-effectiveness turns upon a variety of variables, some readily quantifiable, others more abstruse. The most central of these variables are the scale of a formation's establishment, the frequency of its employment, the utility of its actions, and both the operational and nonoperational costs of its development and use. The interplay between these variables was unique to every formation, and it thus becomes extremely difficult, if not impossible, to compare in detail the cost-effectiveness of each unit. How can, for example, the relative cost-effectiveness of the handful of men in the Special Boat Sections be adequately compared to a unit the likes of Merrill's Marauders, a unit undertaking a dramatically different task with an establishment of approximately twenty-five hundred men? It is thus necessary to address the themes of cost-effectiveness in broad terms, drawing upon specific examples for the illustration of argument.

One of the key theoretical benefits to special operations is that they have the promise of reaping disproportionately favorable results commensurate with neither the expenditure of men nor materials taken up in their conduct. While this notion was certainly not universally applicable, in a number of instances it holds clear resonance.

For the British there is no better example of a cost-effective specialist formation than the Long Range Desert Group (LRDG). The virtuosity and value of the unit has been well emphasized in preceding chapters, but when it is also considered that the unit remained of a very modest size throughout the war—never exceeding an operational strength of 250 men (and often working with considerably fewer); that the unit made no outrageous demands on equipment or resources; and that the unit was almost continually employed—there being a total of only five months in its existence during which no operational patrols were active, a very favorable impression of cost-effectiveness becomes apparent. Julian Thompson has thus suggested that the LRDG should be considered "the yardstick by which one should gauge those that came after them."[2] Within the American example, a comparative "yardstick" is found in the Alamo Scouts. Mirroring the successes and the flexibility of deployment of the LRDG, the unit was also widely and consistently utilized, conducting some 106 missions during its one and a half years of operational existence. It also made as few demands on resources or on personnel—consisting of no more than 140 men during the war—and, unlike even the LRDG, would sustain no losses while on operations.[3]

Because their notable achievements and consistent employment came at a very low cost, the LRDG and Alamo Scouts can, perhaps equally, be viewed as paragons of cost-effectiveness. It would, however, be quite fallacious to assume that all specialist formations were able to match the record of the LRDG or Alamo Scouts, to assume that formations were always kept to a modest scale, were consistently deployed, or were as successful. While even the most ardent critic of specialist formations would have difficulty in arguing against the merits and value of units such as the LRDG and Alamo Scouts, there remain numerous critics of the general proliferation of irregular formations during the war who contend that, as in the words of Field Marshal William Slim, special forces were "expensive, wasteful, and unnecessary."[4]

The Drain on Manpower

One of the most acute criticisms leveled against specialist formations was directed at the demands they made on scarce manpower reserves, which, it is claimed, deprived the conventional arms, most particularly the infantry, of large numbers of good men. John Terraine criticized all specialist formations, or "private armies," as being a "not legitimate, or even sensible" drain on manpower. He believed that the Commandos were the "most famous" of the "offenders"; saw the Chindits as an "aberration . . . allowed to spoil a whole Division"; viewed the Airborne Forces as "the worst of all"; and was equally dismissive of the LRDG and SAS, believing that, though few in numbers, they helped to "compound the felony."[5] John Peaty, in a PhD thesis studying the British Army manpower shortage of 1944, similarly claimed that the proliferation of special forces "distorted the British Army's manpower distribution and contributed to its manpower problems," and that "on any rational assessment the inflated and under-employed Special Forces which the British Army possessed during WWII were not cost-effective. Quite simply, the benefits did not match the costs."[6]

Such arguments are, however, distorted by two principal factors: their reliance upon rather simplistic conclusions about the value and achievements of specialist formations (which commonly ignore many of their more intangible benefits) and, more significantly, the tendency to adopt overwhelmingly broad definitions of what constituted "special forces" that regularly encompass, in addition to the commandos and special forces of this work, the airborne forces, mountain units, specially-trained "regular" battalions, and the Chindits. Using such an expansive definition, Peaty misleadingly estimated that in 1944 within the British Army there was a total of 91 battalions of special forces, equating to some 25 brigades or 10 infantry divisions worth of men.[7] If the definition of specialist formations is restricted to those commando and special forces units inclusive of this work, the "drain" on manpower becomes significantly lessened. Using these narrower definitions, it is estimated that by mid-1944 the British had an "on the books" maximum of approximately 13,000 men tied up in commando and special forces. The United States, at this time, had a slightly smaller figure of approximately 10,000 men involved in specialist formations. (See appendix B for a breakdown of these estimates and those for other stages of the war.) At the height of the Allied manpower shortage, therefore, an approximate 23,000 Allied servicemen were in specialist units, enough manpower (at the average figures of the day) to have formed slightly under two infantry divisions. Although this number remained a noteworthy drain on manpower reserves, when taken alongside an understanding of the wider achievements of special operations, these figures dramatically lessen the weight of argument against their proliferation.

The divisive issue of the "drain" caused by specialist formations is not, however, solely focused on the quantity of manpower consumed but also embraces the quality of personnel absorbed.[8] Because of three things—the distinctive missions undertaken by these formations; the process of volunteerism, so often central to the recruitment processes for these units; and the physical demands of training and the necessity of finding the right man for the job—specialist formations tended (and continue) to attract "warriors," enterprising men of initiative, physically and mentally fit individuals who wanted to see action, many of whom would likely have made excellent NCOs or junior officers had they served in more regular formations.[9] This "leadership drain," aggravated by the perpetual risk of high casualty rates, serves, in the opinion of Roger Beaumont, to create a "selection-destruction cycle" that leads to depletion of hard-to-replace assets and resources.[10] In a postwar assessment of the utility of the Commandos, Lieutenant Colonel Joseph Patrick O'Brien-Twohig, who in the war had served alongside Commandos and Yugoslav partisans in the Adriatic, stressed how unfavorable this was and emphasized the "many shambles" that had occurred during the war resulting from the lack of good leaders. He argued that the "gallantry and skill the Commandos displayed did not compensate for the dearth of good junior leaders to which their existence was a big contributing factor."[11] Similar arguments were advanced in the United States, particularly over the establishment of the Raiders at a time when the USMC was desperately "struggling to flesh out the rapidly expanding divisions on a meager skeleton of experienced men."[12]

That specialist formations drained a proportion of talented individuals who would have been of good service elsewhere is not in dispute, but at least some diversion of such personnel was a natural and unavoidable concomitant to the decision to create new formations. Although the process of volunteerism, endemic to the creation of many specialist formations, often attracted the most keen "warriors" and weeded out those physically and mentally unsuitable, for the majority of units, however, being able to "cherry-pick" recruits from existent formations for expansion or reinforcement was a rare privilege. The reinforcement and replacement of highly trained personnel was a perennial problem for wartime specialist formations. High attrition in protracted operations made certain that the "problem of reinforcement was often paralysing to the Commandos."[13] The volunteer principle of the Army Commandos and the requirement to provide specialist instruction to any new recruits made reinforcement a difficult prospect. On average only 20 to 25 percent of those volunteering for the Commandos would actually make it through training to be accepted. Despite the problems this caused, for the Army Commandos the volunteer principle remained sacrosanct. As Brigadier Joseph Charles Haydon of the SS Brigade would write, the Commandos "should either consist of volunteers as it does now or be done away with. It is quite fantastic what a fundamental difference it makes and I am certain that the volunteer principle is one to which we simply must adhere."[14] Although the Royal Marine Commandos, which were created (with the exception of A Commando) from direct conversions of Royal Marine battalions, did not adhere to this same volunteer principle, they often faced even greater problems with reinforcement than their Army counterparts, simply because of the more general shortage of available Royal Marine personnel.

American ranger formations also faced particular difficulty both in recruitment and in replacing losses. As General Jacob Devers of AFHQ claimed in reference to Italy: "The greatest obstacle to overcome in the special forces . . . has been the problem of suitable replacements."[15] Although for much of the time ranger units remained as dependent upon the much-despised replacement depots as were the rest of the U.S. Army, from such sources they were, however, generally able to attract the best and most willing available personnel; then, if time constraints allowed, these personnel would commonly be submitted to an extensive "weeding out process." For example, when the 3rd and 4th Rangers were being recruited from these sources, Darby was willing to accept "green troops" but only an approximate 150 men out of every 1,000 volunteers would ultimately be deemed suitable for service in the Rangers.[16]

As the war progressed and as manpower shortages became more acute, the majority of new specialist units, notably the mainstay of the Royal Marine Commandos and the 6th Ranger Battalion, were formed not from volunteers but by direct conversions ("weeding out" inclusive) of existent and generally underemployed units. In such instances the idea of "drain" becomes negligible, and it is easy to advance the case, for example, that the 6th Rangers were of infinitely more use in the Southwest Pacific than they ever were as the 98th Field Artillery Battalion. It should further be recognized that at least a proportion of the personnel attracted to irregular units would have been wasted, if not totally misplaced, within regular units. As M. R. D. Foot asserted, many individuals "were able to achieve a significant role in the war solely because they were in SOE, which provided the unique, unorthodox channel through which their martial abilities could be expressed."[17] Many men within the Anglo-American special forces of the Second World War were not warrior-supermen but gifted amateurs, whose unique knowledge and skills (be it, for instance, a virtuosity in desert travel and navigation, an expertise in swimming or working with small boats and canoes, or an esoteric aptitude for the unconventional) would have been squandered in more conventional formations. As Terence Otway contended: "SAS operations provided an opportunity to exploit the personal independence and initiative of individual leaders who excel in comparatively small actions, apart from the more mass-controlled operations of the main armies. . . . They achieved results out of all proportion to the forces at their disposal and far greater than they would in more regular circumstances."[18]

While this "manpower drain," on occasions exacerbated by heavy casualties, was arguably one of the most notable "costs" in the development and use of specialist formations, so long as the men taken up in these units were adequately employed, the significance of this "drain" is greatly lessened. The manpower consumption of specialist formations should be kept in perspective. During the war, numerous sources absorbed valuable potential infantry recruits, and any assessment of the merits of one branch over another is fraught with difficulty. Cases could certainly be advanced that a greater "drain" came from the Allied air forces, which, while attracting large numbers of what certainly *were* the best and the brightest, also lost large proportions in the costly and indecisive strategic bombing campaigns that, as Steve Weiss stated, "demanded the combined utilization of two limited resources, intelligence, well-trained personnel and sophisticated technology. These shortages in personnel, aircraft and supplies imposed tight restrictions on irregular warfare."[19]

For those special forces that operated at depth there is much potential for comparisons of cost-effectiveness to be made with the use of Allied air power. When not mutually supportive, the parallels between the roles of certain special forces and air power (such as the undertaking of raids, interdiction, harassment, or reconnaissance activities) lend themselves to cost-effectiveness calculations. The limitations, or unavailability, of air power to adequately conduct certain roles— such as beach reconnaissance or long-range intelligence gathering—would, in a number of instances—such as the LRDG, the Combined Operations Pilotage Parties (COPPs), or Alamo Scouts—actually dramatically underline the need for the creation of a special unit in the first instance. In an offensive capacity, too, specialist formations offered the potential for mounting operations against targets that air power could not attack with requisite accuracy or without potentially heavy losses. Such limitations were the prime motivations in using specialist formations for the conduct of such operations as the Commando raid on St. Nazaire or, on a smaller scale, the Operation Frankton raid against shipping in Bordeaux by the Royal Marine Boom Patrol Detachment (RMBPD).

The efficiency of aerial bombardment over the merits of sabotage or *coup de main* attacks by irregular elements is particularly open to debate. Critical of the inaccuracy of aerial bombardment, OSS officer Franklin Lindsay stated that "a large number of bombs had to be delivered to ensure that one or two hit the target.... If one could get next to the target and plant the explosives by hand right on the most vulnerable parts of, for example, a bridge, the probability of its destruction could be increased greatly and the explosives used would be a tiny fraction of that used in aerial bombardment."[20] As well as being potentially more damaging because of its accuracy and offering the benefit of fewer civilian casualties through indiscriminate destruction, sabotage also represented a more moderate outlay in men and materials and had the further advantage, providing insertion of specialist groups and equipment did not greatly imperil aircraft, of offering a lower-risk solution. As Guy Courtney of the Special Boat Section (SBS) emphasized: "Weigh the possible loss of two men in a canoe against one or more bomber aircraft in an attack on a railway bridge and you have an example of cost-efficiency."[21] Despite this, M. R. D. Foot asserted that there were "only a few" instances in which sabotage could be seen to be "a superior instrument to mass bombing," citing the examples of the raid on the Vemork hydroelectric plant (yet even this was eventually repaired and had to be attacked by the USAAF) and the attack on

Montbéliard, where a team of SOE and French partisans did "what several squadrons of bombers could not" and sabotaged a tank turret factory to place it out of action for the duration of the war.[22]

It is neither possible nor practicable to argue that special operations were a superior tool to air power. They had neither the reach nor the destructive potential that mass bombing had. Air power, particularly when superiority was attained in the later stages of war, could reach many targets "both easier and with a much greater devastating effect"—albeit with potentially greater losses—than small groups of men could ever hope to achieve. Allied aerial and naval superiority toward the end of the war were actually a clear reason for a number of special forces—most notably those concerned with maritime sabotage—remaining largely unemployed.[23] Despite these factors, it remains clear that on occasion special operations could provide a potentially less costly and more accurate alternative, or ancillary, to the use of air power. Furthermore, raids and special operations were capable of amplifying the effectiveness of air power by, for instance, drawing out the enemy (as was an explicit motivation behind the Dieppe raid) or by providing targeting information and directing interdiction strikes. Such was part of the inherent value of special operations: they expanded options and increased the Allied repertoire of response.[24] Engaging in such debates over relative merits becomes somewhat redundant, however, when one considers how reliant, particularly in the later stages of the war, specialist formations became on the utilization of aerial and naval resources.

The Demands on Operational Resources

The demands that certain special operations made upon overstretched operational resources were not in any way modest. The strain they placed on shipping, submarines, and aircraft to facilitate transportation, reinforcement, and supply could be quite exacting. The effort taken to mount even a very minor operation could be quite considerable. Operation Anklet of December 1941, for example, was a relatively small diversionary raid undertaken for the benefit of Archery, the larger Lofotens action, and involved three troops of No. 12 Commando and attached Norwegians. Yet to mount this proportionately small operation required the direct committal of one destroyer, one corvette, and one infantry landing ship and their crews, plus a much larger escort to the target comprising one cruiser, seven more destroyers, one more corvette, three minesweepers, two submarines, two oilers, and an additional infantry carrier.[25] Various other special operations, particularly those occurring at depth, required a similar commitment of regular forces to support and facilitate them. Thus, while a special operation may itself involve only a seemingly cost-effective handful of men, there were often numerous "hidden costs" involved that must not be ignored.

The diversion or risk of active-service craft, and their crews, dramatically increased the cost of mounting special operations and at times can be considered to have been counterproductive to their inherently low-cost virtues of execution. Early irritant commando raids of negligible value often did not attain results commensurate with the expenditure and risk of scarce resources utilized in their conduct (the Commandos themselves inclusive). Perhaps the most contentious diversion of active-service craft came in the form of utilizing both submarines and heavy bombers for the transport of special forces, activities that not only placed both the craft and their crews at risk but also diverted them away from their regular activities, which ultimately could be of potentially greater value to the war effort than the special operation they were facilitating. Charles Cruickshank, for instance, went as far as calling Operation Jaywick, the successful September 1943 canoe-based raid on Japanese shipping in Singapore Harbor, carried out by men of the Services Reconnaissance Department of the Australia-based Allied Intelligence Bureau (AIB), both "insignificant" and "counter-productive" because of its diversion of submarines, which at the time were regularly accounting for a greater tonnage of Japanese shipping than the raid itself achieved.[26] Despite this, so long as the submarine was not made subservient to the course of the special operation, such costs were distinctly lessened. Understanding this point, the Admiralty insisted on "combining clandestine operations with normal submarine patrols," so that units such as the SBS (Sections) would be used if and when opportunities presented themselves over the course of a submarine's regular patrol.[27] In this manner specialist units complemented, rather than detracted from, the submarine's own activities.

If opportunities for active-service craft to deploy in their principal occupations were not present, however, their use in special operations was, if no less of a risk, certainly a more tolerable arrangement.[28] The use of dedicated landing craft and transport aircraft, and even the diversion of bomber aircraft in special operations at times when those resources were not required elsewhere, can, providing that they were not lost or diverted for protracted periods, generally be viewed as an acceptable use of resources. Even at those times when these resources had potential use elsewhere, special operations commonly represented only a minor and fleeting diversion of effort. This contention is backed up by a SHAEF report written on the eve of the commencement of D-day, which stated: "While it is undesirable as a general principle to divert strategic air effort from bombing enemy communications . . . the small number of heavy day bomber sorties required for the support of Resistance when taken in relation to the overall air effort available will interfere little, if at all, with the strategic air operations."[29]

In spite of this contention, the active support of armed indigenous guerrilla movements represented the most significant diversion of such resources and the greatest material costs of mounting special operations. Absorbing large amounts of weapons and stores, these activities would also tie up numerous Allied aircraft, crews, and ground personnel in their dispatch. The extensive infrastructure required could dwarf the physical needs of Allied special forces alone. On top of the dedicated "special duty" squadrons—such as No. 38 Group RAF or the Carpetbaggers of the USAAF 801st Bombardment Group (Provisional)—that had been formed, at various times heavy bomber squadrons were also diverted to help supply partisans. For example, in Operation Zebra, occurring on June 25, 1944, some 180 B-17 bombers were used to drop over 2,000 containers of arms and equipment to the Maquis in south central France. This was followed by the even larger Operation Cadillac of July 14, which saw over 320 heavy bombers, escorted by an even greater numbers of fighters, deliver over 3,700 containers to partisans in Vercors.[30]

Because the effectiveness of partisan formations could differ quite considerably, the maintenance and supply of indigenous movements cannot always be considered to have been cost-effective. Confusion in policy over which guerrilla movements to support could lead, as in Greece and Yugoslavia, to a degree of wastage and duplication of effort or, in the worst case, the resources being delivered into enemy hands. In places much time, money, and effort was spent arming indigenous groups whose military impact was negligible at best. In direct contrast to such instances, however, are the successes attained in Burma that provide vivid illustration of the worth of arming indigenous guerrillas. The cost of Detachment 101's operations, for instance, were not in any way immoderate: the dispatch of over 1.5 million pounds of supplies into the field each month required a significant diversion of effort. Yet, given the successes attained, such a commitment certainly appears to have been warranted.[31] Both Detachment 101 and the more than 10,000 Kachin "Rangers" it eventually organized were a sound investment that reaped a disproportionate return. As Roger Hilsman stated regarding his own Kachin Ranger "battalion": "In terms of cost-effectiveness, it cannot be doubted that the guerrilla efforts of OSS Detachment 101 were a resounding success. For our battalion, the cost had been the commitment of three Americans and one Englishman, pay and supplies for 300 guerrillas, C-47s and crews to supply us, and radio and administrative personnel at headquarters. The intelligence we gathered alone would have justified such small costs many times over."[32]

Size of Establishment

The issue of the "cost" of specialist formations, in terms of both manpower and resources, is inherently linked to the issue of scale. An obvious and generally applicable rule is, the larger the unit, the greater the cost. The fact that commando and ranger formations operated in battalion and brigade strength thus inherently opened these larger formations up to more criticism than was commonly directed toward special forces.[33] Even that outspoken critic of specialist units Field Marshal Slim remained optimistic about units that were "designed to be employed in small parties, usually behind the enemy, on tasks beyond the normal scope of warfare in the field. . . . Not costly in manpower, they may, if handled with imaginative ruthlessness, achieve strategic results."[34] Although in operational deployments most special forces remained subservient to tactical maxims dictating only a small-scale commitment of force, it does not necessarily follow that individually and collectively they did not absorb a significant proportion of manpower and resources. Of the previously cited estimates of the numbers of personnel within the Anglo-American specialist forces in 1944 (a total of approximately 23,000 men), special forces accounted for approximately 3,870 men in British units and 4,525 men in American units. The proportion of men in some units, such as the SAS Brigade, OSS Detachment 101, or the Underwater Demolitions Teams (UDTs), would ultimately exceed the numbers of personnel involved in certain commando formations. (See appendix B.)

It is undoubtedly true that the small scale of the LRDG and the Alamo Scouts was a central factor in their exemplary cost-effectiveness. However, to pose a hypothetical question, would this cost-effectiveness have been retained had their establishments been expanded? It would be easy to assume that simply providing more men, vehicles, and weapons to a fully employed and effective force would lead to a proportionate increase in their margin of success. It might be possible to argue, for instance, that the LRDG might have achieved more had the unit been expanded by a patrol or two. Yet such estimates are rarely accurate. To retain overall cost-effectiveness the enlarged formation would have to have been deployed as frequently and with the same margins of success as were the original personnel. One need only look at the underemployed Indian Long Range Squadron at various stages in the Desert War to see that the expansion of the LRDG concept had its limits. There is a definite "cutoff point" in size of establishment, and too much expansion risked these formations becoming less "special" and potentially subverting their inherent virtues of ease of operation, economy of effort, flexibility and autonomy, thus limiting their chances for correct employment. Part of the reason that the LRDG and Alamo Scouts remained so cost-effective was that they were perpetually kept to a modest size.

The SAS provides an ideal case study for an assessment of the relative merits of the expansion of a special force. Within the space of only three years the SAS grew from a tiny force of some sixty men at its inception into a multinational brigade with a strength of approximately twenty-five hundred men by mid-1944. Its earliest operations in the desert were, without doubt, very cost-effective. Its destruction of aircraft alone "far outweighed the personal score achieved by any aircrew, whose training was both long and costly, and who attacked in expensive aircraft maintained by a large number of ground crew."[35] It was these very successes that led to the SAS gaining its regimental establishment in September 1942. Yet in the later stages of the Desert War, as a regiment the SAS began to show diminished results at the expense of higher casualties, David Lloyd Owen of the LRDG would claim that the SAS "balance sheet" began to show "too great an excess of expenditure over achievement."[36] This modest downturn in cost-effectiveness, which in no way subverted the overall value of the unit, was not so much a result of the physical expansion of the unit—although rapid expansion did lead to the cutting of some corners in the training of new recruits—as it was caused by situational changes resulting from a better prepared enemy, shortened enemy lines of communication, and a more hostile environment. Even given their higher losses, these later operations were still generally of value, their results being at least proportionate with investment.

While the achievements of the 1st SAS in the Desert War are hard to dispute, the value of the 2nd SAS Regiment's operations in North Africa, Sicily, and Italy in 1943 are somewhat more debatable. Despite Bill Stirling's optimistic estimates that the widespread deployment of his regiment in small groups would be both "very economical to mount" and capable of dramatic results, the regiment was not given the opportunity to test such theories in any more than token form.[37] Instead, either broadly underemployed or facing employment in a more conventional capacity, the actual value of the 2nd SAS at this time must be regarded as minimal and, in light of this, not particularly cost-effective.

While the expansion of the SAS into brigade strength in preparation for the invasion of France increased their potential for success, it also dramatically increased the "cost" of the unit in terms of personnel, resources, and supporting infrastructure. Nevertheless, the eventual combat record of the SAS Brigade in France makes for impressive reading: excluding many of the more intangible benefits of special operations, over the course of 49 operations, in which 1,987 men were dispatched (850 of whom were British), 7,753 casualties were inflicted on the enemy and 4,764 prisoners were taken (excluding the inflated numbers surrendering in conjunction with larger Resistance activities); over 400 vehicles were destroyed or seized (some accounts place this figure as high as 1,000); numerous railway lines and roads were cut and trains, bridges, and telephone lines thereon destroyed. However, these results were achieved at notable cost to the SAS Brigade, which, excluding 4th SAS, sustained losses of 345 men killed, missing, or captured and 115 wounded in action.[38] Even given these losses and the greater expenditure in manpower and resources taken up, or diverted, in mounting the operations, it is evident that the results achieved justified the expenditure. The SAS remained cost-effective after 1943, even if not as startlingly so as it had been during its first year in the Desert War.

The use of the OSS OGs in France represented a much more modest effort than the employment of the SAS Brigade, but in terms of tangible achievements the units appear to have produced a proportionately similar return. Undertaking only twenty deployments, in which a total of 356 men were employed, the OGs claimed, albeit in conjunction with the Resistance, to have killed 461 of the enemy, wounded approximately the same number again, and to have taken 10,021 prisoners.[39] Compared to the SAS, the OGs achieved these returns at a much reduced cost, sustaining losses of only 8 men killed, 23 wounded, and 1 missing in action.[40] A comparison of the relative achievements of these two units, while not necessarily proper (in light of variations in the methods and manner of their operation—particularly concerning the differing extents to which they were integrated with the Resistance), does, nevertheless, highlight the fact that the expansion of a specialist formation, or at least a moderate increase to brigade strength, did not necessarily result in diminished returns per se but instead indicates that the returns stayed broadly proportionate. In short, the expansion of a specialist formation, so long as this occurred in response to a clear need with there being a definite potential for deployment, was not necessarily to the detriment of cost-effectiveness.

The Relationship between Proliferation and Opportunity for Employment

Opportunity for employment is a prerequisite of cost-effectiveness; thus disuse of specialist formations potentially represents the most damning waste of resources. To remain valuable and therefore be cost-effective, specialist formations had to be consistently utilized. That this was not always the case added to the arguments of their detractors. David Thomas, for instance, disparagingly noted the persistent "disparity between the sophistication of commando training and the high quality of commando units, on the one hand, and the insignificance of the objectives assigned to these units and the limited tactical employment of commando forces in general, on the other."[41] The example of the American-Canadian First Special Service Force (FSSF) provides a solid illustration of the complexity of such an argument. Outwardly the results of the force's deployments appear to have been very cost-effective. In addition to facilitating operational manoeuvre in Italy the unit, numbering approximately 2,500 men, has been credited with 12,000 enemy killed and the capture of upwards of 7,000 prisoners. Such figures suggest that one commando force alone accounted for almost the same number of the enemy as the total number of all Allied personnel involved in specialist formations by 1944.[42] In spite of such favorable calculations, it is legitimate to ask, in light of its extensive Arctic, airborne, and amphibious training being of only marginal tangible use (such as in the scaling of Monte la Difensa or in the capture of Ile du Levant and Ile de Port Cros prior to Operation Dragoon), whether the cost and time of this training, which kept the force unemployed for over a year, was worth the outlay. Stanley Dziuban, writing in a special volume of the U.S. Army's official history, doubts it was, highlighting the fact that the force "engaged but little in the highly specialized types of operations for which it had been trained" and concluding that it "represented a costly expenditure of resources and a complex administrative effort, particularly to Canada because of the force's distance from Canadian administrative machinery."[43]

Although the rigorous training that the FSSF underwent was ultimately of little specific application, it was not, however, entirely wasted. Molding the unit into a cohesive whole and endowing the personnel with a high level of skill at arms, this training laid the foundations for the force's successes. Monte la Difensa would certainly not have been taken and held as efficiently as it was had it not been for such intensive training.[44] Cohesion, however, rarely survives attrition. Once the force had sustained heavy casualties its fighting effectiveness, commensurate with that of other formations, such as the 1st Rangers by the Battle of Cisterna, naturally declined. The only way this could have been subverted and the quality of the instrument maintained would have been to take formations out of "the line" for reinforcement and retraining. This was a fact well understood by the British, who expanded their commando organization to specifically provide "sufficient" formations "so as to allow for wastage and rest between operations."[45] However, in light of the exigencies of the battlefield, such a policy was rarely practical.

The value and cost-effectiveness of proportionately much smaller formations is equally reliant upon correct and consistent deployment. There are various examples of special forces that, although remaining of modest scale, can face charges of being expensive, redundant, and underemployed. The excessive proliferation of certain maritime special forces, each with diverse niche roles, in particular, leaves a proportion of them open to such criticisms. The Royal Marine Boom Patrol Detachment (RMBPD) had, in general terms, a somewhat limited operational record and achieved only two notable successes (the crippling of two destroyers to facilitate a raid on Simi arguably being of more significance than the sinking of blockade runners during the audacious Operation Frankton against Bordeaux), and it is thus certainly debatable whether these operations alone justified the time, equipment, and personnel taken up in forming the unit.

Of even less cost-effectiveness was the Sea Reconnaissance Unit (SRU). Despite being one of the smallest independent units created during the war, with just over forty men in its establishment, the unit underwent over two years of expensive training in California, Nassau, and Britain before eventually being sent to Ceylon in October 1944.[46] The outfit was then not operationally deployed until February 1945, and while proving of use, most clearly in performing reconnaissance for XXXIII Corps, was soon made redundant by the crossing of the Irrawaddy River only one month later.[47] Despite its small size, the proportion of time and money spent training the formation negatively contrasted with its modest successes and limited time in the field.

Britain's excessive proliferation of disparate maritime special forces, each with their own niche offensive role, cannot be considered cost-effective. In light of the limited operational deployments of some of these units, it could well be argued that some of the tasks to be undertaken could easily have been catered to by an existent, versatile, and equally small-scale formation like the Special Boat Section (SBS), which certainly was cost-efficient. Furthermore, before becoming centralized under the branches of the Special Boat Unit, Small Operations Group (SOG), or Deputy Director of Operations Division (Irregular), each of these units also made additional demands upon individual training and experimental and administrative resources, and they spent excessive amounts of time and money in efforts to develop new methods and equipment that, for the most part, had little wartime application and can be considered "a complete waste of time."[48] That said, given the potential leverage that might have been gained by a technological breakthrough, some of these activities, when not relying on hindsight, are difficult to actually condemn.

These arguments are not, however, necessarily reserved for Britain alone. Although the American development of *offensive* maritime formations all under the aegis of the OSS Maritime Unit (MU) was certainly more cost-effective than the cumbersome British approach, the wartime application of much of the MU—aside from the "Italian" branch and those later converted to UDTs—was slight. The "London," "North African" and "Far Eastern" branches of the MU, in particular, were constantly hindered by both a lack of opportunity for employment and inadequate transportation to use when opportunity did arise. Illustrative of the frustrations elements of the MU faced are comments made by Lieutenant Commander A. G. Atwater, the ironically named South East Asia Command (SEAC) MU chief, in May 1945: "We have approximately 43 personnel that have been training for over a year. They have been here almost a year and the work has been nil. A certain amount of jobs were found in the Arakan show but it did not require personnel who were trained as specialists; in fact, the specialist training was a drawback due to difficulties in utilising this type of personnel for regular duties."[49]

At practically all times these niche-skilled maritime formations were in stiff competition for employment with other formations with a similar mandate. Redundancy and competition resulted from having too many similar units and not enough opportunity for their employment. Colonel H. T. Tollemache, commanding the SOG in Ceylon, emphasized these problems well when he reflected that "neither functions nor general methods [between units] have been markedly dissimilar. . . . The differences consequent of this independent function, in technique, in composition and in organization have resulted in lack of economy both in personnel and stores due to each type of team 'running its own show' and to maintaining establishments designed for one theater while operating in another."[50]

There existed a thin line between a specialist formation being suitably "specialized," and justifying its existence by fulfilling a role that no other force could perform, and its becoming too specialized as it risked becoming inapplicable to the wider war should the unique circumstances for its use never, or too infrequently, appear. Overspecialized forces are not desirable; they lose their intrinsic flexibility and therefore much of their potential application. As Robert

Laycock wrote after the war, "The answer to the question as to whether or not you require "specialist" troops for raiding is 'Yes.' But the lesson is: don't raise too many; don't form odd units for odd jobs, because if they are worth their salt, they ought to be quite capable of carrying out any particular type of raid."[51]

The "mushroom growth of all sorts of these organizations" during the war risked undermining some of their inherent claims to cost-effectiveness. Too many specialist formations and too little divergence in role meant that resources were wasted as units were not employed as designed.[52] Extensive proliferation not only undermined the strength of the conventional arms but also impacted negatively upon the quality and efficiency of other specialist units, spreading too thin those individuals with a real flair for the conduct of irregular operations and, more significantly, leading to duplication of effort, confusion, and competition for missions and resources. Ideally Britain would have not needed to establish such a diverse range of offensive maritime formations, nor would the United States have needed to create the UDTs, Naval Combat Demolition Units, USMC Reconnaissance Battalions, the Scouts and Raiders (S&R), and elements of the OSS MU, all operating independently with overlapping mandates.[53] That these formations were prone to develop with significant overlap was a natural consequence of adopting small units in an opportunistic or ad hoc manner to deal with the exigencies of a global war. Intertheater requirements and, often more significantly, interservice (or interagency) confusions directly led to a degree of duplication of effort and, therefore, redundancy.[54]

Were Specialist Formations Necessary?

One of the fundamental principles behind the creation of specialist formations was that they were to perform tasks that regular forces either would or could not carry out within the same constraints of time and space or without sustaining disproportionate losses. It follows, therefore, that some of the most acute criticisms of specialist units are based on the assertion that their creation was redundant because, as Field Marshal Slim contended, "Any well-trained infantry battalion should be able to do what a commando can do; in the Fourteenth Army they could and did."[55] When specialist formations undertook more conventional roles, arguments against their proliferation would increase, whether these roles were taken in extremis or not and almost irrespective of any successes they attained in such occupations. For example, as late as May 1945 the War Office stated that if Commandos were to be employed in brigade strength, complete with the attendant administrative infrastructure, it "would appear that normal Infantry Brigades on light scales would meet requirements equally well."[56] When specialist formations sustained heavy casualties by performing tasks for which they lacked the necessary numbers, supplies, and firepower, their detractors received obvious ammunition. It is thus no coincidence that American attitudes toward ranger formations declined appreciably following the high attrition rates these units endured during the winter of 1943–44 in Italy, something that became particularly pronounced after the 1st and 3rd Ranger Battalions were lost at Cisterna. When units such as Merrill's Marauders, which had a very high rate of wastage, are considered, it is hard to avoid the charge that, as General Auchinleck stated in regard to the Chindits, "Infantry in normal formations having proper Artillery and other support are defeating Japs and sustain far fewer casualties."[57]

In Burma there were numerous examples of British and Indian field formations undertaking tasks that approached those conducted by commando formations when the latter deployed more conventionally. As part of the reforms taken after the calamitous First Burma Campaign to train and prepare British and Indian forces in jungle warfare, a number of programs were instigated to teach irregular techniques to field formations. In 1942 the 17th Indian Division, for example, took steps to become a "storm troop division," and requesting COHQ documents to help the process, allotted the 16th, 48th, and 63rd Brigades the specialized roles of acting as "shock troops in support of tanks and against strong points," "jungle warfare shock troops," and "combined operations and river shock troops," respectively. In addition, it was expected that each battalion would form a "shock platoon" from handpicked men who would attend "commando camps" to qualify them for "special tasks."[58] These initiatives should not, however, be viewed as part of any real desire to develop independent irregular warfare capabilities but rather as an effort to better adapt these formations to the requirements of the campaign in Burma, instigate pathfinder and short-range divisional reconnaissance companies, and provide troops with experience and an opportunity to engage with the enemy.

Another good example of an initiative to train regular formations in irregular methods is provided by the V Corps School of Raiding that Brigadier Gerald Templer established (with a meager establishment of two officers and four NCOs as instructors) in Britain in late 1941. Concerned that the Commandos were the only outfits at that time amassing experience in raiding, Templer created this school with the dual intention of training one V Corps infantry company a month in raiding techniques and of providing them with the opportunity to carry out small-scale raids against the French coast. Although staff and students from the school were able to undertake a limited number of forays against France, such as Operation Curlew, a reconnaissance raid on St. Laurent in Normandy on January 18, 1942, it ultimately proved to be a short-lived and distracting enterprise that was disbanded in late September 1942 as COHQ took sole responsibility for coastal raiding.[59]

It was in a similar manner that both the 3rd and 34th U.S. Infantry Divisions would form "raider platoons" among some of their regiments. These platoons, and the likes of the Scout-Sniper platoons as formed by the USMC in Guadalcanal, did not represent specialist units as much as they did a cadre of experienced and willing volunteers who could be called upon to undertake tactically difficult or dangerous—but quite conventional—operations for the immediate benefit of their parent field formations.[60] In fact, because of their volunteer and somewhat ad hoc nature, these groupings were often "over worked," were prone to be "sent on too many missions without adequate rest," and were often called upon to undertake operations hastily, without having had sufficient time to plan and prepare. Furthermore, because these outfits tended to undertake a disproportionate share of the more hazardous tasks assigned to a regiment, the ability for all ranks in that regiment to gain experience was lessened with potentially detrimental ramifications for its quality as a whole.[61]

That conventional formations on occasion sought to develop their own organic elite–light infantry capabilities was largely reactionary to operational requirements and denigrates neither the value nor cost-effectiveness of specialist formations dedicated to undertaking similar activities. In a sense the existence of these kinds of formations among conventional units was a direct complement to specialist formations as innovators. As Eliot Cohen has emphasized, "a light infantry unit may perform tasks similar to those of conventional units, but its separate existence is justified by its ability to inject fresh thinking into the mainstream of military thought."[62] It will not be forgotten that endemic to the U.S. perception of specialist formations was the mentality that once training, and even operational deployment, was completed, the personnel would be returned, either as a whole or on a rotational basis, to conventional units to disseminate information and act as instructional troops. In the case of the 29th Rangers, as well as both the Alamo Scout and S&R Schools, this theory was put into practice.

Scott McMichael argued that because of a "relative scarcity of legitimate missions for specialized forces," the formation of these units should have been limited. He further contended that when "specialized operations are necessary, they can be undertaken by conventional units provided with special training prior to the operations."[63] Although this argument appears to have some resonance when the "misuse" of certain commando-style formations in protracted defensive infantry duties is considered, in application to the majority of specialist tasks, however, it is quite erroneous. To have made widespread use of conventional forces to undertake specialist roles would have taken up a significant proportion of time and resources and would certainly not have been in anyway cost free. Teaching regular formations irregular skills would have been potentially wasteful and risked distracting them from their primary war-winning occupations.[64] In defense of his formation of the Commandos, Dudley Clarke was keen to emphasize that they were initially created as separate units precisely to avoid the disruption or diversion of any normal unit from the then pressing tasks of mainland defense.[65]

Although regular formations could and, with training, did undertake a number of roles synonymous with specialist formations—such as spearheading amphibious landings, performing overland infiltration, or undertaking the occasional raid—it is certainly possible to argue, as Robert Laycock and many others involved in the planning of special operations have, that even these more "simplistic" operations still required "a special technique, a special temperament. . . . Each individual . . . must possess special qualifications which are not normally found in regular units and which it is not really practical to teach them."[66] Furthermore, it is quite incorrect to assume that all regular soldiers with, let alone without, a degree of unique instruction could have been relied upon for the conduct of particularly complex special operations—such as intelligence gathering, beach reconnaissance and pilotage, sabotage in depth, or liaising with partisans—without dramatically sacrificing results. To have relied upon regular formations with only a modicum of extracurricular training for the conduct of specialist operations would likely have resulted in numerous problems. With no standing special operations capabilities, the time taken to have raised organic specialist parties from regular formations in response to a specific opportunity would have dramatically decreased the potential operational speed of response and may well have led to missed opportunities. Peter Young, historian and wartime commander of No. 3 Commando, admitted that "any infantry can do our job" but summed up one of the key benefits of the Commandos by stating that "only we . . . can do it in the time allotted."[67] Thomas Churchill, wartime commander of 2nd SS Brigade, also illustrated this point well with his contention that "a [regular] battalion can, in a month or two, be trained to step out of landing craft and to perform *specific* tasks, on a specific beach . . . but it would require at least a year's training to enable it to compete with successive and differing tasks . . . assigned to the Commandos."[68] While specialist formations traditionally placed a premium on detailed planning and rehearsal, many of the operations they undertook during the Second World War were conducted on comparatively short notice and under conditions whereby "only exceptionally well-trained and cohesive units . . . are likely to succeed."[69]

Utilizing regular elements for the conduct of specialist tasks would have made calling for volunteers essential, and lest mentally and physically unsuited men subvert the chances of success, subjecting those volunteers to a subsequent "weeding out" process would have been desirable. Further, considering the often impromptu manner in which a number of "private armies" were raised during the war, the net result of any attempt to develop specialist capabilities within regular formations in a short space of time would doubtless have resulted in something approaching the earliest specialist formations anyway but likely would also have lacked the so often critical flair and drive provided by an "errant captain" at the helm. Any such regular unit so converted would probably have also lacked a clear mandate and had a more constrained freedom for action; would likely have confused regular command and control channels; and would doubtless have been open to abuse and a misapplication of its budding abilities because of its "regular" identity. In addition, if having performed an operation the personnel were then to be returned to their original company or regiment, experience and esprit de corps would be sacrificed, and should a future requirement for a special operation emerge, it would have been necessary to take the lengthy and wasteful step of having to recruit another band for its conduct.

The potential limitations of using regular forces to undertake specialist roles were most succinctly highlighted by David Lloyd Owen of the LRDG. He stated:

> I would willingly have undertaken many of the tasks we carried out with the men of a regular unit. But I could not have done it without rejecting those who were not physically fit, those who were not temperamentally suited and those who were not prepared to parachute. Then I would have had to train them—for the mental strain of being constantly on the watch is something for which continual training is required. . . . To have tried this type of raid and other tasks without specially trained and selected men would have been madness. For not only would you virtually destroy the structure of a normal unit in transforming it for a specialized task but also you would be diverting it from its main purpose.[70]

That specialist formations arose as they did was no accident. They were created in direct response to the undesirability and limitations of utilizing conventional arms for the conduct of irregular and specialized operations. This point should not be forgotten.

Although not all special operations were of low cost and high value, their conduct did require specially organized formations. Missions such as intelligence gathering or beach reconnaissance, tasks of such great advantage to the application of conventional force, required practitioners trained, equipped, and suited to the particular rigors of that work. Many operations would have been conducted at a disadvantage, or with increased losses, had specialist formations not been formed to facilitate these tasks. Even such tasks as liaising with partisans and performing harassment or interdiction in depth, which although beneficial were not strictly speaking essential, similarly required special selection, temperament, and training. Specialist formations arose to fulfill a genuine need: to conduct operations that regular formations could not adequately undertake in the time available without undue disruption. So long as a requirement for a special operation was identified, there was little alternative to the creation of specialist formations for its conduct. Had regular formations with a modicum of specialist training been relied upon for such purposes, it would have been significantly more costly and would have resulted in much diminished results.[71]

Attitudes toward Disbandment

In 1948 Colonel Twohig claimed that much of the "suspicion" of the "private army" was caused by the "disinclination to disband, and the consequent search for a justifying role."[72] In terms of cost-effectiveness the policy adopted toward the disbandment of formations is almost as significant as the policies of proliferation and expansion. Consistent with their differing military cultures and divergent attitudes toward the establishment of specialist formations, Britain and the United States also had markedly different approaches toward their wartime disbandment. Throughout the war the British steadily increased the number of both commando and special forces within their order of battle, as late as 1943 remaining committed to doubling the number of Commandos and organizing the Royal Marine Commandos for this purpose. Though by 1944 they were content to expand existent formations, such as the SAS Brigade, as late as 1945 they were still establishing new units, such as Royal Marine Detachment 385. The steady growth of British formations is illustrative both of their continued complicity with irregular solutions as well as their propensity for viewing specialist formations as an investment that they were generally unwilling to disband while the war continued.

America, on the other hand, was much more willing to disband its formations once they ceased to be considered cost-effective or when it was believed that conventional operations could proceed reliant on the virtues of mass and firepower, without the need for redundant "sideshows" offered by special operations. As many U.S. formations were established with the clear mandate of being "temporary" or "provisional" in nature, this course of action was as initially intended. Aside from the 2nd, 5th, and 6th Rangers, America disbanded all of its ranger formations well before the closing stages of the war. The reasons behind these decisions varied, but each had at its core a cost-effectiveness calculation. Merrill's Marauders and the

1st, 3rd, and 4th Rangers were each disbanded because they were so mauled in their deployments that it was thought neither practicable nor necessary to re-form the units around the remnants of these formations.[73] The 29th Rangers were disbanded, as intended, to disseminate the experiences of their Commando training to the 29th Infantry Division, although in light of the subsequent creation of the 2nd and 5th Rangers, this move was rather wasteful. The four USMC Raider Battalions were disbanded both because the opportunity for their employment in the Central Pacific was becoming increasingly unlikely and because the manpower they took up—there was a manpower "cap" on the USMC—was impeding the creation of further marine divisions.[74] The FSSF, meanwhile, was disbanded both because of the difficulty in replacing casualties—an exacting complication for the Canadian contingent, whose manpower shortage was particularly acute—and because of the assumption that by late 1944, following successful landings in France and the commencement of conventional operations, there would be no further call for their unique specialities.

Despite having disbanded the Layforce Commandos in 1941 after heavy losses and the lack of opportunity for amphibious raids in the Mediterranean at that time, and having disbanded Nos. 12 and 14 Commandos in early 1944 because of a presumed lack of requirement for small-scale amphibious raids, the British attitude toward the wartime disbandment of commando formations was noticeably more moderate than that of the United States. Heavy casualties and pressing manpower concerns did not necessarily deter the British from reconstituting and reinforcing formations, as seen with No. 2 Commando following losses sustained during the St. Nazaire raid. Furthermore, the commando transition of role to elite light infantry did not provoke the same hostility among the British as it did among the Americans; they were more willing to integrate Commando formations into their order of battle for conventional operations. For the British, a military culture forged in small wars that encouraged decentralized control, their distinct regimental traditions, and the unique relationship between the "errant captain" and "champion" that was so evident in the creation of special forces[75] all combined to ensure what was an almost sentimental unwillingness to dissolve units with a clear identity or esprit de corps.

Throughout the war British Commandos continually outnumbered U.S. ranger formations, and it is apparent that the United

States did not seem to have understood or agreed with the British policy under which these units proliferated. As early as August 1942 OSS commentators touring the Commandos would report that Britain had formed too many Commandos. They would advise that instead of the twelve Commandos which (at that time) had been formed, six would have been preferable and two would have been sufficient. This assessment was made on the basis that after deployment "the units are so badly shot up and lose so much equipment that the needed replacements take months to receive. The result is that the Commando unit makes an average of 2 raids in two years and the men go very sour in the interval. Two units could be kept replaced and kept up in condition."[76] While the transition to spearhead and elite infantry roles, cemented after the Sicilian invasion, prompted the formation of seven additional Royal Marine Commandos it only resulted in the correspondently moderate creation of two more Ranger battalions (excluding the 6th Rangers).

When the 1st and 3rd Rangers were decimated at Cisterna, the U.S. Army took the decision not to reconstitute them and, in so doing, also decided to disband the 4th Rangers. It was believed that the cost of re-forming and reinforcing these battalions was not commensurate with their utility, and that any further requirement for Ranger units was already taken care of by the 2nd and 5th Rangers. Although certain individuals, General Marshall in particular, were keen to retain these battalions, the ultimate decision to disband them was taken on the basis of cost-effective calculations and the belief that at that stage of the war "the general advantage of special trained forces is not worth the effort spent in special organization or training."[77] The conclusion of a feasibility study on Rangers, tellingly made on the eve of D-day and arguably the most significant Ranger contribution of the war, outlined perfectly the general perception of them being contrary to the "American way of war": it stated that offensive warfare required not heavily specialized groups but the "maximum use" of infantry battalions "adapted to varied and sustained action." The study concluded that "limited possible employment for Ranger Battalions in present and prospective operations, special replacement problem, and consideration of manpower make the reactivation of these Ranger Battalions at this time a questionable investment in manpower."[78] America appears to have been much more conscious of the costs of specialist formations than was Britain, and its decision to discontinue ranger formations once their utility or purpose was called into question was arguably a more rational approach than that pursued by the more sentimental British.

Without foresight, however, the decision to disband such formations was by no means an easy one. Disbandment invariably ruins well-trained, cohesive, and potentially experienced assets, and if future utility exists, it is almost always a waste. On the other hand, should no such obvious future employment exist, then disbandment is sometimes the only possible course of action lest a potentially large number of personnel be left unemployed, incapable of having impact on the course of the war, or else risk being wasted in unsuitable tasks if deployment for the sake of employment occurs. Thus the decision to disband the FSSF, for example, following the successful invasion of France and the development of conventional offensives can, in light of the declining potential for such light infantry formations by the end of 1944, be considered a reasonable and cost-effective decision. However, at that stage the war in the Far East was far from resolved, and given the likely importance of amphibious actions in future operations against the Japanese, there was definite risk in prematurely disbanding well-motivated, cohesive, and experienced personnel that had already been of proven value in support of such activities.

Even if specialist formations were facing disuse or an alteration of role, in an unclear strategic situation not to disband could be considered the more prudent decision. For instance, while it certainly would have been wasteful and time consuming to have formed a special force to perform the reconnaissance roles that the SAS was undertaking in northwestern Europe in 1944–45, to have retained an existent and available formation for such deployments was quite legitimate. To have not used, or to have disbanded, this experienced and cohesive force at a time when a task existed that the unit was both willing and capable of undertaking would not have been making best use of its abilities. That the SAS continued to be deployed right up until the end of the war in Europe highlighted its versatility and its continued return on initial investment. The fact that such units were consistently employed, even in a climate of diminishing opportunities toward the end of the war, certainly helps justify the British decision to retain many of their special forces until the cessation of hostilities.

Assessing the value of specialist formations will always be fraught with problems. Within cost-effectiveness debates it is hard to avoid dubious "what if . . . ?" scenarios whereby conjectural questions—such as, What if the Commandos had not been created?—only serve to promote further inquiry: Would the personnel taken up in their establishment have been better employed elsewhere? or Would the results and benefits they accrued have been achieved more effectively by other means? Although specialist formations had a definite, albeit token, impact on the course of events in the Second World War, these were not achieved without cost. Specialist formations did not offer a "free lunch."[79] On occasion specialist formations could reap significant returns for very little cost, in terms of both personnel absorbed and diversion of effort; at other times they took time and money to establish, consumed manpower and resources that could have been of benefit elsewhere, were underemployed or unsuccessful in endeavors of little value. The value and cost-effectiveness of specialist formations varied widely and turned on many calculations, yet it is both proportionality—in the number of formations raised and the scale of each—and utility—the frequency, duration, and significance of their use—that are perhaps the most significant considerations.

It is likely that specialist formations were not employed as much as they could have been during the war, and had there been more sensible tasking, it is certainly arguable that more value could have been gained from these units. With this in mind, it is equally true that too many varieties of specialist formations were created, each often possessing a very specific niche specialization that likely only served to further impede their wider application. Special forces, particularly those maritime examples, although generally not taking up as many resources per unit as the commando formations, were not always cost-effective, and their drain on personnel and resources was not always commensurate with results attained. Often rising as ad hoc expedients, as "private armies," the earliest specialist formations commonly developed without a rational plan for their structure or organization. That their proliferation, utility, and retention did not proceed along the most cost-conscious lines was hardly surprising in light of their embryonic nature. That there were flaws in their proliferation was inevitable, particularly for the British. Entering the war later and benefiting from the British example, the United States was able both to develop a more rational view of specialist formations and to follow a more sensible, or professional, route to their proliferation that identified what the requirements were and resulted in the creation of a minimum of organizations for their conduct.

Had the concept of specialist formations or irregular warfare been a clearly established precedent before the war, and had commanders and practitioners alike had a doctrinal point of reference upon which to refer, a more sensible procurement policy for specialist formations may have occurred. As it turned out, however, specialist formations first emerged as a coherent genus during the Second World War, all stages of the development and use of these nascent creations forming part of an evolutionary learning curve. Special formations arose at different times, in different theaters, and because of different circumstances to fulfill a range of varied roles. Their procurement, organization, and use was thus not always undertaken in the most rational or cost-effective manner. As such, when addressing the proliferation of these units in the Second World War, it is important not to impose, or assume, the existence of a rational or more "modern" procurement policy forged with a clear knowledge of specialist forces and their missions and tempered by the exigencies of peacetime budgets.

At times specialist formations were certainly expensive, prone to misuse and disuse, and were ineffective. These problems were not, however, exclusive to specialist formations. War is a wasteful endeavor, and specialist formations were certainly no more wasteful in terms of "costs" than various other undertakings whose contributions are potentially more debatable. The fact nonetheless remains that specialist formations were often able to remain true to the theory behind their existence and carry out important and force-magnifying actions that reaped significant returns disproportionate to investment. Although not all formations were equally as cost-effective, taken as a whole the investment that Britain and the United States made in the establishment and use of specialist formations was worthwhile. In regard to the damage inflicted upon the enemy and benefits accrued to the Allies, specialist formations were cost-effective. Simply put, their "return" was greater than their "investment."

Conclusion

Having taken a holistic view of the rise, application, and value of the Anglo-American commandos and special forces of the Second World War, it is evident that extensive innovatory and evolutionary processes were at play. Prior to the outbreak of war neither Britain nor the United States had any coherent concept of special operations or any consistent plans to develop organizations or formations for its conduct. Aside from a handful of prewar investigations on the subject, irregular warfare remained a generally ignored and often distasteful phenomenon thought to be confined to past colonial wars and frontier campaigns. It is, however, misleading to view the absence of prewar studies and initiatives in these fields as neglect; broadly considered, there was simply no preexistent body of knowledge or practicable experience to neglect. Specialist formations arose during the Second World War, not because of any preexisting concept, but instead from innovation (or assimilation) in response to opportunity and exigency. The absence of prewar ideas and concepts would ultimately prove to be an impediment to neither Britain nor America's ability to successfully—independently and jointly—conceive, develop, and utilize an extensive range of specialist formations during the course of the war.

The first British specialist formations had their origins in the desperate summer of 1940. Innovation and ad hoc experimentation was a result of frustration and conventional weakness. Within a short space of time, and illustrative of the British enthusiasm toward these units, a number of "errant captains" had swiftly proposed, and "champions" supported, various unorthodox solutions to the problems then faced. Specialist formations were naturally attractive. They offered a proportionately low-cost means through which the strategic initiative could be regained; they provided a mechanism though which experience—particularly in combined operations—could be attained, and they offered a focal point for the fortification of popular morale. The development of the Commandos, the

Special Operations Executive (SOE), and the "private armies" of the Long Range Desert Group (LRDG) and Special Boat Sections (SBS), all in the summer of 1940, was of paramount importance in laying the foundations for the successes that followed. The years 1940–41 were, however, part of a formative learning period, and many problems and limitations with the development and application of these formations were clearly evident. While units such as the LRDG and SBS, and emergent units such as the Special Air Service (SAS), were certainly showing potential, this period also witnessed Commando formations experiencing a fair few failures and frustrations. Many of these early tribulations were inevitable, stemming from both inexperience and a more general inability to project force; they were broadly symptomatic of a sharp learning curve about virtually every aspect of the composition, organization, and use of irregular units. Britain was learning its trade and would surmount these difficulties only by trial and error.

In mid-1941 the still neutral United States began its first tentative moves toward developing irregular warfare, clandestine intelligence, and special operations capabilities. These investigations and developments, most significantly the creation of William Donovan's Coordinator of Information (COI) organization, were noticeably aided and influenced by the British example and would serve as a stepping-stone for the development of the first American specialist formations soon after Pearl Harbor. In the overall evolution of specialist formations, 1942 would prove to be a critical year, one that witnessed the apex of the amphibious raid with such ambitious actions as Vaagso, St. Nazaire, and, in the American instance, Makin, occurring alongside numerous smaller pin pricks executed by, for example, No. 12 Commando and the Small Scale Raiding Force. In spite of this, the year also bore witness to a more general decline of such operations, as the commando and ranger role evolved away from independent raiding activities and toward directly supporting the amphibious landing of conventional arms. August 1942 was a turning point, with the likes of the Dieppe raid and the USMC landings against Tulagi highlighting the potential of commando formations for undertaking spearheading, flank guard, and shock troop tasks. By the end of the year, the invasion of North Africa, Operation Torch, had crystallized this transition of the commando and ranger role.

With commando formations being gradually drawn away from raiding activities, the mantle of special forces began to expand. By the end of 1942 special forces had become a clearly definable genre. Perhaps more than any other factor, it was the widespread successes and versatility of the LRDG and SAS in the Desert War and of the SBS in the Mediterranean that would lead to the expansion and legitimization of units heretofore regarded as "private armies." These units had gradually illustrated their cost-effective potential in successfully conducting a range of tasks both offensive and nonoffensive with versatility and speed. Following the gradual development of dedicated command and control structures, which managed to successfully coordinate the activities of such highly individualistic bodies, these units began to escape the stigma of the "private army" and became increasingly well integrated into the objectives of the overall military campaign.

The year 1943 was one of change and reorganization for virtually all specialist formations, as they began to alter their structures and methods to provide for transitions in the overall strategic picture. By this stage of the war, commandos and rangers had proven their application in amphibious assaults, and with the ever-looming invasion of France at the forefront of Allied minds, the desirability of retaining, and even expanding, these formations had become solidified. The experience of North Africa and Sicily would nevertheless prove that in order to remain viable these elite light infantry formations had to be prepared to undertake post-assault operations, even if that meant utilizing them, however distastefully, at the front in conventional infantry duties. To cater to such a requirement, both the Commandos and Rangers would make alterations to their establishments. Broadly considered, the British were more amenable than the Americans in facilitating this reorganization and in granting their Commandos a margin of legitimacy. Significantly, ranger formations were adversely affected by an unwillingness to create a structure comparable to the effective British SS Brigades that helped to ease the integration of Commandos into the regular battle while still enabling the conduct of more independent activities where necessary. In direct contrast to the lessons emerging in Europe about the value of commando formations at this time, however, was the situation in the Pacific that saw the USMC Raiders becoming increasingly marginalized within the firepower-oriented amphibious doctrine as practiced by the U.S. Navy and Marine Corps.

For the various special forces the year of 1943 was also a period of transition and change. Following the rushed development of tentative measures before the Anglo-American invasion of North Africa, the increasing volume and significance of amphibious operations at this time virtually guaranteed the steady proliferation of a variety of maritime-oriented specialist formations. Operation Husky against Sicily would mark the first concerted use of special forces both before and during a landing to provide for hydrographic and beach intelligence, pilotage, approach demolitions, and deception activities. Yet in spite of these activities and the consistent deployments of the LRDG and SBS (Squadron) in the Aegean, or those of OSS Detachment 101 in Burma, 1943 was a proportionately fallow year for special forces as they began to adjust to the requirements of supporting the Allied offensives in depth. Nascent American units like the OSS Operational Groups (OGs) were still learning their trade, while more experienced British units such as the SAS needed to familiarize themselves with new methods and different operational environments. Three principal factors impeded the widespread employment of special forces at this time: a lack of knowledge about their capabilities; a lack of means to facilitate their deployment; and, perhaps most significantly, a lack of practicable opportunity for their use. Despite the idealistic expectations of certain protagonists, the situation on the ground in most theaters in 1943 was simply not ready for the committal of large numbers of uniformed special forces in depth.

The year 1944 represented the zenith of the use of specialist formations as a direct ancillary to conventional Allied strategy. The operations of Anzio, Normandy, Anvil/Dragoon, and Luzon all saw commando and ranger formations work in support of conventional amphibious landings in either a spearheading capacity, or as was becoming more common at this stage of the war, to secure flanks or important outlying objectives. Following such undertakings, however, once beachheads had been secured, American enthusiasm toward ranger formations (with the exception of Merrill's Marauders and the 6th Rangers) declined, as problems were faced in accommodating these units in post-assault tasks. Britain, on the other hand, faced no comparable difficulties and continued to utilize their Commandos broadly, in a wide variety of important tasks, until the end of the war.

It was in 1944 that, in contrast to the gradual downturn in ranger deployments, special forces really began exhibiting their potential in both independent operations and working in direct support of conventional forces. The invasion of France, the Italian campaign, the peripheral actions in Greece and Yugoslavia, the offensives in Burma, and the Central and Southwest Pacific amphibious drives would all witness the concerted application of special forces. From the summer of 1944 onward, the distinct acceleration in the activities of partisan movements in support of major Allied offensives resulted in a concomitant increase in the application of special forces to harness, control, and aid these indigenous elements. As this occurred, greater controls and increasingly centralized, often inter-Allied, command structures developed to provide for the increased volume and complexity of operations. The development of various "special operations" branches under both theater and subordinate commands from 1944 on increased the effective application of these units and serves as evidence of a marked evolution in the acceptance and integration of special forces into Allied operations and strategy. By the later stages of the war both Britain and America exhibited a definite proficiency in employing specialist formations. This gradual increase in aptitude occurred in tandem with a more general growth of martial abilities, for, as General Frederick Browning would state, only a "real expert who has behind him the basic and fundamental experiences of his trade can afford unorthodox methods. . . . Only the real expert can depart from comparative orthodoxy."[1]

This growth in abilities notwithstanding, it is evident that there were certain limitations to the development and employment of specialist formations during the war: the proliferation of these units was occasionally eccentric; command and control mechanisms could be cumbersome, confused, and marred with animosity; and misuse and disuse was clearly evident. Such factors were, however, to be expected as being endemic to the units' nascent nature. These varied formations managed to conduct a myriad of complicated activities across a wide range of different operational environments with little or no formal preexistent doctrine to guide them—a notable achievement that perhaps should not be unfairly judged using the same criteria with which one might assess professional modern-day Special Operations Forces. It is, as S. J. Lewis stated in reference to the Jedburgh Teams, not "surprising that new organizations breaking new ground would encounter unforeseen difficulties."[2] Problems were part of the evolutionary learning curve, and by the end of the war many had been overcome, a result of amassing practical experience; of developing efficient command structures; and of possessing a growing body of knowledge about, and an appreciation of, specialist capabilities.[3]

It is abundantly clear that in a number of places the Anglo-American alliance was an absolutely central factor in the wartime development, evolution, and use of specialist formations. Such a close relationship, reflective of the broader military, diplomatic, and political links existing between Britain and the United States during the Second World War, was an essential ingredient for the successful conduct of coalition special operations lest they be hindered by confusion, competition for missions and resources, and counterproductive duplications of effort. Though both partners would ultimately benefit from this mutually supportive alliance, it is fair to suggest that the Americans profited more from this close relationship than did the British. At a time when the United States first began considering irregular warfare, Britain had already developed an extensive range of specialist units and was amassing an ever-increasing body of practicable operational experience in their application. British willingness to share their established model and guide their new ally in this field propelled the American adoption of these units and enabled the United States to hit the ground running to develop an extensive range of specialist formations, all within the first six months of 1942.

For the United States such rapid learning was not, however, without cost. The fee was that it had to firmly accept its position of student and sacrifice a margin of control by bowing to British experience. Had the British not been willing to share their knowledge or accommodate American requests for information and assistance, then it is likely that the Americans would have faced a longer and more troubled path toward the creation of these units than they ultimately did. The delayed U.S. adoption of the formations did, however, ensure that by studying the British model they could avoid many of the pitfalls and administrative and interagency problems that the British experienced in their awkward "private army" and "mobs for jobs" formative stages. This learning period made certain the development of many American formations on more formal, or centralized, lines than did the majority of the British units. That many American special forces developed under the aegis of the same body that was responsible for providing for clandestine subversion, sabotage, and espionage was certainly of benefit. Notwithstanding the fact that OSS control could, as the OGs found before their "militarization," occasionally impede smooth relations between specialist units and field commands, this arrangement can generally be regarded as a positive advantage that had obvious benefits for the economical proliferation, administration, and command and control of American irregular units.

Though owing much to the British example, American perceptions and motivations behind the creation of ranger formations contained notable differences from those of the British. The Commandos, as was SOE, were conceived at a time of strategic desperation and were viewed as an important means of waging offensive war at a time of conventional impotence. As such, Britain viewed these units as an important striking arm, placing some gravitas behind their creation. American ambitions for ranger formations, conceived at a time when the strategic situation had been stabilized (if not quite reversed), were much more subdued. Ranger formations were perceived as temporary expedients, as a mechanism for gaining and disseminating combat and amphibious experience, and as a means to facilitate the conventional battle, which was to be fought with mass and firepower. Once these goals had been attained, once conventional formations had gained experience and were able to conduct operations of the required scale and duration, there was a definite awkwardness (with the exception of the 6th Rangers) in the ability and willingness of the United States to adapt ranger formations to alternate applications. Once these units began to sustain casualties, were faced with disuse or the undertaking of more conventional tasks, the U.S. military was quick to justify their disbandment in cost-effectiveness terms. The British, on the other hand, were much more inclined to retain the services of trained and cohesive units, adapting them according to the requirements of the operational situation, rather than resorting to disbandment.

The American adoption of special forces units was far less reliant on the British example than was the case with their ranger formations. In spite of this, between the Anglo-American special forces there would ultimately be much greater commonality, not to mention a much greater level of cooperation in the field, than there ever was between the Commandos and the ranger formations. However, in light of the broadly independent paths through which these units were created, there could be noteworthy differences in the composition, methods, and roles of the respective British and U.S. special forces. Most significantly, there would be no direct American equivalent to units such as the SAS, which placed a premium on autonomous small-scale mobile harassment, and no British efforts to emulate either the composition or methods employed by the bilingual OSS OGs or those of the extensive Underwater Demolition Teams (UDT) organization. Such diversity should perhaps be expected as being a consequence of the fundamentally different military cultures of the two allies.

Although British influence and aid to America was understandably most prevalent in the earlier stages of the war when their ally was still learning, British patronage and assistance and their provision of instruction, training, and operational transport continued to be of great importance even in the later stages of the war. When the field of specialist formations is viewed through the lens of the Anglo-American alliance it is apparent that the more general trend of U.S. military dominance toward the end of the war is broadly reversed. British hegemony in the field of specialist formations largely outlasted the declining significance of their overall strategic contribution.

With the exception of northern Burma, China, and the Southwest Pacific, as a whole it would not be until mid- to late 1944 that the United States in any way began to approach the British volume of special operations. In these later stages of the war, however, it is most useful to regard the Anglo-American alliance as mutually beneficial and supportive. Once mobilized, American proficiency in these fields increased, and as it did so information and knowledge was increasingly shared between the Allies. Moreover, the burden of mounting and providing for operations—especially orchestrating the supply of indigenous partisan movements—began to be lifted from the shoulders of the British. It is thus unnecessary to dwell excessively upon such notions as the origins of innovation or cultural ownership. The fact remains that in the field of specialist formations at the strategic, operational, and tactical levels of war, Britain and America developed a relationship that was close, harmonious, and mutually supportive.

From the outset this work has highlighted the undesirability of making the assumption that the Anglo-American wartime development of specialist formations was in any way based either on prewar attitudes and experiences of irregular warfare or upon national strategic cultures. Although culturally and historically speaking the

British were amenable to the use of irregular methods, their adoption of such measures during the Second World War owes much more to the unique conditions, requirements, and opportunities that confronted them in 1939–45 than it does to any esoteric national predisposition. Before the war America certainly had both less familiarity and less cultural inclination toward these units than did the British, and during the war the traditional American "way of war" would certainly appear to have been an obstacle toward the development of specialist formations: such units went against a traditional antipathy toward elite units, were ill suited to their homogenous "production-line" approach to mobilization, and were alien to a big-unit orientation toward mass and concentration. Though suppressed in the early stages of the war, such factors ultimately impeded the American adoption and use of ranger formations. It is not, however, warranted to assume that they were in any way a similar obstacle for the development of special forces. Although America had difficulty utilizing and accepting commando-style formations to the same extent as did Britain, U.S. special forces would ultimately proliferate in numerical terms as extensively and in practical terms as effectively as they did among the more culturally predisposed British. One only needs to examine the record of the OGs, the Alamo Scouts, Detachment 101, or the UDTs to find vivid illustration of American innovation, adaptability, and virtuosity in these fields, which was certainly comparable to that of the oft-regarded British "masters." Special forces found a role within the broader American "way of war" and the likes of Roosevelt, Marshall, Eisenhower, and Donovan all developed at least an appreciation of how the application of minimal force in the right places could recoup advantages for their application of maximum force.

It is apparent that the conduct of special operations during the war was not subject to the same obstacles and common strategic dilemmas of politics, diplomacy, or geography that affected the employment of conventional arms. Specialist formations presented a means of applying force on a global scale, offering the Allies a sense of ubiquity by enabling operations to be undertaken in theaters in which it was politically or militarily impossible, unacceptable, or unwarranted to conventionally deploy. The employment of specialist formations could thus both circumvent and reinforce national strategic policies: they offered Britain a medium through which its more ambitious tangential "Churchillian" strategies could be embraced without significant diplomatic backlash and afforded the United States the opportunity to undertake operations in peripheral theaters ostensibly so abhorrent to conventional American strategy. Specialist formations were also a great political device. By providing evidence of activity and aggression they helped Britain overcome the common criticism that they were too indecisive and circumspect. And by providing evidence that Americans were capable of finesse in the professional use of minimum force, they similarly helped the United States to overcome criticisms that it was inexperienced, undisciplined, and too reliant on mass and firepower.

Although this volume has rendered a favorable overall verdict upon the impact and value of the Anglo-American specialist formations of the Second World War, it is important to note that shortly before, or soon after, the cessation of hostilities both Britain and the United States would disband and demobilize the overwhelming majority of their commandos and special forces. The British policy toward the retention of the Commandos after the war reflected the general enthusiasm with which they had embraced the conception and utilization of these formations during the war. Britain had come out of the Second World War with a clear impression of the value of utilizing Commandos to prosecute amphibious assaults. Their experience with amphibious operations was honed in the Mediterranean and European theaters, where the virtues of speed and surprise (over the application of massive supporting fire) had created a clear role for specialist amphibious shock troops, spearheaders, and flank guards in the prosecution of landings. In mid-1944 a committee under the chairmanship of Air Marshal Sir Norman Bottomley was established to consider future interservice responsibilities for amphibious warfare, paying particular attention to the role of the Royal Marines therein. One of the conclusions reached by this committee held that the Royal Marines should be given sole responsibility for the maintenance of postwar specialist formations connected with amphibious activities.[4] Given such an amphibious-oriented justification for their retention, it was only natural that the Royal Marines be granted the postwar responsibility for the Commandos. Thus while all British Army Commandos were disbanded by the end of 1945, the Royal Marines were permitted to retain a permanent (albeit somewhat scaled-down) establishment of one Commando brigade, ultimately made up of three individual Commandos.

Given the difficulties the United States had in accepting ranger formations during the war, it is perhaps not surprising that the Americans did not seek to retain, in the same manner as did the British, any of these formations immediately after the war. Two principal factors reinforced this decision. First was the fact that in the later stages of the war not only had many ranger formations already been decimated by casualties and subsequently disbanded, but those that had been retained (aside from the 6th Rangers) were infrequently used at best. Secondly, and more significantly given the key British justification for the retention of the Commandos, was the fact that in the American mindset any benefits that ranger units were assumed to have had in aiding the prosecution of amphibious assaults were overshadowed by the dominant amphibious doctrine of the USMC/ U.S. Navy. The Pacific war had been successfully prosecuted following the tenets of mass and firepower of "amphibious blitzkriegs" and without any clear need for elite light infantry formations. For all the successes of commandos and rangers in aiding amphibious assaults, it should not be forgotten that, as Otto Heilbrunn reminds us, one "could possibly draw up an impressive list of coastal operations in which Commandos and Rangers did not take a leading part. Such incidents in particular led to the widespread belief that Commandos had no special function to perform."[5]

Immediately after the end of the war, the only special forces that Britain and the United States would directly retain were similarly influenced by calculations of their potential value in future amphibious operations. In the American instance, only the UDTs would be retained, albeit at a dramatically reduced scale of only two understrength teams (one each for the Pacific and Atlantic coastlines). The extensive UDT organization, which by early 1945 had already assimilated large numbers of personnel from other wartime maritime special forces, was the obvious choice for retention. Even in the firepower-centric doctrine of amphibious landings as exhibited in the Central Pacific, the UDTs had proven their value and necessity. At the end of the war, as the commander of UDT 6 would emphasize, these teams had come to be "considered an integral and essential part of amphibious warfare . . . regardless of advancements made along more scientific lines; . . . hand placed demolition charges and reconnaissance will be necessary in securing many beachheads."[6]

Britain was similarly motivated. With no desire to lose the knowledge and experience gained during the war and not wishing to be "caught unprepared in any future war," it was agreed as early as October 1944 that Britain should retain a proportion of its special maritime capabilities after the war.[7] In doing so, however, it was made abundantly clear that the many disparate specialist maritime units that had existed during the war would need to be rationalized. Immediately after the war, therefore, in continuation of a policy that had been steadily implemented from late 1944 onward, each of the heretofore independent maritime formations were disbanded and a new one, the Combined Operations Beach and Boat Section was established under the Admiralty. Various Royal Navy and Royal Marines personnel who had served in units such as the Combined Operations Pilotage Parties, Royal Marine Boom Patrol Detachment, and Sea Reconnaissance Unit during the war would be integrated into this new section, while those British Army personnel involved in such units (most obviously those in the SBS) were either returned to their parent units or demobilized.[8] However distasteful this might have been to some of the Army personnel involved, such a move was, as with the disbandment of the Army Commandos, a sensible precaution against those interservice and interorganizational problems that had existed during the war.

Despite various other Anglo-American specialist formations having amassed impressive wartime records, neither Britain nor the United States chose to retain any other wartime specialist formation at the end of the war. The abiding impression was that these units were wartime expedients that would have little place in lean and professional peacetime armed forces. The outbreak of peace ensured that the majority of formations, almost irrespective of any wartime successes, became regarded as surplus to requirement. For all of the achievements of these units, it was clear that the war had not ultimately been won by such ephemeral means. Victory was gained not in the shadows but in the application of mass and firepower. Nagasaki and Hiroshima punctuated this point, serving as an expression of force so powerful and so destructive that it would dwarf anything that specialist formations could hope to achieve. Although during the war specialist warriors fought many pitched battles to justify the retention, or even expansion, of their establishments, at the close of the war the number of such irregular voices to argue for postwar establishments was distinctly lessened. Few of the men within wartime specialist formations were prewar professional soldiers, and there were definite tendencies for personnel to regard their wartime exploits merely as adventures and not recognize, or lobby for, any long-term continuation of such means. The majority of these men were as happy to be demobilized at the end of the war as were the bulk of other service personnel. Conversely, those truly irregular characters who had found a home in undertaking irregular activities during the war would often find themselves having great difficulty adjusting to the idea of garrison life in the peacetime military, just as the military itself would find problems in accommodating such individualistic personalities.

Within a relatively short period of time, however, both Britain and America would face various political and military challenges that would compel a readoption, or redevelopment, of dedicated specialist formations. The gradual, and at times tumultuous, revival of specialist capabilities would draw greatly upon the experiences of the Second World War, which had opened up minds to the potential of irregular formations and set a precedent for how future units should be organized, utilized, and controlled. Although not all postwar units arose as direct lineal descendants of wartime formations, the overwhelming majority of the later units would remain greatly influenced by, or even be formed around, a cadre of experienced wartime veterans. The very existence of modern Special Operations Forces and elite light infantry units thus owe a great deal to their wartime forebears, and, in many regards the seemingly ever-increasing prominence of such units in modern force structures serves as testimony to the successes of those units arising in the Second World War.

Appendix A

Organizational Charts

284　APPENDIX A

Figure A.1. Special Service Brigade Organization, November 1940

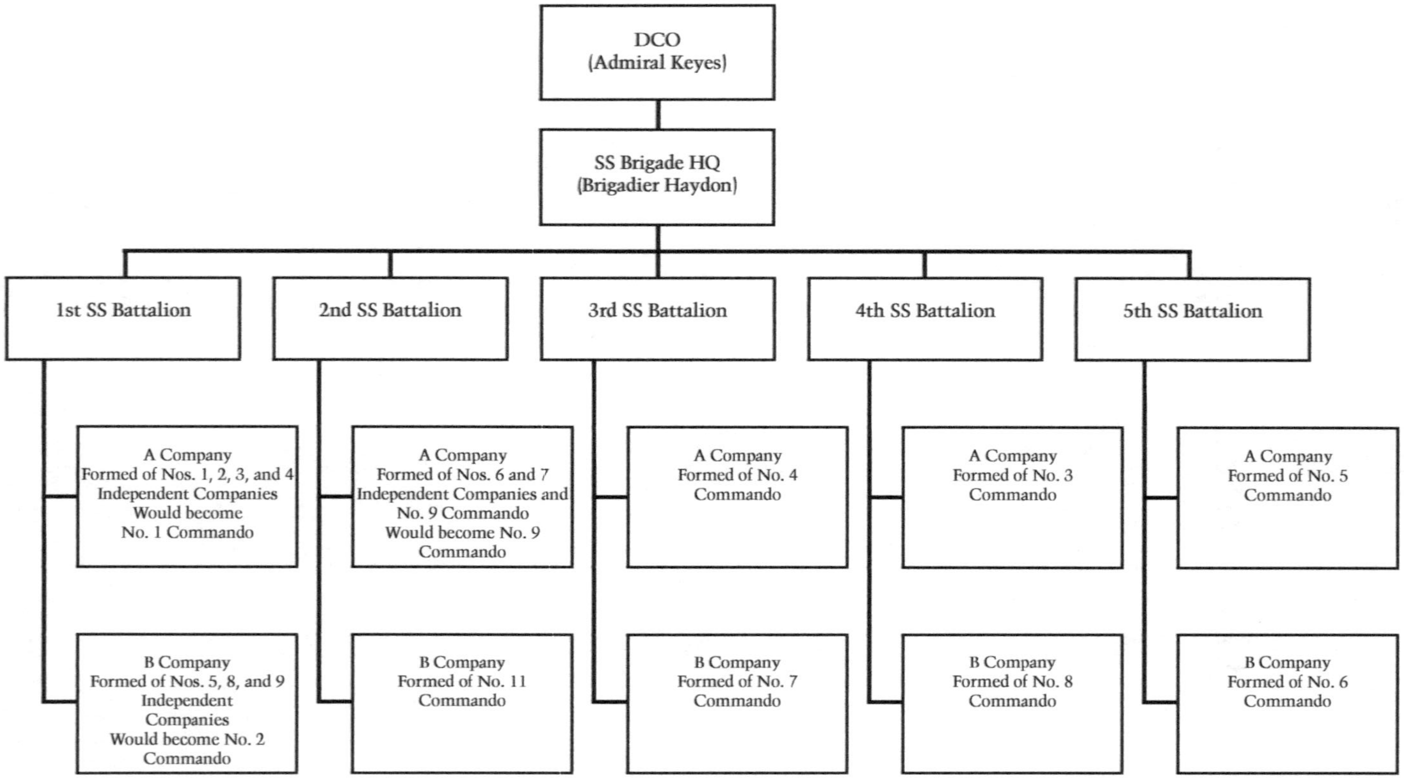

- DCO (Admiral Keyes)
  - SS Brigade HQ (Brigadier Haydon)
    - **1st SS Battalion**
      - A Company — Formed of Nos. 1, 2, 3, and 4 Independent Companies. Would become No. 1 Commando
      - B Company — Formed of Nos. 5, 8, and 9 Independent Companies. Would become No. 2 Commando
    - **2nd SS Battalion**
      - A Company — Formed of Nos. 6 and 7 Independent Companies and No. 9 Commando. Would become No. 9 Commando
      - B Company — Formed of No. 11 Commando
    - **3rd SS Battalion**
      - A Company — Formed of No. 4 Commando
      - B Company — Formed of No. 7 Commando
    - **4th SS Battalion**
      - A Company — Formed of No. 3 Commando
      - B Company — Formed of No. 8 Commando
    - **5th SS Battalion**
      - A Company — Formed of No. 5 Commando
      - B Company — Formed of No. 6 Commando

APPENDIX A 285

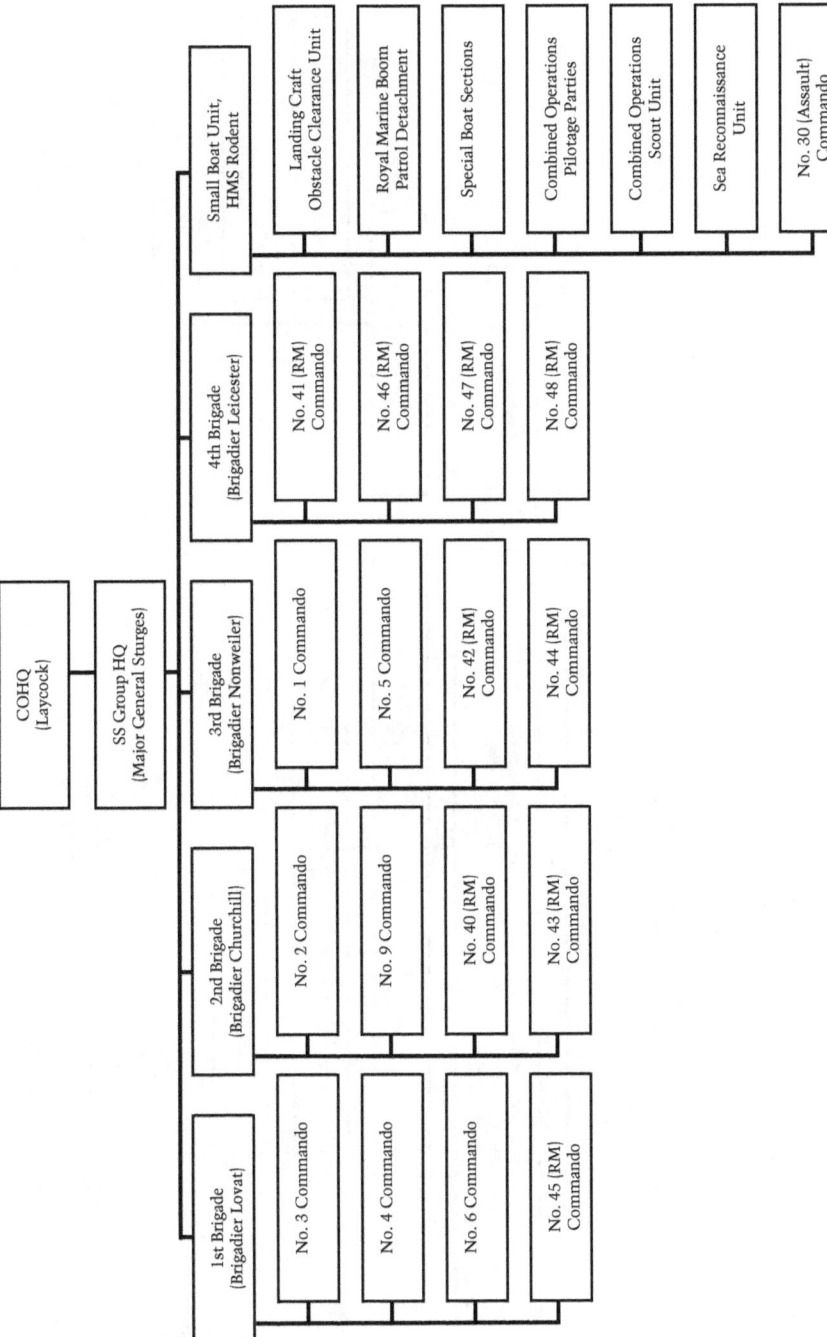

Figure A.2. Special Service (Commando) Organization, February 1944

286 APPENDIX A

Figure A.3. Command Arrangements for Specialist Formations, Mediterranean Theater, April 1944

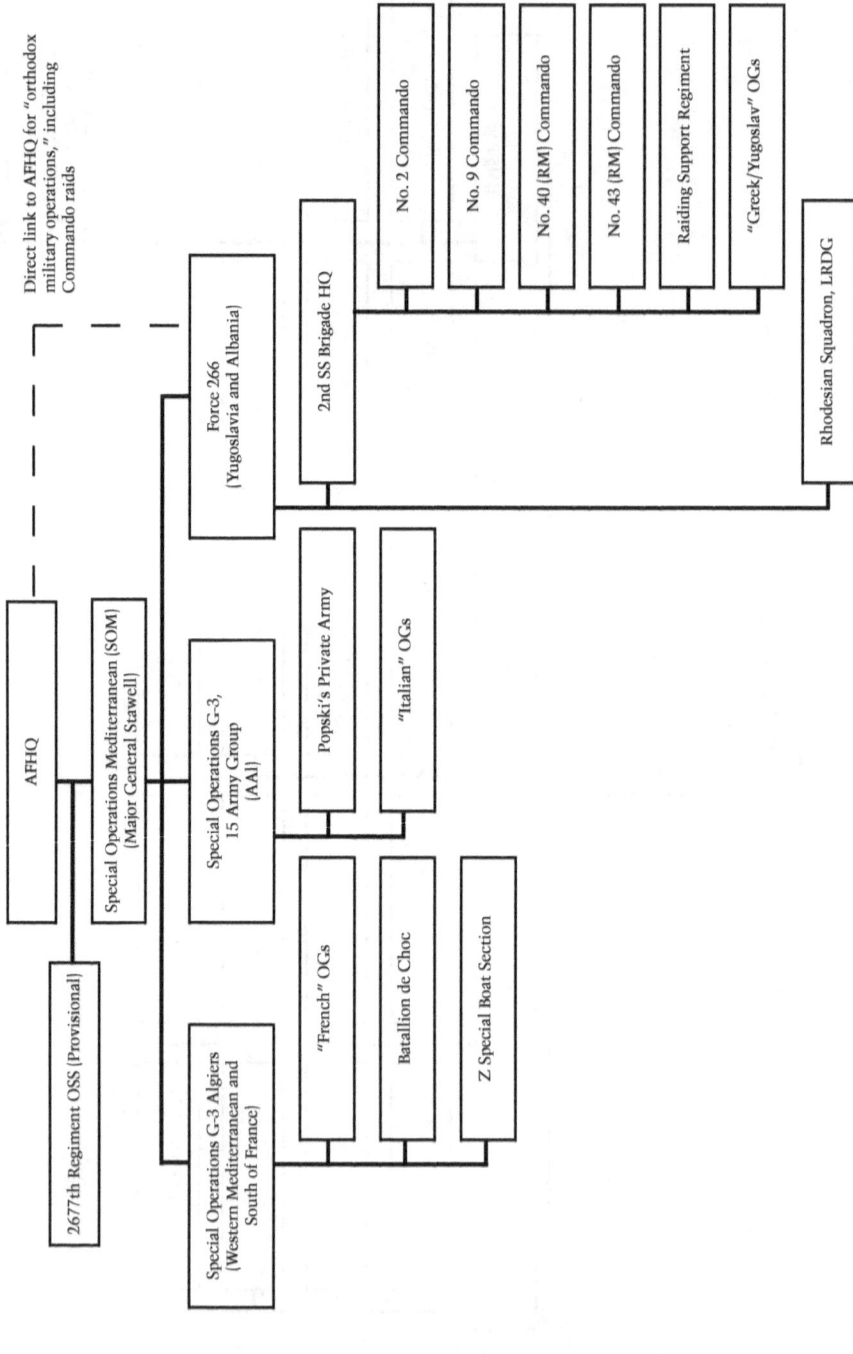

APPENDIX A 287

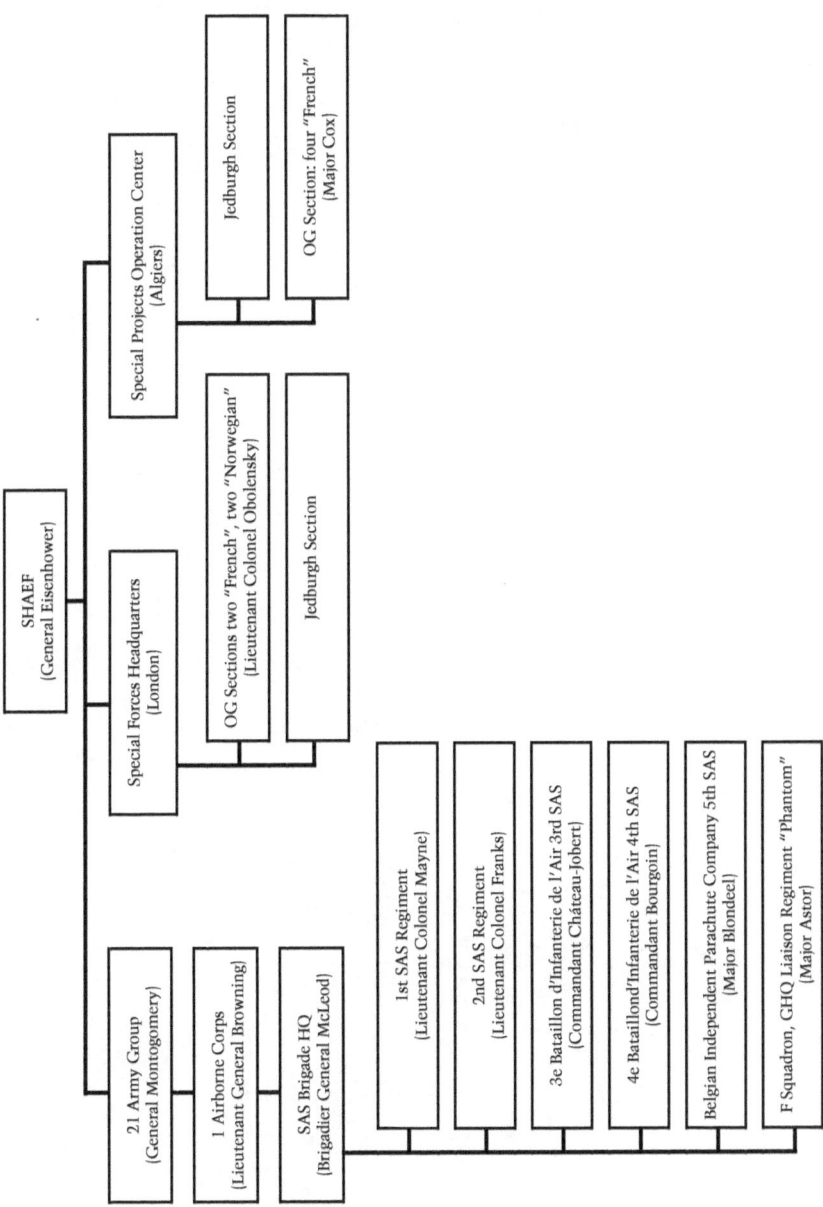

Figure A.4. Anglo-American Special Forces Command Organization for the Invasion of France, June 1944

APPENDIX B

ESTIMATES OF MANPOWER WITHIN ANGLO-AMERICAN SPECIALIST FORMATIONS

The following tables are based on the maximum establishment, the "on book" strengths, of these units. In many instances, however, these are estimates, and the disparity between what a force was entitled to have and what it actually had could be acute. Because of difficulties with recruitment and casualties, formations were rarely the size they were authorized to be. For example, in mid-1943 the Commandos had a base figure (as stipulated in these figures) of 7,000 men (based on 5,000 Army and 2,000 Royal Marine Commandos); yet Ladd in *Commandos and Rangers* (p. 167) estimates that at this time there were not more than 3,700 Commandos. As the disparities between listed and actual strengths are hard to ascertain, these figures, while estimates, err on the side of maximum totals. Further, these figures are made on the basis of combatant personnel and do not take into account the by no means moderate numbers of administrative, planning, logistics, and support personnel so essential to the application of the formations.

Late 1940

	Total personnel
Special Service Troops (Commandos and Independent Companies)*	5,000
Long Range Desert Group	200
Special Boat Section, No. 8 Commando	30
101 Troop, No. 6 Commando	30
	5,260

*On the basis of five "SS Battalions," each consisting of two "companies" each of approximately 500 men. See appendix A for organizational chart.

Comparison between Personnel in Commando, or Ranger, Formations and Those in Special Forces

Commandos	5,000
British special forces	260

Mid-1941

	Total personnel
Army Commandos	6,500
Long Range Desert Group	200
L Detachment Special Air Service Brigade	60
1st Special Boat Section	30
101 Troop No. 6 Commando	30
	6,820

Comparison between Personnel in Commando, or Ranger, Formations and Those in Special Forces

Commandos	6,500
British special forces	320

Mid-1942

British

	Total personnel
Army Commandos[1]	5,000
Royal Marine Commandos	500
Royal Navy Commandos	608
Long Range Desert Group	200
L Detachment Special Air Service Brigade	200
Indian Long Range Squadron	100
Libyan Arab Force Commando	25
Small Scale Raiding Force	50
No. 30 (Assault) Commando	250

British total personnel (cont.)	
Special Interrogation Group	30
1st Special Boat Section	30
2nd Special Boat Section	30
Sea Reconnaissance Unit	40
Royal Marine Boom Patrol Detachment	60
	7,123

United States

	Total personnel
U.S. Army Rangers	450
First Special Service Force[2]	1,500
USMC Raiders	1,800
Scouts and Raiders	150
OSS Detachment 101[3]	100
Navy Group China (SACO)	200
	4,200

Comparison between Personnel in Commando, or Ranger, Formations and Those in Special Forces

Commandos	6,108
U.S. rangers	3,750
British special forces	1,015
U.S. special forces	450

Mid-1943

British

	Total personnel
Army Commandos	5,000
Royal Marine Commandos	2,000
Royal Navy Beach Commandos	608
Long Range Desert Group	200
2nd Special Air Service Regiment	450
Special Raiding Squadron	250
Special Boat Squadron	250
Popski's Private Army	100
No. 30 (Assault) Commando	250
Z Special Boat Section	30
2nd Special Boat Section	30
Combined Operations Pilotage Parties	100
Sea Reconnaissance Unit	40
Royal Marine Boom Patrol Detachment	60
Combined Operations Scout Unit	120
Landing Craft Obstacle Clearance Unit	440
V Force[4]	100
	10,028

United States

	Total personnel
U.S. Army Rangers	1,350
29th Rangers	180
First Special Service Force	1,500
USMC Raiders	3,600
Scouts and Raiders	150
OSS Detachment 101	200
Navy Group China (SACO)	200
Beach Jumpers	200

United States total personnel (cont.)	
OSS Operational Groups	210
OSS Maritime Unit	100
USMC Reconnaissance Company	200
Naval Combat Demolitions Unit	60
	7,950

Comparison between Personnel in Commando, or Ranger, Formations and Those in Special Forces

Commandos	7,608
U.S. rangers	6,630
British special forces	2,420
U.S. special forces	1,320

Mid- to Late 1944

British

	Total personnel
Army Commandos	4,000
Royal Marine Commandos	4,500
Royal Navy Beach Commandos	608
Long Range Desert Group	200
Special Air Service Regiments[5]	900
Special Boat Squadron	250
Popski's Private Army	100
30 Assault Unit	200
Raiding Support Regiment	600
Z Special Boat Section	30
2nd Special Boat Section	30
Combined Operations Pilotage Parties	200
Sea Reconnaissance Unit	40
Royal Marine Boom Patrol Detachment	60

British total personnel (cont.)	
Combined Operations Scout Unit	120
Landing Craft Obstacle Clearance Unit	440
V Force	600
Jedburghs (British)	100
	12,978

United States

	Total personnel
U.S. Army Rangers	1,350
First Special Service Force	1,500
Merrill's Marauders	2,500
Scouts and Raiders	150
OSS Detachment 101	800
Navy Group China (SACO)	800
Beach Jumpers	480
OSS Operational Groups	455
Alamo Scouts	140
OSS Maritime Unit	200
USMC Reconnaissance Battalion	400
Underwater Demolition Teams	1,000
Jedburghs (U.S.)	100
	9,875

Comparison between Personnel in Commando, or Ranger, Formations and Those in Special Forces

Commandos	9,108
U.S. rangers	5,350
British special forces	3,870
U.S. special forces	4,525

Early and Mid-1945

British

	Total personnel
Army Commandos	4,000
Royal Marine Commandos	4,500
Royal Navy Beach Commandos	608
Long Range Desert Group	200
Special Air Service Regiments	900
Special Boat Service	250
Popski's Private Army	100
30 Assault Unit	200
Raiding Support Regiment	600
Z Special Boat Section	30
Special Boat Sections[6]	90
Combined Operations Pilotage Parties	200
Sea Reconnaissance Unit	40
Royal Marine Detachment 385	130
Royal Marine Boom Patrol Detachment	60
Landing Craft Obstacle Clearance Unit	440
V Force	600
Jedburghs (British)	50
SAARF (British)	100
	13,098

United States

	Total personnel
U.S. Army Rangers	1,350
Scouts and Raiders	150
OSS Detachment 101	1,000
Navy Group China (SACO)	1,000
Beach Jumpers	480
OSS Operational Groups	350

United States total personnel (cont.)	
Alamo Scouts	140
OSS Maritime Unit	100
USMC Reconnaissance Battalion	400
Underwater Demolition Teams	3,000
Jedburghs (U.S.)	50
SAARF (U.S.)	100
	8,120

Comparison between Personnel in Commando, or Ranger, Formations and Those in Special Forces

Commandos	9,108
U.S. rangers	1,350
British special forces	3,870
U.S. special forces	6,770

1. Including, in this assessment, the 1st SS Regiment (or Middle East Commando).
2. FSSF estimates for these figures are made on the basis of American personnel only; there were an additional estimated 1,000 Canadian personnel in the force.
3. Not all OSS Detachment 101 and SACO personnel were operational, but due to the difficulty of making a distinction, the figures for these units include other nonoperational American personnel employed.
4. Estimates are inclusive of the Assam Rifle personnel employed but do not include the indigenous partisans raised.
5. In addition, the British 1st and 2nd SAS were joined in the SAS Brigade by 1,000 French and 500 Belgian personnel.
6. Including A, B, and C Groups sent to SEAC.

APPENDIX B 297

Figure B.1. Comparison of Manpower in Commando (or Ranger) Formations and Special Forces

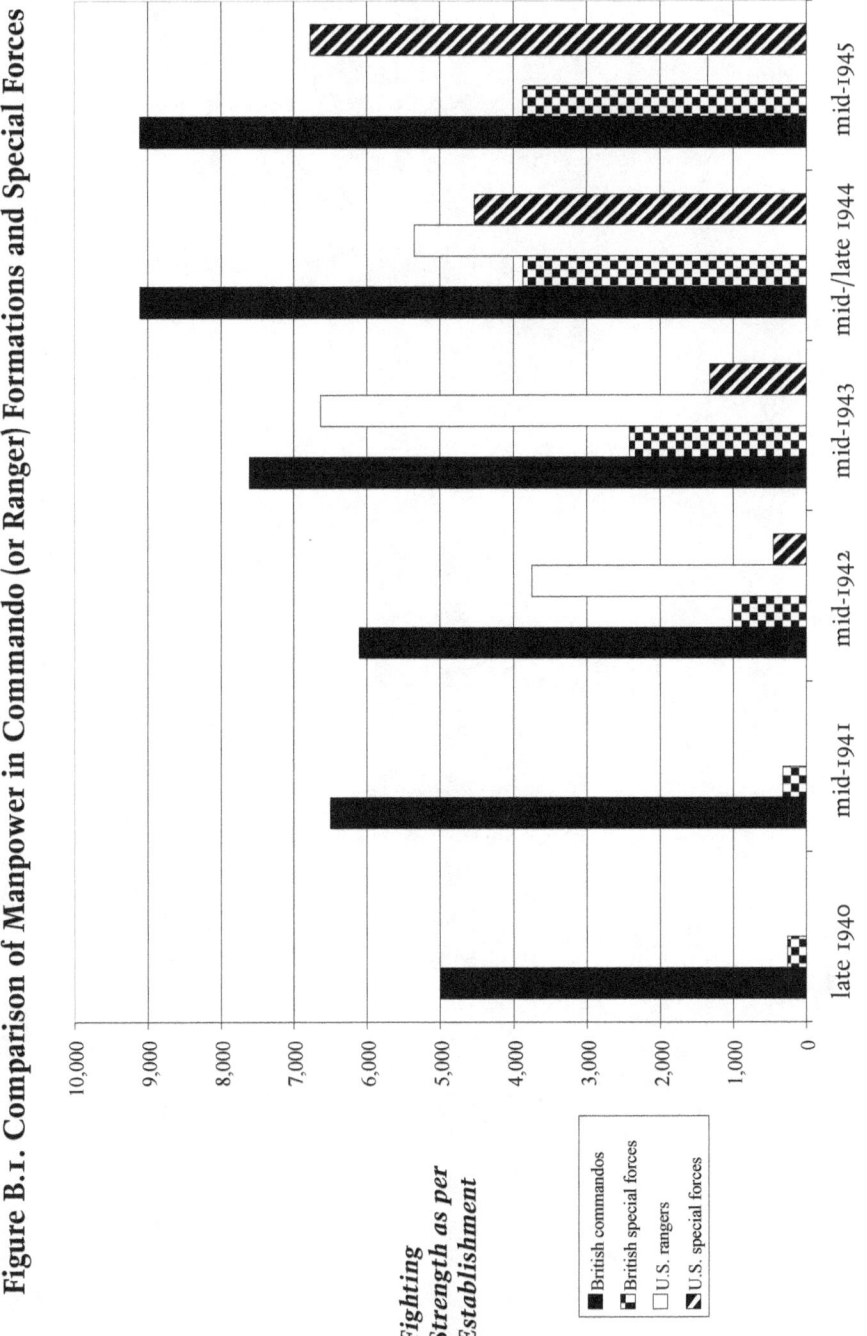

APPENDIX B 299

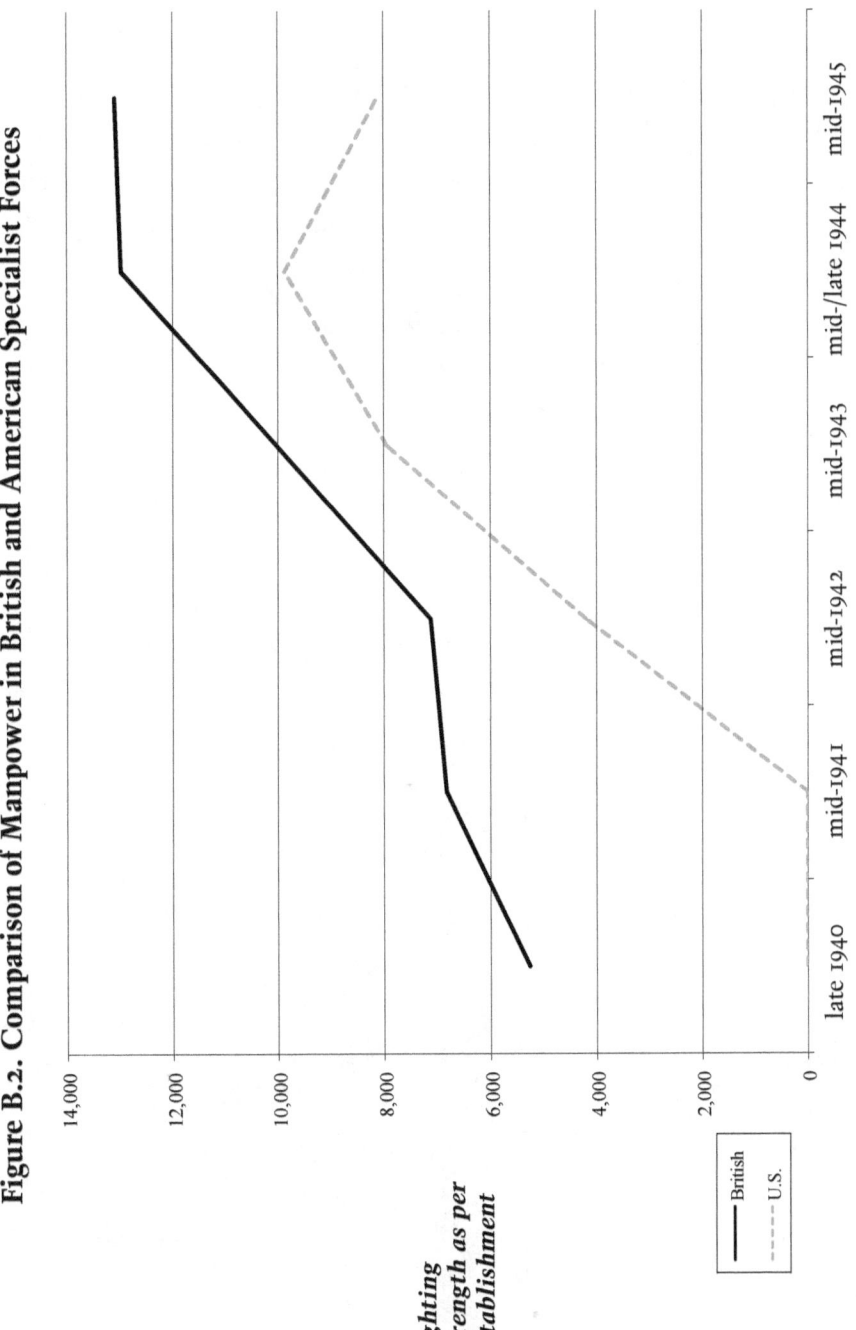

Figure B.2. Comparison of Manpower in British and American Specialist Forces

Notes

Introduction

1. As Russell F. Weigley tellingly commented, "American military historians have mirrored the tendency of the United States Army itself to prefer preparation for and study of conventional war—to say nothing of waging it—far above examination of irregular war." Weigley in foreword to Heaton, *German Anti-Partisan Warfare*, 9.
2. Gray, *Explorations in Strategy*, xvi; see also Kiras, *Special Operations and Strategy*.
3. For the British perspective, see Thompson, *War behind Enemy Lines*; Warner, *Secret Forces of World War II*; and Morris, *Churchill's Private Armies*. For the U.S. perspective, see Paddock, *U.S. Army Special Operations*, and Hogan, *U.S. Army Special Operations in World War II*.
4. Mockaitis, *British Counterinsurgency*, 1.
5. Gray, *Explorations in Strategy*, 144.
6. U.S. Joint Chiefs of Staff, *Doctrine for Joint Special Operations*, Joint Publication 3-05, December 2003.
7. Gray, *Explorations in Strategy*, 152.
8. See Beaumont, *Military Elites*.
9. Cohen, *Commandos and Politicians*, 17–18.
10. Gordon, *Other Desert War*, xix.
11. On November 21, 1940, the approximately five hundred personnel of No. 2 Commando were converted into a unit originally known as 11 Special Air Service Battalion (not to be confused with the later SAS). This group would go on to become the nucleus of 1st Parachute Battalion in September 1941. Otway, *Airborne Forces*, 31–32.
12. These were Operation Colossus, a raid against an aqueduct in southern Italy in February 1941; Operation Biting, a raid on radar infrastructure at Bruneval in February 1942; and Operation Freshman, a glider-borne raid against the Norwegian heavy water plant at Vemork in November 1942. Ibid., 63–73.
13. Greenacre, "Development of Britain's Airborne Forces."
14. Frost, *A Drop Too Many*, 118.
15. Otway, *Airborne Forces*, 51, 231.
16. Heilbrunn, *Warfare in the Enemy's Rear*, 166–67.
17. Thompson, *War Behind Enemy Lines*, 256.
18. McMichael, *Historical Perspective on Light Infantry*, 13.
19. Bidwell, *The Chindit War*, 25.
20. Ogburn, *The Marauders*, 33.
21. Neillands, *In the Combat Zone*, 31.
22. Gordon, *Other Desert War*, xvii.

23. Adrian Weale contended that the "Great Game" was where "the real roots of modern Anglo-American-influenced special forces lie." Weale, *Secret Warfare*, 8–9.
24. Arquilla, *From Troy to Entebbe*, 11–12.
25. Mackenzie, *Secret History of S.O.E.*, 3.
26. Callwell, *Small Wars*; Anglim, "Callwell versus Graziani," 588–608; Reitz and Smuts, *Commando*; Jones, *SAS Zero Hour*, 57–63.
27. Weale, *Secret Warfare*, 30.
28. Bidwell, "Irregular Warfare," 80.
29. For an overview of the array of works on Lawrence, see Holden Reid, "T. E. Lawrence and His Biographers."
30. Mockaitis, *British Counterinsurgency*, 146; Bidwell and Graham, *Firepower*, 224.
31. French, *British Way in Warfare*, xv.
32. See Liddell Hart, *Future of Infantry*, 62–63.
33. Gray, *Explorations in Strategy*, 155; See also Grenier, *First Way of War*.
34. Such was the legacy of Rogers's Rangers that the modern U.S. Army Rangers (somewhat inaccurately) consider them their spiritual forebears and continue to cite a modified version of Rogers's 28 "Rules of Ranging" in their standing orders.
35. Weigley, *American Way of War*, 18–39.
36. Zedric and Dilley, *Elite Warriors*, 84.
37. Mackey, *The Uncivil War*; Sutherland, *A Savage Conflict*; Millett and Maslowski, *For the Common Defense*, 180–81.
38. Adams, *U.S. Special Operations Forces*, 27.
39. The U.S. Army's use of Indian scouts in the Indian Wars provides a good indication of such adaption; see Dunlay, *Wolves for the Blue Soldiers*. For a definitive discussion of the U.S. Army's ability to deal with an unconventional foe in the Philippines War, see Linn, *U.S. Army and Counterinsurgency in the Philippine War*, and Linn, *The Philippine War*.
40. Weigley, *American Way of War*, 313.
41. Weigley, *History of the United States Army*, 543.
42. Foot and Langley, *MI 9*, 31.
43. For copies see IWM Gubbins 04/29/8 6/1 and 6/2.
44. For a good summary of the work of these departments, see Mackenzie, *Secret History of S.O.E.*
45. Thompson, *The Royal Marines*, 227–28.
46. The 1935 manual was revised and published as the seminal *Small Wars Manual* in 1940.
47. Isely and Crowl, *U.S. Marines and Amphibious War*, 4–5.
48. Clifford, *Three against Rommel*, 167.
49. David Thomas (who used the term "commando operations" to embrace the actions of both special forces and commando units) erroneously asserted that the "American Army . . . never grasped the concept of commando operations, or attached any value to commando forces." He claimed that during the Second World War only the armies of Britain,

Germany, and the Soviet Union developed "a coherent, if practical and improvisational, concept of commando operations informing the operational deployment of commando forces." Thomas, "Importance of Commando Operations," 690–91. Similar reckoning caused Adrian Weale to contend that the United States did not create a *"military* special operations unit during the war"[original emphasis]. Weale, *Secret Warfare*, 147.
50. Gray, "Handfuls of Heroes," 4.
51. Weiss, *Allies in Conflict*, 2.
52. Weigley, *History of the United States Army*, 479.

Chapter 1

1. French, *British Way in Warfare*, 201.
2. Posen, *Sources of Military Doctrine*, 47.
3. The Fifth Battalion Scots Guards predated the Independent Companies. Having a somewhat irregular mandate, the battalion was formed in January 1940 to act as an elite ski troop to aid Finland in the Winter War. An ill-conceived and desperately ad hoc expedient designed to fight in the wrong war, fortunately for the British it was swiftly disbanded in March before ever having been operationally deployed. In historical terms the most notable fact about this formation was that various personnel who had trained in the battalion went on to play prominent roles in the subsequent creation of other specialist formations. Erskine, *The Scots Guards*; Calvert, *Fighting Mad*.
4. Major General Richardson, Director of Military Training, to Divisional Commanders, 24 April 1940, WO 106/1889; and various documents in WO 260/32. One might be reminded how closely these qualities corresponded to Basil Liddell Hart's prewar predictions about the future of infantry: Liddell Hart, *Future of Infantry*, 62–63.
5. Brigadier Colin Gubbins, "Observations on the organisation, equipment, training and discipline of the British Army, based on the recent fighting in Norway," 13 June 1940, IWM Gubbins 04/29/8, 2/3.
6. Morris, *Churchill's Private Armies*, 34; reports on Independent Companies in Norway, CAB 106/1155.
7. Another MI(R) initiative directed against Norway was the planned dispatch of smaller parties, via submarine, to sabotage railways and arm partisans. As it turns out, transportation problems led to the abortion of this mission. Many of the personnel earmarked for these operations (such as Peter Fleming and Bill Stirling) would, nevertheless, subsequently help establish the Irregular Warfare Training School near Lochailort in Scotland. This school provided some of the training that various Commando units received before the centralized Commando Training Centre was established at Achnacarry in 1942.
8. Colonel Clarke, "Start of 'Commandos,'" 30 October 1942, DEFE 2/4.
9. Clarke, *Seven Assignments*, 207.
10. Churchill, *Second World War*, 2:217–18.
11. Stafford, *British and European Resistance*, 206.
12. Stafford, *Churchill and Secret Service*, 400.

13. Although Germany used small numbers of the Brandenburg Regiment and specially trained Fallschirmjäger airborne units in their early blitzkrieg victories, popular perception in Britain in 1940 would dramatically exaggerate the prevalence and value of such forces. For a good debunking of such perceptions, see De Jong, *German Fifth Column*.
14. Churchill, *Second World War*, 2:147. Despite Churchill's remarks it should be made clear that the German "storm troopers" of the 1918 offensives were conventional forces conducting a new form of regular combined arms warfare and cannot be cited as examples of specialist forces.
15. Ibid., 413.
16. Although it was not carried out under Keyes's tenure as DCO, the March 1942 Commando raid on the drydock of St. Nazaire holds clear similarities to the 1918 Zeebrugge Raid. See Karau, "Twisting the Dragon's Tail," 478.
17. Colonel Clarke, "Start of 'Commandos,'" 30 October 1942, DEFE 2/4.
18. Lieutenant General R. H. Haining, DCIGS, to Lieutenant General Sir A. F. Brooke, C in C Southern Command, 6 July 1940, WO 199/1849.
19. At this time it had also been proposed that the Marines should form a 1,800-man "striking force." Thompson, *The Royal Marines*, 227–28; Ladd, *By Land, By Sea*, 59.
20. Fergusson, *The Watery Maze*, 261; Morris, *Churchill's Private Armies*, 81.
21. Minutes of DCO meeting on "Means of Assisting Home Forces with SS Troops," 30 January 1941, WO 199/604; Churchill, *Second World War*, 2:147, 217–18.
22. Colonel Clarke, "Start of 'Commandos,'" 30 October 1942, DEFE 2/4; War Office Commando Training Instruction No. 1, 5 August 1940, File 101/G/2 in LHCMA: GB 0099 KCLMA Montanaro.
23. Major General R. H. Dewing, Director of Staff Duties, "Formation of Commandos," 23 June 1940, WO 199/1849.
24. See reports on Operation Collar, WO 106/1740.
25. Durnford-Slater, *Commando*, 32; report on Operation Ambassador, WO 106/2958.
26. Churchill, *Second World War*, 2:572.
27. See various documents in IWM Haydon 93/28/4, JCH 2/6.
28. Dunstan, *Commandos*, 23.
29. Although the Litani River Battle was characterized by a number of misfortunes that can mostly be attributed to general inexperience, Laycock stated that it "may be taken as a very fair example of a Combined Operation involving the opportune use of Special Service troops in a suitable role." Précis of lecture given by Laycock on the Litani River Battle, March 1942, CAB 106/389.
30. General Auchinleck, C in C MEF, "Future of 1st SS Regiment," 24 and 26 July 1942, WO 201/728.
31. Young, *Commando*, 42.
32. General Paget, C in C Home Forces, to CCO, 7 June 1943, WO 106/4158.
33. Messenger, *The Commandos 1940–46*, 409.

34. Brian Villa offered one of the most scathing treatments of the raid, claiming that "Dieppe is a classic example of military failure—in decision-making, in planning, and in execution—that has its roots in an intricate network of motives that almost defies analysis by the historian or political scientist." Villa, *Unauthorized Action*, 248.
35. Buckley, *Norway, The Commandos, Dieppe*, 229.
36. See Fowler, *Commandos at Dieppe*.
37. Lessons from No. 4 Commando's attack were subsequently turned into a War Office training manual: "Destruction of a German Battery," Notes from Theaters of War No. 11, February 1943, WO 208/3108.
38. War Cabinet to JCS, 21 August 1942, RG 218, Geographical File 1942–45, Box 58; Folder CCS 350.05 Dieppe.
39. Lieutenant Colonel T. Ely, Office of DCO, to Major Daniell, War Office, 31 July 1941, WO 193/405.
40. Ladd, *Commandos and Rangers*, 95.
41. Garrett, *The Raiders*, 204.
42. Mattingly, *Herringbone Cloak—GI Dagger*.
43. Stafford, *Roosevelt and Churchill*, 3.
44. Hoffman, *From Makin to Bougainville*.
45. Ibid.
46. Darby and Baumer, *Darby's Rangers*, 3; Harrison, *Cross-Channel Attack*, 15–16.
47. Major General Chaney, Adjutant General, to GOC, USANIF, 1 June 1942, RG 407, Entry 427, Box 21066, Folder INBN-1-0; Black, *Rangers in World War II*, 3.
48. Truscott, *Command Missions*, 38.
49. Black, *Rangers in World War II*, 8–9.
50. Burhans, *First Special Service Force*, 8–10; Adleman and Walton, *Devil's Brigade*, 17.
51. Dziuban, *Military Relations Between the United States and Canada*, 259.
52. Adleman and Walton, *Devil's Brigade*, 44–46; Beaumont, *Military Elites*, 52.
53. Major General Chaney, Adjutant General, to GOC, USANIF, 1 June 1942, RG 407, Entry 427, Box 21066, Folder INBN-1-0.
54. HQ USANIF, "Commando Organization," 7 June 1942, RG 407, Entry 427, Box 21066, Folder INBN-1-0.
55. Lewis, *Omaha Beach*, 70.
56. Lieutenant General Alfrey, GOC V Corps, to Nos.1 and 6 Commandos, April 1943, DEFE 2/43.
57. No. 1 Commando War Diary, DEFE 2/37; Parker, *Commandos*, 130.
58. Major General R. H. Dewing, Director of Staff Duties, "Formation of Commandos," 23 June 1940, WO 199/1849.
59. Lieutenant Colonel Darby to Adjutant General, 1 January 1943, RG 407, Entry 427, Box 21066, Folder INBN-1-0.
60. Stewart, "Ranger Force at the Battle of Cisterna," 17; King, *Rangers: Selected Combat Operations*, 14.

61. Lieutenant Colonel Darby to Adjutant General, 4 March 1943, RG 407, Entry 427, Box 21066, Folder INBN-1-0; Darby and Baumer, *Darby's Rangers*, 67; King, *Rangers: Selected Combat Operations*, 74.
62. Hoffman, *From Makin to Bougainville*.
63. Brigadier W. H. Rupertus, Assistant Divisional Commander, to GOC, 1st Marine Division, 29 September 1942, RG 127, USMC Geographic Files, Guadalcanal, Box 40, Folder: 1st Marine Division, Tulagi.
64. C in C Pacific Fleet to C in C U.S. Fleet, 20 October 1942, RG 127, USMC Geographic Files, Makin, Box 183.
65. USMC Historical Branch Accounts of the Makin Raid, RG 127, Entry 46B, Box 100.
66. Captain Harry L. Torgerson, USMC Parachute Battalion, report on Tasimbako Raid, RG 127, USMC Geographic Files, Guadalcanal, Box 44, Folder A36-1; Macksey, *Commando Strike*, 120.
67. Lieutenant Colonel Carlson to GOC, 1st Marine Amphibious Corps, RG 127, USMC Geographic Files, Guadalcanal, Box 44, Folder A39-1.
68. Isely and Crowl, *U.S. Marines and Amphibious War*, 155.
69. Minutes of Fourth Commanding Officers' Conference at SS Brigade Headquarters, 15 January 1943, File 24, KCLMA Laycock.
70. Lieutenant Colonel Macdonald, War Office, to COSSAC Operations Branch, 4 June 1943, WO 106/4158.
71. CCO, "Note on Reorganization of Commandos," March 1943, WO 32/10416; Brigadier Robert Laycock, OC SS Brigade, "Reorganisation of SS Brigade," 1 April 1943, DEFE 2/1051.
72. Darby and Baumer, *Darby's Rangers*, 94.
73. General Marshall to General Eisenhower, 19 April 1943, RG 407, Entry 427, Box 21066, Folder INBN-1-0.
74. King, *Rangers: Selected Combat Operations*, 2–3, 13.
75. Ladd, *Commandos and Rangers*, 129.
76. Brigadier Laycock to Major General Haydon, 8 August 1943, File 23 in KCLMA Laycock.
77. Lieutenant Colonel Darby, Field Order No. 1, 1 July 1943, RG 407, Entry 427, Box 21071, Folder INBN-1-3.9; Major Herman W. Dammer, CO 3rd Ranger Battalion, to Adjutant General, 31 July 1942, RG 407, Entry 427, Box 21074, Folder INBN-3-0.3.
78. War Office memorandum, "Points Brought Out in Ops. 'Husky,'" WO 201/799.
79. Durnford-Slater, *Commando*, 171.
80. Brigadier-General Norman D. Cota, COHQ G-3, "Observation of Operation Husky," August 1943, RG 165, Entry 418, Box 1249, Folder OPD 381 ETO (Section V) Cases 108–37; Cota to GOC ETOUSA, 10 August 1943, RG 407, Entry 427, Box 24157, Folder 534.
81. Darby to General Eisenhower, 10 August 1943, RG 407, Entry 427, Box 21066, Folder INBN-1-0.
82. Hogan, *Raiders or Elite Infantry?*, 37.
83. Durnford-Slater, *Commando*, 171.
84. Laycock, "Reorganisation of SS Brigade," 1 April 1943, DEFE 2/1051.

85. Hogan, *U.S. Army Special Operations in World War II*, 23.
86. Darby and Baumer, *Darby's Rangers*, 140–41.
87. Report on operations of SS Brigade in Termoli, October 1943, WO 204/7222; also WO 204/8277.
88. Thompson, *War Behind Enemy Lines*, 275.
89. 21 Army Group Staff Study No. 8 "Employment of Commandos and Rangers," 27 December 1943, RG 331, Entry 199, Box 32, Folder 322 Rangers.
90. "History of the Commandos in the Mediterranean, September 1943 to May 1945," DEFE 2/700.
91. Minutes from COS Committee meetings, 17 and 25 November 1942, WO 193/74; and DEFE 2/4.
92. McMichael, *Historical Perspective on Light Infantry*, 172.
93. Major General Lowell W. Rooks, Assistant Chief of Staff G-3 Section, AFHQ, to Chief of Staff, 3 September 1943, WO 204/1532.
94. General Wilson to AFHQ, 10 September 1943, WO 204/1532; various documents in RG 218, Records of the JCS, Geographical File 1942–45, Box 158, Folder 381 Norway.
95. AGWAR to Combined Chiefs of Staff, 7 September 1943, WO 204/1532; Lieutenant Colonel T. J. Conway, G-3 Plans AFHQ, memorandum on deployment of "Plough Force," 4 October 1943, WO 204/1532.
96. McMichael, *Historical Perspective on Light Infantry*, 184–85.
97. Adleman and Walton claim that during the attacks on Monte la Difensa and Monte la Remetanea 532 men were killed or wounded, a third of the FSSF's fighting strength. See Adleman and Walton, *Devil's Brigade*, 134–36.
98. "History of the Commandos in the Mediterranean," DEFE 2/700.
99. Ranger Force (Provisional) Field Order No. 2, 29 January 1944, RG 407, Entry 427, Box 21067, Folder INBN-1-0.3; Beaumont, *Military Elites*, 50. For an assessment of the Rangers at Cisterna, see Stewart, "Ranger Force at the Battle of Cisterna."
100. Lieutenant Colonel Roy A. Murray, Jr., CO 4th Ranger Battalion, report of action for March 1944, 26 March 1944, RG 407, Entry 427, Box 21075, Folder INBN-4-0.1.
101. Springer, *Black Devil Brigade*, 142.
102. Adleman and Walton have misleadingly asserted that in such deployments the force operated "as guerrillas." This was not the case; the FSSF were only undertaking activities, albeit with great flair, of the variety regularly performed by conventional infantry units seeking to gather intelligence or gain the moral ascendancy. Adleman and Walton, *Devil's Brigade*, 162.
103. Hogan, *Raiders or Elite Infantry?*, 61.
104. Summary of FSSF operations 1–30 June 1944, RG 407, Entry 427, Box 23274, Folder SSFE-1-0.3.
105. 21 Army Group Staff Study No. 8, "Employment of Commandos and Rangers," 27 December 1943, RG 331, Entry 199, Box 32, Folder 322 Rangers.

106. 1st SS Brigade War Diary, DEFE 2/53.
107. Major General de Guingand, Chief of Staff 21 Army Group, to SHAEF, 7 June 1944, WO 205/136.
108. Thompson, *The Royal Marines*, 341.
109. 1st Commando Brigade Operation Orders, March–April 1945, DEFE 2/53; Samain, *Commando Men*, 138.
110. 21 Army Group Staff Study No. 8, "Employment of Commandos and Rangers," 27 December 1943, RG 331, Entry 199, Box 32, Folder 322 Rangers.
111. U.S. War Department, *Small Unit Actions*, 1–63.
112. Hogan, *U.S. Army Special Operations in World War II*, 43.
113. Henry S. Glassman, "'Lead the Way, Rangers,' A History of the Fifth Ranger Battalion," RG 407, Entry 427, Box 21076, Folder INBN-5-0, p. 38.
114. "A Narrative History of the Second Ranger Infantry Battalion, 1944," RG 407, Entry 427, Box 21072, Folder 23745, INBN-2-0.3, ch. 8, p. 3.
115. Henry S. Glassman, "'Lead the Way, Rangers,' A History of the Fifth Ranger Battalion", RG 407, Entry 427, Box 21076, Folder INBN-5-0, pp. 56–57.
116. FSSF Summary of Operations, August 1944, RG 338, Entry 37042, Box 459.
117. Hogan, *U.S. Army Special Operations in World War II*, 28; FSSF Summary of Operations, October 1944, RG 407, Entry 427, Box 23275, Folder SSFE-1-0.3.
118. Memoirs of Captain J. E. C. Nicholl, IWM Nicholl 78/43/1, p. 186; "History of the Commandos in the Mediterranean," DEFE 2/700; also various documents in WO 204/1527.
119. Joint Planning Staff report on employment of Commandos, January 1945, WO 203/2102; HQ 3rd SS Brigade War Diary, DEFE 2/53.
120. No. 1 Commando War Diary, DEFE 2/37; Colonel Peter Young, "The Battle for 170," 11 February 1945, WO 203/1792.
121. Historical summary of No. 10 (IA) Commando, May 1946, DEFE 2/780; history of No. 3 Troop No. 10 (IA) Commando, 25 April 1946, DEFE 2/977; Dear, *10 Commando*.
122. Good examples of such undertakings are Operation Chess, a reconnaissance raid near Ambleteuse in July 1941, and Operation Anklet, a December 1941 diversionary action for the larger Archery raid against Vaagso. See reports in DEFE 2/45 and WO 106/4116.
123. Brigadier Durnford-Slater, "Report on Manacle and Hardtack Operations—December Dark Period," 18 January 1944, DEFE 2/57.
124. See operational reports in DEFE 2/57; WO 106/4290; and RG 331, Entry 12, Box 14, Folder SHAEF/6RX/INT.
125. Brief on "Arctic Commandos" for CCO, 25 November 1942, DEFE 2/4.
126. No. 14 Commando War Diary, DEFE 2/45.
127. Unpublished memoir of Colonel N. A. C. Croft, IWM Croft 03/54/1, p. 136.
128. Minutes of meeting on future of 14 Commando and other small forces, 22 February 1943, DEFE 2/742; Melville, *Story of the Lovat Scouts*, 84.

129. Elements of No. 30 Commando occasionally undertook roles that bore greater similarities to the undertakings of various special forces units than they did to their Commando brethren. In February 1945, for example, personnel of 34 (Army) Troop operated with partisans in protracted behind-the-lines operations in Italy. Nutting, *Attain by Surprise*, 56–59.
130. Lieutenant Commander Glanville, "History of No. 30 Commando," 1947, ADM 223/214.
131. GOC SS Group paper on administration of SBU, 28 October 1943, DEFE 2/1035.
132. Nutting, *Attain by Surprise*, 15; Lieutenant Commander Riley, Intelligence Division, SACSEA, to BGS(I) 11 Army Group, 26 August 1944, KCLMA Riley; memorandum on Special Engineering Unit "Objects and Possibilities," 4 November 1943, DEFE 2/742.
133. In addition to the aforementioned units, there were also the Royal Navy Commandos (later known as the Naval Beach Control Parties), which acted as beachmasters during amphibious assaults, and the RAF Servicing Commandos, which had the role of servicing newly captured airfields. Nomenclature aside, these units were quite distinct from other specialist formations. Messenger, *The Commandos, 1940–46*, 139.
134. RG 127, USMC Geographic Files, Russell Islands, Box 315, Folder A10-1; and Bougainville, Box 2, Folder A3-1; Hoffman, *From Makin to Bougainville*.
135. Illustrative of this point is the manner in which the Raiders struggled at Bairoko on New Georgia because of the absence of supporting arms.
136. Lieutenant Colonel Carlson to GOC, 1st Marine Amphibious Corps, RG 127, USMC Geographic Files, Guadalcanal, Box 44, Folder A39-1.
137. Hoffman, *From Makin to Bougainville*.
138. History of the King II Operations of 6th Ranger Battalion, October 1944, RG 407, Entry 427, Box 21079, Folder INBN-6-0.3; King, *Rangers: Selected Combat Operations*, 55–56; Black, *Rangers in World War II*, 250.
139. "Combat History of 6th Ranger Battalion," January 1945, RG 407, Entry 427, Box 21079, Folder INBN-6-0.
140. Hogan, *U.S. Army Special Operations in World War II*, 88; Black, *Rangers in World War II*, 332; and various documents in RG 407, Entry 427, Box 21079, Folder INBN-6-0.3.
141. U.S. War Department, *Merrill's Marauders*, 7; See various documents in RG 407, Entry 427, Box 213211, Folder INRG-5301-1.13.
142. Ogburn, *The Marauders*, 33.
143. Heilbrunn, *Warfare in the Enemy's Rear*, 92–93.
144. U.S. War Department, *Merrill's Marauders*, 15.
145. Ibid., 92–113.
146. Prefer, *Vinegar Joe's War*, 155.
147. See various documents in RG 407, Entry 427, Box 213211, Folder INRG-5301-1.13.

Chapter 2

1. For further discussion of this, see Hargreaves, "Advent, Evolution and Value of British Specialist Formations."
2. Lieutenant General Sir John W. Hackett in foreword to Heilbrunn, *Warfare in the Enemy's Rear*, 9.
3. Posen, *Sources of Military Doctrine*, 47.
4. Millett and Murray, *Military Innovation in the Interwar Period*, 409.
5. Kelly, *Hunt for Zerzura*, 136.
6. Bagnold, *Sand, Wind and War*.
7. When Bagnold's proposal was submitted to General Hobart (himself often regarded as being something of a military "maverick"), he was impressed and forwarded the scheme to GHQ, which subsequently rejected it. That this occurred is illustrative of the fact that the presence of an "errant captain" with an idea (Bagnold) and an innovative and unorthodox senior officer willing to serve as "champion" (Hobart) was not itself sufficient to warrant the inception of a specialist formation. Exigency or great opportunity was an essential ingredient in propelling acceptance. Neither factor was present in sufficient quantities while Italy remained neutral. LRDG War Diary and Narrative—Chapter I "Formation of the Long Range Patrol—Organization and Activities Up to September 1st, 1940," WO 201/807.
8. Jenner, List, and Badrocke, *Long Range Desert Group*, 5; Lloyd Owen, *Providence Their Guide*, 7.
9. Maule, *Out of the Sand*, 84.
10. Raugh, *Wavell in the Middle East*, 22; Lewin, *The Chief*; Woollcombe, *The Campaigns of Wavell*.
11. Wavell continued to have a massive influence on Wingate's career. In both late 1940 in the Middle East and later, in early 1942, in the Far East, Wavell personally summoned Wingate to serve under him as his "expert in guerrilla operations." Rooney, *Wingate and the Chindits*, 34; Bidwell, *The Chindit War*, 25.
12. Playfair, *History of WWII—The Mediterranean and Middle East*, 1:295.
13. Shaw, *Long Range Desert Group*, 27.
14. Kelly, *Hunt for Zerzura*, 136.
15. Bagnold, *Sand, Wind and War*, 123–24.
16. Timpson and Gibson-Watt, *In Rommel's Backyard*, 17.
17. Brigadier T. S. Airey, DMI, notes on LRDG Road Watch, 14 December 1942, WO 201/771.
18. GHQ MEF to Bagnold, 10 July 1941, WO 201/754; LRDG War Diary, September 1940, WO 201/807.
19. Shaw, *Long Range Desert Group*, 91.
20. Maule, *Out of the Sand*, 83; various documents, WO 201/808.
21. Bagnold, *Sand, Wind and War*, 124.
22. LRDG operations in support of Eighth Army, 8 December 1941, WO 201/811; Wynter, *Special Forces in the Desert War*, 99.
23. Rooney, *Wingate and the Chindits*, 48.
24. Bagnold, "Modified Wingate Scheme," 30 October 1940, WO 201/807; Bagnold, memorandum, 22 December 1940, WO 201/808.

25. Not all elements of the Wingate-Bagnold schemes were flawed. It was clearly possible for brigade-sized formations to operate at depth in the desert. In November 1941, for example, Brigadier Reid's "Force E," made up of a battalion of the 2nd Punjab Regiment, the 6th South African Armored Car Regiment, and some field and antiaircraft gunners, seized, in a manner analogous to Leclerc's attack on Kufra and in cooperation with the LRDG, the Jalo Oasis. From this position, Reid's force would subsequently undertake a number of larger operations. There was, nevertheless, a wealth of difference between such actions and the depth and nature of special operations conducted by irregular formations. See Lloyd Owen, *Providence Their Guide*, 69.
26. LRDG War Diary and Narrative, April–August 1941, WO 201/809.
27. Major W. McCoy, CO ILRS, report on deployments, 5 June 1943, WO 201/797.
28. Whittaker, *Some Talk of Private Armies*, 36.
29. Stirling was, in a way that Bagnold was not, a member of the societal elite, and the likes of Michael Asher and Tim Jones recently debunked many myths by suggesting that Stirling had "deliberately targeted" Ritchie, who was a friend of the Stirling family. Asher, *Get Rommel*, 77; Jones, *SAS Zero Hour*, 29.
30. Jones, *SAS Zero Hour*, 19.
31. Otway, *Airborne* Forces, 102.
32. Morgan, *Daggers Drawn*, 21.
33. Lieutenant Deane-Drummond, report on Colossus, 19 December 1942, CAB 106/8.
34. These are examined in detail in Jones's *SAS Zero Hour*. One of the more interesting observations is the Stirling family's historical legacy of being permitted to form their own unique formations, it being Simon Fraser, the fourteenth Lord Lovat and uncle of David Stirling, who established the Lovat Scouts for small-party reconnaissance in the Boer War.
35. See "Report on First Parachute Jump in the Middle East," May 1941, WO 218/173; Jones, *SAS Zero Hour*, 160; 166.
36. Hoe, *David Stirling*, 73.
37. See Lewes, *Jock Lewes*, 247.
38. Asher, *The Regiment*, 35.
39. Hoe, *David Stirling*, 90.
40. Stirling, "Origins of the SAS Regiment," 8 November 1948, KCLMA McLeod; Thompson, *War Behind Enemy Lines*, 50.
41. Windmill, *Gentleman Jim*, 77.
42. Both David Stirling and David Lloyd Owen, an LRDG patrol commander, would later claim responsibility for this idea. The truth, as with all such processes, is likely that the idea arose as a result of collective discussion.
43. Morgan, *Sting of the Scorpion*, 96; Weale, *Secret Warfare*, 101.
44. Morris, *Guerrillas in Uniform*, 72–73.
45. Maclean, *Eastern Approaches*, 193–94.
46. Hastings, *The Drums of Memory*, 45; Lloyd Owen, *Providence Their Guide*, 103.

47. General Auchinleck, C in C MEF, "Future of 1st SS Regiment," 26 July 1942, WO 201/728.
48. To cope with evolving enemy tactics for airfield defense, the SAS had to remain flexible in its methods of attack. The most notable departure from the on-foot, hand-planted demolitions approach was the July 26, 1942, massed-jeep attack on the airfield of Sidi Haneish near Fuka. This innovative, but more risky, approach succeeded in destroying some forty aircraft, but would not again be repeated. The experiment was, however, illustrative of Stirling's perceptual search for diverse tactical approaches. As Asher has claimed, "Stirling's genius as a special forces commander lay in the elasticity of his intellect: he saw his campaign as an elegant mental dance with the enemy." Asher, *The Regiment*, 141.
49. Pitt, *Special Boat Squadron*, 25.
50. Colonel T. S. Airey, GS, to Brigadier G.M.O. Davy, DDO, 1 April 1942, WO 201/732.
51. Miller, *The Commandos*; Francis Mackay doubts this view and has emphasized a potentially more plausible scenario by contending that the Derna operation was compromised as early as June 11 by intercepted signals emanating from the U.S. Military Attaché in Cairo, Colonel Bonner Fellers. Mackay, *Overture to Overlord*, 82. Michael Asher similarly argues that treachery was not involved, instead asserting that the operation was compromised from the outset by the Abwehr's "Rebecca" spy ring in Cairo. Asher, *The Regiment*, 122.
52. German special forces undertook similar approaches during the war, most notably in the 1944 Ardennes offensive. During the postwar war crimes trials, a number of Germans, most notably Otto Skorzeny, were charged with violating these laws but were subsequently acquitted, not least of all because Wing Commander F. F. E. Yeo-Thomas, a former SOE officer, testified about having done precisely the same thing against the Germans.
53. "Brief History of 'L' Detachment SAS Brigade and 1st SAS Regiment 1941–1942," WO 201/721.
54. Kemp, *The SAS at War*, 37.
55. General Arthur Smith, DCGS, to General Ritchie, March 1942, WO 201/731; Windmill, *Gentleman Jim*, 116.
56. Stirling to GHQ MEF, 3 May 1942, WO 201/732.
57. "Brief History of 'L' Detachment SAS Brigade and 1st SAS Regiment 1941–1942," WO 201/721; Mackay, *Overture to Overlord*, 87; Otway, *Airborne Forces*, 107.
58. Seymour, *British Special Forces*, 266.
59. Peniakoff, *Popski's Private Army*, 61–62.
60. Ibid., 127.
61. Foot and Langley, *MI 9*, 96.
62. Historical summary of No. 1 Demolition Squadron PPA, December 1945, WO 106/2332.
63. Peniakoff, *Popski's Private Army*, 210.
64. Yunnie, *Fighting with Popski's Private Army*, 10.

65. Peniakoff, *Popski's Private Army*, 210, 226.
66. War Diary of No. 1 Demolition Squadron, PPA, March 1943, WO 169/11083; historical summary of No. 1 Demolition Squadron, PPA, December 1945, WO 106/2332.
67. GHQ MEF Operational Instruction No. 145 to G1(RF), 28 September 1942, WO 201/743; Lieutenant General R. L. McCreery, CGS, to C in C MEF, September 1942, WO 201/732.
68. With fond memories of serving alongside Theodore Roosevelt's "Rough Riders" in the Spanish-American War, Knox was largely supportive of unconventional methods and remained a strong advocate of Donovan.
69. Casey, *Secret War Against Hitler*, 16.
70. Harris Smith, *OSS*, 1.
71. Paddock, *U.S. Army Special Operations*, 36.
72. Major A. Peter Dewey, "OG History," 13 June 1945, RG 226, Entry 99, Box 98, Folder 5, p. 8.
73. Roosevelt, *War Report of the OSS*, 1:80.
74. Donovan to War Department, 1 August 1942, RG 226, Entry 136, Box 140, Folder 1464.
75. This pattern certainly correlates with G. J. A. O'Toole's arguments that despite a frequent distaste for the irregular, "clandestine activities are as American as apple pie or the bald eagle. Espionage and subversive warfare are part of a venerable American tradition that dates back to George Washington. . . . The thesis that clandestine things are somehow against the American grain, a transplanted organ rejected by the national body, flies in the face of the obscure but demonstrable two-hundred-year history of American intelligence, espionage, and covert action." See O'Toole, *Honorable Treachery*, 403–405; 493.
76. Stimson to Donovan, 8 July 1942, RG 226, Entry 136, Box 140, Folder 1464.
77. JCS Directive 155/4/D, "Functions of the OSS," 23 December 1942, RG 218, Records of the JCS, Central Decimal File 1942–45, Box 372, Folder CGS 385 Sec. 1 Pt. 3.
78. OSS/London War Diaries, Vol. 8, KCLMA MF 208.
79. Obolensky, *One Man in His Time*, 275; Casey, *Secret War Against Hitler*, 93.
80. Lieutenant Colonel Ellery C. Huntington, Jr., to Major General W. B. Smith, Chief of Staff AFHQ, 1 February 1943, RG 218, Geographical File 1942–45, Box 153, Folder CCS 385 North Africa.
81. Director OSS Special Order No. 21, 13 May 1943, RG 226, Entry 136, Box 140, Folder 1460.
82. Personnel for Polish and Danish OGs were also recruited but never operationally deployed. See various OSS correspondence, RG 218, Records of the JCS, Central Decimal File 1942–45, CCS 385, Box 372, Folder CCS 385 Sec.1 Pt. 5.
83. Gordon, *Other Desert War*, 179.
84. Brigadier Davy, DMO, future policy for LRDG, 7 March 1943, WO 201/797.

85. Report of Lieutenant Colonel Prendergast, CO LRDG, August 1943, WO 201/797.
86. Captain G. W. Read (ed.),"Raiding Forces—the Story of an Independent Command in the Aegean, 1943-1945," WO 201/2836, p. 14.
87. GHQ MEF directive to Brigadier Turnbull, OC Raiding Forces, November 1943, WO 201/797.
88. See LRDG Operational Instructions, WO 204/6810.
89. Pleydell, *One Doctor's War*, 110 in IWM Pleydell 90/25/1.
90. Morris, *Guerrillas in Uniform*, 163.
91. Brigadier F. W. de Guingand, Chief of Staff, Eighth Army, to GHQ MEF, 16 February 1943, WO 201/771.
92. Brigadier Davy, DMO, to No. 1 Planning Staff, 24 February 1943, WO 204/7960.
93. Mortimer, *Stirling's Men*, 109.
94. Durnford-Slater, *Commando*, 153.
95. GHQ MEF to Brigadier Turnbull, November 1943, WO 201/797.
96. Warner, *Special Air Service*, 97; and various reports in WO 170/4012 and WO 201/2831.
97. Lloyd Owen, David, "The Larder Was Often Bare—The Story of the Long Range Desert Group, 1943-1945" (unpublished memoir, 1955) in IWM Lloyd Owen, PP/MCR/C13, Reel 4; Brigadier Davy, CO LFA, to Brigadier J. Napier, AFHQ, 18 September 1944, KCLMA Davy.
98. For a good appraisal, see Dear, *Sabotage and Subversion*, 61-69; Appleyard, *Geoffrey*, 71-78.
99. Mountbatten to COS, 19 February 1942, WO 106/4117.
100. The SSRF was occasionally referred to as both the Small Scale Raiding Company or by the cover name, No. 62 Commando.
101. C in C Plymouth to Secretary of the Admiralty, 4 November 1944, ADM 116/5112.
102. Appleyard, *Geoffrey*, 123-27.
103. Ibid., 134.
104. Kemp, *The SAS at War*, 97; Mackay, *Overture to Overlord*.
105. See various COHQ correspondence, January 1943, DEFE 2/957.
106. Appleyard, *Geoffrey*,172; and various operational reports, WO 204/1950.
107. W. Stirling, "Appreciation of 2 SAS Regiment," 29 April 1943, WO 204/7960.
108. W. Stirling to 15 Army Group, 1 July 1943, RG 226, Entry 97, Box 41; Folder 713.
109. Mortimer, *Stirling's Men*, 97; Major A. R. W. Low, AFHQ General Staff, "Note on Special Operations for Husky," July 1943, WO 204/7960.
110. Warner, *Special Air Service*, 128; Strawson, *A History of the SAS Regiment*, 143.
111. W. Stirling to 15 Army Group, 1 December 1943, WO 204/1949.
112. Colonel Franks, Report on SAS Regiment in Italy, period Taranto-Termoli, WO 218/176.
113. Strawson, *History of the SAS Regiment*, 139-43; Thompson, *War Behind Enemy Lines*, 276-81; Farran, *Winged Dagger*, 158.

114. Corvo, *The OSS in Italy*, 72;90.
115. History of Company "A," 2671st Special Reconnaissance Battalion, RG 226, Entry 143, Box 11, Folder 146; Obolensky, *One Man in His Time*, 279.
116. Hogan, *U.S. Army Special Operations in World War II*, 28–29.
117. The French *Bataillon de Choc* comprised some 500 tri-service volunteers who had escaped France through Spain. It was created "for the purpose of bringing specifically military-style assistance to the Resistance organizations inside France" and in the interim mounted a limited number of operations from Corsica against Western Mediterranean islands. Gaujac, *Special Forces in the Invasion of France*, 303–17.
118. MEDTO "Pouch Reviews" and "Cable Reports" for 1944–45, RG 226, Entry 99, Box 35; Reports on "Italian" OGs, RG 226, Entry 99, Box 45, Folders 6 and 7; various documents, RG 226, Entry 97, Box 40; 226, Entry 143, Box 10; and PRO: WO 204/12836.
119. Peniakoff, *Popski's Private Army*, 353.
120. General L. C. Hollis to Prime Minister, 27 January 1944, WO 106/4158; SHAEF memorandum, "NEPTUNE—Action of SAS Troops," April 1944, WO 218/189.
121. Lieutenant Colonel Collins, GSO-1 (SAS), "Notes on the Organization, History and Employment of SAS Troops," May 1945, KCLMA McLeod.
122. AFHQ summary on 2nd SAS Regiment, 24 January 1944, WO 204/10242.
123. AFHQ, "Scope, Employment and Organization of SAS Troops," 13 February 1944, WO 204/1949.
124. Lieutenant General Browning, GOC Airborne Troops, to Chief of Staff, 21 Army Group, 8 May 1944, WO 218/189.
125. Ford, *Fire from the Forest*, 36; Otway, *Airborne Forces*, 240–59.
126. Lieutenant Colonel Collins, "Notes on the Organization, History and Employment of SAS Troops," May 1945, KCLMA McLeod.
127. Hastings, *Das Reich*, 209; John Hislop, who served alongside the SAS as an F Squadron (Phantom) signaler, expressed similar reservations about Operation Loyton, of which he was part. Dispatched into the Vosges area of France from August 1944, thirty-one men out of ninety-two deployed were killed (the majority executed after capture) when the mission was compromised, attacked, and dispersed by a superior enemy force. See Hislop, *Anything but a Soldier*, 167.
128. Ford, *Fire from the Forest*, 100.
129. Major General Richard Gale, Commander HQ 1 British Airborne Corps, to SHAEF G-3 Ops C, 23 December 1944, RG 331, Entry 30, Box 146, Folder 370-30.
130. Ford, *Fire from the Forest*, 117; 145–50.
131. See Asher, *Get Rommel*.
132. Colonel H. V. White, Assistant Chief of Staff, G-2, Sixth Army, to General Krueger, 22 May 1944, RG 338, Records of Sixth Army G-2 Section, Box 1.
133. Zedric, *Silent Warriors of World War II*, 143–45.
134. "Operations of the 4th French Parabattalion" (4th SAS), KCLMA McLeod; documents of Oswald Cary-Elwes, KCLMA Cary-Elwes; Hue and Southby-Tailyour, *The Next Moon*, 67.

135. Brigadier McLeod, "Employment of SAS Troops," 17 June 1944, WO 218/194.
136. In August 1940 Mission 101, led by Colonel Daniel Stanford, began operating with a mandate to assist and foster an Ethiopian revolt against the Italians. In so doing, Stanford sought to utilize small groups of officers and NCOs to supply arms to and train Ethiopian "patriot" forces. In November 1940 Major Orde Wingate had joined this mission and proposed leading a regular force (which became known as Gideon), made up of two battalions of Sudanese and Ethiopian troops, to harass and raid in support of the main effort.
137. SOE document, "Co-ordination of Activities behind the Enemy Lines with the Actions of Allied Military Forces Invading N.W. Europe," 6 April 1943, HS 8/288; Foot, *SOE*, 190.
138. OSS/London War Diaries, Vol. 1, KCLMA MF 204.
139. JCS memorandum on Jedburghs, 28 August 1942, RG 218, Central Decimal File 1942–45, Box 8, Folder CCS 000.5, Subversive Activity.
140. SOE, "History of Jedburghs in Europe," HS 7/17.
141. Ibid.
142. SOE/OSS memorandum on Jedburghs, 10 March 1944, KCLMA MF 209.
143. OSS/London War Diaries, Vol. 4, KCLMA MF 206; For individual team reports see RG 226, Entry 103, Boxes 2 and 3; and RG 226, Entry 154, Box 56, Folder 945.
144. It is interesting to note that some Jedburghs considered it a "great mistake" that they were not encouraged to go into action themselves. Major Marten was of the impression that "after leading a successful military action and demonstrating one's own military prowess, the maquis were far more inclined to obey orders and held the team in greater respect." Major H. N. Marten, "Report on Jedburghs (Zone Sud)," 6 October 1944, RG 226, Entry 154, Box 56, Folder 945.
145. "The Role of Jedburghs in the Invasion of N.W. Europe," 6 June 1943, HS 8/288.
146. It was with obvious bias that SOE/SO London reported: "In comparison with the SAS, the OGs represented a more versatile and highly-trained body of men, having greater resources at their disposal for the conduct of fighting." OSS/London War Diaries, Vol. 4A, KCLMA MF 207.
147. "Summary of Origin and Development of Resistance in France," RG 226, Entry 190, Box 741, Folder 1469; Foot, *SOE in France*, 401–402.
148. The term "Special Forces" within the modern U.S. military is commonly taken to refer directly to the U.S. Army Special Forces, the so-called Green Berets, which was created in 1952 with the principal role of working with indigenous populations conducting "unconventional warfare."
149. OSS Planning Group, "Implementation Study for Special Military Plan for France (North African Theater)," 7 September 1943, WO 204/12980.
150. OSS/London War Diaries, Vol. 3, KCLMA MF 204.
151. Ibid., Vol. 4A; memorandum on employment of OGs in the ETO and procedure for their dispatch, 6 June 1944, KCLMA MF 209; various OG operation reports, RG 226, Entry 143, Box 11; and Entry 148, Box 83.

152. "Jedburgh Team Chronologies," RG 226, Entry 190, Box 740, Folder 1462.
153. Ford, *Fire from the Forest*, 32.
154. "Jedburgh Team Chronologies," RG 226, Entry 190, Box 740, Folder 1462; see also Kehoe, "An Allied Team with the French Resistance."
155. Mackenzie, *Secret History of S.O.E.*, 605.
156. "Jedburgh Team Chronologies," RG 226, Entry 190, Box 740, Folder 1462.
157. SAS Brigade "Sitreps," December 1944–March 1945, RG 331, Entry 30, Box 135, Folder 370.2-4; Thompson, *War Behind Enemy Lines*, 333.
158. Lieutenant Colonel Collins, "Notes on the Organization, History and Employment of SAS Troops," May 1945, KCLMA McLeod.
159. Farran, *Winged Dagger*, 279; Further exception can be noted with the deployment of the French SAS Battalions, via parachute, in small groups into Holland to aid the advance of the First Canadian Army. The depth of these operations were, nevertheless, far shallower than those in France had been.
160. Summary of Jedburgh Operations, RG 226, Entry 101, Box 1; Brown, *The Jedburghs: A Short History*, in IWM Brown 03/24/1, p. 16; Thompson, *War Behind Enemy Lines*, 404.
161. OSS/London War Diaries, Vol. 8, KCLMA MF 208.
162. History of "Italian" OGs, RG 226, Entry 143, Box 11, Folder 146; Obolensky, *One Man in His Time*, 279; MEDTO "Pouch Reviews" and "Cable Reports" for 1944–45, RG 226, Entry 99, Box 35; reports on "Italian" OGs, RG 226, Entry 99, Box 45, Folders 6 and 7; various documents, RG 226, Entry 97, Box 40; 226, Entry 143, Box 10; and WO 204/12836.
163. History of "Italian" OGs, RG 226, Entry 143, Box 11, Folder 146, p. 17; reports of "Italian" OGs in WO 204/7289.
164. Major General W. B. Smith, Chief of Staff, to OSS Italy, 3 October 1943, WO 204/10392.
165. Major Fred Bielaski, CO "Greek" OG, operational reports, 24 December 1944, RG 226, Entry 99, Box 45, Folder 4.
166. GHQ MEF to Brigadier Turnbull, November 1943, WO 201/797.
167. RSR and Force 399 situation reports, 1944, WO 170/1364.
168. OSS/London War Diaries, Vol. 8, KCLMA MF 209.
169. For more on this theme, see Morris, *Guerrillas in Uniform*.
170. The Royal Marines' Mobile Naval Base Defense Organizations 1 and 2 were established in 1939, with a focus on establishing and defending far-flung bases. Their establishment was short lived, with many of their personnel ultimately being drawn into the Royal Marines Commandos.
171. Hampshire, "Exploits of Force Viper," 41–50.
172. Documents of Major Duncan Johnston, KCLMA Johnston D.
173. For a personal account of such actions, see Chapman, *The Jungle Is Neutral*.
174. Lieutenant Colonel Peers, CO, "History of OSS Detachment 101," November 1944, RG 407, Entry 427, Box 70, Folder 92-TF-1-0.2; Hilsman, *American Guerrilla*.
175. Dennis J. Roberts, Acting Chief MU, to Major Carl O. Hoffmann, 28 October 1943, RG 226, Entry 92, Box 490, Folder 27; OSS Planning Group,

"Over-all and Special Programs for Strategic Services Activities in SEAC," 24 May 1944, RG 226, Entry 144, Box 70, Folder 630.
176. Hilsman, *American Guerrilla*, 125.
177. Ibid., 232.
178. SAARF War Diary, RG 226, Entry 101, Box 2, Folder 48; report on SAARF, 10 July 1945, WO 193/673; various documents, RG 331, Entry 56, Box 158, Folder 322 SAARF.
179. See Dear, *Sabotage and Subversion*, 197–208.
180. Major Adam M. Wyant, Operations Officer, "History of Detachment 404 Operations," 21 September 1945, RG 226, Entry 99, Box 64.
181. War Diary of HQ 3rd SS Brigade, DEFE 2/53, Folder 1; Bowen, *Undercover in the Jungle*, 102; Seymour, *British Special Forces*, 58; Thompson, *War in Burma*, 94, 138.
182. "Notes of a Report on the China Commando Group," 9 April 1942, HS 1/164.
183. Thompson, *War Behind Enemy Lines*, 133.
184. Zedric and Dilley, *Elite Warriors*, 167.
185. For information see RG 226, Entry 154, Box 162, Folder 2760; Lieutenant Colonel Alfred T. Cox, CO reports on activities of OG Command, 7 October 1945, RG 226, Entry 154, Box 162, Folder 2762; also see RG 226, Entry 154, Boxes 162–66.
186. Historical record, RG 338, Records of Sixth Army G-2 Section, Box 7, pp. 12–13.
187. Hogan, *Raiders or Elite Infantry?*, 82.
188. Krueger, *From Down Under to Nippon*, 29.
189. Zedric, *Silent Warriors*, 41; 51.
190. Shelton, "Alamo Scouts," 29–30.
191. Breuer, *MacArthur's Undercover War*, 147; Zedric, *Silent Warriors*, 150–51.
192. For information on operations, see RG 338, Records of Sixth Army G-2 Section, Box 7, pp. 13–16; Zedric, *Silent Warriors*, 75; McRaven, *SPEC OPS*, 152–254; Hogan, *U.S. Army Special Operations in World War II*, 82.
193. Courtney, *SBS in World War Two*, 23.
194. Parker, *SBS*, 18.
195. The "folbot" was a form of folding canoe. It is occasionally referred to as a folboat or a foldboat.
196. Parker, *SBS*, 26. During the war two distinct units used the designation SBS: the Special Boat Section(s) (which first originated in 1940 and over the course of the war included the following groups: 1st, 2nd, Z, A, B, and C) and the Special Boat Squadron (which was established in early 1943 from a nucleus of the SAS and 1st Special Boat Section personnel). In late 1944 the Squadron was renamed Special Boat Service.
197. For various SBS operations, see DEFE 2/970.
198. Thompson, *War Behind Enemy Lines*, 74.
199. Papers of Brigadier Gerald Montanaro, KCLMA Montanaro; "Past, Present, and Future Activities of the Special Boat Section," 23 November 1943, DEFE 2/740.

200. Captain R. P. Livingstone, SBS to Captain (S) 8th Submarine Flotilla, 30 March 1943, DEFE 2/740; reports for the historical record of SBU, 26 January 1944, DEFE 2/1035; Major G. B. Courtney, OC Z SBS reports of Mediterranean operations, September 1943, DEFE 2/1036.
201. "Report of Activities of 'B' Group Special Boat Section Attached to 21 (East African) Brigade," 25 November 1944, DEFE 2/970.
202. Major G. B. Courtney, Z SBS, to COHQ, 14 April 1944, DEFE 2/970.
203. Admiralty report on RMBPD, June 1944, ADM 1/21986; Laffin, *Raiders*, 128.
204. Major H. G. Hasler, OC RMBPD, "General Situation," 14 September 1943, DEFE 2/742.
205. Lieutenant Colonel H. F. G. Langley, Commandant CODC, to CCO, 12 May 1942, DEFE 2/988.
206. COHQ Docket, "Command and Administration of RMBPD," 22 November 1942, DEFE 2/953; RMBPD War Diary, ADM 202/310.
207. Major G. C. S. Montanaro to Lieutenant General R. P. Pakenham-Walsh, 10 September 1950, File 101/Gs/1 in KCLMA Montanaro.
208. The only operations of a vaguely similar nature were Operations Jaywick and Rimau, conducted by the predominantly Australian "Z Special Unit" of the Services Reconnaissance Department (SRD) of the Allied Intelligence Bureau (AIB) against Singapore in September 1943 and September 1944, respectively. Courtney, *Silent Fleet*; McDonald, *New Zealand's Secret Heroes*.
209. Lucas Phillips, *Cockleshell Heroes*, 59.
210. The classically named Greek Sacred Squadron had been formed from escaped Greek military personnel in 1942 during the Desert War. During this campaign, it was attached to David Stirling's SAS and later became part of Raiding Forces Aegean, where it worked closely with the SBS (Squadron) and the LRDG. See Joint Operational Staff minutes on Commanders in Chief Committee meeting on employment of raiding forces in Eastern Mediterranean, 5 January 1944, WO 201/2202.
211. Pitt, *Special Boat Squadron*, 149; reports on Operation Tenement, July 1944, WO 201/2831.
212. Major Hasler to CCO, 16 August 1942, DEFE 2/988.
213. This unit was also briefly known as the Sea Reconnaissance Section.
214. Wright, *Frogmen of Burma*, 20–35.
215. GOC SS Group, "Administration of SBU," 28 October 1943, DEFE 2/1035.
216. Wright, *Frogmen of Burma*, 71.
217. Minutes of 260th SEAC meeting, 8 July 1945, WO 203/131; Wright, *Frogmen of Burma*, 104.
218. GOC Royal Marines, Administrative Instruction No.252 on formation of RM Detachment 385, 2 March 1944, DEFE 2/1203; Oakley, *Behind Japanese Lines*, 11.
219. CCO brief on Special Parties in SEAC, October 1944, DEFE 2/1035; record of SOG, SEAC, March 1946, DEFE 2/1747.
220. SEAC OG operational narratives, RG 226, Entry 144, Box 70.
221. History of the OSS MU, RG 226, Entry 99, Box 98, Folder 4, p. 5.

222. Ibid., p. 16.
223. Ibid., p. 19.
224. History of the OSS MU in the Middle East, July 1943 to March 1945, RG 226, Entry 99, Box 54, Folder 4; Benyon-Tinker, *Dust Upon the Sea*, 13–14.
225. Lieutenant C. Gilpatric, Executive Officer, MU London, to Lieutenant D. J. Roberts, Chief MU, 23 January 1944, RG 226, Entry 144, Box 72, Folder 4; Lieutenant Commander R. R. Guest, Chief MU London, "The L-Unit," 10 March 1944, RG 226, Entry 148, Box 83, Folder 1200.
226. History of the OSS MU, RG 226, Entry 99, Box 98; Folder 4, 18–19.
227. The San Marco Battalion was an Italian special forces unit comprising two elements, one trained in underwater sabotage swimming and the other in small boat operations, surface swimming, and the attack of land-based targets. In mid-1944 those Italian personnel willing to cooperate were attached to the Allies. The underwater specialists were sent to work with COHQ and SOE, while those focused on small-boat and overland deployments were predominantly attached to OSS. Lieutenant William H. Pendleton, Chief MU NATO, "MU Report for Period 16–30 April 1944," RG 226, Entry 143, Box 5, Folder 77.
228. Colonel William P. Davis, Chief of Operations, to OSS Italy, 13 November 1944, WO 204/12984; Lieutenant Kelly, Chief MU AAI, report on Ossining, 30 June 1944, RG 226, Entry 143, Box 5, Folder 77.
229. Lieutenant Pendelton to Chief MU Washington, 28 June 1944, RG 226, Entry 143, Box 5, Folder 77; Lieutenant Kelly, "Operational Report, February 1945," 2 March 1945, RG 226, Entry 143, Box 6, Folder 96.
230. Thompson, *War Behind Enemy Lines*, 46.
231. Ladd, *Commandos and Rangers*, 58.
232. Outline history of COPPs prepared for War Diary, 26 November 1943, DEFE 2/1116.
233. Fowler, *Commandos at Dieppe*, 47.
234. The SBS took umbrage at the formation of a separate and hurriedly formed unit for these purposes and believed that they, with two years' operational experience, were more than capable of these tasks. Captain G. B. Courtney, SBS, to Brigadier Laycock, September 1942, File 9 in KCLMA Laycock.
235. Lieutenant Commander Willmott to Naval Commander in Chief, Expeditionary Force, 20 September 1942, DEFE 2/741.
236. Outline history of COPPs prepared for War Diary, 26 November 1943, DEFE 2/1116.
237. Minutes of COHQ meeting, 27 November 1942, DEFE 2/4.
238. Reports for the historical record of SBU, 26 January 1944, DEFE 2/1035.
239. COPP War Diary, DEFE 2/741; documents in ADM 179/347; DEFE 2/1101.
240. Outline history of COPPs prepared for War Diary, 26 November 1943, DEFE /1116; Lieutenant I. Morison, CO COPP 9, Report on "Natkan," 17 April 1945, DEFE 2/1204.
241. Dwyer, *Scouts and Raiders*, 3–4.
242. This school would subsequently relocate to the Fort Pierce, Florida, ATB. Ibid., 5–6.

243. Commander J. C. Hammock, USNATB, Fort Pierce, Florida, "Training Activities," RG 24, Historical Records of Navy Training Activities, 1940–45, Box 28, Folder ATB Fort Pierce, Florida.
244. Marquis, *Unconventional Warfare*, 21.
245. Admiral B. H. Ramsay to CCO, 11 December 1943, RG 331, Entry 12, Box 14, Folder SHAEF/6RX/INT.
246. See Dwyer, *Scouts and Raiders*, 28–31, 83–91; Cunningham, *Frogmen of World War II*, 152; Zedric and Dilley, *Elite Warriors*, 128–29.
247. Cunningham, *Frogmen of World War II*, 13.
248. Dwyer, *Scouts and Raiders*, 34, 135, 143.
249. Colonel G. B. Erskine, corps intelligence order 4-42 "Reconnaissance Patrols Landing on Hostile Shores," 29 October 1942, RG 127, History and Museums Division, Subject File Relating to World War II, Box 46, Folder 7.
250. Correspondence between V Amphibious Corps and Reconnaissance Company, RG 127, USMC Geographic Files, Gilberts, Box 27, Folder A6–9.
251. Meyers, *Fortune Favors the Brave*, 8.
252. Interservice tensions and confusion over the responsibility for shoreline and high-water mark demolitions had caused the U.S. Army's Corps of Engineers to parallel a number of NCDU developments. As early as 1923 the U.S. Army had been responsible for constructing beach and underwater defenses and had begun experiments in their destruction two months before the instigation of the U.S. Navy's program. Unlike the Navy, however, the Army assigned this role to existent combat engineer units and did not form any dedicated specialist units for the task. O'Dell, "Joint-Service Beach Obstacle Demolition in World War II," 36.
253. Admiral E. J. King to U.S. Fleet Commands, 6 May 1943, RG 80, Formerly Security-Classified General Correspondence of the CNO/Secretary of the Navy, 1940–47, Box 1009, Folder S76-3–S76-5.
254. CNO to BuPers, 25 November 1943, ibid.
255. Marquis, *Unconventional Warfare*, 2; Dwyer, *Scouts and Raiders*, 31. After the UDTs had been established Kauffman was sent to the Pacific, where he would be operationally deployed in the Marianas campaign as commander of UDT 5.
256. Rear Admiral C. S. Daniel, "Establishment of a Boom Commando," 25 June 1943, DEFE 2/963.
257. COHQ Docket, "Establishment of a Boom Commando, 27 September 1943, ADM 1/12848.
258. Zedric and Dilley, *Elite Warriors*, 174; Supplemental Plan to V Corps NEPTUNE Plan, 26 March 1944, RG 407, Entry 427, Box 24369, Folder 601.
259. O'Dell, "Joint-Service Beach Obstacle Demolition in World War II," 36.
260. Zedric and Dilley, *Elite Warriors*, 163.
261. Alexander, *Storm Landings*, 29.
262. Fane and Moore, *The Naked Warriors*, 15.
263. Rear-Admiral Turner to CNO, 26 December 1943, RG 80, Formerly Security-Classified General Correspondence of the CNO, 1940–47, Box 1764, Folder S76-3/A-ZZ; VAC study of conditions at Tarawa, January 1944, RG 127, Records of U.S. Marine Corps, USMC Geographic Files, Gilberts, Box 36.

264. W. B. Phillips, Administrative Commander, VAC, to Chief of Naval Personnel, 28 March 1944; CNO to BuPers, 2 May 1944, RG 80, Formerly Security-Classified General Correspondence of the CNO, 1940–47, Box 1452, Folder S76-3.
265. Admiral R. K. Turner, Commander Fifth Amphibious Force, to Admiral Nimitz, 14 March 1944, ibid.
266. Various documents, RG 226, Entry 139, Box 73, Folder 73.
267. War Diary of COSU, DEFE 2/740; "Directive for the Camouflage Training and Development Center 'B,'" 19 May 1942, DEFE 2/740.
268. In September 1944 responsibility for the unit passed from COHQ to the Royal Navy, and the unit was subsequently renamed Navy Scout Unit.
269. Admiral Mountbatten, CCO, to Colonel C. D. Barlow, CO "Camouflage . . . 'B,'" 5 July 1942, DEFE 2/740.
270. Dwyer, *Seaborne Deception*.
271. Ibid., 48.
272. Mackenzie, *Secret History of S.O.E*, 41.
273. EMFFI Operational Brief No. 3, Operation Antagonist, 8 August 1944, RG 226, Entry 148, Box 83, Folder 1205.
274. Foot, *Resistance*, 53.

Chapter 3

1. Eisenhower, *Allies*, xxi.
2. Reynolds, *The Creation of the Anglo-American Alliance*, 294.
3. Stafford, *Roosevelt and Churchill*, 56.
4. Roosevelt, *War Report of the OSS*, 1:12.
5. Roosevelt, *War Report of the OSS*, 2:viii, 3.
6. Stafford, *Camp X*, 12, 61.
7. Yu, *OSS in China*, 19; Stafford, *Churchill and Secret Service*, 153.
8. Harris-Smith, *OSS*, 32–33.
9. Lieutenant Colonel T. Ely, Office of DCO, to Major Daniell, War Office, 31 July 1941, WO 193/405.
10. Mountbatten to COS Committee, 23 January 1942, CAB 121/177.
11. Durnford-Slater, Commando, 56; No. 3 Commando War Diary, 1941, WO 218/23; Vice Admiral R. L. Ghormley, U.S. Special Naval Observer London, to CCO, 21 January 1942, CAB 121/177.
12. Major General Chaney, Adjutant General, to GOC, USANIF, 1 June 1942, RG 407, Entry 427, Box 21066, Folder INBN-1-0.
13. Ibid.
14. Black, *Rangers in World War II*, 17.
15. Dudley Clarke, GHQ Cairo, to Major A. W. E. Daniell, War Office, 10 July 1941, WO 193/405.
16. Major A. W. E. Daniell, War Office, to Lieutenant Colonel T. Ely, Office of DCO, 23 July 1941, WO 193/405.
17. Stacey Lloyd to Major Bruce, "Commando Training and Operations," 5 August 1942, RG 226, Entry 92, Box 111, Folder 49.
18. For a copy see DEFE 2/849.
19. Stacey Lloyd to Major Bruce, "Commando Training and Operations," 5 August 1942, RG 226, Entry 92, Box 111, Folder 49.

20. As Lord "Shimi" Lovat, wartime commander of No. 4 Commando (and later 1st SS Brigade) commented, "The severity of commando training, rather than its diversification and originality, have . . . been taken out of context and exaggerated. All ranks took pride in physical fitness, knew how to swim, handle explosives and sail boats, and expected to live dangerously. None were supermen: until they had received specialist training few showed exceptional skills in the arts of war." Lovat, *March Past*, 149.
21. History of the OSS MU, RG 226, Entry 99, Box 98, Folder 4.
22. Dennis J. Roberts, Acting Chief MU, to Ensign Putzel, 28 October 1943, RG 226, Entry 92, Box 490, Folder 26.
23. OSS MU ETOUSA to Lieutenant D. J. Roberts, Chief MU, 18 December 1943, RG 226, Entry 144, Box 72, Folder 4, London.
24. Lieutenant Commander Guest, Chief MU London, to Colonel D. K. Bruce, 8 November 1943, RG 226, Entry 148, Box 83, Folder 1200.
25. Minutes of COHQ Amphibious Warfare Sub-Committee, 4 January 1944, DEFE 2/1035.
26. Lieutenant C. Gilpatric, Executive Officer, MU London, to Lieutenant D. J. Roberts, Chief MU, 23 January 1944, RG 226, Entry 144, Box 72, Folder 4.
27. Minutes of COHQ meeting, 31 March 1944, RG 226, Entry 148, Box 83, Folder 1200.
28. MU London War Diary, RG 226, Entry 148, Box 83, Folder 1199; Commander Lester Armor, Deputy Director OSS ETO, to Captain F. A. Slocum, RN, DDOD(I), 13 November 1944, RG 226, Entry 148, Box 83, Folder 1200.
29. Historical summary of CCOR, Washington D.C., DEFE 2/780.
30. Wright, *Frogmen of Burma*, 39–40.
31. General H. M. Smith, "Equipment for Amphibious Reconnaissance Company, FIFTHPHIBCORPS," 31 August 1943, RG 127, History and Museums Division, Subject File Relating to World War II, Box 7, Folder 9.
32. History of the OSS MU, RG 226, Entry 99, Box 98, Folder 4, p. 21.
33. Lieutenant Commander Wright to CCO, DEFE 2/741.
34. H. G. A. Woolley, CCO/OSS Liaison Officer, to Laycock, 15 December 1943, DEFE 2/741.
35. Laycock to Admiral King, 13 November 1943, DEFE 2/741.
36. Wright, *Frogmen of Burma*, 97.
37. O'Dell, *Water Is Never Cold*, 7.
38. MU report on NCDU, 2 September 1943, RG 226, Entry 92, Box 534, Folder 8; joint report of Major C. E. Kennedy and Major R. R. Fairbairn to Commander, Amphibious Forces, U.S. Atlantic Fleet, 5 August 1943, RG 218, Central Decimal File 1942–45, Box 281, Folder CCS 370.03.
39. Rear Admiral C. S. Daniel, "Establishment of a Boom Commando," 25 June 1943, DEFE 2/963; OSS MU ETOUSA to Chief MU, 18 December 1943, RG 226, Entry 144, Box 72, Folder 4.
40. See, for example, reports on Leyte operation, DEFE 2/963.
41. OSS/London War Diaries, Vol. 1 Chief of Staff, KCLMA MF 204.
42. Roosevelt, *War Report of the OSS*, 1:206–207.

43. "Summary of Agreement between British SOE and American SO," September 1942, HS 1/165.
44. JCS 86/1 "Agreements between OSS and British SOE," 26 August 1942, RG 218, Central Decimal File 1942-45, Box 369, Folder CCS 385 (8-6-42).
45. Stafford, *Churchill and Secret Service*, 224-25.
46. OSS/London War Diaries, Vol. 1 Chief of Staff, KCLMA MF 204.
47. Illustrative of OSS gradually matching SOE's operational contribution is the fact that in March 1944 the British contribution to supply sorties into France was ten times as much as OSS, but by May a larger OSS allocation of aircraft ensured that OSS was matching British involvement. Harris-Smith, *OSS*, 174; Roosevelt, *War Report of the OSS*, 2:4; Hogan, *U.S. Army Special Operations in World War II*, 48.
48. "SOE/OSS Relations in North Africa," "AMF" to "CD" [Gubbins], 27 September 1943, HS 3/57.
49. Harris-Smith, *OSS*, 174.
50. Quoted in Briscoe, "Major Herbert R. Brucker SF Pioneer," 72-85.
51. Quoted in ibid.
52. Bank, *From OSS to Green Berets*, 6-9.
53. Colby, *Honorable Men*, 36.
54. Brown, *The Jedburghs: A Short History*, in IWM Brown 03/24/1, p. 5.
55. Papers of Colonel Sir Thomas Macpherson, IWM Macpherson 05/73/1.
56. Foot, *SOE*, 151.
57. Yu, *OSS in China*, 271.
58. "Chronology of Detachment 101 to August 31, 1944," RG 226, Entry 92, Box 192, Folder 1, 13982-3, pp. 1-2.
59. Also ceding to 101's control at this time was "Dah Force," a British military mission that sought to raise Kachin guerrillas in support of the Chindits' second expedition, Operation Thursday. Peers and Brelis, *Behind the Burma Road*, 120, 147.
60. Roosevelt, *War Report of the OSS*, 2:369-92.
61. Thorne, *Allies of a Kind*, 228.
62. Roosevelt, *War Report of the OSS*, 2:393.
63. Cruickshank, *SOE in the Far East*, 173; also various documents, WO 106/6092.
64. Roosevelt, *War Report of the OSS*, 2:393-405.
65. Although initially supportive of OSS, as evidenced by the actions of Sir William Stevenson and his New York–based "British Security Coordination Agency," the Special Intelligence Service's relationship with their American counterparts had begun to sour by 1943. Becoming broadly distrustful of American anti-imperialistic sentiments, Sir Stewart Menzies, heading SIS, began to impose increasingly strict limits on cooperation with OSS.
66. Harris-Smith, *OSS*, 34.
67. Previously withdrawn OSS NATO documents, RG 226, Entry 210, Box 72, Folder 3.

68. Ibid.
69. Eisenhower, *Allies*, 121.
70. Reynolds, *Rich Relations*, 342.
71. CMP to CCO, 6 January 1943, DEFE 2/957.
72. History of OSS Cairo, RG 226, Entry 99, Box 54, Folder 2.
73. Brigadier General John R. Deane for JCS to Donovan, 7 September 1943, WO 201/2263.
74. Hogan, *U.S. Army Special Operations in World War II*, 48–49.
75. Bradley, *A Soldier's Story*, 59.
76. Quoted in Lindsay, *Beacons in the Night*, 205.
77. Reynolds, *Rich Relations*, 327.
78. Obolensky, *One Man in His Time*, 301.
79. Black, *Rangers in World War II*, 46.
80. Ibid., 33.
81. Captain Roy A. Murray to Darby, CO 1st Ranger Battalion, 26 August 1942, RG 407, Entry 427, Box 21066, Folder INBN-1-0.
82. King, *Rangers: Selected Combat Operations*, 9–10.
83. For instance, see Exercise PEP, September 1942, RG 407, Entry 427, Box 9575, Folder 334-INF(168)-0.3 October–December 1942.
84. Eastern Assault Force Administrative Order No. 2, 4 October 1942, RG 407, Entry 427, Box 9575, Folder 334-INF(168)-0.3 October–December 1942; Berens, "First Encounters," 45–48.
85. No. 1 Commando War Diary, 9 December 1942, DEFE 2/37; No. 6 Commando War Diary, DEFE 2/43.
86. Lieutenant Colonel Trevor, CO No. 1 Commando, report on Operation Bizerte, December 1942, KCLMA Allfrey.
87. Captain Philip Dunne to Brigadier Laycock, undated, KCLMA Laycock File 16.
88. No. 1 Commando War Diary, 31 January 1943, DEFE 2/37.
89. The few secondary sources citing this arrangement are prone to assume, erroneously, that the RCT men were U.S. Army Rangers.
90. "History of the Commandos in the Mediterranean," DEFE 2/700 p. 37; Darby and Baumer, *Darby's Rangers*, 143.
91. Major Richard P. Fisk, Assistant Adjutant General, to Adjutant General, Washington, 2 December 1942, RG 407, Entry 427, Box 24157, Folder 534.
92. Black, *Rangers in World War II*, 65.
93. Ibid., 72.
94. Macksey, *Commando Strike*, 165, 183.
95. Black, *Rangers in World War II*, 113.
96. Ibid., 125.
97. Lieutenant General Morgan, COSSAC, to CO ETOUSA, 14 December 1943, WO 219/481.
98. Macksey, *Commando Strike*, 181.
99. "A Narrative History of the Second Ranger Infantry Battalion, 1944," RG 407, Entry 427, Box 21072, Folder 23745, INBN-2-0.3 ch. 1, pp. 1–3.
100. Brigadier Durnford-Slater, "Report on Candlestick and Hardtack

Operations—January Dark Period," 17 February 1944, DEFE 2/57; also WO 106/4290.
101. Henry S. Glassman, "'Lead the Way, Rangers,' A History of the Fifth Ranger Battalion," RG 407, Entry 427, Box 21076, Folder INBN-5-0, pp. 12–13.
102. Lieutenant Colonel Rudder to GOC V Corps, 20 April 1944, RG 407, Entry 427, Box 24385, Folder 731.
103. Obolensky to Colonel Edward J. F. Glavin, CO 2677th HQ Company Experimental [OSS], 8 December 1943, RG 226, Entry 97, Box 41, Folder 713. This was not the first contact that OSS had had with the 2nd SAS. Prior to Husky, the OSS Secret Intelligence (SI) branch had attached some Italian-speaking personnel to the regiment to aid their operational deployments. See Corvo, *OSS in Italy*, 61–62; 80.
104. Lieutenant Colonel Russell B. Livermore, CO OGs MEDTO, to Glavin, 10 January 1944, RG 226, Entry 143, Box 11, Folder 143; semimonthly OG reports, 29 March 1944, RG 226, Entry 143, Box 11, Folder 143.
105. Lieutenant Colonel Russell B. Livermore, CO OGs MED, to Colonel Glavin, 10 January 1944, RG 226, Entry 143, Box 11, Folder 143; Lieutenant Emileo T. Caruso, Liaison Officer, semimonthly OG reports, 29 March 1944, RG 226, Entry 143, Box 11, Folder 143; Kemp, *The SAS at War*, 110–12.
106. Obolensky to Colonel J. F. Glavin, CO 2677th HQ Company Experimental [OSS], 8 December 1943, RG 226, Entry 97, Box 41, Folder 713.
107. Colonel Glavin to G-3 AFHQ, 11 December 1943, WO 204/12980; Colonel Glavin and Lieutenant Colonel Stirling to Assistant Chief of Staff, G-3, AFHQ, 13 December 1943, WO 204/12837.
108. Colonel B. M. Archibald, AFHQ G-3, "Command of Special Raiding Forces," 13 January 1944, WO 204/1565. At the end of the war in Europe, when David Stirling was freed from Colditz prison, he resurrected similar ideas and proposed to Donovan that he be permitted to command a joint OSS OG/SAS Brigade for action against Japan. David Stirling quoted in Stevens, *The Originals*, 317–18.
109. OSS/London War Diaries, Vol. 2, KCLMA MF 204.
110. Reports on Operation Percy Red, RG 226, Entry 148, Box 83, Folder 1212; Dear, *Sabotage and Subversion*, 179.
111. See RG 226, Entry 144, Box 70, Folders 635 and 639/A.
112. McConville, *Small War in the Balkans*, 118.
113. For information see RG 226, Entry 144, Box 68, Folder 586.
114. Excerpt from USAFIME Accomplishment Report, 1 January 1944 to 30 June 1944, RG 226, Entry 144, Box 68, Folder 590.
115. "History of the Commandos in the Mediterranean," DEFE 2/700, pp. 162–69; Major Philip G. Lovell, CO "Greek/Yugoslav" OGs, to Lieutenant Colonel Paul West, Chief Operations Officer Special Bari Section, 1 April 1944, RG 226, Entry 144, Box 68, Folder 598.
116. See various OG reports, RG 226, Entry 144, Box 68, Folders 591–92.
117. Major Philip G. Lovell, CO "Greek/Yugoslav" OGs, to Lieutenant Colonel Paul West, Chief Operations Officer Special Bari Section, 1 April 1944, RG 226, Entry 144, Box 68, Folder 598.

118. No. 2 Commando War Diaries, 1944, WO 218/64; Major Samuel C. King, Jr., Executive Officer "Greek/Yugoslav" OGs, "Report for Period 1–15 November 1944," RG 226, Entry 144, Box 68, Folder 597.
119. Captain Richard R. Quay, Executive Officer "Greek" and "Yugoslav" OGs, to CO OG MED, 15 June 1944, RG 226, Entry 144, Box 68, Folder 598.
120. For reports, see RG 226, Entry 99, Box 45, Folders 4 and 5; also RSR situation reports, WO 170/1364.
121. Captain Cronje to OC RSR, 2 August 1944, WO 170/1364.
122. Major Fred Bielaski, CO, report on "Greek" OG operations, 24 December 1944, RG 226, Entry 99, Box 45, Folder 4.
123. Lieutenant John Giannaris, "Report on Operations and Conditions in Greece at Kirkstone," 28 October 1944, RG 226, Entry 144, Box 68, Folder 587.
124. See, for example, LRDG Operation Instruction No. 140 (A Sqn), 2 September 1944, AIR 23/7802; and various documents in WO 204/10306.
125. For a personal account of RSR and OG cooperation in Greece, see Reid, *Resistance Fighter*, 95–98.
126. Lieutenant William H. Pendelton, Chief MU NATO to Chief MU Washington, D.C., 28 June 1944, RG 226, Entry 143, Box 5, Folder 77.
127. Lieutenant (jg) Bennett M. Cave, OSS, to Lieutenant Pendleton, Chief MU NATO, 11 August 1944, RG 226, Entry 143, Box 5, Folder 77.
128. Lieutenant Kelly, MU operational reports, February–March 1945, RG 226, Entry 143, Box 6, Folder 96.
129. Lieutenant Kelly to OSS AFHQ, 3 October 1944, RG 226, Entry 143, Box 5, Folder 77. In what was probably a reciprocal arrangement, two LRDG officers were sent to America to observe and advise the Americans on their activities. See Thompson, *War Behind Enemy Lines*, 358–59.
130. COS Eighth Army to OSS AFHQ, 27 June 1945, WO 204/12982. In various deployments PPA had close relations with this MU. Illustrative of the bond that developed between the two units are PPA captain John Campbell's recollections of Kelly, commanding the MU, as being one of "the best friends I have ever had." Campbell, *Green Box*.
131. Commander R. Davis Halliwell to Mr. J. M. Scribner, 12 January 1944, RG 226, Entry 92, Box 49, Folder 15.
132. Lieutenant Commander R. R. Guest, Chief MU London, to Mr. Scribner and Lieutenant Roberts, 19 February 1944, RG 226, Entry 148, Box 83, Folder 1199, MU War Diary Part I.
133. Report on MU in SEAC, RG 226, Entry 99, Box 64, Folder 5, p. 14.
134. See, for example, report on Operation Target, HQ 1st OG SEAC, January 1945, RG 226, Entry 144, Box 70, Folder 637.
135. Dwyer, *Scouts and Raiders*, 21.
136. Macksey, *Commando Strike*, 148.
137. Minutes of COHQ meeting, 27 November 1942, DEFE 2/4.
138. O'Dell, *Water Is Never Cold*, 20.
139. C in C Mediterranean to First Sea Lord, 1 May 1943, DEFE 2/741.
140. Lieutenant N. T. McHarg, CO COPP 4, to OC COPP Depot, 2 August 1943, DEFE 2/741.

141. Cunningham, *Frogmen of World War II*, 180.
142. Courtney, *SBS in World War Two*, 118; Dwyer, *Scouts and Raiders*, 55.
143. Minutes of COS (X) meeting, 17 September 1943, ADM 179/347; Trenowden, *Stealthily by Night*, 93.
144. Lieutenant Commander F. M. Berncastle, "Sounding in the Dark—The Hydrographic Surveying of Beaches for Use by Assault Craft and Prior to the Landings on the Coast of Normandy, 1944," IWM Berncastle 02/56/1; Admiral B. H. Ramsay to CCO, 11 December 1943, RG 331, Entry 12, Box 14, Folder SHAEF/6RX/INT.
145. Dwyer, *Scouts and Raiders*, 69.
146. Trenowden, *Stealthily by Night*, 140.
147. Reynolds, *Rich Relations*, 15.
148. Danchev, "Great Britain: The Indirect Strategy," 6.
149. Casey, *Secret War Against Hitler*, 31.
150. Reynolds, *Rich Relations*, 15.
151. See Eisenhower, *Allies*, 394.
152. Mackenzie, *Secret History of S.O.E.*, 393.
153. Macksey, *Commando Strike*, 210.

Chapter 4

1. Fleming, "Unorthodox Warriors," 381.
2. Asprey, *War in the Shadows*, 299.
3. Admiralty paper, "Transfer of Unorthodox Offensive Units to the Control of DDOD(I)," 30 July 1944, ADM 1/16957.
4. Gray, *Explorations in Strategy*, 183.
5. Brigadier Martin to CGS, AFHQ, 16 June 1943, WO 204/1949; David Lloyd Owen, CO LRDG, to Guy Prendergast, 3 March 1944, IWM Lloyd Owen, PP/MCR/C13, Reel 2.
6. Beaumont, *Special Operations and Elite Units*, 7; Bidwell, "Irregular Warfare," 80.
7. Churchill, *Second World War*, 2:413.
8. Stirling to 15 Army Group, 1 July 1943, RG 226, Entry 97, Box 41, Folder 713.
9. Hogan, *Raiders or Elite Infantry?*, 29.
10. Adleman and Walton, *Devil's Brigade*, 154–55.
11. Cohen, *Commandos and Politicians*, 53.
12. Gray, *Explorations in Strategy*, 167.
13. Ibid., 150–51.
14. COS Committee directive to ACO, 17 October 1941, CAB 80/31/29.
15. Ladd, *Commandos and Rangers*, 27; Seymour, *British Special Forces*, 15.
16. Hughes-Hallett, "Mounting of Raids," 580.
17. Quoted in Lovat, *March Past*, 223.
18. Mountbatten to COS Committee, 21 March 1942, CAB 80/35/57.
19. Mountbatten to Secretary, COS Committee, 23 July 1942, WO 106/4117.
20. Mountbatten to COS Committee, 9 May 1942, CAB 80/62/55.

21. Force J was a naval command formed immediately after the Dieppe raid to provide COHQ with a force capable of brigade-size lift.
22. Hughes-Hallett, "Mounting of Raids," 587.
23. This occurred despite the fact that the original personnel of SSRF, formerly of *Maid Honor* Force, remained jointly administered by SOE and COHQ. CO SSRF to Mountbatten, 1 January 1943, DEFE 2/957.
24. Minutes of COS Committee meeting, 4 January 1943, DEFE 2/1093.
25. Tensions between SIS/SOE activities and military raids were prone to flare up in any theater where the two occurred in close proximity. For instance, in early 1944 SOE took umbrage at the activities of Raiding Forces Aegean, which, they claimed, not only made clandestine intelligence gathering more difficult but also increased the enemy presence, encouraged reprisals against friendly populations, and more generally limited the number of available "hiding places" its agents could use. See various documents in HS 5/445.
26. G. E. Wildman-Lushington, COS for CCO, to Secretary of the Admiralty (M Branch), 20 September 1943, DEFE 2/741; Dwyer, *Scouts and Raiders*, 41.
27. Minutes of Reconnaissance Committee, 6 November 1943, WO 106/4117.
28. Admiral Ramsay to Secretary of the Admiralty, 5 November 1943, ADM 1/13228.
29. Laycock, "Reorganization of SS Brigade," 1 April 1943, DEFE 2/1051.
30. Mountbatten to CIGS, 4 May 1943, WO 32/10416.
31. Major General de Guingand, COS 21 Army Group, to SHAEF, 7 June 1944, WO 205/136; Samain, *Commando Men*, 44.
32. 21 Army Group Staff Study No. 8, "Employment of Commandos and Rangers," 27 December 1943, RG 331, Entry 199, Box 32, Folder 322 Rangers.
33. "History of the Commandos in the Mediterranean," DEFE 2/700, p. 397.
34. For an excellent overview of such issues, written by the commander of the 2nd SS Brigade, see Churchill, *Commando Crusade*.
35. The importance of this point should not be underestimated. Toward the later stages of the war Commando Brigades, when working closely with conventional arms, commonly had various other formations placed under their command. For instance, during Operation Roast to cross Lake Comacchio in April 1945, No. 2 Commando Brigade, which was operating under V Corps of Eighth Army, had under its command an Italian partisan brigade, M Squadron SBS, two RSR batteries (75 mm and 4.2 inch mortars), a 6 pounder AT battery, storm boats, LVTs, DUKWs, one troop of Kangaroo armored personnel carriers, B Squadron of the North Irish Horse, two forward squadrons of 6th Armored Division, and a number of other miscellaneous groups. In its deployment it would have support from the HQ Royal Artillery 56th Division with its numerous batteries, a field ambulance group, a radar unit, and an RAF controller. Commando Group Monthly Letter No. 17, April 1945, ADM 202/446.

36. HQ SACSEA to GHQ India, 3 May 1945, WO 203/4594.
37. Laycock to Under Secretary of State, War Office, 10 October 1944, WO 32/10415.
38. Laycock to Brigadier Mills-Roberts, 28 March 1945, KCLMA Mills-Roberts Folder 3/17.
39. Darby to Eisenhower, 10 August 1943, RG 407, Entry 427, Box 21066, Folder INBN-1-0.
40. Major Murray to General McNair, 28 November 1943, RG 407, Entry 427, Box 21075, Folder INBN-4-0.1.
41. Darby to Eisenhower, 10 August 1943, RG 407, Entry 427, Box 21066, Folder INBN-1-0.
42. Correspondence between Patton and Eisenhower, 12 August 1943, RG 407, Entry 427, Box 21066, Folder INBN-1-0.
43. Correspondence between "AWG" and Clark, 14 October 1943, RG 407, Entry 427, Box 21066, Folder INBN-1-0.
44. Report of action, 22 January 1944–45 February 1944, RG 407, Entry 427, Box 21067, Folder INBN-1-0.3.
45. "A Narrative History of the Second Ranger Infantry Battalion, 1944," RG 407, Entry 427, Box 21072, Folder 23745, INBN-2-0.3, ch. 1, p. 8.
46. Hogan, *U.S. Army Special Operations in World War II*, 90–91; 138.
47. Chae, "Roles and Missions of Rangers," 47.
48. Springer, *Black Devil Brigade*, 67, 123.
49. Lieutenant Colonel Carlson to GOC, 1st Marine Amphibious Corps, RG 127, USMC Geographic Files, Guadalcanal, Box 44, Folder A39-1.
50. Twining, *No Bended Knee*, 178–79.
51. In doctrinal terms the command arrangements for Carlson's "long patrol" were not unprecedented. The 1940 edition of the USMC *Small Wars Manual* stated: "It is sometimes desirable to organize a few permanent combat patrols with roving commissions throughout the theater of operations, irrespective of area boundaries or other limitations. These patrols should be as lightly equipped as possible commensurate with their tasks. Authority should be granted them to secure from the nearest outpost or garrison such replacements of personnel, animals, equipment, and rations as may be required. Aviation is normally their main source of supply while in the field." USMC, *Small Wars Manual—1940 Edition*, para. 6–12, 9.
52. Hoffman, *From Makin to Bougainville*.
53. Twining, *No Bended Knee*, 184.
54. As specialist formations increased in establishment and as operations became increasingly complex, the distinction between command and leadership could become problematic. As one staff officer wrote in June 1943 in reference to the 2nd SAS Regiment: "There seems to be an urgent need to have somewhere in the unit an experienced and relatively senior officer, capable of command and administration, and of planning this type of operation. . . . he need not be operational. . . . The point really is that the qualities which make a successful leader of a small party of raiders do not always include those who are essential for good CO and HQ Staff." Brigadier Martin to CGS, AFHQ, 16 June 1943, WO 204/1949.

55. Bagnold, *Sand, Wind and War*, 125.
56. Hackett., "Employment of Special Forces," 34.
57. David Stirling, "Origins of the SAS Regiment," 8 November 1948, KCLMA McLeod; Hoe, *David Stirling*, 61–63; Strawson, *History of the SAS Regiment*, 38.
58. For the first three months of their existence, Bagnold's Long Patrols had worked under the Intelligence staff. The patrols ceded to the control of DMO in October 1941.
59. Brigadier J. F. M. Whiteley, DDO, to Eighth Army, 11 October 1941, WO 201/731.
60. CGS MEF document, 17 November 1942, WO 201/752.
61. Macksey, *Commando Strike*, 165.
62. "LRDG's Part in the 8th Army Operations, April 19th–May 26th," 7 June 1942, WO 201/813.
63. Minutes of GHQ MEF conference, 23 August 1942, WO 201/732.
64. Lieutenant Colonel Graham to GHQ MEF, 8 August 1942, WO 201/732.
65. Major Randolph S. Churchill to Winston Churchill, 24 June 1942, File 24 KCLMA Laycock.
66. Hoe, *David Stirling*, 148.
67. David Stirling to the Prime Minister, 9 August 1942, WO 201/728.
68. General McCreery to General Alexander, September 1942, WO 201/732.
69. Hackett in foreword to Messenger, Young, and Rose, *Middle East Commandos*, 9; GHQ MEF to Hackett, 28 September 1942, WO 201/743; Fullick, *Shan Hackett*, 57–62.
70. For an account of this operation, see Landsborough, *Tobruk Commando*.
71. Miller, *The Commandos*, 87.
72. Lloyd Owen, *Providence Their Guide*, 104.
73. Pitt, *The Crucible of War*, 201.
74. Gilbert, *Desert War*, 197–98.
75. Lessons of Bigamy and Nicety, October 1942, WO 201/748.
76. However, examining the SAS Bigamy attack on Benghazi, Asher makes the intriguing comment that no intelligence leak was ever proven and that the blunder in this operation "lay in Stirling's failure to send a recce party, to make a through survey of the route," and of Stirling's mistaken "decision to concentrate on a roadblock rather than go for an assault from several directions." He claimed that "Bigamy went wrong not because of a security leak, but through a lack of precision and planning by Stirling." Such an opinion certainly serves to highlight the fact that in the early stages of special operations everyone, including "founding father" practitioners, had much to learn about their nascent art. Asher, *The Regiment*, 173–74.
77. "Operation—Agreement, Lessons from the Military Aspect," undated, WO 201/745; Lessons of Bigamy and Nicety, October 1942, WO 201/748.
78. Gordon, *Other Desert War*, 187–88.

79. Churchill, *Second World War*, 2:413.
80. Gordon, *Other Desert War*, 156.
81. GHQ ME directive to Lieutenant Colonel Cator, 8 March 1943, WO 201/2202.
82. Raiding Forces Aegean comprised, at different stages, the LRDG, SBS [Squadron], the Raiding Support Regiment, the Raiding Forces Holding Unit, elements of No. 30 Commando, the RMBPD, the Levant Schooner Flotilla, the Greek Sacred Squadron, and the Kalpaks (the latter being a unique formation made up of approximately twenty Kurds, about which the Raiding Forces Aegean War Diary remarks: "A less gently mannered age than this would have called these enthusiasts thugs, we politely say they showed a marked disregard for the sanctity of human life."] See "Composition, Organization and System of Command and Administration of Raiding Forces," 11 November 1943, WO 204/10242; Captain G. W. Read (ed.),"War Diary of HQ Raiding Forces, 1943–1945 in the Aegean," WO 169/19917, p. 5.
83. Guy Prendergast, CO LRDG, to "Nicholson," 12 October 1943, WO 201/796.
84. Report by CO LRDG, 24 November 1943, IWM Lloyd Owen, PP/MCR/C13, Reel 2.
85. Lloyd Owen, *Providence Their Guide*, 138.
86. Gooderson, "Shoestring Strategy," 10.
87. COI memorandum to War Department, May 1942, RG 226, Entry 136, Box 140, Folder 1464.
88. Casey, *Secret War Against Hitler*, 5; Harris Smith, *OSS*, 2.
89. Yu, *OSS in China*, 13.
90. Hogan, "MacArthur, Stilwell," 104–105; Breuer, *MacArthur's Undercover War*, 33–34; Manchester, *American Caesar*, 439.
91. History of the OSS MU, RG 226, Entry 99, Box 98, Folder 4, p. 146.
92. Harris Smith, *OSS*, 244; Hogan, "MacArthur, Stilwell," 106.
93. OSS reasserted its independence in China in early 1944 with the establishment of Detachment 202 that was administratively independent of SACO. Roosevelt, *War Report of the OSS*, 2:361–63; Hogan, "MacArthur, Stilwell," 106; Yu, *OSS in China*, 52–53.
94. Eifler to Donovan, 24 November 1942, RG 226, Entry 99, Box 65, Folder 3.
95. Ibid.
96. Peers and Brelis, *Behind the Burma Road*, 117–18.
97. Roosevelt, *War Report of the OSS*, 2:143
98. Ibid., 2:6–7.
99. Ibid., 2:65.
100. Colonel Ellery C. Huntington, Jr., OC OGs, to Lieutenant Commander R. Davis Halliwell, Chief SO, 22 June 1943, RG 226, Entry 136, Box 140, Folder 1460; SOE document, "Employment of OGs in the ETO and Procedure for Their Dispatch," 6 June 1944, HS 8/288.
101. Major A. Peter Dewey, "OG History," 13 June 1945, RG 226, Entry 99, Box 98, Folder 5, pp. 35–36.

102. History of "Italian" OGs, RG 226, Entry 143, Box 11, Folder 146, p. 13.
103. Livermore to Lanier, 12 June 1944, RG 226, Entry 99, Box 34, Folder 7.
104. The Kommandobefehl, issued in October 1942, was an order contradicting the Geneva Convention that called for the execution of all persons caught conducting irregular warfare behind the enemy's line irrespective of uniform.
105. For information see RG 226, Entry 143, Box 11, Folder 138; and RG 226, Entry 97, Box 2, Folder 9.
106. Donovan, "Activation of OG Command," 27 November 1944, RG 226, Entry 136, Box 140, Folder 1460.
107. AFHQ Algiers to War Office, 30 April 1944, WO 193/620.
108. "AFHQ History of Special Operations: Mediterranean Theater," WO 204/10392.
109. Ibid.; AFHQ memorandum, "Functions of G-3, Special Operations," 8 February 1944, AIR 51/105.
110. "Channels of Command for Special Operations and SOE/OSS Activities in the Mediterranean Theater," April 1944, WO 193/620.
111. AFHQ instructions to Major General Stawell, 14 April 1944, WO 204/10392; Beevor, *SOE Recollections and Reflections*, 85.
112. LFA Commander's Report, May 1945, WO 204/10429.
113. Foot, *SOE in France*, xxii.
114. Macksey, *Partisans of Europe in World War II*, 192.
115. Funk, *Hidden Ally*, 74.
116. Lewis, *Jedburgh Team Operations*; Ford, *Steel from the Sky*, 29–30.
117. Major A. Peter Dewey, "OG History," 13 June 1945, RG 226, Entry 99, Box 98, Folder 5.
118. Major H. N. Marten, "Report on Jedburghs (Zone Sud)," 6 October 1944, RG 226, Entry 154, Box 56, Folder 945.
119. Arthur Brown, "Some Notes on Jedburgh 'Quinine,'" in IWM Brown 03/24/1, p. 3.
120. Ford, *Steel from the Sky*, 153.
121. Otway, *Airborne Forces*, 107; 229.
122. Warner, *Special Air Service*, 145.
123. Otway, *Airborne Forces*, 231–32.
124. Kiras, *Special Operations and Strategy*, 110–11.
125. HQ Airborne Troops to Commander SAS Troops, 4 June 1944, HS 6/604.
126. Ford, *Fire from the Forest*, 32; Ford, *Steel from the Sky*, 106; Funk, *Hidden Ally*, 74; OSS/London War Diaries, Vol. 2 Planning, KCLMA MF 204.
127. Wing Commander R. Hockey, "Notes on SAS Operations," 11 June 1944, AIR 20/8945.
128. "Jedburgh Team Chronologies," RG 226, Entry 190, Box 740, Folder 1462.
129. Lewis, *Jedburgh Team Operations*.
130. Mountbatten to Admiralty, 21 June 1943, ADM 116/5112.
131. Willmott to COHQ, February 1943, DEFE 2/1111.
132. SBU would administer the LCOCUs, RMBPD, SBS, COPPs, COSU, SRU, and No. 30 (Assault) Commando.
133. COHQ Docket, "Liaison between COPP Units and C in C's and Force Commanders," 11 October 1943, ADM 1/13228.

134. DDOD(I) paper, "Transfer of Unorthodox Offensive Units to the Control of DDOD(I)," 30 July 1944, ADM 1/16957; Office of Allied Naval Commander to SHAEF, 2 February 1944, RG 226, Entry 148, Box 83, Folder 1200.
135. Parker, *SBS*, 127; Clifford, *Amphibious Warfare Development*, 217.
136. Ultimately comprising the COPPs, SBS, SRU, and RM Detachment 385.
137. Record of SOG, March 1946, DEFE 2/1747; Minutes of SEAC meeting on formation of SOG, 3 February 1944, WO 203/131.
138. CCO to Secretary of the Admiralty, 28 February 1945, DEFE 2/1203.
139. DCO, "Notes on SBS," March 1944, DEFE 2/1036.
140. CCO to Major General G. E. Wildman-Lushington, Advance HQ, SEAC, 22 May 1944, DEFE 2/1203.
141. This was in line with Z SBS's earlier deployments in the Mediterranean, which saw the unit avoid the SBU and work directly under submarine flotillas in Malta and for Special Operations G-3, Algiers "as a private army . . . and not as part of any larger organization." Note on SOG and SBS, April 1944, DEFE 2/1036; Major G. B. Courtney, CO Z SBS, to CCO, 26 April 1944, DEFE 2/1203.
142. CCO brief on Special Parties in SEAC, October 1944, DEFE 2/1035; Colonel Tollemache, SOG Bulletin No. 1, 31 July 1945, DEFE 2/1203; Record of SOG, March 1946, DEFE 2/1747.
143. SACSEA Directive, 18 December 1943, RG 226, Entry 92, Box 491, Folder 15.
144. Captain Alfred M. Lichtman, MU Area Operations Officer, to Lieutenant William H. Pendelton, Chief MU NATO, 12 April 1944, RG 226, Entry 143, Box 5, Folder 77.
145. Admiral Cunningham, C in C Mediterranean, "U.S. Navy 'Special Operations' Units," 7 March 1944, WO 204/8425.
146. Commander E. D. Brewster, UDT 1, report on Operation Flintlock, 8 February 1944, RG 38, World War II Action and Operational Reports, Box 787.
147. Commander UDT Squadron 2 to C in C U.S. Fleet, 31 August 1945, RG 38, World War II War Diaries, Box 535.
148. Captain B. Hall Hanlon, Commander UDTs, "After Action Report, Iwo Jima Operation," 12 March 1945, RG 38, World War II Action and Operational Reports, Box 787.
149. UDT Squadron Two War Diary, RG 38, World War II War Diaries, Box 535.
150. Slim, *Defeat into Victory*, 548–49.
151. Major Ian G. Collins to CCO, 30 December 1942, DEFE 2/957.
152. Foot, *SOE in France*, 404.
153. Churchill, *Second World War*, 5:182.

Chapter 5

1. Gray, *Explorations in Strategy*, 164.
2. Ibid., 149.
3. Captain Philip Dunne to Brigadier Laycock, undated, KCLMA Laycock, File 16.
4. Laycock, "Reorganisation of SS Brigade," 1 April 1943, DEFE 2/1051.

5. "History of the Commandos in the Mediterranean," DEFE 2/700.
6. Lloyd Owen, *Providence Their Guide*, 46.
7. Ralph Bagnold to Guy Prendergast, 24 September 1941, WO 201/810.
8. Crichton-Stuart, *G Patrol*, 87.
9. Zedric, *Silent Warriors*, 114.
10. Major Murray, CO 4th Rangers, to General McNair, 28 November 1943, RG 407, Entry 427, Box 21075, Folder INBN-4-0.1.
11. Hogan, *Raiders or Elite Infantry?*, 26.
12. Stewart, "Ranger Force at the Battle of Cisterna," 46–50.
13. Ibid., 49; Truscott, *Command Missions*, 314.
14. Gray, *Modern Strategy*, 290.
15. Ford, *Fire from the Forest*, 22.
16. Hogan, *Raiders or Elite Infantry?*, 18.
17. McMichael, *Historical Perspective on Light Infantry*, 35.
18. After the war, however, the resurgence of U.S. special forces capabilities would stem from "founding fathers" who had learned their craft during the Second World War. Fine examples are provided by Aaron Bank (a Jedburgh), "the father of U.S. special forces," and Russell Volckmann (a leader of guerrillas on the Philippines), who together helped develop the U.S. Army Special Forces in 1952; Roger Hilsman (a Marauder and in OSS Detachment 101), who, working for the State Department, became Kennedy's adviser on irregular warfare and assistant secretary of state for Far Eastern affairs; or William Colby (Jedburgh and later leader of NORSO group), who later became head of the CIA.
19. Quoted in Parker, *Commandos*, 35–36.
20. Lindsay, *Beacons in the Night*, 248.
21. Churchill, *Commando Crusade*, 139.
22. McConville, *Small War in the Balkans*, 108–109; 174; Maclean, *Eastern Approaches*, 410–12.
23. Laycock in SS Brigade War Diary, 8–15 August 1943, DEFE 2/55.
24. "As one wag remarked, 'Second Raiders will never need any artillery support. Carlson's always got twenty-one guns in his hip pocket.'" Twining, *No Bended Knee*, 178.
25. McMichael, *Historical Perspective on Light Infantry*, 211.
26. Gray, *Explorations in Strategy*, 167.
27. Laycock, "Reorganisation of SS Brigade," 1 April 1943, DEFE 2/1051.
28. Captain Dunne to Brigadier Laycock, undated, KCLMA Laycock, File 16.
29. Anderson to Mountbatten, 23 May 1943, WO 32/10416.
30. Hogan, *Raiders or Elite Infantry?*, 26.
31. Quoted in Bjorge, *Merrill's Marauders*, 2.
32. Prefer, *Vinegar Joe's War*, 71–72.
33. Bjorge, *Merrill's Marauders*, 23.
34. Hogan, "MacArthur, Stilwell," 110; Larrabee, *Commander in Chief*, 565.
35. Bjorge, *Merrill's Marauders*, 3, 44.
36. Hogan, *Raiders or Elite Infantry?*, 44.
37. Ibid., 88–90.

38. Laycock, "Reorganisation of SS Brigade," 1 April 1943, DEFE 2/1051.
39. Bradley, *A Soldier's Story*, 132.
40. LRDG War Diary, September–November 1943, WO 201/818.
41. Lloyd Owen, "The Larder Was Often Bare" (unpublished memoir), in IWM Lloyd Owen PP/MCR/C13.
42. "LRDG Operations in Aegean, 11/9/43 to 30/11/43", in IWM Lloyd Owen PP/MCR/C13. For more general information about the Aegean campaign, see Rogers, *Churchill's Folly*, and Gooderson, "Shoestring Strategy."
43. Stewart, "Ranger Force at the Battle of Cisterna," 70.
44. Bradley, *A Soldier's Story*, 139.
45. Captain G. W Read (ed.), "Raiding Forces—the Story of an Independent Command in the Aegean, 1943–1945," WO 201/2836, p. 7.
46. Lieutenant Colonel Lumsden to Adjutant General Royal Marines, 20 July 1943, ADM 202/103.
47. "Past, Present, and Future Activities of the Special Boat Section," 23 November 1943, DEFE 2/740.
48. Gray, "Handfuls of Heroes," 2.
49. McConville, *Small War in the Balkans*, 232–33.
50. Messenger, Young, and Rose, *Middle East Commandos*, 120.
51. Brigadier Davy, DDO, to CGS, 25 April 1942, WO 201/732.
52. Reports of Lieutenant Colonel John Graham, CO 1st SS Regiment, to GHQ MEF, 13 July 1942, WO 201/732.
53. Eighth Army to GHQ MEF, 7 May 1942, WO 201/2624.
54. General Auchinleck, C in C MEF, "Future of 1st SS Regiment," 24 and 26 July 1942, WO 201/728.
55. Laycock, "Note on Commandos," 11 September 1941, WO 201/731.
56. Minutes of COS Committee meeting, 2 August 1941, WO 193/405.
57. Field Marshal Dill, Joint Staff Mission Washington, to War Cabinet, 3 March 1943, WO 106/1974.
58. COS to Dill, 5 March 1943, WO 106/1974; Minutes of COS Committee meeting, 16 December 1942, WO 106/1974; Lieutenant General F. M. Andrews, USFOR London, to AGWAR, 12 February 1943, RG 218, Central Decimal File 1942–45, Box 285, Folder CCS 370.5.
59. Wright, *Frogmen of Burma*, 71–77.
60. CCO brief on Special Parties in SEAC, October 1944, DEFE 2/1035; Major General G. E. Wildman-Lushington, SEAC, to CCO, 19 June 1944, DEFE 2/1203.
61. Lieutenant Commander A. G. Atwater, Chief MU, to Colonel Bigelow, Washington, 26 May 1945, RG 226, Entry 92, Box 491, Folder 16; Major Alfred M. Lichtman, MU Area Operations Officer, Washington, to Colonel Richard F. Heppner, G-3, USAFCBI, 17 October 1944, RG 226, Entry 92, Box 491, Folder 15.
62. SACSEA staff meeting, 10 February 1944, WO 203/4796.
63. Lieutenant Dennis Roberts, Chief MU Washington, to Donovan, 21 July 1944, RG 226, Entry 139, Box 73, Folder 73.
64. Mountbatten to Army Commanders in Chiefs, 2 August 1943, DEFE 2/1116.

65. History of COPPs, 1942–45, DEFE 2/1116.
66. Colonel Tollemache, "Lessons Learnt from Formation of SOG," 1 October 1945, DEFE 2/1203.
67. Minutes of COS meeting, 8 June 1943, WO 106/4117.
68. CCO to Admiral Hughes-Hallett, 14 January 1943, DEFE 2/957.
69. Warner, *Special Air Service*, 145.
70. Memorandum of "HQ Airtps," 28 December 1944, WO 219/2877; Funk, *Hidden Ally*, 73–74.
71. Team Cecil reports, "Jedburgh Team Chronologies," RG 226, Entry 190, Box 740, Folder 1463.
72. Major H. N. Marten, "Report on Jedburghs (Zone Sud)," 6 October 1944, RG 226, Entry 154, Box 56, Folder 945.
73. Major Alfred T. Cox, comments in "History of [OG] Operations in Southern France," 20 September 1944, RG 226, Entry 143, Box 11.
74. Lieutenant General Browning to SHAEF, 17 November 1944, WO 205/92.
75. Lieutenant McKenzie III, comments in "History of [OG] Operations in Southern France," 20 September 1944, RG 226, Entry 143, Box 11.
76. Ford, *Steel from the Sky*, 29–30.
77. SOE, "History of Jedburghs in Europe," HS 7/18, p. 11.
78. Thompson, *War Behind Enemy Lines*, 414.
79. HQ SAS Brigade meeting, 19 November 1944, WO 218/189.
80. Major General R. N. Gale, Commander 1 British Airborne Corps, to GOC, First Allied Airborne Army, 18 January 1945, WO 219/2877. In support of Operation Market Garden, seven Jedburgh Teams were attached to the Allied Airborne Divisions. See summary of Jedburgh Operations in RG 226, Entry 101, Box 1.
81. Morris, *Guerrillas in Uniform*, xvi.
82. Hogan, *Raiders or Elite Infantry?*, 18.
83. Hoe, *David Stirling*, 94–95.
84. Ibid., 194.
85. Windmill, *Gentleman Jim*, 259.
86. Thompson, *War Behind Enemy Lines*, 334.
87. OSS/London War Diaries, Vol. 8, KCLMA MF 209.

Chapter 6

1. Foot, "Was SOE Any Good?"
2. Colin S. Gray, in an excellent and all too uncommon treatment of the subject, claims that the "master claims" to the "strategic utility" of special operations are that they provide "economy of force" and "expansion of choice." Their "other claims" are "innovation," "morale," "showcasing of competence," "reassurance," "humiliation of the enemy," "control of escalation," and "shaping of the future." Gray, *Explorations in Strategy*.
3. Holden Reid, "Introduction: The Operational Level of War and Historical Experience," in Mackenzie and Holden Reid (eds.), *The British Army and the Operational Level of War*, 7.
4. Gray, *Explorations in Strategy*, 148.

5. Ibid., 148.
6. Ibid., 165.
7. Churchill, *Second World War*, 4:106.
8. Gray, *Explorations in Strategy*, 142.
9. McRaven, *SPEC OPS*, 43, 230.
10. Otway, *Airborne Forces*, 63–73.
11. Cookridge, *Inside SOE*, 516–24.
12. Stafford, *Churchill and Secret Service*, 298.
13. Cookridge, *Inside SOE*, 524.
14. Macksey, *Commando Strike*, 139; Morris, *Churchill's Private Armies*, 204–205; Young, *Commando*, 127.
15. Thompson, *War Behind Enemy Lines*, 7.
16. Gray, *Explorations in Strategy*, 148–49.
17. Kiras, *Special Operations and Strategy*, 61.
18. The significance of this achievement is put in better perspective when Axis aircraft strengths in North Africa are considered. In June 1942 it was estimated that there were a total of 183 German and 248 Italian frontline aircraft in the North African theater, a figure that had risen to 375 and 283 aircraft respectively by November 1942. Ellis, *World War II Databook*, 232.
19. Thompson, *War Behind Enemy Lines*, 420; David Stirling, "Origins of the SAS Regiment," 8 November 1948, KCLMA McLeod.
20. GHQ MEF, "Brief history of 'L' Detachment SAS Brigade and 1st SAS Regiment," WO 201/721.
21. Liddell Hart, *Rommel Papers*, 393.
22. Morgan, *Daggers Drawn*, 14–15.
23. Hastings, *Das Reich*, 187.
24. Thompson, *War Behind Enemy Lines*, 308.
25. Ford, *Fire from the Forest*, 75–76.
26. Ibid., 56.
27. War Office memorandum, "Points Brought Out in Ops. 'Husky,'" WO 201/799.
28. Vagts, *Landing Operations*, 629.
29. Hogan, *U.S. Army Special Operations in World War II*, 32.
30. Dunning, *Fighting Fourth*, 57.
31. Major General Haydon to Captain J. H. Devins, 13 February 1962, IWM Haydon 93/28/4; JCH 2/6; Mann, "Combined Operations," 492.
32. Lewis, *Omaha Beach*, 40.
33. Ferris, "Intelligence-Deception Complex," 731.
34. Timpson and Gibson-Watt, *In Rommel's Backyard*, 17.
35. Brigadier T. S. Airey, DMI, notes on LRDG Road Watch, 14 December 1942, WO 201/771.
36. Constable, *Hidden Heroes*, 141.
37. Jenner, List, and Badrocke, *Long Range Desert Group*, 35–36.
38. Kelly, *Hunt for Zerzura*, 187.
39. Hunt, *A Don at War*, 132.
40. General Montgomery to Lieutenant Colonel Prendergast, CO LRDG, 2 April 1943, WO 201/816.

41. Morris, *Guerrillas in Uniform*, 153.
42. HQ BAF to AFHQ G-3, 17 January 1943, WO 204/1564.
43. Zedric, *Silent Warriors*, 251.
44. See RG 338, Records of Sixth Army G-2 Section, Box 7.
45. Krueger, *From Down Under to Nippon*, 189.
46. Colonel Peers, "Detachment 101 ATB," RG 226, Entry 161, Box 8, Folder 86; Hogan, "MacArthur, Stilwell," p. 111.
47. Peers and Brelis, *Behind the Burma Road*, 184. It is, nevertheless, interesting to note Charlton Ogburn's claim that for all of the intelligence that Detachment 101 amassed, little of it reached Merrill's Marauders in the field. He claims to have been unaware of the actions of the "Kachin Rangers" in his area of operations and was surprised not to have witnessed a "sanguinary collision" between the two groups in the field. Ogburn, *The Marauders*, 139.
48. Millar, *Bruneval Raid*.
49. Jones, *Most Secret War*, 316.
50. Brigadier Haydon, Report on Claymore, 13 March 1941, DEFE 2/54; also see various in WO 231/2; Durnford-Slater, *Commando*, 54; Weale, *Secret Warfare*, 65.
51. For a good discussion of this point, see Mann, "Combined Operations," 477.
52. Thompson, *War Behind Enemy Lines*, 319; Warner *Secret Forces of World War II*, 107; Yunnie, *Fighting with Popski's Private Army*, 128–29; 177.
53. Thompson, *War Behind Enemy Lines*, 420.
54. Admiral Nimitz to Admiral King, 22 August 1944, RG 38, World War II Action and Operational Reports, Box 789.
55. Thompson, *War Behind Enemy Lines*, 8.
56. Keegan, *Second World War*, 495.
57. Vercors, near Grenoble, witnessed a large-scale Resistance uprising following proclamations made on the eve of D-day. On June 8 Jedburgh Team Veganin was deployed, and the Resistance grew steadily. On June 28 OG mission Justine was dispatched to the area, and extensive air drops were arranged. On July 19 the Germans undertook a massive counteroffensive, employing over 10,000 troops, including gliders, which landed on strips the Maquis had prepared for the Allies. Resistance casualties were extensive, and the partisan groups had to disperse. The criticisms with this uprising were that it was undertaken too early and too far away from the main landings (and the distractions of the front), and that the French partisans had simply been too impetuous.
58. Keegan, *Second World War*, 484–85.
59. Casey, *Secret War Against Hitler*, 69.
60. Ibid., 122.
61. Dear, *Sabotage and Subversion*, 188.
62. SOE, "History of Jedburghs in Europe," HS 7/18, pp. 4–5.
63. Summary of Jedburgh Frederick, HS 7/19.
64. SOE, "History of Jedburghs in Europe," HS 7/18, p. 9.

65. Macksey, *Partisans of Europe in World War II*, 190; Gaujac, *Special Forces in the Invasion of France*, 401.
66. OG Command, "History of Operations in Southern France," 20 September 1944, RG 226, Entry 143, Box 11.
67. Asprey, *War in the Shadows*, 318.
68. Kiras, *Special Operations and Strategy*, 84–85.
69. Ibid., 111.
70. Hogan, *U.S. Army Special Operations in World War II*, 32–33.
71. Heaton, *German Anti-Partisan Warfare in Europe*, 88.
72. Pitt, *Special Boat Squadron*, 163; IWM Lloyd Owen, PP/MCR/C13, Reel 2; HQ BAF to AFHQ G-3, 17 January 1943, WO 204/1564.
73. Major Richard R. Quay, Reports Officer "Greek" and "Yugoslav" OGs, to OG HQ, August 1944, RG 226, Entry 144, Box 68, Folder 588. The employment of No. 30 (Assault) Commando from Vis was also impeded by Tito's suspicions of an "intelligence" unit. Lieutenant Glanville to OC No. 30 Commando, 7 November 1943, KCLMA Riley.
74. Special Operations Committee memorandum, "Employment of Personnel of the American Greek Battalion," 5 September 1943, WO 201/2263.
75. Kehoe, "1944: An Allied Team with the French Resistance."
76. Farran, *Winged Dagger*, 234–35.
77. Lieutenant Grahl H. Weeks, CO OG Section PEG, OG Command, "History of Operations in Southern France," 20 September 1944, RG 226, Entry 143, Box 11.
78. Cited in Heaton, *German Anti-Partisan Warfare in Europe*, 53.
79. War Office, "Notes from Theaters of War, No. 22: Long Range Desert Group," December 1945, WO 231/28, p. 37.
80. Churchill, *Commando Crusade*, 240–41.
81. General Clark, commendation of "Italian" OGs, May 1945, RG 226, Entry 99, Box 42, Folder 3.
82. Clark to CO, "Italian" OGs, May 1945, RG 226, Entry 143, Box 11, Folder 146.
83. Intercepted telegram from Field Marshal Kesselring to Field Commands, 26 February 1945, RG 226, Entry 99, Box 42, Folder 3.
84. Colonel Peers, "Detachment 101 ATB," RG 226, Entry 161, Box 8, Folder 86; Hogan, "MacArthur, Stilwell," 111; Roosevelt, *War Report of the OSS*, 1:114.
85. Peers and Brelis, *Behind the Burma Road*, 142.
86. Ibid., 184.
87. Dear, *Sabotage and Subversion*, 208.
88. Zedric and Dilley, *Elite Warriors*, 166–67.
89. Asprey, *War in the Shadows*, 444.
90. Gray, *Explorations in Strategy*, 170.
91. Bagnold, *Sand, Wind and War*, 125.
92. Wavell to Bagnold, 1 October 1940, WO 201/807.
93. Hackett, "Employment of Special Forces," 28.
94. HMSO, *Destruction of an Army*, 58–59.

95. War Office, "Notes from Theaters of War, No.22: Long Range Desert Group," December 1945, WO 231/28, pp.37–38.
96. Lieutenant General Bourne, DCO, to COS Committee, 10 July 1940, CAB 80/14/60.
97. General Haining, Vice-CIGS, memorandum on revised DCO directive, 30 October 1940, WO 216/54.
98. Reynolds, *Rich Relations*, 91; Harrison, *Cross-Channel Attack*, 15–16.
99. Churchill to Roosevelt, 1 April 1942, NARA: Franklin D. Roosevelt Library, FDR-MR: Papers as President, Map Room File, 1939–45.
100. Pitt, *Special Boat Squadron*, 146.
101. "History of the Commandos in the Mediterranean," DEFE 2/700; pp. 296–97.
102. Mann, "Combined Operations," 477–78, 495.
103. Keegan, *Churchill*, 129.
104. Quoted in Young, *Commando*, 87–88.
105. Minutes of Admiralty meeting, 4 November 1942, ADM 116/5112.
106. Correspondence between COSSAC and G-3, SHAEF, January 1944, RG 331, Entry 29A, Box 120, Folder SHAEF/17225/Ops.
107. COSSAC, "Raids and Reconnaissance Programme," 20 January 1944, RG 331, Entry 12, Box 14, Folder SHAEF/6RX/INT.
108. Correspondence of General de Guingand, 27 January 1944, DEFE 2/1093.
109. Admiral Nimitz to Admiral King, 20 October 1942, RG 127, USMC Geographic Files, Makin, Box 183.
110. Alexander, *Storm Landings*, 26–27.
111. Macksey, *Commando Strike*, 120.
112. COHQ to Director of Plans, 24 December 1942, ADM 116/5112.
113. Crowl and Love, *Seizure of the Gilberts and Marshalls*, 62–63.
114. Minutes of COS meeting, 13 October 1942, ADM 116/5112.
115. Kiras, *Special Operations and Strategy*, 3.
116. Quoted in Stevens, *The Originals*, 290.
117. Captain G. W. Read (ed.), "Raiding Forces—the Story of an Independent Command in the Aegean, 1943–1945," WO 201/2836, p. 35.
118. Foot, *SOE*, 81.
119. Seymour, *British Special Forces*, 13.
120. Lucas Phillips, *The Greatest Raid of All*, 259; Saunders, *Green Beret*, 98.
121. Such resentment also emanated from other irregular organizations. For example, a remarkable lack of interagency coordination before a 1943 raid against Simi by Raiding Forces Aegean led to a general upheaval, during which the abbot of Panormiti, a close SOE collaborator, was killed and an SOE radio operator captured. Commander F. G. Pool to Force Commander, 28 February 1944, HS 5/445.
122. Lieutenant Hamilton to SSO Bari, 10 May 1944, RG 226, Entry 136, Box 19, Folder 197.
123. Newsinger, *Dangerous Men*, 12.
124. Gray, *Explorations in Strategy*, 175.
125. Ibid., 175.

126. Hughes-Hallett, "Mounting of Raids," 580–81.
127. Stacey Lloyd to Major Bruce, "Commando Training and Operations," 5 August 1942, RG 226, Entry 92, Box 111, Folder 49.
128. Beaumont, *Joint Military Operations*, 87.
129. Notes on conference with Admiral Nimitz and General Megee, 24 April 1957, RG 127, Entry 46B, Box 100.
130. USMC Historical Branch accounts of the Makin Raid, RG 127, Entry 46B, Box 100.
131. Black, *Rangers in World War II*, 47.
132. Robertson, *Dieppe*, 195–96, 460.
133. Sides, *Ghost Soldiers*, 63.
134. Ibid., 65.
135. Mucci, "Rescue at Cabanatuan," 19.
136. 6th Ranger Battalion combat history, January 1945, RG 407, Entry 427, Box 21079, Folder INBN-6-0.
137. Villa, *Unauthorized Action*, 166.
138. Churchill, *Second World War*, 5:64.
139. Tuchman, *Sand Against the Wind*, 432–33.
140. Minutes of 121st COS(O) Meeting, 8 June 1943, WO 106/4117.
141. Churchill, *Second World War*, 4:789.
142. Linderman, *The World Within War*, 230.
143. Timpson and Gibson-Watt, *In Rommel's Backyard*, 12.
144. Slim, *Defeat into Victory*, 547.
145. Gray, *Explorations in Strategy*, 143–44.
146. Fleming, "Unorthodox Warriors," 387.

Chapter 7

1. Thompson, *War Behind Enemy Lines*, 7.
2. Ibid., 33.
3. Zedric, *Silent Warriors*, 11.
4. Slim, *Defeat into Victory*, 548.
5. Terraine, *Right of the Line*, 642.
6. Peaty, "British Army Manpower Crisis," 101, 137.
7. Ibid., 103–104.
8. Many senior officers, even those who had championed certain irregular groups, remained conscious of this cost. For example, Claude Auchinleck, who had given license to the SAS while serving in Cairo, would later state: "'I have always been rather sceptical (hidebound—I suppose!) of the value of these specialized small units. I feel that the officers and NCOs they absorb would be of much greater value training and leading regular units on which we must rely to win the battle finally.'" Quoted in Warner, *Auchinleck*, 78.
9. For a good discussion of the "warrior" and the implications of this for modern SOF, see Henriksen, "Warriors in Combat."
10. See Beaumont, *Military Elites*, and Bounds, *Notes on Elite Units*.
11. Twohig, "Are Commandos Really Necessary?" 88.
12. Hoffman, *From Makin to Bougainville*; Isely and Crowl, *U.S. Marines and Amphibious War*, 155.

13. "History of the Commandos in the Mediterranean," DEFE 2/700.
14. Major General Haydon to Major General J. S. Steele, Director of Staff Duties, War Office, 13 October 1943, WO 32/10417.
15. General Jacob Devers, AFHQ, to War Department, 13 March 1944, RG 165, Entry 418, Box 682, Folder OPD 320.2.
16. Brigadier General Norman D. Cota, "Observation of Operation Husky," August 1943, RG 165, Entry 418, Box 1249, Folder OPD 381.
17. Foot, *SOE*, 249.
18. Otway, *Airborne Forces*, 258.
19. Weiss, *Allies in Conflict*, 122.
20. Lindsay, *Beacons in the Night*, 72.
21. Courtney, *SBS in World War Two*, 279.
22. Foot, "Was SOE Any Good?," 176.
23. OSS Executive Committee recommendations, "OSS Underwater Swimming Activities in UK," 22 June 1944, RG 226, Entry 148, Box 82, Folder 1198.
24. Gray, *Explorations in Strategy*, 169.
25. Admiralty orders for Anklet, December 1941, ADM 116/4381.
26. Cruickshank, *SOE in the Far East*, 250.
27. Roosevelt, *War Report of the OSS*, 2:397.
28. 260th SEAC Meeting, 8 July 1945, WO 203/131.
29. SHAEF, "Development of Resistance in France," 4 July 1944, AIR 20/8945.
30. As David Oliver reminds us, "To put the cost of supporting Churchill's undercover army of resistance fighters into perspective: for every SOS, SIS or OSS agent who lost his or her life in the field—more than 400—at least one RAF or USAAF airmen was killed while flying Special Duties operations." Oliver, *Airborne Espionage*, 237. See also Sacquety, "Supplying the Resistance," and documents in AIR 20/8945.
31. Hilsman, *American Guerrilla*, 297–98.
32. Ibid., 289–90.
33. Gray, *Explorations in Strategy*, 167.
34. Slim, *Defeat into Victory*, 548.
35. Thompson, *War Behind Enemy Lines*, 420.
36. Lloyd Owen, *Providence Their Guide*, 120.
37. For an example of Stirling's estimates, see W. Stirling to 15 Army Group, 1 December 1943, WO 204/1949.
38. "Summary of Casualties Inflicted on the Enemy by SAS Troops during Operations in 1944," KCLMA McLeod; and Lieutenant Colonel Collins, "Report on SAS Operations," 1 December 1944, WO 204/2020.
39. At this late stage in the war in Europe, "surrender" tallies should be taken in moderation. Often they are less a reflection of any particular virtuosity on the part of the Allies than they are a comment on the declining morale of the enemy.
40. OG Command, "History of Operations in Southern France," 20 September 1944, RG 226, Entry 143, Box 11.
41. Thomas, "Importance of Commando Operations," 696.

42. McMichael, *Historical Perspective on Light Infantry*, 209; Springer, *Black Devil Brigade*, 255–56.
43. Dziuban, *Military Relations Between the United States and Canada*, 267–68.
44. Springer, *Black Devil Brigade*, 68; 84–85.
45. War Office memorandum, "Points Brought Out in Ops. 'Husky,'" WO 201/799.
46. Wright, *Frogmen of Burma*, 158.
47. 260th SEAC Meeting, 8 July 1945, WO 203/131.
48. Thompson, *War Behind Enemy Lines*, 420; Parker, *SBS*, 99.
49. Lieutenant Commander A. G. Atwater to Colonel Bigelow, Washington, 26 May 1945, RG 226, Entry 92, Box 491, Folder 16.
50. Colonel Tollemache, "Lessons Learnt from Formation of SOG," 1 October 1945, DEFE 2/1203.
51. Laycock, "Raids in the Late War," 528–40.
52. David Lloyd Owen, "The Larder Was Often Bare" [unpublished memoir], in IWM PP/MCR/C13.
53. O'Dell, *Water Is Never Cold*, 21.
54. Ibid., 36–40.
55. Slim, *Defeat into Victory*, 546–47. It is interesting to note that commando formations would occasionally direct similar sentiments toward special forces. Prior to the formation of the 2nd SAS Regiment, for example, the SS Brigade had claimed "we cannot agree that the role of SAS differs from that which could be fulfilled by any well trained Commando." General Haydon to CCO, January 1943, DEFE 2/957.
56. War Office to C in C India, May 1945, WO 203/4594.
57. C in C India to SACSEA, January 1945, WO 203/3426.
58. 17th Indian Division Training Instruction No. 2, 24 June 1942, WO 172/475; 63rd Indian Brigade Training Instruction No. 4, 4 September 1942, WO 172/601.
59. In its brief existence the school also gave instruction to some of the participants of both the Bruneval and Dieppe raids. Bill Westcott, "My War" [unpublished memoir], April 1998, in IWM Westcott 99/19/1, pp. 9–15.
60. Twining, *No Bended Knee*, 134.
61. Ranger Training Center Staff Study, "Ranger Type Units," 26 December 1950, RG 319, G-3 Operations Records Section, Decimal File, 322 Ranger, Box 380.
62. Cohen, *Commandos and Politicians*, 31–32.
63. McMichael, *Historical Perspective on Light Infantry*, 211.
64. Laycock, "Raids in the Late War," 529.
65. Colonel Clarke, "The Start of 'Commandos,'" 30 October 1942, DEFE 2/4.
66. Laycock, "Memorandum on Reorganization of Commandos," 13 November 1941, WO 201/731.
67. Quoted in Saunders, *Green Beret*, 350.
68. Churchill, "Value of Commandos," 87.

69. King, *Rangers: Selected Combat Operations*, 75.
70. David Lloyd Owen, "The Larder Was Often Bare" [unpublished memoir], in IWM PP/MCR/C13.
71. Such logic had continued resonance after the Second World War. Examining various failings with American efforts to undertake strategic special operations at various points between 1960 and the early 1990s, Lucien Vandenbrouke argued that "the history of strategic special operations in the past thirty years makes clear that relying on ad hoc groups and forces to plan and carry out these missions invites problems and, ultimately, failure." He further stated that "success in special operations requires, besides proficient and cohesive forces, personnel who are bold, self-reliant, flexible and good at improvising, adept at using and exploiting deception and surprise. This is a combination of traits that many otherwise well-trained and capable military personnel do not necessarily have." Vandenbroucke, *Perilous Options*, 171.
72. Twohig, "Are Commandos Really Necessary?" 88.
73. That said, it was common for the personnel of disbanded units to be kept together following dissolution. As such, the disbanded Ranger formations provided reinforcement for the First Special Service Force, while some of the Marauders fought on in Burma as part of the Mars Task Force.
74. Hogan, *Raiders or Elite Infantry?*, 83.
75. As Thompson has claimed, "The personality of the commander of the force was often a deciding factor in prolonging a special unit's existence well beyond its useful operational life." Thompson, *War Behind Enemy Lines*, 421.
76. Stacey Lloyd to Major Bruce, "Commando Training and Operations," 5 August 1942, RG 226, Entry 92, Box 111, Folder 49.
77. General Jacob Devers, AFHQ, to War Department, 13 March 1944, RG 165, Entry 418, Box 682, Folder OPD 320.2, AFRICA Cases 584–616.
78. Major General Thos. T. Handy, Assistant Chief of Staff, "Disposition of Ranger Battalions," 5 June 1944, RG 165, Entry 418, Box 682, Folder OPD 320.2, AFRICA Cases 584–616.
79. Gray, *Explorations in Strategy*, 147–48, 155, 169.

Conclusion

1. Lieutenant General F. A. M. Browning, CO Airborne Troops, memorandum, 1944, DEFE 2/56.
2. Lewis, *Jedburgh Team Operations*, 59.
3. Certain limitations, however, appear to be endemic to the nature of special operations and have arguably never been satisfactorily resolved. Grievances over the misuse and disuse of specialist assets; problems with rigid definitions of roles and responsibilities; debates over autonomy versus control; interservice and interagency conflicts of responsibility; and ignorance or antipathy from conventional bodies remained perennial concerns of postwar SOF.
4. Brigadier L. C. Hollis to Churchill, 21 August 1944, DEFE 2/1325.
5. Heilbrunn, *Warfare in the Enemy's Rear*, 48.

6. Carl P. Hagensen, Report on UDT 6, 30 September 1945, RG 38, World War II Action and Operational Reports, Box 788,
7. DDOD(I) docket on SS Establishment—HMS Mount Stewart, 29 October 1944, ADM 1/26900.
8. Thompson, *The Royal Marines*, 419; various documents, DEFE 2/988.

Bibliography

Primary Material
Unpublished: Official Documents

Liddell Hart Centre for Military Archives, King's College London

HISTORY OF 30 ASSAULT UNIT, 1942–46; GB99 KCLMA History of 30 Assault Unit, 1942–46.

OSS/London: Special Operations Branch and Secret Intelligence Branch War Diaries; GB99 KCLMA MF 204-211.

The National Archives, Public Record Office, Kew

ADM Series: Records of the Admiralty, Naval Forces, Royal Marines, Coastguard, and Related Bodies

RECORDS OF THE NAVY BOARD AND THE BOARD OF ADMIRALTY

ADM 1/12848   COMBINED OPERATIONS (47): Clearance of enemy underwater defenses during combined operations: use of Boom Commando and departmental allocation of responsibilities.

ADM 1/13185   COMBINED OPERATIONS (47): Army and Royal Marine Commands: organization into Special Service Group.

ADM 1/13228   COMBINED OPERATIONS (47): Liaison between pilotage party units, Cs in C and force commanders: proposals.

ADM 1/13232   COMBINED OPERATIONS (47): Raids on Norway by special service forces: policy on use of Norwegian personnel and buildup of force.

ADM 1/15639   ADMIRALTY (5) and COMBINED OPERATIONS (47): Future control of Combined Operations Pilotage Parties: Administration of personnel.

ADM 1/15713   ADMIRALTY (5) and FOREIGN COUNTRIES (52): Activities of U.S. Pacific Fleet in various fields including submarine warfare and combined operations. Admiralty comments.

ADM 1/16232   ADMIRALTY (5); DEFENCES–UNITED KINGDOM (32) and COMBINED OPERATIONS (47): Functions of R.M. Boom Patrol Detachment: control of RMBPD transferred from Chief of Combined Operations to Admiralty.

ADM 1/16248   ADMIRALTY (5) and COMBINED OPERATIONS (47) and NAVAL STATIONS (50) and FOREIGN COUNTRIES (52): Formation of Small Operations Group to obtain additional intelligence in respect of enemy-occupied coastlines in South East Asia Command.

ADM 1/16957 RN OFFICERS (71): Instructions to acting Captain T. B. Brunton DSC RN Commanding Officer Designate of Special Service establishment to assume control of units engaged on unorthodox offensive warfare.

ADM 1/16961 FOREIGN COUNTRIES (52): Question of required employment of the Royal Boom Patrol in Southeast Asia detachment.

ADM 1/21986 ADMIRALTY (5): Royal Marine Boom Patrol Detachment: history: transfer to Admiralty controls.

ADM 1/26900 Unorthodox offensive warfare units: proposed war establishment and postwar future of Special Service Establishment HMS Mount Stewart.

ADMIRALTY: RECORD OFFICE: CASES

ADM 116/4379 Raids on French, Belgium, and Dutch Coasts: directives to Commanders in Chief.

ADM 116/4381 Operation Anklet: (combined Allied raid on Lofoten Islands, Norway).

ADM 116/5112 Review of policy concerning operations of small-scale raiding force and establishment of Special Boat Unit.

ADMIRALTY: PORTSMOUTH STATION: CORRESPONDENCE

ADM 179/254 Establishment of raiding force on South Coast: administration of Force J: minutes of meetings.

ADM 179/347 Employment of X craft working with COPP units to carry out reconnaissance of French coast.

ADMIRALTY AND MINISTRY OF DEFENCE: ROYAL MARINES: WAR DIARIES, UNIT DIARIES, DETACHMENT REPORTS, AND ORDERS

ADM 202/87	40 Commando.
ADM 202/103	41 Commando.
ADM 202/104	46 Commando.
ADM 202/105	46 Commando.
ADM 202/310	Boom Patrol Detachment (for Operation Frankton).
ADM 202/311	2nd Special Boat Section.
ADM 202/446	Special Service/Commando Group: monthly letters.

ADMIRALTY: NAVAL INTELLIGENCE DIVISION AND OPERATIONAL INTELLIGENCE CENTRE: INTELLIGENCE REPORTS AND PAPERS

ADM 223/214 Appendix 1 (Part 5): History of 30 Commando (later called 30 Assault Unit and 30 Advanced Unit).

ADM 223/683 Operation Pitch: Commando raid on Castelorizo Island, Eastern Mediterranean.

ADM 223/697 Operation Hardtack: intelligence gathering raids on the Channel Islands.

AIR Series: Records Created or Inherited by the Air Ministry, the Royal Air Force, and Related Bodies

AIR MINISTRY AND MINISTRY OF DEFENCE: DEPARTMENT OF THE CHIEF OF THE AIR STAFF: REGISTERED FILES

AIR 8/1751   Mediterranean: control of special operations by air.

AIR MINISTRY: BOMBER COMMAND: REGISTERED FILES

AIR 14/2413   Special operations.
AIR 14/2414   Special operations and instructions.

AIR MINISTRY AND ADMIRALTY: COASTAL COMMAND: REGISTERED FILES

AIR 15/444   Cooperation with Special Forces.

AIR MINISTRY AND MINISTRY OF DEFENCE: PAPERS ACCUMULATED BY THE AIR HISTORICAL BRANCH

AIR 20/8174   OPERATIONS: France and Low Countries CODE 55/2/3: improvements in Special Air Service operations.
AIR 20/8413   OPERATIONS: Central Europe CODE 55/2/1: Balkan Air Force: reorganization of special operations.
AIR 20/8819   OPERATIONS: General (Code 55/1): SOE and SAS operations: planning and control.
AIR 20/8822   OPERATIONS: General (Code 55/1): SOE and SAS operations: matters arising from operations reports.
AIR 20/8823   OPERATIONS: General (Code 55/1): Special operations: SAS policy.
AIR 20/8945   OPERATIONS: France and Low Countries CODE 55/2/3: SAS troops: operation instructions.
AIR 20/8948   OPERATIONS, France and Low Countries CODE 55/2/3: SOE and SAS: planning and control of operations.

AIR MINISTRY AND MINISTRY OF DEFENCE: ROYAL AIR FORCE OVERSEAS COMMANDS: REPORTS AND CORRESPONDENCE

AIR 23/1678   AFHQ: weekly reports of special operations.
AIR 23/1781   Special operations.
AIR 23/2140   Small Operations Groups: policy.
AIR 23/2147   Small Operations Groups: operational and training experience.
AIR 23/7787   Island of Vis: policy.
AIR 23/7802   Special Boat Service and Long Range Desert Group: operation instructions and orders.
AIR 23/7935   "S" Squadron SBS (Special Boat Squadrons): outline plan for employment.
AIR 23/8125   Land Forces Adriatic: operation instructions.
AIR 23/8155   Long Range Desert Group (LRDG) Patrols Northern Adriatic: commanders' conferences.

AIR MINISTRY AND MINISTRY OF DEFENCE: FLYING TRAINING COMMAND AND TECHNICAL TRAINING COMMAND: REGISTERED FILES AND REPORTS

AIR 32/2   Provision of an airborne force.

AIR MINISTRY, DIRECTORATE OF INTELLIGENCE, AND RELATED BODIES: INTELLIGENCE REPORTS AND PAPERS

AIR 40/2564   Special operations: official histories; proposals, policy and arrangements.

AIR MINISTRY: COMBINED OPERATIONAL PLANNING COMMITTEE: PAPERS

AIR 42/18   Special operations: suggestions.

MEDITERRANEAN ALLIED AIR FORCES: MICROFILMED FILES

AIR 51/105   Special operations: policy: Parts 1–5.
AIR 51/288   Intelligence section: Special Boat Service reports.
AIR 51/394   AEAF Air Staff files: Employment of SAS troops.

CAB Series: Records of the Cabinet Office

COMMITTEE OF IMPERIAL DEFENCE, HISTORICAL BRANCH AND CABINET OFFICE, HISTORICAL SECTION: WAR HISTORIES: DRAFT CHAPTERS AND NARRATIVES, MILITARY

CAB 44/151   Section V, chapter T: history of the Long Range Desert Group in the Middle East, 1940–1943, by Brigadier H. W. Wynter.
CAB 44/152   Section V, chapter U: history of Commandos and Special Service troops in the Middle East and North Africa, 1941 Jan.–1943 Apr. by Brigadier H. W. Wynter.
CAB 44/153   Section V, chapter V: history of the Commandos in the Mediterranean, 1943 Sept.–1945 May, by Combined Operations Headquarters.

WAR CABINET AND CABINET: MINUTES (WM AND CM SERIES)

CAB 65/20/7   3. The Commandos.

WAR CABINET AND CABINET: CHIEFS OF STAFF COMMITTEE: MINUTES

CAB 79/7/45   1. RAIDING OPERATIONS. Memorandum by Director of Combined Operations discussed.
CAB 79/20/28   2. FORMATION OF COMMANDOS OF ALLIED FORCES.
CAB 79/20/49   5. OPERATION "RUTTER."
    6. FORMATION OF COMMANDOS OF ALLIED FORCES.
CAB 79/21/16   4. CHIEF OF COMBINED OPERATIONS—VISIT TO UNITED STATES.
    5. UNITED STATES COMBINED OPERATIONS TRAINING.

7. AIR SUPPORT FOR RAIDING OPERATIONS.
CAB 79/59/45   1. French Resistance in National Territory. COS(43)120(O).
                2. OSS Operations in Norway. COS(43)117(O).
CAB 79/70/2   4. Commandos for "Overlord."
CAB 79/70/8   3. Commandos for "Overlord."
CAB 79/70/16   1. Combined Operations—Visit of Liaison Officers to USA.
                2. Employment of Greek Troops.
                3. U.S. Aircraft for SOE purposes.
                4. Commandos for "Overlord."

WAR CABINET AND CABINET: CHIEFS OF STAFF COMMITTEE: MEMORANDA

CAB 80/10/57   NORWAY. INDEPENDENT COMPANIES. Memorandum by CIGS covering draft message to F.O., Narvik.
CAB 80/14/60   RAIDING OPERATIONS POLICY. Memorandum by Director of Combined Operations.
CAB 80/21/23   RAIDING FORCES REQUIREMENTS. Report by Director of Combined Operations.
CAB 80/31/24   COMBINED OPERATIONS AND RAIDS. Draft Directives to Adviser on Combined Operations and C in C, Home Forces.
CAB 80/31/29   COMBINED OPERATIONS AND RAIDS. Directive to Adviser on Combined Operations.
CAB 80/32/38   RAIDS BY C IN C, HOME FORCES. Memorandum by Adviser on Combined Operations.
CAB 80/35/57   RAIDING OPERATIONS. PROCEDURE FOR: Note by Chief of Combined Operations.
CAB 80/56/62   SPECIAL SERVICE TROOPS: RAISING NEW COMMANDOS. Note by Secretary.
CAB 80/58/41   RAIDS. Copy of Minutes Dated 18 July 1941 from Director of Combined Operations to Chiefs of Staff Committee.
CAB 80/59/6   RAIDS. Copy of Minutes Dated 2 August 1941 from Director of Combined Operations to Chiefs of Staff Committee.
CAB 80/61/30   RAIDS ON NORWAY. Note by Adviser on Combined Operations.
CAB 80/61/35   PROPOSED RAID ON NORWAY. Note by Adviser on Combined Operations.
CAB 80/61/46   PROPOSED RAID IN THE BAYONNE AREA. Memo by Adviser on Combined Operations.
CAB 80/62/55   MINOR RAIDS. Memorandum by Chief of Combined Operations.
CAB 80/66/50   LIMITATIONS OF SMALL SCALE RAIDING. Memorandum by Chief of Combined Operations.
CAB 80/66/67   SMALL SCALE RAIDING. Memorandum by Chief of Combined Operations.
CAB 80/76/72   SMALL SCALE RAIDS: RESPONSIBILITY FOR PLANNING AND MOUNTING. Note by Combined Operations Headquarters.
CAB 80/78/56   PROVISION OF COMMANDOS FOR "OVERLORD." Memorandum by Chief of Combined Operations.

CAB 80/78/77   COMMANDO RAIDS ON "CROSSBOW" SITES.
Memorandum by Chief of Combined Operations.

WAR CABINET AND CABINET OFFICE: HISTORICAL SECTION: ARCHIVIST AND LIBRARIAN FILES

CAB 106/8   Account of Operation Colossus, Combined Operations Raid in Italy, 10 February 1941, by Lieutenant A. J. Dean Drummond.
CAB 106/389   Syria: Report on Commando Operations in Litani River Battle.
CAB 106/1155   Accounts of Actions of Independent Companies, May 1940.
CAB 106/1216   Operations by Long-Range Desert Group in Aegean Sea During Autumn/Winter 1943.

CABINET OFFICE: SPECIAL SECRET INFORMATION CENTRE: FILES

CAB 121/177   Mobile Naval Base Defence Organisation, Royal Marine Group, Special Troops and Commandos.

WAR CABINET AND CABINET OFFICE: BRITISH JOINT STAFF MISSION AND BRITISH JOINT SERVICES MISSION: WASHINGTON OFFICE RECORDS

CAB 122/1328   U.S. Liaison Officers to Combined Operations Headquarters, London.

DEFE Series: Records of the Ministry of Defence

COMBINED OPERATIONS HEADQUARTERS, AND MINISTRY OF DEFENCE, COMBINED OPERATIONS HEADQUARTERS, LATER AMPHIBIOUS WARFARE HEADQUARTERS: RECORDS

DEFE 2/4	Headquarters.
DEFE 2/37	No. 1 Commando.
DEFE 2/37	No. 2 Commando.
DEFE 2/38	No. 3 Commando.
DEFE 2/40	No. 4 Commando.
DEFE 2/43	No. 6 Commando.
DEFE 2/43	No 7 Commando.
DEFE 2/45	Commando Bombardment Units: progress reports.
DEFE 2/45	Holding Operational Commando.
DEFE 2/45	No. 10 Commando.
DEFE 2/45	No. 12 Commando.
DEFE 2/45	No. 14 Commando.
DEFE 2/45	No. 2 Special Service Battalion.
DEFE 2/45	No. 3 Special Service Battalion.
DEFE 2/45	No. 4 Special Service Battalion.
DEFE 2/45	No. 5 Special Service Battalion.
DEFE 2/46	No. 4 Commando Brigade.
DEFE 2/48	No. 1 (RM) Commando.
DEFE 2/48	No. 40 (RM) Commando.

DEFE 2/48	No. 41 (RM) Commando.
DEFE 2/48	No. 42 (RM) Commando.
DEFE 2/53	Commando Wing GHQ 2nd Echelon.
DEFE 2/53	HQ No. 3 Special Service Brigade.
DEFE 2/53	No. 1 Special Service Brigade.
DEFE 2/53	No. 1 Special Service Brigade Signal Troop.
DEFE 2/54	Special Service Brigade.
DEFE 2/55	Special Service Brigade.
DEFE 2/56	Special Service Brigade, GHQ 2nd Echelon.
DEFE 2/57	Special Service Brigade, (Main).
DEFE 2/349	Operations Lighter, Copper, Flipper, and Exporter at Bardia and Litani River and translation of paper entitled "The Commandos" captured from the Vichy French in the Middle East c. 1943.
DEFE 2/700	History of the Commandos in the Mediterranean, 1943–45.
DEFE 2/701	No. 4 Commando Brigade chronological history.
DEFE 2/740	Special Boat Unit: reports, diaries, etc.
DEFE 2/741	Special Boat Unit: notes on objectives, reports, etc.
DEFE 2/742	Special Boat Unit (HMS Rodent): minutes of meetings, general correspondence and signals, etc.
DEFE 2/766	The Small Operations Group: handbook.
DEFE 2/780	Histories and accounts of Chief of Combined Operations Representative Washington. No. 10 Inter-Allied Commando and Small Operations Group in Southeast Asia.
DEFE 2/787	Raids and operations in the Middle East: reports.
DEFE 2/843	Commando casualties 1940–45. Incomplete returns.
DEFE 2/849	Special Service Brigade: equipment, appointments, standing orders, and instructions.
DEFE 2/927	Special boat unit organization: minutes of meetings, formation of unit, functions, provision of headquarters, and reorganization of Royal Marine and Army Commandos.
DEFE 2/952	RM Boom Patrol Detachment: reports on operations.
DEFE 2/953	RM Boom Patrol Detachment: formation.
DEFE 2/957	Small Scale Raiding Force: procedures, responsibility, etc.
DEFE 2/960	Special Service Brigade: recruitment standards, reorganization, wearing of flashes, etc.
DEFE 2/961	Royal Naval Beach Commandos: complements, organization, reports, and policy.
DEFE 2/963	Clearance of underwater obstacles: organization of landing craft Obstruction Clearance Units.
DEFE 2/970	Special Boat Unit operations: reports.
DEFE 2/971	Combined Operations Pilotage Parties: brief on information required, establishment, function, and use.
DEFE 2/977	History of 46 (RM) Commando. Activities of No. 10 (Inter-Allied) Commando.
DEFE 2/987	History of Naval Beach Control Parties (formerly Royal Naval Beach Commandos).
DEFE 2/988	Royal Marine Boom Patrol Detachment.

354 BIBLIOGRAPHY

DEFE 2/1016   Deployment of Troops in No. 10 (1.A) Commando.
DEFE 2/1035   Special Boat Unit organization: proposals, requirements, and administration in South East Asia Command; disbandment and recommendation for awards.
DEFE 2/1036   Special Boat Unit organization: proposals, requirements, and administration in South East Asia Command; disbandment and recommendation for awards.
DEFE 2/1041   Royal Marine Commandos: formation, reorganization, move of 3 Special Service Brigade overseas.
DEFE 2/1051   Special Service Brigade: role, reorganization, etc.
DEFE 2/1073   Special Service Group: monthly letters.
DEFE 2/1074   Special Service Group: monthly letters.
DEFE 2/1091   Commandos in action: reports.
DEFE 2/1093   Small Scale Raiding Force: policy, formation, responsibility, etc.
DEFE 2/1101   Combined Operations Pilotage Parties: composition and movement of teams, complement, requirements for beach reconnaissance, etc.
DEFE 2/1105   Requirement for commandos in India and Southeast Asia.
DEFE 2/1107   30 Assault Unit (formerly Special Engineering Unit, formerly 30 Commando, later 30 Advanced Unit): mobilization, control, disbandment, honors and awards.
DEFE 2/1111   Combined Operations Pilotage parties: progress reports, honors and awards.
DEFE 2/1116   Combined Operations Pilotage Parties: history and reports.
DEFE 2/1134   Training policy for Commandos.
DEFE 2/1152   Combined Operations Pilotage Parties: progress reports.
DEFE 2/1192   Combined Operations Pilotage Parties: use of aircraft for long-range reconnaissance.
DEFE 2/1203   Small Operations Group: formation, organization, stores, appraisal, etc.
DEFE 2/1204   Combined Operations Pilotage Parties: progress reports.
DEFE 2/1214   Combined Operations Pilotage Party: awards and medals.
DEFE 2/1222   Special service group: reorganization for the Far East.
DEFE 2/1223   Special service group: reorganization for the Far East.
DEFE 2/1224   Special service group: reorganization for the Far East.
DEFE 2/1257   Small Operations Group organization.
DEFE 2/1325   Disbandment of the Commando Group: Order of the Day.
DEFE 2/1747   The Small Operations Group, South East Asia Command: formation, composition, and functions; record of operations carried out in Southeast Asia; pamphlet SOG: The Small Operations Group.
DEFE 2/2084   Combined Operations Pilotage Parties.

FO Series: Records Created and Inherited by the Foreign Office
FOREIGN OFFICE: POLITICAL DEPARTMENTS: GENERAL CORRESPONDENCE 1906–66

FO 371/41904   Special operations in France: arming and maintenance of the Maquis.

HS Series: Records of Special Operations Executive

SPECIAL OPERATIONS EXECUTIVE: FAR EAST: REGISTERED FILES

HS 1/164   Commando group.
HS 1/165   OSS/SOE cooperation.
HS 1/212   Liaison SAS/SOE; Force 136; Clandestine ops; SIS reports; SOE reports.
HS 1/279   Military establishments: 92 (Gurkha Force Nucleus) to 94 (Jedburgh operations).
HS 1/287   Jedburghs: personnel.

SPECIAL OPERATIONS EXECUTIVE: GROUP C, SCANDINAVIA: REGISTERED FILES

HS 2/53   SOE/OSS liaison.
HS 2/116   Jedburghs: personnel.
HS 2/134   OSS activities in Norway.
HS 2/219   OSS/SOE coordination.

SPECIAL OPERATIONS EXECUTIVE: AFRICA AND MIDDLE EAST GROUP: REGISTERED FILES

HS 3/15   OSS/SOE coordination.
HS 3/41   French special services.
HS 3/56   SOE/OSS coordination.
HS 3/57   SOE/OSS coordination.
HS 3/229   Projects: sabotage of enemy ships; storage of material for Greek guerrillas; OSS activities.

SPECIAL OPERATIONS EXECUTIVE: BALKANS: REGISTERED FILES

HS 5/87   Resistance movements; partisan groups and forces.
HS 5/445   Syros report; survey of Aegean Islands and political personalities; escaped and enticed caiques; reconnaissance of Aegean islands by St. Nichlos; activities of raiding forces.
HS 5/608   Noah's Ark: infiltration of Raiding Support Regiment (RSR) units; list of area commanders.
HS 5/612   Noah's Ark: operational instructions; infiltrations of RSR detachments and other groups.

SPECIAL OPERATIONS EXECUTIVE: WESTERN EUROPE: REGISTERED FILE

HS 6/218   SAS operations.
HS 6/604   SAS operations under SHAEF control.

SPECIAL OPERATIONS EXECUTIVE: HISTORIES AND WAR DIARIES: REGISTERED FILES

HS 7/2   Special Force headquarters.
HS 7/17 Jedburghs in Europe 1942–44.
HS 7/18 Jedburghs in Europe.
HS 7/19 Jedburghs in Europe.
HS 7/117   Force 136: Special Forces Development Centre 1943–45.

MINISTRY OF ECONOMIC WARFARE, SPECIAL OPERATIONS EXECUTIVE AND SUCCESSORS: HEADQUARTERS: RECORDS

HS 8/288   Overlord: Jedburghs.
HS 8/381   SFHQ (Special Forces Headquarters) operational procedures.
HS 8/833   Selection of title Special Force Headquarters; SO/SOE London group.

WO Series: Records Created or Inherited by the War Office, Armed Forces, Judge Advocate General, and Related Bodies

WAR OFFICE AND SUCCESSORS: REGISTERED FILES (GENERAL SERIES)

WO 32/9729   ARMY ORGANIZATION: General (Code 14 [A]): Reorganization of Special Service Units to form Commandos.
WO 32/9781   ARMY ORGANIZATION: Airborne (Code 14 [P]): Army Air Corps: formation: Glider Pilot Regiment, Parachute Regiment, Special Air Service Regiment, Airborne Forces Depot, Airborne Forces Holding Unit, Parachute Battalion.
WO 32/10415   ARMY ORGANIZATION: Commandos (Code 14 [Q]): Special Service Brigade.
WO 32/10416   ARMY ORGANIZATION: Commandos (Code 14 [Q]): Commandos: reorganization.
WO 32/10417   ARMY ORGANIZATION: Commandos (Code 14 [Q]): Distribution of and Policy for upkeep of Commandos.

WAR OFFICE: REPORTS, MEMORANDA AND PAPERS (O AND A SERIES)

WO 33/1668   Commando Training Instruction 1.
WO 33/1669   Independent Company Training Instruction 1.

WAR OFFICE: DIRECTORATE OF MILITARY OPERATIONS AND MILITARY INTELLIGENCE, AND PREDECESSORS: CORRESPONDENCE AND PAPERS

WO 106/1665   Minor operations and raids.
WO 106/1672   Special operations: naval role.
WO 106/1734   Special operations: demolitions in France.
WO 106/1735   Special operations: demolitions in St. Malo.
WO 106/1740   Report on Operation Collar; report on a small raid near Boulogne.

WO 106/1829   Independent companies: instructions.
WO 106/1867   Movements; independent companies.
WO 106/1889   Independent companies for Norway.
WO 106/1908   Independent companies: situation reports.
WO 106/1919   Scandinavia Operations: independent companies.
WO 106/1944   Independent companies: formation of and movement to Norway.
WO 106/1974   Plough: special force for reconquest of Norway.
WO 106/2332   Popski's Private Army.
WO 106/2958   CHANNEL ISLANDS: Operation Ambassador, attack by Commandos on Guernsey: report.
WO 106/3946   Chiefs of Staff intelligence reports and special operations.
WO 106/3959   Operations Maple and Baobab: Jan. 1944: report by Lieutenant Worcester, 2nd Special Air Services Regiment.
WO 106/3965B   HQ Special Operations—Mediterranean.
WO 106/3966   Special operations: situation reports.
WO 106/4115   Raid on Dieppe: report by Chief of Combined Operations on lessons learned.
WO 106/4116   "Chess": reconnaissance raid on French coast by commando troops.
WO 106/4117   Reconnaissance and raiding operation's procedure.
WO 106/4158   Commandos and Special Air Services Troops.
WO 106/4194   Rutter: combined operation raid on Dieppe.
WO 106/4290   Dragoon: Operations Hardtack, Candlestick, and Manacle: raids on French coast.
WO 106/4322A   Special operations activities and operational situation reports: France and the Low Countries.
WO 106/4323   Special operations activities and operational situation reports: Middle East and Balkans.
WO 106/4460   Amherst and Keystone: special air services operation.
WO 106/5450   Special operations planning.
WO 106/6092   Liaison between Maj. Eifler of Office of Strategic Services (OSS) and British authorities.

WAR OFFICE: HOME FORCES: WAR DIARIES, SECOND WORLD WAR

WO 166/4111   5 Training Battalion Scots Guards.
WO 166/15539   1 Special Services Bde.

WAR OFFICE: BRITISH FORCES, MIDDLE EAST: WAR DIARIES, SECOND WORLD WAR

WO 169/11083   1 Demolition Sqn.
WO 169/12708   Lt. Repair Sec. att. 1 SAS HQ Raiding Force.
WO 169/17278   Lt Repair Squad Raiding Force.
WO 169/19917   Raiding Forces (Simi).

358 BIBLIOGRAPHY

WAR OFFICE: CENTRAL MEDITERRANEAN FORCES (BRITISH ELEMENT): WAR DIARIES, SECOND WORLD WAR

WO 170/1364   Raiding Support Regt.
WO 170/3962B   1 Demolition Sqn. Popski's Private Army.
WO 170/4012   Special Boat Service.
WO 170/4825   Raiding Support Regiment: Raiding Sup. Regt.
WO 170/7362   1 Demolition Sqn. Special Force.
WO 170/7529   Special Boat Service.

WAR OFFICE: BRITISH AND ALLIED LAND FORCES, SOUTH EAST ASIA: WAR DIARIES, SECOND WORLD WAR

WO 172/475   17th Indian Division G Branch.
WO 172/601   63rd Indian Infantry Brigade.
WO 172/2267   B Special Service Sqn.

WAR OFFICE: WEST AFRICAN COMMAND: WAR DIARIES, SECOND WORLD WAR

WO 173/307   Special Service Bde. Det.
WO 173/308   4 Commando Det.

WAR OFFICE: DIRECTORATE OF MILITARY OPERATIONS AND PLANS, LATER DIRECTORATE OF MILITARY OPERATIONS: FILES CONCERNING MILITARY PLANNING, INTELLIGENCE, AND STATISTICS (COLLATION FILES)

WO 193/74   Institution of Plough specialized units and equipment prepared by Americans.
WO 193/77   Composition and mobilization of Special Forces.
WO 193/384   Independent companies.
WO 193/405   Special Air Service and Special Service activities.
WO 193/620   Reorganization of special operations in Middle East and control of funds.
WO 193/624   Liaison between Special Operations Executive and related organizations.
WO 193/673   General policy, including special Allied Airborne Reconnaissance Force.

WAR OFFICE: HOME FORCES: MILITARY HEADQUARTERS PAPERS, SECOND WORLD WAR

WO 199/604   Special service units.
WO 199/1763   Liaison with Commandos and employment of, in the event of a raid.
WO 199/1849   Formation of Irregular Commandos.
WO 199/1994   Enemy invasion or raids: U.S. Army units operational role.
WO 199/3057   Reports on commando raids: Operations Acid Drop, Archery, and Bristle.

WAR OFFICE: MIDDLE EAST FORCES; MILITARY HEADQUARTERS PAPERS, SECOND WORLD WAR

WO 201/721 Special Air Service (SAS) Regiment: brief history of L Detachment SAS Brigade and 1st SAS Regiment 1941–42. Copy of report in WO 218/98 and WO 218/173.
WO 201/724 Appreciation of Operation Heartless: landing of special force at Derna.
WO 201/727 Raiding Forces: personal file of Lt. Colonel J. E. Haselden.
WO 201/728 REorganization of Special Service.
WO 201/731 Special Forces: operational questions.
WO 201/732 Special Forces: operational questions.
WO 201/735 Reports on operations: Raiding Forces at Benghazi.
WO 201/736 Reports on Operation Anglo by Special Boat Section: attack on airfields at Maritza and Calato, island of Rhodes.
WO 201/738 Long Range Desert Group: report on Section 1 and Section 2 raid on airfield at Benina.
WO 201/739 Report on Operation Caravan: raid on Barce, Benghazi, Tobruk.
WO 201/743 Raiding Forces: personal copies of GHQ operation instructions. Including Operation Longstop.
WO 201/745 Notes and reports on individual raids, including Operation Agreement and Operation Nicety.
WO 201/747 Special Air Service Regiment: battle file.
WO 201/748 Agreement, Bigamy, Nicety: report.
WO 201/752 Raiding Forces: appointment of commander.
WO 201/754 Long Range Desert Groups: operations.
WO 201/756 Raiding Forces: plans for operations.
WO 201/760 Long Range Desert Group: summary of operations.
WO 201/761 Long Range Desert Group: situation report.
WO 201/768 Seaborne raiding operations: Chief of Staff Committee papers.
WO 201/771 Long Range Desert Group and Raiding Forces: general policy and reports.
WO 201/784 Raiding Forces: Operation Hess.
WO 201/785 L Detachment Special Air Service Brigade: Special Air Service Parachute detachment: history.
WO 201/787 Raiding operations in the Aegean: employment of special troops.
WO 201/788 Naval cooperation with First Special Airborne Service and other raiding forces.
WO 201/791 Operation reports of Raiding Forces.
WO 201/792 Operation reports of Raiding Forces.
WO 201/796 Aegean: role of Raiding Forces.
WO 201/797 Reorganization of Raiding Forces. Future of Long Range Desert Group and Indian Long Range Squadron.
WO 201/799 Raiding Forces: operational reports in Aegean.

WO 201/802   Advance Raiding Forces: situation reports.
WO 201/807   Long Range Desert Group: Diary and narrative.
WO 201/808   Long Range Desert Group: Diary and narrative.
WO 201/809   Long Range Desert Group: Diary and narrative.
WO 201/810   Long Range Desert Group: Diary and narrative.
WO 201/811   Long Range Desert Group: Diary and narrative.
WO 201/812   Long Range Desert Group: Diary and narrative.
WO 201/813   Long Range Desert Group: Diary and narrative.
WO 201/814   Long Range Desert Group: Diary and narrative.
WO 201/815   Long Range Desert Group: Diary and narrative.
WO 201/816   Long Range Desert Group: Diary and narrative.
WO 201/817   Long Range Desert Group: Diary and narrative.
WO 201/818   Long Range Desert Group: Diary and narrative.
WO 201/863   Special Services in Levant (Services Speciaux du Levant): personnel.
WO 201/1653   Operations: Raiding Force.
WO 201/1739   GHQME: op instructions and organization of Raiding Force.
WO 201/1755   Dodecanese operations: Raiding Force.
WO 201/2152   Captured enemy report: enemy appraisal of British Commandos.
WO 201/2202   Raiding forces: directive to commanders.
WO 201/2263   Balkans: guerrilla operations special forces.
WO 201/2624   1 Special Service Regiment: provision of personnel for Irregular Commandos.
WO 201/2831   Operation Tenement: attack by raiding forces on the Island of Symi in the Aegean.
WO 201/2836   Raiding forces: history of an independent command in the Aegean.
WO 201/2839   Special operations in Italy January–February 1944.

WAR OFFICE: SOUTH EAST ASIA COMMAND: MILITARY HEADQUARTERS PAPERS, SECOND WORLD WAR

WO 203/131   Special Operations Executive: small group operations.
WO 203/1255   Small operations groups: formation and administrative directives.
WO 203/1263   Small operations group: formation, function, and organization.
WO 203/1740   Commandos: employment in SEAC formations.
WO 203/1792   3 Commando Brigade: report on operations in Arakan.
WO 203/2102   Employment of Commandos: paper No. 94/1.
WO 203/2144   Administration of British Clandestine and Special Forces in SEAC: instruction.
WO 203/3426   Special Air Service Units: employment in SEAC.
WO 203/3437   Small Operations Group: formation and administration.
WO 203/3449   Royal Marine Boom Patrol Detachment.
WO 203/3460   Role of Combined Operations Pilotage Parties.
WO 203/3545   Small Operations Group: formation and organization.

WO 203/3547 Special Service Brigade: proposals for operational employment.
WO 203/3607 Commando brigades: operational requirements.
WO 203/4594 Commando Units: demands.
WO 203/4796 Combined Operations Pilotage Parties: organization and activities.
WO 203/4797 Special Boat Units: organization.
WO 203/4800 Small Operations Groups: policy on formation and dispersal.
WO 203/4802 Employment of Commando Brigades.
WO 203/5416 Joint and Executive Planning Staff papers No. 94 and 94/1 on employment of Commandos.
WO 203/6386 Duties and functions of OSS in SEAC.

WAR OFFICE: ALLIED FORCES, MEDITERRANEAN THEATER: MILITARY HEADQUARTERS PAPERS, SECOND WORLD WAR

WO 204/1527 Commandos: training, deployment, and operational use.
WO 204/1527 Commandos: training, deployment, and operational use.
WO 204/1532 First Special Service Force (trained for operations in snow): proposed employment: movements. Movement of Ranger battalions.
WO 204/1564 Raiding forces: planning and reports.
WO 204/1565 Raiding forces: policy.
WO 204/1949 Raiding forces: policy.
WO 204/1950 Raiding forces: operational planning papers.
WO 204/2020 Special Air Service operations in Italy: planning papers and reports.
WO 204/2030B AFHQ History of Special Operations.
WO 204/6308 HQ Allied Armies Italy: reports from G. Special Operations.
WO 204/6806 Special Forces, Commandos, Long Range Desert Group, Popski's Private Army, etc.: administration, employment, and movement.
WO 204/6807 Special Forces, Commandos, Long Range Desert Group, Popski's Private Army, etc.: administration, employment, and movement.
WO 204/6810 Long Range Desert Group operations in the Balkans: administrative instructions and reports.
WO 204/7222 Special Service Brigade: operations.
WO 204/7289 2671 Special Reconnaissance Battalion, U.S. Army: reports.
WO 204/7577 Report of a raid by 2 Commando on the island of Solta, Dalmation coast.
WO 204/7960 Minor operations and raids in the Mediterranean Theater by Special Forces and Special Air Service units in support of Operation Husky.
WO 204/8277 Operations in Italy: reports of battles at Termoli and on the River Trigno.
WO 204/8397 War establishment: infantry and commando units.
WO 204/8425 Special operations in the Adriatic: policy, planning papers, appreciations, and reports.
WO 204/8426 Special operations in the Adriatic: policy, planning papers, appreciations, and reports.
WO 204/8427 Special operations in the Adriatic: policy, planning papers, appreciations, and reports.

WO 204/8461   Greece: report on the activities of 9 Commando and attached units (Foxforce).
WO 204/8491   Operations in North Adriatic by Long Range Desert Group and Special Boat Service.
WO 204/8500   Long Range Desert Group: policy for employment and miscellaneous correspondence.
WO 204/8512   Long Range Desert Group operations against the Italian, Yugoslav, and Greek coasts: orders and reports.
WO 204/9681   Raiding forces in the Adriatic: narrative of operations.
WO 204/10185   Establishment of Military HQ Balkans Land Forces Adriatic and Balkan Air Force.
WO 204/10242   Raiding forces: availability and employment.
WO 204/10243   Coordination of special forces.
WO 204/10285   Special Air Service: miscellaneous reports and correspondence.
WO 204/10306   U.S. Operational Groups: operation orders, mainland of Yugoslavia.
WO 204/10392   AFHQ. History of Special Operations: Mediterranean Theater.
WO 204/10429   British and United States forces operations June 1944 to May 1945: report by commander Land Forces Adriatic.
WO 204/12836   OSS: operations.
WO 204/12837   OSS: policy.
WO 204/12980   OSS special operations.
WO 204/12981   OSS special operations.
WO 204/12982   OSS special operations.
WO 204/12983   OSS special operations.
WO 204/12984   OSS special operations.
WO 204/12985   OSS special operations.
WO 204/12986   OSS special operations.

WAR OFFICE: 21 ARMY GROUP: MILITARY HEADQUARTERS PAPERS, SECOND WORLD WAR

WO 205/92   Reports on Special Air Service operations.
WO 205/136   Special Service Troops: operational command and control.
WO 205/208   Special Air Services: plans, instructions. Part I.

WAR OFFICE: DIRECTORATE OF MILITARY OPERATIONS AND INTELLIGENCE, AND DIRECTORATE OF MILITARY INTELLIGENCE: MINISTRY OF DEFENCE, DEFENCE INTELLIGENCE STAFF: FILES

WO 208/1262   Infantry; commandos and special tactical units.
WO 208/1866   Report on partisan warfare.
WO 208/2002   Partisan movements; appreciations, historical reports, origin and development, operational reports, etc.
WO 208/2581   Intelligence report file of the Kami organization (Special Service Organization).
WO 208/3108   Notes from theaters of war 1–17, 21.

WAR OFFICE: OFFICE OF THE CHIEF OF THE IMPERIAL GENERAL STAFF: PAPERS

WO 216/54   Reorganization and location of Special Service troops: revised directive to Director, Combined Operations.

WAR OFFICE: SPECIAL SERVICES WAR DIARIES, SECOND WORLD WAR

WO 218/1   HQ Special Service Bde.
WO 218/19   HQ Special Service Bde.
WO 218/20   HQ Special Service Bde. (Det.).
WO 218/23   3 Commando.
WO 218/28   12 Commando.
WO 218/29   HQ Special Service Bde.
WO 218/32   1 Commando.
WO 218/34   3 Commando.
WO 218/35   4 Commando.
WO 218/37   6 Commando.
WO 218/41   12 Commando.
WO 218/42   14 Commando.
WO 218/49   1 Commando.
WO 218/57   12 Commando.
WO 218/58   14 Commando.
WO 218/64   2 Commando.
WO 218/96   1 Special Air Service Regiment. Includes war diary for B Squadron, 1 SS Regiment for October 1942.
WO 218/97   1 Special Air Service (1 SAS Regt) including 1 Special Boat Section. Raiding Forces Headquarters, including Special Boat Squadron and Special Raiding, Squadron, 1 Special Air Service (1 SAS Regt).
WO 218/98   HQ Raiding Force.
WO 218/101   Raiding Support Regt.
WO 218/103   2 Special Boat Sec.
WO 218/104   2 Special Boat Sec.
WO 218/106   M Detachment 1 Special Air Service Regiment and M Detachment, Special Boat Squadron, 1 Special Air Service Regiment.
WO 218/109   HQ Raiding Forces.
WO 218/173   L Detachment SAS Brigade (later 1 SAS Regt): formation, training, and report of operations in Mediterranean area.
WO 218/176   2 SAS Regt: report of operations in Italy from Taranto to Termoli.
WO 218/179   2 SAS Regt: report on operations against enemy lines of communication in Italy between Arcona and Pescarra.
WO 218/189   Operational employment of SAS forces.
WO 218/194   Employment of SAS troops.
WO 218/252   Long Range Desert Group.

WAR OFFICE: SUPREME HEADQUARTERS ALLIED EXPEDITIONARY FORCE: MILITARY HEADQUARTERS PAPERS, SECOND WORLD WAR

WO 219/481 U.S. Rangers: employment.
WO 219/548 1 Special Service Force: disbandment and brief history.
WO 219/1872 Redeployment of commando units from the Mediterranean Theater for use in Overlord.
WO 219/2196 Raids and reconnaissances: reports on minor operations carried out.
WO 219/2329 Liaison with Special Force HQ.
WO 219/2389 Operation Overlord: Special Air Service operations.
WO 219/2398 Strategic planning for resistance and Special Air Service operations.
WO 219/2674 Special Air Service: command and control, war establishments equipment, and deployment, including French and Belgian units.
WO 219/2877 Employment of the Special Air Service units: policy.
WO 219/5304 OSS units.

WAR OFFICE: DIRECTORATE OF MILITARY TRAINING, LATER DIRECTORATE OF ARMY TRAINING: PAPERS

WO 231/2 Operation Claymore (raid on German-held ports in Lofoten Islands): brief account.
WO 231/5 Operation Archery: report of a raid on Vaagso Island, southwestern Norway.
WO 231/28 Notes on the operations of the Long Range Desert Group.

WAR OFFICE: DIRECTORATE OF STAFF DUTIES: PAPERS

WO 260/32 Scissors: formation of special infantry and independent companies: notes on meetings.

WAR OFFICE: HEADQUARTERS ALLIED LAND FORCES NORWAY, WAR CRIMES INVESTIGATION BRANCH: REGISTERED FILES (A/GI/WCI SERIES)

WO 331/14 Operation Musketoon, commando raid on Glomfjord Power Station, Norway: capture of allied personnel and transfer to Germany.
WO 331/16 Operation Freshman, destruction of heavy water plant at Rjukan, Norway: killing of survivors of raid at Stavanger, Norway.

National Archives and Record Administration [U.S.], College Park, Maryland

Record Group 24: Records of the Bureau of Naval Personnel

HISTORICAL RECORDS OF NAVY TRAINING ACTIVITIES, 1940–45

Box 28; Training activities at ATB Fort Pierce, Florida.
Box 34; S&R Training.

BIBLIOGRAPHY

Record Group 38: Records of the Office of the Chief of Naval Operations

WORLD WAR II WAR DIARIES

Box 535; UDTs.

WORLD WAR II ACTION AND OPERATIONAL REPORTS

Boxes 788–91; UDTs.

Record Group 80: General Records of the Department of the Navy, 1798–1947

FORMERLY SECURITY-CLASSIFIED GENERAL CORRESPONDENCE OF THE CNO/SECRETARY OF THE NAVY, 1940–47

Box 1009; S76-2/A9-4 to S76-3/QR9.
Box 1452; S76-2/AVP to S76-3.
Box 1762; S76-1/A9-4 to S76-3.
Box 1763; S76-3.
Box 1764; S76-3/A1-1 to S78.
Box 2148; S76-1 to S76-6.
Box 2414; S76-1 to S76-3.
Box 2415; S76-3 to S78.

Record Group 127: Records of the U.S. Marine Corps

HISTORY AND MUSEUMS DIVISION, REPORTS, STUDIES, AND PLANS RELATING TO WORLD WAR II MILITARY OPERATIONS, 1941–56

Box 5; NND 984110.

HISTORY AND MUSEUMS DIVISION, SUBJECT FILES RELATING TO WORLD WAR II

Box 7; Beach Reconnaissance (General).
Box 13; Coastwatchers.
Box 15; Dieppe.
Box 46; Reconnaissance.
Box 57; Ft. Pierce School.
Box 58; Warfare: Guerrilla.

USMC GEOGRAPHIC FILES

Box 2; Bougainville.
Box 27; Gilberts.
Box 35; Gilberts.
Box 36; Gilberts.
Box 38; Guadalcanal.
Box 39; Guadalcanal.
Box 40; Guadalcanal.
Box 41; Guadalcanal.

Box 42; Guadalcanal.
Box 43; Guadalcanal.
Box 44; Guadalcanal.
Box 45; Guadalcanal.
Box 183; Makin.
Box 315; Russell Islands.

ENTRY 46B: RECORDS OF GROUND COMBAT UNITS

Box 66; 1st Raider Regiment War Diary, 15 March 1943–30 September 1943.
Box 69; 2nd Raider Battalion War Diary, 1 May 1943–31 August 1943.
Box 76; 3rd Raider Battalion War Diary, 15 June 1943–31 June 1943.
Box 77; 4th Raider Battalion War Diary.
Box 78; Fifth Amphibious Force UDT Recommendations Based on Flintlock, 14 March 1944–14 March 1944.
Box 79; V MAC [Fifth Marine Amphibious Corps] Amphibious Reconnaissance Battalion Readiness Reports, April 1944–June 1944.
Box 100; Historical Branch Account of Makin Island Raid, 16 August 1942–18 August 1942.

Record Group 165: Records of the War Department General and Special Staffs

ENTRY 418: OFFICE OF DIRECTOR OF PLANS AND OPERATIONS, SECURITY CLASSIFIED GENERAL CORRESPONDENCE, 1943–45

Box 682; Folder 320.2 Africa, Case 584 to 649.
Box 1249; Folder 381 ETO, Case 108 to 111.

ENTRY 421: RECORDS OF OPERATIONS DIVISION, TOP SECRET "AMERICAN-BRITISH-CANADIAN" CORRESPONDENCE RELATING TO THE ORGANIZATIONAL PLANNING AND GENERAL COMBAT OPERATIONS DURING WORLD WAR II AND THE EARLY POSTWAR PERIOD 1940–48

ABC 381 Bolero (3-16-42) Sec.1; Direction for formation of Commando Unit.

Record Group 218: Records of the Joint Chiefs of Staff

ENTRY 1: CENTRAL DECIMAL FILES 1942–45

Box 8; Folder 000.51; Subversive activity, Jedburghs.
Box 150; Folder 323.361; Command for U.S.-British operations.
Box 151; Folder 323.361; Command for U.S.-British operations.
Box 152; Folder 323.361; Command for U.S.-British operations.
Box 281; Folder 370.03; Development of technique of the passage of underwater and beach obstacles.
Box 284; Folder 370.23 (5-2-44); Coordination of resistance groups.
Box 285; Folder 370.5 (2-2-43); Employment of FSSF.
Box 369; Folder 385 (8-6-42); Agreements between OSS and SOE.
Box 372; Folder 385; OSS.

Box 373; Folder 385; OSS.
Box 374; Folder 385; OSS.
Box 375; Folder 385; OSS.

ENTRY 2: GEOGRAPHIC FILES 1942–45

Box 13; Folder 370.64; Guerrilla operations in the Balkans.
Box 58; Folder 350.05; Dieppe Raid.
Box 153; Folder 385; Special Operations from North Africa.
Box 158; Folder 381 (7-15-42); Employment of FSSF.

Record Group 226: Records of the Office of Strategic Services 1940–46

ENTRY 1: R+A OFFICE OF THE CHIEF, GENERAL CORRESPONDENCE

Box 13; Folder 10; OSS: Maritime Unit.

ENTRY 92: COI/OSS CENTRAL FILES

Box 111; Folder 49; Commando Training.
Box 159; Folders 39–40; OSS: Maritime Units.
Box 160; Folders 1–8; OSS: Maritime Units.
Box 192; Folders 1–5; OSS: History Det. 101.
Box 271; Folders 1–2; OSS: Maritime Unit.
Box 329; Folders 10–12; North Africa OG.
Box 490; Folders 26–28; OSS: Maritime Unit in Asia.
Box 491; Folder 3–7; OSS: Maritime Unit in Europe.
Box 491; Folder 8; SAS Troops.
Box 491; Folders 15–16; OSS: Maritime Unit in SEA.
Box 495; Folder 10; OSS: Maritime Unit in Mediterranean.
Box 534; Folder 8; OSS: Diving Unit.
Box 546; Folders 9–11; OSS: Underwater Operations.
Box 547; OSS: Underwater Operations.

ENTRY 97: ALGIERS FILES

Box 2; Folder 9; OG (Algiers).
Box 40; Algiers.
Box 41; Algiers.

ENTRY 99: OSS HISTORY OFFICE

Box 2; Folder 4; London Office Progress Reports.
Box 16; French Resistance.
Box 17; French Resistance.
Box 28; 2677th Regiment progress reports.
Box 29; 2677th Regiment progress reports.
Box 34; OGs on Vis.
Box 35; OGs (Patch review 2).
Box 36; OGs on Corsica.
Box 42; Reports on value of partisan operations in Italy.

Box 44; Folder 182; MEDTO Co. B. Spec. Recon Bn. Operational Reports 1944.
Box 45; Folders 184-186; MEDTO Greece and Italy OGs.
Box 46; OG in Italy.
Box 54; OG in Balkans and METO MU.
Box 63; Reports on MU [3/4].
Box 64; Det 404.
Box 65; Det 101.
Box 66; Det 101.
Box 67; Det 101.
Box 74; OSS in CBI.
Box 98; History of OG and MU.
Box 118; NORSO.

ENTRY 101: RECORDS OF THE JEDBURGH TEAMS

Boxes 1 and 2.

ENTRY 103: RECORDS OF THE SPECIAL FORCES AND JEDBURGH MISSION REPORTS

Boxes 1-3.

ENTRY 108C: WASHINGTON REGISTRY SI INTEL FIELD FILES

Box 12; Folders 58-59; Operational Groups.

ENTRY 133: WASHINGTON REGISTRY OFFICE CHRONOLOGICAL FILES

Box 16; Folders 12-13; MU (Washington).

ENTRY 136: WASHINGTON AND FIELD STATION FILES

Box 19; Folder 197; MU (Bari).
Box 140; Folders 1460-67; OG (Washington).
Box 141; Folder 1468-69; OG (Washington).

ENTRY 139: WASHINGTON AND FIELD STATION FILES, HONOLULU

Box 73; Folder 710; MU.

ENTRY 143: FIELD STATION FILES: CALCUTTA AND CASERTA

Box 5; Folders 71-83; MU (Caserta).
Box 6; Folders 81-101; MU (Caserta).
Box 7; Folders 102-13; MU (Caserta).
Box 8; Folders 114-19; OG (Caserta).
Box 9; Folders 120-26; OG (Caserta).
Box 10; Folders 127-37; OG (Caserta).
Box 11; Folders 138-48; OG (Caserta).
Box 11; Folder 145; History of 2671 Sp. Rec. Bn.
Box 12; Folders 149-54; OG (Caserta).

Box 13; Folder 154A; OG (Caserta).
Box 14; Folders 155–57; OG (Caserta).

ENTRY 144: FIELD STATION FILES: ALGIERS, AUSTRIA, BARI, BELGIUM, BURMA, CAIRO, AND CALCUTTA

Box 68; Folders 586–99A; OG (Bari).
Box 70; Folders 631–41; OG (Burma).
Box 70; Folder 630; MU (Burma).
Box 70; Folders 642–46; MU (Cairo).
Box 71; Folders 647–62; MU (Cairo).
Box 72; Folders 663–78; MU (Cairo).
Box 73; Folders 679–91; MU (Cairo).
Box 74; Folders 691–710; MU (Cairo).
Box 75; Folders 711–27; MU (Cairo).
Box 76; Folders 728–43; MU (Cairo).
Box 77; Folders 744–50; MU (Cairo).

ENTRY 148: FIELD STATION FILES, CHUNGKING

Box 12; Folders 231–34; Commando Op.
Box 14; Folder 249; OSS: SACO Relationship.
Box 82; Folder 1194; MU (London).
Box 83; Folders 1199–1202; War Diary ETO MU.
Box 83; Folders 1204–12; OG (London).

ENTRY 154: FIELD STATION FILES: KUNMING

Box 56; SO (Caserta).
Box 162; Folders 2760–74; OG (Kunming).
Box 163; Folders 2775–2805; OG (Kunming).
Box 164; Folders 2806–25; OG (Kunming).
Box 165; Folders 2826–45; OG (Kunming).
Box 166; Folders 2846–55; OG (Kunming).

ENTRY 161: SCHOOLS AND TRAINING BRANCH RECORDS

Box 8; Folder 86; Det. 101 ATB.

ENTRY 165A: RECORDS OF OSS OPERATIONS

Box 5; Folder 9; Det. 101 Roster 1944–45.

ENTRY 168: FIELD STATION FILES: CAIRO

Box 6; Folders 105–13; OG (Kunming).

ENTRY 190: FIELD STATION FILES: HISTORY OF OSS AID TO FRENCH RESISTANCE

Box 75; Folder 54; MU.
Box 740; Folders 1462–63; Jedburgh History.
Box 741; Folder 1469; Jedburgh Origin and Developments.

370 BIBLIOGRAPHY

ENTRY 194: WASHINGTON AND FIELD STATION FILES, CAIRO

Box 14; Folders 53–54; MU (Cairo).
Box 19; Folder 71; OG (Caserta).
Box 34; Folder 158; OG (Kunming).

ENTRY 210: PREVIOUSLY WITHDRAWN DOCUMENTS

Box 63; Folders 01521-2; War Diary 2671/CO A.
Box 72; Folder 2537; History, SOE Disagreement.

Record Group 319: Records of the Army Staff

ASSISTANT CHIEF OF STAFF, G-3 OPERATIONS,
RECORDS SECTION

Box 380; Decimal File, March 1950–51, 322 Ranger.

Record Group 331: Records of Allied Operational and Occupation Headquarters, World War II

ENTRY 1: SHAEF OFFICE OF THE CHIEF OF STAFF, SECRETARY,
GENERAL STAFF, DECIMAL FILES

Box 61; 70 Land and Sea Reconnaissance.

ENTRY 2: SHAEF OFFICE OF THE CHIEF OF STAFF, SECRETARY,
GENERAL STAFF, GEOGRAPHICAL CORRESPONDENCE FILE,
1943–45

Box 110; French Resistance.

ENTRY 12: SHAEF GENERAL STAFF, G-2, OPERATIONAL
INTELLIGENCE SUBDIVISION, NUMERIC-SUBJECT FILE

Box 12; German Report on Dieppe Raid.
Box 13; SHAEF Raids and Reconnaissance Committee.
Box 14; SHAEF Raids and Reconnaissance Committee.

ENTRY 23: SHAEF OFFICE OF THE CHIEF OF STAFF, G-3,
GENERAL RECORDS

Box 16; Dieppe Raid, 1942, Operation and Instructions.
Box 17; Dieppe Raid, 1942, Operation and Instructions.
Box 55; SHAEF Raids and Reconnaissance Committee.

ENTRY 29A: SHAEF GENERAL STAFF, G-3, OPERATIONS "A"
SECTION, NUMERIC FILE

Box 120; 17225 Raids and Reconnaissance: Policy and Operations.

ENTRY 30: SHAEF GENERAL STAFF, G-3 "C" SECTION DECIMAL FILES

Box 128; 322-4 Liaison with Special Force HQ.
Box 129; 370-1 SAS Operations Reports.
Box 130; SFHQ and Resistance Documents.
Box 131; 370-30 Strategic planning for Resistance and SAS Organizations.
Box 132; 370-21 Assistance from Special Forces to Operation Eclipse.
Box 133; 370-30 Strategic Planning for Resistance and SAS Organizations.
Box 134; OSS MU Operations.
Box 135; Resistance and SAS Organizations.
Box 136; EMFFI Reports.
Box 137; 370.2-14 Reports on SAS operations.

ENTRY 30A: SHAEF G-3, OPERATIONS "C" SUB SECTION

Box 145; 17240/16 Special Report on Resistance Operations in Brittany.
Box 146; SAS Operations.

ENTRY 30C: SHAEF GENERAL STAFF, G-3, ORGANIZATION AND EQUIPMENT SECTION, DECIMAL FILES

Box 152; 091.411-1 SAS Activities.

ENTRY 56: SHAEF SPECIAL STAFF, ADJUTANT GENERAL'S DIVISION, EXECUTIVE SECTION, DECIMAL FILES 1944

Box 41; 322-1 1st Special Service Force.
Box 60; 370-9 Reconnaissance Operations for Overlord.
Box 81; 370.5-5 30 Assault Commando.
Box 158; 1945: 322 SAARF.

ENTRY 61: SHAEF SPECIAL STAFF, ENGINEER DIVISION, EXECUTIVE OFFICE, DECIMAL FILE

Box 2; 370-26 Policy on Control of Raids and RECCE.

ENTRY 198: HQ TWELFTH ARMY GROUP, SPECIAL STAFF, ADJUTANT GENERAL SECTION, ADMINISTRATIVE BRANCH, DECIMAL FILES

Box 141; 322 Rangers.

ENTRY 199: HQ TWELFTH ARMY GROUP, SPECIAL STAFF, ADJUTANT GENERAL SECTION, ADMINISTRATIVE BRANCH, TS DECIMAL FILES

Box 30; 322 First Special Service Force.
Box 32; 322 Rangers.
Box 94; 370.2 SAS.

ENTRY 262A: SHAEF AIR STAFF, SHAEF DEPUTY CHIEF OF STAFF (AIR), SUBJECT FILES

Box 28; SAS Jeep Squadron in France.

ENTRY 268: SHAEF A-3, AIR PLANS SECTION, NUMERIC FILES

Box 70; SAS Operations in Support of Overlord.
Box 93; Employment of SAS Troops.

Record Group 338: Records of U.S. Army Operational, Tactical, and Support Organizations (World War II and Thereafter)

ENTRY 37042: UNIT RECORDS, HQ 1ST SPECIAL SERVICE FORCE

Boxes 455–64.

ENTRY 745054: RECORDS OF SIXTH ARMY G-2 SECTION

Boxes 1–27.

Record Group 407: Records of the Adjutant General's Office, 1917–

ENTRY 427: WWII OPERATIONS REPORTS

Box 70; Asiatic Theater, 92-TCC3-0.2 to 92-TF6-3.16.
Box 9575; 34th Infantry Division, 334-INF(168)-0.3.
Box 21066; Infantry INBN-1-0.
Box 21067; Infantry INBN-1-0.3.
Box 21068; Infantry INBN-1-0.7.
Box 21069; Infantry INBN-1-0.12 to INBN-1-1.14.
Box 21070; Infantry INBN-1-3.7.
Box 21071; Infantry INBN-1-3.9 to INBN-1-3.13.
Box 21072; Infantry INBN-2-0 to INBN-2-0.3.
Box 21073; Infantry INBN-2-0.3 to INBN-2PA-0.2.
Box 21074; Infantry INBN-3-0 to INBN-3-1.13.
Box 21075; Infantry INBN-4-0.1 to INBN-4-1.14.
Box 21076; Infantry INBN-5-0 to INBN-5-0.3.
Box 21077; Infantry INBN-5-0.3.
Box 21078; Infantry INBN-5-0.3 to INBN-5-1.13.
Box 21079; Infantry INBN-6-0 to INBN-6-0.3.
Box 21080; Infantry INBN-6-0.4 to INBN-6-2.2.
Box 21081; Infantry INBN-6-3 to INBN-6-3.7.
Box 21082; Infantry INBN-6-3.9 to INBN-6-30.0.
Box 21321; Infantry, INRG-5307-1.13 to INRG-7892-1.14.
Box 23274; Special Service Force, SSFE-1-0 to SSFE-1-0.3.
Box 23275; Special Service Force, SSFE-1-0.3.
Box 23276; Special Service Force, SSFE-1-0.3 to SSFE-1-2.1.
Box 23277; Special Service Force, SSFE-1-2.1.
Box 23278; Special Service Force, SSFE-1-3.1.
Box 23279; Special Service Force, SSFE-1-3.2.

Box 23280; Special Service Force, SSFE-1-3.2.
Box 23281; Special Service Force, SSFE-1-3.2 to SSFE-1-3.17.
Box 24157; Pre-Invasion Planning, 525 to 535.
Box 24369; Pre-Invasion Planning, 596 to 615A.
Box 24385; Pre-Invasion Planning, 719 to 734.

Unpublished: Private Correspondence, Diaries, Memoranda, Etc.

Imperial War Museum, London

IWM 02/56/1	Papers of Lieutenant Commander F. M. Berncastle.
IWM 03/24/1	Papers of O. A. Brown.
IWM 97/7/1	Papers of Major General T. B. L. Churchill.
IWM 77/67/1	Papers of Captain N. Clogstoun-Willmott.
IWM 03/54/1	Papers of Colonel N. A. C. Croft.
IWM 05/20/1	Papers of J. R. Davies.
IWM 03/53/1	Papers of F. Enright.
IWM 04/29/8	Papers of Major General Sir Colin Gubbins.
IWM 93/28/4	Papers of Major General J. C. Haydon.
IWM 88/48/1	Papers of Colonel T. B. Langton.
IWM PP/MCR/C13 Reels 1–5	Papers of Major General D. L. Lloyd Owen.
IWM 05/73/1	Papers of Colonel Sir Thomas Macpherson.
IWM 78/43/1	Papers of Captain J. E. C. Nicholl.
IWM 78/1/1	Papers of Captain F. R. J. Nicholls.
IWM 90/25/1	Papers of Captain M. J. Pleydell.
IWM 84/42/1	Papers of Major P. H. B. Pritchard.
IWM 67/253/1	Papers of Captain G. W. Read.
IWM 77/68/1	Papers of Commander J. S. Townson.
IWM 76/143/1	Papers of Lieutenant S. Weatherall.
IWM 99/19/1	Papers of Major B. H. Westcott.
IWM 73/46/1	Papers of Major G. S. Young.

Liddell Hart Centre for Military Archives, King's College London

KCLMA Allfrey   Papers of Lieutenant General Sir Charles Walter Allfrey (1895–1964).
KCLMA Burton   Papers of Captain John George Burton (1921–78).
KCLMA Cary-Elwes   Papers of Lieutenant Colonel Oswald Aloysius Joseph Cary-Elwes (1913–94).
KCLMA Davy   Papers of Brigadier George Mark Oswald Davy (1898–1983).
KCLMA Johnston D   Papers of Major Duncan Johnston (1914–45).
KCLMA Laycock   Papers of Major General Sir Robert Edward Laycock (1907–1968).
KCLMA McLeod   Papers of General Sir Roderick William McLeod (1905–1980).
KCLMA Mills-Roberts   Papers of Brigadier Derek Mills Roberts (1908–1980).

KCLMA Mockler-Ferryman   Papers of Brigadier Eric Mockler-Ferryman (1896–1978).
KCLMA Montanaro   Papers of Brigadier Gerald Charles Stokes Montanaro (1916–1979).
KCLMA O'Regan   Papers of Captain Patrick Valentine William Rowan O'Regan (1920–61).
KCLMA Purdon   Papers of Major General Corran William Brooke Purdon (b 1921).
KCLMA Riley   Papers of Lieutenant Commander Quintin Theodore Petroe Molesworth Riley (1905–80).
KCLMA Street   Papers of Major General Vivian Wakefield Street (1912–70).

Miscellaneous

Campbell, John. *The Green Box*. Privately held unpublished memoir.

Published: Official Documents

Briscoe, Charles H., et al. *All Roads Lead to Baghdad: Army Special Operations Forces in Iraq*. Fort Bragg, N.C: United States Army Special Operations Command History Office, 2006.

Buckley, Christopher. *Five Ventures: Iraq-Syria-Persia-Madagascar-Dodecanese*. London: HMSO, 1977.

———. *Norway, The Commandos, Dieppe*. London: HMSO, 1977.

Crowl, Philip A., and Edmund G.Love. *Seizure of the Gilberts and Marshalls*. Washington, D.C.: Office of the Chief of Military History, Department of the Army, 1955.

Department of the Army. *Field Manual No. 31–21: Guerrilla Warfare and Special Forces Operations*. Washington, D.C.: Headquarters, Department of the Army, 1961.

Destruction of an Army: The First Campaign in Libya: Sept. 1940–Feb. 1941. London: His Majesty's Stationery Office, 1941.

Dziuban, Colonel Stanley W. *United States Army in World War II – Special Studies: Military Relations Between the United States and Canada 1939–1945*. Washington, D.C.: Department of the Army, 1959.

Foot, M. R. D. *SOE in France: An Account of the Work of the British Special Operations Executive in France, 1940–1944*. London: Her Majesty's Stationary Office, 1966.

Harrison, Gordon A. *Cross-Channel Attack*. Washington D.C.: Office of the Chief of Military History, Department of the Army,: 1951.

Hinsley, F. H. *British Intelligence in the Second World War: Its Influence on Strategy and Operations*, vol. 1. London: Her Majesty's Stationary Office, 1979.

———. *British Intelligence in the Second World War: Its Influence on Strategy and Operations*, vol. 2. London: Her Majesty's Stationary Office, 1981.

Historical Division, U.S. War Department. *Merrill's Marauders*. Washington, D.C.: U.S. Army Center of Military History, 1990.

———. *Small Unit Actions*. Washington, D.C.: U.S. Army Center of Military History, 1991.

MacDonald, Charles B. *The Siegfried Line Campaign*. Washington D.C.: Office of the Chief of Military History, Department of the Army, 1963.
Ministry of Information. *Combined Operations, 1940–1942*. London: HMSO, 1943.
———. *The Eighth Army September 1941 to January 1943*. London: HMSO, 1944.
Playfair, I. S. O. *History of WWII: The Mediterranean and Middle East*, vol. 1: *The Early Successes Against Italy*. London: Her Majesty's Stationery Office, 1954.
Playfair, I. S. O., and C. J. C. Molony. *History of WWII: The Mediterranean and Middle East*, vol. 4: *The Destruction of the Axis Forces in Africa*. London: Her Majesty's Stationery Office, 1966.
Roosevelt, Kermit. *War Report of the OSS*, vol. 1. NewYork: Walker and Co., 1976.
———. *War Report of the OSS*, vol. 2: *The Overseas Targets*. Walker and Co.: New York, 1976.
United States Army. *SH 21-76: Ranger Handbook*. Fort Benning, Ga: United States Army Infantry School, July 2006.
United States Joint Chiefs of Staff. *Doctrine for Joint Special Operation*. Joint Publication 3-05, December 2003.
United States Marine Corps. *Small Wars Manual, 1940 Edition*. Washington, D.C.: United States Government Printing Office, 1940.
United States Special Operations Command (USSOCOM). 2006 Posture Statement. http://www.socom.mil/Docs. Accessed June 2007.
Wynter, H. W. *Special Forces in the Desert War 1940–1943*. Kew: Public Records Office, 2001.

Published: Autobiographies and Memoirs

Alsop, Stewart, and Braden, Thomas. *Sub Rosa: The OSS and American Espionage*. New York: Harcourt, Brace and World, Inc., 1964.
Altieri, James. *The Spearheaders*. New York: Bobbs-Merrill Co., 1960.
Bagnold, Ralph A. *Sand, Wind and War: Memoirs of a Desert Explorer*. Tucson: University of Arizona Press, 1990.
Bank, Aaron. *From OSS to Green Berets: The Birth of Special Forces*. New York: Presidio Press, 1986.
Beevor, J. G. *SOE Recollections and Reflections, 1940–1945*. London: The Bodley Head, 1981.
Benyon-Tinker, W. E. *Dust Upon the Sea*. London: Hodder and Stoughton, 1947.
Brown, Arthur. *The Jedburghs: A Short History*. Privately printed, 1991. [Copy in IWM 03/24/1].
Bowen, John. *Undercover in the Jungle*. London: William Kimber, 1978.
Bradley, Omar N. *A Soldier's Story*. New York: Henry Holt and Co., 1951.
Burhans, Robert D. *The First Special Service Force: A War History of the North Americans, 1942–44*. Washington, D.C.: Infantry Journal Press, 1947.
Byrne, J. V. *The General Salutes a Soldier*. London: Robert Hale, 1986.
Calvert, Michael. *Fighting Mad*. Shrewsbury: Airlife Publishing, 1996.

Chapman, F. Spencer. *The Jungle Is Neutral*. London: Granada Publishing, 1977.
Churchill, Thomas B. L. *Commando Crusade*. London: William Kimber, 1987.
Clarke, Dudley. *Seven Assignments*. London: Jonathan Cape, 1948.
Colby, William. *Honourable Men: My Life in the CIA*. London: Hutchinson, 1978.
Cooper, Johnny. *One of the Originals: The Story of a Founder Member of the SAS*. London: Pan Books, 1991.
Corvo, Max. *The OSS in Italy, 1942–1945*. London: Praeger, 1990.
Courtney, G. B. *SBS in World War Two: The Story of the Original Special Boat Section of the Army Commandos*. London: Robert Hale, 1983.
Cowburn, Benjamin. *No Cloak, No Dagger*. London: Jarrolds, 1960.
Crichton-Stuart, Michael. *G Patrol: The Story of the Guards Patrol of the Long Range Desert Group*. London: Tandem, 1958.
Darby, William O., and William H. Baumer. *Darby's Rangers, We Led the Way*. New York: Ballantine Books, 1980.
Dodds-Parker, Douglas. *Setting Europe Ablaze: Some Account of Ungentlemanly Warfare*. Surrey: Springwood Books, 1983.
Dunning, James. *The Fighting Fourth: No. 4 Commando at War 1940–1945*. Gloucestershire: Sutton Publishing Ltd., 2003.
Durnford-Slater, John. *Commando: Memoirs of a Fighting Commando in World War Two*. London: Greenhill Books, 2002.
Farran, Roy. *Winged Dagger: Adventures on Special Service*. Cassell: London, 1998.
Fergusson, Bernard. *The Watery Maze: The Story of Combined Operations*. London: Collins, 1961).
Frost, John. *A Drop Too Many*. London: Sphere Books, 1980.
Hackett, General Sir John. *I Was a Stranger*. London: Chatto and Windus, 1977.
Harrison, Derrick. *These Men Are Dangerous*. London: Blandford Press, 1988.
Hastings, Stephen. *The Drums of Memory: An Autobiography*. Yorkshire: Leo Cooper, 2001.
Hills, R. J. T. *Phantom Was There*. London: Edward Arnold and Co., 1951.
Hilsman, Roger. *American Guerrilla: My War Behind Japanese Lines*. Washington, D.C.: Potomac Books, 2005.
Hislop, John. *Anything but a Soldier*. London: Michael Joseph, 1965.
Hue, André, and Ewen Southby-Tailyour. *The Next Moon: The Remarkable True Story of a British Agent behind the Lines in Wartime France*. Penguin: London, 2004.
Hunt, David. *A Don at War*. London: Frank Cass, 1990.
Krueger, Walter. *From Down Under to Nippon: The Story of Sixth Army in World War II*. Washington, D.C.: Zenger Publishing Co., 1979.
Lawrence, T. E. *Seven Pillars of Wisdom*. Hertfordshire, UK: Wordsworth Classics of World Literature, 1997.
Lloyd Owen, David. *The Desert My Dwelling Place*. London: Arms and Armour, 1986.
———. *Providence Their Guide: The Long Range Desert Group 1940–45*. Barnsley, UK: Pen and Sword, 2003.

Lodwick, John. *The Filibusters: The Story of the Special Boat Service*. London: Methuen and Co. Ltd., 1947).
Lord Lovat. *March Past*. London: Weidenfeld and Nicolson, 1979.
Lindsay, Franklin. *Beacons in the Night: With the OSS and Tito's Partisans in Wartime Yugoslavia*. Stanford, Calif.: Stanford University Press, 1993.
Maclean, Fitzroy. *Eastern Approaches*. London: Webb, Son and Co. Ltd., 1949.
Marks, Leo. *Between Silk and Cyanide: A Codemaker's Story 1941–1945*. London: HarperCollins, 1999.
Masters, John. *The Road Past Mandalay*. London: Cassell and Co., 2002.
Mather, Carol. *When the Grass Stops Growing: A War Memoir*. London: Leo Cooper, 1997.
McConville, Michael. *A Small War in the Balkans: British Military Involvement in Wartime Yugoslavia, 1941–1945*. London: Macmillan, 1986.
Mousalimas, Andrew S. *Greek/American Operational Group Office of Strategic Services: Memoirs of World War II*. Preservation of American Hellenic History Network, 2004, available at http://www.pahh.com/oss.
Neville, Ralph. *Survey by Starlight: A True Story of Reconnaissance Work in the Mediterranean*. London: Hodder, 1949.
Obolensky, Serge. *One Man in His Time*. London: Hutchinson and Co. Ltd., 1960.
Ogburn, Charlton. *The Marauders*. New York: Harper and Brothers, 1959.
Owen, Ben. *With Popski's Private Army*. Wolverhampton, UK: Astrolabe Publishing, 1993.
Peers, William R., and Brelis, Dean. *Behind the Burma Road*. London: Robert Hale, 1964.
Peniakoff, Vladimir. *Popski's Private Army*. London: Cassell, 2003.
Pleydell, Malcolm James. *Born of the Desert: With the S.A.S. in North Africa*. London: Greenhill Books, 2001.
Purdon, Corran, *List the Bugle: Reminiscences of an Irish Soldier*. Greystone Books: Antrim, N.I.: Greystone Books, 1993.
Reid, Francis. *Resistance Fighter*. London: Brown, Watson Ltd., 1957 [previously published by W. and R. Chambers Ltd. as *I Was in Noah's Ark*].
Reitz, Deneys, and Smuts, J. C. S. *Commando: A Boer Journal of the Boer War*. Londdon: Faber and Faber, 1929.
Samain, Bryan. *Commando Men: The Story of the Royal Marine Commando in World War Two*. Barnsley, UK: Pen and Sword Military Classics, 2005.
Shaw, W. B. Kennedy. *Long Range Desert Group: The Story of Its Work in Libya, 1940–1943*. London: Collins, 1945.
Slim, Field Marshal Sir William. *Defeat into Victory*. London: Cassell, 1956.
Strong, Kenneth. *Intelligence at the Top: The Recollections of an Intelligence Officer*. London: Cassell, 1968.
Thompson, Robert. *Make for the Hills*. London: Pen and Sword Books/Leo Cooper, 1989.
Timpson, Alistair, and Gibson-Watt, Andrew. *In Rommel's Backyard: A Memoir of the Long Range Desert Group*. Barnsley, UK: Leo Cooper, 2000.
Truscott, Lieutenant General Lucian King, Jr. *Command Missions: A Personal Story*. New York: E. P. Dutton and Co., 1954.

Twining, Merrill B. *No Bended Knee: The Battle for Guadalcanal*. New York: Ballantine Books, 1996.
Wellsted, Ian. *SAS with the Maquis: In Action with the French Resistance, June–September 1944*. London: Greenhill Books, 1997.
Wright, Bruce S. *The Frogmen of Burma: The Story of the Sea Reconnaissance Unit*. William Kimber: London, 1970.
Yunnie, Robert Park. *Fighting with Popski's Private Army*. London: Greenhill Books, 2002 [published in 1959 as *Warriors on Wheels*].

Secondary Sources
Books

Adams, James. *Secret Armies: The Full Story of SAS, Delta Force and Spetsnaz*. London: Hutchinson, 1987.
Adams, Thomas K. *U.S. Special Operations Forces in Action: The Challenge of Unconventional Warfare*. London: Frank Cass, 1998.
Adleman, Robert H., and Walton, George. *The Devil's Brigade*. London: Corgi Books, 1968.
Alexander, Joseph H. *Storm Landings: Epic Amphibious Battles in the Central Pacific*. Annapolis, Md.: Naval Institute Press, 1997.
Ambrose, Stephen E. *Pegasus Bridge–D-Day: The Daring British Airborne Raid*. London: Pocket Books, 2003.
Anglim, Simon. *Orde Wingate and the British Army, 1922–1944*. London: Pickering and Chatto, 2010.
Appleyard, J. E. *Geoffrey, Being the Story of "Apple" of the Commandos and Special Air Service Regiment*. London: Blandford Press, 1946.
Arnold, R., *The True Book about the Commandos*. London: Muller, 1954.
Arquilla, John (ed.). *From Troy to Entebbe: Special Operations in Ancient and Modern Times*. Lanham, Md.: University Press of America, 1996.
Asher, Michael. *Get Rommel: The Secret British Mission to Kill Hitler's Greatest General*. London: Cassell, 2004.
———. *The Regiment: The Real Story of the SAS*. London: Penguin, 2007.
Asprey, Robert B. *War in the Shadows: The Guerrilla in History*. New York: William Morrow and Company, 1994.
Barbey, Daniel E. *MacArthur's Amphibious Navy: Seventh Amphibious Force Operations 1943–1945*. Annapolis, Md.: U.S. Naval Institute Press, 1969.
Barnett, Frank R., Hugh B. Tovar, and Richard H. Shultz (eds.). *Special Operations in U.S. Strategy*. Washington, D.C.: National Defense University Press, 1984.
Beaumont, Roger *Military Elites*. London: Robert Hale and Co., 1974.
———. *Special Operations and Elite Units: A Research Guide*. Westport, Conn: Greenwood, 1988.
———. *Joint Military Operations: A Short History*. Westport, Conn.: Greenwood, 1993.
Beckett, Ian F.W. *Modern Insurgencies and Counter-Insurgencies: Guerrillas and Their Opponents Since 1750*. London: Routledge, 2001.
Beevor, Antony. *Crete: The Battle and the Resistance*. London: Penguin Books, 1991.

Bennett, Ralph. *Ultra and the Mediterranean Strategy 1941–1945*. London: Hamish Hamilton, 1989.
Bidwell, Shelford. *The Chindit War: The Campaign in Burma 1944*. London: Book Club Associates, 1979.
Bidwell, Shelford, and Dominick Graham. *Firepower: British Army Weapons and Theories of War 1904–1945*. London: George Allen and Unwin, 1982.
Bierman, John, and Colin Smith. *Alamein: War Without Hate*. London: Penguin Books, 2002.
Bjorge, Gary J., *Merrill's Marauders: Combined Operations in Northern Burma in 1944*. Fort Leavenworth, Kans.: Combat Studies Institute, U.S. Army Command and General Staff College, 1996.
Black, Robert W.,*Rangers in Korea*. New York: Ballantine Books, 1989.
———. *Rangers in World War II*. New York: Ballantine Books, 1992.
Bond, Brian (ed.). *The First World War and British Military History*. Oxford: Clarendon Press, 1991.
Bounds, Gary L. *CSI Report No.4: Notes on Elite Units*. Fort Leavenworth, Kans.: Combat Studies Institute U.S. Army Command and General Staff College, 1984.
Bradford, Roy, and Martin Dillon. *Rouge Warrior of the SAS: Lt-Col. "Paddy" Blair Mayne*. London: John Murray, 1987.
Breuer, William B. *MacArthur's Undercover War: Spies, Saboteurs, Guerrillas, and Secret Missions*. Chichester, UK: John Wiley and Sons, 1995.
Butler, Rupert. *Hand of Steel: The Story of the Commandos*. London: Severn House Publishers, 1981.
Callwell, C. E. *Small Wars: Their Principles and Practice*. University of Nebraska Press: Lincoln, 1996.
Campbell, John P. *Dieppe Revisited: A Documentary Investigation*. London: Frank Cass, 1993.
Carrell, Paul. *The Foxes of the Desert*. London: Macdonald, 1960.
Casey, William. *The Secret War Against Hitler*. London: Simon and Schuster, 1990.
Chappell, Mike. *Army Commandos 1940–1945*. London: Osprey Publishing, 1996.
Churchill, Winston S., *The Second World War*, vol. 1: *The Gathering Storm*. London: Cassell, 1948.
———. *The Second World War*, vol. 2: *Their Finest Hour*. London: Cassell, 1950.
———. *The Second World War*, vol. 3: *The Grand Alliance*. London: Cassell, 1950.
———. *The Second World War*, vol. 4: *The Hinge of Fate*. London: Cassell, 1951.
———. *The Second World War*, vol. 5: *Closing the Ring*. London: Cassell, 1952.
Clancy, Tom, Carl Stiner, and Tony Koltz. *Shadow Warriors: Inside the Special Forces*. London: Sidgwick and Jackson, 2002.
Clausewitz, Carl von. *On War*. Hertfordshire, UK: Wordsworth Classics of World Literature, 1997.
Clayton, Peter. *Desert Explorer: Biography of Colonel P. A. Clayton*. Cornwall, UK: Zerzura Press, 1998.

Clifford, Alexander. *Three against Rommel: The Campaigns of Wavell, Auchinleck and Alexander.* London: George G. Harrap and Co., 1943.
Clifford, Kenneth J. *Amphibious Warfare Development in Britain and America from 1920 to 1940.* New York: Edgewood, 1983.
Cocks, A. E. *Churchill's Secret Army 1939–45.* Lewes, UK: Book Guild, 1992.
Cohen, Eliot A. *Commandos and Politicians: Elite Units in Modern Democracies.* Cambridge, Mass.: Harvard Studies in International Affairs No. 40, 1978.
Collins, John M. *Special Operations Forces: An Assessment*, Washington D.C.: Institute for Strategic Studies. National Defense University Press, 1994.
Constable, Trevor James. *Hidden Heroes: Historic Achievements of Men of Courage.* London: Arthur Barker, 1971.
Cook, Graeme. *None but the Valiant.* London: Rupert Hart-Davis, 1972.
———. *Small Boat Raiders.* London: Hart-Davis, MacGibbon, 1977.
Cookridge, E. H. *Inside SOE: The Story of Special Operations in Western Europe, 1940–45.* London: Arthur Barker, 1966.
Courtney, G. B. *Silent Fleet: The History of "Z" Special Operations, 1942–45.* Melbourne: R. J. and S. P. Austin, 1993.
Cowles, Virginia. *The Phantom Major.* London: Armarda, 1989.
Cruickshank, Charles. *Deception in World War II.* Oxford: Oxford University Press, 1979.
———. *SOE in the Far East.* Oxford: Oxford University Press, 1983.
Cunningham, Chet. *The Frogmen of World War II: An Oral History of the U.S. Navy's Underwater Demolition Teams.* New York: Pocket Star Books, 2005.
Danchev, Alex. "Great Britain: The Indirect Strategy." In David Reynolds, Warren F. Kimball, and A. O. Chubarian, (eds.), *Allies at War: the Soviet, American, and British Experience, 1939–1945.* New York: St. Martin's Press, 1994.
Dear, Ian. *Sabotage and Subversion: The SOE and OSS at War.* London: Cassell, 1996.
———. *Ten Commando.* London: Pen and Sword, 2010.
Devins, Joseph H., Jr. *The Vaagso Raid: The Commando Attack That Changed the Course of World War II.* London: Robert Hale, 1967.
Dugan, Sally. *Commando: The Elite Fighting Forces of the Second World War.* London: Channel 4 Books, 2001.
Dunlay, Thomas W. *Wolves for the Blue Soldiers: Indian Scouts and Auxiliaries with the United States Army, 1860–90.* Lincoln: University of Nebraska Press, 1982.
Dunstan, Simon. *Commandos: Churchill's "Hand of Steel."* Surrey, UK: Ian Allan, 2003.
Dwyer, John B. *Seaborne Deception: The History of U.S. Navy Beach Jumpers.* London: Praeger, 1992.
———. *Scouts and Raiders: The Navy's First Special Warfare Commandos.* London: Praeger, 1993.
Eisenhower, John S. D. *Allies: Pearl Harbor to D-Day.* New York: Da Capo Press, 2000.

Elliott-Bateman, Michael (ed.). *The Fourth Dimension of* Warfare, vol. 1: *Intelligence, Subversion, Resistance*. Manchester, UK: Manchester University Press, 1970.

Ellis, John. *The World War II Databook: The Essential Facts and Figures for All the Combatants*, 2nd ed. London: Aurum Press, 2003.

Erskine, David. *The Scots Guards 1919–1955*. London: William Clowes and Sons, 1956.

Fane, Francis Douglas, and Dan Moore. *The Naked Warriors*. London: Allan Wingate, 1957.

Fenby, Jonathan. *Alliance: The Inside Story of How Roosevelt, Stalin and Churchill Won One War and Began Another*. London: Simon and Schuster, 2006.

Foley, Charles. *Commando Extraordinary: Otto Skorzeny*. London: Cassell. 1987.

Foot, M. R. D. *Resistance: An Analysis of European Resistance to Nazism 1940–1945*. London: Eyre Methuen, 1976.

———. *SOE: An Outline History of the Special Operations Executive 1940–46*. London: BBC, 1984.

Foot, Michael, and J. M. Langley. *MI 9: The British Secret Service that fostered Escape and Evasion: 1939–1945 and Its American Counterpart*. London: The Bodley Head, 1979.

Ford, Roger. *Fire from the Forest: The SAS Brigade in France, 1944*. London: Cassell, 2003.

———. *Steel from the Sky: The Jedburgh Raiders, France 1944*. London: Cassell, 2004.

Fowler, Will. *The Commandos at Dieppe: Rehearsal for D-Day*. London: HarperCollins, 2002.

French, David. *The British Way in Warfare, 1688–2000*. London: Unwin Hyman, 1990.

Fuller, J. F. C. *Lectures on F.S.R. III (Operations between Mechanized Forces)*. London: Sifton Praed and Co., 1932.

Fullick, Roy. *Shan Hackett: The Pursuit of Exactitude*. Barnsley, UK: Leo Cooper, 2003.

Funk, Arthur Layton. *Hidden Ally: The French Resistance, Special Operations, and the Landings in Southern France, 1944*. London: Greenwood, 1992.

Garrett, Richard. *The Raiders: The World's Elite Strike Forces*. Devon, UK: David and Charles, 1980.

Gaujac, Paul. *Special Forces in the Invasion of France*, trans. Janice Lert. Paris: Historie et Collections, 1999.

Geraghty, Tony. *Who Dares Wins: The Story of the SAS 1950–1992*. London: Warner Books, 1993.

Gilbert, Adrian. *The Imperial War Museum Book of the Desert War*. London: Sidgwick and Jackson, 1992.

Gilmore, Allison B. *You Can't Fight Tanks with Bayonets: Psychological Warfare against the Japanese Army in the Southwest Pacific*. Lincoln: University of Nebraska Press, 1998.

Gordon, John W. *The Other Desert War: British Special Forces in North Africa 1940–1943*. London: Greenwood, 1987.

Gray, Colin S. *Explorations in Strategy*. London: Greenwood, 1996.
———. *Modern Strategy*. Oxford: Oxford University Press, 1999.
———. *Another Bloody Century: Future Warfare*. London: Weidenfeld and Nicholson, 2005.
Grenier, John. *The First Way of War: American War Making on the Frontier, 1607–1814*. Cambridge: Cambridge University Press, 2005.
Handel, Michael I. (ed.) *Intelligence and Military Operations*. Oxon, UK: Frank Cass, 1990.
Harris Smith, Richard. *OSS: The Secret History of America's First Central Intelligence Agency*. Berkeley: University of California Press, 1972.
Hastings, Max. *Das Reich: Resistance and the March of the 2nd SS Panzer Division through France, June 1944*. London: Michael Joseph, 1981.
Hawes, Stephen, and Ralph White (eds.). *Resistance in Europe 1939–1945*. London: Butler and Tanner, 1975.
Heaton, Colin D. *German Anti-Partisan Warfare in Europe*. Atglen, Pa.: Schiffer Publishing, 2001.
Heilbrunn, Otto. *Partisan Warfare*. London: George Allen and Unwin, 1962.
———. *Warfare in the Enemy's Rear*. London: George Allen and Unwin, 1963.
Heimark, Bruce H. *The OSS Norwegian Special Operations Group in World War II*. London: Praeger, 1994.
Hoe, Alan. *David Stirling: The Authorised Biography of the Creator of the SAS*. London: Warner Books, 1992.
Hoffman, Bruce. *Commando Raids: 1946–1983*. Santa Monica, Calif.: RAND Corporation, 1985.
Hoffman, Jon T. *From Makin to Bougainville: Marine Raiders in the Pacific War*. Washington, D.C.: Marine Corps Historical Center, 1995.
Hogan, David W., Jr. *Raiders or Elite Infantry? The Changing Role of the U.S. Army Rangers from Dieppe to Grenada*. London: Greenwood, 1992.
———. *U.S. Army Special Operations in World War II*. Washington D.C.: Department of the Army, Center for Military History, 1992.
Holden Reid, Brian. "T. E. Lawrence and His Biographers." In Brian Bond (ed.), *The First World War and British Military History*. Oxford: Clarendon Press, 1991).
Holland, Jeffrey. *The Aegean Mission: Allied Operations in the Dodecanese, 1943*. Westport, Conn.: Greenwood, 1988.
Holt, Thaddeus. *The Deceivers: Allied Military Deception in the Second World War*. London: Scribner, 2004.
Hooton, E. R. *Eagle in Flames: The Fall of the Luftwaffe*. London: Brockhampton Press, 1997.
Horner, David *SAS: Phantoms of the Jungle; A History of the Australian Special Air Service*. London: Allen and Unwin, 1989.
House, Jonathan M. *Combined Arms Warfare in the Twentieth Century*. Lawrence: University Press of Kansas, 2001.
Howarth, Patrick (ed.). *Special Operations*. London: Routledge and Kegan Paul, 1955.
———. *Undercover: The Men and Women of the SOE*. London: Phoenix Press, 2000.

Hoyt, Edwin P. *Airborne: The History of American Parachute Forces*. New York: Stein and Day, 1978.
Ireland, Bernard. *The War in the Mediterranean 1940–1943*. London: Arms and Armour, 1993.
Isely, Jeter A., and Philip A. Crowl. *The U.S. Marines and Amphibious War: Its Theory and Its Practice in the Pacific*. Princeton, N.J.: Princeton University Press, 1951.
Jenner, Robin, David List, and Mike Badrocke. *The Long Range Desert Group 1940–1945*. Osprey New Vanguard Series no. 32. Oxford: Osprey Publishing, 1999.
Jewell, Derek (ed.). *Alamein and the Desert War*. London: Sphere Books, 1967.
Jones, R.V. *Most Secret War: British Scientific Intelligence 1939–1945*. London: Hodder and Stoughton, 1979.
Jones, Tim. *Postwar Counterinsurgency and the SAS, 1945–1952: A Special Type of Warfare*. London: Frank Cass, 2001.
———. *SAS Zero Hour: The Secret Origins of the Special Air Service*. London: Greenhill Books, 2006.
De Jong, Louis. *The German Fifth Column in the Second World War*. London: Routledge and Kegan Paul: London, 1956.
Keegan, John. *The Second World War*. London: Hutchinson, 1989.
———. *Churchill*. London: Weidenfeld and Nicholson, 2002.
Kelly, Saul. *The Hunt for Zerzura: The Lost Oasis and the Desert War*. London: John Murray, 2002.
Kemp, Anthony. *The SAS at War: The Special Air Service Regiment, 1941–1945*. London: John Murray, 1991.
Keyes, Elizabeth. *Geoffrey Keyes V.C.* London: George Newnes, 1956.
King, Michael J. *Rangers: Selected Combat Operations in World War II*. Fort Leavenworth, Kans.: Combat Studies Institute, U.S. Army Command and General Staff College, June 1985.
Kiras, James D. *Special Operations and Strategy: From World War II to the War on Terrorism*. New York: Routledge, 2006.
Kolenda, Christopher (ed.). *Leadership: The Warrior's Art*. Carlisle, Pa: Army War College Foundation Press, 2001.
Ladd, James, *Assault from the Sea, 1939–45: The Craft, the Landings, the Men*. Newton Abbot, UK: David and Charles, 1976.
———. *Commandos and Rangers of World War II*. London: MacDonald and Jane's, 1978.
———. *SBS—The Invisible Raiders: The History of the Special Boat Squadron from World War Two to the Present*. London: Arms and Armour, 1983.
———. *By Sea, by Land: The Royal Marines 1919-1997 An Authorised History*. London: HarperCollins, 1998.
———. *SAS Operations: More than Daring*. London: Robert Hale, 1999.
Laffin, John. *Raiders: Great Exploits of the Second World War*. Gloucestershire, UK: Sutton Publishing, 1999.
Lamb, Richard. *War in Italy 1943–1945: A Brutal Story*. London: John Murray, 1993.

Lankford, Nelson Douglas (ed.). *OSS against the Reich: The World War II Diaries of Colonel David K. E. Bruce*. Kent, Ohio: Kent State University Press, 1991.

Landsborough, Gordon. *Tobruk Commando: The Raid to Destroy Rommel's Base*. London: Greenhill Books, 1989.

Lane, Ronald L. *Rudder's Rangers*. Manassas, Va.: Ranger Associates, 1979.

Langelaan, George. *Knights of the Floating Silk*. London: Hutchinson, 1959.

Larrabee, Eric. *Commander in Chief: Franklin Delano Roosevelt, His Lieutenants, and Their War*. London: Andre Deutsch, 1987.

Last, David, Bernd Horn, J. Paul de B. Taillon (eds.). *Force of Choice: Perspectives on Special Operations*. Montreal: McGill-Queens University Press, 2004.

Lewes, John. *Jock Lewes: Co-Founder of the SAS*. Barnsley, UK: Leo Cooper, 2000.

Lewin, Ronald. *The Life and Death of the Afrika Korps: A Biography*. London: B. T. Batsford, 1977.

———. *The Chief: Field Marshal Lord Wavell*. London: Hutchinson, 1980.

Lewis, Adrian R. *Omaha Beach: A Flawed Victory*. Chapel Hill: University of North Carolina Press, 2001.

Lewis, Jon E. (ed.). *The Mammoth Book of SAS and Special Forces: True Stories of the Fighting Elite behind Enemy Lines*. London: Robinson, 2004.

Lewis, Laurence. *Echoes of Resistance: British Involvement with the Italian Partisans*. Kent, UK: Costello, 1985.

Lewis, S. J. *Jedburgh Team Operations in Support of the 12th Army Group, August 1944*. Fort Leavenworth, Kans.: Combat Studies Institute, 1991.

Liddell Hart, B. H. *The Future of Infantry*. London: Faber and Faber, 1933.

——— (ed.) *The Rommel Papers*. London: Collins, 1953.

Linderman, Gerald F. *The World Within War: America's Combat Experience in World War II*. Cambridge, Mass.: Harvard University Press, 1997.

Linn, Brian McAllister. *The U.S. Army and Counterinsurgency in the Philippine War, 1899–1902*. Chapel Hill: University of North Carolina Press, 1989.

———. *The Philippine War, 1899–1902*. Lawrence: University Press of Kansas, 2002.

Lucas, James. *War in the Desert: The Eighth Army at El Alamein*. London: Arms and Armour Press, 1982.

———. *Kommando: German Special Forces of World War Two*. New York: St. Martin's Press, 1985.

Lucas Phillips, C. E. *Cockleshell Heroes*. London: Pan Books, 1956.

———. *The Greatest Raid of All*. London: Pan Books, 2000.

Mackay, Francis. *Overture to Overlord*. Barnsley, UK: Pen and Sword, 2005.

Mackenzie, William. *The Secret History of S.O.E.: Special Operations Executive 1940–1945*. London: St. Ermin's Press, 2002.

Mackenzie, J. J., and Brian Holden Reid (eds.). *The British Army and the Operational Level of War*. London: Tri-Service Press, 1989.

Mackey, Robert Russell. *The Uncivil War: Irregular Warfare in the Upper South, 1861–1865*. Norman: University of Oklahoma Press, 2004.

Macksey, Kenneth. *The Partisans of Europe in World War II*. London: Hart-Davis, MacGibbon, 1975.
———. *Commando Strike: The Story of Amphibious Raiding in World War II*. London: Leo Cooper, 1985.
Manchester, William. *American Caesar: Douglas MacArthur 1880–1964*. New York: Dell Publishing, 1978.
Marquis, Susan L. *Unconventional Warfare: Rebuilding U.S. Special Operations Forces*. Washington, D.C.: Brookings Institution, 1997.
Marrinan, Patrick. *Colonel Paddy: The Man Who Dared*. Belfast: Pretoni Press, 1983.
Marshall, Bruce. *The White Rabbit*. London: Cassell, 2000.
Mattingly, Robert E. *Herringbone Cloak—GI Dagger: Marines of the OSS*. Quantico, Va.: USMC Command and Staff College, 1979.
Maule, Henry. *Out of the Sand: The Epic Story of General Leclerc and the Fighting Free French*. London: Odhams Books, 1966.
McDonald, Gabrielle. *New Zealand's Secret Heroes: Don Stott and the "Z" Special Unit*. Auckland, NZ: Reed Books, 1991)
McMichael, Major Scott R. *A Historical Perspective on Light Infantry*. Combat Studies Institute Research Survey no. 6. Fort Leavenworth, Kans.: U.S. Army Command and General Staff College, 1987.
McMillan, Richard. *Rendezvous with Rommel: The Story of Eighth Army*. London: Jarrold's, 1945.
McRaven, William H. *SPEC OPS—Case Studies in Special Operations Warfare: Theory and Practice*. Novato, Calif.: Presidio Press, 1995.
Mead, Peter. *Orde Wingate and the Historians*. Devon, UK: Merlin Books, 1987.
Melville, M. Leslie. *The Story of the Lovat Scouts 1900–1980*. Edinburgh: St. Andrew Press, 1981.
Messenger, Charles. *The Commandos 1940–46*. London: William Kimber, 1985.
Messenger, Charles, George Young, and Stephen Rose. *The Middle East Commandos*. Northamptonshire, UK: William Kimber, 1988.
Meyers, Bruce F. *Fortune Favors the Brave: The Story of First Force Recon*. Annapolis, Md.: Naval Institute Press, 2000.
Miksche, F.O. *Secret Forces: The Technique of Underground Movements*. London: Faber and Faber, 1950.
Millar, George. *The Bruneval Raid: Stealing Hitler's Radar*. London: Cassell, 2002.
Miller, Russell *The Commandos*. Chicago: Time-Life Books, 1981.
Millett, Allan R., and Williamson Murray (eds.). *Military Effectiveness*, vol. 3: *The Second World War*. London: Allen and Unwin, 1988.
———. *Military Innovation in the Interwar Period*. Cambridge: Cambridge University Press, 1996.
Millett, Allan R., and Peter Maslowski. *For the Common Defense: A Military History of the United States of America*, rev. and exp. ed. New York: Free Press, 1994.
Mockaitis, Thomas R. *British Counterinsurgency, 1919–1960*. London: Macmillan, 1990.

Moreman, Tim. *British Commandos 1940–46*. New York: Osprey Publishing, 2006.
Moore, Robin. *Task Force Dagger: The Hunt for Bin Laden*. London: Macmillan, 2003.
Moorehead, Alan. *African Trilogy: The North African Campaign 1940–43*. London: Cassell, 1998.
Morgan, Mike. *Daggers Drawn: Second World War Heroes of the SAS and SBS*. Gloucestershire, UK: Sutton Publishing, 2000.
———. *Sting of the Scorpion: The Inside Story of the Long Range Desert Group*. Gloucestershire, UK: Sutton Publishing, 2003.
Morris, Eric. *Churchill's Private Armies: British Special Forces in Europe 1939–1942*. London: Hutchinson, 1986.
———. *Guerrillas in Uniform: Churchill's Private Armies in the Middle East and the War against Japan 1940–1945*. London: Hutchinson, 1989.
Mortimer, Gavin. *Stirling's Men: The Inside History of SAS in World War II*. London: Weidenfeld and Nicolson, 2004.
Nagl, John A. *Learning to Eat Soup with a Knife: Counterinsurgency Lessons from Malaya and Vietnam*. Chicago: University of Chicago Press, 2005.
Neillands, Robin, *In the Combat Zone: Special Forces Since 1945*. New York: New York University Press, 1998.
Newsinger, John, *Dangerous Men: The SAS and Popular Culture*. London: Pluto Press, 1997.
Nutting, David (ed.). *Attain by Surprise: The Story of 30 Assault Unit Royal Navy/Royal Marine Commando and of Intelligence by Capture*. Chichester, UK: David Colver, 1997.
Oakley, Derek. *Behind Japanese Lines: The Untold Story of Royal Marine Detachment 385*. Portsmouth, UK: Royal Marines Historical Society, 1996.
O'Carroll, Brendan. *Bearded Brigands: The Diaries of Trooper Frank Joplin*. Dublin: O'Brien Press, 2002.
O'Dell, James Douglas. *The Water Is Never Cold: The Origins of the U.S. Navy's Combat Demolition Units, UDTs, and SEALs*. Washington, D.C.: Brassey's, 2000.
Oliver, David. *Airborne Espionage: International Special Duties Operations in the World Wars*. Gloucestershire, UK: Sutton Publishing, 2005.
O'Neill, Richard. *Suicide Squads*. London: Salamander/Lansdowne, 1981.
Osanka, Franklin Mark (ed.). *Modern Guerrilla Warfare: Fighting Communist Guerrilla Movements, 1941–1961*. New York: Free Press of Glencoe, 1962.
O'Toole, G. J. A. *Honorable Treachery: A History of U.S. Intelligence, Espionage, and Covert Action: From the American Revolution to the CIA*. New York: Atlantic Monthly Press, 1991.
Otway, T B. H. *The Second World War, 1939–1945: Airborne Forces*. London: Imperial War Museum, 1990.
Overy, Richard. *Why the Allies Won*. New York: W. W. Norton and Company, 1995.
Paddock, Alfred H., Jr. *U.S. Army Special Operations: Its Origins*, rev. ed. Lawrence: University Press of Kansas, 2002.
Parker, John, *SBS: The Inside Story of the Special Boat Service*. London: Headline, 1998.

———. *Commandos: The Inside Story of Britain's Most Elite Fighting Force*. London: Headline, 2000.

———. *The Paras: The Inside Story of Britain's Toughest Regiment*. London: Metro Publishing, 2002.

Perrett, Bryan. *Desert Warfare: From Its Roman Origins to the Gulf Conflict*. Northamptonshire, UK: Patrick Stephens, 1998.

Perry, F. W. *The Commonwealth Armies: Manpower and Organisation in Two World Wars*. Manchester, UK: Manchester University Press, 1988.

Pitt, Barrie: *The Crucible of War: Western Desert 1941*. London: Jonathan Cape, 1980.

———. *The Crucible of War: Year of Alamein 1942*. London: Jonathan Cape, 1982.

———. *Special Boat Squadron: The story of the SBS in the Mediterranean*. London: Century Publishing, 1983.

Porch, Douglas. *Hitler's Mediterranean Gamble: The North African and the Mediterranean Campaigns in World War II*. London: Weidenfeld and Nicolson, 2004.

Posen, Barry R. *The Sources of Military Doctrine: France, Britain, and Germany Between the World Wars*. London: Cornell University Press, 1984.

Prefer, Nathan N. *Vinegar Joe's War: Stilwell's Campaigns for Burma*. Novato, Calif.: Presidio Press, 2000.

Rankin, Nicolas. *Churchill's Wizards: The British Genius for Deception, 1914–1945*. London: Faber and Faber, 2008.

Raugh, Harold E. *Wavell in the Middle East 1939–1941: A Study in Generalship*. London: Brassey's, 1993.

Reynolds, David. *The Creation of the Anglo-American Alliance: A Study in Competitive Cooperation*. London: Europa, 1981.

———. *Rich Relations: The American Occupation of Britain, 1942–1945*. London: HarperCollins, 1996.

———. *In Command of History: Churchill Fighting and Writing the Second World War*. London: Penguin Books, 2005.

Reynolds, David, Warren F. Kimball, and A. O. Chubarian (eds.). *Allies at War: the Soviet, American, and British Experience, 1939–1945*. New York: St. Martin's Press, 1994.

Rhodes-James, Richard. *Chindit*. London: John Murray, 1980.

Robertson, Terence. *Dieppe: The Shame and The Glory*. London: Pan Books, 1965.

Rogers, Anthony. *Churchill's Folly— Leros and the Aegean: The Last Great British Defeat of World War Two*. London: Cassell, 2004.

Rooney, David. *Wingate and the Chindits: Redressing the Balance*. London: Arms and Armour, 1994.

Rottman, Gordon L. *U.S. Special Warfare Units in the Pacific Theater 1941–45: Scouts, Raiders, Rangers and Reconnaissance Units*. New York: Osprey Publishing, 2005.

Royle, Trevor. *Orde Wingate: Irregular Soldier*. London: Phoenix Giant, 1995.

Saunders, Hilary St. George. *The Green Beret: The Story of the Commandos 1940–1945*. London: Michael Joseph Ltd., 1949.

Schrijvers, Peter. *The Crash of Ruin: American Combat Soldiers in Europe during World War II*. New York: New York University Press, 1998.
Seymour, William. *British Special Forces: The Story of Britain's Undercover Soldiers*. Barnsley, UK: Pen and Sword Military Classics, 2006.
Sheffield, G.D. (ed.). *Leadership and Command: The Anglo-American Military Experience Since 1861*. London: Brassey's, 1997.
Sides, Hampton. *Ghost Soldiers: The Forgotten Epic Story of World War II's Most Dramatic Mission*. New York: Doubleday, 2001.
Springer, Joseph A. *The Black Devil Brigade: An Oral History*. New York: ibooks, inc., 2001.
Stafford, David. *British and European Resistance, 1940–1945: A Survey of the Special Operations Executive, with Documents*. Toronto: University of Toronto Press, 1980.
———. *Camp X: SOE and the American Connection*. London: Viking, 1988.
———. *Roosevelt and Churchill: Men of Secrets*. London: Abacus, 1999.
———. *Churchill and Secret Service*. London: Abacus, 2000.
———. *Secret Agent: The True Story of the Special Operations Executive*. London: BBC Worldwide Limited, 2000.
Strawson, John. *A History of the SAS Regiment*. London: Grafton Books, 1986.
Stevens, Gordon. *The Originals: The Secret History of the Birth of the SAS, in Their Own Words*. London: Ebury Press, 2005.
Sutherland, Daniel E. *A Savage Conflict: The Decisive Role of Guerrillas in the American Civil War*. Chapel Hill: University of North Carolina Press, 2009.
Sutherland, Jonathan. *Elite Troops of WWII*. Shrewsbury, UK: Airlife Publishing, 2003.
Swinson, Arthur. *The Raiders: Desert Strike Force*. Campaign Book no. 2 of Purnell's *History of the Second World War*. London: Macdonald, 1968.
Terraine, John. *The Right of the Line: The Royal Air Force in the European War 1939–1945*. London: Hodder and Stoughton, 1985.
Thompson, Julian. *Ready for Anything: The Parachute Regiment at War, 1940–1982*. London: Weidenfeld and Nicolson, 1989.
———. *The Imperial War Museum Book of War Behind Enemy Lines*. London: Sidgwick and Jackson, 1998.
———. *The Royal Marines: From Sea Soldiers to a Special Force*. London: Pan Books, 2000.
———. *The Imperial War Museum Book of the War in Burma, 1942–1945*. London: Sidgwick and Jackson, 2002.
Thompson, Leroy. *U.S. Special Forces of World War Two, Uniforms Illustrated 1*. London: Arms and Armour Press, 1984.
———. *U.S. Special Forces, 1941–1987*. Poole, UK: Blandford Books, 1987.
———. *America's Commandos: U.S. Special Operations Forces of World War II and Korea*. London: Greenhill Books, 2001.
Thorne, Christopher. *Allies of a Kind: The United States, Britain and the War against Japan, 1941–1945*. Oxford: Oxford University Press, 1978.
Trenowden, Ian, *Stealthily by Night—The COPPists: Clandestine Beach Reconnaissance and Operations in World War II*. Manchester, UK: Crécy Books, 1995.

Tuchman, Barbara. *Sand Against the Wind: Stilwell and the American Experience in China*. London: Macmillan, 1971.
Tulloch, D. *Wingate in Peace and War*. London: Macdonald, 1972.
Vandenbroucke, Lucien S. *Perilous Options: Special Operations as an Instrument of U.S. Foreign Policy*. New York: Oxford University Press, 1993.
Vagts, Alfred, *Landing Operations: Strategy, Psychology, Tactics, Politics, from Antiquity to 1945*. Washington D.C.: Military Service Publishing Company, 1946.
Van der Bijl, Nick, *No. 10 (Inter-Allied) Commando 1942–45: Britain's Secret Commando*. New York: Osprey Publishing, 2006.
Van Wagner, R.D. *Any Place, Any Time, Any Where: The 1st Air Commandos in WWII*. Atglen, Pa.: Schiffer Publishing, 1998.
Vaughan-Thomas, Wynford. *Anzio*. London: Longmans, 1961.
Villa, Brian Loring. *Unauthorized Action: Mountbatten and the Dieppe Raid 1942*. London: Oxford University Press, 1989.
Warner, Philip., *The Special Boat Squadron*. London: Sphere Books, 1983.
———. *The Special Air Service*. London: Sphere Books, 1986.
———. *Auchinleck: The Lonely Soldier*. London: Cassell, 2001.
———. *Secret Forces of World War II*. Barnsley, UK: Pen and Sword, 2004.
Weale, Adrian. *Secret Warfare: Special Operations Forces from the Great Game to the SAS*. London: Hodder and Stoughton, 1997.
Weigley, Russell F. *History of the United States Army*. London: B. T. Batsford, 1967.
———. *The American Way of War: A History of United States Strategy and Policy*. London: Collier Macmillan Publishers, 1973.
Wienberg, Gerhard L. *A World at Arms: A Global History of World War II*. Cambridge: Cambridge University Press: 1994.
Weiss, Steve. *Allies in Conflict: Anglo-American Strategic Negotiations, 1938–44*. London: Macmillan Press, 1996.
Whiting, Charles. *The Battle of Hurtgen Forest*. London: Pan Books, 2003.
Whittaker, Len. *Some Talk of Private Armies*. Hertfordshire, UK: Albanium Publishing, 1984.
Windmill, Lorna Almonds. *Gentleman Jim: The Wartime Story of a Founder of the SAS and Special Forces*. London: Constable and Robinson, 2001.
Woollcombe, Robert. *The Campaigns of Wavell 1939–1943*. London: Cassell, 1959.
Young, Peter. *Commando*. London: Pan/Ballantine Books, 1969.
Yu, Maochun, *OSS in China: Prelude to Cold War*. New Haven, Conn.: Yale University Press, 1996.
Zedric, Lance Q. *Silent Warriors of World War II: The Alamo Scouts behind Japanese Lines*. Ventura, Calif.: Pathfinder Publishing, 1995.
Zedric, Lance Q., and Michael F. Dilley. *Elite Warriors: 300 Years of America's Best Fighting Troops*. Ventura, Calif.; Pathfinder Publishing, 1996.

Articles

Absalom, Roger. "Hiding History: The Allies, the Resistance and the Others in Occupied Italy 1943–1945." *Historical Journal* 38, no.1 (March 1995): 111–31.
Andrews, R. D. A. "Special Boat Section: Royal Marines." *Marine Corps Gazette* 39, no. 12 (December 1955): 48–52.
Anglim, Simon. "MI(R), G(R) and British Covert Operations, 1939–42." *Intelligence and National Security* 20, no. 4 (December 2005): 631–53.
———. "'Callwell versus Graziani: How the British Army Applied 'Small Wars' Techniques In Major Operations in Africa and the Middle East, 1940–41." *Small Wars and Insurgencies* 19, no. 4 (December 2008): 588–608.
Arnoldt, Robert P. "The Dieppe Raid: A Failure That Led to Success." *Armour* 900, no. 4 (July–August 1981): 12–191.
Asprey, Robert B. "Special Forces: Europe." *Army*, January 1962, 56–61.
Bailey, Roderick. "OSS-SOE Relations, Albania, 1943–44." *Intelligence and National Security* 15, no. 2 (2000): 20–35.
Berens, Robert J. "First Encounters." *Army* 42, no. 7 (July 1992): 45–48.
Bidwell, Shelford. "Irregular Warfare: Partisans, Raiders and Guerrillas." *Journal of the Royal United Services Institute for Defence Studies* 122, no. 3 (September 1977): 80–81.
Brailey, Malcolm. "The Transformation of Special Operations Forces in Contemporary Conflict: Strategy, Missions, Organisation and Tactics." In *Land Warfare Studies Centre, Working Paper no. 127*, November 2005.
Briscoe, Charles H. "Major Herbert R. Brucker SF Pioneer, Part III: SOE Training and 'Team HERMIT' into France." *Veritas: Journal of Army Special Operations History* 3, no. 1 (2007): 72–85.
———. "Major Herbert R. Brucker SF Pioneer, Part IV: SO Team HERMIT in France," *Veritas: Journal of Army Special Operations History* 3, no. 2 (2007): 3–16.
Burton, Chris. "The Eureka-Rebecca Compromises: Another Look at Special Operations Security during World War II." *Air Power History*, Winter 2005, 24–37.
Churchill, T. B. "The Value of Commandos." *Journal of the Royal United Service Institution* 65, no, 577 (February 1950): 85–90.
Clancy, James, and Chuck Crossett. "Measuring Effectiveness in Irregular Warfare." *Parameters*, Summer 2007, 88–100.
Colby, William E. "OSS Operations in Norway: Skis and Daggers." *Studies in Intelligence*, Center for the Study of Intelligence, Winter 1999–2000.
Dodson, Charles A. "Special Forces." *Army* 11, no. 11 (June 1961): 44–58.
Drysdale, D.B. "Special Forces." *Marine Corps Gazette* 38, no. 6 (June 1954): 49–53.
Ferris, John. "The Intelligence-Deception Complex: An Anatomy." *Intelligence and National Security* 14, no. 4 (October 1989): 719–34.
Finlayson, Kenneth, and Robert W. Jones Jr. "Rangers in World War II: Part II, Sicily and Italy." *Veritas: Journal of Army Special Operations History* 3, no.1 (2007): 49–58.

Fleming, Peter. "Unorthodox Warriors." *Journal of the Royal United Service Institution* 104, no. 616 (November 1959): 378–89.
Foot, Michael R. D. "Was SOE Any Good?" *Journal of Contemporary History* 16, no.1 (January 1981): 167–81.
Freeman, Paul J. "The Cinderella Front: Allied Special Air Operations in Yugoslavia during World War II." A research paper submitted to the Research Department Air Command and Staff College, March 1997.
Funk, Arthur L. "American Contacts with the Resistance in France, 1940–1943." *Military Affairs* 34, no. 1 (February 1970): 15–21.
Gleason, Frank A. "Unconventional Forces: The Commander's Untapped Resources." *Military Review* 39, no. 7 (October 1959): 25–33.
Gole, Henry G. "Bring Back the LRRP." *Military Review* 61, no. 10 (October 1981): 2–10.
Gooderson, Ian. "Shoestring Strategy: The British Campaign in the Aegean, 1943." *Journal of Strategic Studies* 25, no. 3 (September 2002): 1–36.
Gray, Colin S. "Handfuls of Heroes on Desperate Ventures: When Do Special Operations Succeed?" *Parameters*, Spring 1999, 2–24.
Gubbins, Sir Colin. "Resistance Movements in the War." *Journal of the Royal United Service Institution* 93, no. 570 (May 1948), 210–23.
Hackett, J. W. "The Employment of Special Forces." *Journal of the Royal United Service Institution* 97, no. 585 (February 1952): 26–41.
Hampshire, A. Cecil. "The Exploits of Force Viper." *The Royal United Service Institution Journal*, February 1968, 41–50.
Hanrahan, G. Z. "Guerrilla Warfare." *Marine Corps Gazette* 40, no. 3 (March 1956): 26–31.
Hargreaves, Andrew L. "The Advent, Evolution and Value of British Specialist Formations in the Desert War, 1940–43." *Global War Studies* 7, no. 2 (2010): 7–62.
Henriksen, Rune. "Warriors in Combat: What Makes People Actively Fight in Combat?" *The Journal of Strategic Studies* 30, no. 2 (April 2007): 187–223.
Hogan, David W., Jr. "MacArthur, Stilwell, and Special Operations in the War Against Japan." *Parameters*, Spring 1995, 104–15.
Horan, R. H. E. "Combined Operations, 1939–45." *Journal of the Royal United Service Institution*, February 1953.
Hughes-Hallett, Rear Admiral J. "The Mounting of Raids." *Journal of the Royal United Service Institution*, 95, no. 580 (November 1950): 580–88.
———. "The Mounting of Raids." *Military Review* 31, no. 2 (May 1951): 85–93.
Isenberg, David. "Special Forces: Shock Troops for the New Order." *Middle East Report no. 177: Arms Race or Arms Control in the Middle East?*, July–August 1992, 24–27.
Karau, Mark. "Twisting the Dragon's Tail: The Zeebrugge and Ostend Raids of 1918." *The Journal of Military History* 67, no. 2 (April 2003): 455–82.
Kehoe, Robert R. "1944: An Allied Team with the French Resistance: Jed Team Frederick." *Studies in Intelligence*, Center for the Study of Intelligence, Winter 1998–99.
Kutger, Joseph P. "Irregular Warfare in Transition." *Military Affairs* 24, no. 3 (Autumn 1960): 113–23.

Laycock, R. E. "Raids in the Late War and Their Lessons." *Journal of the Royal United Service Institution* 92, no. 568 (November 1947): 528–40.
Maloney, Sean M. "Who has seen the wind? An Historical Overview of Canadian Special Operations." *Canadian Military Journal*, Autumn 2004, 39–48.
Mann, Christopher. "Combined Operations, the Commandos, and Norway, 1941–1944." *The Journal of Military History* 73, no. 2 (April 2009): 471–95.
Melillo, Michael R. "Outfitting a Big-War Military with Small-War Capabilities." *Parameters*, Autumn 2006, 22–35.
Mucci, Henry A. "Rescue at Cabanatuan." *Infantry Journal* 56, April 1945: 15–19.
Nickerson, H. Jr. "Force Recon: by Land, Sea, and Air." *Marine Corps Gazette* 43, no, 2 (February 1959): 44–48.
O'Dell, James Douglas. "Joint-Service Beach Obstacle Demolition in World War II." *Engineer*, April–June 2005, 36–40.
Sacquety, Troy J. "Supplying the Resistance: OSS Logistics Support to Special Operations in Europe." *Veritas: Journal of Army Special Operations History* 3, no.1 (2007): 37–48.
———. "A Special Forces Model: OSS Detachment 101 in the Myitkyina Campaign—Part I." *Veritas: Journal of Army Special Operations History* 4, no.1 (2008): 30–47.
———. "Wings Over Burma: Air Support in the Burma Campaign." *Veritas: Journal of Army Special Operations History* 4, no. 2 (2008): 30–43.
Shaw Close, C. C. "An Early Attempt at Combined Operations." *Journal of the Royal United Service Institution* 99, no. 594 (May 1954): 267–70.
Shelton, George R. "The Alamo Scouts,' *Armor* 91, September–October 1982: 29–30.
Spearin, Christopher. "Special Operations Forces a Strategic Resource: Public and Private Divides." *Parameters*, Winter 2006–2007, 58–70.
Stiner, Carl W. "U.S. Special Operations Forces: A Strategic Perspective." *Parameters*, Summer 1992, 2–13.
Thomas, David. "The Importance of Commando Operations in Modern Warfare 1939–82." *Journal of Contemporary History* 18, no. 4 (October 1983): 689–717.
Tompkins, Peter. "The OSS and Italian Partisans in World War II: Intelligence and Operational Support for the Anti-Nazi Resistance." *Studies in Intelligence*, Center for the Study of Intelligence, Spring 1998.
Twohig, J. P. O'Brien. "Are Commandos Really Necessary?." *Army Quarterly* 57, no. 1 (October 1948): 86–88.
Wheeler, Mark. "The SOE Phenomenon." *Journal of Contemporary History* 16, no. 3 (July 1981): 513–19.
Williams, Colonel R. C. Jr. "Amphibious Scouts and Raiders." *Military Affairs* 13, no. 3 (Fall 1949): 150–58.
Wyatt, Thomas C. "Butcher and Bolt: The Case for Strategic Offensive and Reconnaissance Troops, Trained to Execute Special Missions." *Army* 10, no. 10 (May 1960): 37–45.

Theses

Chae, Chelsea Y. "The Roles and Missions of Rangers in the Twenty-First Century." Thesis, U.S. Army Command and General Staff College, Fort Leavenworth, Kans., 1996.
Greenacre, John William. "The Development of Britain's Airborne Forces during the Second World War." PhD thesis, University of Leeds, 2008.
Peaty, John Robert. "British Army Manpower Crisis 1944." PhD thesis, King's College London, 2000.
Rhyne, Richard G. "Special Forces Command and Control in Afghanistan." Thesis, U.S. Army Command and General Staff College, Fort Leavenworth, Kans., 2004.
Stewart, Jeff R. "The Ranger Force at the Battle of Cisterna." Thesis, U.S. Army Command and General Staff College, Fort Leavenworth, Kans., 2004.
Wenner, Randall D. "Detachment 101 in the CBI: An Unconventional Warfare Paradigm for Contemporary Special Operations." Thesis, U.S. Army Command and General Staff College, Fort Leavenworth, Kans., 2010.
Winters, Edward G., and Paro, Kent A. "The Misuse of Special Operations Forces." Thesis, Naval Postgraduate School, Monterey, Calif., 1994.

Index

Abwehr, 312n51
Abwehrkommando, 46
Achnacarry, Scotland (Commando Training Center), 113, 115, 130–31, 211–12, 303n7
Adachi, Hatazo, 81
Advance A Force. *See* MI9
Aegean campaign, 71–72, 74, 95, 97, 161, 176, 190–91, 228–29
A Force (deception), 105
Agheila, Libya, 63
Agreement, Operation (raid on Tobruk, Libya, 1942), 65, 157–59
Airborne forces, 26, 36, 41–42, 61, 65–66, 190, 216, 243, 301nn11–12; as distinct from specialist formations, 6–7
Airey, Terence S., 213
Alamo Scouts, 196, 204, 278; cost-effectiveness of, 242, 252; creation of, 91, 101, 106, 138, 162, 247; deployment in New Guinea, 81, 92, 182; deployment in Philippines, 92, 152, 215, 236; role of, 91–92, 109, 182, 215; value of, 215–16, 239
Alamo Scouts Training Center, 91, 109, 261
Aleutian Islands, 39
Alexander, Harold, 75, 186
Alexandria, Egypt, 94
Allen, Terry, 188
Allied Air Forces, 220, 250, 343n30; cost-effectiveness of, 246–48
Allied Force Headquarters (AFHQ), 70, 75–76, 79, 125, 166
Allied Intelligence Bureau, 162, 249, 319n208
Ambassador, Operation (commando raid on Channel Islands, 1940), 23–24, 114

American Civil War, 12
American-Indian wars, 12–13, 302n39
American War of Independence, 11
AMF (SOE section), 120
Amphibious operations: American approaches toward, 14, 28–29, 47–48, 104, 109, 272, 280; British approaches toward, 10–12, 22, 109, 212, 279; maritime special forces roles in, 99–107, 118, 136, 174, 217, 273, 280–81; specialist formations role in spearheading, 25–27, 36–38, 41–42, 51, 73, 210–12, 261–62, 267, 271–73, 279
Amphibious Reconnaissance Company/Battalion (USMC), 9, 101–104, 117, 258
"Amphibious Roger." *See* Scouts and raiders
Amphibious Scouts and Raider School, 101. *See also* Scouts and raiders
Amphibious Training Bases: Fort Pierce, Florida, 101–102, 104, 118, 320n242; Little Creek, Virginia, 100; Solomons Island, Maryland, 100, 102, 118
Andartes partisans, 87, 134–35, 222–24
Anderson, Kenneth, 187–88
Andrews, Frank M., 194
Anglo-American relations, 4, 29–30, 50, 97, 109–11, 127, 282; American aid to Britain, 116–18, 130–31, 140, 276–77, 324n47; animosity in, 90, 120–27; British aid to America, 113–16, 121, 138–39, 275–78; COHQ-OSS relationship, 113–16; differences in approaches to specialist

395

formations, 16, 81, 83, 97, 108–109, 113, 126, 130, 177–78, 184–85, 219, 264–69, 272–73, 276–82; pre–Pearl Harbor relationship, 111–13; significance of in the development of specialist formations, 4, 27–28, 138–41, 275–78; SOE-OSS relationship, 111–12, 118–20, 324n47
Anklet, Operation (Commando raid on Norway, 1941), 248–49, 308n122
Antagonist, Operation (OG mission in France, 1944), 108
Anvil/Dragoon, Operation (Allied landings on the South of France, 1944), 43, 133, 197, 220, 255, 273
Anzio, Italy, 40–41, 77, 132, 137, 233, 273
Aola Bay, Guadalcanal ("long patrol"), 33, 153–54, 330n51
Apamama Atoll, Gilberts Islands, 102
Arab Revolt (1916–18), 10
Arab Revolt in Palestine (1936–39), 19, 57
Archery, Operation (Commando raid on Vaagso Island, Norway, 1942), 24, 26, 114, 144, 212, 229, 231, 271, 308n122
Area D, Virginia (COI training facility), 97, 115
Arzew, Algeria, 32, 136
Assam Organization. *See* V Force
Assam Rifles, 89
Assassination, 80–81, 109
Atwater, A. G., 257
Auchinleck, Claude, 61, 63–64, 182, 193, 259, 342n8
Auxiliary units, 18
Avalanche, Operation (Allied landings on Salerno, Italy, 1943), 37, 76–77, 129, 137

Bagnold, Ralph, 55–57, 59–61, 94, 105, 155, 182, 310n7, 311n29, 331n58
Bairoko, New Georgia, 309n135
Balkan Air Force, 166, 215

Bank, Aaron, 121, 224, 335n18
Bardia, Libya, 25, 189
Battle of France (1940), 17
Beach Jumpers (U.S. Navy), 105, 173, 196
Beach reconnaissance and assault pilotage, 98–101, 107, 217
Benghazi, Libya, 64, 66, 93, 157–58, 200, 331n76
Berneval, France, 27
Bigamy, Operation (SAS raid on Benghazi, 1942), 158, 200, 331n76
Bizerte, Operation (Commando landings in Tunisia, 1942), 129
Black, Edwin, 133
Boer War, 10, 311n34; use of *Kommando*s in, 19
Bône, Algeria, 129
Boom Clearance Parties. *See* Landing Craft Obstacle Clearance Units (LCOCUs)
Boom Commando. *See* Landing Craft Obstacle Clearance Units (LCOCUs)
Boom Patrol Boat, 95
Bottomley, Norman, 279
Bougainville Island, New Guinea, 47
Boulogne, France, 95
Bourat, Libya, 93
Bourne, Alan, 21, 228
Braç Island, Adriatic Sea, 134, 192
Bradley, Omar, 126, 190–91
Bradshaw, Frederick, 91
Brandenburg Regiment, 304n13, 312n52
Brest, France, 43
Bright, George, 136
British: pre-WWII impressions of irregular war, 10–16, 302n23; thoughts on special operations, 71, 83, 105, 107, 126, 143, 264–67, 276–82
British Army: I Airborne Corps, 169, 176; 1st Airborne Division, 78, 169; First Army, 67, 187; 1st Parachute Battalion, 301n11; 2nd Parachute Battalion, 216; 2nd

Punjab Regiment, 311n25; 4th Light Brigade, 214; V Corps, 260, 329n35; Fifth Battalion Scots Guards, 303n3; 6th Airborne Division, 41; 6th Armored Division, 329n35; 6th South African Armored Car Regiment, 311n25; 7th Armored Division, 56; Eighth Army, 58, 60, 67, 78, 135, 155, 160, 200, 215, 329n35; X Corps, 37; Fourteenth Army, 90, 226, 258; XV Corps, 172; 17th Indian Infantry Division, 88, 259; 21 Army Group, 149, 190, 200, 230; 22nd Guards Brigade, 214; 25th Indian Division, 44, 211; XXX Corps, 199; XXXIII Corps, 256; 36th Infantry Brigade, 32; 56th Division, 329n35; 78th Division, 38; Argyll and Sutherland Highlanders, 158; GHQ Home Forces, 145–46; GHQ India, 123; GHQ MEF, 59–60, 65, 99, 143–44, 155–56, 161, 166, 207; Northern Irish Horse, 329n35
British Security Coordination Agency, 324n65
Brittany, France, 81, 85, 133, 147, 219–20
Brook, Robin, 82
Brooke, Alan, 25
Browning, Frederick, 169, 197, 274
Brucker, Herbert, 121
Bruneval, France, 45, 216, 301n12, 344n55
Buck, Herbert, 65
Bulbasket, Operation (SAS mission in France, 1944), 80, 84, 209–10
Burma campaign, 44, 50, 88–90, 94, 96, 100, 122–24, 160, 216, 259; Arakan, 44, 172, 211, 236, 257; Burma Road offensive, 88, 163, 211, 225–26; Myitkyina, 50, 211, 226
Burma "Commando," 88
Buttercup, Operation (2nd SAS raid on Lampedusa, 1943), 75

Cabanatuan, Philippines, raid on, 49, 92, 152, 236
Cadillac, Operation (USAAF air supply of French Resistance, 1944), 250
Calvert, Michael, 88, 90, 185
Camouflage Training and Development Center B, 105
Campbell, John, 327n130
Camp Edwards, Massachusetts, Amphibious Training Center, 31
Camp Forrest, Tennessee, 37
Camp Pendleton, California, 117
Camp X, 112, 123
Canadian Army, 30, 46, 235–36; 2nd Canadian Division, 26, 128
Candlestick, Operations (Commando reconnaissance raids on French coast, 1943–44), 45, 131, 230–31
Cape Murro di Porco, Sicily, 73
Caravan, Operation (LRDG raid on Barce, Libya, 1942), 158
Carlson, Evans F., 29, 184–85, 231, 235, 330n51, 335n24; experience with Chinese guerillas, 28; ideas for raiders, 33, 47–48; long patrol of, 153–54
Casablanca Conference (Symbol, 1943), 73
Casey, William, 139
Cator, H. J., 160
Ceylon, 88, 98, 133, 256–57
Châtellerault, France, 209–10
"Champions," role in the creation of specialist formations, 20, 48, 55, 57, 61, 91, 105, 143, 155, 265, 270, 310n7, 342n8
Character, Operation (SOE operation in Burma 1945), 89, 226
Chariot, Operation (commando raid on St. Nazaire, France, 1942), 24, 45, 114, 144, 191, 247, 265, 271, 304n16; reprisals after, 233–34; value of, 205–206
Chennault, Claire Lee, 226
Cherbourg Peninsula, France, 74
Chess, Operation (commando raid near Ambleteuse, France, 1941), 308n122

398 INDEX

Chestnut, Operation (SAS raid against Sicily, 1943), 76
Chief of Combined Operations Representative, Washington, D.C., 116–17
Chiefs of Staffs (British), 145–46
Chieti, Italy, 132
China-Burma-India theater, 88, 90, 123–24, 153
Chindits, 49, 59, 88, 243, 259, 324n59; as distinct from specialist formations, 7–8
Chinese commandos, 90–91
Chinese guerrillas, 28, 90, 101, 226
Choate, Arthur O., 195
Church, Benjamin, 11
Churchill, Jack, 133, 185–86
Churchill, Randolph, 157, 186
Churchill, Thomas, 133–34, 185–86, 224, 262
Churchill, Winston, 125–26, 143, 156–57, 159, 176, 186, 194, 206, 219, 228, 232, 278; on specialist formations, 19–20, 24, 144, 236–37; role in creation of commandos, 19–20
Cisterna, Italy, 40, 183–84, 191, 255, 259, 266
Clark, Mark, 39, 94, 144, 152, 189, 224–25
Clarke, Dudley, 19–20, 23, 61, 113–14, 261
Claymore, Operation (commando raid on Lofoten Islands, Norway, 1941), 24, 26, 144, 238, 248; lessons learned from, 212; value of, 216–17
Clayton, Pat, 57
Clogstoun-Willmott, Herbert Nigel, 98–100, 171
Coastwatchers, 91
Cochrane, Thomas, 9
"Cockleshell Heroes." See Royal Marine Boom Patrol Detachment
Colby, William, 121, 200, 335n18
Collar, Operation (Independent Company raid on Pas-de-Calais, France, 1940), 23

Collins, Ian, 169, 176
Colossus, Operation (British airborne raid on Tragino aqueduct, Italy, 1941), 6, 61, 63, 301n12
Comacchio, Lake, Italy, 74, 135, 329n35
Combined Chiefs of Staff, 116
Combined Operations Beach and Boat Section, 281
Combined Operations Development Center, 94–95, 97
Combined Operations Headquarters (COHQ), 21, 24, 96, 105, 114, 117, 131, 161–62, 170–71, 177–78, 185, 212, 232, 320n227, 329n23; American tours of, 27, 29–30, 111, 113, 115–16; responsibilities of, 145–48, 228, 260
Combined Operations Pilotage Parties (COPPs), 115, 136, 148, 171–72, 204, 247, 281, 333n132, 334n135; creation of, 99–100; deployments of, 100–101, 135–38, 171, 194–96; role of, 99–100; value of, 217
Combined Operations Scout Unit (COSU), 105, 333n132
Command and control: development of, 142–79, 274; higher commands' thoughts on special operations, 21, 77, 142–45, 150, 162, 177, 181, 242, 342n8; in France, 84, 133, 149, 166–70, 221–22; in the Desert War, 155–60; of amphibious raids, 145–48; problem of, 142, 159–60, 165–66, 169–71, 173, 175–79, 180–81, 229–30, 272, 274, 330n54, 345n3
Commando brigade(s). See Special Service Brigade(s)
Commando Order (Kommandobefehl), 165, 232, 333n104
Commandos (British): cost-effectiveness of, 243, 245, 249, 259, 261–62; creation of Army Commandos, 18–22, 31, 185–86, 261, 270–71, 276; creation of Royal Marine Commandos, 22,

36, 148–49, 245, 279; deployment during advance on Germany, 42; deployment in Adriatic and Greece, 44, 86–87, 133–34, 186, 192, 234; deployment in Burma, 44, 211; deployment in France, 41–42; deployment in Italy, 37–39, 40, 44, 129, 135, 329n35; deployment in North Africa, 32, 128–29, 148, 181, 187–88; deployment in Sicily, 35–36, 181–82; disbandment of, 45–46, 265, 279, 281; Layforce, 25, 61–62, 67–68, 93, 189, 193, 265; links with U.S. Army, 127–32; links with USMC, 27–29, 112–13; Middle East Commandos (Nos. 50, 51, and 52), 24–25, 65, 189; misuse of, 25, 181–82, 187–89, 191–92; No. 1 Commando, 32, 44, 128–29, 136, 181, 187–88; No. 2 Commando, 86–87, 129, 134, 186, 191, 207, 265, 301n11; No. 3 Commando, 23, 26–27, 32, 35–38, 73, 113, 128, 262; No. 4 Commando, 26–27, 128, 130–31, 211, 305n37, 323n20; No. 5 Commando, 26, 44; No. 6 Commando, 32, 93, 128–29, 181, 187–88; No. 7 Commando, 25; No. 8 Commando, 92; No. 9 Commando, 38; No. 10 (IA) Commando, 44–45, 130; No. 11 Commando, 25, 81; No. 12 Commando, 45, 75, 130, 248, 265, 271; No. 14 Commando, 46, 87, 130, 265; No. 30 (Assault) Commando, 46–47, 216, 309n129, 332n82, 333n132, 340n73; No. 40 (RM) Commando, 26, 35, 37–38, 73; No. 41 (RM) Commando, 35, 129; No. 47 (RM) Commando, 41; recruitment and reinforcement of, 244–45; reorganization of, 34, 36, 148, 181–82, 264; roles of, 6, 22–27, 32, 34, 35–38, 43–44, 47, 50–52, 61–63, 73, 150, 189–90, 201–202, 210–11, 227–32, 271–74, 304n29; training of, 24, 28–29, 113–14, 128, 303n7, 323n20; value of, 205–206, 210–12, 216–17, 227–33, 235, 239, 271. *See also* Special Service Brigade(s)

Compass, Operation (British offensive in Libya, 1940–41), 227

Coordinator of Information (COI), 27–28, 68–69, 97, 111–13, 115, 162, 271. *See also* Donovan, William J.

Confederate Partisan Ranger Act (1862), 12

Corsica, 77, 86, 108, 315n117

Cost-effectiveness of specialist formations, 241–69, 276; and demands of specialist formations on resources, 248–51; and disbandment, 264–67; drain of specialist formations on manpower, 242–48; frequency of employment, 254–58; relative to size of establishment, 251–54

COSSAC (Chief of Staff to Supreme Allied Commander), 131, 148, 230; Raids and Reconnaissance Committee, 148, 231

Cota, Norman D., 36–37

Coultas, William B., 103

Courtney, Guy, 94, 172, 185, 247

Courtney, Roger, 92–94, 99, 105, 185

Cox, Alfred T., 197

Creagh, Michael O'Moore, 56

Crete, 18, 24–25, 185, 189

Crichton-Stuart, Michael, 182

Croft, Noel Andrew, 46

Cronje (OSS OG captain), 134

Crusader, Operation (British offensive in Libya, 1941), 59, 61, 63, 144, 201

Curlew, Operation (V Corps reconnaissance raid on St. Laurent, France, 1942), 260

Cyrenaican Arabs, 66

Dah Force, 324n59
Dakar, 22
Darby, William O., 37, 128, 184–85, 191, 199, 245; on Cisterna, 183–84; reorganization of the Rangers, 35, 48, 151–52, 154
Davy, George Mark Oswald, 166
DCO. See Combined Operations Headquarters (COHQ)
D-day. See Overlord, Operations (OSS MU operations in Italy and Istria, 1944)
Deception operations, 104–105, 107, 229
Defoe, Operation (SAS operation in France, 1944), 80
Demolitions, 102–103, 107
Demolitions Unit No. 1 (U.S. Navy). See Naval Combat Demolitions Units
Dempsey, Miles, 186
Deputy Director of Operations Division (Irregular) branch, (DDOD[I]), 171, 173, 256
Derna, Libya, 65, 312n51
Desert War, the, 71, 88, 252–53, 272; command arrangements in, 155–60, 175; creation of special forces in, 54–60, 63–68; value of special forces in, 208–209, 212–15, 227–28, 338n18
Detachment 101 (OSS), 50, 90, 98, 139, 173, 273, 278, 324n59; command and control of, 162–63; cost-effectiveness of, 250–52; creation of, 88; links with British, 123–24, 324n59; links with SACO, 162–63; roles of, 89, 216; value of, 216, 225–26, 239, 339n47
Detachment 404 (OSS), 90, 98, 124, 133, 173, 236
Devon, Operation (British landings on Termoli, Italy, 1943), 38–39, 73, 77, 211
Dieppe, France (raid, 1942), 32, 45, 51, 99, 127–28, 212, 217, 236,
248, 271, 305n34, 344n55; No. 3 Commando in, 26–27; No. 4 Commando in, 26–27, 211, 305n37; publicizing of, 235–37; Royal Marine A Commando in, 26; U.S. Army Rangers in, 31–32, 51, 128
Dill, John, 19, 194
Dinagat Island, Philippines, 48
Dingson, Operation (SAS deployment in France 1944), 85
Disbandment of specialist formations, 264–67, 279–82, 345n73
Djebel el Ank, Tunisia, 32
Donovan, William J., 27–28, 68, 105, 115, 126, 161–62, 165, 271, 278, 313n68, 326n108; as COI, 69–70, 162; ideas for "guerilla battalions," 69–70, 114–15; and Mountbatten, 117, 124, 135–36; opposition toward, 69–70, 162; relations with British, 111–14, 119, 126
Doolittle raid, 235
Dragoon, Operation. See Anvil/Dragoon, Operation (Allied landings on the South of France, 1944)
Drake, Francis, 9
Dugi Otok Island, Adriatic Sea, 234
Dunkirk evacuation, 17–18, 23
Dunne, Philip, 129
Dunning, James, 211–12
Durnford-Slater, John, 23, 45, 73, 128

Easonsmith, Jake, 191
East African campaign, 24
EDES (National Republican Greek League), 224
Edson, Merritt, 29, 33, 153, 184
"Edson's Ridge," Guadalcanal, 33–34, 189
Egyptian Desert Survey, 58
Eifler, Carl F., 163
Eisenhower, Dwight D., 70, 75, 125–26, 131, 151, 278
El Agheila, Libya, 214
El Alamein, Egypt, 67, 160, 214, 237

ELAS (Greek People's Liberation Army), 224
Elbe River, Germany, 42, 100
Electra House, 13
Elite units, 6–7, 143
El Qubba, Libya, 66–67
Ely, Lewis B., 100–101
Enterprise, Operation (Crossing of Elbe River, Germany, 1945), 42
"Errant captains," role in the creation of specialist formations, 54–56, 60, 62, 66, 92, 94, 105–106, 155, 159, 184–85, 262, 265, 270, 310n7
Etat-major des Forces Françaises de l'Intérieur (EMFFI), 166

Fairbairn, R. R., 118
Fairbanks, Douglas, Jr., 105
Faroe Islands, 22
Farran, Roy, 80, 223
Fellers, Bonner, 312n51
First Special Service Force (FSSF), 202, 307n97, 345n73; command and control of, 153, 177–78; cost-effectiveness of, 254–55; creation of, 30–31, 49, 194; deployment in France, 43; deployment against Kiska, 39; deployment in Italy, 38–41, 144, 211, 233; disbandment of, 43, 52, 265, 267; role of, 38–40, 87, 189, 194–95, 211, 307n102
1st Special Service Regiment, 68, 156–58
First World War, 10, 12, 20–21, 234 Corps School of Raiding, 260
5307th Composite Unit (Provisional). See Merrill's Marauders
5332nd (Provisional) Brigade. See Mars Task Force
Fleming, Ian, 46
Fleming, Peter, 143, 239, 303n7
Flintlock, Operation (American landings on Marshall Islands, 1944), 104, 174
Flipper, Operation ("Rommel Raid," Libya, 1941), 81, 185

"Folbot" section. See Special Boat Section(s)
Foot, M. R. D., 176
Forbes, Charles, 230
Force 266, 166
Force Viper, 88
Forfar, Operations (Commando reconnaissance raids on French coast, 1943–44), 45, 131, 230–31
Fortitude North, Operation (deception scheme), 229
Franks, Brian, 185
Frankton, Operation (RMBPD raid on Bordeaux, France), 95, 247, 256
Fraser, Simon, 311n34
Frederick, Robert T., 30–31, 41, 153, 185
Free French Forces, 58–59, 214; Bataillon de Choc, 77, 133, 315n117; 1 Infantérie de l'Air, 64–65
French Resistance, 79–82, 84–85, 167, 197–98, 210, 219, 248, 253–54, 339n57; value of, 219–24
Freshman, Operation (SOE raid against Vemork, Norway, 1943), 206, 301n12
Fuller, J. F. C., 57

G (Raiding Forces), 157–61
Gaff, Operation (SAS deployment in France, 1944), 80
Galahad. See Merrill's Marauders
Garigliano River, Italy, 38
Garnons-Williams, G. A., 173
Gazala, Libya, 63, 199
Gela, Sicily, 36
German military: Afrika Korps, 59, 66–67; Brandenburg Regiment, 304n13, 312n52; 1st Fallschirmjäger Division, 217, 304n13; SS Das Reich Division, 209–10; "Storm troopers" (1918), 20, 304n13
Gideon Force, 82, 316n136
Ginny II, Operation (OSS raid on railways near La Spezia, Italy, 1944), 165

Giraud, Henri, 94
Glavin, Edward, 166
Goodfellow, Millard Preston, 69
Graham, John A., 156–57
Grant, Ulysses S., 12–13
Graziani, Rodolfo, 227
Great Game, the, 9, 302n23
Greek Civil War, 224
Greek Resistance, 222–24, 250
Greek Sacred Squadron, 95, 228–29, 319n210, 332n82
Greene, Nathanael, 11
Greene, W. M., Jr., 28
Griffith, Samuel B., 28–29
Grouse, Operation (SOE raid against Vemork, Norway, 1943), 206–207
GS(R). *See* MI(R)
Guadalcanal campaign, 33–34, 144, 153–54, 231, 260
Guam, 217
Gubbins, Colin, 13, 18–19, 143
Guingand, Francis de, 230–31
Guiuan Island, Philippines, 48
Gulf of Martaban, Burma, 88

Hackett, John "Shan," 157, 159–61
Haft, Operation (SAS deployment in France, 1944), 80
Haiti, 14
Hall Hanlon, B., 174
Hambro, Charles, 119
Hamilton, John, 234
Hardtack, Operations (Commando reconnaissance raids on French coast, 1943–44), 45, 131, 230–31
Haselden, John Edward, 157–58
Hasler, H. G. "Blondie," 94–96, 105, 172
Hastings, Ismay, 20
Hawthorn, Operation (SAS raid against Sardinia, 1943), 76
Haydon, Joseph Charles, 245
Hayes, Graham, 74
Hewitt, Henry Kent, 105
Heydrich, Reinhard, 81
Hill 170, Burma, 44, 211
Hill 400 ("Castle Hill"), Germany, 43–44

Hilsman, Roger, 251, 335n18
Hislop, John, 315n127
Hitler, Adolph, 126, 165, 206, 229, 232
HMS *Rodent*. *See* Small Boat Unit
Hoague, George, 136
Hobart, Percy, 56, 310n7
Hoel, Alfred G., 118
Holcomb, Thomas, 28, 34
Holland, J. C. F., 13
Homonhon Island, Philippines, 48
Horrocks, Brian, 186
Hughes-Hallett, John, 147
Hunter, Charles, 188
Huntington, Ellery C., 119–20
Husky, Operation (Allied invasion of Sicily, 1943), 35–36, 73, 77–78, 105, 148, 272; beach reconnaissance and demolitions before, 102–103, 107, 118, 136–37, 139, 171, 273; use of commandos in, 35–36, 40, 47, 148–49, 182, 210, 272; use of rangers in, 35–36, 51, 151, 210, 272; use of SAS in, 75–76, 144; use of SRS in, 73
Hvar Island, Adriatic Sea, 134

Iceland, 22
Ile de Port Cros, France, 43, 255
Ile du Levant, France, 43, 255
Independent Companies, 21–22, 82; creation of, 18; misuse of, 19, 187; No. 11 Independent Company, 23; in Norway, 18–19
Indian Long Range Squadron (ILRS), 60, 214, 252
Intelligence gathering, 58–59, 72, 74, 78, 91, 144, 147, 230–31; value of, 212–18
Inter-Service Training and Development Center (ISTDC), 14
Irish War of Independence, 9–10
Irrawaddy River, Burma, 88, 94, 256
Irsch-Zerf road, Germany, 43, 191
Italian Army, 56
Italian campaign, 75–76, 132, 224–25; Anzio, 40–41, 77, 132, 137; Bernhardt Line, 39–40, 211;

Salerno, 37, 76–77, 129, 137; Taranto, 78; Termoli, 37–38, 73, 77
Italian maritime special forces, 94–95, 98, 320n227
Italian partisans, 86, 224–25, 309n129, 329n35

Jalo, Libya, 158, 311n25
Japanese Army, 15th Division, 89
Jaywick, Operation (SRD raid on shipping in Singapore Harbor, 1943), 249, 319n208
Jebel Akhdar, Libya, 66, 214
Jedburgh Teams, 86, 89, 121, 219, 274; command and control of, 167–70, 176; creation of, 81–82; deployment in Burma, 198; deployment in France, 82, 84, 167–70, 176, 197, 219–23; deployment in Holland, 337n80; relationship with SAS, 84–85; role of, 82, 84, 108, 316n144; Team Cecil, 197; Team Frederick, 85, 220, 223; Team George, 85; Team Hugh, 84; Team Veganin, 197, 339n57; value of, 219–20
Jellicoe, George, 73, 108
Johnston, Duncan, 88
Joint Chiefs of Staff, 70, 126
Jones, James Logan, 101
Jonquil, Operation (SAS deployment in Italy, 1943), 132

Kabrit, Egypt, 65, 93
Kachin "Rangers," 50, 88, 225–26, 250–51, 324n59, 339n47. See also Detachment 101 (OSS)
Kai-shek, Chiang, 90, 226
Kalpaks, the, 332n82
Karen guerillas, 89, 226
Kastelorizo Island, Aegean Sea, 25, 189
Kauffman, Draper L., 102, 321n255
Kehoe, Robert, 223
Kelly, Richard, 98, 135, 327n130
Kennedy, C. E., 118
Kesselring, Albert, 39, 225

Keyes, Geoffrey, 81
Keyes, Roger, 21, 93, 162, 228, 304n16; dismissal of, 145–46
Kidnapping, 80–81, 109
King, Ernest J., 102, 105, 117
Kirkstone, Operation (OG/RSR raids on rail networks in Greece, 1944), 134
Kiska, Aleutian Islands, 39, 194
Knowlton, Thomas, 11
Knox, Frank, 68, 313n68
Koenig, Marie-Pierre, 167
Kommandobefehl. See Commando Order (Kommandobefehl)
Koodoo/Inhuman, 99–101, 136. See also Combined Operations Pilotage Parties (COPPs)
Kreipe, Heinrich, 81
Krueger, Walter, 106, 178–79; and Alamo Scouts, 81, 91, 215–16; and 6th Rangers, 48, 152
Kufra, Libya, 59, 182, 311n25
Kwajalein, Marshall Islands, 104

Land Forces Adriatic, 166
Landing Craft Obstacle Clearance Units (LCOCUs), 103–104, 118, 138, 333n132
Lawrence, T. E., 10, 20, 57, 234
Laycock, Peter, 45
Laycock, Robert, 45, 115, 117, 181, 185–86, 190, 193, 257–58, 261, 304n29; and Layforce, 25; on raiding, 37; and SS Brigade, 34–35, 148, 151
L Detachment SAS. See Special Air Service (SAS)
Leclerc, Jacques-Philippe, 59–60, 311n25
Leese, Oliver, 186
Leflesen (OSS lieutenant colonel), 201
"Leopards," 20, 22
Leros Island, Aegean Sea, 72, 191
Levant Schooner Flotilla, 97, 332n82
Levitha Island, Aegean Sea, 72, 190–91
Lewes, John Steel "Jock," 62
Leyte, Philippines, 48, 92, 174

404 INDEX

Li, Tai, 90, 163, 226
Libyan Arab Force, 66
Libyan Arab Force Commando, 58, 66–67
Libyan campaign. *See* Desert War, the
Liddell Hart, B. H., 10–11, 57, 303n4
Light Car Patrols, 56
Light infantry forces (general), 7, 11–12, 260–61
Light Scout Car Training Center. *See* Camouflage Training and Development Center B
Lindsay, Franklin, 127, 185–86, 247
Lingayen Gulf, Philippines, 174
Litani River, Lebanon, 25, 304n29
Livermore, Russell, 164–65
Lloyd Owen, David, 143, 161, 182, 190, 252–53, 263, 311n42
Lochailort, Scotland, Special Training School, 75, 303n7
Lofoten Islands, Norway. *See* Claymore, Operation (commando raid on Lofoten Islands, Norway, 1941)
Long Range Desert Group (LRDG), 99, 143, 193, 196, 204, 237, 263, 327n129; command and control of, 155–56, 161, 166, 331n58, 332n82; cost-effectiveness of, 242–43, 252; creation of, 55–57, 59, 91, 94, 247, 271, 310n7; deployments in the Desert War, 57–61, 63–64, 67, 144, 158, 182, 212–15, 227–28, 272, 311n25; deployments in Greece and the Aegean, 71–72, 74, 135, 161, 190, 215, 228–29, 273, 319n210; deployments in Yugoslavia, 72, 74, 135, 215, 223; misuse of, 182, 190–91; road watches, 58–59, 212–14; role of, 57–59, 65–66, 71–72, 89, 91, 106, 108, 182; value of, 208–209, 212–15, 227–28, 239, 272
Long Range Patrols. *See* Long Range Desert Group (LRDG)
Lovat, Lord "Shimi," 323n20

Lovat Scouts, 46, 311n34
Lovell, Phillip G., 134
Loyton, Operation (SAS deployment in France, 1944), 315n127
LRDG. *See* Long Range Desert Group (LRDG)
Lumsden, Bruce, 192
Luzon, Philippines, 48, 174, 215, 273

MacArthur, Douglas, 162, 179, 236
Maclean, Fitzroy, 81, 157, 185–86
Madagascar landings, 26
Madden, Charles, 14
Madden Committee, 14, 22
Maid Honor force, 74, 329n23. *See also* Small Scale Raiding Force (SSRF)
Makin, Gilbert Islands: consequences of raid on, 231–32; invasion of, 103; publicity of raid on, 235, 237; raid on, 33–34, 51, 153, 271
Manacle, Operations (commando reconnaissance raids on French coast, 1943–44), 45, 131, 230–31
Maquis. *See* French Resistance
March-Philipps, Gustavus, 74
Mareth Line, 214–15
Marion, Francis, 11
Maritime Unit (OSS), 104, 162, 258; command and control of, 166, 173, 178, 196; cost-effectiveness of, 257; creation of, 97, 115, 138; deployment from Britain, 98, 115; deployment in Burma, 89, 98, 135–36; deployment in Greece and Aegean, 97; deployment in Italy, 98, 135; deployment in the Pacific, 195; links with British, 115–17, 135–36, 327n130; roles of, 97–98, 195
Market Garden, Operation (Allied airborne operation in Holland, 1944), 199, 337n80
Marshall, George C., 29–30, 35, 106, 126, 194, 266, 278; COHQ tour, 29–30; on raids, 31, 228
Mars Task Force, 50, 345n73

Marten, H. N., 197, 316n144
Mayne, Robert Blair "Paddy," 72–73
McConville, Michael, 133, 192
McCreery, Richard L., 156
McHarg, Neville Townley, 137
McKenzie, William H., 198
McLeod, Roderick W., 81
McNair, Lesley J., 151
Menzies, Stewart, 324n65
Merrill, Frank, 184, 188, 226
Merrill's Marauders, 8, 88, 184, 188, 226, 236–37, 241, 273, 339n47; command and control of, 153, 177–78; cost-effectiveness of, 259; creation of, 49; disbandment of, 50, 264–65, 345n73; misuse of, 188–89; role of, 49–50, 211
MI(R), 13–14, 18–19, 303n7
MI9, 58, 66, 89, 132, 135, 156
Middle East Commando. *See* 1st Special Service Regiment
Miles, Milton E., 90, 163, 226
Military innovation, 17–18, 55, 270
Mills-Roberts, Derek, 185
Milton Hall, England, 121
Misuse of specialist formations, 201–202, 261, 269, 274, 276, 345n71, 345n3; because of exigency, 187–92; command misapplication, 180–86; disuse of, 192–96, 202, 254–57; of airborne forces, 7; opportunities and means for employment of, 196–201, 221, 273
Mljet Island, Adriatic Sea, 134
Moari, New Guinea, 92
Mobile Naval Base Defense Organization (MNBDO), 88, 317n170
MO9, 20–21
Montbéliard, France, 247–48
Monte la Difensa, Italy, 39–40, 144, 211, 255, 307n97. *See also* First Special Service Force (FSSF)
Monte la Rametanea, Italy, 39, 144, 211, 307n97. *See also* First Special Service Force (FSSF)
Montgomery, Bernard L., 78–79, 215

Morgan, Frederick E., 230
Mosby, John S., 12
Mountbatten, Louis, 34–35, 95–96, 117, 170–72, 175–76, 187, 194–95, 232; appointment as CCO, 21, 146; plans for raids, 74, 146–47, 232; at SEAC, 124, 135–36, 171–73
Mucci, Henry, 152, 236
Murray, Roy, 128, 151
Murzak, Libya, 59
Musketoon, Operation (commando raid on Glomfjord, Norway, 1942), 207
Mussolini, Benito, 56
Myebon Peninsula, Burma, 44, 100
Myitkyina, Burma, 50, 211, 226

Narcissus, Operation (SAS deployment in Sicily, 1943), 76
Nassau, Bahamas, 96, 98, 117, 194–95, 256
Naval Beach Control Parties. *See* Royal Navy
Naval Combat Demolitions Units, 102, 104, 116, 118, 138, 140, 258, 321n252
Nazira, India, 163
New Georgia, Solomon Islands, 47
New River, North Carolina, landing exercises on, 100
New Zealand Division, 57, 214–15
Nicaragua, 14
Nicety, Operation (Sudan Defense Force raid on Jalo, Libya, 1942), 158
Nimitz, Chester W., 103, 153, 162, 235
Noah's Ark, Operation (harassment of German forces in Greece, 1944), 87, 134
NORSO Group, 87, 121, 200–201. *See also* Operational Groups (OSS)
North-West Frontier (campaigns), 9–10
Norway: Norwegian Campaign (1940), 18–19, 99, 187, 303n7;

raids against, 30, 38–39, 46, 87, 130, 146, 194, 200–201, 206–207, 229. *See also names of operations in Norway*
Nygaardsvold, Johan, 229

Obolensky, Serge, 108, 127, 132, 168
O'Brien-Twohig, Joseph Patrick, 244
O'Daniel, John "Iron Mike," 114
Office of Strategic Services (OSS), 28, 68–69, 81, 100, 124, 161–64, 167–68, 172, 178, 224–25, 276, 320n227, 326n103, 332n93; creation of, 70, 112, 114, 186; impressions of commandos, 114, 266; London Branch, 163–64; opposition toward, 69–70, 162–64; relations with COHQ, 113–16; relations with SIS, 124, 324n65; relations with SOE, 118–24, 127, 140; Special Operations branch, 70–71, 77, 97, 119–21, 164–67, 220. *See also* Detachment 101 (OSS); Detachment 404 (OSS); Jedburgh Teams; Maritime Unit (OSS); Operational Groups (OSS)
Ogburn, Charlton, 49, 339n47
Oiustreham, France, 41
Okinawa, 104
Omaha Beach, France, 41–42
101 Troop (No. 6 Commando), 93–95
Operational groups (OSS), 107, 125, 165, 185, 219, 273, 276, 278; command and control of, 164–70, 173, 176, 178; cost-effectiveness of, 254; creation of, 69–71, 115, 138, 164, 313n82; deployment in Adriatic, 86–87, 133–34, 223; deployment in Burma, 89–90, 96, 133; deployment in France, 83–84, 108, 133, 167–70, 176, 197–98, 220–21, 223–24, 254, 339n57; deployment in Greece, 134–35; deployment in Italy and Western Mediterranean, 77, 86, 108, 132–33, 165, 225; "French" OGs, 83, 86–87, 127, 133; "Greek" OGs, 86–87, 133–35, 215, 223–24, 236; "Italian" OGs, 86, 133; links with Commandos, 133–34; links with SAS, 132–33, 316n146, 326n108; "Norwegian" OGs, 83, 87, 127, 200–201; role of, 70–71, 82–84, 86, 88, 90, 108–109, 316n146; value of, 220–21, 224–25, 254; "Yugoslav" OGs, 86–87, 133, 192, 223, 234, 236. *See also* NORSO Group
Ossining, Operations (OSS MU operations in Italy and Istria, 1944), 98
Overlord, Operation (Allied invasion of France, 1944), 132, 139, 219–22, 230, 266, 273; beach reconnaissance and demolitions before, 100, 103, 138; use of commandos in, 41–42; use of Jedburghs in, 81–85; use of rangers in, 42, 152, 211, 266; use of OSS OGs in, 83–85, 254; use of SAS in, 78–80, 82–85, 209–10, 253–54

Partisans: Allied attitude toward, 126, 219; resources required to support, 250–51; specialist formations working alongside, 19, 69–70, 77, 79–83, 86–88, 107–108, 218–26, 274, 316n144. *See also* Andartes partisans; Chinese guerrillas; French Resistance; Greek Resistance; Italian partisans; Kachin "Rangers"; Karen guerillas; Yugoslav partisans
Patch, Alexander McCarrell, 220
Patton, George S., 36, 151, 219
P Division, 124, 172–73, 179
Peers, William R., 163, 216
Peg, Operation (OSS OG deployment in France, 1944), 223
Peniakoff, Vladimir "Popski," 66–67, 78, 217
Peninsular War, 9, 11
Philippine-American War, 12, 302n39

INDEX   407

Philippine guerrillas, 49, 92, 162, 236
Picton-Phillips, Joseph, 26
"Plough" Force. *See* First Special Service Force (FSSF)
Pointe du Hoc, France, 42, 211
Ponte di Malati Bridge, Sicily, 36
Popski's Private Army (No. 1 Demolition Squadron), 83, 89, 109, 196, 217; in Desert War, 66–67; in Italy, 78; and OSS MU, 135, 327n130
Po River, Italy, 135
Port-en-Bessin, France, 41
Prendergast, Guy, 57, 161
"Private armies," 18, 55, 60, 81, 87–88, 172, 178, 262, 268, 271, 275, 334n141; evolution into special forces, 68, 272; opposition toward, 70, 106, 155, 243, 264
Psychological impact of special operations, 232–33
Publicity of special operations, 10, 23, 143, 201, 234–37
Pyke, Geoffrey, 30

Quantrill, William C., 12
Quebec Conference (Quadrant, 1943), 49, 124
Queen Elizabeth (battleship), 94

Raider battalions (USMC), 9, 33, 117, 144, 184, 237; command and control of, 153–54, 177–78; cost-effectiveness of, 244; creation of, 27–29, 34, 113; deployments of, 33–34, 47, 231–32, 235, 309n135, 330n51; disbandment of, 48, 52, 102, 154, 265; roles of, 33–34, 47–48, 50–52, 81, 228, 272
Raiding Forces Aegean, 72, 233, 319n210, 329n25, 332n82, 341n121; limitations of, 161
Raiding Forces Middle East, 87, 95, 160–61
Raiding Support Regiment (RSR), 87, 108, 134–35, 166, 224, 329n35, 332n82
Raids, 5–7, 22–24, 29, 37, 51–53, 106, 131; attitudes toward, 144, 146; controls on, 148, 229–30, 341n121; planning and direction of, 145–48, 262; value of, 205–212, 227–32, 238
Ramsay, Bertram, 148
Rangers (U.S. Army): command and control of, 150–52, 177–78; creation of 1st Battalion, 27, 29–31, 51, 106, 113; creation of 2nd and 5th Battalions, 37, 101, 130–31, 265, 266; creation of 3rd and 4th Battalions, 34–35, 245, 266; creation of 6th Battalion, 48, 106, 162, 245–46; deployment from Britain, 131, 230, 235–36; deployment in France, 42–43; deployment in Germany, 43, 191; deployment in Italy, 37, 40, 129, 182–83, 255, 259; deployment in North Africa, 32, 136, 144, 188; deployment in the Philippines, 48–49, 92, 152, 189–90, 236, 273; deployment in Sicily, 36, 151; disbandment of, 52, 264–66, 345n73; links with commandos, 127–32, 139; misuse of, 182–84, 188–91, 199; pre-WWII origins, 11–12; Ranger Force, 129, 151–52, 182–83; roles of, 6, 31–32, 34–38, 41, 43, 47–49, 50–52, 81, 182–83, 210–11, 230, 271–74, 276; 29th Ranger Battalion, 129–30, 261, 265; value of, 210–11, 239
Reid, Denys Whitehorn, 311n25
Reprisals, 233–34, 341n121
Rhine River, crossing of, 42, 100, 211
Rhodes, 99, 108
Rimau, Operation (SRD raid on shipping in Singapore Harbor, 1944), 319n208
Ritchie, Neil, 61, 311n29
Roast, Operation (Eighth Army offensive crossing Lake Comacchio, Italy, 1945), 74, 329n35

Rogers, R. H., 174
Rogers, Robert, 11, 302n33
Roi Namur, Marshall Islands, 104
Romania, 122
Rommel, Erwin, 66–67, 158, 207
Roosevelt, Franklin D., 28, 68, 111, 126, 228, 278
Roosevelt, James, 28–29, 69, 186, 235, 335n24
Roosevelt, Theodore, 313n68
Royal Air Force (RAF): Desert Air Force, 208; No. 4 Parachute Training School RAF, 66; No. 38 Group, 250; operations, 72, 214; Royal Air Force Servicing Commandos, 309n133. *See also* Allied Air Forces
Royal Marine Boom Patrol Detachment, 96, 115, 171, 196, 281, 332n82, 333n132; cost-effectiveness of, 255–56; creation of, 94–95; deployments of, 95; role of, 94–97, 247
Royal Marine Detachment 385, 96, 106, 264, 334n135
Royal Marine Engineer Commandos, 103
Royal Marines, 279, 304n19; 11th Royal Marine Battalion, 158; pre-WWII responsibilities, 14, 22; Royal Marines Division, 22. *See also* Commandos (British); Mobile Naval Base Defense Organization (MNBDO); Royal Marine Boom Patrol Detachment; Royal Marine Detachment 385
Royal Navy, 249; 1st Submarine Flotilla, 93; 10th Submarine Flotilla, 93; 12th Submarine Flotilla, 206; 712th LCP Survey Flotilla, 137; Eastern Fleet, 172; Force J, 147, 329n21; Royal Navy Commandos, 309n133
Rudder, James Earl, 42, 131, 152, 185
Russell Islands, 47

Rype, Operation (NORSO raid on rail networks in Norway, 1945), 200–201

Saipan, Marianas Islands, 195
Salerno, Italy. *See* Avalanche, Operation (Allied landings on Salerno, Italy, 1943)
Samos Island, Aegean Sea, 233
Samwest, Operation (SAS deployment in France, 1944), 85, 220
San Marco Battalion. *See* Italian maritime special forces
San Mollarella, Sicily, 36
Santiago Island, Philippines, 48
Sardinia, 77, 108
SAS. *See* Special Air Service (SAS)
Schneider, Max, 152
Scouts and raiders, 104, 136, 148, 173, 258, 261; creation of, 100–101; deployments of, 101, 105, 136–38; links with British counterparts, 136–38; roles of, 90, 101; value of, 217
Sea Reconnaissance Unit (SRU), 281, 319n213, 333n132, 334n135; cost-effectiveness of, 256; creation of, 96; deployments in Burma, 96; links with U.S. formations, 96, 98, 104, 117, 140; role of, 96, 194–95
Secret Intelligence Service (SIS), 13, 58, 156, 163, 172; relations with America, 111–12, 124, 324n65; relations with special forces, 147, 329n25
Section D, 13–14
Seekings, Reg, 233
Services Reconnaissance Department, 249, 319n208
Shaw, Bill Kennedy, 57
Sicilian campaign. *See* Husky, Operation (Allied invasion of Sicily, 1943)
Sidi Haneish, Egypt, 312n48
Simi Island, Aegean Sea, 74, 95, 256, 341n121

Sino-American Cooperative Organization (SACO), 90, 101, 216, 332n93; links with OSS, 162–63; value of, 226
Sirte, Libya, 63
Sixth Army Special Reconnaissance Unit. *See* Alamo Scouts
Skorzeny, Otto, 312n52
Slim, William, 175, 237, 242, 251, 258
Slovakia uprising, 219
Small Boat Unit, 171–73, 256, 333n132
Small Operations Group (SOG), 172–73, 179, 196, 256–57
Small Scale Raiding Force (SSRF), 196, 271, 314n100, 329n23; creation of, 74–75, 106, 147; roles of, 74–75, 147
Smith, E. H. "Dutch," 117
Smith, Holland M., 28
Smith, Julian, 113–14
Snapdragon, Operation (2nd SAS raid on Pantellaria, 1943), 75
Solborg, Robert, 69
Solta Island, Adriatic Sea, 134
SO/SOE Agreement, 119, 122
Source, Operation (midget submarine attack on the *Tirpitz*, 1943), 206
South East Asia Command (SEAC), 89, 124, 136, 257
Sparks, Bill, 95
Spartan, SOE exercise (1943), 82
Special Air Service (SAS), 107, 194, 196, 234, 273; command and control of, 155–57, 167–70, 176, 330n54; cost-effectiveness, 243, 246, 252–54; creation of L Detachment, 60–61, 68, 106, 155, 271–72; creation of SAS Brigade, 78, 264; creation of 2nd SAS Regiment, 73–75, 125, 344n55; deployments in Belgium and Holland, 86, 198–99, 317n159; deployments in Desert War, 58, 63–65, 72, 74–75, 93, 157, 176, 199, 201, 208, 227–28, 252–53, 312n48, 319n210; deployments

in France, 79–81, 84, 133, 167–70, 176, 184, 197, 209–10, 219–22, 267, 315n127; deployments in Sicily and Italy, 75–77, 85, 132–33, 253; links with OSS, 132–33, 326n103, 326n108; role of, 62–66, 72–73, 75–79, 82–86, 89, 108, 198–99; value of, 203, 208–10, 219–22, 227–28, 252–54, 272, 276. *See also* Special Raiding Squadron
Special Allied Airborne Reconnaissance Force (SAARF), 89, 106
Special Boat Section(s), 115, 158, 172, 175–76, 192, 241, 249, 281, 318nn195–96, 320n234, 333n132, 334n135; cost-effectiveness of, 256; creation of, 92–94, 271; deployment in Burma, 94; deployment in Mediterranean, 93, 98–99, 272; links with SAS, 64, 93, 156–57; roles of, 92–94, 99, 106; Z SBS, 94, 97–98, 137, 172, 334n141
Special Boat Service. *See* Special Boat Squadron
Special Boat Squadron: creation of, 73, 318n196; deployments in Greece and the Aegean, 71–72, 95, 108, 228–29, 273, 319n210, 332n82; operations, 74, 135, 215, 223, 329n35; roles of, 73–74
Special Force. *See* Chindits
Special Forces Detachments, 170
Special Forces Headquarters (SFHQ), 120, 133, 167–70
Special Interrogation Group (SIG), 65, 109, 158
Specialist formations: definition of, 6–9, 54, 243, 316n148; drain on manpower, 242–48; as innovators, 35, 55, 95, 97, 105, 140–41, 211–12, 239–40, 256–57, 260–61; need for, 258–64; post-WWII resurgence, 282, 335n18; reasons for creation of, 17–18, 31, 54–55,

87–88, 92, 105–107, 185–86, 263–64, 269–70; relationship between commandos and special forces, 4–5, 8, 52, 54, 73, 105–106, 271–72; relationship with other elite units, 6; size of establishment, 7–8, 52, 104, 106–107, 243–45, 251–54; value of, 4, 203–40, 268–69, 281–82
Special Night Squads, 57
Special operations: conventional forces used in a specialist capacity, 258–64, 345n71; definition of, 5; pre-WWII history of, 9–13, 270
Special Operations Executive (SOE), 13, 18, 20, 58, 74, 81, 111–12, 147, 156, 162, 165, 167–68, 171, 206–207, 224–25, 248, 271, 276, 320n227, 329n23, 329n25, 341n121; Force 133, 87; Force 136, 89, 94, 98, 172, 216, 226; Mission 101, 82, 316n136; Mission 204, 90; No. 101 Special Training School (Malaya), 88; relations with COI/OSS, 112, 115, 118–24, 127, 135, 140; value of, 219–20. *See also* Jedburgh Teams
Special Operations G-3 Algiers, 166–68, 334n141. *See also* Special Projects and Operations Center
Special Operations G-3 15 Army Group, 166, 173
Special Operations Mediterranean (command branch), 166, 172
Special Projects and Operations Center, 167–70
Special Raiding Squadron, 37–38, 73, 77–78, 169. *See also* Special Air Service (SAS)
Special Service Battalions. *See* Commandos (British)
Special Service Brigade(s), 30, 34, 36, 149–52, 161, 177, 185, 192, 272, 329n35; 1st Brigade, 41–42, 149, 211, 323n20; 2nd Brigade, 43–44, 133, 149, 186, 224, 262, 329n35; 3rd Brigade, 44, 149–50, 211; 4th Brigade, 41–42, 149; SS Brigade Group, 148–49; SS Brigade Headquarters, 113, 130, 145, 148–49, 245, 344n55
Special Service Unit 1 (7th Amphibious Force), 101, 103
Stanford, Daniel, 316n136
Station de Sened, Tunisia, 32
Stawell, W. A. M., 166
Stevenson, William, 324n65
Stilwell, Joseph, 88, 153, 216, 225–26, 236; and British, 123–24; and OSS, 162–63; use of Marauders, 50, 184, 188
Stimson, Henry L., 69–70
Stirling, (Archibald) David, 75, 105, 185, 199–200, 311n42, 312n48, 326n108, 331n76; capture of, 72, 200; and Churchill, 157; and creation of SAS, 61–62, 65–66, 155–56, 311n29, 311n34
Stirling, William "Bill," 72, 143–44, 185, 303n7; cooperation with OSS, 132–33; on role of 2nd SAS, 75–76, 78–79, 144, 253
St. Nazaire, France. *See* Chariot, Operation (commando raid on St. Nazaire, France, 1942)
Strategy, 10, 15–16, 20–21, 50–51, 125–26, 141, 160, 170, 273–74, 276, 278–79; strategic utility of special operations, 31, 204–205, 207–208, 221–22, 227, 238–40, 337n2
Street, Vivian, 186
Sturges, Robert, 149
Sudan Defense Force, 158
Sumter, Thomas, 11
Supreme Headquarters Allied Expeditionary Forces (SHAEF), 80, 120, 133, 167, 222, 250
Swallow, Operation (SOE raid on Vemork, Norway, 1943), 206–207
Swayne, Ronald, 185

Tamet, Libya, 63
Taranto, Italy, 78
Tarawa, 102–103, 217, 231
Tasimboko village, Guadalcanal, 33
Technological advances, 17, 94–95, 97, 140, 211
Templer, Gerald, 260
30 Assault Unit, 47, 216. *See also* Commandos (British)
Timpson, Anthony, 212, 237
Tirpitz (battleship), 206
Titanic, Operation (SAS deployment in France, 1944), 80
Tito, Josip Broz, 186, 192, 340n73
Tmimi, Libya, 63, 199
Tobruk, Libya, 18, 62, 65, 157–59
Tod, John Frederick "Ronnie," 38
Tollemache, H. T., 172, 196, 257
Torch, Operation (Allied invasion of French North Africa, 1942), 107, 271–73; pre-invasion beach reconnaissance and pilotage in, 99, 136; use of commandos in, 32, 34, 47, 128–29; use of rangers in, 32, 34–35
Truscott, Lucian K., 29, 36, 113, 116, 183
Tulagi Island, Solomon Islands, 33–34, 144, 153, 271
Turnbull, D. J. T., 161
Turner, Richmond Kelly, 103–104, 174
2671st Special Reconnaissance Battalion Separate (Provisional). *See* Operational Groups (OSS)
Tyson, John, 121

"Ultra" intelligence, 213–14, 216–17
Underwater Demolition Teams (UDT), 118, 140, 204, 257–58, 276, 278; command and control of, 173–75, 178–79; cost-effectiveness of, 252; creation of, 103–104; deployments of, 104, 174, 321n255; postwar retention of, 280; roles of, 101, 104, 107, 109; UDT 10, 104; value of, 217

United States: attitudes toward specialist formations, 16, 29, 35–37, 51–52, 68–71, 81, 83, 105–107, 97, 126, 130, 143, 152, 177, 184–85, 228, 259, 261, 264–67, 276–82, 301n1, 303–304n49; pre-WWII impressions on irregular war, 12–16, 302n39, 313n75
United States Army: I Corps, 182; 1st Infantry Division, 32, 188; 3rd Infantry Division, 40, 183, 260; Fifth Army, 189; Sixth Army, 91, 152, 182, 189–90; Seventh Army, 151, 220; 27th Infantry Division, 232; 29th Infantry Division, 130, 265; 33rd Infantry Division, 49; 34th Infantry Division, 30, 128, 260; 83rd Chemical Mortar Battalion, 35, 129; 98th Field Artillery Battalion, 48, 246; 168th Regimental Combat Team, 128–29, 325n89; 475th Infantry Regiment, 50; 504th Parachute Infantry Regiment, 40; Army Ground Forces, 151; Corps of Engineers, 103, 321n252
United States Army Air Force (USAAF), 126; 801st Bombardment Group (Provisional), 250; operations, 81, 207, 248–49. *See also* Allied Air Forces
United States Marine Corps (USMC), 8–9, 52, 102, 144, 265; 1st Marine Division, 28, 153–54; 2nd Marine Division, 231; 4th Marine Division, 48; 5th Marine Regiment, 28; amphibious doctrine, 14, 48, 104, 109, 272, 280; links with British, 27–29, 112–13, 117; pre-WWII activities, 14; "Rubber boat" companies, 28; Scout-Sniper platoons, 260
United States Naval Group China, 90, 163. *See also* Sino-American Cooperative Organization (SACO)

United States Navy: Eighth Fleet, 173; Pacific Fleet, 153; Task Group 80.4, 173

Vaagso Island, Norway. *See* Archery, Operation (commando raid on Vaafso Island, Norway, 1942)
Valiant (battleship), 94
Vandergrift, Alexander, 154
Varengeville-sur-Mer, France, 27
Vemork, Norway, 206–207, 238, 248, 301n12
Vercors, France, 219, 250, 339n57
V Force, 89–90, 123, 172, 216, 226
Vis Island, Adriatic Sea, 44, 86–87, 133–34, 186, 229, 340n73
Volckmann, Russell, 335n18

Walawbum, Burma, 188
Walcheren, Netherlands, 42
Wallace-Hardy, Operation (SAS deployment in France, 1944), 80
Warsaw uprising, 219
Washington, George, 11
Waterlily, Operation (SAS deployment in Genoa, Italy, 1943), 76
Wavell, Archibald, 55–57, 59, 61, 143, 155, 227, 310n11
Widgeon, Operation (commando crossing of Rhine River, Germany, 1945), 211
Wilder, Nick, 214
Wilkinson, Peter, 82, 127
Wilson, Henry Maitland, 39, 166, 190
Wingate, Orde, 7–8, 49–50, 57, 59, 185, 310n11, 316n136
Winter War, the, 303n3
Wolfe, James, 9
Woolley, H. G. A., 97, 115
Wright, Bruce S., 96, 105, 117

X-Craft submersibles, 100, 137, 206

Yamamoto, Isoroku, 81
Yeo-Thomas, F. F. E., 312n52
Young, Peter, 262
"Y" Service, 213–14
Yugoslav partisans, 39, 72, 74, 87, 186, 192, 250; value of, 222–23, 228–29

Zahidi, Fazlollah, 81
Zebra, Operation (USAAF air supply of French Resistance, 1944), 250
Zeebrugge Raid (France, 1918), 21, 304n16
Zerzura Club, 56
Z Special Unit, 319n208

www.ingramcontent.com/pod-product-compliance
Lightning Source LLC
Chambersburg PA
CBHW021333230426
43666CB00006B/278